The Making of King James II

*The Formative Years of a
Fallen King*

THE MAKING OF KING JAMES II

The Formative Years of a Fallen King

John Callow

SUTTON PUBLISHING

First published in 2000 by
Sutton Publishing Limited · Phoenix Mill
Thrupp · Stroud · Gloucestershire · GL5 2BU

British Library Cataloguing in Publication Data
A catalogue record for this book is available from the British Library.

ISBN 0-7509-2398-9

Typeset in 10/12pt New Baskerville.
Typesetting and origination by
Sutton Publishing Limited.
Printed and bound in England by
J.H. Haynes & Co. Ltd, Sparkford.

Contents

Acknowledgements

Firstly, I owe a very great debt of gratitude to Professor E.J. Evans whose wealth of knowledge, acute perception and constant good advice did so much to shape my studies at Lancaster University as both a postgraduate and an undergraduate. Without his unfailing interest, energy and support this project would simply not have been possible in its present form. Secondly, I am extremely grateful to Professor Ronald Hutton from the University of Bristol, for all of his help, kindness and generosity, and for allowing me to draw freely upon his enormous and quite unparalleled knowledge of the entire Restoration period.

Many thanks also go to Professor R.M. Bliss – especially for his many impromptu seminars on American colonial history – to Dr M. Mullett, for imparting his deep understanding of seventeenth-century Roman Catholicism and for letting me raid his bookshelves from time to time, and to Professor J.K. Walton for all his encouragement and good cheer.

Thanks are also due to the staff of the following research libraries who have been unfailingly helpful: the Bodleian Library, Oxford; the British Library, London; the John Rylands Library, Manchester; the National Maritime Museum Library, Greenwich; the Victoria & Albert Museum, London; and the Witt Library lodged in the Courtauld Institute, London. A very big 'thank you' is also extended to the staff of Lancashire County libraries – and in particular to that of the Garstang branch – who managed to hunt down volume after volume of texts for me with good grace and humour through the public inter-library loan system. I am similarly grateful to Mr and Mrs R.G. Reynolds, of Leighton Hall in Lancashire, who allowed me access to the relics of King James II held in their possession.

Lastly, my heartfelt thanks go to the British Academy – without whose award the doctoral thesis upon which this book is based could never have been begun, let alone completed – to Jane Crompton, the Senior Commissioning Editor at Sutton Publishing, for all of her help and interest, and above all to my Dad, to whom I owe far more than I can ever hope to repay and who is everything to me.

List of Illustrations

FIGURES AND MAPS

Figures

Maps

A Note on Dating

Although many European nations had adopted the Gregorian Calendar over the course of the seventeenth century, Britain was to remain stubbornly loyal to the Julian Calendar until 1752. The result was that the British calendar lagged ten days behind that which was generally used on the continent; in 1700 this difference increased to eleven days.

All of the dates used in the text are Old Style, unless the events recorded occurred after 1752. For events on the Continent, both Old and New Style dates are given. As in modern usage, the new year is taken as beginning on 1 January and not 25 March.

CHAPTER ONE

The Lost Memoirs

I

As a servant of the Church, Monsieur Charpentier knew full well that, in the year 1793, the journey from the great Benedictine Houses of Paris to the coast of England would prove both difficult and dangerous. For almost a century the Order had acted as custodian to the relics of the last Stuart King of England: raising shrines to the memory of James II and housing his voluminous writings in their archives. However, with the onset of the French Revolution, the establishment of a republic and the outbreak of war, all of this was to change. James's tomb was ransacked by soldiers, who came looking for the lead from his coffin to mould into musket balls. The dusty velvet canopies which had swathed his monument were torn down and a wax death mask of the exiled king was trampled and smashed underfoot.

The monks, who tended to his chapel, wisely abandoned their practice of holding masses for his departed soul, while their superiors, frightened by recent events, had already sought to preserve their wealth and authorized the dispersal of their treasures. Foremost among these were the memoirs of the dead King himself, and a plan to smuggle them out of the country was quickly formulated. The final inglorious collapse of the Jacobite movement, and the assured extirpation of the direct bloodline, had robbed them of their symbolic value and removed the need for their contents to be kept a secret. All that mattered now was the survival of the documents and it was thought that a ready market for them existed at the Hanoverian Court at Windsor. No longer troubled by the fear of Jacobite conspiracies, the English ruling class and the Prince of Wales, in particular, were anxious to stress the continuity and virtue of the monarchical system, at the expense of the vibrant new brand of democracy championed so forcefully by France. The return of King James's memoirs could only serve to enhance Hanoverian prestige, and to bolster the regime's claims to both political and dynastic legitimacy.[1]

With anticlerical mobs roaming the streets of Paris, the English Benedictines decided that Charpentier, as a layman travelling privately with his wife, would attract far less attention from the *sansculottes* than any priest, and could pass more easily through the paramilitary checkpoints which now ringed the capital. Having removed volume after volume of the King's works from their library shelves, Charpentier, now acting as the emissary of the Benedictine Order, bundled the books up among his own belongings and set out on the long road north. He had hoped to break his journey at the religious college at St Omer, where he would have been provided for by the Brothers and could have arranged his passage across the Channel in relative safety. However, on reaching the town his luck ran out and he was detained by a routine patrol. Fearing that the books, which bore the Royal Arms of England embossed on their leather covers, would be used to incriminate them both as spies, his wife attempted to hide them and buried them in the garden of her lodgings. With the authorities seemingly unconvinced by the couple's story, and with no sign of her husband's early release, Madame Charpentier took matters into her own hands and decided to rid herself of her unwelcome charge. Uncovering the heavy volumes, she burned them page by page, probably on a domestic hearth, and the memoirs of King James II ended their travels in a cloud of thick black smoke.[2]

II

Given the importance that James Stuart had attached to them and the care he had taken in assembling them, it is deeply ironic to consider that the most complete set of his writings were destroyed in such a manner. For few kings had sought to bequeath to posterity so many, and so varied, literary remains. Among British monarchs only his grandfather, James VI and I, and Alfred the Great could come close to matching him in terms of the volume of work produced. Not only did he write nine volumes of memoirs, but he also kept copies of his letters and was the author of books of spiritual and political advice for his son. James had a profound sense of the value of history, and recommended its study to the young in particular as a useful and diverting discipline.[3] Moreover, he seems to have been acutely aware of his own place within history and wanted a record kept for future generations of his thoughts, words and deeds.

From the time of his service in Flanders, in the early 1650s, James had begun to collect together material with the express intention of writing an autobiography. According to Bishop Gilbert Burnet, the Duke kept 'a journal of all that passes, of which he shewed me a great deal'. This was confirmed years later by the Cardinal de Bouillon, who added that as King he had 'written pretty exactly year by year in English the memoirs of his own life'.[4] Each night, it was said, James sat down and recorded the happenings of the day in his journal. However, the nature of his duties meant that it was often hastily written up against the background of a bustling camp or court, and took the form of scrappy or even ungrammatical notes. Consequently, when he had the time and leisure, James made several attempts to have his jottings set down in a more conventional and coherent style, as an official memoir. Each time he employed a new editor, and it was this practice which gave rise to many of the textual discrepancies that beset his 'official' biography. His first wife Anne Hyde, 'for she wr[ote] very correctly', and Charles Dryden, the son of the poet laureate, were both employed to transcribe portions of the memoirs, with the result that they built up a very considerable source of documentation running into many volumes.[5]

James was justly proud of his literary work and was at great pains to preserve it for posterity. When his frigate, the *Gloucester*, ran aground off the Norfolk coast in 1682 he saw to it that a strongbox containing all of his papers was salvaged from the wreck before abandoning ship himself. 'There were things of such consequence' among his writings, he told his friend George Legge, 'that he would hazard his own life' rather than let them be lost. Later, as all around him descended into chaos and he was forced to flee England at the Glorious Revolution, James made meticulous arrangements to smuggle his papers out of the country. They were entrusted to the Tuscan Ambassador, Francesco Terriesi, who eventually managed to get them to the safety of the exiled court of St Germain, via Leghorn.[6]

James continued adding to these manuscripts for the rest of his life, occasionally dusting off and re-editing some of his older works. When the Cardinal de Bouillon began to collect materials for a biography of his uncle, Marshal Turenne, he turned to the old King for advice. James had always held his former Commander-in-Chief in great affection, and took every opportunity to retell the stories of his campaigns and battles in exhaustive detail. His courtiers, and the younger generation in particular, had quickly tired of hearing these accounts and so James was only too glad to help, and flattered at the prospect of having a new audience for them.[7] He personally supervised the collection and revision of the relevant papers, and presented a copy of his early memoirs to the Cardinal in January 1696.

This document, which was never incorporated into the collection held by the Benedictines, was first published in 1735 as an appendix to A.M. Ramsay's *Histoire du Vicomte Turenne*. It was subsequently lost, but upon its rediscovery in the 1950s it was edited by A.L. Sells and republished in its entirety, under the somewhat misleading title of *The Memoirs of James II*. Although this work only covered the period of James's service with the armies of France and Spain from 1652 until 1659, it provides the most readable, systematic and satisfying account of all the writings directed under James's own hand, and has done much to define his posthumous image as Duke of York.[8]

After the death of the King in September 1701, a stream of books, prints and pictures were issued in both Britain and France to commemorate his life. In order to capitalize on this reawakening of interest in his father's career, the Old Pretender decided that James's papers should be brought together to form a standard, 'official' biography. To this end William Dicconson, a clerk at St Germain, was employed and began to sift through the accumulated manuscripts.[9] What confronted him in the late King's archive was little more than a snowstorm of papers, jumbled notes on religious and military matters, mixed in with casual thoughts and autobiographical materials. Dicconson gave these fragmentary writings a coherent shape, providing them with a prologue and an epilogue in order to record James's childhood and latter years. He also filled in the gaps in the narrative to the best of his ability, where James's interest had waned, or where his memory found events too painful or damaging to recall. This editorial process, completed in 1707, is crucially important to our understanding of the King's 'official' biography.

Many later commentators have been led astray in searching for a complete, authoritative and original text, which was authored solely by James. This quest would seem to imply a thoroughly modern conception of the art of autobiography, which fails to take into account either James's erratic methods of work or his personal objectives in setting down his memoirs. In light of the surviving, scattered and often confused source material it would appear that a single definitive text based along such lines never, in point of fact, existed. Rather, Dicconson's volumes of officially sanctioned work, once completed, simply took their place in the Stuart archives alongside James's original letters and papers. It was this large corpus of material which was shown to later visitors and which came to be known by the collective, if erroneous, title of James's 'life'.[10]

These volumes remained at the Jacobite Court for some years before being transferred to the care of the Benedictines at the Scots College, in the University of Paris. Their destruction, at the hands of Madame Charpentier, would have inflicted a devastating blow upon all of James's subsequent biographers had it not been for several writers, who managed to gain access to the manuscripts before they were consigned to the flames. These visitors to the College were able to copy out large extracts from the King's papers and transcribed the totality of Dicconson's work, to use in conjunction with their own researches. These rough notes were to form the basis of two very different books: James Macpherson's *Original Papers Containing the Secret History of Britain*, published in 1775, and James Stanier Clarke's *The Life of James the Second . . . Collected out of Memoirs Written of His Own Hand*, published in 1816.

Macpherson claimed to have seen James's 'memoirs' and, although this is sometimes disputed, he certainly had had access to the work of Thomas Carte, an Anglican clergyman and Jacobite sympathizer, who had

Figure 1 The Provenance of J.S. Clarke's *The Life of James the Second*

BOUILLON MS
Military Memoirs
1. Pub. by Ramsay (1735) and Sells (1962)
2. 1652–9 (Ramsay), 1652–60 (Sells)
3. *c.* 1652–60, re-edited by James, Jan. 1696

JAMES'S OWN WRITINGS
Autobiographical works, conduct books, Military and Religious Writings
1. Destroyed 1793
2. *c.* 1642–98
3. *c.* 1652–98

DEVOTIONS
James's Religious Writings
1. Published by Davies (1925)
2. *c.* 1692–8
3. *c.* 1692–8

C.J. FOX
Only saw the Mss
1. Alluded to his History (1808)
2. 1685
3. *c.* 1765–71, 1802

DICCONSON MSS
James's own writings edited together with new material by Dicconson at St Germain
1. Unpublished *c.* 14 vols Probably destroyed 1793
2. 1633–1701
3. 1707

CARTE MS
Notes only for a history of the reign
1. Preserved at the Bodleian Library
2. 1642–88
3. 1741

J.S. CLARKE
Edited the copy of the Dicconson Mss bought by the Prince Regent in 1813 from the estate of Charlotte, Duchess of Albany, and the English Benedictines
1. Published in his *The Life of James the Second* (1816)
2. 1633–1701
3. Edited 1816

MACPHERSON
Used Carte's journals as a source for his wider history of Britain, 1660–1725
1. Published his *Secret History* (1775)
2. 1660–98
3. *c.* 1770s

Key:
1. Year and details of the manuscript's first publication
2. The period of James's life covered by the work
3. The date when the manuscript itself was originally written

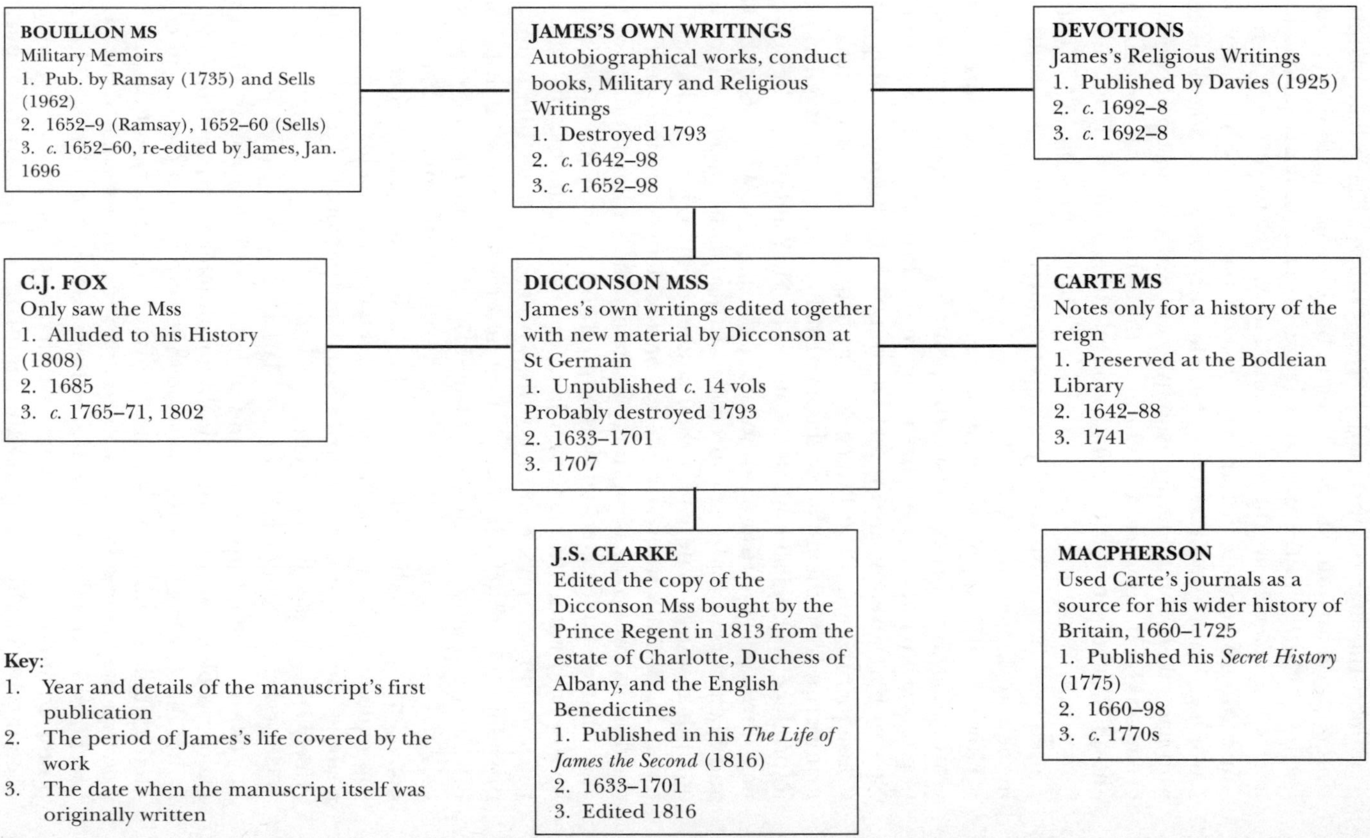

examined the manuscripts at the Scots College. Carte had planned to write his own account of James's reign, but his early death prevented this. He left behind him, instead, a large correspondence and copious notebooks taken from Dicconson and James's own writings.[11] It was this source that Macpherson harvested for his own history. However, while Carte had been a respected scholar, Macpherson was a notorious forger who had taken in the literary establishment with *Ossian*, an allegedly epic cycle of Gaelic poetry. He claimed that these works were of great antiquity, when in truth he had written them himself, from the 1760s onwards, to meet the demands of his Edinburgh publisher.[12] This has caused many later historians, perhaps not surprisingly, to avoid citing him in their work.

However, if Macpherson's book has been largely discounted, then Clarke's *Life* remains as the starting point for any serious study of James. Clarke was a naval chaplain and friend to the Prince Regent, whose life of Nelson had already distinguished him as a fashionable biographer. Consequently, when the Prince Regent acquired a copy of Dicconson's manuscript from the estate of the late Duchess of Albany, it fell to Clarke to produce an English edition.[13] Guided by Sir Walter Scott, he spent the next three years sorting and collating the papers. Whereas both Carte and Macpherson had been interested in using the memoirs only as an additional source material for their studies of the reigns of Charles II and James II, Clarke's interest centered on the actual manuscript itself. He checked its provenance thoroughly against the earlier findings of Carte and Charles James Fox, and attempted to produce the most comprehensive and authentic text from James's extant memoirs. His edition of Dicconson's writings embraced the whole of James's life and career, providing the reader with the clearest and most faithful rendition of the King's autobiography that could be hoped for, in the absence of the original (see Figure 1, p. 5). It is hardly surprising, therefore, that consideration of this single work has assumed a dominance in every subsequent assessment of James's character and activities, fundamentally shaping the nature of the debate about his personal objectives, and his effectiveness as a political and military leader.[14]

However, it is important to read Clarke's *Life* critically, and to be sure in one's own mind just what kind of literature it represents. One of the major problems we face when dealing with later interpretations of James is that the *Life* has been read as though it were all of a piece, and constituted a single continuous narrative. This is emphatically not the case. The *Life*, as it has come down to us, encompasses a diverse collection of highly specialized works, which reflect different types of writing. They were produced at different times and for different purposes. In some areas the account bears the unmistakable imprint of James's own personal experience, while in others the narrative appears to have been stitched together, from more general works, by Dicconson during the editorial process. Although the majority of the material included is biographical, there are sections taken directly from James's campaign journals, spiritual meditations, and his last political testament: a book of *Advice to his Son*. This has served to produce an uneven effect, the quality, tone and depth of writing varying throughout the book. Even the perspective of the narrative shifts between passages, with the author writing sometimes in the first person, and sometimes in the third. It is these inherent strengths and weaknesses in the literature, which have helped to establish the accepted picture of James during his formative years, and which have led to such vivid contrasts being drawn between his early career as a professional soldier and his later, disastrous, reign as King.

III

Like any historical figure, James Stuart cannot be seen to have existed in a vacuum. Shaped as he was by his own social position, the conventions of a court society and by the often grim political realities of the day, his career as Duke of York was inextricably linked to many of the most significant developments and crises of the second Caroline period: whether the Dutch Wars, Exclusion, or the framing and operation of the Settlement Restoration itself. Consequently, how we perceive the Restoration as a whole will profoundly influence our judgements about the nature of his activities. We need, therefore, to put in place an interpretative framework against which to view his actions and on which to ground any conclusions that we might make.

The background literature for the period does, however, present the reader with certain problems and difficulties. Not least of these is the fact that until very recently the Restoration and later Caroline period was a relatively unfashionable area for serious academic study. There were two main reasons for this. In the first place, its popular image, attested to by a range of contemporary memoirs and stage plays, is that of an age of frivolity, licence and cynicism.[15] While this has held appeal for literary and theatrical critics, it has tended to discourage some political and economic historians from looking any further. The second and more serious reason lies in its position, situated between the dramatic events of the English Civil Wars and the Republic on the one hand, and the Glorious Revolution and the foundation of the Constitutional Monarchy on the other. The attention of the historian is focused on these seminal developments in an attempt to explain such thorough-going change. By way of contrast, the Restoration, itself, does not seem to fit in well with the dominant patterns of historiography. The return of a monarchical form of government allied to gentry rule in the countryside and a large measure of mercantile support in the urban areas, following on from an innovatory experiment in republicanism, can be seen by some, and by Marxist historians in particular, as a total anomaly. It defies simple class analysis and runs contrary to mainstream economic determinism. For this reason, the Restoration did not receive the same level of attention accorded to other areas of early modern, or modern, history by the enormously influential post-war generation of Marxist historians. For the most part they chose to ignore it, although there have been sporadic attempts to bring the Restoration back within the Marxist canon, most notably through Iris Morley's evocation of the radical underground, William Thompson's article on Samuel Pepys, C. Mooers' study of the formation of the early modern state and C.B. Macpherson's work on political theory; none received widespread acceptance or significantly enlarged the parameters of study.[16]

The absence of a strong Marxist critique has also rendered the more virulent forms of revisionism redundant. The period, therefore, remains without the strong theoretical background and the clearly defined academic battle lines which characterize the rest of the seventeenth century, and the English Civil Wars and Interregnum in particular.[17] One unforeseen consequence of the lack of these ideologies, and their competing theories, has been the survival of the Whig and Tory schools of history, which have been largely abandoned elsewhere. As we shall see in the course of this chapter, they retain far more importance and weight than they would otherwise have been accorded. Nowhere is this seen more clearly than in the varying perceptions of the Duke of York, where both interpretations still have the power to inform and influence the debate, and where even an emotional and anachronistic appeal to Jacobite sentiment can still have a place.

As a fallen King, James has not enjoyed a particularly favourable press. The eclipse of the English Tories after 1692 deprived him of the support of his most powerful and persuasive advocates, while the need to legitimize William III's seizure of power, combined with the threat of prolonged Jacobite activity, led writers sympathetic to the Revolution Settlement to attempt to blacken his name. From Bishop Burnet's *History of My Own Times* (6 vols, Oxford, 1833) and White Kennett's *A Complete History of England* (3 vols, London, 1706) through to Macaulay's *History of England* (5 vols, London, 1848–61) and Trevelyan's *The English Revolution* (London, 1938), Whig historians attributed the worst of all possible vices and the most sinister of motives to the hapless James. For them, he was the King who had tried to overturn the Constitution and all the laws of the land in his pursuit of absolute power; the head of the Church of England who had attempted to forcibly reimpose Roman Catholicism upon his unwilling and commendably Protestant people. His rule appeared to combine all that was most disturbing and hateful to the English *psyche*, and its guiding spirit of tolerance and moderation, while his personality was that of a stupid and clumsy despot.[18]

This was a picture that sat well with the Victorian and Edwardian certainties of Empire and political dominance. Against a background of European war and revolution, first Macaulay and then Trevelyan – his kinsman and spiritual heir – provided a reassuring vision of, and plausible justification for, Parliamentary democracy based upon the English model. In order to chart the growth of this high level of political stability, both stressed the legacy and advantages of the Constitutional Settlement of 1689. However, the concept of the nation's continual advancement, allied to and benefiting from, an inviolable and unchanging political accord held ever less attraction and became increasingly irrelevant as the twentieth century progressed. A serious blow had already been struck by the publication of Butterfield's *The Whig Interpretation of History* (London, 1931), but more damaging still were new ideas challenging the desirability of Empire, the redefinition of the nation as the British Isles – rather than simply as England – and finally a loss of power and self-confidence following the enormous human and financial cost of waging two world wars. These developments, when combined, poignantly demonstrated the emptiness of a Whig triumphalism.[19]

The Whig tradition did, however, significantly alter in two major respects the way in which James was perceived by later historians. Their interest, as has already been discussed, was primarily in the political and constitutional history of England and they sought to demonstrate James's failings at the key junctures of the period, namely at the Exclusion Crisis and the Glorious Revolution. Consequently, it was James's character and record as King which were most vigorously and successfully attacked. His early record, and participation in the events of the Restoration, were largely ignored and only considered when they were felt to have had a direct bearing on later events. This interpretative practice has created significant gaps in our knowledge of James as Duke of York, and has reduced more than a quarter of a century of active political life to little more than a prelude to a three-year reign.

Secondly, while the judgements of Whig writers have largely been discounted by modern political and constitutional historians, their influence is unduly and disproportionately exerted in other areas. This is particularly the case where sharply focused specialist studies seek to unravel the wider strands of policy. As a result of this, and the accompanying lack of historiographical theory for the Restoration period, the unwitting economic, colonial or military historian may feel constrained to offer conclusions that, from another quarter, would appear curiously out-dated. This trend is all the more marked because of Macaulay's skill as a writer. His faculty for description, mastery of the English language and damning use of the invective, produced one of the most devastating and enduring critiques of James as both man and King, when he wrote of his narrow understanding, obstinate will and unforgiving temper.[20] These verdicts have been picked up and echoed down the years, uniting a diverse cross-section of historians whose chosen fields of study, use of methodology and political purpose held little else in common. In this way, Chandler's study of seventeenth-century warfare, Churchill's biography of Marlborough, Webb's work on the colonies, and Bryant's prolific output on the Restoration and the creation of the Navy Office, came to form a common and consistent picture of James as Duke of York.[21]

This is not to say that this vision achieved total dominance, or went completely unchallenged. From the late eighteenth century onwards, there were several writers who cut completely against the grain and operated largely free from the constraints of both Traditional Whiggism and narrow Jacobite propaganda. One early writer, characteristically out of step with the Whig tradition, in this area as in much else, was Charles James Fox. His *A History of the Early Part of the Reign of James the Second* (London, 1808) was the product of much original research and provided a fresh interpretation of the man and his methods, which in many respects is thoroughly vindicated by modern scholarship. Fox was interested in the deeper, underlying causes which helped to precipitate James's fall, rather than in his personality itself. He thought that he had discovered these in the nature of the restored monarchy. In this light, James cannot be dismissed as being simply a rogue element, irrevocably opposed during his brother's reign to the spirit of the Restoration Settlement. He was, instead, an integral part of it, and a manifestation of merely one aspect of its many injustices. In Fox's view, it was actually Charles II who emerged as the villain of the piece, due to his persecution of the Scottish Covenanters for the free practice of their faith.[22] Significantly, Fox, an advocate of religious toleration, rejected the view held by both Whig and later Tory writers alike that Roman Catholicism had systematically destroyed the Duke's political judgement, and pointed to the long list of Protestant lords who had willingly assisted him in his own Scottish campaigns.[23]

It seems strange, therefore, that Fox's analysis was largely ignored by subsequent Georgian and Victorian authorities. This can be explained by the nature of the work itself. Fox died before its completion, and in its published form it represented only a fragment of what had been originally intended, thus significantly reducing its impact.[24] Furthermore, the absence of biographical detail, and the failure of the narrative to continue on to the events of 1688–9, served to dissuade many Whig historians from according it anything more than a passing inspection, while those on the political right tended to dismiss it out of hand, on the grounds of its author's partisanship and alleged bias. In the twentieth century, the writers of more specialized works have found little use for Fox, as his lifelong preoccupation with domestic politics and profound opposition to the expanding British Empire led him to ignore altogether the colonial and imperial dimension.

Following on from Fox, the first serious attempts at a reassessment of James's reputation were undertaken by an influential group of English Catholic writers. They were anxious to redress some of the worst slanders directed against their religion, and to overcome the centuries of fear, distrust and prejudice which had soured relations between their community and their Protestant fellow countrymen. The leader of this movement was John Lingard, an erudite and liberal priest, steeped in the culture and learning of the Enlightenment, whose *History of England* (vols VIII–X, London, 1855) did much to raise the tenor and quality of debate, while removing many of its more partisan overtones.[25] As a young man, he had begun to write at a time when calls for Roman Catholic emancipation – assisted by the collapse of Jacobitism as both a credible and dangerous political force – had started to gain significant widespread support. Consequently, he was keen to stress the moderation of English Catholics, and their undivided loyalty to both their nation and to their Hanoverian rulers. These considerations undoubtedly shaped his approach to James, as he engaged with much of the Whig critique. Lingard did, however, inject a significant new strand of thought into the historiography by drawing a distinction between James as Duke of York, and James as King. It was this division, allowing for a favourable assessment of his early career – in stark contrast to all that was to follow – that was to be seized upon by Lingard's successors and developed to form the basis for many later apologias.[26]

Unfortunately, as the Cisalpine movement, so dearly espoused and exemplified by Lingard's life and works, was swept away by the First Vatican Council, so too did the writing of English Catholic history undergo a profound change of direction, which was maintained from the late nineteenth century well into the twentieth. A more strident and sectarian tone appeared, replacing the former more outgoing, receptive and conciliatory attitude. This trend was often accompanied by, and allied to, the resurgent attachment to the Jacobite cause, sanitized and made acceptable by the Romantic Movement, and popularized by the adventure stories of Walter Scott, Harrison Ainsworth and Robert Louis Stevenson.[27] In order to justify such an emotional involvement and to underpin their conclusions about the undesirable nature of society post-1688/9, these new pseudo-Jacobite historians needed a recourse to the movement's ultimate source of authority and legitimacy. This could only be achieved through a full-scale reassessment of the character of 'Jacobus', that is, James himself.

Without a historian of the stature of Fox, Lingard or Macaulay to champion them, this group lacked the skill needed to challenge the Whig Tradition outright, or the vision necessary to dramatically reinterpret events and to present an alternative framework for them. As a result, they confined their attacks to those aspects of the period which had been relatively untouched by the Whig consensus, or where their own arguments could be deployed to the maximum effect. Thus, although the established view of James's reign appeared unassailable, his early career as Duke of York seemed to offer much. It had been largely overlooked by previous generations of historians and yet provided an exciting and appealing picture of a young Prince who had served his King and country faithfully. If James had been such a fine and noble Prince, so ran the argument, then he surely could not have been such an unprincipled and disastrous King. These inconsistencies in the picture the Whigs had painted of the young James, when compared to his old self, were forcefully exposed in Hilaire Belloc's *James the Second* (London, 1928). This often impressionistic and very personal account of James's life, concentrating disproportionately on his early years, set both the terms and the tone for many subsequent assessments of the Duke.

Belloc chose to emphasize the Duke's military career, paying particular attention to his bravery, professionalism and love of England. His time as Lord High Admiral was fully explored in the text and he received fulsome praise for his patronage of Pepys and his work in the strengthening of the battle-fleet.[28] In Belloc's eyes, James had little use for power for its own sake. He was the dedicated servant of the State, promoting new schemes for trade and Empire in order to foster the national good, but all the time acting within the sight of God and observing his stringent commandments. Written at the high tide of the British Empire, the work sought primarily to demonstrate the manner in which his labours as Duke of York had benefited England and laid the foundations for her future greatness. However, its religious remit, which sought in no uncertain manner to proselytize for the Roman Catholic faith, injected an element of tragedy and personal suffering into James's story, which had been wholly absent from the dominant literature since the campaign for his canonization had faltered at the Vatican, more than 150 years before. Belloc's James, like King Lear before him, reaped nothing but scorn and ingratitude from those he had done so much to help. Unable to set aside his conscience, his fall from power was occasioned solely by his steadfast adherence to Catholicism. His eldest daughters are thought to have betrayed him, while the English nation, which had once adored him, turned comprehensively against him, stripped him of his rightful titles and cast him out into exile.

This new perspective, emphasizing the positive attributes of James as Duke of York was most clearly and succinctly expressed by Charles Petrie, in his article 'James the Second. A Revaluation' (*Nineteenth Century*, vol. 114, Oct. 1933, pp. 475–84), and by M.V. Hay in his *The Enigma of James II* (London, 1938). However, there are substantial problems involved with accepting this interpretation at face value. Few writers have approached the Restoration with such a fixed and highly politicized agenda, or applied such methods of enquiry to it, as did Belloc, Hay and Petrie. Their work was not the product of original research, and was often impressionistic or polemical in tone, while their arguments were couched in strident and often violent terms.[29] James was viewed with hindsight, with little feel for the realities and concerns of the seventeenth century. The great claims made for the breadth of vision that he displayed as Duke, in creating the Royal Navy and fashioning the Empire, assumed that both institutions were inseparable from the pursuit of English power and had enjoyed a continuity of identity and purpose, which had grown and endured without challenge or interruption, from the 1660s right up to the 1930s. Thus, the exciting and appealing picture of the young warrior Prince was allied to that of the dedicated and prescient states-man, who laboured tirelessly as his brother's most steadfast subject.

In a similar fashion, the problems of contemporary politics loomed large for these authors in their considerations of the past. James was thoroughly reconstructed by them in the form of a modern man: a figure who held a direct and potent relevance for the 1930s. All of these writers were dissatisfied with post-war democracy and, in common with many more recent writers of Jacobite history, sought to hold back its extension, and with it the encroachment of technology and the modern world. In this light, James as Duke of York can become a proto-fascist role model, with his zest for military glory taken to be the highest form of human virtue. His figure was effectively distorted to fit the paradigm, and the implicit hope was expressed that monarchy and Empire could be bound together in a single person. By following the example of his illustrious forebear, Edward VIII might combine together the qualities of both Mussolini and Victor Emmanuel II and, like Franco in Spain, attempt to restore the lustre of former days.[30]

These unpalatable associations and their accompanying lack of any grounding in academic research were not lost upon professional historians, such as Maurice Ashley and David Ogg, or upon such a great wordsmith as Winston Churchill. Each in his own way struck at the very heart of this insidious brand of revisionism, but it was the publication of Churchill's own life of *Marlborough* (4 vols, London, 1933) which ironically threw them a lifeline and ensured that their vision of James would endure, largely untroubled, for the space of a further generation.[31] This masterly exercise in the art of biography was put together with the assistance of Maurice Ashley, who would later work on his own study of James, and served to present a very unflattering portrait of the Duke of York over the course of its first volume.[32] Petrie and Hay were keen to leap to the defence of their hero, and for a time a heated debate raged between the two parties. Somewhat surprisingly, the arguments put forward by James's supporters held up well, with Hay in particular being able to expose serious flaws in Churchill's thesis. In his guide to the controversy, tellingly entitled *Winston Churchill and James II of England* (London, 1934) as though to impute the politician's patriotism, Hay took issue with the criticisms levelled by Churchill, and sought to refute them point by point. What made this work so successful was its selective line of attack, which ran at a tangent to Churchill's main purpose. While Churchill had taken on vast sweeps of history, supported by an enormous and diverse range of source materials, Hay kept to his chosen ground, concentrating on James's record as Duke of York and using small-scale case studies to bring out inconsistencies in the primary literature. He devoted particular attention to the Duke's rule in Scotland and effectively demolished his opponent's view of James's establishment of an exceptionally brutal and tyrannical regime in the northern kingdom. Churchill can be seen here at his weakest. He was hampered by his reliance on Macaulay's earlier narrative, and constrained by his own motivations in writing the book. He aimed to present Marlborough's brilliant victories as being the culmination of a long and principled stand against the ruthless expansionism of Louis XIV's France. Therefore, in order to exonerate his ancestor from the charge of first serving and then deserting his pro-French master, he was forced to locate a rupture between the two following James's assumption of viceregal powers in Scotland. However, the absence of firm evidence for any such breach having occurred in the early 1680s, and the failure of Churchill to directly link James with the atrocities allegedly committed in his name, gifted a victory to Hay and his supporters, who then used it as a Trojan Horse to discredit, by implication, the value of Churchill's work as a whole.[33]

In the long term, the effect of this controversy was to confer a new importance upon the role played by James during his brother's reign. Although they had failed to dent the Whig interpretation of James as King, Belloc, Petrie and Hay, had provided the only lengthy or specialist studies of his early career, and had been able to outline a plausible version of the Duke's activities which was in line with the broad gist of the primary sources. Moreover, their authority in this area seemed to have been confirmed by their success in confronting a major figure like Churchill. This ensured them an acceptance, and a wider audience, that they would not otherwise have enjoyed. As a result of this, and in the absence of a more up-to-date appraisal, their view of the young James passed into the mainstream, profoundly influencing works as diverse as Higham's engaging, if at times idiosyncratic, *King James the Second* (London, 1934), Haswell's straightforward military life of *James II. Soldier and Sailor* (London, 1972) and Trevor's popularist *The Shadow of a Crown. The life story of James II of England and VII of Scotland* (London, 1988).

However, the outstanding difficulty in advancing this very positive image of the Duke of York still lay in the apparent transformation of his character following his accession. The issue had never satisfactorily been explained because James's defenders had consistently avoided direct engagement with the problems of his reign, while the Whigs themselves have never studied his early career in its own right or in any great depth. This meant that the two schools of thought appeared to be thoroughly irreconcilable. Attempts to marry them together only made matters worse and produced some decidedly odd results. Haswell, echoing Belloc, chose to portray James as a brilliant but naive professional soldier who found himself suddenly out of his depth in power politics, being cruelly betrayed by those like Marlborough who owed him the most. Higham, while similarly impressed by the exploits of the young James, and prepared to chronicle his series of naval victories in glowing terms and to stress his commitment to religious toleration, still determined to approach her material through the perspective of the Whig Tradition.[34] Her attachment to the terms of the English Constitution meant that she could not ultimately conclude in James's favour, creating an inbalance between her early findings and her final summary. This did much to harm the narrative structure of the book, producing an uneven and frequently contradictory picture which never managed to come to grips with James's character.

Given the pronounced failure of historians to reach common ground, a fresh approach was required before any further advance could be made in analysing the relative effectiveness, personality and objectives of James as Duke of York. The problem had always been that James's critics and apologists had always been far more preoccupied with the nature of his 'character' than with the significance of his actions and accomplishments. This had led them up a series of blind alleys, and into making value judgements which serve to tell the modern reader rather more about the social and political concerns of their own day, rather than those of the mid–late seventeenth century. Although many extravagant and conflicting claims had been put forward to suggest the Duke's greatness, or total lack of it, and while his participation in naval reform, trade and empire had been well attested to, these assertions had never been taken any further than a simple bald statement of fact.[35] All of this was, however, to change as the result of the patient researches of F.C. Turner.

IV

In his *James II* (London, 1948), Turner delivered the first recognizably modern and comprehensive academic appraisal of James's life and reign. This weighty biography was to serve as the standard reference work for the next thirty years, and still retains much of its value today. Turner was the first of James's biographers to fully shake off the influence of Macaulay, while having little time for the King's more outspoken partisans. He benefited greatly from the resurgence of interest in the late seventeenth century that was being generated by a new wave of historians, led by David Ogg, Esmond De Beer and Sir Keith Feiling, and this fresh climate of ideas and enthusiasm undoubtedly helped to shape his own work.[36] He made full use of the available printed source materials and undertook a careful study of the most important manuscript collections. Unlike many earlier biographers, Turner had set out to present an account of James's life that stretched from cradle to grave. To this end, he divided his book into two distinct, but roughly equal, parts. The first dealt with James as Duke, and the second with him as King. Though he did not particularly care for his subject and accused him of trying to import absolutism, as a foreign and totalitarian institution, uncritically into England, Turner did show James to have been a brave and capable Commander, the victor of the Battles of Lowestoft and Sole Bay, and an invaluable Staff Officer to Marshal Turenne. He did, however, choose to reject the more extravagant claims made for the Duke's ability and foresight as a great naval administrator. James was seen as being little more than a figurehead at the Admiralty, presiding over the hard work of others, and it was Samuel Pepys, and not he, who was for Turner the heroic figure, grasping at the significance of naval power and seeking against the odds to build up a formidable fleet.[37] Since he was the first historian to look at the archival evidence in great detail in order to substantiate his claims and displayed an impressive mastery of the sources available to him at the British Library, Turner's judgements concerning the Duke's administrative abilities and military acumen have carried a great deal of weight. However, in his final evaluation of James's early career, he may well have been unduly influenced by the powerful interpretation of the evolution of the civil service and the rebuilding of the Royal Navy advanced by Sir Arthur Bryant, in his seminal works on the life of Samuel Pepys.[38] As with Churchill, Bryant's genius lay in his ability to produce scholarly research of the highest order and to combine it with an engaging prose-style that was able to convey quite complex ideas with an appealing clarity. It was small wonder, therefore, that his books should be so influential or that Turner should have consulted them as the latest, and most significant interpretative works on the Restoration Navy then available to him.

It must also be remembered that in order to preserve the continuity and focus of his narrative, Turner could not afford to devote equal time and attention to every one of the Duke's interests. He was also heavily constrained in his examination of James's attempts at Empire building by the simple fact that colonial history was still very much in its infancy. These factors effectively limited the parameters of his study, and caused him to do little more than to outline James's involvement with commerce and the colonies. He recognized the Duke's commitment to the merchant community, his connections with the promotion of foreign trade and the seizure of New York, but was generally dismissive of his overall impact. Turner's James was a dilettante prince, more concerned with the profit motive than with dreams of national greatness.[39] This brief treatment was censured by Florence Higham in a review article, but it is not hard to see why he constructed his book in the way that he did.[40] Turner's brief was to provide a concise, single-volume, guide to James as both Duke and King. He was, therefore, forced to concentrate on those areas that he felt to be the most important: those which held a long-term significance for, and a direct bearing on, the later events of James's reign. Consequently, it is no surprise that the momentous political events of the Restoration era, namely the Popish Plot and the Exclusion Crisis, which very nearly cost Charles II his throne and the Duke his life, should be expanded upon at the expense of James's own, very personal, interests in trade and Empire.

The most significant development, from our own point of view, in Turner's treatment of James, was his ability to unite both periods of his subject's life, both pre- and post-1685, in order to form a coherent and plausible whole. Previously, the discrepancy in the dominant historiographies between the young Duke, an active, courageous and naturally talented soldier, and the old King, an indecisive, cruel and increasingly bigoted statesman, had seemed as startling as they were inexplicable. Turner now achieved a satisfactory solution to account for this apparently devastating change in personality by suggesting that James, at some unspecified time in the 1670s, had contracted a debilitating strain of syphilis.[41] The idea of a dramatic collapse in James's personality and will, or else of their erosion over time by either a physical or a mental degeneration, was not, however, entirely new and had deep roots in several previous accounts of his life and reign. For the Whig historians of the nineteenth century, it was the corrosive effects of fundamentalist religion, and of Roman Catholicism in particular, which had destroyed his resolve.[42] Writing in a less sectarian and more sexually liberated age, Turner's suggestions have been eagerly adopted and embellished by a succession of more recent historians, keen to locate James's failures and disappointments in terms of a tragic personal decline rather than through external factors, or his consistent inability to successfully shape and guide policy.[43]

These ideas were not without their foundation in contemporary gossip. Allegations that James was a syphilitic had circulated freely around the Restoration Court. Samuel Pepys heard several stories about a wronged husband who allowed his wife to infect James, on purpose, as a revenge for his cuckolding, while Lorenzo Magalotti, a Florentine traveller, gave the tale another – wholly improbable – twist. He reported that James had given the disease to Anne, his first Duchess, after she had poisoned one of his mistresses in a fit of jealous rage. This would seem to be a particularly self-defeating form of retribution in any age, and have rightly been dismissed as being merely salacious tittle-tattle. However, Bishop Burnet's assertion that James had 'pursued many secret pleasures . . . and . . . is ever going from one intrigue to another, though it is generally thought that these have been very fatal to him, and that the death of so many of his children is owing to that', has gained a far greater currency among later historians.[44] Although it is true that the high level of perinatal infection, when combined with poor midwifery techniques, did claim several of James and Anne's children in the 1660s, and wiped out Mary of Modena's progeny in the 1670s and early 1680s, it was the smallpox virus – rather than syphilis – which would seem to have been the real killer. The fact that two of his daughters, from his first marriage, reached adulthood and suceeded to his throne, while his surviving son, by his second wife, lived to a ripe if unrewarding old age, would seem to negate the theory of a hereditary affliction. Moreover, James, as Duke of York, sired a number of illegitimate children, who survived into middle age and raised healthy families of their own.[45] The existence of so many strong and active children – both legitimate and illegitimate – who were born over several decades, can only serve to throw even more doubt over the hypothesis of James's degeneration. However, the most conclusive evidence for the soundness of James's constitution comes, ironically, from the *sansculottes* who forced open his tomb.

Anxious to see the body of a King, their Royalist prisoners clustered round the shattered sarcophagus and paid them so that they, too, might view the corpse. One Irish monk attempted to prise out a tooth as a keepsake, but found that 'The corpse was beautiful and perfect. The hands and nails were fine. I moved and bent every finger. I never saw so fine a set of teeth in my life . . . I tried to get one out . . . but could not, they were so firmly fixed.'[46] Had James been infected with syphilis, a disease which was virtually untreatable, then among his first symptoms would surely have been bloodied and receded gums, which in time would have resulted in the loss of most of his teeth.

One unintentional result of Turner's forceful postulation of the 'degeneration thesis' was that, with the notable exception of John Miller's study, the debate has been allowed to drift back once more on to the 'character' of James, in a manner which would have been almost unthinkable for the serious treatment of any other major political figure. Thus, Maurice Ashley's biography of *James II* (London, 1977) grew out of his earlier revisionist article 'Is there a Case for James II?' (*History Today*, vol. 13, 1963, pp. 347–52) in which he reopened the discussion on the 'tragedy' of James's career and concentrated the attention of the reader upon his achievements as a young man. Moreover, since his collaboration with Churchill, he had taken on board many of the criticisms which had been levelled against his earlier work by Hay, and now presented a broad thrust of argument which combined elements of Turner's 'degeneration thesis' with the apologists' glowing findings about the efforts of James as Duke of York. In attacking the now moribund Whig Tradition he was, to some degree, already pushing at an open door but, through his careful use of original sources and undoubted scholarship, the notion of James as a swordsman and military genius, whose early promise had gone largely unfulfilled, received a fresh injection of life.[47]

Turner's great work had carried such authority that no further attempt had been made to study James for a generation. However, during the 1970s, dramatic new research challenged the established view of the Revolution of 1688–9 and provided the impetus for a renewed enquiry by John Miller. As the causes of James's fall and the workings of his government came to be examined in increasing detail, the need for a reappraisal of the monarch, the central figure around whom the State apparatus functioned, became increasingly apparent. In his *James II. A Study in Kingship* (London, 1978), Miller delved far deeper into the archives than any of James's previous biographers, and was especially interested in relating the records of central and local government to the implementation of royal policy. Through his mastery of these often highly specialized sources, it was possible for him to reveal the extent of James's system of military and electoral patronage, his massive debts run up as Duke by his opulent lifestyle and his need to secure a substantial new source of income with which to repay his creditors. Unfortunately, like Turner and Ashley before him, he only touched briefly upon the Duke's involvement with trade and the plantations, and viewed them largely in the context of James's naval office, his appetite for hard work and the pressures generated upon him by the Dutch Wars.[48]

This is perhaps not too surprising an approach to his subject, given that Miller's primary objective in writing was identical to that of Turner: to explain the causes of instability within the administrations of Charles II and James II, and to account for the toppling of the latter sovereign from power through an account of his life and reign. As a result, the constitutional struggles that had enveloped England from the 1640s onwards loomed large in their analyses, and both writers sought to explain James's failures primarily in terms of his conception, and practice, of kingship. What is surprising is that, despite the overall soundness of his treatment, the thoroughness of his research and his careful deployment of well-reasoned argument, Miller never came to terms with the thesis of James's degeneration or delivered a definitive verdict upon the nature and scope of his early career. Though casting doubt upon a diagnosis of syphilis, he lent tacit support to the belief that James experienced a physical and emotional decline which contributed to his fall, and portrayed his last years as being marked by a 'fatalism and passivity' which would have unthinkable for him in his youth.[49]

Consequently, while Turner, Ashley and Miller differ from one another in their fundamental aspects – in terms of their literary style, analyses, aims and ideas – when they came to consider James as Duke, they shared much that was in common. Where differences do arise, they are matters of emphasis and style rather than of content. This would seem to be a very interesting and significant, if somewhat unexpected, development in the historiography. We have already demonstrated the way in which every generation, since the early eighteenth century, has sought to redefine its vision of James as man and as King, yet it seems that we have never been able to identify a similar major revision of James's role as Duke. We need to ask ourselves, therefore, why this has been the case and how such a remarkable consensus of opinion has been achieved in modern times, over this single aspect of so controversial a career. Either historians have thoroughly exhausted their subject, comprehensively worked and reworked their sources to arrive at a definitive conclusion, which would hold good for all time, or else there have been some other, as yet unknown, influences operating upon them in order to standardize their findings. I will argue that the answer can be found in this latter area, and that the problem lies partly in the type of questions James's biographers have been asking themselves about his early career and partly in the nature of the literature they used in order to explain, and account for, them.

As has already been seen, historians had initially approached the Duke's career through an analysis of his character. This all changed with the work of Turner, who effectively reconciled the two conflicting halves of James's life and public record, and made any further re-examination of his personality and early career redundant. The theory of James's degeneration gained widespread currency and appeared to remove the need for a closer study of his activities as Duke, as this period of his life was no longer seen to have had such a fundamental bearing upon his later actions. Thus, when Ashley and Miller came to explore James's style of kingship and conception of power, there was little need for them to devote a great deal of time and effort to reappraising an area which was already thought to have been ploughed out, and which would not directly serve to influence their findings. The resulting change of emphasis served to marginalize James's years as Duke and to discourage any further study of them, significantly distorting the historiography of the period. His major biographers have, through assumption and omission, presented us with no single definitive account of his early career and there is little in the way of consensus in the area of his overall administrative impact or effectiveness. This comparative neglect is all the more striking when we come to consider the wealth of general biographical material for James and the proliferation of small-scale studies of far more obscure, near-contemporary figures. Consequently, although Henry, Prince of Wales, has been studied in depth and even the little Duke of Gloucester, the longest surviving son of Queen Anne, has his own biographer, James, Duke of York, still remains to be studied in his own terms and awaits re-assessment.[50]

If all of our ideas about the Duke's activities have stemmed from the need to explain his character and later kingship, then there is a pressing need to investigate the marked similarities to be found in all the accounts of his early life. I will argue that this consensus of opinion was the product of an over-reliance on one particular primary source material, J.S. Clarke's edition of *The Life of James the Second*, which we shall now return to, and that, moreover, the unseen hand scripting and shaping the development of the historiography, and setting the parameters of the debate, is that of James himself.

V

The first section of Clarke's work, dealing with James's early life up until the Restoration of 1660, presents us with an extremely full and clear account of his campaigns in France and Flanders. This was the time that James came to look back upon with the greatest satisfaction, and had recorded for the Cardinal de Bouillon. Dicconson in this case appears to have had direct access to the manuscript written in James's hand and his account, as rendered by Clarke, closely matches those given by Ramsay and Sells, as it continually refers back to the page numbers of the original source.[51] It is here that we can see James's strengths as a writer displayed to their best effect. He benefits from being familiar with his subject: as a professional soldier he is entirely at home with tales of battles and sieges, relatively uncomplicated and straightforward stories, unclouded by the complexities and ambiguities of his later political career. Moreover, in contrast to previous military writers active during the Civil Wars, his writings are very personal and can appear to be strikingly modern. He managed to impart something of himself in his descriptions of marches and counter-marches; desperate charges with the shock and dislocation of sudden – murderous – combat; tales of meetings with fortune-tellers in camp, and the sight of frozen corpses lining the roads in deep mid-winter.[52] If his descriptions are dramatic and evocative, then they are also romantic; James, at this time, had youth and the glamour attached to high social position on his side. It is this heroic image, so forcefully expressed, which attracted so many writers in the mould of Belloc, Petrie and Hay to both his person and his cause, and which profoundly affected Haswell and Ashley's treatment of their subject.

However, while we can admire James's military memoirs as compelling literature, we must be aware of their limitations. They covered only a short period of time spent as a soldier of fortune prior to the Restoration, and have led many historians – and James's apologists in particular – to draw from them far-reaching conclusions about his later motives and aspirations, which have little foundation in the wider historical record. Moreover, there has been a tendency to project the activities of the exiled Duke of York forward into the Restoration period itself, where his role and responsibilities were of a markedly different nature.[53] This action was forced upon them, to a large degree, by the structure of the *Life*, which does not provide such a comprehensive explanation for all of James's subsequent actions as Duke.

It is important to note that, in contrast to the earlier passages, the *Life* is far more problematical in its account of James's activities from 1660 to 1685. The marginal references to James's own memoranda stop and the events described are now related in the third person throughout. In this crucially important section, the *Life* takes on the appearance of a formal history rather than that of an autobiography. This is particularly frustrating given the scope of this present study, but it has also had a wider significance in that it has, in the past, thoroughly discouraged a full examination of James's career from the time of the Restoration through to the Popish Plot. These years saw him, as Duke of York, establishing his position within the restored monarchy and operating at the heart of the governmental machine, with a series of the most important state depart-ments functioning directly under his control. Unfortunately, we will learn precious little about his administration and workload from the pages of the *Life*. James was, it seems, directly involved in the writing up of only those events which he considered to be of particular value. Thus, he saw to it that the papers relating to his naval battles were carefully gathered together, and proudly recalled his victories at Lowestoft and Sole Bay in highly graphic and detailed accounts.[54] However, when it came to writing about those major political and colonial developments with which he was not personally involved, James's interest in his memoirs began to flag. On these occasions he contented himself with providing only a rough sketch of events, leaving the detail to be filled in at a later, unspecified, date by his editors. This was the case when he set down a brief summary of the capture of New Amsterdam by his forces, and explains the omissions and elementary mistakes which litter its text. It seems inconceivable, otherwise, that given his thorough-going knowledge of navigation, James could have so spectacularly misplaced Long Island in the West Indies or that he would have seen fit to describe his friend, Colonel Richard Nicolls, who commanded the expedition simply as 'Nicholas'.[55] If the colonies offered little more than a footnote to the official account of his career, then the humdrum commerce of the boardroom was not rated as being worth a mention. His business interests and activities as Governor of the Hudson Bay and Royal African Companies were almost totally ignored.

These omissions reflect not only the weaknesses of the editorial process, but more importantly the preoccupations of James himself. When he put pen to paper it was in his capacity as a Prince of the blood, anxious to show the world that he had lived up to the highest and most chivalrous ideals traditionally attached to royalty. Although these concepts of the wise and clement prince, who possessed grace and exercised skill at arms, were coming to seem more than a little outdated in the late seventeenth century – with the rise of professional armies, new social classes and the expansion of global trade – they were still the attributes that James prized most dearly and sought to perpetuate. Consequently, when reading the *Life* we can detect the increasing gap between the image and the reality of what it meant to be the Duke of York. James might well have been a very progressive figure with real organizational flair, sitting on a multitude of governmental committees and the boards of the new joint-stock companies, but the *Life* does not reflect these facts and we have no way of substantiating James's claims to effectiveness from its text. What James and editors chose to emphasize, instead, was his pursuit of personal glory. By highlighting this particular area at the expense of all others, they established a frame of reference which later writers have followed all too closely. This has limited the discussion of James's activities as Duke to a simple appraisal of his military effectiveness, often couched in his own terms, which has ruled out any consideration of the wider – and perhaps more important – issues surrounding his political role in governance, trade and Empire.[56]

The quotations from James's own writings begin again when the *Life* reaches the year 1678, and continue in one form or another until the late

1690s. The years prior to his accession are treated more fully, but it is the Duke's time in Brussels and Scotland, and his escape from the wreck of the *Gloucester*, which receive the greatest attention. Significantly, the majority of the original documents cited are extracts from James's correspondence and later memoranda, rather than his own personal reminiscences. This once again constrains the style and immediacy of the writing, breaking up the flow of the narrative and rendering it of less interest to historians than otherwise might have been the case. It is not important here to catalogue all the writings covering the period after James came to the throne, except to pick out two of his thematic and reflective works – his *Devotional Papers* and his *Advice to his Son* – which were included in the *Life*, and which have a direct relevance for our own study.

James's *Devotional Papers* were written during the last decade of his life, when religious matters began to weigh increasingly heavily upon his mind. He intended them not only to demonstate his own faith, but also to inform and educate as many people as possible about the truths – as he saw them – of Roman Catholicism. These are the only remnants of James's authorized biography to have survived in their original form, and in the King's own hand. Extracts from them were incorporated into the *Life*, while the full text was republished in 1925.[57] They are of use to us in several ways. First, they demonstrate how James came to form his strong religious beliefs and provide us with the fullest account of his conversion experience of 1669–72. Second, because they survive in James's own handwriting, they can reveal the manner in which he worked. His *Devotions* consist of odd scraps of paper with ideas randomly jotted down, as and when they occurred to him. Consequently, his writings lack a clear structure and a strong central theme. His thoughts are seldom fully explored and are never pursued for more than a few pages, at any one time. This *ad hoc* practice of note-making goes a long way to explain the variable quality of the *Life*, and necessitated the many editorial revisions and additions made to James's original writings. Lastly, if James's literary style had made the role of the editor essential, then the survival of the *Devotional Papers* should allow us to gauge Dicconson's authenticity as a transcriber: allowing us to compare the original texts with those set down in the *Life*. As the two sources match up very well we have some grounds for believing, that in this section at least, Dicconson's citations were accurate copies from the original memoirs.[58]

In his *Advice to his Son*, James set down all those qualities which he believed that a successful prince should possess. To his mind, a ruler should labour tirelessly for the benefit of the nation: seeking every possible opportunity to enrich it and to expand its frontiers, while protecting the people from all forms of foreign aggression and domestic discord. He laid great stress upon virtue, urging his son to be a faithful and constant Prince who should, on no account, abandon the Roman Catholic faith. Although the public duties and proper concerns of a king and the art of statecraft were discussed at length, it is interesting to note that among these traditional admonitions James should now pay considerable attention to the question of trade and how best to foster it. After emphasizing his own role in encouraging commerce, James urged his son to 'study the Trade of the Nation and encourage it by all lawful means, tis that which will make you at ease at home and considerable abroad'. Moreover, in highlighting the need for a strong navy in order to 'preserve the mastery of the seas', James had, if nothing else, managed to recognize the crucial link between trade and sea-power. Implicit in his argument is the need for an effective administrative system in order to implement the wishes of the monarch and a large, and powerful, naval establishment with which to enforce them. Dicconson, as the probable compiler of the notes, expands upon these themes in his final summary of James's character, claiming that trade 'was so peculiarly his care, that never Prince understood it better'.[59]

This would seem, at first sight, to make a powerful case for James's direct involvement as a patron of trade and these passages have certainly been seized upon as conclusive evidence for his support of the mercantalist system. However, the source of these claims can be found in the writings of a series of Tory propagandists and pamphleteers operating from the 1690s through into the early years of the eighteenth century. For the most part these were the works of dispossessed placemen, written against the background of high levels of taxation levied to pay for William III's foreign wars, and were often published with the help and guidance of the exiled Jacobite court. They were aimed at a mixed audience and catered for the nostalgia of the older generation for a lost world, and for the curiosity of the younger age groups, who remembered little about the last of the Stuart Kings. They were united by their intensely nationalistic tone and in their attempts to establish James's military credentials as the benchmark by which all other, subsequent, kings of England should be judged. Their approach and emphasis served to reinforce the consensual view of James's interests in trade and Empire, which was adopted by Dicconson. This, too, has been picked up once again and channelled, sometimes a little uncritically, by the King's modern apologists.[60]

These statements on their own are clearly not enough to substantiate James's claims to military and commercial pre-eminence, one way or the other, and need to be investigated further. Before we do so, we need to ask ourselves why James himself should want to talk up his successes in these fields. It must be remembered that when James was writing these passages he did so, not as the Duke of York but as an exiled King, in the wake of his disastrous naval expedition of 1692. Forced into print by essentially pragmatic reasons, the *Advice to his Son* was intended to serve as James's last political testament: a justification of his own actions, a manifesto for his supporters and a conduct guide for his little son. After his failure to recapture the Crown, and with French support on the wane, James had given up all hope of returning to the throne himself. Yet he continued to believe that his son might be restored at a later date, and aware that he might not live long enough to raise his young second family, he wanted to guarantee that his heir was brought up according to his wishes and as befitted his station. To this end James was writing with the benefit of hindsight, not only of his own failings – which he might have wished to disguise – but also of the trade boom of the late 1680s and 1690s. Having led the Navy for most of the two previous decades and directed national policy over the middle years of the 1680s, James might, with some justification, have felt cheated of the credit due to him for an unprecedented financial and commercial expansion, which rested squarely upon the performance of the maritime trades. It seemed to James and to many of his supporters, including the prolific Mr Pepys, that William of Orange had undeservedly inherited such a promising economic situation. It was, therefore, with an eye to redressing the balance in this particular area, and to make explicit his claim to having governed as a financially prudent King, that James sat down to compose this section of his memoirs in the winter of 1692.[61]

If we accept that James's work was politically motivated by considerations far removed from those of the 1660s and 1670s, then we also need to be aware of the fact that his idea of compiling a book of instructions for his heir was by no means an original concept by the closing years of the seventeenth century. Louis XIV had written a similar work for the Dauphin, and the Sun King's style of writing and method of keeping little notes, or 'carnets' which could be added to later, mirrored James's practice exactly. It seems more than likely that during the time of his last exile, which he spent as Louis's pensioner and confidant, James could not have failed to have been influenced by the example of his more illustrious cousin. Furthermore, it appears that James followed the broad plan and chapter headings of Louis's work and that in some places the *Advice to his Son* is highly derivative, with homilies and commonplaces culled from the standard conduct books of the day. The experience of living and working in close proximity to the highly centralized government of the French State, which was then at the zenith of its power, may also have coloured James's thoughts. Therefore as with the purely narrative accounts included in the *Life*, the *Advice to his Son* can be seen as telling us far more about his ideas at a later, rather than an earlier, stage of his intellectual development.[62]

However, given the destruction of the majority of James's original papers, and despite its drawbacks in covering the years 1660–78, the *Life* has to assume a primary importance in our study of his time spent as Duke of York. No other source can claim a similar wealth of biographical detail, or comes as close to portraying his thoughts and actions as he himself had wished them to be seen. Every one of his subsequent biographers has drawn upon it extensively and, as has been already demonstrated, its emphasis and wilful omissions have done much to shape their approach to, and understanding of, James's early career. James's motivations for writing in the first place, and his son's for collating the material into its present form, have never been properly examined and as a result its role as propaganda has often been ignored. This has led to an unquestioning acceptance of the *Life* as representing an accurate picture of James's actions and motivations as Duke. This is far from being the case. Moreover, it is clear that any fresh study of the Duke of York cannot progress any further without moving outside of the narrow interpretative guidelines provided for it by James and his editors. There is a pressing need, therefore, to look elsewhere for information to supplement our existing knowledge of the Duke's activities, and the range and scope of his commitments.

VI

Our task in reconstructing James's career is helped immeasurably by the nature of his political and social position, and also by the sheer length of time he spent at the heart of government. This allows us to chart the long-term growth of policy advanced under his direction and ensures that there is a wealth of documentary evidence – from official reports, memoranda and letters, to personal diaries and narratives – at our disposal. As a major figure, constantly in the public eye, popular interest in his naval reforms, military experience and commercial ventures manifested itself in a stream of ballads, broadsides and invitations to participate in the flotations of those joint-stock companies which he sponsored.[63] Moreover, the benefit of hindsight may be largely exorcised by referring to James's extant correspondence and comparing the evidence of his day-to-day concerns, contained therein, with the summary of his interests and achievements set down, during his last years in exile, in the pages of the *Life*. It is extremely fortunate, therefore, that James was a diligent letter writer and that his nephew, William, had both the presence of mind and the sheer political acumen to file them away upon receipt, thus preserving them for his own future reference and for the benefit of a wider posterity. As a result, a great deal of James's private correspondence still survives, with the largest number of his letters, written to the Prince of Orange – from February 1674 to February 1679 and then again from October 1682 through to his accession and the final rupture in their relations – being held at the Public Record Office in Kew. Another portion of this correspondence, running from late October 1678 to the beginning of November 1679, was bought up by a private collector in the eighteenth century and was reprinted by the Historical Manuscripts Commission, as *The Manuscripts of the Right Honourable F.J. Savile Foljambe of Osberton* (London, 1897).[64]

Many of the surviving personal letters exchanged between Charles II, his natural daughter, the Countess Litchfield, and James were transcribed by Viscount Dillon and published at the turn of the century in the *Archaeologia* journal (vol. LVIII, 1902, pp. 153–88). Other sizeable collections of the Duke's letters are to be found in the Bodleian Library, Oxford, and at the British Library in London.[65] However, even though James appears to have been a very prolific letter writer, these sources have been somewhat neglected by his biographers.[66] This is largely due to the nature of the letters themselves. James wrote only when he felt it to be absolutely necessary, in order to address a particular topic, voice a grievance, or to achieve a purpose. Consequently, his letters are brief, straightforward, and have a highly factual content, which, in stark contrast to the *Life*, reveals little that is dramatic or personal. These sources do, however, tell us a great deal about James's interests and anxieties, revealing his concern about the underground republican movement of the 1660s, his desire for a field command a decade later, and his thoughts on the politics of the court.[67] If his later correspondence contained in these collections has been used successfully in order to examine the issues surrounding the Revolution of 1688/9 and to throw light upon his destructive relationship with his nephew, once he had become King, then there is no reason why the earlier – and less well-known – sections of James's letters should not be thoroughly employed in order to inform our own conception of his aims and objectives as Duke of York.

In addition to his writings, the financial accounts for James's household also exist, and though they do not provide us with a continuous run or inventory, they do provide snapshots of the life and evolution of his personal establishment at its significant junctures. The earliest records running from the early to the late 1660s are kept at the John Rylands Library in Manchester, the next series covering the Duke's Commission of Revenue in the 1670s are at Cambridge University, while the later period from 1677 until 1682 are covered by two account books held in the British Library.[68] These are invaluable as they enable us to reconstruct the nature and rhythms of James's household, enabling us to see how it was administered, and providing us with lists of the Duke's companions and dependants.

Having thus gauged the complexion of James's circle of friends and clients, it is also possible to investigate their thoughts and recollections by consulting their own written records and memoirs. Churchill, Coventry, the younger Jermyn, Legge, Littleton and Talbot all left behind them significant caches of papers.[69] To these can be added the literary remains of James's immediate family: his wives, his eldest daughter Mary, his natural son the Duke of Berwick, and his father-in-law the Earl of Clarendon.[70] Then there are the works and reminiscences of many of his placemen, who served him in differing capacities throughout his career. Amongst these Samuel Pepys and William Petty are the outstanding examples, as they compiled not only biographical materials but also detailed accounts of their services at the Admiralty and reflections upon the methods, and abilities, of the Duke himself.[71] Finally, there are the more general observers of events with whom James had contact; these included such vitally important writers as John Evelyn, Lorenzo Magalotti, John Reresby and, of course, Bishop Burnet.[72]

It is important to remember that the sheer range and scope of the Duke's commitments, which encompassed everything from official imperial and naval duties to purely private and mercenary financial concerns, requires the historian to make use of a similarly diverse collection of source materials in order to be able to chart them effectively. There is no single, well-trodden, archive or set of papers that will provide the reader with a definitive account of all of his interests as Duke. This is one very significant deterrent that may have prevented previous researchers and biographers from looking any further into James's early career. Fortunately, although this makes the task much harder, it is by no means impossible. As a public figure, the Duke's actions, and the official publications issued under his hand as Lord High Admiral and proprietor of New York have been preserved among the State papers held at the Public Record Office, the British Library and the National Maritime Museum.[73] A large number of these documents, including some items which exist only in American and Canadian research institutions, have been reprinted by the Naval Records Society, the New York Historical Society and the Champlain Society.[74] Copious manuscript sources exist covering the operation of the different joint-stock companies in which James invested, and the Royal African and Hudson's Bay Companies in particular. These are to be found in the Company Registers at the Public Record Office. The foundation charters of these organizations are reproduced in C.T. Carr's *Select Charters of the Trading Companies* (London, 1913), while the originals of these, together with many seventeenth-century advertisements and tracts discussing the projects sponsored by the joint-stock companies, are to be found in the British Library.[75]

With recourse to these sources, a new examination of James's formative years, from his birth to his accession to the throne, can not only be made possible but can also seek to place the Duke of York firmly back within his own historical context; and to study him in his own terms, free from later accretions and the hindsight provided by the knowledge of the events which toppled him from power in 1688–9. In this light, it will become clear that the accepted view of James's early career, enshrined by the text of the *Life*, has thoroughly distorted the later historiography of both Prince and period, and bears little relation to the wider historical record. Stripped of the protection of his own words, and those of his hired propagandists and modern apologists, the Duke's legacy can be seen to become altogether darker and more questionable. Furthermore, through the use of case studies which examine James's impact as soldier, administrator, imperialist and entrepreneur, it will become apparent that the career of the Duke of York, throughout the whole of the Restoration period, was characterized by a remarkable continuity of both executive decision and practical action: shedding new light on the long-term objectives of this fascinating – if troubled – individual, and examining those courses of action open to him as both Prince and politician.

CHAPTER TWO

The Child of State

On 24 November 1633, candles burned brightly in the chapel of St James's Palace as a new royal baby was baptized. The winter's gloom was all but forgotten as courtiers and aldermen pressed forward to offer their gifts and to watch as the diminutive figure of William Laud, Archbishop of Canterbury, anointed the child. Named in honour of his grandfather, and bestowed with the dukedoms of York and Albany in order to symbolize the union of the English and Scottish Crowns, little Prince James had already survived the first few perilous weeks of childhood and had quickly been judged to be a fair and 'lusty' infant, capable of reaching maturity.[1]

Even though he had no way of knowing it at the time, the circumstances surrounding his baptism reflected, in microcosm, many of the political and doctrinal conflicts which were to dominate his entire adult life. The sumptuous chapel at St James's had been newly redecorated in keeping with the Archbishop's radical reforms of the Church of England; elaborate choral music accompanied the bearing of the child to the font, while Laud's own vestments spoke – louder than any words – of a determination to implement thorough-going change in both the liturgy and religious practice of the established Church. Although, as yet, the Archbishop's personal ambition and energetic championing of the Arminian cause had met with only scattered, and ill co-ordinated resistance, the choice of godparents for the child cradled in his arms was a symptom of the deeper religious tensions which tore at the fabric of European society and which had already plunged much of the continent into a cycle of bloody sectarian wars.

To the delight of the Londoners, who pealed their church bells to mark the occasion and fired salvos from the decks of the merchantmen moored in the Thames, Prince James's godparents were emphatically Protestant, chosen from the small, and increasingly beleaguered, section of continental royalty which still espoused the Reformed faith. His aunt, Elizabeth the 'Winter' Queen of Bohemia, had been toppled from her throne by the armies of the Counter Reformation, while her son, Charles Louis – who also stood as sponsor to the child – sought in vain for English troops and ever-increasing subsidies with which to continue the struggle. Frederick Henry, Prince of Orange, stood as the last of the child's godparents. He too was beset by the affairs of State and, like his co-sponsors, chose to send deputies to the christening in his place. Significantly, to the minds of Protestant Englishmen, the Dutch Republic – over which he presided – offered the prospect of religious liberty and a proud tradition of successful resistance against Catholic Spain. In such a light, it might almost seem as if the fortunes of Stuart and Orange were to be linked, inextricably, from the very first.[2]

Noticeably absent from the proceedings were the parents of the new Duke of York. Although James was to be presented to them later in the day, both King Charles I and his consort, Queen Henrietta Maria, had already set the pattern for their future relationship with their second son. While it has become fashionable to stress the stable and loving family background enjoyed by the children of Charles and Henrietta Maria, the concept of the royal household as a 'closely knit' and decidely modern 'nuclear family', is both inaccurate and grossly misleading. For the most part, the King and Queen appeared only as distant figures to their children, far removed from the concerns of the nursery; to be seen on great State occasions and always in the presence of other people: namely nursemaids, tutors and courtiers. It was determined, therefore, that James was to be raised, along with his elder brother Charles, the Prince of Wales, in the relative seclusion of a separate 'children's' Court at Richmond in Surrey.[3] There, troubled only by a brief controversy over the faith professed by one of his wet nurses, he disappears from our view under the capable – and perhaps more importantly Protestant – care of his governess, the Countess of Dorset.

When he does re-emerge it is as a plump-faced infant in the huge canvasses of Van Dyck, hemmed in on either side by his numerous brothers and sisters. However, despite this relatively passive and undistinguished introduction to public life, he quickly acquired a well-defined personality of his own. The hopes of court hagiographers, such as Herrick, who sought to weave pastoral verses about his childish exploits were to be dashed all too soon. The hope that James would grow: 'Like t' a Rose of Jehrico', with even the fall of his soft foot being the occasion for gardens of flowers to spring up and bloom in the wilderness, was pushed aside and was replaced by an altogether more robust and practical vision of the Prince's achievements.[4] This change in emphasis may well have been in line with conscious royal policy. Henrietta Maria had informed the Savoyard Ambassador of her husband's displeasure at the unveiling of Van Dyck's first great portrait of their children, in 1635. Depicted in childish clothes and naive postures, the infants appeared to have been brought straight from the laps of their nursemaids to the artist's studio.

Unfortunately, while the composition might have the power to charm the modern observer, for a Stuart sovereign conscious of the need to protect the quasi-divine aura of monarchy this attempt at naturalism was

wholly inappropriate and fundamentally unacceptable. In evoking the
cult of the family, Charles I desired that the presence of his children in
official portraiture should augment his own image of regal solemnity,
underline the permanence of his dynasty and serve as living proof of the
bounty and fruitfulness of his reign. Consequently, in later canvasses the
mistake was corrected. All childish allusions were banished, and the little
Princes and Princesses assumed the attitude and demeanour of their
elders. Henceforth they would appear as though they were miniature
adults, fully formed in terms of their interests and intellects, if not in
their exact physical proportions.[5] As a result, James can be seen to stare
out of his early portraits with a wisdom and a self-awareness which far
exceeds his years. However this thoughtful disposition, which sometimes
appears to verge upon the melancholic, would often seem to be wholly at
odds with the strenuous activities in which he is shown to be engaging.
The first engravings of the Duke, printed to commemorate his actions,
reveal him to have been an extremely active child who, in the words of
one contemporary, 'cared not to plod upon his games; for his active soul
was more delighted with quick and nimble recreations, as running,
leaping [and] riding'. A work by Mesians shows him at play on a real
tennis court, racket in hand, while Hollar drew him as a child-General,
old beyond his years, galloping out at the head of his own regiment (see
Plate 2). In the light of this evidence, there would seem to have been the
intention from the very first that James should pursue a military career.
This feeling is positively reinforced by the existence of a pair of matching
portraits, of the Prince of Wales and the Duke of York, commissioned
from Cornelius Johnson around 1639–40.[6] While Prince Charles is shown
as a civilian gentleman, relaxed and thoroughly at ease with his sur-
roundings, James clutches at a miniature pistol as huntsmen pursue a
stag to its destruction.

The problem of finding a suitable career for the King's younger son
was one which had perennially taxed ruling dynasties from the Bourbons
and Stuarts, in the West, to the Ottomans and Moghuls in the East.
Religion and warfare provided fitting opportunities for advancement in
the service of the monarchy, but for the overlooked or under-employed
Prince, rebellion could soon prove attractive and beckon. However, in
the case of Charles I and the Duke of York, it was a dilemma which was
easily solved by the fortunate conjuncture of hard political realities with
the boy's own lively predisposition. The post of Lord High Admiral,
created by the Tudors and strengthened by the Stuarts, had fallen vacant
after the assassination of the Duke of Buckingham and was known to be
coveted by Algernon Percy, the young and ambitious Earl of
Northumberland. With his naval reforms frustrated by the seeming
inability of the local authorities to collect the projected 'ship monies',

and with localized resistance to this new form of taxation rising, Charles I looked to Northumberland to rebuild his battle fleet and to provide the energetic leadership necessary to halt the depredations of the North African pirates who were raiding the South coast, virtually at will. The King knew Percy to be both able and charismatic, but feared the might of this powerful and singularly well-connected Northern magnate. Eager to bind him more closely to the politics of the Court and to ensure his long-term loyalty, Charles I chose to revive the title of Lord Admiral and to settle the command of the battle fleet upon him.[7] However, whereas all previous appointments to the post had been made for life, the King now decided to limit Percy's tenure of office and to make it wholly conditional, and dependent upon, his own royal 'pleasure'. In order to lessen the impact of this very public snub, it was felt that a distinction should now be drawn between the ranks of Lord Admiral and Lord High Admiral. If a decidedly uncontroversial figure, with no strong political following, could be found to fill the latter, more senior, office – and to hold it in a purely titular capacity – then the security of the Crown and the pride of the Percy family could both be guaranteed. The King's second son, who had barely been breached, seemed to present the ideal candidate and was duly raised to the Lord High Admiralcy at a session of the Privy Council in April 1638.[8] The appointment of a four-and-a-half year old child to such a prestigious office was quite unprecedented, but was a compromise measure which initially worked well and satisfied the competing factions at Court. Moreover, the implicit understanding that Percy was to hold the Navy in trust for the Duke of York, and that the practical administration of the service could be transferred to James once he had reached his majority, served to effectively limit the nobleman's room for manoeuvre while reinforcing the power of his sovereign to control and direct military affairs.

Well provided for by Charles I, with both a source of future income and an important role in the defence of the kingdom, there is no reason to accept at face value Bishop Burnet's famous assertion that James was a: 'prince . . . much neglected in his childhood, during the years of his father's care'. He was taught to write legibly and could spell adequately enough, acquiring, under the tutelage of the elderly Marquis of Hertford, many of those social skills thought necessary for his exalted social station. A generous allowance provided him with fencing, archery and dancing masters; while, besides his brother Charles, he found ready playmates in the shape of George and Francis Villiers. The orphaned sons of the Duke of Buckingham had been declared royal wards and were raised, on the orders of King Charles I, alongside his own boys at Richmond.[9] However, while the Prince of Wales struck up a firm friendship with the elder boy which continued into adulthood, James does not seem to have formed a close or lasting attachment to either of his noble companions at this time, and in later years would come to hate and fear the influence of George Villiers upon the councils of State. Acutely aware of his brother's more important status within the monarchy, as heir to the throne, James was already prepared to stand on ceremony in order to ensure that his 'rights' were preserved and displayed a keen competitive edge in all of his dealings with Prince Charles. When Nicholas Ferrar, one of Archbishop Laud's most creative and capable protégés, presented a richly illustrated Bible to the Prince of Wales in Holy Week 1640, it was left to the little Duke of York to strike an awkward note. While his brother excitedly unwrapped his gift and leafed absently through its pages, James asked where his own present was and enquired of Ferrar if he, too, could have a Bible made for him that would be the equal of Charles's.[10]

It would seem, therefore, that – sibling rivalry aside – the two royal brothers, raised and educated together, were subject to the same set of early formative influences. However, it is significant that at precisely the time when he might have been expected to reap the full benefits of a comprehensive social and political education at the court of Whitehall, the storm clouds of civil war began to gather and threatened James's hitherto cosseted existence. While news of the Prayer Book Rebellion and the defeat of his father's armies in Scotland found only a distant echo for James, at play in Richmond, he could not hope to ignore the sound of the great popular tumults emanating from London. The townsfolk, spurred on by gangs of sailors and crop-haired apprentice boys, attempted to storm William Laud's palace at Lambeth, while within the year – across the river at Westminster – the newly reconvened Parliament sat in judgement upon both the King's Chief Counsellor, the Earl of Strafford, and his divisive Archbishop. As the political situation deteriorated month by month, a popular rising by the Gaelic Irish devastated the plantations worked by the new settlers and threatened to sweep away English rule in Ireland altogether. Rumours of plots and counter-plots circulated freely in London, as the crowds – unappeased by the death of Strafford and the imprisonment of Laud – thronged the streets and called for the King to take firmer action against the Irish rebels. Deprived of his most able adviser – whom he had forsaken – and abandoning the more thoughtful and temperate courses of action left available to him, Charles I now attempted a *coup d'état* in order to rid himself of his most vehement Parliamentary critics. His disastrous military intervention on the floor of the House of Commons on 4 January 1642 meant that, even as the Five Members were being spirited away to safety, moderate parliamentary opinion turned decisively against him and his tenuous hold on the governance of the City was lost.

Henceforth, the capital no longer provided a safe haven for the royal family.[11] To avoid a possible upsurge in violence, the King removed himself to Hampton Court before embarking on a long journey, in search of fresh support, to the North. He took with him the Prince of Wales and dispatched the Queen, a particular target for popular hatred on account of her aggressive and proselytizing Roman Catholicism, on an arms-buying mission to France. The younger royal children were, however, simply transferred from their apartments in Whitehall to the comparative safety of St James's Palace, there to wait upon events. Amid the confusion, the fate of the Duke of York was initially overlooked. James was taken back to his own household at Richmond, and it was not until March 1642 that the King thought to send word for his second son to join him. By early spring, Charles I laboured under few illusions about the need to try to preserve the peace in England. He had busied himself raising and arming troops in Yorkshire, and had attempted to reassert his control over the local militias. Convinced that his quarrel with Parliament could only be resolved through force, he now sought to take James back into his care, lest the boy should be seized by his enemies and used as a bargaining counter against him. Parliament had, in fact, issued orders to the Marquis of Hertford for him to confine the Duke of York to Richmond.[12] However, he ignored them and chose instead to answer the King's summons, setting off to accompany James on the long road to York.

The safe arrival of James and his tutor at the Northern city was the cause of great celebration; bonfires were raised by the King's supporters and Charles I chose to mark his reunion with his son by investing him with the Order of the Garter.[13] Moreover, as a mark of his increasing importance to the royal cause, and as an indication of the mounting dangers he faced, a personal escort was assigned to protect him. Unfortunately, the value of these gentlemen recruits was shown to be sadly lacking at their first test. During the Scots wars the port of Hull had served as an enormous supply depot for arms and munitions, and the King was not slow to realize its potential value for equipping an army. Spurred into action by Parliament's demands that the arsenal should be broken up and shipped back to London and the Tower, for safe-keeping, Charles I determined to seize it for himself. Maintaining the pretence that he wished only to reinforce troops already destined for service in Ireland, he arrived outside Hull's Beverley Gate and sent the eight-and-a-half year old Duke of York on ahead to parley with the Governor. King Charles had good reason to think that his pre-emptive strike, combining diplomacy with the veiled threat of physical force, would meet with every success. The Lord Mayor and the majority of the citizens of Hull were known to harbour strong Royalist sympathies, and had already tried to resist the garrisoning of the fortress by Parliamentarian troops. Furthermore, although he had been appointed to his office by the Commons, the position and loyalty of the Governor, Sir John Hotham – as regarding his sovereign – was extremely ambiguous. The appearance of the Duke of York inside the city walls was, therefore, calculated to allay his fears and to preserve an illusion of normality in deeply troubled times.[14]

However, Charles I had seriously miscalculated and while James and his companions sat down to dinner, the city gates were firmly locked and barred behind them. An attempt by the Lord Mayor to throw the keys to the fortress down to the King's men was prevented by the prompt action of the garrison, who sounded the alarm and turned out on to the walls, fully armed and prepared to resist any attempt to take the ramparts by storm. The resolve of the soldiers, in effectively taking matters into their own hands, ruled out the chance of a negotiated settlement and forced the Governor's hand. To the fury of the King, Hotham politely explained that he held the city in the name of Parliament and could not possibly grant him, and his numerous followers, entry to the place. Without a siege train with which to enforce his will upon the rebellious garrison, Charles I was forced to set up camp within sight of the gateway and to embark upon a humiliating round of negotiations aimed at securing the freedom of his son. It was some hours before James and his companions, who included his godfather Prince Charles Louis, came to realize the seriousness of their predicament.[15] Though treated with the utmost courtesy and respect by Hotham, the two days spent under protective custody at Hull came as a great shock to the Duke of York. He reflected in later years that his father should have moved more decisively at the first hint of trouble, entrusting the Duke's own equerries to seize the walls and to 'secure' Hotham, or else to have him murdered and quietly disposed of. Although James confidently asserted that 'Either would have done the work', given the presence in the city of a well-trained and highly motivated group of soldiers whose only opposition consisted of a handful of courtiers and Yorkshire gentlemen, this would seem to have been a particularly high-risk strategy and one which would, almost certainly, have led to disaster.[16] The danger of losing both his young son and the Elector Palatine in what might have quickly degenerated into a bloody street brawl, or worse still a summary lynching, was too dreadful for King Charles to even contemplate. The need for patient diplomacy was lost on James and he took away from the incident an exaggerated belief in the efficacy of military action to solve any given problem. It is noticeable that the *Life* in concluding its account of the action at Beverley Gate delights in the details of Hotham's subsequent fall from grace with Parliament, and the execution of him and his son as traitors to their cause.[17] While James may have felt that a peculiar form of justice had been served upon the pair for their earlier disobedience to their King, the fact remains that at the time of their death both of the Hothams were conspiring to actively aid the Royalist war effort. James's personal animus towards the father and son overrode the wider consideration of their political usefulness, and all thoughts of conciliation and long-term gain. Only the memory of a personal slight and a first, unwelcome, taste of imprisonment endured with him into adulthood.

With the release, one by one, of the Duke and his companions, it was a humbled King Charles who abandoned his positions outside the fortress and withdrew to the town of Beverley for the night. He had quickened the pace of events and raised the political stakes only to lose out in the initial test of strength with an increasingly militant Parliament. For the remainder of the spring, and throughout the summer months, the Duke of York followed in the wake of his father and the embryonic Royalist Army, scouring Yorkshire, the Welsh borders and the Midlands in the search for weapons – to replace those denied to them at Hull – and for new recruits. He saw the Royal Standard unfurled at Nottingham, signalling the commencement of hostilities, and in late October 1642 – from a vantage point high up on the slopes of Edgehill – he witnessed the opening battle of the English Civil Wars. Excited by the prospect of a decisive encounter, he rode forward with the Prince of Wales: mingling with cheering troops until ordered to retire by the King.[18] Narrowly avoiding capture at the hands of a body of Parliamentarian horse, who had broken through the Royalist lines at the onset of the fighting, James could only watch as the battle degenerated into a series of localized clashes, spread out right across the Warwickshire plain. As the two sides fought each other to a standstill, James later recalled that: 'The foot being thus ingaged in such warm and close service, it were reasonable to imagine that one side should run and be disorder'd; but it happened otherwise, for each as if by mutuall consent retired some few paces, and . . . stuck down their coulours, continuing to fire at one another even till night.' The 'rawnes and unexperience of both partys had not furnished them with skill to make the best use of their advantages' and any chance of a conclusive victory, which would end the war and send the King back in triumph to his capital, was lost in the evening chill amid the screams of the wounded and the dying.[19]

The impact of the battle affected Charles I and the Duke of York in very different ways. While James came to regard the action as his baptism of fire, an occasion for glory and heroism, the King perceived it to be a tragedy and dwelt, gloomily, upon the loss of so many of his friends. Wrapped up in his coach against the frost, Charles rejected calls from Prince Rupert and his commanders to follow up their 'victory' and to pursue the enemy all the way back to London. As the Earl of Essex slipped away, with the bulk of the Parliamentarian Army still intact, the

King squandered his initiative and – checked at Turnham Green – was obliged to regroup his forces in the centre of his kingdom. With London denied to him, King Charles chose Oxford as his new capital. Commanding the major road networks, the city was surrounded by fertile arable land, capable of supporting a large – and rapidly increasing – civil and military population for the duration of the conflict.

It was here, amid the cloisters and grand public buildings of the medieval university, that James was to spend the overwhelming majority of the next three-and-a-half years. However, the Prince's stay at Oxford was to be anything but secluded and scholarly. The College greens resounded to the noise of drilling troops, horses were stabled in the lodgings of the dons and artillery pieces were cast afresh, from bronze church bells, in buildings which until recently had been home to the School of Rhetoric. An unwilling citizenry, opposed to the university and the Royalist soldiers alike, were forced to work long hours at strengthening the city's defences. Trees were felled in order to gain an improved field of fire and an impressive earthen bulwark was thrown up at St Giles's, as the city came more accurately to resemble an armed camp rather than a refined seat of learning. The residential areas soon became overcrowded with place-seekers, soldiers and refugees, and Oxford society became a veritable melting pot of people and ideas.[20] Gentlemen who had previously been separated by geography and confined to a narrow parochialism by the politics of their own communities, found common ground in the service of their King. United by the personal and financial losses they had had to suffer in order to fully prosecute the war, and to demonstrate the strength of their loyalty to Charles's person, the brand of High Anglican, ultra-Royalist, politics espoused by these Cavaliers quickly came to dominate the intellectual life of wartime Oxford. It would be surprising, indeed, if every new defeat had not hardened their resolve or if James himself had not been influenced by both their thinking and their eventual plight.

Although Charles I had appointed a succession of worthy and learned tutors to the Duke, there is little evidence to suggest that either Bishop Duppa or any of his successors, drawn from among the Fellows of the Oxford colleges, had any lasting or significant impact upon James's character and intellectual development. For a Prince who never 'minded to make study his business, being so averse from prying upon his book', lessons and the protracted lectures delivered by his tutors came off a poor second best to the exciting tales of the latest daring cavalry raid, or infantry skirmish, to be had from officers returning from the fray.[21] If James was still too young to lead, in person, the regiments which bore his name, then sports and hunting, in particular, offered a welcome release for his pent-up energy and aggression. Charles I wrote despairingly that he hoped that, in the future, the boy would 'ply his book more and his gun less'. Doubtless this well-meaning piece of advice was as roundly ignored as all the other, highly moralistic, admonitions which punctuated the King's correspondence to his sons. Away on campaign for long periods of the year, his time thoroughly consumed by the grim necessities of fighting a civil war, Charles remained a remote figure to James. Unwilling to jeopardize the safety of his son, the King preferred to keep him rooted at Oxford – the most secure of all the great Royalist cities – far removed from the dangers of the battlefield and the squalor of a tented camp.[22] The exception to this policy came in the summer of 1643, when James accompanied his father to the siege lines before Gloucester.

With the storming of Bristol, success in the field, and the capitulation of a series of Parliamentarian strongholds in the West, the Royalist cause had reached its highwater mark. Weakened by internal divisions, the Commons seemed to be losing its grip on military affairs with the result that a significant number of its senior commanders now looked to secure terms from the King, while they still had both the time and the freedom to be able to negotiate from a position of strength. Nathaniel Fiennes had already been seen to lead the way in surrendering to Prince Rupert, and – like the Hothams before him – Edward Massey, the Governor of Gloucester, was now fully expected to swing his allegiance firmly behind the King. Believing that Massey's allegiance had already been won, and that the surrender of the city would be little more than a formality – to be accomplished by the issuing of a summons and through the stroke of the pen – it was with every confidence that Charles I led his Army out of their quarters in Oxford and set them upon the road West. He knew full well that the fall of Gloucester would send shock-waves through the Parliamentarian cause, prompting more desertions and removing the last obstacle to the Royalist Field Armies from moving unchallenged between their new conquest of Bristol and their valuable recruiting grounds in South Wales. Moreover, a propaganda triumph could be achieved in the staging of a magnanimous entry into the city, in the company of his two eldest sons. The virtue of monarchical principles could be restated and the unity of the dynasty displayed, while – in offering the citizens clemency – the King could send a powerful message of support to those Londoners whose loyalty to Parliament had begun to waiver.

Then, as now, Massey's primary motivation for entering into negotiations with the Royalists remains unclear. It may well have been that he was doing no more than toying with King Charles, hoping to delay his march until such a time as a Parliamentarian Army could come to his aid. However, his later conduct and ultimate defection to the Royalists does tend to suggest that he seriously contemplated shifting his allegiances in July and August of 1643. What caused him to break off negotiations and to decide to mount a vigorous defence of the city is equally unclear. He was not subject to the same pressure from an unruly garrison as Sir John Hotham had been, and it may well be that it was the combination of a failure by Charles I to offer him sufficiently attractive concessions and the promptings of his own strong Presbyterian faith which finally led him to embark on such a decisive course of action.

On 10 August, the overtures made by the King's messengers were rejected out of hand by two men of 'lean, pale, sharp, and bald visages', chosen specifically to represent the united interests of the soldiers and citizens of Gloucester.[23] Even though the royal courtiers could afford to mock their shabby appearance, they were no longer left in any doubt as to the resolve of the local Parliamentarians to hold the city until the very end. Assaults were launched upon the suburbs immediately after the rejection of terms and, having been beaten back from the city walls, the Royal Army was forced to settle down to the unwelcome business of conducting a protracted siege. Denied permission to launch a full-scale assault, Prince Rupert sulked about the camp while the King's sons were confined at Matson House, for their own safety. Kept well away from the fighting, closely supervised and denied the company of boys their own age, the siege of Gloucester came to represent a dull affair for both brothers and for James, in particular. He found the thrill of battle, which he had experienced at Edgehill, noticeably lacking in the routine work of throwing up escarpments and digging trenches. In contrast to his powerful description of the first battle that he had witnessed, James – and his editors in the *Life* – chose to pass quickly over the events which transpired at Gloucester and revealed nothing of his thoughts, and feelings, as he waited passively upon events. It would appear that he, and the Prince of Wales, were so thoroughly bored with their situation that they tried to amuse themselves as best they could, and settled down to carving their names into the hard panelling of the great hall.[24]

The monotony was broken, after a fortnight, by a sudden downpour and the unwelcome news that the Earl of Essex was approaching with a strong relieving force. Any chance of a speedy and successful assault was lost overnight, as rains washed away the tunnels dug underneath the walls of the fortress and flooded out the mines which had been laid within. While the garrison took heart in the knowledge that they had gained valuable time, the King was left to survey the muddy ruins of his encampment and to ponder his next course of action. If Gloucester was to fall it would now be as the result of a full-scale confrontation between the Royalist and Parliamentarian Armies. However, an initial trial of strength between Rupert's cavalry and the vanguard of Essex's Army did not prove encouraging, and the King's resolve faltered and failed. Not wishing to hazard everything upon one single clash of arms, he raised the siege and reluctantly withdrew his forces. Denied the chance of seeing another battle with the army of Essex unfold before him, James was seemingly unable to comprehend the failure of his father's campaign. Rather than as the 'boy General' of the popular print, it was as a frightened and bewildered child that he was observed on the Oxford road, begging to know of King Charles when they might cease from their travels and return 'home' to London.[25] Unfortunately for James, his father could offer few words of comfort and 'home' was to remain entirely elusive. There was to be no joyous return to the capital and to the easy comforts, and privileges, of pre-war life. Oxford, as opposed to London, was to form the centre of his world: and it was there that he was to remain lodged until the end of the First Civil War, as a passive witness to the collapse of the Royalist war effort under the weight of comprehensive military defeats and fruitless political recriminations.

While the Prince of Wales was allowed an increasingly independent role, raising morale among the troops and sitting in on the deliberations of the Privy Council, James's existence was far more marginal and his influence extended no further than taking his seat at the shadow Royalist assembly, which convened at Oxford in January 1644. This body, which drew together 83 members of the Lords and 175 MPs who had fled Westminster, was aimed at reinforcing the constitutional legitimacy of the Royalist cause and sought to establish its own authority as a Parliament over that of its rival, and parent body, which sat in London. Unfortunately the assembly's minutes were destroyed lest they fell into enemy hands, along with many other records of the Royalist occupation, when the garrison surrendered in 1646.[26] As a result it is impossible to reconstruct the daily workings and debates of the assembly, or to gauge the levels of James's attendance at it. However, it would appear that the need to serve with the Army or return to their own localities to oversee the war effort there, effectively denuded the body of its members and placed a check upon its exercise of central authority. These constraints, when taken together with its failure to provide an original and independent voice, allowed Parliamentarian writers to dismiss it, all too easily, as a meaningless cipher which existed only in order to implement the wishes of the King. James's first experience of serving on a representative body would, therefore, seem to have been neither auspicious nor particularly rewarding.

As the grip of the Parliamentarian Army on the supply routes into Oxford began to tighten, the role of the assembly became increasingly redundant and news of serious Royalist defeats began to filter through the lines. The Duke of York's regiment of horse was badly mauled at Marston Moor in July 1644, while his regiment of foot was destroyed at Naseby in the June of the following year. With the loss of such a high proportion of his officer corps, and the virtual annihilation of the seasoned infantrymen who formed the backbone of his Army, the King was finally forced to acknowledge the possibility of defeat. A further crushing blow was dealt at the end of the formal campaigning season by Prince Rupert's decision to surrender Bristol to the New Model Army. Believing that Rupert should have done far more to hold on to his prize, the King considered that the port had been 'basely' yielded and broke decisively with his nephew. Fearing treachery from within his own household, he abandoned his former policy over the safe-keeping of his second son and considered how best to have him evacuated from the Royalist capital. Confiding to his Secretary of State that 'none can blame me to venture my children in an army, rather than to be besieged', King Charles urged him to instruct the Duke of York that he was in no way to follow Rupert's ill-example. 'Tell my son', ordered the King, 'that I should be less grieved to hear that he is knocked on the Head, than he should do so mean an action.'[27]

This stern injunction and the growing realization that he was trapped in a stricken city, did much to concentrate James's mind and to strengthen his determination to obey his father's will at all costs. In facing his ruin, this sad and foolish King stood more acutely than ever upon his dignity, and offered defiance to his enemies even as he intrigued with them and attempted to play them off, one against the other. It was this image of the sovereign betrayed, rather than of the mighty European Prince seated at his Court in Whitehall, with which James was familiar and which remained with him into his adult life. The legacy of Charles I as a fallen King, and ultimately as a martyr, was far more potent to his son than that of his achievements during the period of his personal monarchy: a time which James could simply not remember. During the darkest days of the Exclusion, when the Duke had been driven into a second exile by his enemies, he would continue to urge strong action and urged his friends to: 'Remember [the fates of] Edward 2, Richard 2, and the king my father'.[28]

Hoping to gain fresh allies in the form of the Gaelic Irish, King Charles offered to send James to them, in December 1645, as an envoy and a guarantee of his good faith. However, the renewed attempts by local Parliamentarian forces to take Chester and the subsequent fall of the city in February 1646, made both the Duke's flight and the successful landing of an Irish Army quite impossible. A further plan to spirit James out of the country and to deliver him to the safe custody of his mother, in France, was briefly touted before being similarly shelved. While units of the New Model Army closed in around Oxford and began to harry the garrison's outlying pickets, the King placed his last hope for salvation in the ability of Jacob, Lord Astley, to fight his way South, through hostile countryside, and to break the enemy encirclement. Astley and his raw Welsh levies slipped out of Worcester and forded the River Avon, undetected. However, their luck ran out less than a day's march from Oxford, when they were surprised and routed by a better-trained Parliamentarian Army. This defeat effectively set the seal on the city's fate. With no army left in the field to offer the prospect of relief, Charles I now turned to Scotland for support and prepared to abandon the Oxford garrison to its fate. In the early hours of 27 April 1646, having shed his finery and disguised himself as a lowly groom, he rode over Magdalen Bridge and out of Oxford for the last time. His flight to the Scots Commissioners, camped before Newark, had been kept a closely guarded secret even from members of his Privy Council who awoke to find him gone. Furthermore, while he had taken with him two of his closest friends, he had not thought to make provision for the rescue of the Duke of York, and James later wrote – with more than a touch of bitterness – that 'the King had it once in his thoughts to have carried the Duke along with him, but did not'.[29]

Left to fend for himself, James could only watch and wait for the end, as the New Model Army dragged up its heavy siege artillery and prepared to bombard the city into submission. However, both sides realized that the war was already won and lost, and were anxious to avoid the enormous loss of human life which would inevitably result from the storming of such well-defended positions. Consequently, negotiations were quickly entered into and Sir Thomas Fairfax, the Commander-in-Chief of the New Model Army, was prepared to show evidence of his goodwill towards his defeated adversaries.

Food shortages had been a way of life for the citizens of Oxford and starvation was a constant fear. As a result the well-publicized decision to halve the Duke of York's rations had offered Royalist propagandists valuable copy and had signalled James's willingness to endure the same hardships as the common soldiery. In authorizing the despatch of wagon-loads of lamb, butter and game into the city, as a present for the Duke of York, Fairfax aimed, therefore, to do far more than to merely supplement James's diet. While the sight of over-loaded carts rumbling through the streets spoke eloquently to the garrison and citizens, alike, of the ability of the New Model to provision itself effectively during a long siege, Fairfax's gesture of friendship towards the Duke was calculated to bring him within the Army's sphere of influence. The adolescent James was still an unknown quantity who might be moulded to fit the requirements of England's new masters. Moreover, in the absence of his elder brother – who had found a safe haven in the Channel Isles – and of the King himself, who was being held captive by his prospective Scottish allies, James represented an enormously valuable prize.[30] The death of the

Prince in an unnecessary cannonade, or in the uncontrollable fury of a storm, could only serve to redound to the detriment of the New Model Army and its Commanders. It was thus with an eye to the future, rather than out of the exaggerated sense of deference to his office, which James thought he detected, that Fairfax and Cromwell played suit to the Duke of York.

While Prince Rupert and his brother, Maurice – who might have been expected to stand trial for war crimes – were allowed to retire to the Continent and an honourable exile, the terms for the surrender of Oxford demanded that James should be placed under the unconditional control of Parliament. This led to an immediate upheaval in his personal life, with all of his old servants – including a little dwarf to whom he had become particularly attached – being dismissed, and replaced by Parliamentarian nominees whose loyalty was not held in doubt, and who might be expected to exert a far more 'favourable' influence upon his intellectual growth and development. Brought back to London, he was entrusted to the care of Algernon Percy, the Earl of Northumberland, whose good faith had long ago been called into question by Charles I. The King's suspicions had been proved to have been only too well grounded when, at the outbreak of the Civil War, the Earl had proved instrumental in securing the Navy for Parliament. Even though he had been quickly relieved of his command, he had managed to emerge from the conflict with his honour still intact and this factor, when allied to his high social status, enabled him to be presented as the ideal choice for James's Governor.[31] He had already assumed the custody of the Duke's younger siblings, Elizabeth and Henry, and had St James's Palace put at his disposal: to serve as both the children's official residence and *de facto* prison.

It would seem that Percy was equally aware of the enormous opportunities and the dangers which Parliament's bequest had placed upon him. In dealing with his young charges he had to balance the need for their security – from both Royalist and Army plotters, alike – against providing for their comfort and well-being. At the same time, he had to recognize the possibility that political fortunes could change very rapidly and that in years to come any one of his royal wards might find themselves occupying the English throne. Indeed, no sooner had James been handed over to the Earl, than rumours of a plan to crown him as King began to circulate freely. Even Charles I, now removed by his Scottish captors to Newcastle-Upon-Tyne, received word of one such proposition and reacted angrily to the suggestion that he might effect a lasting constitutional settlement – and bring the troubles to an end – by abdicating in favour of the Duke of York. Given the great importance now attached to James by the State, Percy clearly needed to proceed with caution and to avoid offering unnecessary offence to any of the parties concerned. Consequently, he did everything in his power to make James's captivity as comfortable, and as dignified, as was possible under such straitened circumstances. Even though Parliament had granted him ample funds for the maintenance of the Duke, he still chose to assign additional sums from his own private fortune to provide James with the luxury items which he so desired.[32] It was, therefore, highly unfortunate that the Earl's attempts to win the friendship of his charge were almost destroyed by the boy's inability to moderate his temper. Upon learning of his father's imprisonment in Carisbrooke Castle from one of Percy's servants, and having been subsequently rebuked by him for using strong language to greet the unwelcome news, the Duke snatched up a longbow and would have killed the man on the spot had he not been tackled from behind, and wrestled to the floor by other members of the household. The attempted murder of an employee was something which Percy could not simply overlook and, maddened by James's violent behaviour, he threatened to have him whipped like any disobedient scullion. Although it is extremely doubtful if such a punishment was ever carried out, and James maintained a complete silence about the episode in his own writings, it reveals much about the strength of his resentment at the treatment meted out to himself and his father. He keenly felt that the natural social order had been inverted and smarted under the knowledge that the 'rogues' who sat at the Westminster Parliament controlled his fate.[33]

This sense of burning injustice was only fuelled by a series of interviews with his father, which were conducted between June and November 1647, at Hampton Court Palace. King Charles had been moved there in order to facilitate negotiations with the Long Parliament, and Percy – hoping that a settlement was in sight – pushed for visiting rights to be granted to his children. When these were forthcoming, he went even further and offered to remove his wards back from St James's Palace to Syon House, on the outskirts of London. However, while St James's was considered to be the property of the State, Syon House was the Earl's own private residence. It is conceivable, therefore, that behind Percy's stated concern for the royal children to be brought into closer contact with their father, lay the aim of bringing them further under his own control at the expense of Parliamentary authority. Aware of the dangers inherent in loosening their hold over James and his siblings, and the possibility of Percy assuming the mantle of 'kingmaker', the Commons rejected the Earl's offer but allowed the planned visits to go ahead, unhindered. For the first time, James came into close personal contact with his father, unmediated by the need for formality or the adherence to the strict rituals demanded by Court protocol.[34]

The impact of these long interviews upon the Duke of York cannot be overstated. Twice, or even three times a week, he was ushered into the presence of the King and was offered a degree of intimacy, and an insight into the private thoughts of the fallen monarch, which previously would have been unimaginable. The cult of the royal family was firmly re-established as Percy employed Sir Peter Lely to produce a series of paintings to commemorate their meetings, and as Charles I seized the opportunity to stress the need for his family to remain united in the face of adversity (see Plate 3). Realizing that his circumstances might deteriorate at any moment and that he might be called to account for the part he had played in the Civil War, the King 'took great care to instruct his children how to behave themselves, if the worst should befall him'.[35] In this atmosphere of fear and foreboding, Charles's advice to his second son all too easily assumed the form of a dying testament. James was constantly entreated to remain loyal to his elder brother and to obey his wishes without question. He was urged to search for a means of escape at the first possible opportunity and to always hold true to the doctrine – and teachings – of the Church of England, maintaining its rights and preserving the purity of its liturgy. This last admonition was particularly close to the King's heart, as he tried to rationalize his own death and to conceive of it as being a sacrifice offered up for the sake, and preservation, of the Anglican faith. Given James's undoubted love for his father and his willingness to carry out his other commandments to the letter, it would seem surprising that he chose not to follow in the King's devotion to the Established Church. Certainly, Edward Hyde sought after the Restoration to contrast the response of Henry of Gloucester, James's shadowy – and by that time safely dead – younger brother, with the Duke of York's own abandonment of Charles I's religious teachings. While both brothers are shown to have received the same set of instructions, only Henry receives glowing praise for his constancy and virtue in adhering to them. James's response to his father's advice, even though he 'was then about 15 years of age, and so capable of any information or instruction the King thought fit to give him', passes entirely without comment.[36] Rather than accepting that the close confinement – and the subsequent martyrdom – of Charles I was the product of a clash of ideologies, with the King's theology representing a vital element in the unfolding tragedy, it would seem that James's response to the collapse of his father's fortunes was to be couched only in the terms of sheer emotion. It was the experience of seeing the King humbled before his subjects and his willingness to accept his fate with dignity, which struck a deep chord with James. The imprisonment of Charles I had served to win his respect for his father's actions and to reinforce his hatred of the 'popular party' – who had sought to overturn the existing social order – however, the upheavals of the Civil War had not become synonymous, for James, with the fate of Anglicanism. His primary attachment remained to his father and to the

Stuart dynasty, rather than to an abstract set of principles which had been imperfectly transmitted to him by a succession of uninspired tutors.[37]

With the blessing of the King and the valuable assistance of a series of Royalist spies, and sympathizers, James now attempted to effect his escape from Northumberland's custody. Early attempts had already foundered as the result of bad luck and the Duke's ill-health, but matters became far more serious upon the discovery of the secret correspondence which James had maintained with his parents throughout his imprisonment. One of these letters, written to his father at the beginning of 1647, was so well encoded that it could not be cracked by Percy or by any of his servants. James was brought before the Earl, to give an account of his actions, but instead of submitting to his Governor's close questioning he adopted a defiant attitude and refused – under any circumstances – to surrender the key to his cipher. His determination to stand firm and to protect his contacts was, however, to be short-lived and his nerve failed him upon the first serious test. On hearing of the Duke's truculence, the Commons debated how best to proceed against him. He had previously been considered to be no more than a child, who might be manipulated at will and coached to avoid the mistakes of his father, but the receipt of this evidence put an entirely different complexion upon matters. James, like Charles I before him, had gained for himself a reputation for duplicity and wilfulness, and henceforth could not be trusted. Lamenting the failure of any of the royal 'brood' to negotiate fairly or to com-promise, one Member of Parliament was forced to conclude that 'like father, like sons, there is no truth in any of them'.[38] Only the strongest of measures, it was thought, would be effective in bringing the Duke back to obedience. It was, therefore, suggested that he should be removed from Northumberland's care and confined to the Tower of London. Half fortress-half prison, the Tower struck terror into James's heart like no other place in the kingdom. He knew how many politicians, pronounced 'traitor', had met their ends on Tower Hill and how many dispossessed royals had vanished from sight, forever, behind its high walls. Even though James had been quite prepared to recommend a similar fate for Sir John Hotham, with apparently no qualms of conscience, the fear of being summarily dispatched by his enemies – out of public view – filled him with a horror which was every bit as vivid in 1647 as it was in 1688–9. Quickly abandoning his former position, James now begged Parliament to allow him to remain in the Earl's charge and offered up his code books and ciphers, for the scrutiny of the Members.[39]

This setback, however traumatic, did little to dissuade the Duke from seeking a new method of escape. Indeed, the rationale for his flight into exile became even more pressing as the Army Council – struggling to maintain the balance of power with the civilian leaders in the House of

Commons – renewed their calls for the deposition of the King, the disinheritance of the Prince of Wales and the crowning of the Duke of York, in their place. At the same time as these measures were being discussed, the House was receiving a steady stream of intelligence reports which attested to the existence of a number of well-organized Royalist plots aimed at securing James his freedom. The revival of the threat to discipline the Duke was enough, in itself, to persuade him to swear an oath to the Speakers of both Houses of Parliament that he would never again conspire in such a business. However, despite pledging in all honour and faithfulness to remain true to his word, within a matter of weeks James would have fled England's shores for the safety of the Hague and his sister's court.

The manner of his successful flight from London, disguised as a young girl, has entered Royalist folklore and has taken its place alongside other Stuart escape narratives. The genre had its roots in Charles I's failed attempt to break out of Carisbrooke Castle and found its most satisfying expression in the tales of Charles II's escape after the battle of Worcester, which were set down by Samuel Pepys at the insistence of James, himself.[40] Similar motifs would later attach themselves to the accounts of Monmouth's capture after Sedgemoor and to the flight of the Old Pretender from Montrose in 1716, and flourished, for one last time, in the heavily romanticized stories of the Young Pretender's escape from Culloden Moor and his subsequent preservation, in the Highlands and Islands in 1746, through the sacrifices of Flora MacDonald, Cluny Macpherson and a small but dedicated band of loyal adherents. In this context, the accounts given by James in the *Life* and by his accomplices in their own writings can be viewed as conforming to an already well-established literary convention that had wide dramatic appeal and the power to endure, through its many guises, as a propaganda tool in the armoury of the House of Stuart for more than a century. While acknowledging that the Duke of York faced very real dangers in embarking upon this course of action, it is worth emphasizing that his escape from St James's Palace might not have been such an unexpected occurrence or one which owed quite so much to his individual initiative. The arrangements for snatching James away from his captors had been laid well in advance, with the prior knowledge and consent of the King, while the role played by the Earl of Northumberland in events was anything but transparent. Although the escape has been consistently portrayed – in line with James's own account – as a maverick operation conducted with assistance of only a handful of agents, significant doubts as to Northumberland's continuing commitment to the imprisonment of the Duke need to be raised.[41] He had already wrung a concession out of Parliament that he would not be held responsible if James did, indeed, succeed in achieving his freedom and had taken few precautions to ensure that he had closed off as many avenues of escape as were humanely possible to his troublesome charge. Moreover, it is unthinkable that any governor – intent on keeping his prisoner secure – would have made him the present of a coach, with which to drive through the undulating territory of St James's Park, in and amongst its copses, water features and deer pens, almost at will. It is similarly remarkable that for the weeks immediately prior to James's flight, he acquiesced in allowing the boy to play at hide-and-seek, always at dusk, in and around the palace grounds. Whether we are to conclude that Northumberland was prepared to turn the other way while an escape attempt was mounted or if he was simply negligent and complacent in the performance of his duty, the fact remains that through his behaviour the Commons lost control of a prisoner of immense importance, second only in value to the King himself. All hopes of Parliament bestowing the crown upon James were lost at a stroke, as on the night of 20 April 1648 the barge on which he was travelling dimmed its lights, and slipped unnoticed in between the blockhouses, which guarded the River Thames, and out towards the open sea.[42]

CHAPTER THREE

The Bitter Bread of Exile

I

Stepping ashore onto Dutch soil, the Duke of York faced an uncertain future. His deliverance from imprisonment may have appeared to him as being little short of the miraculous, but it also created a new set of tensions among the Royalist exiles – who now jockeyed for position around his person – and afforded the boy a level of freedom and influence which he could previously have only dreamt of.[1] With the King absent – still held as a captive by his Parliament – and with access to his counsels denied, the leadership of the Royalist movement was effectively split. Competing factions, centering around Henrietta Maria and the Prince of Wales at the Court of Paris, sought to exercise their authority independently – and often to the detriment – of the other. In this climate, personal, political and religious jealousies ran high among the extremely heterogeneous, and increasingly impecunious, elements which made up the Royalist diaspora. The devotion to the Church of England, and the legalistic respect for constitutionalism which so embodied Sir Edward Hyde's conception of Royalism, might easily be scoffed at and considered anathema by the elder Henry, Lord Jermyn, who sought to firmly harness the Roman Catholic interest and to effect a return to authoritarian power, with as few restraints placed upon the royal prerogative as was humanly possible. The arrival of the Duke of York, at his sister's Court at The Hague, introduced another factor into this already complicated equation. He brought with him Colonel Joseph Bampfield, an Officer who had fought in the South-west under Prince Maurice and Sir Ralph Hopton during the First Civil War and who, despite frequent professions of Presbyterian faith, had slipped all too easily into a career of deceit and subterfuge with the Royalist secret service. It had been Bampfield who had both masterminded and effected James's dramatic escape from England. Consequently, it was no difficult task for him to assume the mantle of the Duke's closest confidant and mentor, during the early days of their exile. James, who had been deprived of affection and praise during his captivity, instinctively warmed to a man who combined military expertise with the observance of all the courtesies and deferences which he held to be due to himself, as a Prince. For his own part, Bampfield recognized the value of having

James's ear and set about constructing an embryonic household around the Duke, which was broadly sympathetic to his own political viewpoint and aspirations.[2]

Shortly after their arrival in The Hague, an incident occurred which allowed James the chance of assuming independent responsibility for the first time in his life; and which offered Bampfield the prospect of becoming a major power-broker in any subsequent attempt to restore the monarchy. The mutiny of a squadron of Parliamentarian warships, stationed off the Downs, in May 1648 coincided with a fresh outbreak of pro-Royalist risings across England and Wales. The possession of a small fleet made it possible to plan for the successful landing of an exiled Army, in support of the insurgents, anywhere in the British Isles. Previously such an ambitious project, aimed at the reopening of hostilities, could not have been seriously contemplated by the Royalist war councils, much less embarked upon with any real prospect of success. The key difference now lay in the shift in the balance of power within Parliament and also, though to a far lesser degree, in the changing nature of the naval command and of the elevation of the Duke of York's own position.

James, as we have already seen, had been far too young to have been placed at the head of the Admiralty in the autumn of 1642. As a child, he was wholly unable to present himself as a serious alternative source of authority when the allegiance of the battle-fleet was threatened by Northumberland's defection to Parliament. Both Percy and Robert Rich, the Earl of Warwick – who succeeded him in his post in December 1643 – had been able to consolidate their hold upon the Navy and to use the fleet as a vital weapon in prosecuting the war against the King. Parliamentarian ships blockaded Royalist ports, resupplied their own beleaguered coastal garrisons and guaranteed that the City of London would not be cut off from its vital trade routes with the North-East, the Hanseatic cities and the colonies of the New World. With the London merchants assured of their profits, and with Warwick quickly proving himself to be a competent and popular Commander-in-Chief, the allegiance of the Navy was virtually assured throughout the course of the First Civil War.[3] However, as attempts at compromise between the King and his captors foundered in late 1647 and early 1648, cracks began to appear in the uneasy Parliamentary alliance between the Presbyterians and Independents, which threatened to plunge the nation into a renewed conflict. These differences in outlook and in the direction of policy were easily exploited by the King. The Navy, in particular, was becoming increasingly susceptible to Royalist propaganda and the dis-affection which had been sown was only further exacerbated by replacement of many of the high-ranking Naval Commanders, who had led the service throughout the Civil War years, with untried appointees handpicked by the Independent party. Warwick had already been forced into temporary retirement by the provisions of the *Self-Denying Ordinance*, but it was the summary dismissal of William Batten which provoked ten of the warships under his command to declare themselves for the King and to set course for Holland.

The arrival of Batten and his small armada off the Dutch coast was the cause of great excitement among the Royalist exiles at The Hague. Seizing the moment and acting under Bampfield's advice, James rushed to join the squadron. He arrived as the ships dropped anchor at Helvoetsluys and lost no time at all in attempting to assert his authority over the sailors and in installing himself at their head.[4] However, in embarking upon this course of action, James had taken a great deal for granted. Having clung on tenaciously to the title of Lord High Admiral during the war years and throughout his term of imprisonment, he naively assumed that his elder brother would confirm him in his post, automatically, and would grant him leave to take the ships back out to sea at the first available opportunity. Unfortunately, James had not counted upon the absolute horror with which the Prince of Wales would receive the news of his rash and precipitous behaviour. Charles and his advisers had fundamental doubts about the ability of a fifteen-year-old boy, no matter how royal and how gifted he believed himself to be, to impose any sort of order upon the hardened and mutinous crews. The Prince's worst fears were realized when, in July 1648, he arrived from Calais to find the fleet in a deplorable condition. While Bampfield and the Duke's other servants 'lorded' themselves over the Naval Officers, Batten had begun to bitterly regret his defection from Parliament and now longed to return to England – upon terms – at the first available opportunity. To make matters worse, it transpired that the common seamen had not revolted out of a sense of duty to the King; but out of a desire to shake off harsh naval discipline and to seek redress about their grievances over pay. However, if the London Parliament – backed by the City merchants – could not have managed to pay their wages on time, the Duke of York and his threadbare household, subsisting largely on a pension from the Prince of Orange, had little or no hope of giving them satisfaction. Consequently, it was an unruly and totally demoralized squadron which turned out to greet the Prince of Wales upon his arrival.[5]

Charles moved quickly to dismiss Bampfield, relieved the Duke of his self-appointed command, and entrusted the charge of the little fleet to Prince Rupert, who had by now been thoroughly rehabilitated and reconciled to the Royalist service. As a seasoned veteran of countless battles and skirmishes, Rupert was still at the height of his powers and possessed the necessary experience – and personal toughness – to be able to weld such a troublesome command into a unified, effective fighting force. However, while Charles's Privy Council might have agreed that Rupert was the natural choice for such a prestigious and vitally important command, James did not choose to view the appointment of his cousin in quite the same light. For him, it was not the question of merit but one of rank and social position which was of central importance. He steadfastly maintained that the post of Lord High Admiral was his by right, and that his father had always intended that he should have control over any ships which had defected to the Royalist cause. He wrote angrily that his brother's actions had stripped him of his birthright 'much to his mortification', and complained that he was not even to be 'trusted with himself', reflecting bitterly that he was now no freer than he had been as the prisoner of Parliament.[6] A compromise solution accepted by the Prince of Wales, by which James might have been allowed to set sail under Rupert, was rejected outright by the Duke when he discovered that the destination of the fleet was to be Ireland.

Given James's undoubted thirst for action and his enormous impact upon the development of the Irish nation, in later life, this decision may be viewed as being both strange and extremely surprising. However, it must be remembered that while James had servants and friends of Irish origin, he consistently failed to show any great attachment to – or concern for – the Irish people. As both Duke and King, he conceived of himself as being wholly English and regarded Ireland as being only the junior partner in the union of the three crowns. Moreover, at the prompting of Bampfield, he may well have come to fasten all of his hopes for success upon a sudden descent on the English coast. In this light, Rupert's expedition to support the Earl of Ormonde and the Irish insurgents could have appeared to him as being little more than a dangerous, and a thoroughly disagreeable, side-show.[7] The decision of the Prince of Wales to confine him to the shore, while the fleet underwent sea-trials in September 1648, set the seal upon the quarrel and may have served to confirm James in his opinion that the acceptance of any position under Rupert would have amounted to an unacceptable loss of face.

The real casualty of this dispute, however, was Colonel Bampfield. His influence in the counsels of the Duke of York was destroyed and, upon this loss of his royal protection and favour, he began to treat with the representatives of successive Republican governments, eventually serving as one of Thurloe's secret agents. His defection allowed him, with the full benefit of hindsight, to be scapegoated for all of the troubles which beset the Royalist fleet. Clarendon attacked his 'restless, unquiet spirit' which had filled the Duke with so many 'intrigues and desires', while James – seeking to exonerate his own conduct – blamed him for 'tampering with the seamen even while the duke was on board with them, and driving on a Presbyterian interest to the great disturbance of his majesty's [i.e. Charles I's] service'. Thus, Bampfield 'lost all the advantages that he might have reasonably expected from those services which he had lately performed' and earned the undying hatred of the Duke of York; forced into exile at the Restoration he considered it prudent to remain abroad while his former friend and master had power in the land.[8]

A much more serious consequence of James's rift with Charles was the propaganda gift which it presented to their enemies in London. Henceforth any hint of discord between the two royal brothers was seized upon, to be used to advantage not only by their own placemen but also by the agents of the English Republic, operating out of Paris and The Hague. At times of crisis, when Charles accepted the terms of the National Covenant in order to be crowned King at Scone, or when he was thought to have been drowned *en route* for Scotland, discontented elements in the exiled Royalist community would now automatically cluster around James's person in the hope of advantage and reward. While it cannot be denied that Charles and James experienced a difficult and strained relationship during their years of exile, there is little to suggest that the Duke of York actively encouraged the schemes for him to usurp his brother. Although James was quite prepared to enhance his own reputation at Charles's expense and to entertain advantageous offers of marriage, this in no way amounted to disloyalty. It is clear that Charles was equally prepared to visit his own spite and jealousy upon his younger sibling, regardless of the political cost, and it can be fairly concluded that even though they were acutely conscious of their own status – relevant to one another – the royal brothers never once deviated from their common cause. The restoration of the monarchy and the hereditary principle figured uppermost in their thoughts throughout their long years of exile.

The ties that bound them together were further strengthened by the news that King Charles I had finally been held to account, by his own subjects, for the bloodshed of the Civil Wars. Tried before a court of law, held culpable and sentenced to death before representatives of the Army and his own Parliament, Charles I's public execution generated shockwaves which radiated out from Whitehall and reverberated across the whole continent of Europe. While other kings had been killed in battle or murdered by their nobles, never before had a monarch been subjected to moral scrutiny and the judgment of his own people. It was thus the manner of his death – as opposed to its actual occurrence – which made the execution of King Charles I appear to be nothing short of a hideous and terrifying crime for the other crowned heads of Europe. However, while diplomats from the Escorial to the Kremlin filed their letters of complaint and threatened dire retribution, James remained completely silent about his father's death. He had received word of the execution upon his arrival in Paris and although he donned the official black dress of mourning, highlighted only by his jewelled Garter Star, no record of his immediate reaction to the news exists. He certainly did not greet it with the very public outpouring of emotion exhibited by many Royalist exiles and chose not to indulge in the form of swooning histrionics and maudlin sentimentality, as practised by the Marquis of Montrose. His memoirs give us no clue to his thoughts or feelings, and in later life he was extremely reticent about the form of his father's 'martyrdom' and the political uses to which it was put by the membership of the Anglican Church.[9] This is not to suggest that the death of Charles I did not strike James to the core of his being, or act as a seminal influence upon his emotional and political development. Rather, it impacted upon him as an intensely personal tragedy, so keenly felt that it could not be commented upon or easily refashioned for the purposes of public consumption and propaganda.

James, however, was not slow to draw political conclusions from the fate of his father. He came to believe that it was the willingness of Charles I to compromise at key junctures in his reign, with Pym over the trial of Strafford and with the Army leaders over the form his government should take, which had been the cause of all of his misfortunes. It was strength and the willingness to exercise overwhelming force which, James rationalized, were the hallmarks of stable and effective governance. Given his unfortunate experiences at London – when he had been forced to flee the City, following his father's attempt to arrest the Five Members – and at Hull and Gloucester, when the threat of such a force had failed entirely to cow his enemies into submission, it might have been thought that James would have already had enough evidence to perceive the fundamental flaws in his argument. However, while his elder brother had been able to take many of the lessons of the Civil Wars to heart – becoming flexible through necessity and experience – James's own character, which was nothing if not rigid, would not permit him to learn from the mistakes of the past. The humiliation which he had felt as a prisoner of Parliament, a fate which the Prince of Wales had never had to endure, outweighed all other considerations of polity. Furthermore, the very fact that he had twice been held captive as a child and had gone into exile as an adolescent meant that his experience of English society and politics was, at best, limited. The subtle shifts of ideology during the war years, and the varying levels of opposition to the government of Charles I, effectively passed him by.[10]

There is little in his writings to suggest that he ever understood the complex, and often mutually antagonistic, natures of the various factions which comprised the Long Parliament. He made no clear distinction between the Presbyterians and the Independents, branding them equally as traitors and 'republicans', who had desired the death of the King from the very first. Later, as Exclusion threatened, James would seek to go even further; attributing all of the troubles in England to the covert machinations of bands of 'insolent republicans'. In his eyes, the world was polarized between the forces of monarchy – which enshrined law, order and obedience – and Republicanism, which only served to act as a corrosive upon the very fabric of society. If given the chance, such a system would inevitably result in widespread criminality: the violation of traditional rights of property and heredity, and the destruction of the existing – and divinely ordained – social relationships and hierarchies. However, James's constant warnings of an omnipresent Republican menace, continually at work upon the consciousness of the English people, was – certainly by the 1670s – a gross distortion of the political realities. In attempting to remove religion entirely from the equation, and to continually equate dissent with disloyalty and an abstract form of Republicanism, James was doing little more than to provide himself and his closest followers with a comforting fiction. Although the English Republic had indeed been established over the broken body of his father and consigned him, personally, to exile for more than a decade, James was to allow his formative experiences and prejudices to dominate his entire political outlook. Even after the elections of 1661, when the *axis mundi* had decisively shifted, leaving the 'Good Old Cause' to contract until it embraced no more than a handful of plotters, and religious and social visionaries, James continued to ascribe to it a vastly inflated importance and a uniquely malign significance. In locating all of the nation's ills in one stream of political thought and in effectively dehumanizing individual members of the Republican movement, James had already – after the death of his father – set the interpretative pattern upon which all of his later political judgements were to be formed.[11] When combined with his inability to tolerate the opinions of others and to acknowledge the centrality of religious practice in the everyday lives of the English people, he had done no more than to establish his capacity for self-deception and had begun the long process of elevating it to its final position as the guiding force in all of his affairs.

II

The immediate consequence, for the exiled Royalist community, of Charles I's untimely death was the concentration of power and moral authority in the hands of his eldest son. From the outset, Charles II made it plain that it was he who would one day return to England as King. He alone had inherited his father's mantle and it was to him that Charles's scattered supporters should look for help and guidance. The hopes of Henrietta Maria, that she might formulate policy in the name of her son, were confounded and the career of her favourite, Henry, Lord Jermyn went into eclipse. For his part, James backed his brother to the best of his abilities. Never close to the Dowager Queen, he was stung by her slight regard for him and his abilities, and fully comprehended the need for Charles II, as the new and rightful King, to assert his own privileges.

However, while Prince Rupert was free to range the shipping lanes of the world, in search of English merchantmen to plunder, James could only shuttle between Paris and The Hague in the pursuit of useful employment; he was afforded ample enforced leisure to ponder upon the exploits of his lost fleet. A sojourn in Jersey quickly palled, in the early months of 1650, as Charles II left for Scotland and entrusted him with the defence of the Channel Islands. James had enjoyed spending the autumn and winter months of 1649 with his brother, at Elizabeth Castle, filling his days with shooting parties and sailing lessons. Unfortunately, Charles's sudden departure deprived him of a confidant and foisted upon him an unwelcome level of responsibility. The routine work of resupplying the garrison, maintaining morale, and of soothing the easily frayed tempers of a large train of courtiers and hangers-on, held little interest for him. In time, even the drilling of his soldiers grew burden-some and he wrote to his brother asking if he might be relieved of his command. With no imminent threat of invasion by Commonwealth forces, James had no scope for proving himself in a desperate defence of the Islands and he looked further afield, to Sweden and to France, in search of action and excitement. Even though he had previously refused the offer of service under Prince Rupert, he now changed his mind, upon hearing of his glorious exploits, and pleaded in vain with Charles II to be allowed to rejoin the fleet.[12] Effectively barred by his brother from the negotiations with the Scottish commissioners, and denied service in the campaigns of Dunbar and Worcester, he was left to his own devices and sought to reshape his household in the light of his personal preferences. Surrounded constantly by an ever-changing circle of highly practised and self-interested courtiers, who 'agreed well in the design of making the Duke of York discontented and weary of his condition', James sought to enhance his own prestige by making and breaking friendships, and alliances, almost at will. Showing little time or respect for Henry Bennet, who had been appointed as his secretary by Charles II, he ran through a succession of governors and favourites, before a rumour that the King had been lost at sea reached him. He immediately determined to set out for Brussels, in order to 'provide for himself' and to take service with the Duke of Lorraine, who might not only be 'able to give [James] good counsel, but the assistance to make it effectual'.[13]

With the French Royal Armies simultaneously embroiled in fighting the rebels of the Fronde at home and the might of Spain abroad, James's decision placed his mother in a very difficult and embarrassing situation. As a pensioner of the Court of Paris, dependent upon the goodwill of Mazarin and Louis XIV for her continued maintenance and diplomatic recognition, Henrietta Maria could ill afford to see her son publicly offering his sword to one of France's most implacable enemies. However, James 'very obstinately' informed her that his mind was made up and set out for Flanders in the company of a small band of followers. Having been deprived of his father's advice, it may be assumed that he perceived Charles of Lorraine to be a possible mentor and role model, drawing strong parallels between the Duke's situation and his own. Stripped of his lands and driven into exile by Cardinal Richelieu, Lorraine had won a formidable reputation for himself as a soldier of fortune, who had 'by his own activity and virtue, made himself so considerable, that Spain depended upon his army, and France itself would be glad of his friendship'. Consequently, while a disconsolate Henrietta Maria was left to fret about her son's activities and was forced to write to Mazarin – abasing herself – and disclaiming all responsibility for them, James spent the autumn and winter months of 1650–1, cheerfully enough, in the pursuit of preferment among the armies of Spain. To begin with, everything went well; the Duke of Lorraine proved to be a courteous host, who oversaw the lodgings of James and his servants in Brussels, and lent the Prince a considerable sum of money in order to cover their expenses. There was talk of making the command of eight regiments in Lorraine's army over to James and of giving him a General's rank. Even when it became clear, soon after James's arrival, that the rumours of Charles II's disappearance had no foundation in fact and that the King was actually safe and sound in Edinburgh, his position did not significantly alter. However, as the months dragged on, James's financial position worsened and it became increasingly apparent that the Duke of Lorraine had little intention of delivering on his promises. The rudeness and profligacy of James's servants, when combined with the growing realization that he was operating purely upon his own initiative with no substantial backing from the wider Royalist movement, began to seriously undermine his position. Duke Charles 'grew colder in his respects' and in a desperate attempt to revive their flagging fortunes, James's friends suggested that he might become the husband of Lorraine's illegitimate daughter.[14] This scheme, which was to prove unacceptable to all of the parties involved – with the notable exception of James himself – succeeded only in briefly uniting Charles II and Henrietta Maria in their common opposition to it, and was dismissed out of hand by the Duke of Lorraine, the moment that he discovered that James was acting without the permission of his elder brother. With his loan long since spent and with no other source of available income,

James was at last forced to accept that an offer of employment with the armies of Spain would not be forthcoming. However, he did not leave Brussels with an air of contrition or regret. His first taste of independence, away from the formalities and duties of Court life, had proved to be agreeable and he 'was rather delighted with the journeys he had made'. Never for a second did he consider 'that he had not entered upon them with reason enough', while his experiences 'had [only] fortified him with a firm resolution, never to acknowledge that he had committed any error'.[15]

Returning to his sister's Court at The Hague, James found that his position there had changed very much for the worse since his last visit. The sudden death of the Prince of Orange had deprived the Royalist cause of a valuable ally and had transferred power back into the hands of the States of Holland, which openly espoused a brand of bourgeois republicanism. With civic pride and public virtue at a premium, the arrival of a wandering prince was particularly unwelcome and singularly ill-timed. The newly widowed Princess Mary lobbied hard for her brother; but the suggestion that James should be granted asylum at The Hague and should receive a handsome pension from the coffers of the States General fell upon stony ground. Worse still, the memory of James's previous bad behaviour while residing in Holland had done little to endear him to the Dutch people, or to any of the burghers and merchants who still waited in vain for the repayment of his outstanding debts. Before his death, even the Prince of Orange had been given cause to remark upon the 'impertinence and insolence of [James's] train' and had breathed an audible sigh of relief at the passing of the Duke of York and his 'uneasy family [i.e. household]' from out of his lands.[16]

Forced to leave The Hague, James stayed on only long enough to take his leave of his sister and to coddle her newborn child. William, the posthumous son of the Prince of Orange, was an undersized and sickly infant whom the physicians did not expect to live. Given such a bleak prognosis, it is doubtful if James – having returned the infant to his nurses – ever expected to see his nephew again; still less could he have conceived that the frail infant who had struggled in his arms would one day grow into the formidable European captain who would strip him of his throne, and condemn him to the dark despair of a final exile at the court of Louis XIV from 1690 until 1701.

With nowhere else to go, James now attempted to negotiate a return to his mother's Court in Paris and to salvage as much of his dignity as he could under the circumstances. It was left to Sir Edward Hyde to bring him back to obedience, but the future Earl of Clarendon was horrified to discover upon his arrival that the Duke's household was on the verge of collapse 'in all the confusion imaginable, in present want of everything and not knowing what was to be done next'. James, quite overawed by his predicament, stood on ceremony but gave no lead to his followers. 'They all censured and reproached the counsel by which they had been guided', Clarendon recalled, 'and the counsellors as bitterly inveighed against each other.' Under the careful auspices of Hyde, a formula was worked out by which the Duke and his increasingly ragged train of servants might return to the Louvre with their dignity still intact. No acts of contrition were demanded from James and his mother put on a show of welcome for him, that was unmarred by reproaches from either side.[17] However, having once tasted a measure of personal freedom, the re-imposition of the constraints on his conduct by his mother and her willingness to withhold monies from him, in order to modify and condition his behaviour, came as something of a shock to James and were resisted at every opportunity. Consequently, he attempted to carve out a place for himself at the Court of King Louis XIV that was independent of Henrietta Maria's patronage. Despite his halting grasp of the French language, he was able – through the fortunate combination of his royal birth, 'comeliness and personal dexterity' in sports – to gain acceptance in this narrow and exacting society. By July 1651, scarcely a month after his arrival back in Paris, he was already negotiating for command of a troop of horse in the French Royal Army. Rumours spread that he was to be found a permanent place at Court as a functionary, with his further education as a Prince to be overseen by no less a personage than the Regent Anne, and negotiations for his marriage to the daughter of the Duc de Longueville were entered into, during the following winter months. Unfortunately, his progress as a would-be courtier and diplomat was interrupted by events over which he had simply no control. The news that Cromwell had destroyed Charles II's field army at the battle of Worcester, combined with the arrival of the King in person – after six weeks spent as a hunted fugitive across half of the length of England – radically altered perceptions of the exiled Stuarts on the Continent. The decisive nature of their defeat at the hands of the Commonwealth had destroyed all hope that they might be restored to power in the immediate future. As the last remaining Royalist strongholds in the Isle of Man and the Channel Islands capitulated one by one, the military and political ascendancy of Parliament was complete, and many of the King's erstwhile followers thought it prudent to reach an accommodation with the masters of the vigorous new Republic.[18]

These developments, worrying enough in themselves, now served to seriously compromise James's position in the minds of his prospective French backers. As the younger brother of a King who ruled in name alone, there was little advantage to be gained in openly supporting him and only danger to be sought in antagonizing the all-powerful

Commonwealth. Moreover, with no obvious source of income with which to support him, other than the *largesse* of the French crown, he constituted as both a creditor and as a suitor a singularly risky and unattractive prospect. Worse still, the rebellion of the Prince de Condé in August 1651 had reignited the flames of civil war in France and driven the Royal Court to seek sanctuary far to the west, in the relative safety of Angers. In such perilous times, when the ambitions of the house of Condé threatened to pull down the Bourbon monarchy, the preferment of a foreign Prince – who had few powerful friends and no proven skills of any kind – took a poor second best in the deliberations of the Regent Anne and her advisers. With no other opportunities presenting themselves, James once more determined upon pursuing a life as a soldier. This time, with his importance to his brother's cause greatly diminished and 'with great violence' threatening 'so much toil, and blood' across the kingdom of France, he chose exactly the right moment to press his case and his appeals met with success.[19] Sir Edward Hyde took up his cause with Henrietta Maria, and by a judicious sleight of hand – whereby he was presented as a gentleman volunteer rather than a commissioned officer – he was accepted into the French royal service, without fear of enraging English opinion or causing embarrassment to his hosts. Having secured a loan from a Gascon mercenary who had served under his father, James purchased arms and armour, and hired half a dozen servants and footmen to attend him on his campaigns. His friends, Sir John Berkeley and Colonel Robert Werden, were chosen to accompany him as they had seen extensive action during the English Civil Wars, and had had experience of both staff work and independent command. Although they brought with them their own horses, James still felt moved to complain that 'Nothing was so rare as money' and to lament that neither he, nor his noble companions had a spare set of mounts. The transportation of their servants was provided for, when Charles II donated to them six undersized horses, which had proved to be thoroughly inadequate for the pulling of his coach; and a pair of mules were also found to carry James's cumbersome camp bed and provisions on the trek south.[20] The only obstacle which remained to them was to absent themselves from Henrietta Maria's household at St Germain, where they were nominally watched over by James's uncle – Gaston, Duke of Orléans – a Frondeur Prince. This was successfully accomplished under cover of a hunting party organized at the behest of Charles II. As soon as they were safely beyond the walls of the old castle, and out among the forests and parkland which surrounded it, the two brothers took leave of one another and James set off on the road for Chartres, eager to reach the encampment of the French Royal Army and to embrace the dangerous – yet exciting – existence of a soldier of fortune.[21]

III

The vast majority of the evidence attesting to the Duke's early promise and later degeneration rests upon his record as a military commander, which commenced immediately upon his arrival at the camp of Marshal Turenne in late April 1652. Fortesque, in his *History of the British Army*, thought that James was 'a man of stronger military instincts than any English [prince] since Henry the Eighth. He . . . served through four campaigns under Turenne and through two more with the Spaniards, and . . . had studied the military profession with singular industry and intelligence of observation.' Dorothy Middleton sought to further attest to his 'valour and resource in youth', but remarked sadly that he seemed 'to have declined from his early promise, to have lost the fervour and elasticity of youth somewhere in the middle years of his life without gaining any of the compensating virtues of age. His early exile and the attacks of his political enemies in later life acted like acid on his spirit and loosed the springs of self-pity and self-distrust; as his courage faded with advancing time he had no defences against the fates.'[22] At first sight this plausible and confident diagnosis might appear to have been the case. The contrast between the gallant young Officer – always ready to hazard his life on the most dangerous of reconnaissance missions or to charge home, time and again, into the ranks of his enemies at the Battle of the Dunes – and the cowardly old General – prone to nosebleeds, who fussed so ineffectually about Salisbury Plain in 1688 while his Army disintegrated around him, or who fled the Boyne and abandoned his Irish allies in 1690 – could not be clearer. However, upon a closer examination of the key developments in James's military career and of his independent commands in particular, we can begin to see how these old stereotypes begin to break down.

James would come to regard the four years that he spent as an Officer in the French Royal Army as constituting the happiest, most carefree and personally fulfilling period of his life. His memoirs lovingly record his youthful exploits on the battlefield as an energetic cavalry Officer, and came to reflect his growing admiration and respect for his Commander-in-Chief, Henri La Tour d'Auvergne, the Marshal Turenne.[23] There is ample evidence, both from the pages of James's own writings and from those of his comrades-in-arms, that he was often where the fighting was at its thickest and that his own physical courage, when under fire, proved to be of the very highest order. However, it is important to remember that throughout the majority of this time, James was only serving in the capacity of a junior Staff Officer and *aide de camp*. He was responsible for delivering messages to divisional Commanders and for scouting out the enemy's lines in order to gain intelligence as to their dispositions. It was not, therefore, altogether surprising that he saw a good deal of action or that he frequently engaged in furious hand-to-hand combats. What is noteworthy, however, is that while he always posed as a scientific soldier, James – together with the succeeding generations of his apologists, who took their cues directly from the descriptions of battle contained in the *Life* – chose to cast himself in a faintly chivalric light, as though he were a second Bayard fighting in order to redeem his own personal honour.[24] This somewhat anachronistic approach to the subject, in an age that was increasingly coming to be dominated by long-range artillery fire, also serves to reflect the fact that before the morning of the Boyne, James had never led a field army into a pitched battle. He had held charge of the administration of the French Army during the occasion of Turenne's absences from camp, but it is important to remember that during the whole of his time with the armies of France – and later with those of Spain – the Duke of York was never tested as a General by being given a truly independent command. Moreover, it is significant that it was not primarily for his knowledge of military affairs or for his personal insights into the development of new tactics that he was originally attached to the French staff. He was there as the result of his own breeding and his great natural skill as a horseman, a combination of traits which became increasingly useful to the chain of command as the eyesight of the French Marshal began to fail. We are told that Turenne kept James at his side for he 'saw not clearly at a distance, [and as he] would not trust his own eyesight, he therefore desired the Duke to observe' the movements of the enemy and to report back to him about their intentions. As Turenne's sight deteriorated even further, James was given the job of escorting him around the battlefield and was charged with the responsibility of ensuring the Marshal's safety.[25]

Much has been made of Turenne's affectionate remark that the young James 'was the greatest prince and like to be the best general of his time', but if this reveals anything more than the state of conventional flattery, then it is surely bound up solely with the nature of their personal relationship. These two men, despite the differences in their age, shared much in common. Both were still essentially considered to be 'foreign princes', though serving the French Crown, and as the younger sons of two great royal houses, whose lustre had been dimmed by the changing fortunes of war and by the first encroachments of the power of the nation state, both were exceptionally conscious of their rank and protective of their few remaining prerogatives. Having failed to cultivate the Duke of Lorraine, James was delighted to find a patron who accorded 'him a reception suitable to his birth; and endeavoured, by all possible proofs of affection, to soften the remembrance of his [i.e. James's] misfortunes'.[26] Moreover, Turenne had married late in life and as middle age encroached upon him, it may have appeared to the childless General that James held many of the attributes of the son he had wished for, but never had. There can be little doubt that Turenne was a far more awkward and socially isolated individual than has often been suggested. Away from the battlefield he lacked self-confidence, had few close friends and chose to live with the greatest simplicity. Though he proved to be a kind master to his servants, he gained a reputation as a haughty nobleman, inordinately proud and supremely conscious of any slight – no matter how small – to his reputation. Given James's similar problems in forming and sustaining human relationships, it may well be that these two supremely awkward and difficult men recognized something of their own nature in the other, and that this realization was to prove to be the foundation upon which their friendship was to be built.

Although one would not appreciate it from a reading of the *Life*, Turenne was an intensely political figure whose career in the service of the Bourbon monarchy had been chequered in the extreme and was punctuated by periods of rebellion against his sovereign. Indeed, in the spring of 1652, he had only been reconciled to the French Court for a matter of months. His jealousy of Condé's advancement, seemingly at the expense of his own house, had finally outweighed both his distrust of Mazarin and his concern to protect the rights of his fellow Huguenots. Moreover, the refusal of his own soldiers to follow him *en masse* into the rebellion of the Princes, had given him serious cause to reconsider his own relationship with the French people and with the State itself. He had always prided himself in the love and devotion shown to him by the rank and file of the Army, but the discovery that their primary loyalties now lay with their King and country – rather than with their feudal lords and regions – came as a profound shock to him.[27] His subsequent *rapprochement* with the agencies of central government, his attachment to the person of Louis XIV, and his ability to harness the administrative reforms conducted by Mazarin and Le Tellier, in order to ensure sweeping victories in the field, made a deep impression upon James. He had witnessed the genesis of the French Royal Army, an increasingly professionalized force, which over the course of the next fifty years would achieve an almost unbroken string of successes and would come to dominate the strategic thinking of statesmen right across the continent of Europe. James could not fail to be aware of the advantages which a standing army could bestow upon the power of the State and was not slow to recognize the positive benefits which a displaced Prince might also accrue, to himself, in the pursuit of military glory in such a service. He proved himself to be an eager pupil of Turenne, hanging on to every word of the older man and supporting him, unconditionally, at every opportunity. When before the enemy lines at Arras, the will of the French war council faltered in August 1654, James was one of only two Senior Officers to back Turenne's plans and to urge an all-out assault upon Condé's entrenchments, regardless of the cost.[28] However, while Turenne's genius lay in the lightning speed of his marches, his ready grasp of the most intractable problems, and in his ability to wrong-foot and to completely outmanoeuvre his opponents, James's accounts of his campaigns focus largely upon other matters. Turenne's physical bravery and dedication to duty impressed the Duke greatly, but we learn far less about his thought processes and strategic mastery. Those areas of his command with which James was familiar, at a brigade level and below, are those which are most clearly delineated. We learn much about his methods of reconnoitering the positions of his foes, slipping out of his quarters every morning 'by sunrise, slenderly attended' to receive intelligence reports from his scouts and to probe the enemy's picket lines, yet the uses to which this information was put are almost invariably skirted over. Similarly, it is the onset of battle, rather than the political or military objectives which occasioned it, which is of interest to James. It was enough for him that a stronghold had been taken or that a siege was successfully raised. Whether in the suburbs of Paris – where 'men heaved stones at each other, fired pistols and thrust their swords through the holes' in the garden walls – or in the fire and smoke of the ditches before Ligny Castle – when the '[i]ce broke under' the Duke's men – it is the description of the action, rather than the use to which a victory was put, which engages the passions but not the the intellect of the author.[29] This absence of a true critical analysis is a remarkable and constant theme of James's military memoirs, and becomes all the more marked in his evaluation of his own worth, and that of Turenne.

After the Restoration of 1660, Sir William Coventry had lectured an interested audience about the Duke's virtues and abilities. His master, so he claimed, was 'a man naturally Martiall to the highest degree, yet a man that never in his life talks one word of himself or service of his own; but only that he saw such or such a thing, and lays it down for a maxime that a Hector can have no courage'. However, if James chose to make Turenne – and not himself – the central figure around which his military memoirs are based, he does benefit considerably from his close association with the great Commander and basks in the reflected glory which surrounded him. It is understood implicitly, throughout his writings, that Turenne can do no wrong; for he 'consider'd nothing but the public good, and the carrying of the King's Ser[v]ice'. His failures and defeats are always the fault of others, whether the French Court or his subordinate commanders, who had 'by-ends and interests of their own'. He himself is presented as an infallible source of authority: 'the greatest Captain of this and perhaps of any age', and 'the greatest and most perfect man [James] had ever known . . . the best friend he had ever had'.[30] In this light, the Marshal's frequent – and often lavish – praise for the Duke of York can assume an altogether exaggerated importance. Indeed, in later years, Bishop Burnet was to sneer that 'Turenne was so much taken with his application, and the heat that he shewed, that he recommended him out of measure', magnifying James's abilities purely on account of his courage and dedication.[31] For his own part, the Duke was keen to portray himself as being a figure who was indispensable to the Marshal's successful prosecution of the war. Throughout his memoirs he conveys the impression that he acted as Turenne's 'right hand' and was the one Officer who did not seek to frustrate his master through jealousy or ill will. James tells us that the Marshal 'was not a little delighted in having so illustrious a person for his Schollar in the discipline of warr' and that the Duke 'was used to speaking in confidence of his affairs with Monsieur de Turenne'. Furthermore, the Marshal had even considered pawning his own plate in order to finance a projected invasion of England under James's command. Every word of praise for his protégé that Turenne had uttered was lovingly set down and preserved for posterity. Whether or not James would have considered himself to be an Achilles rather than a Hector, his modesty did not prevent his demonstrating to his readership that Turenne's trust in him had been well placed and that even his enemies thought him to be a valiant soldier. James points out that after a dangerous reconnaissance mission, it had been: 'The Duke [who] was the first to advise him that they [i.e. Condé's men] were entrenching themselves', and that even the Governor of a frontier town had gained a hard-won respect for him and his abilities. Even though he had had the Duke of York in his sights, the Governor of the rebel citadel at Mouzon had recognized him on account of the Garter Star sown on to his cloak and had forbidden his soldiers to open fire. James declared that this was 'a respect very usuall beyond [the] Sea', but noted by way of contrast that the Governor 'had not the same consideration for those afterwards who were commanded to repair' the trench wall, and that 'severall of those [common soldiers] who were employed in that work were slayn, and others hurt'.[32]

Under Turenne's patronage, promotion came quickly and after only two years' service James was promoted in 1654 to the rank of Lieutenant General. Still not quite twenty-one, he was proudly to recall that he had taken 'my day according to the date of my Commission as the youngest [general] who serv'd in that Army'. News of his exploits on the battlefield began to filter back to the exiled English Court, and the Duke's achievements as a soldier were widely held to have started to eclipse those of his brother, as politician and King. While Charles II had allegedly idled away his time in the Low Countries with his friends and mistresses, James was seen to have been actively fighting for the Royalist cause. Sir George Radcliffe reported that the 'Duke of York hath gotten a great reputation and power in the French army', and even Sir Edward Hyde thought that he had 'much grown and improved' over recent months; having earned 'much esteem' while under arms.[33] The potent myth of James's military genius has its roots firmly embedded in these times, yet his tenure of command was remarkably short-lived. After barely four campaigning seasons with the French Royal Army, the international situation shifted once again, with new alliances being formed between the great powers. James was forced to relinquish his commission, break with Turenne, and seek service with his former enemies: the Spanish.

IV

Spain had not been slow to take advantage of the social, economic and military dislocations generated by the Frondes. It regained the great Flanders ports of Gravelines, Mardyck and Dunkirk, redoubled its efforts against the rebellious Catalans and Portuguese, and threw cavalry patrols out across the River Somme and on into the heartlands of the French countryside. Only when Turenne's victories began to bring the rebellious Princes to heel, could Mazarin afford to entertain measures designed to curb their depredations. To this end, he sought out and forged a pragmatic trade alliance with the English Republic in the autumn of 1655, which was later expanded to include offers of military assistance. Under the provisions of the initial trade agreement, James was named – along with seventeen others – as an undesirable and was obliged to leave France with all possible haste. However, having at last found a firm friend and a career that proved agreeable to him, James was loath to give up his hard-won privileges and contrived to stay in France for another ten months. He was helped in his resolve by Mazarin himself. The Cardinal had recognized that the presence of the Duke of York in the French Army had attracted considerable numbers of similarly displaced Royalists, of English, Scottish and Irish origins, into the service of his master: Louis XIV. With James gone, there would be nothing to bind them to the French Crown and an enormously valuable reservoir of highly trained and motivated manpower would be lost. Worse still, if the Duke obeyed the commands of his brother and accepted a commission with the Spanish Army in Flanders, his regiments would be sure to follow him. Consequently, Mazarin looked for a compromise solution by which James might continue to serve France, but would do so from beyond its borders. It was suggested that he should take charge of one wing of the French and Savoyard Army, stationed beyond the Alps in Piedmont, and expressing his 'strong inclination to get more and more experience in arms', James leaped at the chance. Unfortunately, the Duke of Savoy had little respect for either his person or his abilities, and vetoed the appointment.

Following Charles II's removal from Cologne to Brussels, and his initiation of talks aimed at securing Spanish backing for his cause, the Duke of York's position in France became ever more tenuous. Despite appeals for guidance from his Irish Officers, James still believed that he could keep his regiments together under the command of Turenne and forbade his colonels from letting 'their soldiers . . . pass into Flanders piecemeal or in small parties, although the Spaniards might invite them, on the occasion of the King's having retired into their country'.[34] In negotiating his treaty with the Spanish, Charles II had consciously overlooked James's position, believing that his brother would be able to achieve far greater concessions for himself and his followers if he treated with them separately. However, James chose to ignore the reality of the Spanish alliance and claimed that as he was not named in the treaty, he could not be bound by any of its provisions. Moreover, he suggested that as both Charles II and Prince Henry were already at Bruges and had been contracted to the service of Spain, King Philip IV could not possibly begrudge the French Crown for bargaining for – and making use of – his talents as the one remaining Stuart Prince whose employment had not so far been guaranteed. Although James was to claim that Marshal Turenne had colluded with him in formulating this line of argument, it did little to impress King Charles and the Spanish diplomats with whom he was currently engaged. If the Duke's refusal to heed the counsels of his brother had raised alarm in the minds of some Royalist exiles, then his willingness in May 1655 to countenance an assassination plot aimed at Oliver Cromwell had already proved his predispostion for casuistry.

While Charles II and his remaining adherents had been prepared to back numerous schemes to topple the Republican government and to secure Cromwell's death, there was a general realization among them that assassination was a clumsy and unpredictable weapon. Such a desperate measure, which attested to the weakness rather than to the strength of the Royalist cause, might be effective if it was carried through by one of the Lord Protector's erstwhile comrades in the Presbyterian or Leveller parties. Loyal Anglicans might also be seen to have been pursuing justifiable vengeance for the execution of their 'Sovereign Saint', but the murder of the head of the English State at the hands of Roman Catholic conspirators was completely unacceptable to every shade of Protestant opinion. It would have brought memories of the assassinations of William the Silent and Henry of Navarre back to prominence, and easily conformed to the stereotype of the disaffected and treasonous Roman Catholic, who lurked like a cancer in the body politic. Such tales of Jesuit spies, sent in to the country by foreign powers, and native insurgents, bent on violence, had been the common coin of Protestant folklore in England since before the time of the Gunpowder Plot. However, James, in seeking Cromwell's death by any means necessary, was prepared to approve just such an endeavour and to agree to a reward being given to the 'four Roman Catholics that have bound themselves in a solemn oath to kill Cromwell', on the completion of their act.[35] Had this deed been successfully accomplished, then the political and social repercussions for the law-abiding Roman Catholic community would have been devastating in their swiftness and totality. The injustices of the Penal Code and the Popish Plot would have been as nothing when compared to the reprisals undertaken in the name of Cromwell, the Protestant champion and martyr. Moreover, it would have alienated moderate Anglicans and Presbyterians from both their Roman Catholic neighbours and King Charles II, and would have made the Royalist cause forever synonymous with that of a narrow and unforgiving brand of religious extremism. James, in considering such a wild scheme and in recommending it to his brother, had shown himself to be impervious to the diverse nature of Royalist support and blind to the concerns and prejudices of the English people.

Although Charles II's response to this plan has not survived, the project was denied the support and authority of his council. Without official backing and the necessary financial resources, it could not flourish and was left to quietly wither away, unseen and unlamented by all. In the intervening months, however, the Duke of York had given little indication that he had learned by his mistakes. Thus, when Sir Henry Bennet was dispatched by the King with orders to bring James back into line and to return him to the Court at Bruges, there was only a slight chance of a quick and painless resolution of the question of the Duke's equivocal status in France. James received his secretary coldly and made it abundantly clear that he preferred the company of his newfound friends – John and Charles Berkeley, and the younger Henry Jermyn – to that of his brother's appointee. He disliked the officious Bennet, with his exaggerated regard for formality and bogus war wound, and ignored his presence as much as was humanly possible: 'not at all look[ing] on [him] unless with an ill eye'.[36] For his own part, Bennet had long since ceased to regard himself as being primarily the Duke's servant and was now committed to carrying out the King's instructions, to the letter. While his secretary vainly protested at his delays, James continued to find reasons for prolonging his stay in France and chose to ignore the mounting pile of correspondence from his brother, urging him to leave immediately for Flanders. However, the Duke could not maintain this level of opposition forever and after ten months of flouting the King's will, he was finally forced to realize that his position in Paris had been fatally compromised. The courtiers and citizens, who had once praised him for his bravery under Turenne, now viewed him with suspicion as an enemy alien and shunned his company. With creditors circling once again about his lodging place and with Bampfield making an unwelcome attempt to return to his favours, James rejected forcing an outright breach with his brother and set about negotiating for an advantageous return to Flanders.

Determined to win the trust of his Spanish allies, Charles II did everything in his power to make the Duke's journey out of France and his reception in Bruges as welcome and dignified as was possible. 'In all places', orders were given out, 'for his reception [to be as grand] as if the King of Spain . . . had been there in person', and ample funds were put at his disposal, upon his arrival in the city, to enable him to pay his servants and clear some of his outstanding debts. Unfortunately, these measures proved insufficient to mollify the Duke and to restore his followers to good order. Negotiations aimed at securing him the independent command of a Spanish Army came to nothing, and he found himself excluded from the private councils of Charles II and Sir Edward Hyde. More disturbingly, his choice of household officers and attendants was once more called into question. In leaving France, he had disobeyed the King and brought with him Sir John Berkeley, a figure who, while beloved of the Duke, was almost universally detested by the Court at Bruges. Amid mounting criticism of Berkeley's thoughtless and heavy-handed behaviour, Bennet moved to have Charles II dismiss him from James's service, on the pretext that his outspokenly francophile views would fatally weaken the relationship between the exiled Royalist community and their new hosts.[37] Distraught at the depths to which his influence had, seemingly, declined, James resolved to defend his servant to the last and to reaffirm his rights to maintain an independent household, separate from that of the King. Crucial to this dispute was the extent of Charles II's prerogative powers in enforcing discipline among the junior members of the House of Stuart, and his ability to make unilateral decisions about the selection of their advisers and staff. He held that it had been customary for English Kings, from time immemorial, to oversee the development of every arm of the royal household, while James contended that this rule had only applied to the children of the ruling sovereign. He claimed that both he and Charles had been models of obedience to the wishes of King Charles I in the establishment and governance of their households, during his lifetime. However, once their father had died there was nothing to subordinate the wishes of the younger Stuart siblings to the will of their eldest brother. Through this attractive defence of their 'rights', James was able to enlist the support of his sister, Mary, Princess of Orange, in this struggle and to make common cause with Henry of Gloucester. Unwilling to set a dangerous precedent in his dealings with his family and to divide up his authority between the individual members, Charles II stood firm and evoked the memory of Charles I – as a patriarch – in a bid to restore discipline among his troublesome kin and to remind them that it was division, and dissent, which had ushered in the Civil Wars and brought them to such a low ebb. Without a kingdom, or even the military and financial resources with which to retake it, all that Charles II had left to him was his title and his personal authority. If he could not maintain his control over his own family, there was little hope that he could impress upon the Spanish the need to act decisively in his interests.[38] James, however, saw the dispute purely in domestic terms and regarded his brother's actions as being an unwarranted infringement upon his own liberties. Having been allowed to act for himself during his military service, and with the praises of a great French General still ringing in his ears, it was a bitter blow for the Duke to have to once more submit to the commands of his own brother.

With the argument turning against him, James decided upon a desperate course of action and fled the Court at Bruges in January 1657, with only Charles Berkeley and Henry Jermyn for companions. Picking up Sir John Berkeley, the source of all their troubles, *en route*, they rode hard for Utrecht. However, James's hopes of securing a passage to France were dashed by a hard frost, which slowed their progress on already pitted roads, and by the presence of English warships which prowled the coast of Flanders and blockaded the port at Veere. While the Duke crossed into Holland and took up lodgings first in Zulestein and then in Breda, the news of his 'unimaginable sally' broke over his brother's household and caused Charles II to fear the very worst. No one knew where James and his companions had fled to, and it was widely supposed that he had already returned to France and re-enlisted under Turenne's colours. Pawning his remaining finery, Charles II despatched the Earl of Ormonde and numerous couriers in an attempt to discover his whereabouts; he reproached Princess Mary for encouraging her brother in his disobedience and appealed to the Commander-in-Chief of the Spanish forces in the Netherlands to act as an intermediary 'and piece up so unlucky a breach'. Don Juan-José of Austria, who it was whispered was the natural son of King Philip IV, wrote to James offering to expedite his return 'with honour' and to secure him a commission, as befitted his station, in the Spanish Army; but to no avail. Encouraged by his mother to believe that France would receive him with open arms, the Duke retorted that Don Juan had taken league with his brother and George, Lord Digby – a courtier whom he vehemently hated – to 'tear' from him all of his most trusted and 'valued' servants.[39] The loss of his Lieutenant-Generalcy still pained him, and he protested that he had been pledged to the service of Spain before there was any justifiable reason for him 'to command against the army under M. Turenne, who is one of the men in the world I am the most obliged to and have the greatest value for'.[40] Without the resources, or seemingly even the moral authority, to compel his brother to return to Bruges, Charles II was forced to give way to James on all points and to effect a humiliating climb-down. In February 1657, the Duke of York presented the terms on which he would consider making his return to court. Having conceded only that he would no longer turn to his mother for political advice and having participated in a highly stage-managed show of 'reconciliation' with Digby, James was given complete autonomy over the governance of his own household. Sir Henry Bennet was dismissed from his service and packed off on a diplomatic mission to Spain, while Sir John Berkeley was allowed to return to court in triumph and was later rewarded for his 'industry', with the title of Lord Berkeley of Stratton.

With the immediate crisis in the royal family resolved, Ormonde encouraged Charles II and Sir Edward Hyde to settle James into the service of Spain, as quickly as was possible and with the minimum of fuss. 'The Duke of York will take exceedingly in the army', he confided, and went on to express his hopes that once James had adjusted to his new situation he would prove as 'little troublesome as a prince can be'. However, he had not reckoned with the strength of the Duke's continuing attachment to his old Commander and to his brother Officers, against whom he was now forced to fight. While James thought that 'the Spaniards are the [best] disciplined foot in the world [and] will refuse no extraordinary service if commanded', he had nothing but contempt – which he all too thinly disguised – for their leaders and Staff Officers.[41] He had already been irritated by the boast of one of Condé's Captains that he would soon replace the Vicomte de Turenne in his 'good graces' and ignored his advice to temper his praise of French military practices. Remember always, the Comte de Marsin warned him, that the Spanish were 'a jealous people'. It was highly unfortunate, therefore, that the Duke did nothing to put his new masters at ease. The English and Irish troops under his command were not slow to pick fights with their Spanish allies, and in August 1657 he lambasted Don Juan, the Marquis of Caracena and the Prince de Ligne for their overcaution in committing their troops to an attack upon an enemy supply convoy. Worse still, during the following month at the siege of Mardyck, James infuriated his superiors by fraternizing openly with the French pickets. He had already been censured for a similar indiscretion after the skirmish at Montbernanson, but on this occasion he strayed out far beyond the safety of the Spanish lines. When challenged by soldiers from the Regiment of Picardy, who had been out foraging, shots were exchanged and it looked certain that bloodshed would surely follow. However, the French Officers recognized the 'big greyhound' which had loped out after the Duke and which had run to the fore as soon as the fighting had begun. Asking if James was with the enemy patrol, they were answered in the affirmative and immediately set about arranging a truce with their foes. The word spread quickly among the French cantonments that the Duke of York was there and some 'two or three hundred officers . . . most of the persons of quality and notable officers in the French army' left their duties to flock around him. Amid this carnival atmosphere, James waived aside the concerns of his Spanish aides – who feared that the courtesies extended to a prince might not be so forthcoming to them, once they were surrounded by their foes – and proudly declared that 'although in the service of Spain, [he] had no fewer friends in the French army'. His old comrades 'alighted from their horses . . . and . . . conversed together [with him] for nearly an hour until Monsieur de Turenne [restored discipline] and ordered them to come back' to their own regiments. Despite James's delight at his popularity and the 'civility' shown to him by his brother Officers, it is notable that his friend and former Commander-in-Chief took no part in these proceedings, and clearly disapproved of them.[42] Turenne's overriding sense of professionalism and dedication to duty had compelled him to place the hard necessities of war, and the need to maintain the fighting spirit and common will of the Army, over and above his private feelings for one single individual. Even though James continually stressed his adherence to the maxims of Turenne, and in later years would come to repeat them *ad infinitum,* there is little evidence from incidents in the field to suggest that he fully understood their significance or that he was capable of applying the teachings of his master to real situations, when forced to think and act for himself.[43] Furthermore, if James might have been a little disappointed by the failure of the Marshal to make his re-acquaintance, he was thoughly bemused and saddened by the inability of his Spanish hosts to delight in his adventures. Riding back to his own lines, he thought only of the extent to which his fame and personal importance had risen, as the consequence of his recent actions. Refusing even to conceive that his conduct might have been open to question, he was so insensitive to the concerns and feelings of his new comrades that he could afford to claim that 'The Duke of York does not positively know whether the Spaniards took umbrage at these courtesies; but at the end of the campaign Monsieur de Marsin advised him, personally, to abstain from them henceforth. He told him that the Spanish character is . . . circumspect; and that although they gave no sign of it, they might not be at all satisfied.'[44]

'The Spaniards', James considered, were 'accustomed to flattering themselves easily on the success of their enterprises'. Unlike the French

Commanders, who constantly exerted themselves in their care for their troops and in rigorously surveying the terrain of the battlefield, the Spanish Staff Officers were models of sloth and irresolution. If Turenne was portrayed as the embodiment of wise judgement and decisive action in James's military memoirs, then Don Juan-Jose and Caracena act as his foils. Despite the honours and kindnesses they heaped upon the Duke of York, they appear in his writings as insubstantial figures: dilettantes, more concerned with court etiquette and the taking of their siestas at the appointed hour, than with correctly ordering their Army before a battle or with pressing home an obvious advantage.[45] This damning evaluation of the effectiveness of the Spanish military has gone largely unchallenged, but it bears no relation to the actual position of Spain in the mid-seventeenth century, as both a major European power and the world's greatest colonial Empire. Similarly, it totally disparages the dedication and professionalism of the Spanish High Command which, although eclipsed since the Battle of Rocroi by French arms, was still capable of delivering a stunning victory at Valenciennes in 1656. In this light, James's criticisms – and his failure to deliver a thorough appraisal of the Prince de Condé's somewhat ambiguous conduct during the campaigns of 1656–8 – carry rather less weight than has previously been thought and begin to take on the appearance of a racist slur. It is significant that Spanish writers were unimpressed by the Duke's posturing as a great military authority and condemned him for his 'rashness' and impetuosity in the field.[46] Their criticisms were echoed by George, Lord Digby, who – although he was generally perceived to be no advocate of either James's intelligence or his abilities – had, nevertheless, witnessed his conduct in Flanders at first hand. In the late summer of 1657, he wrote to Charles II urging him 'to chide the Duke of York for exposing himself to so much danger'. 'It may do well for once to purchase so great applause', Digby noted, 'but should he doe it a second time, as he did on this occasion of [the siege of] Ardres, instead of being admired as he is, he would be censured.' During the siege, James had incurred the wrath of Don Juan by throwing himself needlessly forward into the advance trenches and was rebuked by the Spanish staff for acting unwisely. Although he claimed that he was merely following the precedent set by the Prince de Condé and was obeying, to the letter, the lessons about the value of a thorough reconniassance which he had learned as *aide de camp* to Turenne, there is sufficient doubt to question the wisdom of his conduct. James was no longer a Junior Officer, free to move about the battlefield at will and able to engage in individual combats in order to boost his own reputation. As the Commander of the Anglo-Irish contingent in the allied Army, he was obliged to preserve the chain of command, to report back to his superiors, to submit to their orders without question and to operate as part of a unified team. However, there is nothing in James's accounts of his two campaigns, spent with the Spanish Army in Flanders, to suggest that he ever understood the importance of playing down the national and regional differences of the troops under his command, or of sublimating his own desires in order to promote the common good. Rather, it would seem that his determination to assert his own authority, independently of the other commanders of foreign regiments, helped to fuel the endemic rivalries which already existed between the Spanish nationals, the German and Walloon mercenaries, and the contingents of English, Irish and French exiles who served alongside them.[47] In a patchwork army, such as that led by Don Juan, individual prejudices could divide the command: hindering effective co-operation between different wings and fatally impairing the overall fighting efficiency of the army. This is precisely what happened at the Battle of the Dunes in June 1658.

With the Navy of the Protectorate blockading the Spanish coast and delaying the arrival of payment for the Army of Flanders, Turenne stole a march on his enemies, slipped through their lines, and laid siege to the port at Dunkirk. Outmanoeuvred and thoroughly dismayed, the Spanish Commanders determined to relieve their stranded garrison and to present such a show of force before the French camp that they would feel compelled to withdraw from their positions, rather than risk a decisive and potentially fatal engagement. Confident of the quality of their veteran infantry and sure in the knowledge that their cavalry were well-mounted, and far more numerous than their opponents, Caracena and Don Juan began their advance to the sea. Their plans, however, did not proceed smoothly. Their artillery train lagged far behind the main body of the Army and, not wishing to be slowed further, the Spanish Generals allowed it to become completely detached in their haste to raise the siege. With their supply routes over-extended and straining under the pressure of a forced march, through a countryside already swept clean by Turenne's dragoons, the pride of Don Juan's army – his heavy cavalry – were forced to disperse in search of forage for their horses. More seriously still, the jealousies which had sapped at the vitality of their Commanders throughout the campaign simmered at the council table and boiled over at the very moment that their scouts first began to push at the outposts of Turenne's Army. Don Juan and Caracena sniped incessantly at one another, while Condé openly mocked their battle plans and abrogated his responsibility for the failure which he thought would surely follow. Even before the opening French cannonades ripped through the closely packed ranks of Spanish troops lining the soft sands before Dunkirk, he had been prepared to countenance the possibility of defeat and had communicated his fears to James and his junior officers. Instead of sweeping around the French siege lines to the West, where the ground was open and flat, the Spanish had pushed forward along a narrow coastal strip, that was broken by banks of steep and rolling sand dunes.[48] To their right they were threatened by fire from a squadron of English frigates who patrolled close into the shoreline, while on their left they were bounded by the deep channel of the Furnes–Bruges Canal which limited their ability to fully deploy on the plain. While Lockhart's brigade of Redcoats, drawn from some of the Lord Protector's best regiments, marched on through the night towards the sound of the guns, the Spanish High Command still clung to their belief that their enemies might use the cover of darkness to make good their retreat.

At supper with the Marquis of Caracena, James voiced his opinion that, rather than fleeing, Turenne might venture an immediate attack upon their scattered and largely unprotected bivouacs. Although not unprecedented, Caracena knew that such a hazardous operation was probably beyond the capabilities of any seventeenth-century army and saw no reason why the French should venture to abandon their carefully chosen positions without a clear chance of success. Nightfall could hide the passage of an army, but it could also hinder the secret mustering of troops, delay commands and fatally confuse friend with foe, once battle had been joined. Moreover, the Spaniards, while respectful of the remarkable qualities of the French Marshal, were mindful not to turn him into a deity and to accord him supernatural abilities. With their pride injured by the Duke's constant lectures on the superiority of Turenne's military genius, which served little purpose other than to erode the morale of the men under their command, Caracena and his Staff Officers resolved to show their mettle and bit back that they very much hoped that the French Commander would accept battle at the first possible opportunity, as the Spanish would be more than ready for him. Smarting at their refusal to accept without question the soundness of his every judgement, James refused to cheer his comrades in the face of adversity and retorted, with an air of petulance, that he 'knew Mons[ieu]r de Turenne So well, as to assure them they should ha[v]e that Satisfaction', before taking his leave of the assembled dignitaries and returning to his own billet.[49]

Though the night passed without incident, at dawn the drums of the French Army beat the call to arms and Lockhart's brigade surged forward on to the sands, under the cover of the frigates' guns. Highly visible on his thorough-bred, Turenne noted 'on the faces of all our troops a cheerful expression that was of good omen for the success of the day' and galloped down the length of his advancing line, shouting encouragement to his soldiers and reordering the dispositions of his regiments, accordingly. Pausing only briefly to send his compliments to Major-General Morgan, he drew rein and dropped back behind the leading formations, so that he might better observe the progress of the English regiments under his command, who were the first to make contact with the enemy. Outstripping their French allies, the Redcoats swarmed over the sandbanks and crashed through the Spanish line with a great roar, which was taken up and made 'generall from all their foot'.[50] Recoiling in horror, the men of Boniface's Regiment were pushed back off the summit of the dunes, while their Officers fell in a desperate defence of their colours. Seeing his right wing faltering under the English onslaught, Don Juan sent James hurrying across the battlefield with reinforcements, determined to plug the gap in the line. Plunging into the midst of his foes, James was beaten back and was left to rue that 'all who were at the head of my own Troope, were either killed or wounded; of which number I had been one, had not the goodness of my armes preserv'd me'. Rallying his own horse guards and a handful of Don Juan's household troops, who had escaped being cut to ribbons on the English pikes, he attempted to stem the flight of Boniface's men. In the midst of the confusion, he came upon the Marquis of Caracena who demanded to know why he had not already charged the enemy. 'I answered him', the Duke recalled, that 'I had already done it, and [been] worsted for my paines; farther telling him, That considering the present posture of the Enemy, it was impossible to be done.' Yet even as the two Field Officers remonstrated with one another, and spat out accusations about the misconduct of their affairs, Morgan was leading his soldiers on again into the heart of the Spanish line. In order to relieve the pressure on the infantry, James consented to charge once more at the head of forty of his bodyguards 'and charg'd that Battalion So home, that I broke into them, doing great execution upon them', and managing to fell one unfortunate musketeer 'by a stroke I gave him with my sword over the face, which layd him along upon the ground'.[51]

Ever afterwards, James would cling to the belief that had he been properly supported by his fellow Officers he might yet have carried the day, but this was almost certainly not the case. Right across the battlefield, the regiments of Spain and her allies were already breaking up, with the whole 'Army . . . in rout . . . scatter'd, and every man endeavour'd to gett off, which few of them were so lucky as to perform'. To the far left of the Duke's position, the French had already cleared the remaining mercenaries from out the watermeadows which bordered the canal, while the remaining supporters of the Prince de Condé were in headlong flight, having seen their Captain unhorsed and lost from view amid the mêlée. In the centre, Don Juan fought with the utmost bravery, despite several of his battalions not 'Staying to be thoroughly charg'd; which cowardise of theirs, and the defeat of Boniface['s] . . . Regiment . . . strook such a terrour into our horse . . . that the greatest part of them . . .

ran away without being charg'd, or even without seeing an Enemy.' Even on the extreme right, where James and his companions had managed to ride in among those companies of musketeers who had been disordered by a hard climb over the shifting sands, they failed to break the resistance of the Protectorate troops. One observer thought that they fought 'like wild beasts', while James dryly noted that 'not so much as one single man of them ask'd quarter, or threw down his armes; but every one defended himself to the last: so that wee ran as great danger by the butt end of their musketts, as by the volley which they had given us'. After almost four hours of fighting, 'the Regiments of Picardy and Turenne . . . were as far advanced as where our men had been incamped the night before', and James decided that he 'was obliged to make what hast[e] I could to get away', as 'I thought it but reasonable to endeavour my own escape'.[52] Beside him, the Duke of Gloucester had had his sword struck from out of his hand and Charles Berkeley – the Captain of his horseguards – had been wounded. With only a handful of troopers left to escort him from the field, James did not attract the attention of the enemy and was able to pass himself off as a French Officer when questioned. Avoiding the wreckage of the Spanish Army and the bottlenecks created by anxious footsoldiers, who jammed the mainstreets of the little villages which lined his route east, James picked up the main highway and was reunited with Don Juan and his shattered command. They halted at Furnes, where they regrouped around their artillery and baggage trains, and were spared a fresh pursuit only by Turenne's decision to break off contact and return to his primary objective, the capture of Dunkirk.

On receiving the news that the town had fallen, the Spanish Army withdrew to the relative safety of Nieuport where its leaders met for one last council of war. It was to be a heated affair, more suited to the settling of scores than to the accomplishment of anything that was positive and practical. Don Juan presided over a command that was fatally weakened and divided. Condé, who had only narrowly escaped from the battle with his life, may already have begun to question his future in the service of Spain and to examine the possibility of negotiating a return – upon almost any conditions – to his homeland. Caracena remained unreconciled to his Commander-in-Chief, and James's biting criticisms of superiors only served to inflame an already volatile situation and to destroy any remaining chance of holding the Army together. Indeed, the Prince de Condé was so shocked by the intemperate language of the Duke that he asked him why he would venture to destroy the last vestiges of Don Juan's authority, in front of his own general staff. What right, the Frenchman asked, did he have to contradict, and upbraid, the son of a King and a superior Officer to the detriment of the entire Army? James's reply, when it came, was as blunt as it was revealing: 'I answer'd him,

Because I had no desire to be forced to run again, as wee had done so lately at Dunkirk.'[53] Injured pride and the fear of failure far outweighed his sense of duty, and James – who demanded total obedience from others – can be seen to have offered his only conditionally. With the fragile unity of the Spanish and their heterogeneous allies shattered, the Army broke up into its constituent parts and went its separate ways. Unable to face the French in the field, detachments were sent to reinforce the barrier fortresses of Flanders. Condé set out for Ostend, the Prince de Ligne for Ypres, and Don Juan returned to Bruges, while James was left behind at Nieuport with only the disagreeable Marquis of Caracena for company.

Yet if the Duke of York could only watch as successive Spanish strong-holds fell to the might of Turenne's guns, and feel a pang of sullen resentment at the Marshal's unstinting praise for the bravery of his English allies, he chose to view the débâcle of the Battle of the Dunes as being nothing short of a personal triumph: a vindication of his courage and strength in arms. That the last regiments of Royalist exiles, preserved for so long by Charles II as testament to his commitment to Spain and in the hopes of one day launching a fresh assault upon the British Isles, had been broken and irredeemably lost, featured little in James's calculations. The praise of his father's old adherents, who rejoiced in his brisk charge and gallantry, and the selfless love which parties of Royalist gentlemen had displayed in scouring the field for his person when they believed that he had been lost or taken, served to confirm the Duke in his belief in his own worth. Moreover, while his factual account of the battle did not significantly differ from that given by Turenne, the purpose and tone of his writings are far removed from the terse and saturnine descriptions provided by his idol. Where Turenne was self-effacing and the master of understatement – writing to his wife only, that: 'The enemy came to us and God be praised they have been defeated: I was pretty busy all day, which has fatigued me: I wish you good night' – James sought to recreate every sight and sound that he had experienced that day, and to chart his every movement on the field.[54] The recollection of the exhilaration he felt at the charge and the brutal excitement of battle, lends his account a unique colour and sense of immediacy, which finds no echo in the Marshal's objective and dispassionate assessments. While Turenne sought to praise every one of his own captains who had 'done his best', and paid a generous tribute to his foes: 'Don John and the Marquis of Caracena, the Duke of York, and the Duke of Gloucester . . . [who] behav'd themselves very well', James's major concern was to justify his own actions and to apportion the blame for the defeat among his senior Com-manders.[55] It is significant that it was this pursuit of personal glory which animated his undeniable skills as a writer, while it was the grim necessity and the human cost of achieving victory, in the name of the State, which proved to be the hallmarks of Turenne's reflections. While the Marshal lamented the deaths of the common footsoldiers, to whom he felt a responsibility, James delighted in the business of killing. He recorded, without emotion, the names of all the noblemen and dignitaries who had fallen in the engagement but passed no comment upon the slaughter of the rank and file, admitting only that: 'I cannot say what Captains and other inferiour Officers were made prisoners.'[56] This inability to recognize the human suffering of others, allied to the single-minded pursuit of his own military advancement, would do much to determine and define James's conception of the art of war.

Having failed to force a general engagement with the French troops sent to harry his positions, it was at Nieuport in September 1658 that the Duke of York learned of Cromwell's death. Pleading that 'the Season of the year being too far spent . . . there was not any need of my presence at the place of my Command', James abandoned his post and 'made what haste [he] could to Bruxelles', in order to take advantage of this sudden and unexpected crisis at the heart of the Republican government. During the following summer, the rising in Cheshire – led by Sir George Booth – united old Royalists with discontented Presbyterians, and gave the exiled Stuarts renewed hope for an 'alteration of [their] affaires'.[57] James left his brother's court and crossed the French border, in an attempt to seek out his old Commander and to solicit his help in organizing an invasion of England. At Amiens, he came to Turenne 'in disguise' and was gratified to discover that the Marshal was prepared not only to renew their friendship, but also to authorize a descent upon the coast which was not dependent upon either the approval of Cardinal Mazarin or the Court at Paris. Concerned at the behaviour of 'the multitude of sects that overspread Great Britain', Turenne pushed aside all thoughts of his government's commitment to the alliance with the English Republic and reasserted the traditional 'rights' of his family as a Prince of Sedan.[58] Determining to do 'the Royal House of Stuart a considerable piece of service', he allowed James to draw upon his own credit and offered him the command of over twelve hundred men: comprising the Regiment of Turenne and the Scottish Gendarmes of the *Maison du Roi*. An artillery train was assembled and thousands of surplus weapons were loaded aboard ship, which could be used to arm new recruits to the fledgling army, once they had landed before Dover. Unfortunately, their preparations were disturbed by the news that the rising in Cheshire had collapsed in the most ignominious of fashions and that Booth had been taken, disguised as a woman, at an inn at Newport Pagnell. With Lambert's troopers hunting down the fugitives along the Welsh border and opposition to the government of the Commonwealth spluttering out across Surrey and Oxfordshire, Turenne

decided that despite the 'great . . . stir in England . . . that defeat
overturns at present all my projects', and moved to have the whole
operation aborted.[59] James, however, was not so easily dissuaded and
tenaciously hung on to his dreams of leading an army back into England.
To command alongside Turenne, once more, and to seek to overturn the
military verdict of the entire English Civil Wars was such an alluring
prospect that he was loathe, under almost any circumstances, to give it up.
Not knowing what preparations Charles II had made to support Booth's
rising and having lost track of his brother's movements entirely, since he
had left Brussels, James pleaded with the Marshal to set sail immediately
for the Cinque Ports. Although he had no evidence with which to back up
his claims, James was convinced that the King had already landed in either
the South-West or in Wales, and was in very great danger. If they failed to
act now, he argued, they would have permanently ceded the initiative to
the Commonwealth cause and would have been guilty of failing in their
duty to King Charles II, having allowed him to be delivered up into the
hands of his enemies, without a blow being struck. If there was still the
slightest chance of establishing a bridgehead at the port of Rye and of
raising the South for the King, then, he suggested to Turenne, they were
already morally obliged to act in his defence.

Had Charles II indeed left for England, as he had originally planned,
James may well have had a strong case but the intelligence reports which
filtered back from the coast of Brittany suggested otherwise to the French
Commander. Turenne was in no doubt that the King had been unable to
obtain a passage aboard ship and 'was not gone for England', and chose
to make it plain to James 'that tho he were, it was not reasonable for the
Duke to hazard himself, when there was no probability of Success'.[60]
Thoroughly dejected, James returned to Brussels having obtained only a
pass through the French lines and a loan of a further 300 *pistoles* from the
Marshal, with which to ease his journey. He had not, however, thought to
abandon his plan to invade England and began to muster those remnants
of his command at the Battle of the Dunes who had managed to struggle
back to the gates of Brussels, and who now sought useful employment on
every street corner of the city. Assuring both his brother's servants and
the Royalist underground at work in London, that he 'was very resolute
to put himself into action at the first opportunity', he ordered his scratch
force out on to the road for St Omer. His intended passage through the
flat, open countryside of Flanders, which had been so deeply scarred in
recent years by the continual movements of rival armies, left nothing to
secrecy and word of the plan came quickly to the attention of the Spanish
authorities. Having confined his own troops to their winter quarters, Don
Juan had returned to his father's court at Madrid and had conferred his
command of the province to Caracena. The Marquis, mindful of the

slights he had suffered at James's hand, cast dark and 'dry looks' over his latest venture and confined his soldiers to their barracks, firmly refusing the Duke of York his permission to proceed any further.[61] He feared the possible breaches in security that might be occasioned by the continual recrossing of the front line, and was reluctant to let bands of trained soldiers – whose services had already been pledged to the Spanish Crown – renegotiate the terms of their employment and fraternize with the enemy, almost at will. At this point, both the Spanish authorities and their French counterparts seem to have finally tired of James's free-booting. With peace talks underway, aimed at bringing the conflict between the two great powers to a satisfactory conclusion, neither side wanted to provoke fresh trouble or to give unnecessary offence to the other. As a result, James's spurious pleas that Marshal Turenne had provided him with a warrant which authorized all of his actions, fell upon stony ground and he was forced to disband his remaining troops. The signing of the Peace of the Pyrenees, in November 1659, dealt a further blow to his military career as, at a stroke, the fighting in the Low Countries was brought to an end and the Prince de Condé facilitated his return to France by breaking up his Army, and paying off his foreign regiments.[62] Having thrown over his Spanish commission in his haste to take command of the projected invasion force, the Duke was now once again unemployed, wholly unable to pay his soldiers what was owed to them and totally dependent upon the scant resources of Charles II's tattered little court for his own subsistence.

James's reappearance at Bruges, therefore, did little to raise the morale of the exile community and threatened to rekindle discord among his brother's councillors. Even though, by his own admission, the Duke's fortunes had been 'reduced to the lowest ebb', he continued to refuse to rule out the military option and to accord a greater value to diplomatic overtures which were being made to the increasing number of special interest groups within the English Republic, who had viewed the collapse of the Protectorate with dismay.[63] These groups – comprising those Presbyterian grandees excluded from the Commonwealth Parliaments, frustrated placemen, disaffected soldiers and City merchants, fearing for their profits – if they could be correctly harnessed, offered constitutional Royalism enormous reservoirs of previously untapped popular support. To this end, Sir Edward Hyde charted a careful and deliberate course; holding up the promise of a stable monarchical government bounded by the Parliamentary reforms of 1640–1, and reinforced by the re-establishment of an inclusive national Church. His attempts to allay the fears of those who had taken up arms against their sovereign at the outbreak of the Civil Wars, did not, however, find sympathy with the Duke of York. Although the failure of Booth's rising had demonstrated, beyond all doubt, the futility of unilateral military action against the might of the Commonwealth, James was unwilling to see the struggle against the Republic in anything other than military terms. Final victory, he believed, could only come through the battlefield. The Berkeleys picked fights with the King's civilian counsellors and crudely contrasted James's skill as a soldier with the supposed sloth, and passivity, of his elder brother. With the Duke's blessing, members of his household targeted Hyde for censure and equated him with all the troubles which had afflicted their cause.[64] In this version of events, it was the failure of the Royalist movement to unanimously endorse James's invasion of England, and not the inability of Booth and his partisans to garner sufficient support, which had undermined the recent struggles for a Restoration. With external assistance, in the shape of French and Spanish troops, becoming an increasingly remote possibility, and with peace returning to the states of central and western Europe, James had to face the prospect of his exile becoming permanent and to accept, henceforth, that his livelihood would depend solely upon his removal to the very margins of the Continent, in order to seek what employment he could, as an itinerant mercenary soldier.

CHAPTER FOUR

The Brother of the King

I

In the spring of 1660, James Stuart found himself to be just one more young Prince among the growing band of minor royals who, having been dispossessed by the wars and revolutions of the previous thirty years, were forced to take service with foreign powers as and when they could, jostling for appointments and preferment around the Courts of Europe. In this struggle, James was admittedly more fortunate than most. His reputation for bravery under fire had been confirmed by his conduct at the Battle of the Dunes, and spread abroad by his friends and propagandists, while the association of his name with the exploits of both Turenne and Condé ensured not only that he won the respect of his peers, but that he also assumed the mantle of an able and experienced Field Commander, which was to remain unchallenged for almost thirty years. Despite the animosity of Caracena, the Spanish authorities were still bound by the spirit of their treaty commitments to the exiled Royalist Court to assist James in securing fresh employment. If the war in Flanders had ceased, then Spain was still fighting to put down a rebellion by the Portuguese. The sheer weight of the Duke's patronage was more than enough to ensure that he would have little trouble in finding a command in the forthcoming campaigning season, but the memory of the divisive role he had played in the Low Countries led him to be offered a post which although prestigious, was also likely to be devoid of any real authority. While James proudly recalled that the post of High Admiral of Spain 'was never given to any but the King's Sons or near Relations, and whoever enjoys it . . . wherever he lands [in the colonies] . . . commands as Vice Roy of the Country whilst he stays in it', there is good reason to believe that he would never have gone to sea at the head of a Spanish fleet. Such an exalted position in the service of Spain could only be held, actively, by a practising Roman Catholic. During this period, there is nothing in James's make-up to suggest that he held a deep affection for the Roman faith, beyond a broad respect for individual Catholics and an acceptance of the justice of the argument for tolerating their personal beliefs. Moreover, any change in the Duke's religion would have been rigorously opposed by Charles II and would have been greeted with absolute horror by the overwhelmingly Anglican constituency, which comprised his father's most devoted followers. With little evidence to suggest that James was actually prepared to take this drastic step, it seems likely that his title would have been an empty one and that he would have been consigned to the periphery of the Spanish Court. He himself hinted at the truth of the matter, when he admitted that it was not the prospect of immediate military action which had drawn him to accept this position but rather the status it bestowed, 'as a very honourable post' which kept alive his pretensions to the Lord High Admiralcy of England, and the large financial remuneration which came from the settling of a fifth of all Spanish prize money upon his person. It was 'also a very advantageous one even as to profit', James confirmed, 'which was what the Duke then wanted'.[1]

With his future income apparently guaranteed, an advance guard of Staff Officers was quickly dispatched to Spain in order to prepare James's way. However, even then things did not go quite according to plan, as the offer of the Duke's naval command was subtly, but significantly, amended by Caracena to extend only as far as a detachment of the fleet stationed off the coast of Flanders. These ships could, in theory, be used as the nucleus of a new armada with which to launch an invasion of England, but in practice the resources which were to be allocated to James were wholly inadequate to the task at hand. As the political situation in England suddenly deteriorated, it was important for King Philip IV to be seen to be working in Charles II's interests and to be honouring the provisions of the treaty of 1656. With the minimum of outlay he might seek to enhance his position as an arbiter of European affairs, gain an invaluable advantage from the possible upturn in the fortunes of King Charles II, and also manage to keep a troublesome and noisy Prince in profitable employment. The quickening pace of events, however, overtook all of his plans and James's voyage to Spain, in order to discuss the terms of his service, 'was happily prevented by the wonderful changes, which were almost daily produced in England'. As the Commonwealth threatened to disappear under the weight of its own debts and Republican opinion fractured, General Monck led his army south from Scotland to reimpose order and to usher in a 'Free Parliament', comprising all those members who had been excluded from the chamber during the previous twelve years. 'And when the motion [of these events] was once begun', James commented with almost an air of disbelief, 'it went on so fast, that [the royal brothers were] almost in [their] own Country, before those abroad, especially the Spaniards, would believe there was any Revolution towards it.'[2]

The English Republic, which until recently had seemed to be impregnable, suddenly fell in on itself and collapsed with the merest whimper. Although groups of soldiers hurried from their garrisons to muster on the slopes of Edgehill in a symbolic act, to proclaim the onset of a new struggle and to draw strength from the knowledge of their past endeavours, their leader – General Lambert – was seized by one of his old comrades and hauled off back to London in disgrace. With the Army thoroughly purged by Monck of its natural leaders and religious visionaries, the great Presbyterian landowners who had dominated Parliament throughout much of the First Civil War returned to prominence and took their seats upon the Council of State. While the City of London rejoiced, and mobs of apprentices and drunken soldiers dealt out hard blows to any Quaker or servant of the old regime who was unlucky enough to cross their paths, this elite caucus aimed to hold the balance of power and to negotiate the return of the King, under their own terms. Those nobles, like the Earl of Northumberland, who from 1641 to 1648 had chosen to act out of duty to their conscience rather than out of loyalty to their sovereign, now came to realize that their dreams of a limited monarchy, acting under the advice and with the consent of Parliament, was at last within their grasp. The stream of letters and the famous Declaration of Breda, that flowed out to them from the industrious pen of Sir Edward Hyde, served to allay their fears of Royalist reprisals and to confirm them in their belief that religious comprehension, based around a rejuvenated Presbyterian Church, was possible. However, even as they prepared the ground for the King's return and reaped the benefits of high office so long denied to them, they fatally misjudged the mood of the country. Rather than marking a return to the allegedly halcyon days of the Elizabethan Church and sparking a renaissance in their affairs, the early months of 1660 represented no more than a watershed for the Presbyterian grandees and their preachers, a brief 'Indian Summer' before terminal decline and disillusion set in. Having first harnessed and then released the forces of reaction which had lain dormant at the heart of English society, they were completely unable to control them. The radical reforming appeal of Calvinism among the gentry and county elites was rapidly fading, eclipsed by the zeal of the sectaries, on the one hand, and by the social conservatism of resurgent Anglicanism, on the other. Unable to compete, the Presbyterian party watched as their candidates were swept aside in successive elections to the Parliaments of 1660 and 1661, by some of Royalism's most uncompromising partisans. Thus, while it was the spirit of Hyde's patient and conciliatory statesmanship which had effected the act of Restoration itself, the new style of politics ushered in by the return of King Charles II was to be governed by men who were thoroughly in tune with many of James's overriding prejudices about the nature of political sovereignty and the need for retribution against their former enemies. Assisted by the final implosion of the organized Republican movement, as its remaining adherents failed to agree about either a common manifesto or a consistent course of action, Charles II was restored on a wave of genuinely popular support, with the bare minimum of constraints and preconditions placed upon him and his ministers. Although the grosser abuses of the royal prerogative, such as the Star Chamber and the Court of Wards, were not revived, the House of Lords was reconstituted along its pre-war lines and the Church of England was restored to prominence, recovering much of its lands and all of its self-confidence in the process. Reanimated with a militant and unforgiving spirit, Anglicanism would become the driving force behind the new Cavalier Parliament of 1661 and would do much to define the dominant political climate in England, for more than the next half-century.[3]

Even though James had played little part in these events, and his prognostication of a military rather than a political defeat of Republicanism had proved to be entirely misplaced, these dramatic and wholly unexpected events had fundamentally altered, and suddenly redefined, his own position as a Prince of the blood. During his years of exile, he had fought for the Crown in foreign wars in an attempt to bolster its flagging prestige, to provide for his own subsistence, and to maintain the pretence that there was still a Royalist Army in the field. As a result, while he had been an important instrument of his brother's cause, he had been ultimately expendable in the pursuit of its wider aims. However, now that the Restoration had been accomplished, without the foreseen levels of bloodshed and social dislocation, the rationale behind his military career and relative freedom of action had dissolved, almost overnight. The Duke of York now found himself to be a central pillar of a youthful, and as yet insecure, ruling dynasty: a mere heartbeat away from the throne itself. The simple, and self-evident, fact of his royal birth ensured that not only his preservation but also all of his subsequent activities held a vital importance for the survival and perpetuation of the system of monarchy. It was James's dynastic significance and his unique position within the fabric of the restored monarchy which accounted for the distinctive flavour of his new public appointments, and which contributed a great deal to the unprecedented scope of his powers, and to the wide range of his interests and influence as Duke of York.[4]

II

When King Charles II had stepped ashore at Dover, in May 1660, to the sound of saluting cannon, cheering crowds and loyal addresses, he was accompanied by both of his younger brothers. This was in itself a remarkable feat, for no brother of a reigning English monarch had managed to survive into adulthood since the late Middle Ages. However, the presence of not one but two royal Dukes, at the side of the throne, generated a new set of problems for the House of Stuart, that needed to be quickly resolved after the return to England. Appointments had to be found for York and Gloucester, and revenues settled upon them. Most importantly of all, there was the need for them to be successfully accommodated within the political settlement. As there was no existing precedent with which to gauge the limits of their powers, or to define their roles within the monarchy, one had to be forged over the course of the decade, largely on the basis of expediency, trial and error. In the ordinary course of events this process would have been of secondary importance, but the failure of the direct line of succession made it an altogether more pressing concern.

Charles II had come to the throne as a relatively young and active man, and as such there was no reason to suppose that, having already fathered a string of natural children, he would not marry and produce a legitimate heir of his own. However, as the years passed by, it became increasingly clear that his marriage to Catherine of Braganza would not result in the birth of a healthy child. It was not until 7 May 1668 that the King wrote to his sister, the Duchess of Orléans, that his wife had conceived only to have miscarried 'a perfect child', of about ten weeks old. A year later, stories began to circulate around the Court and the City of London that Catherine was again pregnant. However, on 7 June the King wrote that his wife 'after all our hopes, has miscarried', and that this had taken place 'without any visible accident'. He, thereafter, became increasingly sceptical about the ability of the Queen to have any children at all, telling his sister that 'The physicians are divided whether it were a false conception or a good one.' Catherine was never again able to conceive, but equally significant was the popular assumption that she was barren, a belief that was not only voiced in the press but was also daubed on the walls of the capital city.[5]

The failure of the bloodline threw the succession into doubt, creating a problem which was to become increasingly important as the reign progressed and which, in the form of the Exclusion Crisis, was to threaten the very existence of the monarchy itself. This potentially dangerous situation was still further exacerbated by Charles II's own actions. He showed little concern for the need to consolidate the position of his own House and to ensure a smooth transfer of power, to a designated heir, after his death. Instead of resolving the matter beyond all shadow of doubt, he chose to play off the different factions at Court, one against the other, introducing an air of ambiguity and uncertainty into any discussion of the royal succession. In the short term, this ploy worked very well for the King. It enabled him to leave all of his options open until the very last minute and to always keep his opponents guessing about his true intentions and as to his real favourites. When his heart dictated, or when the Whig opposition appeared to be in the ascendant, he was free to indulge the ambitions of the Duke of Monmouth or to condone projects aimed at his own remarriage. Conversely, for the greater part of his reign, he was able to follow his natural political instincts and to uphold the law of primogeniture, lending his strong backing to the principle that James, under whatever circumstances, still retained the right to succeed him in due course. Unfortunately, while this policy enabled Charles II to effectively trim his sails and weather the political storms of the 1670s and early 1680s, it also created long-term instability at the heart of the political nation and threw the junior members of his family into a starker prominence than they would otherwise have enjoyed. If this were not bad enough in itself, Charles had been prepared to ignore popular concerns and to countenance two potentially disastrous marriages for his brother, James.

The first, to Sir Edward Hyde's daughter – Anne – in 1660, brought with it no material or political gains for the House of Stuart, and served only to compromise the position of the Lord Chancellor, in the eyes of his peers, and to fully expose James's own weaknesses of character. Though his memoirs recalled only that he had met Anne in Paris, while she had been serving as a maid of honour to his sister – the Princess of Orange – in 1656, it seems likely that James embarked upon an affair with her soon afterwards and gave her his promise to marry her, at the first available opportunity. With the strict moral code which had sought to govern the Court of King Charles I no more than a distant memory to his sons, and with the open enjoyment of their sexuality at a premium for the royal brothers – as yet unencumbered for James, by responsibility or by the proscriptive mores of organized religion – such matters were of little consequence.[6] During their exile, the Royal Court had often taken on the character and appearance of an armed camp. It was frequently on the move, perennially short of money and necessarily informal; it survived only to protect the person of the King and to attempt to engineer his return to the throne. While marriages with foreign heiresses consistently eluded the royal brothers, Charles II took a series of lovers – girls from relatively modest backgrounds – who were pursued solely in the cause of pleasure and whose passing from the Court signified next to nothing. Having undergone the privations of exile, when Charles II finally did take possession of his crown, at the comparatively late age of thirty, his tastes and attitudes had been fully formed and he found it difficult to abandon many of the habits he had acquired as a 'private' gentleman. He was determined to enjoy being King, and to seize upon all the opportunities for comfort and personal gratification that his office afforded him. Thus, Charles II's mistresses, even after the Restoration, came to be viewed as an accepted – if not universally approved of – part of the life of the Royal Court. Yet, if the King was able to cheerfully father a whole string of illegitimate children, without incurring an overwhelming chorus of disapproval, then James – through his inability to either settle upon a life with Anne or to set her firmly aside – contrived to break the taboos of his age.

Shortly after their return to England, Anne had announced to him that she was pregnant with his child and, despite the discrepancies in their social status, James had rushed to his brother to beg, upon his bended knees, that he might have 'his majesty's leave and permission . . . "that he might publicly marry her"'.[7] However, having once gained the consent of the King, James experienced a change of heart which was as rapid as it was complete. Reviled for his stupidity, by both Henrietta Maria and by the Princess of Orange, James was urged to remember that he was a Stuart Prince and should act accordingly. In an act of contrition, he resolved to abandon Anne and, encouraged by Sir Charles Berkeley, he allowed several of his closest companions to claim that they too had slept with the girl. With the child's parentage called into doubt, and with Anne's character blackened beyond all recognition, James hoped that the contract would be easily set aside. In this, he found an unexpected ally in the form of Anne's own father, the newly enobled Lord Clarendon, who had few illusions about either James's political acumen or his personal immaturity, and who viewed the royal marriage as no more than a dangerous liability. However, despite James's pleadings that he would 'never . . . see the woman again, who had been so false to him' and the advice of his chancellor, that he should imprison Anne for her temerity or else marry her off to a private gentleman, the King contrived to undo all of their plans.[8] In a rare display of prudery, which reflected both his annoyance at James's vacillation and his abiding delight in the misfortunes of others, Charles II announced that the child was undeniably his brother's and that, as such, the contract between him and Anne was both just and legally binding. With James reconciled to his betrothed and with the fears of Clarendon – that 'the whole kingdom would be inflamed to the punishment of it' – largely dispelled, the marriage ceremony was conducted at the dead of night, on 5 September 1660, with only the son of the Duke of Ormonde and one of Anne's maids in attendance.[9]

While James's union with the Lady Anne would raise no more than a brief ripple of amused gossip at Court, his actions in seeking to avoid the match had revealed that particularly volatile combination of uncontrollable sexual energy, followed by feelings of guilt and revulsion, which underpinned all of the Duke's physical relationships and which surfaced, in the form of indecision and self-doubt, at particular moments of strain. Indeed, during his final exile in the 1690s – as age finally blunted the edge of his sexual desire – James would go so far as to attribute all of his misfortunes to his early infidelities, which he thought had turned the favour of God decisively away from him.[10] This need to attribute his failures to his own lust and to the malice of others, speaks not of a tragic degeneration and a dissolution of his powers but of a fundamental inability to control his urges, to reconcile his feelings of guilt, and to rationally appraise his own abilities, which was an ever-present feature of his character throughout his entire adult life. Consequently, Lorenzo Magalotti's scurrilous observation, that 'In his inclination towards sensuality he is the opposite of the King, since he cares little for the more innocent preparations for tenderness, and longs for the occasion for the release of a vicious brutality', and Charles II's pointed jest that his brother had his priests pick out his mistresses for him as a special form of penance, may have a particular poignancy and resonance about them. Just as he was to retreat into himself upon Salisbury Plain in the winter of 1688, in an attempt to ignore the pressing realities which shook his throne, so too, in the summer of 1660, Clarendon had noticed that James – when under stress – had grown 'melancholic and dispirited, and cared not for company, nor those divertisements in which he formerly delighted'. Moreover, the Lord Chancellor was surprised to discover that James had managed to blank any thought of his predicament from his mind and 'that, in all that time, the duke never spake one word to him of that affair'.[11]

The memory of James's disreputable conduct over his marriage to Anne Hyde, had, however, made a particularly strong impression upon Charles II and coloured his attitudes to all of his brother's subsequent requests to be allowed to remarry after the death of his first Duchess, in 1671. James had wasted no time in searching for a new bride, but his petition for leave to marry Susan Bellasyse – another commoner – drew only scorn from the King. Curtly informing his brother that 'he could not play the fool again at his age', Charles II set about scouring Europe for a purely dynastic alliance with a foreign Princess, who would bring with her new allies and fresh subsidies for the English Crown. Unfortunately, while Susan Bellasyse had been a Protestant, the list of eligible royals presented to James, for scrutiny as possible brides, included only Roman Catholics. Having passed over a selection of French and southern German princesses, as well as the little nieces of the Vicomte de Turenne, James finally settled upon Mary d'Este, the eldest daughter of the Dowager Duchess of Modena, as his second wife. This match, which received the full blessing of Charles II, was not only curiously ill-timed but brought with it few obvious advantages and many, all too apparent, dangers. Modena was no more than a pocket state, a narrow fertile plain in the north of Italy, sandwiched in between the Alps and the Apennine

Mountains, and surrounded on almost every side by its more illustrious neighbours: Florence, Genoa, Milan and the Papal States. It had survived, so far, by drawing upon the support of the great European powers and playing off each, in turn, against their rivals. It was now fully committed to the France of Louis XIV for both its inspiration and continued protection, and, to the informed observer, seemed to offer England no more from an alliance than a further strain upon her already overstretched resources. If this were not deterrent enough, then the effect upon domestic public opinion of a marriage between an heir to the throne, who was already suspected of having converted to Roman Catholicism, and an Italian Princess, who had grown up steeped in the traditions of the Counter Reformation, should have set warning bells ringing in the head of any astute English politician.[12] That Charles II should have allowed Henry Bennet, now ennobled as the Earl of Arlington, and James's envoy, the Earl of Peterborough, to proceed with such a fool-hardy alliance is testament to the extent to which the King was prepared to sit back and let events take their own course.

The arrival of Mary of Modena at Dover, on 21 November 1673, did little to allay the suspicions of Protestant England that their Prince was in league with Rome, or that their King was preparing to sell them to France. At the same time as Charles II had finally been forced to prorogue the Cavalier Parliament, amid calls for the Duke of York to be stripped of his commands, the appearance of a deeply pious foreign Princess, who brought with her train a Roman Confessor and who made no secret of her desire to have entered a convent, seemed to confirm the worst fears of Anglican and Dissenter alike. There could now be little doubt as to the nature of James's chosen religion and the prospect of his young bride presenting him with a son and heir, who might be raised as a Roman Catholic, opened up before them. Although not widely reported, the fact that Louis XIV had paid for Mary's dowry in an attempt to bind English and French foreign policy more closely, served to further disquiet some of the Stuarts' most loyal servants. Consequently, the great nobility chose to stay away from the wedding celebrations and, as before, only a handful of important guests were there to cry out the foreign-sounding '*vivats*', which announced the confirmation of the legally binding marriage ceremony. For James's part, as far as can be discerned, he seems to have considered that his marriages were private or purely family affairs, which had little immediate impact upon the workings of the State or upon the sensibilities of his own countrymen. In this context, he could be forgiven for choosing to ignore the complaints of those MPs and Lords who equated his marriage with the French alliance and with the burden of extra taxation levied to pay for an increasingly unpopular war with Holland. Similarly, the absurdity of popular rumours about Roman

Catholic risings and plots to secure the Crown, was clearly apparent to James and his followers when confronted by the reality of a shy, and frightened, fifteen-year-old girl who trembled and wept openly on first catching sight of her middle-aged husband.[13] Unfortunately for James, his every initiative as heir presumptive was open to scrutiny, discussion, and to a wide range of conflicting interpretations. The admonition of his paternal grandfather, that 'the prince's actions are those set up upon a stage', held true for a seventeenth-century audience who were well versed in symbolism and who looked primarily to their Princes to uphold the existing social order. In challenging the assumptions of Protestant England and in seeking to upset, however unwittingly, the status quo, James had managed to elevate the question of the succession to one of national importance. It was no longer the sole preserve of the ruling dynasty, but a matter which seemed to directly affect the lives and prosperity of all Englishmen regardless of their social status. Charles II's failure, in the 1660s and 1670s, to provide for and to clearly determine a single male heir, when combined with James's suspected Catholicism and his Italian marriage, thus created the conditions of deep unease and suspicion about the future course of English governance which struck at all levels of society, and which exploded with such popular force in 1678 as the Popish Plot.[14]

It can be clearly seen, therefore, that the circumstances which surrounded both of James's marriages should have combined to totally undermine his prestige as heir presumptive. However, this was not to be the case, due to the conjunction of a number of entirely unforeseen circumstances, which actually served to reinforce his position within the Restoration monarchy. The smallpox epidemic, which swept across Europe in 1660, deprived the Royal House of two of its youngest members: the King's sister Mary, Princess of Orange, who died at the age of twenty-nine, and his brother Henry, Duke of Gloucester, who died unmarried at the age of twenty (see Figure 2, p. 95). Gloucester's premature death, in particular, had deep repercussions for the Stuarts and served to focus even greater attention upon the issue of the succession. Henry garnered many fulsome obituaries from his contemporaries and Clarendon thought fit to describe him as being 'in truth the finest youth and of the most manly understanding that I have ever known'. It was significant that at the time of his death he was a Protestant, and this single fact has been seized upon by several modern writers to suggest that had he survived he might later have emerged as a popular rival to the Catholic James.[15] However, this is a point which has been somewhat overstretched. A young life cut short always appears to offer the promise of a great talent unfulfilled and similarly extravagant – and unfounded – claims to greatness have been made on behalf of a long

Figure 2 The House of Stuart

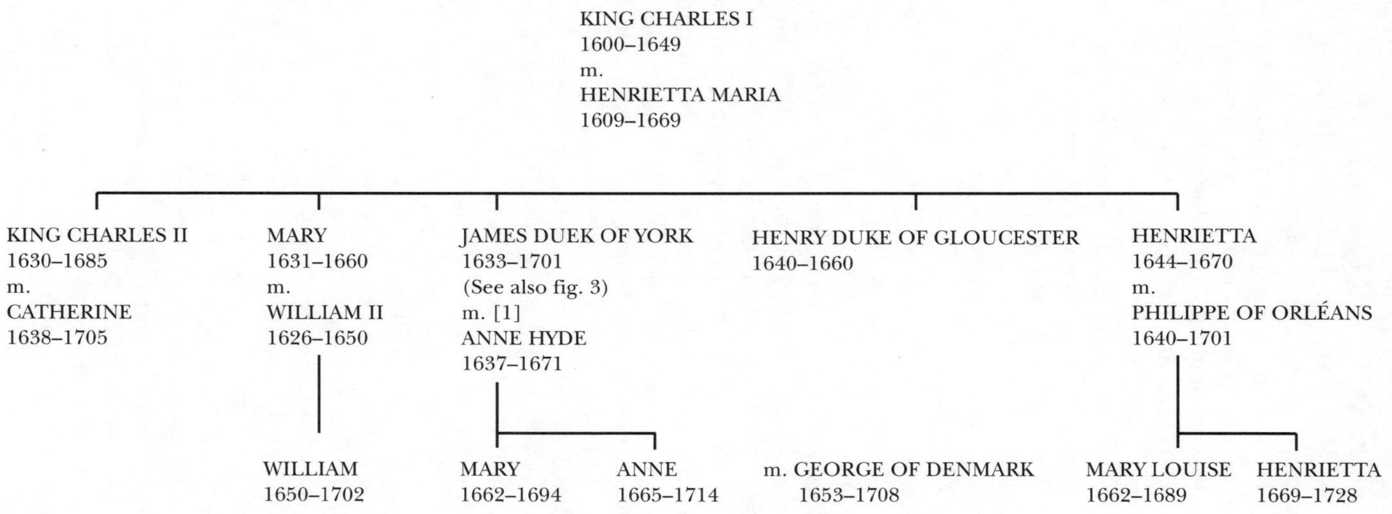

KING CHARLES I
1600–1649
m.
HENRIETTA MARIA
1609–1669

KING CHARLES II
1630–1685
m.
CATHERINE
1638–1705

MARY
1631–1660
m.
WILLIAM II
1626–1650

JAMES DUKE OF YORK
1633–1701
(See also fig. 3)
m. [1]
ANNE HYDE
1637–1671

HENRY DUKE OF GLOUCESTER
1640–1660

HENRIETTA
1644–1670
m.
PHILIPPE OF ORLÉANS
1640–1701

WILLIAM
1650–1702

MARY
1662–1694

ANNE
1665–1714
m. GEORGE OF DENMARK
1653–1708

MARY LOUISE
1662–1689

HENRIETTA
1669–1728

line of English royalty who died before their time, stretching from the Black Prince in the Middle Ages right down to Diana in the present day. The truth is that we can never hope to know what Henry would, or would not, have done. He remains a shadowy and largely anonymous figure, who speaks to us in only a handful of early letters and who stares out, rather dolefully, from a single unattributed canvas kept at the National Portrait Gallery. Even Clarendon's fulsome praise, written at a later date and with the benefit of hindsight, took the form of a standard Court eulogy rather than that of an original, or enlightening reminiscence of the Duke of Gloucester. Had fate been a little more discerning and had it been James, and not Henry, who had perished in 1660, history would also have remembered the Duke of York in similar, and perhaps in even more glowing, terms as an unequivocally Protestant prince.[16]

If the Duke of Gloucester was not destined to provide the King with an alternative choice of heir to James, then there were few other satisfactory candidates (see Figures 2 and 4, p. 95 and p. 99). The Duke of Monmouth was merely the natural son of Charles II, and the various schemes put forward to legitimize him had always proved far too damaging to countenance for long. By the early 1680s these had run out of steam with both the King and his Court, and Monmouth was to look increasingly to the world of plots and opposition politics to keep his hopes of the crown alive. The King's nephew, William of Orange, managed to survive a traumatic childhood but grew into a frail and asthmatic youth, who came to be considered as a serious candidate for the throne only in the closing years of the reign; while his cousin, Prince Rupert, showed little intention of marrying and was suffering from the debilitating results of an old headwound. Pepys was singularly unimpressed by his conduct and recorded that he did 'nothing but swear and laugh a little, with an oath or two'.[17] Consequently, the levels of national prestige and dynastic importance enjoyed by the Duke of York could not fail to be enhanced by the death of his younger brother. He was left, as Antonia Fraser has rightly pointed out, as the only heir to King Charles II who was male, legitimate and was perceived to be wholly English.[18]

Furthermore, even his politically damaging marriages seemed to benefit his importance to the succession in the long run. While Charles's union with Catherine had remained barren, Anne Hyde fell pregnant to James at regular intervals throughout their life together and gave birth to healthy babies at the rate of almost one a year. Although Lorenzo Magalotti could poke fun at the Duchess' 'fecundity' and claim that it was merely the result of her natural promiscuity, having been bred 'from a lower class' than was normal among the wives of princes, the growing number of children who swelled the royal nurseries at Richmond and St James's Palace underlined the importance of an existing line of succession,

Figure 3 The House of York

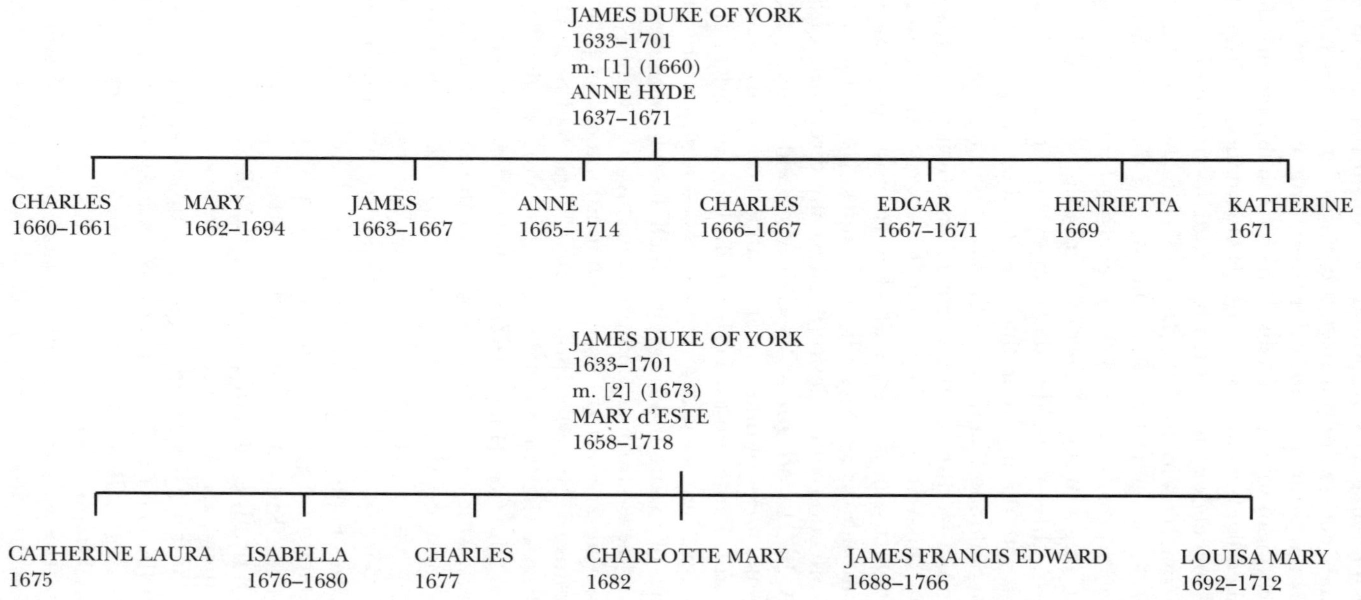

JAMES DUKE OF YORK
1633–1701
m. [1] (1660)
ANNE HYDE
1637–1671

CHARLES	MARY	JAMES	ANNE	CHARLES	EDGAR	HENRIETTA	KATHERINE
1660–1661	1662–1694	1663–1667	1665–1714	1666–1667	1667–1671	1669	1671

JAMES DUKE OF YORK
1633–1701
m. [2] (1673)
MARY d'ESTE
1658–1718

CATHERINE LAURA	ISABELLA	CHARLES	CHARLOTTE MARY	JAMES FRANCIS EDWARD	LOUISA MARY
1675	1676–1680	1677	1682	1688–1766	1692–1712

through the Duke of York, which had no obvious rivals.[19] In total, Anne bore James eight children over the course of eleven years of marriage: four sons and four daughters. Of these, only two of the boys, James and Edgar, who took the title of the Duke of Cambridge in quick succession, ever looked likely to survive the perils of childhood. Although, in the end, neither succeeded, it is still important to remember that during the period from 1663 to 1671 the Duke of York always had at least one male heir (see Figure 3, p. 97). Courtiers rushed to pay their compliments to the little Princes, in the hope of securing future patronage or posts in their growing retinues. James of Cambridge received the Order of the Garter as a three-year-old and was given the titular command of his own regiment, with the provision that he should one day 'break forth from the clouds of childhood' and 'prove the wonder of his age'.[20]

To emphasize further the dynastic significance of this new House of York, the Duke named his progeny with a careful eye to the future. He initially selected those names which were most closely associated with his immediate family: such as Charles, James, Henrietta and Anne, out of respect, affection and a desire to stress the direct line of Stuart descent. However, he also sought to lay claim to a wider source of legitimacy by evoking memories of other, earlier, ruling houses. In choosing the names of Mary and Katherine to recall the Tudors, and Edgar from among the West Saxons, he was attempting to send out powerful signals about the continuity of royalty and kingship which, he felt, were eternal institutions stretching back – through an unbroken line of descent – into the mists of time. They also reflected the status and aspirations of James himself, and the Marquis of Worcester thought that Edgar had been chosen in order to emphasize the Duke's claims to naval glory, as that distant monarch had been 'the first [English] King that had dominion of the seas'.[21] In later years, with James's remarriage and the raising of his second family, this tried and tested formula was to change slightly as more cosmopolitan names, such as Isabella, Laura and Charlotte, were introduced in order to respect Mary of Modena's lineage and the traditions of Continental royalty (see Figure 3, p. 97). However, when another son was born in 1677, James once again decided to have him christened in honour of his brother, the King. Even after the deaths of his sons, the Duke's line remained firmly established in the form of his daughters Mary and Anne. In time they were to become the best hopes for a Protestant succession, but the controversies surrounding their upbringing and education, not to mention the careful thought shown by Charles II in the arrangements of their marriages, demonstrated that by the 1670s they were already figures of national importance.

It is little wonder, therefore, that within a few years of the re-establishment of the monarchy, the Duke of York – as Charles II's most

Figure 4 The House of Stuart – Collateral Branches

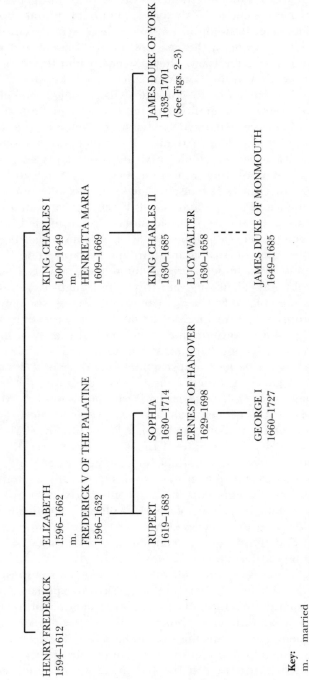

Key:
m.   married
=   denotes a union outside marriage
——   denotes a legitimate line of descent
- - - denotes an illegitimate line of descent

likely successor and the would-be father of future generations of kings and queens – came to be viewed as a figure of central importance to the government of Restoration England. These dynastic considerations and his unique position at the heart of the royal family, did much to shape James's career after 1660. They prevented him from ever renewing his military service on the Continent and caused the King to relieve him of his naval command in 1665, for fear that he might be killed in action.[22] Similarly, during the outbreak of the Great Plague in that same year, the two brothers were separated as a matter of policy in order to diminish the chances of the epidemic striking both of them down at once. However, if his role as the King's single surviving brother placed constraints upon James's behaviour, then it also might have been felt to have raised new dangers for Charles II himself, dangers which were not so pressing with the presence of a large number of direct heirs or with a more extended family unit. In France a similar situation had existed, but Louis XIV's younger brother – Philippe, Duke of Orléans – had been consciously raised by Anne of Austria and Cardinal Mazarin to be a laughing-stock, who could never hope to present himself as a serious threat to the King. This cold and calculating, not to mention high-risk, strategy was never even contemplated by Charles I and would in any case have been entirely inappropriate for an English monarchy forced to fight through three Civil Wars for its very survival. As we have already seen in the course of Chapter 2, the Long Parliament had toyed with the idea of forcing the abdication of Charles I, and stripping the Prince of Wales of his rights, in favour of James at several critical junctures during the late 1640s. This same fantasy of replacing Charles II with James was briefly revived during the darkest days of their exile and was given credence by the allegations of Titus Oates during the Popish Plot, and by Shaftesbury's Whig propagandists at the time of the Exclusion Crisis.[23] It is, therefore, undeniable that the potential for trouble between the royal brothers always existed, but that it was never successfully exploited during the Restoration era represents the single most striking fact of James's public career. Although rumours of Charles's illness or death always brought the provident and the place-seekers scurrying to his side, as happened in 1650–1 and 1681, the Duke continued to remain true to his brother and dutifully – although sometimes grudgingly – continued to obey his wishes. This strong sense of loyalty and common purpose which united Charles and James was born out of the shared experience of bereavement at their father's death and was further strengthened by the shame, and penury, that followed from the loss of their birthright and their subsequent exile. It was this overriding sense of allegiance to the Crown, as personified by his elder brother, that enabled James to pursue such an active political career at the Restoration and which ensured him a continuity, and stability, of office that few other statesmen could ever have hoped to enjoy. At the same time it also conferred upon him an unprecedented degree of personal authority within the governmental machine and allowed Charles II to grant him so many vitally important offices of State, without the fear of treachery. Many of these appointments were specifically tailored to suit James's own abilities, as well as to the needs of defence and internal security which were fundamental to the survival of such a new, and as yet untried, regime.

III

Charles II confirmed James in his post as Lord High Admiral on 16 May 1660, as the English fleet was gathering off the coast of Holland in order to spirit them back home. This appointment, for which the Duke of York had hungered and fought during the early part of his exile, was now to constitute the single most important position that he was to hold over the course of the next twenty-five years. Although the full implications of his tenure of office as Lord High Admiral will be discussed in Chapter 7, it is enough here to point out that, at a stroke, James had been given charge of the largest and most important department under the direct control of central government. It carried with it the subsidiary appointments of Governor of Portsmouth, Warden of the Cinque Ports and Constable of Dover Castle. These were crucial strategic centres for the defence of the British Isles in the event of a foreign invasion; Portsmouth was emerging as the most important naval base on the South coast, the Cinque Ports were strategically placed to protect the mouth of the Thames and the vulnerable South-East, while Dover Castle commanded the straits and was known as the 'Key to England'. Whoever held Dover, it was felt, held the whole kingdom. In order to fulfil his duties, James was granted permission to raise independent companies of soldiers with which to garrison these strongholds, as well as his own Lord High Admiral's Regiment, a regular standing force, from which drafts of maritime troops could be drawn to fight with the fleet as required.[24]

These commissions seem to have particularly pleased the Duke for they allowed him to return to soldiering, his first choice of profession, albeit on a small scale. Even though he was to command at a series of naval battles and to throw himself whole-heartedly into an attempt to reform the Admiralty, James continued to define himself primarily as a soldier throughout the Restoration period. Sir William Coventry, appointed as the Duke's Secretary after the Restoration, talked a great deal about his master to Samuel Pepys, and considered James to be 'a man naturally Martiall to the highest degree', adding 'that he is more himself, and of judgment is at hand in him, in the middle of a desperate service then at other times – as appeared in the business of Dunkirke [i.e. the Battle of the Dunes]'. There can be little room for doubt that the post that he really desired throughout this period was the command of an army. This would seem to be borne out by the speed of his decision, following his accession to the throne in 1685, to combine the commands of both the Army and the Navy under his own person. Unfortunately for him, that prize was well beyond his grasp in the immediate aftermath of the Restoration, as it had already been settled upon George Monck. It was Monck, soon to be ennobled as the Duke of Albemarle, who had secured the loyalty of the Army of the Commonwealth for the Stuart cause on the long march south from Coldstream, and had used his soldiers to forcibly usher in the new order. His position at the head of the newly re-created Royal Army ensured a continuity of leadership in a period of rapid transition, the lack of which might otherwise have led all too easily to instability and dissension in the ranks.[25] While Monck had no ambition to play any further part in politics, his one request to Charles II as a return for his services was to be confirmed in his office as Lord General. This was an offer that the King simply could not afford to refuse.

For the time being, therefore, James had to content himself with taking charge of a number of policing actions aimed at rooting out the plots and conspiracies organized by the radical Republican underground, before they could mature into full-scale risings. The political climate was still extremely volatile in the early 1660s, old Commonwealth men were reported to be distributing powder among their supporters in the North, informants claimed that a rebellion was being planned in Wrexham to coincide with the anniversary of Cromwell's death and it was said that even the 'pulpits blew sparks'. On the night of 6 January 1661, a small band of Fifth Monarchists – a radical millenarian sect – led by Thomas Venner penetrated the defences of the City of London in an attempt to bring the reign of King Charles II to an end, and to establish the reign of 'King Jesus' upon Earth. They got as far as St Paul's Cathedral before they were beaten back, but for the next three nights they managed to wreak havoc across the length and breadth of the capital. James took part in the mustering of troops to suppress Venner's men but – to his evident disappointment – by the time he and his horsemen had arrived on the scene, the fighting was long since over and the remaining rebels had been mopped up by the Lord Mayor and the City Militia.[26] However, the outbreak of fighting had proved such a shock to the establishment that Parliament was prompted to authorize the raising of a second troop of horseguards for the protection of the Duke of York and to lay down the foundations for a far stronger regular army than had been originally intended.

The outbreak of war with Republican Holland four years later revived fears of a Northern rising, backed this time by substantial Dutch military support. Consequently, in early August 1666 after the campaigning season had drawn to a close, Charles II dispatched his brother North in order to keep a watchful eye upon events. James, still chafing at having been denied a new command in the war, was mollified at the prospect of being able to render the King a valuable service and to pursue those elements in society which, he believed, presented the most dangerous, and pernicious, threat to public order and royal authority. However, the balance of power in England still remained delicately poised, with the monarchy still attempting to push down firm roots after almost a decade of stable Republican government, and James was given the strictest of instructions not to provoke further trouble or to do anything that might inflame the situation. As a result, the Duke on his arrival in York was careful to avoid an unnecessary show of force, which might have alarmed the townsfolk, and went out of his way to stress in his overtures to the local nobility that he did not wish to 'put the Country to more trouble then shall be of necessity to the King's service, and their owne safety'. He mounted a charm offensive with the help of his wife, Anne, who paid court to many of the local magnates on his behalf, while he toured the houses of the remainder of the county elites in person. James was particularly successful in gaining the support of Thomas, Lord Fairfax, who, although crippled by ill health and war wounds, might still have proved a popular hero for the Republican forces to rally around. Even though he proceeded cautiously, and displayed a rare degree of tact and diplomacy in his public pronouncements and dealings, the Duke of York remained firmly committed to the principle of applying force to stamp out the causes of dissension and used the time he had gained, by his manoeuverings, to prepare for the fight to come. To this end, he began his stay by dashing off a series of letters to all of the major figures in local government across the North-East of England, advising them to take preventative action in case of an outbreak of disturbances. The militias should be properly drilled, ready to muster at designated strong-points, and able to 'upon short warning draw together' to crush the rebel forces. In addition, the Duke encouraged the local authorities to intercept mail, and to use a network of informers to spy upon all known 'dangerous men' and 'Phanatiques'.[27]

In the end, all this careful preparation proved unnecessary, as the Republican threat evaporated without Dutch men and munitions to back it up, and with the stories of the movements of large bodies of former Cromwellian soldiers proving to be largely illusory. The backbone of the resistance movement had been comprehensively broken the year before and the Duke's secretary, Sir William Coventry, was able to write that 'there was no danger of risings since the most dangerous men were [already] secured'. 'If London do not lead the dance, in this distracted time', he concluded, then the rest of the country would not stir. After the initial excitement had died down and the fears of trouble had proved groundless, a feeling of anticlimax set in and James's seven-week stay in York began to take on the aspect of a rather dreary holiday in the far-flung provinces.[28]

If these attempts at grabbing military glory were nowhere near as impressive as he might have wished them to have been, the Duke was still able to cultivate a formidable reputation as an expert in military affairs. He advised the Privy Council on everything from the handover of Dunkirk in 1662, which he co-ordinated with Marshal Turenne, to the war in Scotland, which he eventually oversaw in person from 1681 to 1683, and the evacuation of Tangier in 1684, which was conducted by his protégé George Legge. Following the debacle on the Medway, in June 1667, it was James who directed de Gomme's team of engineers and oversaw the massive scheme to survey and refortify the whole of the South coast. Most importantly of all, he sought to strengthen his hold on the system of patronage which operated at all levels of the Army. Crucial to this process was his position as Commander-in-Chief of the Honourable Artillery Company, to which he had been elected in June 1660. The Company, which had strong links to the corporation of the City of London, became known under James's stewardship as the 'School of War' and served to provide the only available source of professional training for officers in the entire kingdom. As the Company was firmly rooted in the metropolitan community, and enjoyed both a social and a civic function during festivities and public holidays, its existence seemed quite innocuous to Parliament and its growth went ahead unchecked.[29] In the past it had trained gentlemen to serve in the London Trained Bands, but by the late 1660s its role had expanded to embrace Officers from the county militias and the regular Army. It provided a valuable reservoir of military talent and expertise which could be drawn upon in times of trouble, and James and his friends always made a point of attending the Company's annual dinners, and of participating in their manoeuvres and mock battles.[30]

The provisions of the first Test Act of 1673 should have effectively stripped the Duke of his post as the Company's Commander-in-Chief, as they had already done with all of his other official appointments in England. However, this was not to be the case in this particular instance. The Artillery Company's unique position within the City of London and its appeals to customary practice, free from Parliamentary interference, coupled with the simple pretence that James's office was unofficial and largely honorific, enabled the Duke to remain in command without facing a serious challenge until the late 1670s. By that time the Earl of Shaftesbury and his followers had at last woken up to the serious threat posed to them by the Company's military strength, and launched a concerted campaign in order to remove James from his power-base once and for all. Anti-Catholic posters were plastered all over the Company's central hall when the Duke attended a dinner there in October 1679, but in another of his rare displays of tact James pretended not to have noticed them and continued on with his meal regardless, thanking the assembled Officers in the most gracious terms for their continued support and loyalty towards the King. A more serious and tangible threat to his authority arose in February 1681, when Sir Thomas Player, a Whig gentleman, solicited enough support from among the Officers and men of the Company to stand against him in the forthcoming annual elections to the executive. Player's candidature aroused considerable popular interest in the contest and many contemporary writers thought that the Duke would be hard-pressed to escape a humiliating defeat at his hands. The vote, however, was never destined to take place. It was called off at the last minute through the personal intervention of Charles II, who declared that all of the existing Officers should be automatically confirmed in their positions for a further year. This decision constituted a significant victory for the Yorkist party, enabling them to weather the storms of the early 1680s and to build upon their electoral support in the City during the subsequent Royalist reaction. Moreover, it also ensured that at the height of the Exclusion Crisis from 1679 to 1681, a significant reserve of well-trained and well-armed citizens remained firmly under the control of the Duke of York, ready to respond to the King's orders at short notice. That London remained largely free of popular riots and protests during these years may well be attributable, in part at least, to the continued existence and wide-ranging activities of the Artillery Company, whose loyalty to Charles II was guaranteed by the constant presence of his brother, James.[31]

Yet if the Duke of York played a significant part in the training and administration of London's militias, he still hoped for a more prestigious command in the regular Army. The death of the Duke of Albemarle, in January 1670, presented James with just such an opportunity to extend his control over military appointments still further. His supporters had never ceased lobbying for him to be given command of a new army and plans had been put forward for him to lead troops against Scots Covenanters in 1666. It came as no surprise, therefore, that with Albemarle gone, he should once again press for the rank of Lord General.[32] However, against the background of the Secret Treaty of Dover – which in theory committed Charles II to the reconversion of England, with full backing of French arms – and with stories about James's Roman Catholicism beginning to leak out (he had stopped receiving Communion according to Anglican rites after 1669), the concentration of the command of both the Army and the Navy in the hands of one individual became far too contentious an issue for the King to even contemplate. Since there was no other suitable candidate available, the position of Lord General was allowed to lapse and many of its functions were assumed by a new executive committee. This was formed in an attempt to reconcile the various competing factions at Court and consisted of a carefully balanced group of Senior Officers chosen from across the political spectrum, with the Duke of York acting as chairman. Although to begin with this was no more than a nominal body, with the day-to-day administration of the Army being left to the Earl of Arlington and Sir Stephen Fox, the committee did begin to exert a real influence after the outbreak of the Third Dutch War in March 1672 and James moved quickly to establish himself as the guiding force behind its decision-making. Thus, by the early 1670s, at least, the Duke of York had become the chief source of military patronage in the three kingdoms. He had direct control over all the appointments to the six line regiments above the rank of Captain and almost all of the junior Field Officers were his protégés. George Legge, John and George Churchill, Richard Talbot, Sir Charles Littleton, Thomas Dalmahoy, Robert Werden, James Graham, Thomas Dongan, Justin Macarty, Louis de Duras and Henry Jermyn, among a long list of others, all owed their military advancement to the Duke. Indeed, James's interest had become so strong that he could pick out one Officer, whose promotion he had been unable to block, for individual censure. He boasted that his 'Troops that were on foot were . . . well affected, and their Officers, all except Collonel Russel, such as would serve the Crown without grumbling or asking questions'.[33] John Russell had been a well-known Whig and a friend of Lord Shaftesbury, and it seems that even the passage of time could not soften the annoyance felt by James and his secretaries towards this one figure, who had slipped through the net to achieve high command and had intruded on what was felt to be the Duke's own private preserve.

Even the passing of the Test Acts did not do quite so much damage to James's prestige, in this area, as might at first be assumed. Although the provisions of the Acts had forced him to renounce the titles to all his public offices, as a sop to popular opinion, this loss of power turned out to be far more symbolic than real. The bureaucratic system and chain of command that had grown up around the Duke remained virtually unchanged and continued to function largely as before, allowing him to preserve much of his influence at the administrative level and to continue to sit in, informally, upon the deliberations of the war councils. Furthermore, by the simple expedient of changing the names of his regiments and reshuffling his appointments between his closest companions, James was able to retain effective control over a large section of the military establishment. In this way, the Lord High Admiral's Regiment was transformed into the Duke of York's Foot and the governorship of Portsmouth was entrusted to the safe hands of George Legge.[34] These cosmetic changes worked very well, enabling James to maintain an active involvement with the Army and to keep his hopes of a field command alive, while deflecting potentially destructive criticism away from his own person.

The opportunity of active service presented itself again in 1678, when the balance of power in Europe shifted decisively in favour of France and the prospect of a triumphant Louis XIV sweeping all before him in the Low Countries caused Charles II to hastily realign himself with the Dutch. This dramatic change in English foreign policy was, perhaps somewhat surprisingly, embraced wholeheartedly by the Duke of York. He had always been seen as a strong and active supporter of French interests, and this sudden and seemingly inexplicable *volte face* caused considerable consternation among his former friends, and the French Ambassador, Barrillon, in particular. It is not hard, however, to see why he acted in the way that he did. By leading a victorious military campaign against an increasingly powerful and bellicose European rival, James could, at a stroke, hope to restore his popularity with the English people and at the same time forestall any possible attempt to impeach him in the coming Parliament. Moreover, as a soldier, he was well aware that the seizure of the invasion ports by France would carry with it profound implications for the long-term security of the British Isles. The whole of the Channel coast would be thrown open to the possibility of sudden and unexpected attack, regular blockades could be mounted with the aim of restricting commercial traffic and plans for the landing of foreign armies could be pursued with a far greater chance of success.

The resurgence of French power had also coincided with a marked improvement in the relationship between James and the young Prince of Orange, which had developed in the months following the marriage of William to the Duke's eldest daughter, Princess Mary. James seems to have been extremely excited at the prospect of a return to the rigours of campaigning, at the side of one of Europe's foremost captains, and began a lively correspondence with William in the late winter and early spring of 1678, repeatedly assuring him that he was doing everything in his power to further the war effort. 'I am absolutely of [the] opinion, knowing the temper of the french, that we must have a war', wrote James, adding that: 'You may be assured nothing shall be wanting that we can do to support your interest, Commissions are now a giving out to raise more men, and so sone as we can gett a considerable body togather, I intend to go over with them to ajust [affairs] with you.' Although these preparations had to be necessarily low-key and conducted 'with as little noyse as we can', while last-minute diplomatic missions were still being dispatched to the French Court, James confidently predicted that 'no tyme shall be lost when we can once go to worke'.[35]

In order to reassure Parliament, commissions in the newly raised regiments were awarded to prominent civilians, with little or no formal military experience, who could act as watchdogs on the Army commanders. Furthermore, the composition of the staff group who were to take charge of the expeditionary force was designed to reflect the political realities of the day, with a careful balance being struck between old Royalists, Yorkists and Whigs. The Duke of York was to be Captain-General, with James, Duke of Monmouth, acting as his General of Horse. Henry Somerset, the Marquis of Worcester; Charles Gerard, the Earl of Macclesfield, and Colonel John Russell, were to be appointed as Lieutenant-Generals, with Sir Samuel Clerke assuming the rank of Major-General for the duration of the campaign. The plan was to raise an army of 27,000 foot, 4,000 horse and 2,000 dragoons. In addition, William had suggested hiring German mercenaries in an attempt to strengthen the force further but although James had 'shewd his Majesty your [i.e. the Prince of Orange's] letter, [he] bids me tell you he has no mony for it, and that had he any it should be made use on to raise more troups here'.[36] In order to make good these numbers, the Duke was forced to send his favourite, John Churchill, to Brussels and The Hague in order to negotiate with the Spanish and Dutch authorities about settling the level of their contributions to the war chest, and to co-ordinate the actions of the three allied forces over the course of the forthcoming campaign.

Unfortunately, if James had been supremely confident about securing the command of the Army of Flanders, then he was to be gravely disappointed. Charles II had been working towards a very different set of objectives from those of his brother, and wanted to stop short of provoking a full-scale European conflict, hoping that the threat of English arms would be enough on its own to prevent the fall of Ostend, and to secure a well-needed respite for the Dutch Republic. He had no intention of forfeiting his French subsidies, and in an attempt to reassure Barrillon about his motives told him that 'frankly my brother's talk [of war] pains me. We have not a penny for the raising of troops and he speaks as if we had an army. The idea of being a general has gone to his head.'[37]

If James was being carried away by his own enthusiasm to return to the colours, then more damaging still to his ambitions were the provisions of the Test Acts and the growing unwillingness of MPs to fund the war. Parliament had had time to recover from its initial shock at the threat posed by French expansionism and had turned its attention back to events closer to home. Moreover, a significant section of the Commons was deeply disturbed by the prospect of equipping a standing army that could so easily be used against it, and of entrusting this force to the one man who was increasingly coming to represent all that was most hateful to them. As a result, they determined to do all that was in their power to hinder the prosecution of the war and filled up the available debating time in the House with a series of obscure bills, covering everything from the mistreatment of domestic servants to the administration of Crown lands. The raising of an army for Flanders was, thus, effectively sidelined and James was left to lament that 'those who seemed to be most zealous for a war with france last sessions, are those who abstract [i.e. obstruct] most of the giving of a supply'. He simply could not understand the seemingly unpatriotic behaviour of the Members of Parliament and wrote that 'I wish the house of Commons would do their part as we shall do ours, for the carrying it on, for the leveys go on very fast and we are setting out more ships every day, but they have such groundlesse jealousis in their heads, that they make no advances in the providing [of] the rest of the mony.' This increasing sense of frustration and disillusionment became increasingly evident in his letters to William of Orange, as he complained that 'things here go but slowly on' and was reluctantly forced to admit 'that we shall be able to do little this yeare'.[38] The final, and perhaps most damaging, blow to James's hopes came in the form of the objections raised by the Governor of the Spanish Netherlands, the Duke of Villahermosa, about his fitness to act as Commander-in-Chief. The Spaniards, it would seem, had long memories and recalled the insults and jibes he had levelled against them during his earlier service. Accordingly, they voiced their concerns that he might prove to be far too impetuous a General, interested only in the pursuit of personal glory, and that his presence would upset the delicate balance between the different religious denominations in their occupied territories.[39]

His role during this period, as the most prominent and forceful advocate of an aggressive foreign policy at the English Court, had major implications for his subsequent career. He had managed to alienate Louis XIV and had raised questions in the minds of the French about his reliability as an ally, which would come to cost him dear in 1688. At the same time, James's overwhelming desire to relaunch his military career, and his heavy-handed treatment of the Army as his personal fiefdom, had set the seal upon his deepening quarrel with the Duke of Monmouth. He had previously shown his nephew some goodwill and relations between the two had always been cordial, if not particularly close, but while out walking, in the grounds of Windsor, Monmouth had confided to his uncle that he had set his heart on the Generalship. The Duke of York was enraged and told Monmouth that if he accepted a command that he felt to be his own by right, it would spell the end of their friendship.

However, Monmouth took no notice of his ultimatum and, on 13 April 1678, he was rewarded with the Captain-Generalcy of the Army of Flanders. James protested vigorously to the King but all in vain, and although many of his closest friends and confidants – including John Churchill, Thomas Dongan and Justin Macarty – set sail with the expeditionary force, the Duke was left behind in England and had to content himself with saying farewell to his troops at a grand review held on Hounslow Heath.[40]

Thus, at the age of forty-four, when most Generals were just entering into their prime, James was once again deprived of a command. Given that twenty years had passed since he had led an army and six since he had been away at sea, he may well have believed that he was facing the end of his own, once promising, military career. If James's dignity was hurt by these events, and he was forced into assuming an increasingly administrative and advisory role, then there were other avenues left open to him in an attempt to retain his prestige. Through the assumption of the mantle of a great patron of trade and empire, the Duke could hope to acquire new sources of wealth and power with comparatively little risk or effort, while avoiding the controversies which had plagued him at home. These themes will be developed further in Chapters 9 and 10, but for the remainder of this chapter and over the course of the next attention will be focused on perhaps the easiest and most immediate way of projecting James's authority: through the show and display afforded by a large and glittering household, and by the cultivation of a powerful personal image which reflected the uncomplicated soldier, that the Duke had always wished to be.

IV

When the monarchy returned in 1660, it soon became clear that the establishment of a household fit for the heir to the throne could not be achieved overnight, and that the development of a particular distinctive identity and character that was capable of uniting all of the Duke's servants and binding them to his person could only be accomplished with the passage of time. Despite attempts to refashion a court around the person of the Lord Protector and his son, the Commonwealth had managed to sweep away the old Royal Court and had discarded many of the trappings of the monarchy – even the ceremonial regalia and the crown itself had been melted down. The royal estates had either been con-fiscated, redistributed, or sold off into private hands. A whole generation had grown up with little or no memory of the institutions of monarchical government, the House of Lords, and the series of palaces from which patronage and official appointments had been dispensed. However, successive Republican governments had never managed to cultivate a truly popular alternative image or identity for themselves; and this failure, when combined with reappropriation by the Cromwells of some feudal devices, made it far easier for monarchical forms to resurface almost overnight at the Restoration. Although the reappearance of symbols and folk art in the shape of everything from crowned maypoles to commemorative plates and medals helped to ease the passage of the royal brothers home, there were still many difficulties that needed to be resolved before they could establish a firm presence at the heart of affairs.[41]

The fabric of the Court, as we have already seen, had been dissolved over the course of the English Civil Wars, and the complicated rituals and system of etiquette which had grown up around it had fallen into disuse and been forgotten. Few of those who had served Charles I during the period of his personal monarchy, when his Court had been at its most splendid, had continued to serve throughout the rigours of war and exile in order to guide his sons. As a result, Charles II was far less constrained by precedent and tradition than any of his recent ancestors, while James could seek to achieve a fully independent household and to stamp upon it the imprint of his own personality. Consequently, the form assumed by the new monarchy had by necessity to be the product of a conscious decision and to be recreated almost from scratch. It is not inconceivable that the English monarchy could have been re-established on a comparatively modest scale but the size of the Cavalier victory in the election of 1661, when coupled with the predilections of both King and Duke, effectively ruled this out. Charles II and Lord Clarendon worked to emphasize the political legitimacy of the sovereign's position, the timeless quality encapsulated by the continuing existence of a Royal House, and to create a monarchy of truly European importance. They planned, therefore, a return to what had existed before the Civil Wars, with the Court functioning as a separate power base, largely independent of Parliament, and embracing not only the King's immediate family and friends but also a wider network of patronage and kinship. Just as Charles II was determined to rule as well as to reign, then so too the Court was to be not merely a private household but a vehicle through which the grandeur and opulence of the King could be made manifest. In a similar fashion, and despite all appearances to the contrary, it was to transcend its role as the personal plaything of the monarch and to assume an active political function as the centre of government. From the salons and offices at Whitehall the greater part of official appointments were created and distributed, and careers in the royal service were made and broken.

As with the courtiers, the younger royals themselves had also to fit into this scheme of things. James and Henry might have taken up single apartments at Whitehall and become senior members and officials of the

King's own household, but it became clear from the time of their first
arrival back in England that they would be granted their own private
establishments and sources of revenue. This was in line with the practice
of the enormously influential French monarchy which the royal brothers
had experienced at first hand, and also served to echo the provisions
made by James VI and I, while in England, for regulating the establishments of his own sons. The Duke of York, spurred on by his closest
friends and by Sir Charles Berkeley in particular, was extremely keen to
push for control over his own palaces and servants, and sought to secure
fresh subsidies in order to gain a large degree of financial independence
from the King. In acknowledging the principle that his brothers were
entitled to a level of autonomy on both the national and domestic stage,
Charles II created the conditions for James to mould his household about
his own image, and allowed him to pursue his own projects and private
interests, throughout the early years of the Restoration, almost at will. As
a consequence, not one but three royal households were initially created,
with those of York and Gloucester acting as the junior branches, providing a pool of talent which could in time feed into the King's larger body.
Prince Henry's establishment was short-lived, barely constituted at the
time of his death, and was swiftly broken up into its constituent parts. His
offices and sinecures were divided between his two surviving brothers,
while many of his servants were subsumed into their larger households
and added a further lustre to the Duke of York's growing retinue.[42]

The Duke's official London residence was St James's Palace, where he
worked and conducted most of his day-to-day business, but he also
occupied a suite of rooms at Whitehall during the winter months and was
granted Richmond Palace by the King, in 1664. Lying 12 miles upstream
from the capital, Richmond acted as the Duke's country retreat and as a
nursery for his children. He also maintained permanent apartments at
Hampton Court, took lodgings at Newmarket during the racing season,
patronized his own company of actors at Lincoln's Inn Fields, and
licensed a bath house at Long Acre – known as the 'Duke's Bagnio' –
which for a time became a fashionable place for young courtiers to be,
and to be seen. In addition, James had a yacht, the *Anne*, fully furnished
and rigged out for short cruises. Yet this was far more than just a pleasure
craft, it was a substantial vessel with eight guns and a crew of thirty, which
served as a floating office for the Duke during his visits to the fleet and
inspections of the Royal Dockyards.[43] However, despite this evidence of
James's several different homes and travels, in his capacity as Lord High
Admiral, it is noticeable that he seldom moved outside the Home
Counties except in times of national emergency. As J.P. Kenyon has
rightly pointed out, the Caroline Court was a very restricted place, firmly
grounded in the cultural and social life of the metropolis. The royal

brothers rarely ventured out of an area defined by an imaginary line drawn from Newmarket through Cambridge, Oxford, Winchester, Portsmouth, Sheerness and back again to Newmarket.[44] At a time when English imperial and commercial interests were beginning to make themselves felt very forcibly in Africa and the North American colonies, and new sea charts littered the Duke's private chambers, James's world view seems to have remained surprisingly parochial with the breadth of his horizons defined by the elite culture of the Court and with his social circle limited to a small group of friends, servants, and acquaintances based in London.

Having convinced Charles II of the need for his separate establishment, the Duke of York came to preside over his own miniature Court which reproduced that of the King, albeit on a far smaller scale. There was a definite hierarchy in James's household, based around a small nucleus of trusted courtiers and civil servants. He appointed his own Treasurer, Attorney and Solicitor-Generals, Almoner and Master of Horse. The most important position, originally occupied by Sir William Coventry and later by Sir John Werden, was that of the Duke's Secretary. There was also a small number of specialists attached to the household who were employed as junior secretaries for translating James's foreign correspondence, or as physicians, surgeons and apothecaries to tend his ailments. Everyone's position within the household was clearly defined, from the Duke's Gentlemen and Grooms of the Bedchamber, to his Pages of Honour and Gentlemen Ushers, and on down to the more junior officials such as the Pages of the Backstairs, Grooms of the Person, Waiters and Yeomen of the Robes.[45]

The household was based, in line with traditional royal practice and according to Biblical precedents, around the model of the family unit. The household was primarily thought to be an extension of James's own family, with the Duke himself acting as the patriarch and his servants being placed under particular duties and obligations to him, but receiving rewards and favours in return for their good behaviour. It was possible, therefore, for an individual to rise quite rapidly in James's employment. The most notable example of this was John Churchill, who entered the Duke's service as a Page and who rose through skill, and not a little luck, to be one of James's closest confidants. Given the supremacy of the idealized family in this equation, it comes as no surprise to discover that husbands, wives, brothers and sisters should all enter into the Duke's service and work together in his household. This is precisely what happened with the Berkeleys of Stratton, the Werdens, the Apsleys, and later the Jennings sisters and the collateral line of the Villiers family. This led to the development of very close relationships and complex kinship networks within the ducal household, which could be further strengthened by advantageous marriages. In this manner, Richard Talbot and John Churchill were not only to become brothers-in-law but also the uncles of James's natural children.[46] In an age of uncertainty and high mortality, the Duke's granting of substantial pensions acted as both rewards for long service, in the political and domestic spheres, and ensured that families stayed together, providing a primitive form of insurance in case of a sudden bereavement. It is interesting to note, however, that while James was prepared to assume the responsibility for the welfare of an extended family of servants and clients, the provisions made for the raising of his own daughters were comparatively modest. Although he provided them with their own dancing, harpsicord and guitar teachers, it cannot be said that they were brought up in the 'hothouse' atmosphere of a Renaissance court. They were taught English and domestic skills, such as sewing and embroidery, at the expense of foreign languages, history and literature.[47]

The surviving account books for the Duke's establishment reveal not only the concerns of running a busy and ever-expanding household, but also the interests of James himself. After 'all his life ha[d] been passed in Arms', soldiering in France and the Low Countries, he quickly tired of Court life and came to dislike 'private ease'. He employed a fencing master shortly after his return to England, but seems to have lost interest in the sport and turned increasingly to hunting instead. This would appear to have been an inspired choice, as it not only provided James with a pursuit which was socially acceptable for a Prince of the blood, but also offered him the chance to escape from his troubles and to sublimate the powerful violent and sexual desires which motivated many of his actions, throughout his youth and middle age. He spent much of his time as Duke in the saddle, riding to the hounds two or even three days a week, and even received the news of his mother's death while out riding in the New Forest with the King. During the height of the Exclusion Crisis, he could not bear the thought of being parted from his favourite sport and insisted that his hunt should follow him into exile in Brussels, in 1679, and that his stables should be moved to Newmarket for the season, in 1682.[48] Magalotti thought that James was 'a very good shot, especially at birds on the wing and almost always when on horseback', and the Duke had a groom to look after his weapons and a 'Gunsmyth to keep your R.H. Gunns and pistols in repair', who was granted an extra allowance so that he could maintain 'a horse to attend your R.H. in shooting'. Yet it was deer and fox hunting, and the actual physical exertion of the chase, that James loved and sought after. Samuel Pepys and his friends, John Creed and Ned Pickering, thought that 'the Duke of Yorke is a very desperate huntsman' and noted that no obstacle, whatever its size, was allowed to impede his progress. However, the headlong pursuit of game was not without its dangers, even for members of the royal family, and in the summer of 1663, Pepys was dismayed to encounter 'the Duke, whom I found with two or three patches upon his nose and right eye, which came from being struck with the bow of a tree the other day in his hunting; it is a wonder it did not strike out his eye'.[49] Time did not seem to diminish James's appetite for the kill, or his stamina in the saddle, and worse was to follow. At the start of the season of 1676, he had to listen, to his intense annoyance, as his doctors confined him to bed with a broken collar-bone, after being pitched from his horse during a chase.

It is no overstatement to suggest that the whole of the ducal household was geared, in terms of both personnel and expenditure, to servicing James's one overriding passion: the hunt. The Duke kept a large stable of more than seventy horses, including fourteen expressly for his own use on the hunting field, and was renowned as a good judge of breeding-stock. John Evelyn recorded James's inspection of three Turkish horses, captured at the siege of Vienna, with rare excitement, declaring that they 'trotted like does as if they did not feele the Ground' beneath them. As the Duke's Master of Horse, Henry Jermyn enjoyed a very responsible and high-profile position within the household. He oversaw the building of a fine new stable block at St James's Palace and accompanied the Duke on his expeditions to buy new horses. He also ensured that there were always enough mounts for the huntsmen, farrier and saddler to follow their master in the chase, and remembered to pay them danger money in case the breakneck speed at which James hunted proved too much for them. As well as the horses, the Duke kept several dog kennels and retained a large, and extremely well-paid, complement of professional huntsmen. However, if it had been decided that James should live in such great state, establish a large household worthy of his position, and pursue a very expensive pastime simply for its own sake, then some means had to be found to pay for this extravagant and largely unproductive lifestyle.[50] This was a problem which increasingly came to preoccupy the Duke and his Commissioners of Revenue throughout the early years of the Restoration.

V

From the time of his return to England in 1660 onwards, James had received frequent and generous settlements from Parliament, which confirmed him in wealth – as well as in status – as being second only to the King, and which made him one of the richest, if not the richest, of his brother's subjects. Two contemporary guesses put the Duke's total income at somewhere between £100,000 and £150,000 per anum, although it should be stressed that there was a wide gap between estimated figures and the actual amount received. Samuel Pepys, for instance, thought that his master's revenue amounted to only £40,000 a year.[51] While it is difficult to arrive at a precise figure we can come close and demonstrate how the returns from the grants conferred upon James, and the rents due to him as a major landlord in both England and Ireland, represented very substantial sums indeed.

The lands settled upon James at the Restoration came primarily from the confiscated estates of all the Regicides and other supporters of the Republic who had been convicted of treason, with the exceptions of John Carew and Robert Tichborne. This was thought to be the simplest and most effective way of raising the maximum amount of capital available for the young Prince, at a single stroke. In this way, James was granted the estates of John Okey in and around Leighton Buzzard, and those of the Cromwell family in Redruth, Surrey and Huntingdonshire, as well as their tenement blocks in Seething Lane, London. He was also given all the manors and lands belonging to Sir Michael Livesey and Sir Henry Vane, the younger, in Kent. In addition to these lands seized from prominent Republicans, he also received the manor at Great Staughton, the revenues from the ferry between Richmond and Twickenham, a large acreage in the Duchy of Cornwall, and all the land reclaimed through sea and fen drainage in Norfolk, Lincolnshire and on the Isle of Ely.[52] Similar expedients were applied to the settling of Irish estates upon the Duke, in his capacity as the Count of Ulster, and large territories were granted to him, in April 1661, from among the lands formerly belonging to those Regicides – such as Henry Ireton, Edmund Ludlow, Daniel Axtell and Miles Corbett – who had made their fortunes from the Cromwellian Plantation. Unfortunately, in both England and Ireland, these measures had been pushed through with little thought for the original proprietors of these estates, prior to the 1650s, and with no recognition of the changes in land tenure which had taken place since that time. As a result, the Duke of York found himself embroiled in a number of unexpected lawsuits with established Royalist families, City of London merchants and Old Irish gentry, over the rights to his properties. It transpired that the Regicides had taken possession of the estates of compounded Royalists, in addition to the Crown lands made available to them, and that the surviving members of loyal families – such as Frances, the widow of 'the martyred' Colonel Penruddock – had discovered to their horror that their dismembered estates were not to be returned to them, as they had been led to believe, but were to be transferred directly to James. In Ireland, the situation was even more complicated as upon the premature death of Henry Ireton, in 1651, all of his lands had been broken up and sold on. The Duke of York had unwittingly stumbled across a grey area of the law, and the Act of Oblivion in particular, as City merchants and members of the Anglo-Irish establishment protested that they had bought the rights to Ireton's estate legally and in good faith. However, while James was not responsible for the situation in which he found himself, he exacerbated matters by his failure to conceive of Ireland as being anything other than a limitless, virgin territory which could be exploited at will and parcelled up into grants of land, which could then be redistributed as rewards for good service. Thus, almost as quickly as they were being granted to him, and without waiting for a definitive legal judgment to be made, James was already promising a share of his new estates to his closest associates, and to his Attorney General, Samuel Clerke, and his friend, Sir Maurice Berkeley, in particular. The result was an undignified dash for land, with an enormous number of claims and counter-claims being filed, and protracted legal actions in the courts which took several years to resolve.[53] Although the Privy Council ruled that the Duke's claims should receive priority treatment, and should be processed and settled before any other cases could be decided upon, James's accounts still suffered a shortfall. This was made good in part by direct subsidies from the English Parliament and also by the institution of a system of 'reprisals', or compensation for his lost lands, under the provisions of the Irish Act of Settlement of 1662. These measures guaranteed James a steady, though uneven, income from agriculture which was consolidated over the course of the 1660s and early 1670s.

In the meantime, however, the Duke turned his attention to commercial concerns, which were less prone to the vagaries of the weather, custom and the laborious operation of the civil courts, and whose primary purpose was the acquisition of hard currency, stocks and shares. The money markets of London and Amsterdam could offer him far higher rewards, and a far quicker return on his investments, than the agricultural sector ever could. It is hardly surprising, therefore, that the Duke showed a far greater concern in pursuing direct Parliamentary grants of cash, and in securing prestigious business monopolies, than he ever did in the administration of his own lands. His private endeavours are looked at in Chapter 9, but it is necessary to outline here the extent of those official sinecures that were granted to him by central government. Foremost among these was the monopoly of the newly nationalized Post Office, bestowed on James and his heirs by an Act of Parliament in 1663, which brought him an estimated £16,000 a year during the 1660s. This figure can be favourably compared to that of less than £13,000 a year, which represented the combined revenues of all of his English manors over the same period of time. In his capacity as Lord High Admiral, he was rewarded by the Prize Courts with a percentage of the value of all foreign ships impounded in British ports, or taken at sea, during wartime. This extraordinary source of income could amount to tens of thousands of pounds over the course of a successful naval campaign, and provided the Duke with a powerful incentive to press for the resumption of hostilities with the Dutch. He also received the profits from the excise trade after 1661, which together with the accompanying wine duties and licences totalled over £17,500 per annum. As we have already demonstrated, James was a major landlord who owned a variety of properties in the capital. He sought to rent these out at a profit and his tenants included grog-sellers and brothel-keepers, who appear to have paid him some form of a 'kick-back' in order to be allowed to continue unhindered in their trades.[54]

The majority of the Duke's income, however, continued to come from direct Parliamentary subsidies. He had been provided with an annual allowance of £20,000 in February 1661, with a further one-off payment of £15,000 to be backdated from the time of his arrival in England the year before. The Convention Parliament had already voted him £10,000 in 1660 with which to establish his own household and to clear up any outstanding debts that he might have had, while a grateful nation was to offer him a further £120,000 in 1665, in recognition of his bravery and in grateful thanks for his naval victories. Through special pleading and sleight of hand, many of the running costs of his household were transferred to the Treasury. In this way, the money for his new building projects at St James's Palace and Whitehall, which included the renovation of his apartments and the installation of an armoury, came from out of the public purse rather than from his own. In a similar fashion, some of his servants' wages and the provisions for their upkeep were also paid for at the public expense, while discretionary grants from the royal household served to keep the Duke's own table, wine cellar and larder well stocked.[55]

Yet despite all of these elaborate provisions for his welfare, by the mid-1660s James found himself facing mounting debts and an impending financial crisis, which threatened to cripple his household and to restrict severely his future activities. Sir Alan Apsley and Sir Thomas Povey had been jointly charged with the administration of his finances at the Restoration, and had produced a set of *Rules Concerning the Management of his R.H. Revenue* in June 1662. Unfortunately, these simple guidelines were to prove inadequate for the task at hand and needed further qualification. Consequently, in the August of the same year, Apsley and Povey sat down to draw up a fresh agreement on how best to collect revenues, audit the accounts, and divide up the profits between them 'for the better avoyding of all differences and disputes that might arise in the obtaining of warrants, assignations, or money towards the payment of the said debts to the advantage of either of them'. It was decided 'that they shall equally share all the fees which shall arise by the said Payments, as they are set down', with Povey receiving a one-off grant of £100 for his subsistence, after which the excess profits from the Duke's income were to be divided up between the two officials in the ratio of 3:1 in Apsley's favour.[56] The system got off to a good start, with Povey duly noting that he had been paid his allowance on time, but it was not long before it started to break down as projected revenues failed to materialize and relations between the two men turned sour. They had seemed ideal choices for their posts: Apsley had distinguished himself as a soldier during the Civil Wars and was highly favoured at Court, while Povey's grandfather had overseen James I's accounts, and he himself had made his name through the energetic promotion of colonial and trading ventures during the Interregnum. However, an element of rivalry quickly developed between the two, motivated by Apsley's higher social status and by their strongly contrasting personalities, which only served to deepen the rift.

From the very outset, the Duke's accounts had simply not balanced and by 1663 he was living far beyond his means, spending almost £75,000 over the course of the year from out of an estimated income of approximately £48,417. He could barely meet the running costs of his immediate household, but any extra outlay could not be met and a shortfall of over £800 was estimated for the interim Michaelmas account alone. To his growing dismay, Povey discovered that new bills were arriving daily, while the cash available to pay them was being frittered away on a variety of inessential and constantly changing products. He complained about the strain of meeting 'the constant and emergent charge of the wardrobe as coaches, horses, sadles, Hangings, Bedds . . . The Charge of building, altering, repairing, [and] beautifying', the ducal residences, but failed to take any practical course of action to remedy matters. In the meantime, the situation had worsened considerably as an estimated income of £1,000 from some of the English manors forfeited by the Regicides failed to materialize. It was frankly admitted that 'nothing will be receivd this year' from that source and, by 4 December, Povey was forced to glumly acknowledge 'that the yearly Revenue of his Royal Highness are not likely to answer with certaine his annual Assignations'.[57]

It had been hoped that the situation would eventually right itself, without external aid or the need for decisive action, but this was to prove to be no more than wishful thinking. The debts of the Duke and his Duchess spiralled out of control and grew to exceed their earnings by more than £20,000 a year in the period from 1663 to 1667. Their household, which had been intended to reflect their splendour, was plunged into a 'horrible disorder' by the mounting wall of debt. James was compelled to embark on a major scheme of retrenchment, as it was feared that 'his poverty . . . will disable him from being able to do anything almost, he being himself almost lost in the esteem of people'.[58] In view of the extremely generous sources of income that had been lavished upon James, and which would have been the envy of all his Stuart forebears, we need to ask ourselves why his finances had collapsed in this manner and why an individual, who has often been regarded as a paragon of financial acumen, should have been brought so low.

One obvious source for this shortfall might have been thought to have been found in the corruption of James's servants. Povey had lamented 'all [the] extraordinary allowances' that he was forced to make 'upon . . . Missages', and it is undeniable that fraud and theft were commonplace. Abraham Biggs, the Clerk of the Kitchen, was dismissed for embezzlement in October 1662, and many other cases were allowed to go on unchecked. In an attempt to stop the casual pilfering of their belongings, the Duke and Duchess had their own monograms stencilled on to their chairs and soft furnishings, while their account books were careful to note the materials used for their picture frames – rather than the subjects of the paintings themselves – so that they would be much harder to steal while they were in transit or storage. Such thefts as did occur were of relatively inexpensive, everyday, items and would seem to have stemmed from the 'neglect and indifference' of the Duke's officials, rather than from a sense of endemic corruption at the highest levels of his household.[59] Unfortunately, this was not the conclusion drawn by many contemporary observers and it was the hapless Povey who bore much of the blame when things started to go wrong. There can be little doubt that he was an incompetent manager of resources, reviled by his contemporaries for his 'prodigality', who neglected the business at hand and farmed out much of his work to unqualified juniors. He seems to have had some difficulty in adding up the Michaelmas statement for 1663, his records were for the most part muddled or incomplete, and he was hard pressed, when called upon by the Duke's Commissioners, to reconstruct a full set of accounts for the period of his office. These factors contributed to his summary dismissal as Treasurer in 1666, but he fought on in a tenacious attempt to clear his name and to hold on to a £400-a-year pension that he had been awarded for his previous services to the Duke, and to the Crown.

Povey mounted a strident defence of his actions before James and his council, at a specially convened hearing on 15 February 1668. Going over the heads of his immediate superiors, he delivered a direct appeal to his royal master, declaring that: 'It is with much griefe, but no mixture of shame that I stand here. . . . But . . . being assured that by the Patience of your Royal Highness, and your equity in judging I shall at last recover a much better opinion than I must lye under.' He carefully hinted that his own situation was not that dissimilar to that of James, himself, beset on all sides by disloyal critics and malicious tongues, and proceeded to stress the legality of his own appointment, which had been 'fairely, openly, and upon good Considerations Obtained by me' from the Duke's hand. He concluded his defence by launching an all-out attack upon the other officials of the ducal household, and targeted Sir Alan Apsley for particular censure. 'The Office of Treasurer and Paymaster as Cofferer, obtained by Sir A. Apsley after my Investiture and Establishment was', he claimed, 'new, unnecessary and inconvenient to his R.H. which might as well at first . . . have been executed in one Person, and upon better Right and Pretension. And that the Consequence thereof hath been more than ten thousand Pounds to the Prejudice of the Duke.'[60] However, although his spirited delivery did much to publicize his case in the short term, it made little impression upon James and may even have been a wholly inappropriate and counter-productive strategy, which served only to confirm his permanent removal from the Duke's employment.

It seems certain that Povey was being made the scapegoat, as he claimed, for a much wider malaise in the administration of the royal finances, and that he fell victim to a whispering campaign at Court. To be fair to him, he had tried to warn the Duke of the precarious state of his finances early on in his stewardship and had begged, in December 1663, 'that his Royall Highness would take consideration of this . . . matter and give him such commands and jurisdictions', so that he might, 'more comfortably discharge his Duty of his . . . for the future'. James, however, chose to ignore him, and when Povey tried to produce a paper outlining the household's debts, he was leant upon by the Earl of Clarendon to suppress it immediately. It would seem, then, that Povey had displayed very poor judgement at his hearing by singling out the Duke's Cofferer for such savage and public criticism.[61] Apsley was, after all, a political insider, who enjoyed James's complete confidence and who had already been rewarded for his loyalty during the Civil Wars with a series of several large grants, and the post of Master of the Duke's Hawks. In contrast, Povey as a newcomer to the Duke's service, handicapped by his inferior social position and tainted by his association with the Commonwealth, stood precious little chance of bringing down his more powerful rival. However, he may well have embarked upon this desperate strategy because, by the beginning of 1668, there were simply no other practical courses of action left open to him.

Although he had appealed in his deposition to the mercy and wisdom of 'Both your R.H.'s at whose feet I shall lay myself', he had attempted behind the scenes to shift much of the blame on to the Duchess of York herself. He was prepared to sail precariously close to the wind in his allegations and claimed that Anne sat imperiously 'with the Duke of York's council [which comprised of the administrators of his private estates], and sees what they do; and she crosses out this man's wages and prices as she sees fit for saving money: but yet . . . she reserves £5,000 a year for her own spending'. Povey had good reason to be jealous of the overmighty Hydes and hated the Duchess for raging like 'a devil against him' for his misdemeanours, but in this case his wild allegations do seem to have a solid basis in fact. He was by no means alone in his criticisms of her spending habits; Pepys had thought her to be 'not only the proudest woman in the world, but the most expenseful', while Lady Peterborough noticed her storing away great piles of jewels and precious stones. Anne certainly ruled her household with a rod of iron and that redoubtable old Cavalier, Sir Winston Churchill, learned to fear her influence, intelligence and quick wit in equal measure.[62] The reports and recommendations of the Duke's Commissioners were initially vetted by his Duchess, before being passed on to her husband, and it appears that much of the day-to-day running and decision-making of the household was actually conducted by Anne, rather than James. This caused the King and his friends considerable amusement, and they teased James mercilessly about his wife's assertiveness, calling him 'Tom Otter' after a particularly henpecked character in Ben Jonson's play *The Silent Woman*. Anne, already struggling under the burden of James's neglect and unfaithfulness, was clearly stung by the barbed comments of courtiers about her relatively humble origins and sought to compensate, through displays of conspicuous consumption and spontaneous generosity. However, even in this she managed to strike a false note and Bishop Burnet, though testifying to her generosity, scoffed that she 'took state on her, rather too much'.[63] The end result was to make her family even more unpopular at Court and to set the seal on her own, albeit splendid, isolation.

It seems fair to suggest, therefore, that the reponsibility for the Yorks' financial crisis lay ultimately with the Duke and Duchess themselves. James had shown himself to be something of a spendthrift and a perennial debtor while in exile, and after his return in 1660 he continued to express his gratitude to those closest to him, such as Jermyn, Talbot and Apsley, primarily in the form of large gifts and generous allowances. In common with his elder brother, it would seem that he simply did not understand the value of money and that he was quite prepared to assign considerable sums, and large tracts of land, several times over in order to please a favourite. Although Anne Hyde might be held to have been principally at fault for the couple's slide into insolvency, the situation was aggravated by the gross mismanagement of Povey and by the cult of denial which had grown up among James and his advisers. No one within the administration of the household was prepared to take responsibility for their own actions or to acknowledge the growing crisis, while the Duke seems to have been extremely reluctant to discuss money matters at all.[64] When combined, these very different factors ensured that the household, despite all its apparent wealth, would sink ever deeper into debt without finding any way to extricate itself. A solution, if it was to be found, was not going to come from inside the existing administrative structures and so a Commission of Revenue was created, in December 1667, to oversee the running of the Duke's affairs, compile an accurate inventory of his goods, and to recommend cutbacks in his expenditure wherever possible. Povey was dismissed from all of his offices and, along with Henry Brouncker, was not called upon to sit on the Commission. However, he still managed to fall on his feet and quickly found a new patron in the shape of Henrietta Maria, the Dowager Queen. She interceded on his behalf with James, and persuaded her son to award him £2,000 as compensation for his loss of position. Sir Alan Apsley fared much better and emerged from the crisis unscathed, with his reputation as one of the most influential members of James's inner circle actually being enhanced amid all of the confusion.[65] He had already been entrusted with the management of the royal game reserves and an increasingly large proportion of the naval budget had come to pass through his hands as the Duke's Deputy, but in addition to these offices he was now rewarded with the posts of Treasurer and Receiver General, which he had always coveted. Ironically, the concentration of financial reponsibility in the hands of just one person did, as Povey had predicted, make for greater efficiency and order in the running of the ducal household, and very soon began to deliver positive results. This point was further underlined by Apsley's appointment, a few months later, as the Treasurer of the new Commission of Revenue. This ensured him an unrivalled position at the head of the administration of all James's finances and guaranteed him a free hand to make whatever changes he wished in its operations. Apsley began by issuing instructions for a retrenchment of the Duke's expenditure in late 1667; James was to live strictly within his income, servants were laid off, and every possible new source of income was examined. Among these, trading concerns with the American colonies and the West Coast of Africa loomed large, and it may well be that his protracted financial problems provided the impetus for James to involve himself far more closely with the emergent joint-stock companies than had previously been the case.[66] This theme is returned to in Chapter 9, but it is certain that the Duke was in dire need of large, regular injections of hard currency by 1666–7 and was likely to have been far more receptive to innovative schemes for money-making then, than at any other time in the course of his early career.

The work of the Commission, accompanied as it was by an upturn in the national economy, began to pay the Duke dividends. The cuts in household expenditure and the premature death of the first Duchess, which ended her extravagance once and for all, did much to balance the books, while James's income began to grow rapidly as the 1670s progressed. This was the result of far better regulation by his officials and the imposition of a much more effective system for the collection of payments. The revenue he derived annually from the granting of the wine licences rose by a third in the period from the 1660s to the early 1680s, while his profits from the Post Office more than doubled over the same timescale. Similarly, the impact of the Dutch wars, and the increasing success of the convoy system against the Barbary Corsairs, ensured that prize monies began to roll in to the Duke at a far more regular rate. This, when taken together with the incoming rents from his lands and properties, enabled him to amass a substantial surplus of capital which could be reinvested in any one of the several monopoly trades over which he had direct control. Moreover, in marked contrast to his earlier account books, the surviving examples from the 1670s and 1680s are carefully ordered and balanced, serving as a model of clarity and gaining the Duke a belated reputation for financial prudence.[67] Thus, as he approached middle age, James was able to maintain his court in a style, and to manufacture an image for himself of gravitas and grandeur, of which he could only previously have dreamt.

CHAPTER FIVE

A Question of Authority

I

In terms of both triumphalist sculpture and great public works, James Stuart left few durable monuments to posterity. Today, no imposing statues look out over New York Harbour or Freetown, Sierra Leone, as they once did on the quayside at Newcastle-Upon-Tyne, to testify to the enormity of his imperial domains or to his breadth of vision. This is perhaps not too surprising given his position as a fallen monarch, who reigned for only a short period of time. Many of his monuments, from his chapels at Whitehall and Holyrood to Sir William Cleagh's brass horseman, were destroyed in the upheavals of 1688–9, and their loss has done much to obscure his use of personal imagery. His connection with trade and empire is now recalled in only a handful of place names confined to North America – New York, Albany and the York River – after the emergent African democracies erased any trace of his influence from the map, while those examples of his portraiture that remain have done little to bolster his cause.

After the end of the Second World War, both James and his modern apologists were held to be tainted by their associations with totalitarian regimes. The European ambitions of Louis XIV could be readily equated with those of Hitler, while Sir Charles Petrie's admiration for Spanish fascism appeared to offer a distant echo of James's own collaborationism with the forces of foreign absolutism. For a democratic government, recollections of an authoritarian and fallen King were something of an embarrassment. Consequently, his statue by Grinling Gibbons was quietly taken down from its pedestal in Whitehall and moved to a far less prestigious site at the side of the National Gallery, where it could no longer give offence to passers-by. The modern fear of militarism and respect for human rights served to give the Whig Tradition of English history one last, and perhaps quite unexpected, flowering in the arts. In the 1960s, the actor John Westwood chose to play James as a grim and haughty master in the BBC's production of the *First Churchills*, while, after staring at a canvas of the unfortunate Duke, one recent biographer came to the conclusion that 'the final effect [was] one of sneering super-ciliousness not unmixed with wanton brutality'. When he was appointed Leader of the House of Commons in 1976, Michael Foot was troubled to find a portrait of James hanging up in his office, a leftover from his predecessor, the Catholic traditionalist Norman St John-Stevas. He immediately ordered that the offending item should be removed, and replaced it – though without any recognizable trace of irony – with that of another Tory, Jonathan Swift. Even in Ulster, where the struggles of 300 years ago still have much contemporary resonance, James's craven figure flutters only on the banners of the Orangemen. He has been effectively exorcized from the Nationalist wall paintings in Derry, as his flight from the Boyne rendered him unsuitable as a Roman Catholic champion, and his place has been taken by far more suitable figures from a mythic past, such as Cuchulainn, or from an all too real present, such as Padraig Pearse and Bobby Sands.[1]

This posthumous collapse of James's symbolism might have come as something of a surprise to his contemporaries, for few seventeenth-century princes had worked so unstintingly to cultivate a particular image of themselves in the popular consciousness. On his return to England in 1660, it was whispered that the Duke looked and acted 'far more the king' than his elder brother, and courtiers were impressed by his ability to speak 'several languages', even though it was noted that he had mastered 'none well'. Despite his poor social skills, he had been able to acquire a veneer of courtly good manners. He could acquit himself well on the dance floor and in moments of relaxation he took music lessons, and strummed upon a guitar. Moreover, whereas Charles II might have been considered to have been indolent and ugly 'if he were a private gentleman', James was active, physically strong, and capable of great feats of endurance. Magalotti, on meeting him in 1667, commented upon his natural athleticism and found him to be a striking, if not conventionally handsome, individual. 'His complexion may be called light in colour', he recorded, 'all the outlines of his face are prominent: a square forehead, the eyes large, swollen, and deep blue, the nose curved and rather large, the lips pale and thick, and the chin rather pointed.' Charles II, perhaps all too well aware of the rather unfavourable comparisons being drawn between them at Court, complained that his own curly black wig cast him, according to the theatrical conventions of the day, as the villain of the piece while his brother's light-coloured wig ranked him firmly on the side of the angels.[2]

However, the concept of the 'ideal prince' for seventeenth-century commentators was to remain a shadowy one, cast by a mixture of medieval chivalric idealism and humanistic rhetoric. If most writers agreed that a prince should be active, wise and clement, possessing grace, charm and skill at arms, then James was only partially blessed. Although he was a firm friend and 'affable and corteous with foreigners', he lacked the politician's gift for easy familiarity and had 'little ability to express himself, or to use gestures'. He was often thoughtless and hurt those closest to him, giving away the expensive gifts that they had just lavished upon him to other, newer favourites within a matter of only a few days. Pepys, as his ablest bureaucratic protégé, came to regard him as being a 'stern' master, while Magalotti spoke of his 'certain fierceness' and 'severe majesty'. When confronted by the sheer weight of evidence, even the editor of James's own memoirs was forced to admit that 'his outward cariage was a little stif and constrain'd . . . and . . . his Temper was naturally hot and colerick'. James had little interest in the Royal Society, read sparingly, and had inherited none of his grandfather's intense curiosity or his father's all-consuming passion for art. He made no attempt to rebuild the fabulous art collection that had been gathered together by Charles I, and dispersed by Cromwell, while his own tastes, as far as they can be discerned, were rather bland. The paintings that hung in his office at St James's Palace were an odd assortment of family portraits, landscapes, religious works and classical scenes. Though he employed a small group of professional musicians in his household, including Francesco Corbetta, the composer of *La Guitarre Royale*, he commissioned no major new works as Duke of York and did little to encourage the development, and repertoire, of the theatrical company which bore his name. He was singularly ill at ease with the Court wits who thronged around his elder brother and the playwright Thomas Hearne thought that 'he would not take a jest'. His interests remained firmly rooted to country sports and one visitor to Whitehall, during the Duke's residence there, was disappointed that in the absence of a truly cultured atmosphere at 'Court they talk . . . of nothing but horses and dogs'. Aside from his insatiable pursuit of game, James enjoyed watching and betting upon cock fights, and during his periods of exile from 1679–82 he showed himself to be adept at mastering and popularizing novel games and exercises. He learned to skate and practised the art on the icy waterways of Brussels, led his courtiers in curling competitions on frozen Scottish lochs, and provided employment for several local boys to act as his caddies upon the golf links at Leith.[3]

Yet if James was never destined to be an art connoisseur or a royal savant, he fitted the traditional role of the prince as warrior perfectly and was blessed with all of the necessary self-assurance with which to carry it off. All his interests – from his hunting and sailing, to his study of mathematics and fortification – were intensely practical and harked back to his days as a soldier. They also fulfilled an emotional need and James, despite his ancestry, always considered himself to be the most patriotic of Englishmen. He saw the successful pursuit of war as the greatest possible service a prince could undertake for his people, and his hagiographers were keen to compare him to Henry V and the Black Prince in their pamphlets and broadsides. James praised the 'naturell courage of English men' and prided himself that ''Tis observed that of all nations the English stick closest to their Officers and tis hardly seen that our common Soldiers will turn their backs, if they who command them do not set them the bad example.' Even when he found himself ranged against his fellow countrymen in battle he found that he could not fail to admire their bravery. At the Battle of the Dunes, as we have already seen, James had been prepared to concede that the regiments of the Protectorate 'came on with great eagerness and . . . rash bravery' and: 'Stopt not till they came to push of pyke', scattering his own troops and wounding Charles Berkeley at his side. The scene was to be repeated more than thirty years later at the Battle of La Hogue, in May 1692. As his invasion fleet burned before his eyes and his last practical chance of being restored to the English throne was lost amid the wreckage, James's excitement got the better of him. Turning to his astonished French allies he cried out: 'Ah! none but my brave English could do such so brave an action!'[4]

The strong code of honour that had been instilled into James as a young Officer was to lend a certain dignity to his character and to invest his later, largely self-inflicted misfortunes with a touch of nobility that they would otherwise have lacked. Having already won so much praise as a soldier during his service with Turenne and Condé, and with no real alternative course of self-expression left open to him, it is hardly surprising to discover that the Duke should continue to stress his military credentials even after 1660. Whereas Charles II had sought to emphasize social stability and the continuity of the monarchical form of government by appearing in civilian dress and quasi-medieval garter robes, which harked back to a mythical golden age, James set out to convey the idea that he was no mere dilettante prince, but a vibrant individual and a scientific soldier who had won his spurs fighting on the continent. Moreover, he employed every conceivable artistic medium in order to communicate his potent message. Sir Peter Lely, an artist who had been out of favour with the Court, was enlisted by the Duke to paint the portraits of the flag-captains who had served under him at the Battle of Lowestoft, while Francis and Thomas Poyntz were commissioned to weave a large series of tapestries to commemorate his part in the Battle of Sole Bay, which were given away to family and friends. James's private apartments were decorated with tapestries and wall-hangings showing classical scenes. The lives of Marcus Aurelius, Eugenia and Alexander the Great – complete with epic battle scenes, imperial eagles and tribal standards – took their place beside other hangings which depicted 'a variety of history', including King David, Hero and Leander. James also, appropriately enough, owned a set of six pairs of 'fine tapestry hangings of Don Quixote', though it is doubtful if he ever compared his own anachronistic knight-errantry with that of the man from La Mancha.[5] Personal devices featured strongly in the ducal household, adorning James's residences and adding to their character, as well as marking out the coats of his servants and everyday items such as silver, fabric and tableware. James's interlocking 'D' and 'Y' initials stamped his belongings, hung from his household standards, sealed his letters and even decorated the borders of his engravings (see Plate 10). The Duke ordered that his retainers should wear his own personal livery and went to some considerable expense to have them fitted out in their yellow coats. Generous allowances were given to his footmen; who received £25 4*s* for their 'Livery Cloakes', £9 'Linen Money', and £8 3*s* 6*d* for their belts and 'Trimmings'; while additional sums were allocated for hangings for James's trumpeters and shirts for his bargemen. Yellow had been chosen as the Duke's colour, in contrast to the red of the King, as it had been thought to signify, in the words of one contemporary writer, 'honour or [the] height of virtue'. It soon became synonymous with James's followers and was later adopted as the coat colour of his own regiment of foot, being carried into battle emblazoned upon the standards of the Lord High Admiral's Regiment.[6]

With the two royal brothers attempting to fashion their own independent imageries, the cult of the wider Stuart dynasty was given precious little scope to flourish after the early 1660s and went into a steep decline. The magnificent mausoleum planned for Charles I at Windsor was abandoned because of a lack of money and those few monuments that actually were raised in celebration of the royal family either never caught hold of the popular imagination, or else were singularly ill-fated. One of the grandest and most intricate public works dedicated to the Stuarts was the sundial erected in the Privy Garden at Whitehall. It was richly inlaid with a series of glass panels depicting the King and Queen, the Duke of York and Prince Rupert. Unfortunately, the glass was prone to frost and cracked after a particularly severe winter. The rest of the structure was destroyed in 1675 when: 'My Lord Rochester in a frolick after a rant did . . . beat downe the dyill . . . which was esteemed the rarest in Europ'.[7]

However, if James was never successfully portrayed within the context of the ruling dynasty, then he was represented as the individual subject of an enormous number of paintings by some of Europe's foremost artists in the period stretching from 1660 to 1685. It would seem that the Duke liked to have his portrait painted and, in later years, Sir Godfrey Kneller commented that he and Mary of Modena had 'sate to me about thirty-six times apiece, and I know every line and bit of their faces. Mine Gott! I could paint . . . James now, by memory.' The most striking feature of the Duke's personal imagery remained the consistency of his own portraiture, with its central theme of James as a soldier. The strident and unambiguous terms in which this vision was couched, over the space of twenty-five years, did much to define public perceptions of the Duke's role within the restored monarchy. Whether in simple folk art, scratched on a window pane; monumental sculpture, intended as the centrepiece for one of the capital's new squares, or in official court portraiture, destined for the salons of the rich and famous, James's image is almost invariably that of an armoured figure ready for action. Popular engravings copied from the canvases of Lely and Kneller were distributed to the mass market, or were issued especially to capture the public mood or to commemorate a particular event. James regularly appears in these works in the guise of a victorious general, as the Lord High Admiral, as the 'Count of Ulster', or as the 'Matchless Leader and Chieftain' of the Artillery Company (see Plate 8). He is often surrounded by a large array of props – such as anchors, drums, great coils of rope, spontoons, powder barrels, demi-culverins and pike-staffs – which effectively served to underline his interests, while background scenes of desperate naval battles or cavalry skirmishes further reinforced the impression, and denoted his service to the nation and exemplary personal courage. The only exceptions to this rule occurred when it would have been wholly inappropriate for the Duke to been portrayed in military costume, such as in the painting of pastoral scenes or during the investiture of the Knights of the Order of the Garter. Even on these rare occasions the novelty of the situation would seem to have been apparent to the artist involved. Anne Killigrew's canvas, showing the Duke walking in parkland, was consciously labelled as representing him 'in ordinary dress' and when Lely came to paint the royal family in their Garter Robes he chose to differentiate the various members from one another. Although Charles II was shown to be unarmed, both James and Rupert were portrayed drawing back their voluminous robes in order to reveal the hilts of their swords poking out from underneath.[8]

However, if we can safely assume that the armoured portrait served as the standard model for the Duke during the Restoration, we can at least detect several distinct stages in its evolution. James is initially shown as a young Officer just returned from the wars, as in Lely's famous canvas from 1661 (see Plate 4). While the composition of the scene is idealized and owes much to classicism, the treatment of the sitter is essentially factual and naturalistic. The Duke carries a wooden baton to denote his rank as a Field Officer, while his practical breastplate, buff-coat and high-topped boots are in keeping with his service as a cavalryman in France and Flanders. There is little to distinguish this work from dozens of other paintings commissioned during the Civil Wars from artists such as William Dobson and John Greenhill. All attempted to record the now largely forgotten achievements of Royalist soldiers for posterity and succeeded in capturing something of the grim realities of wartime on their canvases. What distinguishes Lely's first portrait of the Duke from them, apart from its undoubtedly superior technical merits, is the high status of the sitter and the fact that it became the basis for a series of later paintings which chronicled James's marriage to Anne Hyde and the growth of his own royal dynasty.

These paintings had their genesis in the desire of the Earl of Clarendon to commemorate, albeit somewhat belatedly, his daughter's marriage into the ruling House of Stuart. He commissioned Lely to produce matching portraits of the Duke and Duchess, shortly after Charles II had given official recognition to their union in December 1660, and specified that the artist should display their individual virtues to the best possible effect. Given that their marriage had scandalized the Queen Mother, reflected badly upon the Duke's conduct, and been solemnized in an atmosphere of secrecy and resignation, the job of the artist was a difficult one which required a fair degree of tact and diplomacy. On consideration, Lely opted to show the couple in contemporary dress but with James playing Mars, the Roman God of War, to Anne's Venus, his consort and the Roman Goddess of Love (see Plates 4–5). The Duke's sexual passions, when allied to his martial ardour, could be seen as being far more palatable and understandable when subliminally linked to classical precedents. Thus, Anne's conception of a child out of wedlock, once removed from the strictures of Judeo-Christian morality, might appear to be a far more natural and beneficial occurrence. Venus, as the feminine and sensual counterbalance to her fiery lover, had restored order, soothed the temper of the God of War, and brought forth a bounteous issue. However, when a fresh composition was planned between 1663 and 1664, combining both paintings into one single study of the young couple, the depiction of Anne had begun to significantly alter, while that of James remained fundamentally unchanged. Instead of representing a primarily sensuous figure, she had by this time taken on the more conventional form of the virtuous and dutiful wife, cradling her husband's helm somewhat awkwardly in her arms, rather than languidly dipping her fingers into the jet of an oyster-shaped fountain. The Duke's posture, save for the position of his baton in his left rather than his right hand, is entirely as before. He remains in essence the very model of the professional soldier. However, if the original portrait of James had seemed to suggest that he was a soldier just returned from the wars, then the altogether darker tone of the background in the new composition, complete with flashes of light and foreboding storm clouds, would appear to signify his intent to embark upon fresh campaigns against the Dutch.

In the final version of the scene, copied and produced in the early 1670s by Gennari, the Duke and Duchess of York are joined by their two surviving daughters Mary and Anne (see Plate 6). Although the standard forms of the earlier portraits are still observed, and it is noticeable that the couple have not aged with the passage of time and still wear the fashions of the previous decade, the overall emphasis of the work has once again shifted. It now serves as a family portrait, stressing royal continuity and the strength of the bloodline of the House of York. In this respect it differs little from those earlier depictions of the family of Charles I and Henrietta Maria, and a domestic touch is added through the inclusion of one of the Duke's hunting dogs. It is important to note, however, that James was probably already widowed at the time of its completion and that his own symbolism has undergone one final subtle alteration. Previously he had pointed to either a baton or a laurel wreath in order to underline his martial accomplishments, but now he also indicates towards a globe, which may well represent his interests in the colonies and in mercantile projects. James's fame, it would seem, was now being spread the world over.[9]

This adjustment of the Duke's image, to take into account changing political realities, also found an expression in the way in which his skill as a soldier was variously conveyed to an early modern audience, widely schooled in deciphering complex allegory and symbolism. In March 1665, Pepys, as a civilian, was to express his mixture of horror and surprise at seeing his master abandon the finery of his court dress and 'try on his buff coat and hat-piece [i.e. metal skull cap] covered with black velvet' for the first time. As memories of the Civil Wars faded and military fashions were less in evidence on the streets of the capital, the representation of armour in portraiture became increasingly stylized. While its inclusion still made for a profound visual impact, and harkened back to the days of the courtly romances of Roland and Bayard, armour was increasingly redundant on battlefields dominated by long-range artillery. Consequently, by the time Lely came to paint James again, at the time of the Second Anglo–Dutch War, his armour had undergone a profound change and bore little resemblance to anything that he might have worn in action. James now appeared fully encased in a suit of plate armour, fringed by a chain-mail shirt at the wrists and tassets. This far more elaborate pattern of armour, which was often taken from stock items found lying around the artist's studio, rather than from actual pieces in the Duke's own collection, became the standard costume for the majority of his subsequent portraits. It is noticeable, however, that the new sets of plate he ordered from Richard Hoden after his accession to the throne were of a far more sparse and practical nature, consisting only of a lobster-pot helmet, a breastplate and a long elbow gauntlet to protect his bridle arm in the charge. Moreover, on his last campaigns in 1688 and 1690, he abandoned armour altogether and chose instead to wear the embroidered coat of a Staff Officer.[10]

In a similar manner, James's natural hair was replaced by a series of wigs after 1664, which became ever more extravagant and impractical in their construction as the years went by.[11] Following the fashions set by the French Court, the first wigs were flat on the crown and heavily crimped at the sides in imitation of a natural tangle of curls, but by the early 1670s they had become more obviously artificial, extraordinarily long, piled up and heavily back-combed for added height on the top of the head. As portraiture moved away from recording the actual day-to-day appearance of the subject, and placed a far greater reliance upon allegory and symbolism in order to convey the abstract power held by the individual, classical imagery was to experience a marked resurgence. This new development was seen first in the design of medallions. European princes vied with each other in the production and regular issue of commemorative medals, which could attest to the splendour of their own royal culture and the superiority of their manufacturing techniques. By striking their own profile on to countless dies they could publicize their own image and seek to equate themselves, and their endeavours, with those of the Roman emperors who had already been immortalized on hundreds of coins which had made their way into royal collections right across the length and breadth of the continent. These could be used to record every great event in the life of a prince, and James took advantage of the medium in order to stress his naval victories, his dynastic marriage to Mary of Modena and his miraculous rescue from the wreck of the *Gloucester*. He employed John Roettier and George Bower, his brother's craftsmen, to produce medals recalling the Battle of Lowestoft so that they could be given away to his sailors as rewards for good service (see Plate 7). Later he sought to evoke Britannia in a celebration of his skill as a sailor and his concern for the national interest, though in a moment of hubris he declared in the inscription that: '*Nullum Numen habes, si sit prudentia* [Without prudence you have no presence]'.[12]

James frequently appeared as a Roman General on the reverse of these medallions, but it was in a lifesize canvas by Henri Gascars that his appropriation of classical imagery reached its fullest and most dramatic expression (see Plate 1). The painting was commissioned to commemorate the Duke's victory at the Battle of Sole Bay in May 1672, and the King's subsequent visit to congratulate the fleet. It is distinguished by a rich use of symbolism and by the forceful juxtapositioning of both ancient and modern cultural references. James is once again represented as the Roman God Mars, and is shown arming for war in his tent. He wears a muscled cuirass tied at the waist by a tribune's sash, while a gladius inlaid with precious stones hangs at his side; and lion-headed sandals, recalling the classical deity, adorn his feet. A long staff has replaced the customary military baton and a young squire rushes to hand him an extravagantly plumed helmet surmounted by a sphinx. On one level, the Duke is presented to us as being half-god–half-Caesar, but in the midst of all this arcane imagery we are suddenly reminded that James is still an English Prince of the seventeenth century. He retains his flowing wig, and a suit of Greenwich armour, which had once belonged to his brother and had presumably been passed down to him, lies ready at his feet. The gentle closing of the fingers of his gauntlet around the shaft of a halberd offers an implicit threat, and serves to reinforce the Duke's favourite maxim, proclaiming him to be '*Nec Minor in Terris* [Not less on land]'.

Although the soldiers in the background are dressed as Roman legionaries, they march under the cross of St George, carry pikes and beat dull metallic drums. The message would seem to be that James is the rightful successor to the great Generals of antiquity – such as Scipio Africanus, Julius Caesar, Agricola and Trajan – and that classical Rome has been reborn in Restoration England. Moreover, the presence of the modern battlefleet led by the Duke's flagship, the *Prince*, stretched out along the horizon promises fresh conquest and the dreams of a new empire. In this light, the picture appears as being nothing short of a political manifesto, and a testament to James's will and imperial vision. The whole fleet waits on him, the Dutch foe has been vanquished, their possessions scattered, and whole continents are left open for the taking. The comparison is clear, the nascent British Empire is seen as the true successor to the Roman Empire and the power of the legions has been replaced by the might of the English Navy, which under the Duke of York has secured the seas and imposed a '*Pax Britannica*' on all the nations of the world.[13]

This exceptionally beautiful and self-confident painting was unique in the art of the Restoration. It represented an attempt to introduce French fashions into the English Court and would not have seemed out of place in Louis XIV's Versailles. Very similar works, such as Pierre Mignard's *Louis at Maastricht* and Antoine Cosyevox's *Louis trampling his Enemies*, were to define the genre on the Continent and encapsulated the splendour, glory and naked aggression of resurgent monarchy. Conquest, it would seem, was very much the business of princes and the casual observer might be forgiven for walking away from Gascars' canvas with the impression that it was James, and not Charles II, who was actually the King of England. The work is certainly revealing of James's desire to be considered as one of the great Princes of Europe, a soldier and statesman to be reckoned with, and it is to a primarily elite and foreign audience to which he is addressing himself. While this painting, had it been on public display in England, would have evoked fears of the tyranny of an unbridled and popish monarchy, the grandeur and triumphalism of the piece was carefully calculated to impress upon the diplomats and courtiers who flocked to Whitehall the high status, and very real abilities, of the heir to the throne. The presence of this rich vein of Continental influence in James's portraiture, after the late 1660s, does not, therefore, necessarily mean that he deliberately set out to import French models, uncritically, into England in his headlong pursuit of absolutist power. While Henri Gascars himself, as the protégé of the Duchess of Orléans, was reputed to have been a spy for the French government, there is no question that James intended to be seen as the subservient client of a foreign power. Rather than simply aping Louis XIV, it would seem that James was attempting to appropriate a successful Continental image of royalty, which was couched in the universal language of neo-classicism, and to impose upon it peculiarly English characteristics, in this case the quest for maritime empire.

Furthermore, it would be misleading to attempt to link the motives of taste and artistic convention too closely with the individual politics of a patron. It is conceivable that James had chosen Gascars simply because he was the finest artist operating in England at the time, and it should be remembered that there were solid practical reasons behind his adoption of the guise of a Roman, rather than a contemporary, General. Classical armour was not subject to sudden changes in fashion, being already antique it could not date any further, and this served to convey a timeless quality about the sitter, as well as to prolong the effective life of the portrait. There can be no doubt that the French influence was very strong at the Court of Charles II, and that James's portrait was both ambitious and more than a little tactless in its English setting, but even staunchly Protestant Princes had attempted to reflect the rays of the Sun King and both William of Orange and Charles IX of Sweden felt moved to commission similar works to glorify their own achievements in war.

What was unfortunate in James's own pursuit of political identity was that the symbolism he chose, although potent and easily recognizable, was also utterly inflexible. Indeed, the image of the Duke as an armoured man was to become so fixed in the public imagination that he continued to have works produced in honour of his military exploits, long after the events they recorded had been largely forgotten. *Bas reliefs* of his battles against the Spanish and Dutch were carved on to the black marble base of the statue which was raised to him at Sandhills in Newcastle-Upon-Tyne shortly after his accession, and several of his ducal portraits were speedily altered in early 1685 to take account of the new political realities (see Plate 13). Thus, when Sir Godfrey Kneller began his portrait of James in the winter of 1684, it was only intended to mark the Duke's return to office as Lord High Admiral of England (see Plate 12). Consequently,

James's standard use of symbolism was still very much in evidence. He appeared in the painting in full cuirassier armour, holding his baton of command in a proud salute, while an anchor on the shoreline signalled his return to his post and his flagship, out at sea, delivered a full broadside in celebration of the welcome news. However, the sudden death of Charles II in February 1685 caused the half-finished canvas to undergo a drastic revision. It was quickly retouched and updated in order to reflect James's new position as King. The baton clenched in his right hand was replaced with a sceptre, a long ermine-lined cloak was draped over his shoulders, and the crown jewels were somewhat awkwardly painted in, to one side of his figure. The transition to kingship did not, however, mark a watershed in the development of James's personal imagery and the Kneller portrait was not destined to be the final expression of his military ambitions.[14] Though James would occasionally adopt the Garter Robes, in imitation of his elder brother, his portraiture during his brief reign never fully reconciled his civilian duties with the military role that he so earnestly desired. He continued to appear as a soldier, rather than as a statesman or savant, thus fuelling the hostile propaganda which sought to equate him with a Bourbon or a Habsburg despot.

In conclusion, therefore, James's use of personal imagery can be seen to have been extremely powerful and direct. Unfortunately, it was also blunt and tactless, and failed to keep pace with the reality of the Duke's situation. James's early portraiture had accurately reflected his active foreign service and his interest in the Navy, but after the mid-1670s a widening gap began to open up between the image that he had created for himself and the public perceptions of his role. James was no longer a brave young soldier, but a mature statesman approaching middle age, who had seen no active service over the course of the last thirteen years of his brother's reign. Sidelined from military operations and stubbornly refusing to abandon his increasingly dated and redundant imagery, the Duke had now to content himself with playing at being a soldier, taking part in wargames and grand manoeuvres in a rather empty attempt to recapture his lost youth. John Evelyn was present at one of these mock-battles, which was held in the grounds of Windsor Great Park, in August 1674. 'There was . . . a work with Bastions, Bulwarks, Ramparts, [and] Palisades', he recalled, 'in imitation of the City of Maestricht, newly taken by the French . . . defended against the Duke of Monmouth (newly come from that real siege) who (with the Duke of York) attacked it with a little army, to show their skill in tactics; so on Saturday night, they made their approaches, opened trenches, raised batteries, [took] the counterscarp, shot, mines sprung, parties sent out, attempts of raising the siege, prisoners taken, parleys, in short all the circumstances of a formal siege to appearance, and what is most strange, all without disorder or ill accident, but to the great satisfaction of a thousand spectators, when being night it made a formidable show, and was really very divertisant.'[15] As Evelyn hinted, James was beginning to suffer by comparison with his nephew. While he could only hope to take part in a staged recreation of the action, Monmouth had actually participated in the fighting and had won much praise for himself by storming an outlying redoubt. It was exactly the sort of heroic feat that the Duke of York would have undertaken himself, twenty years earlier, and to make matters even worse Monmouth, in his own pursuit of popularity, had begun to appropriate much of his uncle's own carefully constructed imagery, appearing fully armoured and riding to war in the paintings of both Kneller and Gascars.

It would seem then, given Monmouth's concern to follow in the Duke's footsteps, and notwithstanding Englishmen's long-held objections to standing armies, that James's portrayal of an honest and dedicated soldier could have been a particularly compelling and effective form of expression had it been handled in the right way. The image perfectly conformed to the well-established ideal of the English warrior prince. It had originally been created during the Hundred Years War by Edward III and Henry V, was revived by Henry VIII as a young King, and was successfully employed in the 1610s by Henry Stuart, Prince of Wales. Most notably, it was used selectively and to devastating effect during the Exclusion Crisis, when Charles II chose to abandon the familiar civilian robes of his official portraiture in favour of an uncompromising, and unambiguous, suit of armour. At the Oxford Parliament in 1681, Charles II had been prepared to show that he would countenance military force in defence of his throne, and that the King could be both soldier and sovereign. In remoulding himself, in the last years of his reign, to encompass an element of James's more strident and assertive imagery, he had demonstrated the potential advantages to be derived from directly linking the monarchy with its feudal and chivalric past.[16] There was still much to be said for a physically strong and assertive head of State, in an age when personality influenced policy and the vitality of rulers was held to be synonymous with that of the nation as a whole. The Duke of York was fully aware of these sentiments and had been able to capitalize upon them after his victory at the Battle of Lowestoft, in 1665. Parliament had voted him its thanks for his delivery of the nation from the Dutch, monies were granted to him in genuine recognition of his bravery, and church bells were rung to celebrate his safe return home. However, the popular celebrations and feastings which accompanied the news of his endeavours at sea had the effect of confirming James in many of his assumptions. He was at the zenith of his popularity and his military career appeared to reflect an unbroken string of success. If he had won his first fame as a junior Officer on the Continent, he had now surpassed himself and gained a victory in his own right, which firmly established his claims to being the foremost soldier in the land. Henceforth, he would seek to win popularity primarily through the pursuit of arms and would refuse to abandon his equation of battlefield success with domestic approval, even when all the evidence pointed to a very different conclusion. Despite his return to active service and his valour at the Battle of Sole Bay, in 1672, he was unable to reclaim his earlier place in the affections of the English people. This was largely due to his dramatic conversion to Roman Catholicism between 1668 and 1669, which had set public opinion firmly against him and brought all of his attempts to curry favour with his brother's subjects to nothing. Even as James was dreaming of projecting himself on to the European stage and as Gascars was putting the finishing touches to his masterpiece, Parliament was debating the Test Act which would seek to remove the Duke from his powerbase in the Navy. Today, one cannot view the grand canvas without the thought occurring that it represents no more than an empty monument to the hubris and vanity of princes.

Far more seriously, James's open profession of Roman Catholicism was to expose his chosen role as a soldier to a far harsher criticism, and a more sinister interpretation, than would otherwise ever have been the case. As the pages of the *Life* so eloquently attest: 'Before that time he was looked upon as the darling of the Nation, for having so freely and so often ventur'd his life for the honour and interest of the King and Country. . . . But no sooner was the allarme given of his being turn'd Papist, then all these merites were blotted out of their memory, and he [was] sett upon on every side as the common Enemy.'[17]

II

James's conversion to Roman Catholicism, between 1668 and 1669 came as the defining moment in both his public career and personal life. Indeed, it is no exaggeration to paraphrase Hilaire Belloc and to suggest that his faith ran strong and deep, like a single steel thread, through all of his subsequent thoughts, words and deeds.[18] It was the Duke's Catholicism that rendered him suspect to a large proportion of the English people, and raised questions about the nature of his conduct and the succession to the throne which would destabilize English politics for the next two decades. It caused James to be stripped of all his public offices, to lose custody of his children and to be forced into an ignominious second exile, in Flanders and Scotland. However, if the Duke was utterly taken aback by the venom, spite and opprobrium which greeted his public avowal of his new faith, the overwhelming majority of English Protestant opinion was in no doubt as to why they should be so strongly ranged against him.

Roman Catholicism appeared to many not as a religion, but as a repressive political system. Although it maintained the outward show of Christian practice and belief, it was argued that the Roman Church had become so overlaid with ritual 'Whisperings, Sprinklings . . . and Phantasticall Rites', conducted in a foreign and 'an unknown tongue', that it had abandoned the word of God, and allowed its liturgy to degenerate into the mere 'pranks and ceremonyes of Juglers and Conjurers'. The truly sacred had been abandoned before the secular, and what remained was a single-minded desire for temporal obedience and a marked intolerance of any form of dissent. Protestant Englishmen, whether Anglican, Presbyterian, or Independent, had long memories and were steeped in the same cultural values which emphasized Biblical authority, the primacy of scripture, and personal and national independence from outside agencies. More importantly, the experience of having once been a persecuted minority, reviled as heretics, hunted down and burned upon the orders of a Roman Catholic sovereign, was as potent a folk memory as it was a cohesive factor in the formation of both Protestantism and a sense of nation in the English state. The smell of woodsmoke, rising from the hearth of gentleman and artisan alike, could all too easily evoke the fires of Smithfield and drive home the contemporary resonance of readings from John Foxe's *Acts and Monuments of these latter and perilous days,* more commonly known as the *Book of Martyrs.* Save for the Bible itself, this work was perhaps the single most important text for English Protestants, outlining the evolution of their Church and the sacrifices and dangers which had marked out its early development. Moreover, the book offered a particularly comforting form of social inclusion when war with foreign powers threatened, or at times when civil society seemed to be on the verge of a total breakdown. Even though the National Church, the Presbyterians and the scores of new Independent sects which had grown up since the 1640s, might hold very different and mutually antagonistic ideas about the nature of the episcopacy, and the relationship between the subject and the sovereign, all could conceive of a particular definition of 'Englishness' which equated patriotism with Protestantism, and which attempted to place itself in direct opposition to the Papacy and the great European monarchies which sought to defend it. This particular tradition, which drew strength from the rational knowledge that England was not a formidable power and that European Protestantism had been successfully confined by the Counter Reformation to its northern heartland, also appealed to the basest and most irrational of society's fears: that of strangers, distinct subcultures and foreigners. This fear of external threat and the unknown found further expression in the cycle of the ritual year. *Gunpowder Treason Day* was kept as a national holiday, in order to celebrate the deliverance of a Stuart King and his people from a Roman Catholic plot, and was occasioned by children throwing firecrackers in the streets and by the continuous ringing of church bells. The Pope and the Devil were often paraded in effigy, before being torched on the great pyres which rose every year in the vicinity of Temple Bar, in London. As news of the Duke of York's conversion to Catholicism began to leak out of Whitehall, these festivities took on an altogether darker and more frenzied tone. Fear of a popish successor lent a raw political edge to customary practice – satire, debate and protest could be conducted relatively freely and openly for at least one night in the year.[19]

It mattered little to Protestant England that the assassinations countenanced by the Popes of the Counter Reformation were a thing of the past, that the vast majority of their Roman Catholic neighbours shared in their patriotism and loyalty to the Crown, or that their numbers were actually falling to comprise barely 5 per cent of the total population. For, while many Protestants were tolerant and friendly on a personal level towards those Roman Catholics that they actually knew in their communities, they still maintained a vigorous fear and hatred of 'Popery': an omnipresent and covert force, spearheaded by the Jesuit Order and driven by papal dictat, which could strike without warning at their lives and liberties. This feeling of insecurity was reinforced by the belief that individual, high-profile, Roman Catholics appeared to hold a disproportionate share of political power. The Elizabethan penal laws had effectively clamped down upon the general promulgation of the Roman doctrine and had largely succeeded in expunging the faith from among the labouring and middling classes, but there were still many rich and influential Catholics among the landed gentry, who could afford to pay fines for their recusancy and maintained private chapels for their worship. This was felt to be especially true in the North of the country, where families such as the Blundells, Molyneuxs, Shireburns, Swales and Gascoignes, continued to function among the local elites and provided a sense of much needed social cohesion, and the chance of advancement, for their beleaguered co-religionists.[20] More damagingly, at the national level, from the time of Charles I's marriage to Henrietta Maria, the Court of the Stuart Kings had come to be increasingly associated with the promulgation and practice of Catholicism. Charles II's marriage to the devout Portuguese Princess, Catherine of Braganza, and his marked fondness for taking Catholic mistresses – and the Duchess of Portsmouth, in particular – served to reinforce this link in the popular consciousness. It was hardly surprising, therefore, that many Englishmen reacted with fright and alarm to the news that the heir to the throne had suddenly, and without warning, converted to Rome.

This sense of betrayal was made worse by the fact that James's actions seemed to be entirely out of character with what was publicly known about his own nature and wholly at odds with the set of beliefs that had compelled so many old Cavaliers to fight, and die, for his father. There had been little in his early life to suggest a marked predisposition towards Roman Catholicism, and by way of contrast his Anglican credentials had always been assumed to be of the very highest order. He had never enjoyed particularly close or cordial relations with his staunch and proselytizing Roman Catholic mother, while the strict entreaties of his father, only months before he went to the scaffold, that he should never forsake the Church of England were held to be enough, on their own, to have confirmed him in his Anglican faith. During the course of his first exile, those closest to him were a Presbyterian, Bampfield, a French Huguenot, Turenne, and an Anglican, Sir John Berkeley. Thus, even though he had fought with Catholic armies on the Continent and recruited many individual Irish believers, including Richard Talbot and Justin Macarty, into his service, James still retained his reputation as a 'good' Protestant, and sought to stress his firm resolve to continue in both 'profession and practice' as a communicating member of the Anglican Church.[21] Moreover, on his return to England in 1660, James's unexpected love-match to Anne Hyde brought him into close contact with her father, Lord Chancellor Clarendon, and her brothers, Henry and Lawrence, who were all deemed to be among the most rigorous defenders of the rights of the Church of England. While Clarendon's reverence for established institutions complemented the rigid social ideals instilled into James in wartime Oxford, and fitted in well with the Duke's own high concept of monarchy, the marriage more importantly seemed to fix him permanently within the context of constitutional Anglicanism. Courtiers were to note approvingly that although his initial passion for Anne faded, and though he continued to love 'his wife but does not worship her as he once did', even the mistresses he took, such as Catherine Sedley and Arabella Churchill, held decidedly Anglican sympathies.

Having outlined the public perception of James's career up until 1668, we may now ask ourselves why a man on the threshold of middle age, of such stubborn and fixed opinions, who never normally yielded to fresh ideas and who had read little in the way of theology and Church history, should be so utterly and irrevocably won over to Roman Catholicism. Fortunately, we are helped in this task by a mass of primary evidence set down both by James himself, and by the Hyde family, which record his thoughts on the nature of religion and outline, in several places, the reasons behind his change of faith.[22] It would seem that his conversion was a very gradual and painstaking process, based almost entirely upon personal observation and enquiry. James never found himself on 'the road to Damascus', or underwent a dramatic conversion experience of the kind that became the staple fare for the writers of conventional religious narratives. His change in religion was, however, brought about by two interlocking developments. He first rejected the virulent anti-popery of his youth, and then became convinced of the validity of the arguments in favour of Roman Catholicism. We shall deal with each of these factors in turn.

During the twelve years that he spent in France and the Low Countries, from 1648 until 1660, James had mixed with Catholics of all degrees and had seen at first hand how the fears of 'popery' held in England were both exaggerated and often blatantly absurd. Many of his father's most devoted supporters had been of the 'Old Religion' and, as a soldier, James's comrades in arms had been predominantly of the Roman Catholic faith. He recorded the solemn impression left upon him by the religious exercises of the French Army before going into battle, and noted that all the Catholic converts he met had undergone a miraculous change of behaviour, after their abjuration, abandoning their previous bad conduct to become good and faithful Christians. On the other hand, he came to perceive that Protestant converts only seemed to go from bad to worse, multiplying and revelling in their sins against both God and temporal authority. As a result, James reached the conclusion that both individual Catholics and their religion, as a whole, had been grossly misrepresented and treated most unfairly. 'I became sensible', he wrote, 'by experience, that I had wrong notions given me of the Catholic Religion, and that they were not guilty of several things they were falsely taxed with.' Indeed, in later years as his misfortunes multiplied, James was to take comfort from the belief that God had orchestrated his whole exile so that he could come into contact with Catholics and come to know 'what their religion was', learning all 'the true maxims of it'. It is extremely significant that he was in no doubt that it would have been impossible for him to discover these 'truths' had he remained quietly at home in England, surrounded by his Anglican tutors and nurtured by his father's indulgent and comfortable household.[23]

Bishop Burnet claimed that the Duke had been 'reconciled to the Church of Rome while he was in Flanders, but dissembled the matter long after that', citing as evidence a conversation that he had had with James in 1683, during which he allegedly told him that he had been converted by a nun while he was serving with the Spanish Army. Burnet then pressed the matter and asked if he had been in love with the nun, but James only replied wryly that she was 'no tempting object'. This seemingly conclusive passage would appear to suggest an early date for the Duke's conversion, but Burnet made many additions and changes to his text when he came to revise his *Supplement* in 1705, the most startling of which revealed that James 'never told me when or where he was reconcilled'. The story about the nun does seem to be firmly grounded in fact, as James's official biographer alludes to it in the *Life*, but he chooses to put a rather different gloss upon events. Rather than converting the Duke on the spot, she merely provides him with sage advice and causes him to think more deeply about his faith. This interpretation would seem to be confirmed by Roman Catholic tradition, although many of the later accounts are greatly embellished, taking on something of the quality of folk tales in their transmission, and even seeking to identify the individual nun involved. James for his part never directly mentioned the story in any of his letters or devotional writings, and was to give his conversion a far later date in his own narrative account.[24] This may simply have been done out of desire to protect individual Catholics from the blame for leading him away from the Established Church, but Burnet's contention that James hid his conversion from all those around him for several years would seem quite suspect and wholly out of character for a man who, in the 1670s, made a very public show of his beliefs. He clearly disliked any form of subterfuge and, as his writings eloquently show, longed to bear witness to his new faith and to help others to see the 'truth' precisely as he had done. It would seem fair to assume, therefore, that if James was not converted outright in 1658, then he was certainly won over to the cause of Roman Catholic toleration and had his interest in religious matters awakened.

Although the crisis in James's faith was reached during the winter months of 1668–9, it would seem that religious tensions, centering about his immediate family and friends, had been building over the course of the previous eighteen months and that matters were finally brought to a head by the combination of several largely unrelated events. The first of these was the dramatic fall from power and flight into exile of the Earl of Clarendon, in late 1667, which deprived him of his High Anglican mentor, threatened his own political position, and caused him to turn more earnestly to his wife, Anne, for support and advice. Within a matter of months the surprise news of the conversion of Marshal Turenne, whose faith had always been considered unshakeable, came from the Continent and shook European Protestantism to its very foundations. James cannot fail to have been taken aback by this high-level defection of a close personal friend, but thought he saw in it his old Commander's quest for advancement, personal glory, social stability and the national good. He told Samuel Pepys, in December 1668, 'that Turein being now become a Catholique . . . is likely to get over the head of Colbert, their interests being contrary; the latter to promote Trade and the sea (which, says the Duke of York, is that that we have most cause to fear); and Turin to imploy the king and his forces by land, to encrease his conquests'. Unfortunately, while confirming the Duke's singular commitment to maritime power, the diary entry does not expand further on the religious dimension and we have no way of knowing what James really thought about his friend's change of religion. However, we do know that Charles II and Louis XIV had been particularly keen to make use of the friendship that existed between James and Turenne, in an attempt to circumvent existing diplomatic channels. Their private correspondence had been used as an unofficial means of communication between the two governments, in the early 1660s, in order to open up negotiations over the sale of Dunkirk and to ensure the smooth handover of the port to the French authorities. Thus, the deal struck between the governments of Cromwell and Mazarin, which had been sealed by their soldiers' blood at the Battle of the Dunes, was finally absolved by the pen strokes of these two old friends.[25]

Given that James and Turenne were trusted to pursue national policy aims through their personal correspondence, and that they continued to send each other letters that discussed everything from simple family matters to the high politics of the day, right up until the death of the Marshal in 1675, it would seem quite extraordinary if the subject of Turenne's change of religion had gone entirely without mention throughout all of the intervening years. More significant still, in the context of our own study, was the actual manner of the Marshal's conversion. It was said to have come about through quiet study and contemplative personal reasoning, rather than through a sudden ecstatic vision or flash of insight. Such an account, even allowing for the literary and political conventions of the day, matches perfectly with the gradual process of revelation as outlined by James in his own conversion narrative.[26]

However, it was the Duke's wife, Anne, who made the greatest single impact upon his thinking. She had, according to Bishop Burnet, been 'bred to great strictness in [the Anglican] religion' and wrote in her own account that she was 'as well instructed in the Doctrine of it, (as the best Divines, and her Capacity could make her)'. Although, in her youth, she had been 'one of the greatest Enemies [Catholicism] ever had', she appears to have had serious doubts as to her own religion shortly after her return to England, and converted to Catholicism at some – unspecified – time in the 1660s, almost certainly before her husband. Having read up on all the relevant arguments, both for and against changing her faith, Anne came to the conclusion that the Church of England was not a true church at all, and wrote a short pamphlet to that effect. She based her case solely on the nature of infallibility and argued that history had shown that the Anglicans had no right to claim authority through the apostolic succession. Her ideas struck a deep and immediate chord with her husband, and seem to have prompted him to embark upon his own lengthy study of religious thought and Church history. However, when looking at the theological reasons given by James for his conversion, one must compare them closely with those presented by his wife. There is a remarkable similarity between the two, which extends right down to the use of the same stock phrases and common sources of reference. To all practical considerations they are a part of the same conversion narrative. Anne as the more reflective, curious, and intellectually able partner was probably the originator of their search for spirituality and it is likely that James fully accepted his wife's critique of the Church of England, before expanding upon it in the course of his own, more substantial, writings.[27]

With the close of the Second Dutch War, and with little hope of his securing an active command in the near future, James had both the time and leisure to investigate all of those problems that still troubled him. His wife had raised doubts in his mind about the doctrinal authority of the Anglican faith to which he subscribed and, hating uncertainties, he sought reassurance. He hoped to find eternal truths, and the answers to all of his questions, embodied in the fabric of one infallible and unchanging Church. As a result – spurred on by Anne – he set to work with all the purpose and seriousness of mind that so marked his character, in an attempt to discover why the reformed Churches had broken away. He consulted Richard Hooker's *Of the Lawes of Ecclesiastical Politie* and the Bible, and discussed his concerns in some depth with the leading Anglican divines. However, rather than easing his mind, his researches only served to raise new fears for him about the nature of salvation, and to throw him into an even greater confusion than before. He was absolutely horrified to discover that there had been very worldly reasons for the Church of England's separation from Rome, that seemed to have nothing at all to do with miraculous workings of the Kingdom of God. Up until this time he had firmly believed what his chaplain, Dr Richard Steward, had taught him: that the Anglican Church had derived its authority through the apostolic succession and that the authority of the twelve original apostles chosen by Christ had been transmitted directly down the ages, through generations of bishops, to the present episcopate. The Church of England, which had only a very recent history, had allegedly been called into existence once the Roman Church had begun to degenerate and became increasingly overlaid with superstitions and corrupt practices, from the time of the late Middle Ages onwards. All of its formidable moral authority and spiritual lineage was, thus, held to have been ceded to the Anglicans at the moment of the Henrician Reformation, leaving the Church of Rome, although still a 'true church', seriously compromised and no more than a shadow of its former self. By way of contrast, the Presbyterians and Sectaries, whose existence was even more recent, could have no such claims to authority and had only grown out of the wordly greed and folly of man.[28]

However, through his reading, it now appeared to James that this was not in fact the case. Instead of the Roman Catholic Church losing its way and becoming increasingly greedy, he belived that it was actually the arrogance of the reformers which had brought about the damaging schism. James grounded his arguments primarily in historical terms, taking his lead from Dr Heylin's *Ecclesia Restaurata; or the History of the Reformation of the Church of England*, which he had read shortly after its publication in 1661. Heylin had attempted to provide a scholarly and well-balanced account of the development of the Church of England in his book. Unfortunately, his subtle defence of Anglicanism failed quite spectacularly on the Duke and Duchess of York and they managed to draw exactly the opposite conclusions from his work to those that he had originally intended. After finishing his text, Anne felt that she could find no moral justification at all for the English Reformation, and came to the conclusion that it had come about solely as the result of 'three abominable' reasons. The first of these was the desire of Henry VIII to divorce his wife, Catherine of Aragon; the second was the ambition of the Earl of Northumberland, the Lord Protector, who wanted to plunder the wealth of Church lands, and the third was the need of Queen Elizabeth I to legitimize her unlawful succession to the throne.[29] James, deeply impressed by this exposition, declared that those theologians and courtiers who had advanced the cause of the Protestant Reformation during the reign of Edward VI had born 'no resemblance to those who [sat] in the first Council at Jerusalem'. It was they who acted out of human greed and sin. Consequently, they could not possibly be endowed with the same divine spirit as the fathers of the early Christian Church, and their claims to spiritual authority were clearly spurious at best. In writing to his daughter, Mary, James summarized his arguments and stressed that the Roman Catholic Church was endowed with 'a constant succession from the time of the apostles to the present, [which] should be more in the right than those private men who, under the pretext of reformation, have been the authors of new opinions', and added significantly that: 'It was this consideration which principally led me to embrace the communion of the Roman Church, there being no other which claims, or can claim, infallibility, for there must necessarily be an infallible Church, or otherwise what Our Saviour said cannot be and the gates of Hell would prevail against her.'[30]

In this light, therefore, the Church of England could have no more right to infallibility than the Sectaries that they had so reviled. If man could break away once from the Church of God, so James reasoned, then there was nothing to stop him doing so again, and again, upon any whim that he chose. No one, he wrote, should 'wonder that there are such alternations made in the Church of England as established by Law [rather than by God], every day, since those who come after the first reformers have as much authority to reforme againe as those who began' the process. As a result, the reformed Churches appeared to offer nothing in the way of truth or stability, and could only be viewed as being subversive and socially devisive. According to James 'till they began the Schisme all was quiat as to Religion in our unfortunat country but since all the world sees what disorders it has caused and how our Ilands have been over run with diversites of sects and with ruine and Rebellion in the State' nothing at all had gone right in the affairs of Englishmen. All evils, heresies and schisms sprang directly from the actions of proud individuals like Luther and Calvin, who deluded themselves that they knew God's will better than His own Church.[31]

These certainties which did more than anything else to shape James's adult conception of the world, may, however, appear to us to be based upon an extremely simplistic and superficial analysis of Church history. The Duke and, indeed for that matter, the Duchess seem to have read no further than their two original and oft-quoted sources of Heylin and Hooker. Thus, although they were well acquainted with the circumstances surrounding the English Reformation, they appear not to have known of the earlier schisms that had divided the Church in the fourth, ninth, eleventh and fourteenth centuries. The Earl of Clarendon, writing from exile in Montpellier, took issue with James and Anne on precisely these grounds, and vigorously attacked their 'fallacious Arguement of Antiquity and Universality'. This line of reasoning, 'that there is no salvation out of the Church that there bee but one Church and that the Church of Rome is that only true church', was, he thought, 'Confidently urged by men who know lesse than many of those you are acquainted . . . and . . . is both Irrational and untrue.' 'There are many Churches', he continued, 'in which Salvation may be attained as well in any one of them and were many even in the Apostles time otherwise they would not have directed their Epistles to so many venerable Churches in which there were many different Opinions Received and very different Doctrines taught.' However, James, as far as we know, never chose to reply directly to this criticism and clung doggedly to his position. When tackled upon doctrinal matters, he invariably returned to his bold assertion of the Church's divinely invested authority, which afforded it an unassailable position in the interpretation and promulgation of the Gospels, and which appeared to render other, subtler, points of argument totally irrelevant.

Having convinced himself that his own line of argument was flawless in its logic, James moved swiftly to reconcile himself with the Roman Catholic Church. The pages of the *Life*, edited together at his own request, recorded that he became 'more sensibly touched in conscience and began to think seriously of his own Salvation' at the beginning of 1669, and that shortly afterwards he made contact with Father Simeon, a Jesuit priest, who came to act as his confessor and spiritual guide. Simeon was not just any priest, but a very senior member of the Order's English Province. Renowned for his literary and musical accomplishments, he had served as the Professor of Theology and Philosophy at Liege before being appointed as the Order's foremost representative, or Provincial Anglican, resident in London. More importantly perhaps, from James's own point of view, he was also an Englishman. He had been born Emmanuel Loebb, in Portsmouth, over seventy years before, and as the second son of a poor Protestant family had been sent away to Portugal, while still a child, to gain advancement in foreign trade through the study of languages. However, at Lisbon he forsook the easy life of a merchant and was converted to Roman Catholicism, by another English Jesuit, taking Holy Orders shortly afterwards. Thereafter, he devoted all of his energies to the Order and the records kept by the Jesuits describe him as being bright, brave and disciplined, ranking 'high among the members of the English Province for talent, piety and great usefulness'.[32] He may well have appeared to James as a charismatic personality, a resolute and highly motivated man after his own heart. The Jesuits had already established themselves as chaplains to a whole host of European sovereigns – Louis XIII had had four Jesuit Confessors, while his eldest son had as many as five – and it is significant that, as early as the 1550s, Ignatius Loyola had defined one of the primary objectives of the Order as being to 'win the affection of the great and noble'.[33] Their confessors were tactful and prudent, able to cope with the deep-seated jealousies of courtiers and to arbitrate skilfully between princes. They often adapted their moral stance to fit individual circumstances, and either softened or hardened their line depending upon the social class of the audience to whom they were appealing. Given their relative laxity as confessors – and the Duke's largely futile struggles to suppress his own frenetic sexual energy – it may well be that James found their brand of Catholicism to be particularly attractive and reassuring. Moreover, the very fact that their rule owed much to Loyola's formative experiences as a professional soldier and laid great stress upon the need for commands to be obeyed precisely and without question, combining the virtues of both the priest and the military man, probably served to strike a deep chord with the humourless and unflinching Duke, who prized duty, order and seemliness above all things.

The markedly individual and cosmopolitan nature of the Duke's conversion, owing so much to private study and the inspiration of a largely foreign religious order, did much to set the tone of James's subsequent practice and perception of Roman Catholicism. He never tried to lead a separate religious faction at Court or to become the champion of English Catholicism in the country at large. Indeed, he seems to have had little understanding or knowledge of the everyday concerns of his co-religionists, and had precious little contact with the backwoods gentry and the handful of great magnates who struggled to keep the faith alive outside of the capital. The copious letters and notebooks kept by William Blundell, a prominent Lancashire recusant, hardly mention James at all before his accession, and where his actions are discussed they always are in the context of Court politics rather than spiritual life.[34] The Duke, though cordial to Sir William Howard, Viscount Stafford, did not go out of his way to seek his friendship, while his relationship with Cardinal Philip Howard was formal and frequently strained, rather than close. Furthermore, it is noticeable that it was Loebb, a Continental exile, who received James into the faith, as opposed to Cardinal Howard, the titular head of the Roman Catholic Church in England. Apart from Richard Talbot, an Irishman, Henry Jermyn, an English convert, and his Confessors, it is remarkable how few Catholic friends James actually had. His companions were picked primarily because of their usefulness and congeniality, rather than on account of their religion. Consequently, his household was mainly composed of lay Anglicans such as Lawrence Hyde, George Legge and John Churchill; foreign Protestants, such as Louis de Duras, and the godless, such as Henry Herbert and Percy Kirke.

There is no evidence that the Duke's personal religion ever had a strong political dimension, or that his implementation of policy changed radically after his conversion. Gwatkin's contention, that 'If he had a point of religion, it was the religion of Mary Tudor's kind, which stirred him to cruelty and revenge, and drove him to a career of treason against the religion and freedom of his people', does not seem to be borne out in any of the existing sources, aside from Exclusionist tracts. James's faith, by way of contrast, would appear to have been characterized by a strong, if narrowly conceived, belief in the power of human reason and by an abiding, if rather sickly, brand of sentimentality. He was fond of stories that related the sufferings of saints and martyrs, and placed a great deal of reliance upon the conversion narratives of other believers which echoed his own and attested to the morally improving effects of Roman Catholicism. He was touched to hear of the conversion at Macao of 'a little blinking [Chinese] fellow' named Michael, and sought to make his acquaintance when he toured Europe in 1681. Impressed by the seemingly inevitable march of the Cross into previously inaccessible corners of the world, James employed the new convert in cataloguing the Chinese manuscripts held at the Bodleian Library and commissioned Sir Godfrey Kneller to paint him in his oriental dress, clasping his right hand to his breast and pointing to the crucifix. However, if religion had the power to move James's emotions, then he was still far from being credulous. There is nothing to suggest that he was given over to superstition, and he was extremely wary of stories of miraculous cures and sudden visitations. He dismissed a story about a 'boy who was pretended to have a wanting leg restored to him, so confidently asserted by Fr. de St Clair and others', and said that he would only believe in these tales if he witnessed them himself, and in the company of others who could confirm that he was not suffering from a 'delusion of his senses'.[35] Having been converted, primarily, on an intellectual rather than a spiritual level, James set great store on his own powers of reasoning and believed that if all religious arguments were represented fairly, then an individual could not fail to be convinced by Catholicism in the same manner that he had been. In this light, therefore, there was simply no need for intimidation or coercion. All that was needed was an open mind and an atmosphere of general religious toleration in which debate could flourish. This would seem to explain James's growing belief in the need for a policy of toleration in the 1670s and 1680s.[36]

Before that date, he had strongly opposed any such measure for dealing with Protestant Dissenters, equating them with Republicanism, backing the passing of the Five Mile Act in 1665 and advocating stern action to limit the spread of Quakerism. However, it may well be that as he increasingly came to experience persecution himself, he suddenly realized that his own position as a member of a minority faith was analogous to that of the other noncomformist sects. His burgeoning friendship with the younger William Penn and the overtures he made to other Protestant groupings may well be part of his attempt to forge new political alliances in the wake of his rejection by the wider political nation after 1673. He may also have come to believe that his newfound advocacy of toleration might have practical implications for the wealth of both the fledgling Catholic mercantile community and the English nation as a whole. Like Protestant Dissenters before them, Roman Catholics were increasingly becoming involved with small-scale trading concerns and business projects and the Duke came to fully accept the idea that religious freedom was synonymous with high levels of economic growth. Writing much later, with the positive commercial benefits of William III's grant of religious toleration very much in evidence, James and his editors tried to suggest that 'The encreas of trade and riches he knew was a more durable benefit than an empty fame', and that, 'it was one great motive to his granting of libertie of Conscience [in 1687–88], which brought back accordingly so many Dissenters, who had left England for fear of persecution, and had set up the Woolen Manifacture at Lewardin, Lunenbourg and Freezland . . . [so that] he might draw [the] greatest part of the Trade of Europe into the hands of his Subjects.'[37]

Setting aside the possibility that the reasons, given in the *Life*, for James's acceptance of the principle of toleration may have been simply fabricated with the benefits of hindsight and special pleading, the problem with his mechanistic approach to religion still remains. James was fundamentally unable to accept the validity of opposing convictions, genuinely held by others. If those he lectured failed to be convinced by the straightforward logic of his argument, then it was not James's own reasoning or lack of learning which was at fault, but rather the obstinacy and malignity of the individual who opposed him. Indeed one must wonder what would have happened, in the 1680s, had he remained as King and discovered that his policy of 'a level playing field' for all religious groupings would not have brought about the gradual, but inevitable, reconversion of England as he had hoped. At this distance it is fruitless to speculate whether James would have continued down the path towards an enlightened plurality or reverted to harsh coercion, but it seems fair to suggest that he placed altogether too much store upon his own powers of intellect and persuasion, and that his recorded attempts at proselytizing were curiously hamfisted and singularly ill placed. Shortly after his succession to the throne, he approached Percy Kirke on the subject of his religion, offering him a promotion in the armed forces if he converted to Catholicism. 'Upon which', we are told, 'the colonel began to smile and answered him thus – "Oh, your Majesty knows that I was concerned at Tangier, and being oftentimes with the Emperor of Morocco about the late King's affairs, he oft desired the same thing of me, and I passed my word to him that if ever I changed my religion I would turn Mahometan".' It is sad to relate that James's response to Kirke's rare and ironic appeal to integrity has not been recorded for posterity.[38]

In conclusion, therefore, it seems as if the Duke's conversion was undertaken with little thought to political dogma, or to finding the religion best suited to the propagation of a foreign brand of absolutism. It was instead, a uniquely individual response to a basic quest for truth and scriptural authority, that was totally in keeping with James's serious nature and rather crude conception of all human relationships. There was no room, in his way of thinking, for uncertainties or high-flown debate: things were either right or they were wrong. Similarly, it is important to stress that his conversion experience had little direct impact, in the period from 1669 until 1685, upon his actual personality. There is no suggestion that, while Duke of York, he began to retreat from the world, to abandon his interests in warfare, women and horses; or to adopt a strict regime of prayer and meditation. His pursuit of power, and his love of military and imperial conquests, continued unaffected. At most, it would appear that the hierarchical nature of the Roman Catholic Church, and the authoritarian tone set by its priesthood and teachings, did no more than to provide personal reassurance and to confirm him in his existing prejudices about the maintenance of a conservative social order, in a society where political power ultimately seemed to be derived from, and ordained by, the hand of God.

III

Though startled by the ferocity which greeted the news of his conversion, James was not entirely unprepared for the storm that broke over him once word of his Catholicism began to leak out to the press and the public. While he had probably been received into the Roman Catholic Church at Ghent, at some unspecified time between mid-1669 and early 1670, he had hesitated for some months over his final decision, fearing the consequences of the outpouring of popular disapproval which would surely attend it. He had beseeched Father Simeon to appeal to the Pope on his behalf, 'alledging to him the singularity of his Case', for a dispensation 'for outwar[d]ly appearing a Protestant, at least till he could own himself publickly to be a Catholick, with more security to his own person, and advantage to them.' Such dispensations were not uncommon, and it is unclear as to whether or not Simeon was acting on his own authority in declining such a measure, as Pope Clement did not know for sure of the Duke's conversion until 1676. Nevertheless, James recorded that 'the good father insisted, that even the Pope himself had not the power to grant it, for it was an unalterable doctrine of the Catholick Church, Not to do ill that good might follow', and that, 'these words . . . made the Duke think it high time to use all the endeavours he could, to be at liberty to declare himself, and not to live in so unsafe and so uneasy a [spiritual] condition.'[39]

It was about this time that Charles II held a meeting with James, at which the Lords Arlington, Arundell and Clifford were also present, in order to conclude the details of the Secret Treaty of Dover. All of these men were either Catholics at the time, or else 'fellow travellers' who chose to convert at a later date, and over the course of their discussions they turned their attention to how that religion could best be promoted across all of the King's domains. James, who left the only account of the proceedings, then alleged that his brother pledged his own love for Roman Catholicism 'with great earnestness' and with tears streaming down his face. Whether or not this was actually the case, Charles II was certainly well-disposed to the faith and was to remember his debt of honour to Father Huddleston, who had rescued him from his enemies after the Battle of Worcester, on his deathbed. To James, who was far less flexible in his outlook, there could be no such concealment of his change in religion. Secure in the knowledge that there was a powerful undercurrent of crypto-Catholicism at Court and that his own brother had accepted French subsidies in return for a promise to Louis XIV to embark upon the stealthy reconversion of England, he could not bring himself to dissemble upon matters touching the divine. Consequently, he chose not to take the sacrament, according to Anglican rights, at Easter 1671. Thereafter, although he continued to accompany the King to church, he no longer received Communion. As the winter of 1672–3 approached, Charles II tried in vain to persuade his brother to dispel the rumours which were already circulating about his Catholicism and to attend the Christmas Day service with him. James, however, had clearly made his decision and was henceforth sworn to stand by it. John Evelyn recoiled in horror at his extraordinary behaviour and recorded that, in March 1673, 'I staied to see whither (according to costome) the Duke of York did Receive the Communion, with the King, but he did not, to the amazement of every body; This being the second yeare he had forborn and put it off, and this being within a day of the Parliaments sitting, who had Lately made so severe an Act against the increase of Poperie [the First Test Act], gave exceeding griefe and scandal to the whole Nation; They the heyre of it, and the sonn of a Martyr for the Protestant Religion, should apostasize: What the Consequence of this will be God onely knows, and Wise men dread.'[40]

This idea that James had somehow betrayed his father's memory was an extremely potent one and had been played upon by the Earl of Clarendon, when he wrote to warn his son-in-law of the profound dangers that he was now facing. The execution of Charles I had always been portrayed in Royalist circles as the supreme act of self-sacrifice and Anglican martyrdom, and Clarendon had appealed to James to uphold the honour of 'that church for the purity and preservation whereof your Blessed father made himself a sacrifice'. However, unfortunately for the exiled Earl, James had never viewed his father's death in quite those terms. He had forcefully rejected the Anglican interpretation of events and saw the *Eikon Basilike* as being nothing more than a fraud, since it was most definitely 'not of his father's writing'. As we have already seen in Chapter 2, it was the actual example of his father's willing sacrifice and the experience of seeing him suffer in captivity beforehand, that probably had the deepest effect upon James's psyche. The rather spurious claims of the old Cavalier and Anglican cause, in which he had supposedly died, mattered little to him. This may go some way to account for James's own, rather self-conscious, search for martyrdom during his final exile, from 1690 until 1701, and the Duke of Lauderdale's rather pithy observation that 'if he had the empire of the whole world he would venture the loss of it, for his ambition is to shine in a red letter after he is dead.'[41]

If this line of argument was destined to fail then, tactful as ever, Clarendon shifted his attack and directed the force of his criticism against his daughter. Pretending that he did not know of James's conversion, he wrote that 'those bold whispers which have been long scattered abroad concerning your wife being shaken in her religion', had reached him at last and had started 'to break out into noise', as 'publique persons begin to report that the Dutchesse is turned Roman Catholique'. Having identified Anne, as both the thinking partner and the root cause of all the trouble, he went on 'to beseech [James] to look to the matter in time and to apply some Antidote to expell the poison of it', and begged that, 'with the freedom of a troubled and perplexed father I doe most humbly beseech your Royal Highnesse by your authority to Recieve her from buisying a mischief upon you and herself that can never be unpainted'. It would seem that Clarendon was well aware of the rumours concerning the Duke's own conversion, for he added – by way of a back-handed compliment – that 'Your wife is generally Believed to have soe perfect duty and entire Resignation to will of your Highnesse that any defection in her from her Religion will be imputed for want of circum-spection in you', and urged that James should immediately repudiate all of the charges 'to Remove and dispell these Reproaches (how false so ever) by better evidence than contempt'.[42]

Yet what Clarendon did not know when he was penning these lines was that his daughter was already dead. She had died four days before, eaten up by cancer, after 'A long decay of health came to a quicker crisis', and that 'All on a sudden she fell in agony of death.' Her final deathbed scene was made even bleaker by a boycott of her servants, that had been led by her own brother, Henry Hyde. He had refused to attend on account of her repeatedly spurning the intercessions of her Anglican chaplains, and her frenzied calls for only the administration of Roman rites. Even Lawrence Hyde, her younger brother and the Duke's close companion, had decided that it would be imprudent to associate himself too closely with her apostasy and had foresaken her, making only the briefest of appearances during her last days. However, all thought of James's past indiscretions was forgotten as he maintained a vigil at her bedside, now appearing as the contrite and loving husband. He was there for the bitter end and Anne's edifying death in the Roman Catholic faith, coupled with her final, chill entreaty to him: 'Duke, Duke, death is terrible – death is very terrible!', cannot have failed to have had a far deeper effect upon him, than the entire weight of popular opprobrium and contemplative study, binding him ever closer to Rome.[43]

Over the next two years, James was to be stripped of his rank as Lord High Admiral under the provisions of the first Test Act, which ensured that only communicating members of the Church of England could hold office. This very public humiliation, added to his refusal to take Anglican sacraments alongside his brother, brought his profession of Catholicism out into the open. Moreover, his subsequent marriage to a foreign princess, Mary of Modena, who held rigidly to her Roman Catholic faith, only served to make him even more unpopular and to reinforce the implicit link in the minds of many Englishmen between the Duke and the 'fearful' practices of Continental royalty. James stopped attending Anglican services completely after 1676, and although he continued to appoint Church of England clergy to administer to the needs of his household, it is doubtful if they had much contact with either the Duke or his new Duchess. This very open identification with the Church of Rome left James vulnerable to all manner of attacks, which grew in their boldness and ferocity as the decade wore on. To begin with, the Duke had only been criticized obliquely, with the focus of popular rage directed overwhelmingly against his servants, confessors and the person of his second wife. However, as first the Popish Plot, and then the movement for his exclusion from the throne gained momentum, James himself came to be the primary target for vilification at the hands of a myriad of anonymous ballad writers and pamphleteers.

He became synonymous with Saul and Ahab, the Judean Kings who had abjured God, and with the Roman Emperor Julian II, 'the Apostate', who had allegedly tried to forcibly reimpose paganism upon his subject peoples.[44] It was felt that the English nation had to be saved from 'one man led away with a blind perverseness, renouncing the Religion he knows not why (and so wilfully attaining himself)', who would surely 'expose millions of souls to damnation, and streets to flow with blood by suffering that Religion to creep in, whose reformation (at the mildest rate) will certainly prove Fire and Faggot'. It was predicted that 'The whole Nation must inevitably suffer; Religion subverted, and Property destroyed, and the whole People in danger of their Lives.' Roman Catholicism was seen as a disease striking at the body politic, the epitome of 'Superstition and Tyranny', disabling the heir to the throne as though he were 'rendered . . . uncapable . . . as in cases of Idiocy, Lunacy, or the like, and the Parliament is [consequently honour] bound . . . to place [him] where Religion and Property shall be adjudged most safe'. The theme of a deep-seated plot masterminded by the Duke was forcefully revealed: 'Now no man is safe in his bed . . . for . . . he and his Party (which will increase daily, and the Protestants decline) will soon get an opportunity either by Stratagem, or open Force, to avoid all Laws . . . and therefore it will be impossible to be safe without a Protestant Successor.'[45]

These dire warnings appeared to be increasingly well founded in fact, as news began to break almost daily of alleged plots and attempted *coups d'état*. In November 1675, the capital was shocked by the claims of an unfrocked Jesuit priest, by the name of de Luzancy, who alleged that Mary of Modena's Jesuit Confessor, St Germain, had threatened to kill him for daring to convert to Protestantism. The Society of Jesus had always occasioned fear and distrust in England. The archetypal Jesuit was seen as being the servant of foreign powers, rather than of God. Trained abroad and ruthless in both their cunning and expertise, the popular conscious-ness still recalled their complicity in frequent, and often successful, attempts to take the lives of 'good' Protestant monarchs. Six members of the Order were to be hung, drawn and quartered at Tyburn at the height of the Popish Plot, and while St Germain was able to escape to France, Edward Coleman, as we shall see in the course of the next chapter, was not so fortunate. Amid a climate of mutual terror and misunderstanding, several of James's most trusted servants, including Samuel Pepys, were temporarily abandoned by their master and left to their fate.

These worrying events seemed to call for a major reassessment of the Duke's character, by contemporary writers, and created a demand for new biographies of James in order to satisfy growing public interest. The need for fresh material could, however, produce some very odd results and one pamphlet, *The Memoirs of the Most Remarkable Enterprises and Actions of James Duke of York, Albany and Ulster*, published in London in 1681, was clearly the product of two completely different works written at separate times, and hastily cobbled together by the printer in order to take advantage of the change in political climate. The first half of the pamphlet provided a rough chronological overview of James's life, stressing his military service in the Low Countries and during the Dutch Wars, and seemed to fit in well with the established pattern of the Duke's hagiography. However, the account breaks off suddenly in 1673 with the rather terse statement that: 'Since the Discovery of the Popish-Plot his Highness hath resided much in Scotland.' When the narrative is resumed in the second half of the work, it portrays James's character and activities in a very different light. The Duke is no longer the warrior Prince, but leader of a seasoned 'fifth column' of Roman Catholic agitators who had already been implicated in the murder of the judge, Sir Edmund Godfrey, and in an attempt upon the King's life. James, we are told 'not only having engaged himself solemnly to them for the establishing of their Religion, but also that he would restore them to all their Church-Lands, and other privileges taken from their Church formerly', had 'given good assurance to the Pope, besides being a Prince of that Resolution, that if ever he made any engagement, he would never revoke it, which gave them great hopes of dispensing the dark Clouds of Heresy (as by them called)' from over the whole of England.[46]

If this dramatic sea-change in the public's perception of the Duke was not bad enough, then still more worrying to James was the sudden haemorrhaging of support from his own natural followers, the old Cavaliers and members of the rural Anglican gentry, who controlled many of the springs of local government. The Marquis of Halifax confided to Sir John Reresby that 'Except he [the Duke] became a Protestant, his friends would be obliged to leave him, like a garrison one could no longer defend', while a hardened Royalist, who styled himself as 'Philanax Verax', wrote that although his 'pen is guided by a Heart filled with profound loyalty and most passionate veneration towards all the Royal Family, and a sincere respect and most passionate desire for the particular prosperity (Temporal and Spiritual) of Your Royal Highness . . . every day many hundred thousand Protestants were melted with Tears and Horror on this consideration [of James's change of faith], and lament the same as one of the greatest calamities that has happened in our age.' If the Duke were to continue in his practice and pursuit of Roman Catholicism, then he was simply 'the worst subject, the most unkind brother, the most impolitick Prince, and the maddest, or the most monstrous man in the world'.[47]

An attempt, led by Archbishop Sancroft and Bishop Morley, was made in 1678 in order to diffuse this potentially disastrous situation and to effect a lasting reconciliation between James and the Church of England, to 'recover the Duke out of that foul apostasy into which the bust traitors from Rome have seduced him'. Although James received them politely, and allowed them to deliver a long address to him, nothing came of their plans and he remained as immovable in his faith as ever. Even Bishop Burnet was forced to concede that 'I turned the discourse often to matters of religion. . . . He wished I would let those matters alone: I might be too hard for him, and silence him, but I could never convince him.' The Duke, however, chose to deliver a far more vigorous response to Henry Hyde from his place of exile in Brussels, in 1679, rejecting any suggestion that he should reconvert to Anglicanism as a matter of political expediency. Hyde had argued that an outward show of conformity would do much to restore his fortunes, and would still allow for him to retain his own private beliefs and to continue to receive Communion according to Roman Catholic rites, behind the safety of closed doors. James responded angrily, to his confidant William Legge, that 'I assure you that I will never try that way you mentioned, in yours [i.e. a letter] to Churchill, and which also has been hinted to me by several of my best friends, though I were sure it would restore me into the good opinion and esteem of the nation which I once had; and therefore I desire that neither you nor none of my friends will ever mention it to me, or flatter themselves that I can ever be brought to it; what I did was never done hastily, and I have expected many years, and been prepared for what has happened to me, and the worst that can yet befall me.'[48]

If James, therefore, was resolute in his decision not to return to the Church of England, then he needed to vigorously counteract the barrage of Whig propaganda directed at his person. He and his supporters did attempt to mount their own substantial counter-offensives through the pages of the broadsides and the popular press, most notably after his return to England in 1681 and after his restoration to office three years later.[49] Unfortunately, by this time the Duke's image had become so firmly established that it would not bear a fresh interpretation and it is noticeable that in his devastating attack upon Shaftesbury and his fellow Exclusionists, *Absalom and Achitophel*, not even John Dryden could break new literary ground in his description of James's attributes, preferring for the most part to fight shy of expounding upon them altogether. Consequently, with no other means of expression available to them, scores of lesser authors simply recycled the same old appeals to the Duke's noble birth, manly virtues and martial prowess that had been appearing regularly in conjunction with his official portraiture since the 1660s. One anonymous propagandist was typical of this trend, echoing Dryden's claims that the Duke was 'Still dear to all the bravest and the best', called upon his fellow countrymen to remember James's past victories. 'Witness Spain', he wrote, 'what worthy Praises there his Valliour won, his very name made haughty France to tremble and . . . his Royal courage [should have] . . . procured the name of thunder-bolt in War.' However, while Dryden wrote for an elite and cultured audience, content merely to know that James was both loyal and courageous, the unknown pamphleteer went on to graphically describe the carnage of the Battle of the Dunes, which had taken place more than twenty years before, for his own decidedly popularist readership. The Duke had, we are told, 'with his Sword . . . cut out a lasting name in Characters of Blood . . . Fame owns him for her Son: for like to Mars he fought even in the Mouth of slaughter; whilst heaps of slain like ramparts hemed him in and yet the power of France, nor English Rebels (for at that time they could be term'd no less) there in league durst brave his noble fury, or once so much as hinder his retreat.' This theme of violence and the quest for military glory was returned to, again and again, for 'his Royal Highness did [also] command in chief, whose conduct on the roaling Seas is known unto the utmost limits of the yet known World, how bravely he behaved himself amongst a Thousand Fates: tho dres'd in their most dreadful guises, and for his king's his own and Countries Honour, undauntedly fought whilst swift Wing'd Death Swung around his Royal Head, and Climbing Fires made all the Ocian seem to Blaze, whilst Peals of Thundering Cannons from each quarter Belched distructive Flame, and ruin seemed to cover all.'[50]

Unfortunately, such evocative, if lengthy, reiterations of James's past glories seem to have been singularly ineffective, and may even have been counter-productive. In drawing the attention of the readership to the Duke of York's inherent militarism, these writers were dangerously combining the two great fears of English Protestantism – the standing army and popery – into one, and identifying the person of James Stuart as their prime embodiment. He came to be widely associated with plans for a violent insurrection and John Dutton Colt, the Member of Parliament for Leominster in 1681, confidently asserted that 't'was not long since Queen Mary's days and that, if ever the Duke of York should come to the Crown, t'would be worse than t'was then, for we should see our children's limbs cut off and thrown into our faces.' James's armoured portrait which had hung proudly in the Guildhall was slashed under cover of darkness by an unknown assailant and, despite the offer of a £500 reward by the Lord Mayor of London for the name of the culprit, no one was ever brought to trial.[51] Therefore, it would appear that all of the Duke's efforts in evolving a unique personal symbolism had only served to result in the creation of an imagery which was wholly inappropriate for his own political position and for the highly charged times in which he lived, where religion remained a vital, divisive and potent force. Moreover, his continual need to secure fresh victories in order to maintain his image as an all-conquering hero could not fail, when combined with his open avowal of Roman Catholicism, to play directly into the hands of the Whig propagandists and their tales of dark plots, military conspiracies and papist massacres. James was further handicapped, as we have already demonstrated, by the increasing redundancy of his own chivalric message and its utter incompatibility with his desire to function as a prominent civilian statesman in the sphere of national politics. It was this unfortunate combination of driving personal ambition, with unrealistic policy aims, and an overdeveloped sense of his own worth, which caused so much unwelcome attention to be focused upon James's religion and his position as heir to the throne. Labouring under a cloud of suspicion, it seemed to many that he had consciously chosen to render himself unacceptable to the English people by his own actions. As the lustre attached to his name as a soldier became increasingly tarnished or forgotten, he appeared as a mere caricature of his former self, the 'popish successor', who hovered in the shadows only a heartbeat away from the throne, threatening to overturn the Settlement of 1660, and to reduce the lives and liberties of his brother's subjects to dust.

CHAPTER SIX

The Thrice Noble Duke of York

I

Though by his birth a pawn in the affairs of State, James, Duke of York, had been raised to know and to love only war. His real introduction to English politics came after Charles II's restoration to the throne and, though sworn in to the Privy Council – the senior executive body in the land – in 1660, his first steps upon the national stage were necessarily faltering. The band of rootless career soldiers who had followed him throughout his exile cut awkward and alien figures at the Court of Whitehall, and to many Londoners it seemed as if the Duke had 'none but' swaggering 'Irish rogues about him'. Even his own horse appeared to conspire against him as it faltered, stumbled and then bucked him, on the way to his brother's coronation at Westminster Abbey.[1] Labouring under a cloud, as the result of his scandalous marriage to Anne Hyde, James had to work hard to create a distinctive role for himself in the kingdom's government. Though skilled as a soldier, he lacked experience as a statesman and as a manipulator of party and faction; he initially succeeded only thanks to the happy combination of his royal position and family ties. As the brother of the King and the son-in-law of the Lord Chancellor, he was guaranteed unrivalled access to the councils of State and his influence could not long be ignored by would-be politicians in search of advancement. He moved decisively to purge former Parliamentarians from office in the South-East of England, shortly after his return, and supported moves from the floor of the House of Commons to strip Presbyterian ministers of their parishes. He exercised some direct say in minor ecclesiastical appointments and installed High Anglican clergymen in comfortable benefices, private chaplaincies and in the service of the fleet. A list compiled by Sir Thomas Osborne, the future Earl of Danby, in 1669, reveals nine MPs who were directly dependent upon his support and another forty-five who were, to a greater or lesser extent, regarded as being within his sphere of influence and who were prepared to vote in his interest. The Duke's electoral strength was based predominantly in the West Country, where he owned estates, and in the Cinque Ports, where he had the power to raise taxes and gift naval contracts. However, the majority of his supporters, with the notable exception of Francis, Lord Hawley, did not hail from the top flight of the aristocracy but were drawn, instead, from the middle ranks of the gentry and from local elites. In this way, his servants in the provinces – like Roger Vaughan and Sir Jonathan Trelawney in the South-West, or Sir John Reresby in the North – could continue to maintain close ties with the communities that they represented, while his friends at Court – such as Sir Alan Apsley and Thomas Dalmahoy – could pursue their primary careers in the royal household and, at the same time, maintain a close watch upon the deliberations of the Commons.[2]

James was able to secure the election of his Secretary, Sir William Coventry, for the borough of Great Yarmouth in 1661, which as a seaport was within his gift as Lord High Admiral, and thereafter Coventry and Apsley, who had been similarly returned for the Royal Dockyard at Thetford, were to act in tandem as the chief managers of the Duke's interest in the Commons. Coventry, blessed with strong family con-nexions and an appetite for hard work, which made him indispensable to the Duke's service, soon asserted himself in the lower chamber and carved out a reputation as a skilful and conscientious servant of the Crown. However, James's early success in securing the nomination and election of his clients to Parliamentary seats was deceptively easy, in the wake of the fall of the Puritan Republic, and the methods used by the Duke to win electorate support began to come under greater scrutiny, and criticism, as the 1660s progressed. The public perception of the government's complete mismanagement of the Second Dutch War led to the growing identification of James's followers with a recognizable 'court party' or 'faction', which was by its very nature dissolute, wasteful and irredeemably corrupt. In a wave of disastrous by-election results govern-ment candidates were swept from office right across the board, with James's partisans faring worse than most. Baptist May, one of the Duke's Gentlemen of the Bedchamber, had stood for election at Winchelsea, in October 1666, but things went badly for him from the start. He was reviled by the electorate, who branded him as a 'Court Pimp' and bitterly resented his imposition upon them. In an attempt to bolster his flagging campaign, James made a personal intervention, in his capacity as Lord High Admiral and Prince of the blood, and issued May with a glowing letter of introduction, commending him to the voters. His endorsement was clearly intended to impress the townsfolk and to throw the full weight of the Duke's authority behind his candidate. Unfortunately, it proved to be a wholly counter-productive measure, serving only to further identify May with the system of government which had been thought anathema in the first place. The result was that he suffered an embarrassing defeat at the polls at the hands of a local gentleman, Robert Austin of Tenterden.[3] However, James may well have had far more reason to rue his choice of friends, than he ever did to condemn the obduracy of the electors of this small and declining port, for May was shortly to join together with the core personnel of the Duke's household in a sustained, and remorseless, attack upon the Lord Chancellor which plunged the royal government into its first real crisis and which came close to undermining the position of their own master in the affections of his brother, the King.

Clarendon, who as the architect of the Restoration Settlement had stood supreme among the ministers of Charles II, was distinguished not only by his exceptional intellectual clarity but also by his great practical ability in the formulation, and pursuit, of policy. His relationship with James had not always been easy, but it was cemented through the Duke's marriage to his daughter and by the mutual realization that they held much in common. Hyde's love of England and his stubborn refusal, while in exile, to learn foreign languages, fitted in well with James's own parochialism and sense of strident nationalism. Moreover, in the absence of their father, the older man acted as an uncle figure to both Charles II and the Duke of York, freely advising and directing them in the affairs of State, and delighting in the power and status which their close relationship conferred upon him. In particular, he liked to stress the dependency of James upon his counsels and that 'the duke himself, in the house of peers, frequently sat by him upon the woolsack, that he might the more easily confer with him upon the matters which were debated, and receive his advice how to behave himself; which made all men believe that there had been a good understanding between them.'[4] Unfortunately, the dominance of the Hyde family over James and his household caused many of his servants to feel resentment and hatred towards a clan who were otherwise no more than their social equals. The scholarly, gout-ridden old man, with his constant emphasis upon constitutional legality, the Anglican Church and the seemliness of government, was more than a little out of place among the aggressive sportsmen and soldiers who jostled for position around the Duke. Worse still, the guiding influence of Anne Hyde, who led her husband 'by the nose' 'in all things but in his codpiece', was the cause of complaint not just among frustrated place-men, like the Churchills, but also among the Duke's Clerks at the Admiralty and his Parliamentary managers ensconced in the House of Commons. Sir William Coventry viewed both father and daughter with deep mistrust, and came to believe that they stood in the way of his further advancement.[5] However, while he still enjoyed the confidence of both the King and the Duke, personal criticism of the Chancellor remained largely confined to his rivals and to the Court wits, and his position at the apex of government remained utterly unassailable.

It took a combination of successive and dramatic misfortunes to begin to erode the high levels of trust which had existed between the sovereign and his chief minister. The outbreak of the Second Dutch War, which

Clarendon had done so much to try to prevent, was not attended by the spectacular gains which had been envisaged by the King and his council, and, as defeat and disillusion beckoned, the nation was rocked by the twin visitations of plague and fire. With the public burial grounds overflowing and the City of London reduced to a charred ruin, De Ruyter's audacious raid upon the Royal Dockyards and spiriting away of the fleet came as the final straw. Old allegations of the Chancellor's corruption, treachery and malpractice resurfaced, and were lent a new credibility by the sight of his mansion, 'Clarendon House', rising over the skyline on the edge of the humbled City. All of the nation's woes, from naval disasters to the loss of Dunkirk and the inability of the Queen to produce an heir, were suddenly blamed upon him. As public and Parliamentary criticism mounted, Clarendon's luck and health deserted him. Within a matter of weeks in the late summer of 1667, death robbed him of the Earl of Southampton – the remaining ministerial colleague with whom he had a close affinity – two of his grandchildren, and finally his wife and closest companion, Frances.[6] Devastated, he abandoned his seat on the Privy Council in order to arrange her funeral and confided to the Duke of York that he was weary of the world, his duties and onerous offices. Unfortunately, James chose to take his father-in-law literally at his word. He was unable to recognize that it had been grief and depression, rather than rational consideration, which had coloured the Chancellor's initial outburst, and that he actually intended doing nothing of the kind. Confident that he was acting in Clarendon's best interests, helping him through a time of great trouble, James made free at Court with the news that the Chancellor had decided to seek a means of retiring honourably from public life. This sudden and unexpected revelation dramatically altered the political landscape and was a gift to the King, who had tired of his mentor and needed a scapegoat for his own failures against the Dutch, and to Clarendon's rivals upon the Privy Council, who were anxious to supplant him in their master's affections. Arlington, who had been cut to the quick by the Chancellor's refusal to accept his friendship and by his ill-veiled contempt for his abilities, now made common cause with Sir William Coventry in demanding Clarendon's removal from the King's Council. As both James's appointee and employee, Coventry was in something of an invidious position but drew strength from the knowledge that his own star was in the ascendant. He felt that he had largely outgrown his relatively junior position in the Duke's service and could afford to risk losing it, if he could be sure of securing the favour of his sovereign in his quest for higher office. More importantly, having run the Navy Office he had gained invaluable experience about the workings of government and been charged with a responsibility that was far greater than that held by many of Charles II's senior ministers. He believed himself to be ready and more than able to assume a leading role in the government of the kingdom, and was prepared to act against Clarendon not only out of self-interest but also out of expediency. The success of the Dutch raid upon the Thames and Medway could not easily be rationalized, covered up or explained away. Someone in government, or in the Navy Office, would ultimately have to be held accountable and would probably end their days in the Tower of London under an attainder for treason. If the Duke of York, as the head of the service, had already done everything that he could to disassociate himself from the débâcle, then criticism for the poor performance of the Navy would devolve automatically upon Coventry, as his subordinate. The chance to offload the guilt of failure upon the Chancellor was an opportunity which was too good to miss and one which was already being canvassed by many of James's friends in the royal household, and by Henry Brouncker and Baptist May in particular. Given that the almost universal distaste for Clarendon at both the Court and the meetings of the Privy Council was now backed up by calls for his removal which emanated from the Duke's own confidants, Coventry may well have believed that James might have tacitly approved of his move to rid the King of his troublesome and overmighty subject.[7]

He was helped in this by the ambiguous nature of James's relationship with his father-in-law. While James held Clarendon in respect and pious affection, as an integral part of his own dynasty and as the grandfather of his children, he had often argued with him over his opposition to the Dutch war and resented his failure to secure from Parliament the generous grants, and the command of a standing army, which the Duke believed should have been his by right. Indeed, during his final exile, James was to go further still and blame the Chancellor for laying the foundations for all of the struggles between King and Parliament, during the 1670s and 1680s, through his failure to take full advantage of the climate of popular Royalism, immediately after the Restoration, to browbeat the Commons into a state of permanent subservience and submission to the interests of the Crown.[8] However, James was seldom able to divorce himself from his emotions, and the willingness with which Charles II seized upon the news that Clarendon was prepared to quietly resign and depart from the political arena provoked within the Duke an extreme clash of loyalties. It was the very delicacy of his position, balanced equally between both camps, that prompted the King to try to use James as an intermediary between the Privy Council and Clarendon House, and to persuade the Chancellor to give up his seals and surrender his office with the minimum of fuss. Ever the dutiful brother, James paid a visit upon Clarendon at his Piccadilly home on 25 August 1667, to break the unwelcome news. He may still conceivably have hoped that the old man would obey his sovereign sadly and without question, but if he did then he was in for a rude and uncomfortable awakening. Clarendon informed him that he would not be so meanly treated by a King who owed him much, and that he was resolved to cling on to the helm of state come what may. James beat a retreat to Whitehall without the Chancellor's promised seals and returned to Piccadilly the following day, in the company of Charles II, in order to remonstrate with his father-in-law and to bring him to reason. Clarendon's stubbornness had certainly inflamed the King's passions and firmly set him against him, but it had also served to set James to thinking about his own role in the affair. Surprised by the turn of events, he was extremely reluctant to abandon a member of his family who had given faithful service to both him and the Crown, and – after emotional appeals by both his wife and her father – he determined to do all that he could to save him. Up until this point, Charles II had probably believed that the removal of his Chancellor would be a relatively simple and painless operation, and that, were his fortunes ever to rise again, Clarendon might have been allowed to seek readmittance to government once the memory of the war and the passions of the mob had cooled down. However, the statesman's robust defence of his record in office and James's open avowal of his cause had escalated the stakes and made this clearly impossible.

The ducal household divided along rigidly partisan lines, with the Duke discovering to his acute embarrassment that many of his most able servants were those who took the lead against Clarendon. While Talbot and Jermyn chose largely to refrain from joining in the controversy, Coventry's continued presence as James's secretary became untenable. Pepys reported that the Duchess 'could not . . . endure the sight of him', while the Duke was forced to dismiss him from his post in early September and to try to replace him with Matthew Wren, one of the protégés of the Hyde family.[9] Through daily consultations with Clarendon, James was able to mount a formidable defence of his interests in the Upper House of Parliament. With Coventry gone and the vast majority of MPs largely hostile, the Lords came to be perceived as the natural territory in which the Chancellor might hope to stand and fight his case. The natural conservatism of the peers, their fear of disorder, and the recognition that it was unwise to establish a precedent for the arraignment of one of their most illustrious colleagues, all contributed to their willingness to back Clarendon and James, in the face of the King's marked displeasure and will. Charles II had, in the meantime, tired of waiting for his erstwhile servant to take the hint and bow the knee, and now conceived of him as being entirely irreconcilable and profoundly dangerous. He stripped him of his public offices on 30 August and sought to rehabilitate the Duke of Buckingham, in order to neutralize his influence. Through his vocal and frequently repeated denunciations of government corruption, Buckingham had established a significant popular constituency for himself which was now thought useful by the King. With Arlington, a far more skilful manager of temperaments and factions than Clarendon had ever been, hard at work alongside Coventry in securing support among the Commons, the King and Buckingham, with full blessing of public opinion behind them, began their onslaught upon the Lords. James was not prepared, even now, to back down and threw the slanders that had been levelled against the former Chancellor back in Charles II's face, forcing him to acknowledge their slanderous nature and the impossibility of at least one of them. He also made common cause with Gilbert Sheldon, the Archbishop of Canterbury, and the gifted, diminutive and mercurial figure of Lord Ashley, who having ditched his allegiance to the Protectorate was beginning to exert a personable and persuasive influence upon the world of royal politics. Between them and their supporters, drawn largely from the monarchy's traditional Anglican supporters, they began to inflict a series of damaging defeats and rebuffs to the King and his partisans. Taking heart, Clarendon let it be known that he intended to restate his case at the new session of Parliament, to be convened in the following year, and that he hoped for a victorious outcome and a rapid return to office. Unable to risk defeat, and the erosion of his sovereignty and prerogative powers which would subsequently attend it, Charles II acted to curtail the conflict before it got out of hand. He announced that he was prepared to dismiss Parliament while he nominated a panel of twenty-four peers, doubtlessly led by Buckingham, who would bring Clarendon to stand trial for his life on the charge of treason. Through his steely determination that his will would neither be flouted nor bested, the King had effectively called his opponents' bluff and allowed them to glimpse not only the power of the monarchy, but also the truth that they were playing for very high stakes indeed. With no avenues left open to him, other than to stand trial before a jury rigged against him, Clarendon chose to flee into exile. On 29 November 1667, he secured passage on board a ship bound for France and departed England forever.[10] He left behind him the glorious art collection, assembled as the result of his graft and peculation, and a gang of bemused workmen who were still in the process of setting the wrought-iron gates on to the front of his now deserted mansion.

In a Court that had been frightened by the sudden reminder of the fragility and impermanence of temporal power, a relieved Charles II ordered that no Christmas decorations should be set up and no festivities observed in his presence, as a reminder of this sobering and salutary lesson. His breach with James had not been properly healed and the

Duke's conduct during Clarendon's last days of freedom in England had been extremely problematical. While his supporters fought on in the Lords, James, as in so many times of stress and bitter conflicts, sickened and took to his bed. It may well be that his constitution weakened under the strain of opposing all that he held dear – his elder brother and a significant section of his carefully selected household – and that he became more susceptible to the smallpox virus. As he struggled to recover, Charles II had again approached him to act as an envoy to his father-in-law. Though unable to attend the crucial Lords debates, James was able to rise from his sickbed in order to stress the King's mortal resolve to be rid of his ex-Chancellor and to bid him begone.[11] Faced with the animosity and resurgence of his childhood companion, Buckingham, the Duke of York had no choice but to try to come to the best terms that he could with his brother. He effected a *rapprochement* with Coventry, but would not countenance the return of Henry Brouncker to his service or pay the compensation, for the loss of earnings, that that gentleman had demanded from the King. The crucial difference between the two cases remained, that while Coventry had been careful to stress his continued respect and loyalty towards the Duke, as opposed to his father-in-law, Brouncker – a far less able servant – had revelled in the indignity of the Chancellor's fall and that some of that dishonour had, by association, rubbed off on to James, his master. Yet, despite all the evidence to the contrary, the Duke of York remained reluctant to apportion blame upon his own followers and was wholly unable, as a matter of self-preservation and expediency, to single out the King for particular censure. He had learned that the Anglican bishops presented a powerful constituency within the House of Lords and that they were well disposed towards him, but failed to accurately identify the nature of the forces arrayed against him and the Earl of Clarendon. He blamed the Presbyterians, still tainted by the part that they had played in the late Civil Wars, for all of the troubles and thought that they had acted in order to revenge the penal laws enacted against them by the Chancellor. Such claims were blatantly absurd, especially as the true authors of the Earl's impeachment were far closer to hand, often dining in the Duke's presence or carrying out his orders at the Admiralty buildings. Though many nonconformists had joined in the general chorus of disapproval at Clarendon's conduct, and had cause to angrily recall the part he and James had played in halting moves to make the Church of England a wider and more inclusive body, their role in the crisis had never been a significant or a particularly threatening one.[12] Much more serious for James was the continuing coolness of his brother which could be exploited, to his detriment, by ambitious courtiers anxious to fill the void created by the Chancellor's flight.

In the shadow of the fallen oak small saplings now rooted themselves, and the Duke of Buckingham, fearing retaliatory action from James should he ever become King, cast about for new allies in order to consolidate his hold on power. At the time of the last quarrel between the royal brothers, in the early 1660s, Charles II had used the arrival of his illegitimate son at Court to pull the Duke of York back into line and make him remember his place.[13] Now Buckingham strove to win the friendship of the young Duke of Monmouth, flattered his vanity, and spoke to his father of the possibility of declaring him to be legitimate. The recent deaths of James's two elder sons and the continuing inability of the Queen to give birth to a healthy heir, had focused Charles II's mind upon the succession and his decision to purchase Monmouth an expensive, and high-profile, commission in the Life Guards was intended primarily as a warning shot across his brother's bows. While Clarendon's friends were purged from their positions of authority in government, Buckingham's followers began to co-ordinate attacks upon the alleged corruption of the Duke of York's servants in the Navy Office and drew added strength from the complaints of Rupert and Sandwich's displaced acolytes, who were now distributed throughout the fleet. In the short term, they were an easy target as the natural closeness of the relationship between the Houses of York and Hyde had somewhat blurred the distinction between the identity of their servants. Clarendon's furtive escape to France, and his subsequent banishment for life, had been equated with an admission of guilt in the public consciousness. Consequently, it was all too easy for James's placemen to fall under a similar suspicion of ineptitude and malpractice. With the Duke of York concerned to maintain his colleagues in post at the Navy Office, the campaign to legitimize Monmouth and plans for the King to remarry grew apace and combined in a novel and salacious test case which threatened to pave the way for a royal divorce.[14]

John Manners, Lord Roos, was the undisputed heir to the Earl of Rutland and wished to protect his inheritance from the claims of his estranged wife, and her ever-growing band of suppositious children. The case was clear-cut: he had been mocked, cuckolded and shamefully treated, and so petitioned the House of Lords for a civil divorce in March 1670 with every hope of success. However, the grounds on which he based his appeal to the Lords were unique and especially pertinent to the King and Buckingham. Roos claimed that he wished to remarry specifically in order to beget a legitimate heir and thereby secure the future of his own House. As there was no precedent for this bill in English law, it provoked a far-ranging debate about the nature of marriage and the extents to which an individual could go in order to guarantee the survival of his, or her, bloodline. The political implications of the bill were all too apparent and arguments, for and against, soon transcended the particulars of the actual case itself, as it took on a wider significance and came to be regarded as a debate about the future course of the monarchy, raising the spectre of a new succession crisis. The seriousness of the situation was underlined by the presence of the King in the visitor's gallery. Not since Henry VIII had an English monarch attended the sessions of the Lords, and the regular appearance of a tall, dark stranger, badly disguised, in the visitors' gallery with Buckingham and his friends in close attendance cannot but have turned the thoughts of peers to the fates of successive Tudor queens and left them in no doubt about Charles II's own intentions regarding his wife.

In many respects, the case could not have been better chosen for the purposes of Buckingham and his party. Roos was a likeable character who elicited sympathy for his plight, while the scandalous behaviour of his lady could all too easily be transposed on to the Queen and used to defame her. Despite her Roman Catholicism, Catherine of Braganza had remained a popular figure at Court. She had never sought to interfere in State affairs or to create a particular faction that was sympathetic to her interests. Dutiful, generous and good natured – if thoroughly uninspired – her only true failing was her infertility. It was this, perhaps even more than her religion, which made her the object of scorn and distrust for Protestant England. The idea that she had somehow been foisted upon the English King by a clique of cunning and malignant counsellors, foremost among whom had been Clarendon, who had acted at the behest of foreign sovereigns steeped in the tradition of the Counter Reformation, was an extremely potent one for a people schooled in holding Catholicism to be synonymous with treachery. Rather than being a private tragedy, her barren womb became the symbol of her disloyalty to King and country alike.[15] This might, even then, not have mattered too much had it not been for the growing popular fear and resentment of the Duke of York. His disastrous cultivation of precisely the wrong kind of public image, as we have already seen, had elevated him to such a point whereby almost anything could be believed of him. Although news of his conversion to Roman Catholicism was still not widely known for sure, it was at least suspected and commented upon. The picture of the innocent and trusting King, surrounded on either side by scheming 'popish' relatives who intended to subvert the natural line of succession and to foist the crown upon an unlawful Catholic heir, however laughable it may be to us, was entirely plausible to Protestant Englishmen in the late seventeenth century and thoroughly consistent with what they knew of their rulers and their motivations.

The uncertain future posed by a disputed throne and the desire to please the present monarch motivated not only those militant Protestant lords who had chosen to remain at Court, but also several disaffected Anglican clergymen who feared for the continued survival of the Established Church under a Roman Catholic Governor General. Thus, John Wilkins, the Bishop of Chester and the chief intellectual promoter of the bill, went out of his way to stress that a 'divorce might be [granted] not only in case of adultery but also of the immundicity of the womb, which is given forth to [be] the queen's condition'. His supporters took heart when Charles II seemed to lend them his tacit support, evoking memories of the divorce of his father's old enemy, the Earl of Essex, and Frances Howard in 1613. If a man could be divorced for being impotent, the King had been overheard arguing, then he saw no reason why a woman could not be divorced for being barren. With his inner circle of friends – which at this time included Ashley, Arlington, Lauderdale and Angelsey – beginning to push as hard as they could in order to ease the passage of the bill through the Upper House, the Duke of Buckingham took centre stage and persuasively advocated in the chamber that there should be a general law permitting either partner to obtain a divorce on the grounds of adultery. This, he claimed under the cloak of conventional morality, would impose sexual restraints on men as well as upon women and would ultimately be to the benefit of the whole of society.[16]

As the bill progressed through the House, James reacted with horror to the prospect of losing his position in the succession and was quick to rally to the defence of the Queen. Stressing Catherine's personal integrity and the legality of her marriage to the King, he managed to stitch together a coalition of very disparate forces with which to oppose the bill's passage into law. He secured a very strong ally in the shape of Ormonde, called in a large number of favours from his clients in both the Commons and the Lords, and forged an unlikely alliance with Barbara, Countess Castlemaine, who had helped to pull down Clarendon and who up until that point had been one of James's most implacable foes. However, times had changed and as the King's mistress began to lose her hold over his affections, she increasingly looked to save what influence she could and to provide for her children by him. To her mind, Monmouth was no more or less royal than her own sons and any sudden elevation of his position, to Prince of Wales, would be made to the detriment of her own House. Therefore, she began to lobby on behalf of the Queen and the Duke of York, and in so doing laid the foundations for the acceptance of both her son and her long-suffering husband into James's service.[17] However, friends at Court alone were not enough to ensure the success of the Duke's campaign and, as before, he looked to the High Anglican bishops to deliver him a victory. Archbishop Sheldon joined with him and together they mounted a highly effective counter-attack in the Lords which threatened to derail the legislation altogether. In the end, the crucial debate raged on into the night, with the House bitterly divided between the two opposing camps and a final vote being taken just before ten o'clock. Eighty-three lords were present, forty-one of whom voted for the bill and forty-two against. It could not have been closer and James's party sensed victory. However, the casting of proxy votes overturned their advantage and tipped the scales in the opposite direction, carrying the bill through by a majority of just eight. Although Lord Roos was granted his divorce, and the Duke of York and his 'rainbow' coalition of placemen, disappointed courtiers and High Anglicans had been defeated, the passions that the case had aroused and the strength of the opposition to it, had demonstrated beyond any reasonable doubt that it was politically inexpedient for the sovereign to start tampering with the succession. Charles II quickly backtracked and abandoned any plans for a divorce that he might have harboured. Catherine remained as Queen, Monmouth went unacknowledged, and the temporary ruffle between the King and the Duke of York was smoothed over through the timely intercession of the Countess of Castlemaine. Charles II tried to make light of the whole situation and joked, rather poorly, that he had only gone to watch the debates as they made for far better entertainment than any theatre production. James, however, had emerged much strengthened from the affair. His stature as heir presumptive was undiminished, while his flexing of political muscle, in his capacity as the senior peer in the land, had shown his brother that he was capable of drawing upon large reservoirs of latent support, which had been more than enough to check Buckingham's influence with his sovereign and to scotch his attempts to play kingmaker.[18]

James was also undoubtedly helped by the fact that Buckingham's quick temper and self-destructive nature had already begun to compromise his career in politics. When words failed him in the Lords, he had been prepared to pummel his opponents into submission, and his infamous duel with the Earl of Shrewsbury, in which the Earl and two other swordsmen had been run through, would surely have ended with his committal to the Tower had it not been for the King's pardon. James's decision to lobby hard for the end of duelling and the creation of a government committee to punish swordsmen, despite the fact that among his own friends Talbot, Jermyn, Churchill and Rawlings were all inveterate, if spectacularly unsuccessful brawlers, can only be seen to have been motivated by a strong desire to bring Buckingham down by any means that were at his disposal.[19] However, if James could derive some pleasure from his rival's subsequent misfortune, and made sure that he moved hard and fast to destroy his remaining influence once he came to the throne, then there were far more intractable problems facing him, as the 1670s dawned, which could not be so easily resolved through the correct deployment of the bishops and his allies at Court.

II

While James had been able to harness considerable support in the House of Lords throughout the 1660s, he had failed, largely by default, to build upon his following in the Commons. There is little evidence to suggest that in the absence of 'the most ingenious' Sir William Coventry, the dull Sir Alan Apsley was ever blessed with great gifts of organization or insight. This might not have mattered had James not been blinkered by his utter distaste for the workings of factional politics, and further hampered by his own awkwardness and profound lack of charisma. He had been singularly unable to arbitrate between his closest supporters and his own land agents in Ireland during the late 1660s, and watched – apparently powerlessly – as Captain Thornhill and Sir Winston Churchill cheerfully slandered each other in court, and as Richard Talbot had to be locked up for his own protection after threatening to kill Ormonde, the King's viceroy.[20] However, if the Duke of York had been prepared to lose control of his servants as soon as they left the confines of Whitehall, and to turn a blind eye to their rapacious seizure of lands from the Old Irish, then the Roos divorce case had at least served to identify the Duke's natural constituency of supporters: those among the Anglican gentry and bishops, who desired strong and stable government above all other things, and were prepared to tolerate his desire to centralize the administration of the State in order to achieve it. Given his renewed prestige in the immediate aftermath of the case, it might have been thought that he would have moved swiftly to construct an alternative power-base around himself, by the formidable means already at his disposal. James, however, did nothing of the sort. While retaining a small circle of intimate friends and household servants, he never appears to have attempted to build his own party or factional interest that could have functioned independently of the King's. He never entirely understood the concerns of the rural Anglican squires who pledged loyalty to him as a true-born Stuart Prince but reviled him for his open profession of Catholicism, and was frequently rude and dismissive towards those in the localities who were willing to assist his cause and asked for nothing in return save a little praise and consideration. In the early 1660s, he had amused himself by outpacing one anxious petitioner in the grounds of St James's Park and later snubbed Sir John Reresby and his Northern supporters on his way to Scotland in 1679, turning his nose up at their carefully husbanded gifts and observing that they had not come out in as great numbers to welcome him as he had expected or thought fitting for his station.[21] His household remained a profoundly loyalist institution which always sought to act in the spirit of what it believed to be the best interests of Charles II and the government at Whitehall. In no way did it come to represent, as its Whig detractors claimed, a 'shadow cabinet' which sought to mount an effective campaign against the policies of the King. Factors such as friendship, professional regard and the complex workings of patronage and kinship, were all far more important in the shaping and development of James's household than any conscious, rational or binding sense of purpose to inflict despotic and para-military government, as a first resort, upon England and her American colonies.[22]

Though authoritarian, James was neither calculating nor overly manipulative in his pursuit of personal advancement. Clumsiness, rather than that brand of innate cunning exemplified by his elder brother, was the defining trait of his sporadic ventures into the world of high politics. While he was a difficult, exacting and frequently infuriating master, James was surprisingly dependent upon the advice and guidance of his servants. Magalotti, perhaps better than any other writer, captured that peculiar blend of the rigid and the susceptible which sat awkwardly in the Duke's nature. He was, thought the Florentine, 'very often influenced by people, and once he has chosen them it is not easy for him to free himself from their sway; his mind is always like wax, ready to receive and retain indelibly every slight impression of their ideas, without considering whether these proceed from reason, or from self-interest, or malignity, or ambition. To everyone except those people he is inflexible, no matter if they come armed not only with reason, but with evidence itself.'[23] This reliance upon a handful of individuals, whose preferences and prejudices largely mirrored his own, could result in dissension at the heart of his service, as in the case of the feud between Sir William Coventry and the Hyde family, or in protracted and bitter rivalries, such as that between Sir Alan Apsley and Thomas Povey. Those excluded from the Duke's charmed circle had grounds for bitter regret and violent jealousies. Sir Charles Littleton cursed that John Churchill was the 'only favourite of his master', while Richard Talbot and Lawrence Hyde viewed each other with a deep and lasting suspicion. The positive side of James's over-indulgence towards his handful of favoured clients was that he was able to maintain a hard core of followers among the gentry and a remarkable continuity of personnel among his servants, from the humblest bargemen and domestics right up to senior officials in the Admiralty, who would resolutely cling to his side over the course of twenty-five turbulent years.[24] He refused to abandon incompetents like Jean-Baptiste Du Teil or the Earl of Feversham, and promoted the violent and the unconscionable, such as George Jeffreys, Percy Kirke and John Graham of Claverhouse. Only death in battle robbed him of the services of Charles and William Berkeley, Viscount Muskerry, Richard Nicolls and Matthew Wren, while he was separated from Richard Talbot – albeit for only a short period of time – after he was captured by the Dutch at Sole Bay, in 1672.

In the respect, at least, of stability and loyalty to the sovereign, the administrative framework created by James and his servants bears a favourable comparison with the series of troublesome rival courts which formed around the heirs of the later Hanoverian Kings. It was with sound reason that the editors of James's *Life* went out of their way to stress that 'While the King his Brother lived he was a pattern of Obedience', for the key to all of his public appointments after 1660 was the continued support and favour of Charles II, bestowed as rewards for his usefulness and good behaviour.[25] However, while the Duke's political quiescence at Westminster brought him honours and commands, it also left him vulnerable to attack by the increasing vociferous popular forces arrayed against him, and quite unprepared for the tempests and traumas of the Popish Plot and Exclusion campaign, when he stood at the centre stage of national politics.

III

The rhythm and peace of mind of Charles II's Court was shattered in the late summer of 1678 as the King, while on his customary early morning walk, was waylaid by a stranger and informed that he was in danger of his life. Assassins were said to be lurking in the secluded avenues of St James's Park, ready at any moment to train their muskets upon him and shoot him down. Thankfully, the informant told him, their design had been accidently overheard and reported by the law-abiding rector of the church of St Michael's, in Wood Street, but that other designs to topple the monarchy were still afoot. In an age when conspiracies flourished, and were the stock-in-trade of both Republican and Roman Catholic extremities of the political spectrum, and when intelligence gathering by the agents of the State was still fairly rudimentary, Charles II dare not have scorned such information. Perhaps, more importantly, his curiosity had been aroused and he was 'more surprised with the strangeness of the News, than any Apprehension of the Danger', asking only 'how could that be?'.[26] Arrangements were made for the rector, Dr Israel Tonge, to come to the palace and present his evidence to the King, and as news of the scheme by Catholic agents to murder the sovereign and stage a sudden *coup d'état* began to leak out into the public domain, rumour and counter-rumour flourished, and fed upon one another. Before long, Tonge was joined before the King by his companion, Titus Oates, and between them the pair spun a compelling tale of a highly organized Jesuit plot to infiltrate their agents into the capital city and to bring down the State by any means at their disposal.

Standing before the Privy Council, the two men cut strange and disturbing figures. 'Cynical and . . . shifless in the world', Tonge had seen his once promising academic career frustrated by the return of the monarchy and had lost a comfortable living, when his parish of St Mary Stayning was engulfed by the Great Fire of London. In order to rationalize his misfortunes, he turned increasingly to an intolerant brand of Protestantism, and blamed the machinations of the Roman Catholic Church, and the Jesuit Order in particular, for everything from the onset of the English Civil War to the outbreak of the fire at Pudding Lane. The bovine Oates, if anything, was less personable still. Labouring under a highly repressed and ambiguous sexuality, he had briefly taken instruction from the Jesuits at the English College, Valladolid, after first toying with Anabaptism and Anglicanism, in turn, and managing to get himself expelled from his studies at Cambridge University.[27] It might be thought that this disreputable coupling of a religious zealot with a habitual liar would have been seen through, immediately, and that they would have quickly been returned to the obscurity from whence they came. Their stories altered with every telling. Sometimes the King was to have been pistolled, on other occasions poisoned. In one version the Pope himself was the sole author of the plot, while in another it was the Jesuits themselves who played the leading role, and looked to land an invasion army led by a clique of elderly English peers, with the help of either the Spanish or the French monarchies. The identity of the chosen assailants varied even more widely between members of the Roman Catholic community in London, Irish ruffians and, most improbably of all, the Queen herself. Most damagingly to their case, Charles II had repeatedly exposed the inconsistencies in Oates's testimony, at a session of the Privy Council in September 1678, even as the streets of the capital were being swept for 'papist' agents and as Newgate Gaol was being made ready to receive an influx of unfortunate and bewildered suspects.

However, while a belief in the truth of the plot might appear to be highly irrational to modern sensitivities, it was firmly grounded in the English Protestant tradition which had flourished since the late sixteenth century, and reflected the doubts which many felt about the King's intentions and the ongoing development of royal policy over the course of the 1670s. Viewed from this perspective, the real tragedy of the Popish Plot can be seen to have been that the legitimate fears of a considerable section of the population, about the way in which they were being governed, were manipulated and twisted by a religious zealot and a charlatan, who took advantage of the King's extreme diffidence to proceed against them, and were then able to misdirect all of the nation's pent-up hatred on to their Roman Catholic neighbours, who stood entirely guiltless as charged. Furthermore, even though the Secret Treaty of Dover, signed in December 1670, had remained just that, the fact that Charles II had actually committed himself to proselytizing for the Roman Catholic faith in England and had accepted French bribes in order to do so more effectively, cannot be denied. It matters little whether the King was sincere in his promises to convert, or whether he simply wished to secure his finances without relying upon the traditional recourse to Parliamentary subsidies. What does matter is that the suspicions of many on the fringes of the political nation, that their masters were cosying up to an aggressive and aggrandizing European power, were based upon solid fact. They recognized that the Duke of York favoured a French alliance, that he had been won over to Roman Catholicism and that he was unstinting in his predeliction for the use of physical force. With the armies of France tearing into the heartland of Protestant Holland, and the rights of the Huguenots being constantly eroded by the centralizing drift of Church and State under Louis XIV, it was not difficult to conceive of a 'Prince, to whom the British Sceptre may hereafter devolve, intoxicated with the tinsel glories of the French monarch[']s blustering grandeur, [who] should be so vain, as to hope to subjugate the English liberties, and destroy the Constitution of the best establisht government on earth'.[28] James's love for military imagery and his failure to pay adequate regard to the sensibilities of Protestant England, in his public disavowal of Anglicanism, effectively provided the oxygen on which the flames of the plot might feed. The capture of Jesuit priests, who had actually been at work in the private houses and chapels of London, seemed to lend strength to allegations of a plot involving the Order, while in targeting Edward Coleman, the Duke's former Secretary, for particular suspicion, Oates struck a seam of pure gold.

He cared little for distinguishing between true and false leads, and even less for the lives of scores of innocent English Roman Catholics caught up in the frenzy, but in suggesting almost as an afterthought that Coleman's lodgings should be searched, his intuition, based upon the little he knew of the Duke of York's household, paid immediate dividends and the notion of the Plot gained in credibility and substance. The search party, dispatched by the Privy Council, seized a large correspondence that had been exchanged between Coleman, in his capacity as the Duke's Secretary, and the French Court. Most incriminatingly, many of the letters were in code, had been addressed to leading foreign Jesuits, and some panicked attempts had been made to destroy them in the last minutes before the raid. Their contents, had they been published in full, would surely have brought the Duke of York crashing down. Coleman, buoyed up with self-importance at being entrusted with conducting difficult and dangerous negotiations with the Court of Louis XIV, had thrown caution to the wind. He boasted of having James's complete trust and prayed for the recovery of England from Protestant 'heresy and schism', and for its eventual reintegration with the heartlands of Roman Catholic Europe.[29] Such sentiments were pure treason, in the context of the late seventeenth century, and one wonders at the Duke's wisdom and foresight in allowing delicate negotiations to be handled by a servant who was obviously unequal to the task. Coleman had already come to the notice of the City authorities and the Bishop of London, for his enthusiastic championing of his own conversion to Roman Catholicism, and it was probably this indescretion, rather than any particular insight, which prompted Oates to make his original allegations. With hindsight, James tried to argue that he already perceived Coleman to have been a liability and had taken steps to remove him from his service. However, this is only partly true. Coleman's Catholicism had already rendered him suspect, and the Duke's decision to replace him as his Secretary was not accompanied by any loss of status or a clear attempt to sever his diplomatic links with the continent. The cosmetic nature of his reappointment, in virtually the same job, but as Secretary to the Duchess of York rather than to her husband, was accompanied by a strong defence of his loyalty and usefulness by James. Moreover, while the correspondence seized from his apartment was not new, and dated predominantly from the early to mid-1670s, it left no doubt that Coleman had acted with James's blessing and that he had received a considerable sum of money from Louis XIV's Confessor, the Jesuit Père La Chaise, with which to buy support for the Duke in the English Parliament.[30]

The irony of the situation was that one branch of Charles II's government, acting on purely spurious claims, had begun to investigate the activities of the executive and now threatened to pull down not only the Duke of York, but also the basis upon which monarchical government operated. Examined before the Privy Council and subsequently tried for high treason, Coleman's own words were enough to convict him, but the central fallacy around which the notion of an actual 'plot' was based meant that he could not confess his guilt and save himself, by presenting his prosecutors with a list of fellow conspirators. Broken and utterly forsaken, he submitted to being hung, drawn and quartered at Tyburn, without managing to further implicate his royal master. For this, at least, James should have been greatly indebted to him for his own life and possible arraignment for treason hung in the balance. Fortunately, the Earl of Danby, Charles II's Chief Minister, chose to suppress much of the evidence and released only a heavily edited – but still exceptionally damaging – portion of it to be read in Parliament. His prompt actions undoubtedly saved James and allowed him a respite from attack. So far, Oates's allegations had stopped short of identifying him as an instigator, and prime beneficiary, of the Plot. This was purely because Oates and Tonge did not, as yet, feel strong enough to challenge the Duke's hold on power and had no intention of exposing themselves, in turn, to allegations of treachery or *lèse-majesté*. Instead, they postulated a scenario in which the Jesuits had schemed at the deaths of both brothers, in the knowledge that James would be no more willing to carry out their diabolical commandments than Charles.

However, the pace of events quickened once again with first the unexplained disappearance of Edmund Godfrey, the popular London magistrate who had taken depositions from Oates shortly after the original revelation of the Plot, and then the discovery of his lifeless corpse in a drainage ditch upon Primrose Hill. Though it will probably never be known if Godfrey met his end through murder or suicide, or if his possible assailants were common footpads or men guided by a false sense of loyalty to James and the Crown, he became – almost overnight – a Protestant martyr, a hero for emulation, whose supposed murder cried out for vengeance.[31] He was commemorated in print and popular verse, souvenirs were minted in remembrance of his deeds, wakes were held in his memory, and concerned Londoners could even buy special 'Godfrey' knives – more ornament than use – with which to protect themselves against would-be popish assailants. It was inevitable that the Duke of York, whose 'reputation for bravery' and strong action had 'harmed him much more than the death of his father, his poverty, and . . . exile', came under popular suspicion. As enormous crowds turned out in the streets to chant anti-Catholic slogans and to burn representations of the Pope and his regalia, James became indelibly linked with the prelacy and with infectious conspiracy. It was not long before the mob came to surge around his own coach and escort, identifying the danger he represented by his return to the capital and appealing to other districts of the City for support, with the cry that 'A Pope! A Pope!' was among them.[32]

If popular sentiment was running strongly against the Duke, then his cause was similarly faltering and haemorrhaging support in the twin chambers of Westminster. He had been lucky in establishing an alliance, late in the day, with Danby, as the convergence of their interests and sheer instinct for survival drove them together. James had already wisely, on the advice of the King and the Earl, decided to absent himself from further meetings of the Privy Council and the Committee for Foreign Affairs, but this did little to halt the measures advanced in Parliament, by Shaftesbury and his followers, to both define and limit the Duke's powers within the framework of what would have been a new constitutional settlement. Though holding many of the same ideas about the need for commercial expansion, colonization and even social order, James and Shaftesbury had come to represent, in the words of Professor R.M. Bliss, 'the ultimately incompatible extremes of the restoration concensus'.[33] As an uncompromising opponent of French expansionism, the Roman Catholic Church and absolute government, Shaftesbury had increasingly become the focus around which Parliamentary opposition to the policies of Court solidified and grouped. His political and personal connections, knowledge of the workings of statecraft and administration, and undoubted ability to organize and harness the energy of his supporters, had allowed him to build upon the purely factional interests within Parliament and to create a network of powerbases throughout the kingdom. To speak of a Whig 'Party' in the modern sense of the word is misleading, for it presupposes a level of professionalism, discipline and ideological conformity, which was still well beyond the scope and ability of the disparate collection of disaffected Protestant gentlemen, Presbyterians and radical Republicans, who found common cause under his banner. However, through his skill in manipulating and gauging voting intentions, in co-ordinating Parliamentary and extra-Parliamentary agitation, and in sustaining a prolonged – and single-minded – political campaign with the help of a well-developed publicity machine, there is much that was wholly original and innovatory in Shaftesbury's pursuit of high office.[34]

The old struggles for place and patronage, in the service of the monarchy, paled into insignificance with the Earl's sudden and fundamental questioning of the principles upon which the whole of the Restoration Settlement had been based. The quest for a practical and financially solvent form of government, which commanded loyalty from the overwheming majority of its Protestant subjects, and which had finally seemed to have been achieved in the period from 1660 to 1662, appeared to be under threat of the same sort of catastrophic breakdown as had overtaken and destroyed Charles I's administration in 1640. The signs of similar discontent, and the fracturing of social relations on the periphery of the British Isles, were already apparent to anyone who cared to look for comparisons. In Scotland, Lauderdale was struggling to maintain his hold over the Lowland Presbyterans who regarded the ejection of their own ministers and the imposition of Episcopalian clergymen with thinly disguised hatred, and who talked increasingly of armed resistance to throw off the depredations of the Highland Host which the Edinburgh government had quartered upon them.[35] Moreover, the fashionable taverns, theatres and coffee shops of London, where the nation's political elites met, formed opinion and circulated news and gossip, were increasingly becoming the preserve of Shaftesbury and his partisans. Political societies and clubs sprang up, such as the 'Green Ribbon Club' which consciously played upon romantic, and carefully sanitized, memories of the Levellers and the last great upsurge in radical political activity in the late 1640s and early 1650s. Ghostlike figures from that earlier time, such as Algernon Sidney and Andrew Marvell, had begun to write again and their arguments, widely published and disseminated – though often from the safety of exile or with the cloak of anonymity – struck a level of ferocity and achieved a level of pertinency which had been lacking, or would have been altogether out of place, in the earlier years of the Restoration.[36] The very term 'Whig', which was bandied about as abuse for Shaftesbury's followers, equating them with Covenanter raiders and rebels, betokened a fresh division in the world of politics, where ideology, religion and strong personal convictions once again played the central part. It was not long before the Whigs coined the name of 'Tory', which had originally denoted a notorious Irish Catholic clan of murderers and cattle thieves, and settled it as a blanket term upon all of the Duke of York's followers.

While the City boards, institutions and municipal bodies came increasingly to resemble auxilliary battlegrounds upon which the followers of York and Shaftesbury settled their private and public grievances, the main struggle for political supremacy was fought out in the Houses of Parliament. Support for Shaftesbury and his opposition to France had lain dormant throughout much of the 1670s, and only the detonation of the Popish Plot, at the heart of the Danby administration, had allowed the Earl to return to prominence. Fear that any slackening of the pace of attack would allow James to regroup his still considerable forces, and that such an opportunity to dictate policy and the framework for any future settlement might never come his way again, led Shaftesbury to launch a Parliamentary assault upon the Duke of York and his privileges. Consequently, a series of bills were proposed to debar Roman Catholics from sitting in either House of Parliament and to enforce the penal laws, already in existence, with far greater severity. Realizing at last the serious threat posed by these developments to his personal monarchy, Charles II committed himself to firm action and, with Danby's help, mustered all of his supporters in the Lords and Commons, to first resist and then amend the bills brought before him. Attempts to segregate Roman Catholics from the vast majority of their neighbours, to expel them from the capital city, and to limit their movements to within a 5-mile radius of their homes – which would have placed James under virtual house arrest and destroyed his influence in London – were considerably watered down and ruled not to apply to him, or to anyone associated with the Royal Court. Furthermore, although a Second Test Act was passed through both Houses and became law on 1 December 1678, in order to prevent 'the increase and danger of popery in this kingdom' by disabling any Lord or MP who refused to 'make, subscribe and audibly repeat' the oaths of allegiance and supremacy to the Church of England, two additional and amending clauses were foisted upon the legislation by the King's supporters. The first of these exempted the Queen and her Portuguese attendants from its provisions, while the second, in a brief and terse statement of royal will, acted as a disclaimer to the rest of the legislation, declaring it to be binding: 'Provided always, that nothing in this Act contained shall extend to his . . . Highness the duke of York'.[37] In seeking to protect the vulnerable James, Charles II was motivated not only by fraternal affection but also by the cold realization that any adjustment to the hereditary principle of the succession struck at the root of the royal prerogative and ceded final authority, in the government of the State and in the choosing of the executive, to Parliament. He had no wish, as James had taunted him, to become a figurehead who reigned but did not rule. Nor had he regained his three crowns as King of England, Scotland and Ireland in order to siphon off his existing powers and to slip back into an uneasy dependency upon the whims and pleasures of his Parliaments and his subject peoples. As his brother was keen to point out, a vast gulf separated the Doge of Venice from a king of Britain.[38]

However, if the Duke of York had managed to weather the worst of the storm whipped up by Oates's allegations, then, at the very moment that his Parliamentary partnership with Danby and his supporters was beginning to pay real dividends, it was unexpectedly and conclusively dissolved. Ralph Montagu, an MP, former Ambassador and a cousin of the late Lord Sandwich, made public a series of damning government documents given under Danby's seal, which showed beyond doubt that the Earl had been using the English Embassy in Paris to channel bribes from the French monarch. It mattered little that Danby had consistently opposed any alliance with the France of Louis XIV, that he had been simply acting under orders which came straight from Charles II, or even that Montagu had, at the time, been perfectly prepared to further aid and expedite this policy. Of greater importance was the tangible proof that a minister of the Crown had been prepared to negotiate for a £450,000 bribe, given by a foreign power with the sole intent and condition that the English Parliament, which had sat uninterrupted for seventeen years, should be dissolved. Amid gasps of disbelief, consternation and angry threats, opposition MPs moved for the Earl's impeachment.[39]

If the matter of Coleman's life or death had mattered little to the King and the Duke, then the question of Danby's survival was of utmost importance to both of them. Without him, the Court party would be leaderless and its policies left in tatters. Therefore, in an attempt to forestall the charges brought against him, Charles II rushed to dissolve the Cavalier Parliament in January 1679. It was a move which reflected desperation and uncertainty, rather than strength and careful planning; for, although the Commons looked certain to continue to press for his Treasurer to be tried and convicted, any bill for his impeachment would face a far harder fight to be passed in the Lords. The combination of the King's supporters with those of the Duke and Danby still offered a formidable basis from which a counter-attack could be launched in the new year. The King had recent evidence of the power of the Lords to halt and amend legislation passed in the Commons, in November's debates over the passing of the Second Test Act, and could reasonably have expected the peers to overturn the votes of the MPs and return Danby to favour. Moreover, the time bought by the dissolution of Parliament was comparatively meagre. The raising of troops for the war in Flanders, which had been so energetically championed by James, now rebounded against him and his interests. The cost of equipping, paying and subsequently disbanding them, on the cessation of hostilities, could only be met by Parliamentary levy. Without a sitting Parliament, Charles II had no way of meeting his immediate debts, or of maintaining the state of relative financial solvency brought about by Danby's hard-won reforms.[40] As the warrants were issued for a new election, and Shaftesbury's supporters in both the City and in the provinces began to canvass opinion in earnest, the Court party remained in a state of disarray. James, though he made no effort to present a more compromising and less threatening figure to the electorate, may well have come to regret his oversight in not building a strong and active constituency within the Commons. Similarly, his supporters in the country at large, though surprisingly numerous and hailing from among all social classes, were unskilled in presentation, in lobbying, and in devising and coordinating strategies to keep out Whig candidates. More seriously, they lacked any clear mandate or lead from James, who had become the greatest liability to the election of pro-government candidates. To many, including loyal Anglicans and monarchists such as Philanax Verax, it was hard to find fault with – or to effectively dismiss – Shaftesbury's characterization of the popish heir to the throne, as a 'heady, violent and bloody' man.[41]

The election of February 1679 saw the Whig opposition win a clear majority in the Commons, greatly emboldening Shaftesbury, and sharpening both the scope and the sting of his subsequent legislative campaign. Henceforth, his followers aimed at nothing less than the exclusion of the Duke of York from ever succeeding to the throne, his permanent removal from all of his public offices, and his treatment before the law as a common recusant, liable to the same fines and penalties for non-attendance at church as any private subject.[42] The level of sheer audacity, innovation and radicalism inherent in these proposals was truly breathtaking. Without recourse to civil war or open rebellion, the early Whigs were attempting to redraw the division of powers and responsibilities between sovereign and Parliament, through a legislative *coup d'état*, and to bind any future king or queen into a solid, contractual relationship with their people which was far more inhibiting to them than anything that was either envisaged, or adopted, in the Glorious

'Omnium consensu capax imperii, nisi imperasset/All the world would have thought he had the makings of a king had he never ruled' (Tacitus, Histories, I. 49). James Duke of York as Lord High Admiral. Oil on canvas by Henri Gascars, 1672–3. (National Maritime Museum, London)

The most Illustrious & High borne Prince IAMES
Duke of Yorke &c:

The boy soldier 'even from his childhood in the command in armies'. Etching by Wenceslaus Hollar, c. 1640. (Courtesy of the Director, National Army Museum, London)

United in misfortune. Charles I and the Duke of York as the prisoners of Parliament. Oil on canvas by Sir Peter Lely, 1647. (Courtesy of his Grace, the Duke of Northumberland)

Home from the wars. The young Duke of York. Oil on canvas by Sir Peter Lely, c. 1661. (Scottish National Portrait Gallery)

The marriage portrait of Anne Hyde. Oil on canvas by Sir Peter Lely, c. 1661. (Scottish National Portrait Gallery)

The House of York. The Duke and Duchess of York with their daughters, Mary and Anne. Oil on canvas by Gennari after Sir Peter Lely, c. 1673–5. (The Royal Collection © 2000, Her Majesty Queen Elizabeth II)

'Not less on land'. James as a classical General. Medal by John Roettier, 1665. (© The British Museum)

James as the Captain-General of the Honourable Artillery Company. Engraving by William Vaughan, mid-1660s. (© The British Museum)

James, Duke of York. No portrait better captures either the hardness of his jawline or the unthinking arrogance of his gaze. Miniature by Samuel Cooper, mid-1670s. (The Royal Collection © 2000, Her Majesty Queen Elizabeth II)

James, Duke of York and Albany. Engraving by Richard White, after a portrait by Godfrey Kneller, 1682. (© The British Museum)

His Royall Highnefs
IAMES Duke of YORK
& ALBANY etc
Onely Brother to his Sacred Maty King Charles y IId

The loss of the Gloucester. As the stricken ship flounders on the sandbank, James and his retinue are rowed away to safety. Oil on canvas by Johan Danckerts, c. 1682–3. (National Maritime Museum, London)

Lord High Admiral and King. Oil on canvas by Sir Godfrey Kneller, 1684–5. (By courtesy of the National Portrait Gallery, London)

The Brass Horseman. Statue of James erected at Sandhills, Newcastle upon Tyne, to commemorate his accession to the throne in 1685. (Palace Green Library, University of Durham)

Revolution of 1688–89. Confronted by a far more hostile Parliament than had ever previously been the case, Charles II willingly accepted Danby's resignation as Treasurer and confined him to a long, though by no means harsh, imprisonment in the Tower. If the removal of 'the most hated minister that had ever been about the king' was to help quieten passions for the moment, then foremost in the mind of Charles II was what to do about his brother. The Earl of Conway considered that it was primarily 'Fear of the Duke of York [which] ma[de] them [i.e. the Commons] every day fetter the Crown', and James's repeated calls for a military solution to be applied to all of the monarchy's problems risked confirming all of the worst predictions touted by the Whig pamphleteers. While a recourse to arms was a blunt and indiscriminate method, uncertain of success, it was inevitable its result would be suffering and bloodshed inflicted upon both sides, and that if word of the Duke's intentions spread beforehand, the Whigs would be handed a propaganda triumph which would appear to prove beyond doubt the central allegations of the Popish Plot. If Shaftesbury's partisans were often restrained from decisive action by their memories of the destruction of the English Civil Wars, then it would seem that James had remembered everything, but learned nothing, from his father's botched attempt to arrest the Five Members.[43] The Duke's continued presence in the country, therefore, represented not only a danger to himself but also to the stability and peace of the realm. His refusal to heed the warnings of the profoundly loyal, if ineffective, Archbishop Sancroft to return to the Anglican Church, and his angry response to the suggestion of a compromise, whereby he might pay public lip service to Protestantism while continuing in his private Catholic devotions, appeared to be the decisive factor in making up the King's mind. If James could not be separated from his faith, then he would have to be separated from – and put beyond the reach of – the nation which so thoroughly abhorred him.

James, who at the best of times had been disinclined to trust any institution or system which smacked of democracy, had welcomed the news of the demise of the Cavalier Parliament warmly and had hoped that his brother might seek to rule personally from now on, without the interference of either Lords or Commons, while the Court party regrouped and attempted to regain a popular mandate for its actions. However, the pressing financial need to pay for the Army which he himself had created entirely escaped him, and he became increasingly troubled by the King's reticence towards him, and his outright refusal to heed his advice. He found it 'strange his majesty has not written to me, neither in answer to what I wrote . . . nor now upon breaking the parliament', and complained that 'I am not used like a brother nor a friend'.[44] Charles II's decision to send him into exile, though not entirely unexpected, came as a particularly bitter form of punishment. His youthful wanderings had seemed, in retrospect, like wonderful escapades, crammed with incident and largely free of responsibility, but now on the threshold of middle age, with a family to support and having tasted high office, the prospect of once again becoming an itinerant and stateless royal, eking out an existence on the fringes of the Courts of Europe had little to recommend it. Significantly, he did not for a moment contemplate returning to the military profession which he professed to love and failed to lobby the Dutch, French, or even the Imperial services, for a command, despite the fact that he was prepared to conceive of his exile as being final.[45] Instead, he fought against his banishment until the last possible moment, begging his brother to let him stay in England and bidding him an emotional and, for the Duke's part, a heavily tear-stained farewell.[46]

During the six months of his exile in the Spanish Netherlands, James idled his time away, playing with his hunting dogs and writing an interminable stream of gloomy letters to his friends and supporters, which were hardly calculated to provide them with leadership or to raise their flagging spirits. The seriousness of his situation should not be underestimated: Parliament was preparing to outlaw him, to ban him upon pain of death from ever returning to the shores of England, and Shafesbury's men were successfully ejecting many of his remaining supporters from their positions of authority in the municipalities. However, it is important to recognize that during the critical phases of the Exclusion Crisis from March 1679 to March 1682, the Duke of York was conspicuous by his absence from the English political scene. After his dramatic return from Brussels in September 1679, when the King's life was thought to be in danger through illness, he was almost immediately sent away again, this time to Scotland. Thus, his counsels played very little part in the eventual rout of Shaftesbury and his party, and he was not on hand to observe how the King came first to master, and then to break, dissent.[47]

Charles II's claims to the able and effective practice of kingship rest most soundly upon his record of governance from the summer of 1679 up until his death in February 1685. His liberal use of the prerogative to bring a sudden, and juddering, halt to the proceedings of Parliament, once the Exclusion bills had begun to make headway, gave him time to wait upon events and to search out new allies; while his willingness to bring Shaftesbury and his closest associates into government, in April 1679, and to confer upon them office – though without actual power – not only showed him to be magnanimous and ready to receive the advice of his Protestant critics in the name of the national good, but also served to thoroughly wrongfoot Shaftesbury and to discredit him in the eyes of many of his more militant followers. Moreover, his judicious display of force at the Oxford Parliament in March 1681, when he removed his opponents from their natural environment of Westminster into an ultra-Royalist university town which he then had ringed with some of his best troops, effectively called the Whig's bluff without the need for actual physical violence. For the King, unlike James, could read his opponents and understand something of their motivations. Despite government propaganda, he knew Shaftesbury to be no firebrand Republican but a constitutional politician, committed to the safeguarding of private property and the maintenance of the existing social order. These constraints served to limit the Earl's room for manoeuvre and made the prospect of him seeking to resolve matters through armed struggle, as anything but a last resort, a very remote possibility indeed.[48]

In fact, James's removal from the kingdom had helped to greatly reduce tension and to minimalize the chances of violence breaking out between his personal escort and the crowd. While he had still been resident in London, the City mob had a highly visible figure, who seemed to embody all of the evils of popery, living in their midst. In the absence of real Jesuit plotters, it was a relatively simple matter to blame every failing of the central government, every unexplained murder, every sudden troop movement or the strange appearance by a foreigner on the streets of the capital, upon his baneful influence within the councils of State. Similarly, it was an easy task for Whig writers to define their movement primarily in terms of its standing against the person and policies of James Stuart. As soon as he was safely away from England – out of sight, if not perhaps out of mind – it was far more difficult to maintain momentum and a common core identity, as the various factions within the movement began to strike out in different directions. Their cohesion was further sapped by the frequent prorogation of Parliament and by the feeling that it was one thing to bring down a minister, or to seek to neutralize the influence of the brother of the King, but it was quite another to stand full-square against the sovereign himself, and to risk the long haul to Tyburn and a traitor's death on the scaffold. Few of Shaftesbury's MPs had not at some point in their careers been touched by the royal service, in its many different aspects, and deference and a belief in the natural order of monarchy were hard to shake off overnight. Although he now counted the Earl among his friends and stoutly defended the Whig cause, Sir William Coventry, the Duke's old Secretary, could still not bring himself to vote for the first Exclusion bill, when the moment finally came, and chose to quietly retire from politics.[49] Absenteeism during crucial votes and unexpected fluctuations in support, which went unchecked due to the absence of a modern whipping system, certainly hampered the passage of the bills, but it was

the sudden and overt politicization of the role of the King, who abandoned the search for a consensus and, after the winter of 1680–81,
launched a full-scale offensive against his opponents, which proved fatal
to the morale and cohesion of Whig movement within Parliament.

James derived comfort from his brother's new resolve and may have
flattered himself that his calls for the King to 'take bold and resolut
councells, and stick to them', had finally been answered. However, what
he consistently failed to appreciate was the significant shift in the
monarchy's position which had taken place during his absence in
Flanders and Scotland. The hard truth of the matter, which Shaftesbury
and his cohorts were equally slow to acknowledge, was that the financial
necessity for the King's calling of Parliaments had lessened to the point
that he was no longer dependent upon them in order for the executive to
function. The growth of the carrying trades, access to new markets in the
colonies, and increased profits from tariffs levied upon wines and spirits,
had meant that by the early 1680s the monarchy, unencumbered by the
vast expense of war and set on a firm financial footing by Danby's careful
retrenchment of royal expenditure, was not only solvent but also capable
of waging a protracted and expensive campaign against its internal
political opponents. Charles II could, quite literally, afford to govern
without Parliament. Denied a clear platform, after the dissolution of the
Oxford Parliament, Whig MPs were forced increasingly on to the
defensive.[50] Electoral success had given them both self-confidence and a
belief that they had a strong popular mandate in support of all their
actions. Without access to the floor of the House of Commons, it was
difficult to co-ordinate their assaults upon the prerogative, stay in touch
with other members, and maintain momentum. The problem for them,
in stressing that Parliament ultimately acted as the watchdog for
Protestant England and that it might safeguard its liberties, and contain
the further spread of royal power, primarily through legislative means,
was what to do once that organ had been suddenly called out of
existence. For the next four years, the struggle for the executive power
would shift away from the deliberations of the Commons and the Lords,
to the municipalities, City boardrooms, militias and local governments,
where the manipulation of Parliamentary procedure no longer mattered
and where coercion could more often prove decisive.

Having initiated purges of the judiciary and corporations, and with the
knowledge that the monarchy was still an enormously popular institution
which could, in an overwhelmingly paternalist society, draw upon vast
reserves of sympathy and support, Charles II could now begin to consider
how he might bring James safely back into his service. Those very
characteristics of unyielding strength and harsh principle, which had
threatened to damage him beyond all measure in 1679, could, at a time

of violent reaction, play well with the King's Tory supporters. Charles II had already tested the water for James's return to centre stage. The Duke's rule as Viceroy of Scotland had suggested, to his brother, that he could still work effectively with a noble council and that Episcopalian churchmen were prepared to serve under a Roman Catholic Prince. Moreover, he was useful. If Charles II had been prepared to portray him in the 1660s and 1670s as a dour foil to his own image as the generous and libertine 'Merry Monarch', then he was now able to show James as exemplifying the physical force and sheer durability of the Crown. In the new climate, where the King delivered hammer blows against the Whig bastions of the municipalities, and stripped his own capital city of its ancient charter, it was Tory mobs who now roamed the streets, savaging their opponents and crying out for vengeance.[51] Even allowing for the exaggerations of his own propagandists, the resurgence of the fortunes of the Duke of York appeared remarkable and, he thought, even miraculous. When he slipped back into England, in the summer of 1679, he had had to be carefully disguised, wrapped up in the folds of his cloak, his face hidden by the curls of a heavy black periwig; but now his arrival in Whitehall 'was joyfully welcomed by his Royal Brother, and highly Caressed by all the Nobility, the Vulgar sort for some time after, when at any time he went abroad, Crowded in Multitudes about his Coach, as glad to behold that perfect Patern of true Valour, who shunned no danger to preserve his Country from Insulting Foes, crying with joyful Acclamations, "Long Live the King, and the thrice Noble Duke of York, England's Darling, and the Terrour of our Foes"'.[52]

With James's supporters secure in their control of the Artillery Company, and successful in hounding Shaftesbury's friends from their positions of authority in the joint-stock companies, the nature of the Whig opposition began to change, as its leaders began to become more desperate. Previously, it had been a simple enough matter to rally around calls for the Duke's exclusion from the throne. It was a cause which could be pursued with a veneer of loyalty towards the Crown, and agitation could be conducted within the bounds of Parliamentary privilege and legality. However, as it became increasingly likely that the movement was going to fail and as the Duke – despite all of their best efforts – was restored to his offices, there were those who were prepared to countenance far stronger measures in order to prevent a popish successor from ever coming to the throne.

One of the central questions often posed, but never successfully answered, by the Whigs, was who the actual succession would devolve upon in the advent of James's disinheritance. Mary, the Duke's Protestant daughter, or her Dutch soldier husband, William of Orange, were the obvious candidates. However, Mary's sheltered upbringing and almost total disinterest in politics had meant that she, like her younger sister Anne, represented something of an unknown quantity, while William, though a staunch Calvinist, remained a foreigner whose nation had fought England to a standstill over the course of three bloody and recent wars. Prince Rupert's German relatives offered another possibility, and he had begun to canvass Shaftesbury's support on their behalf, but they were remote and singularly failed to capture the public imagination.[53] The only other serious candidate remained the Duke of Monmouth. He had remained singularly loyal to his father throughout the Popish Plot and the early years of Exclusion, leading the Royal Army to triumph in Scotland against the Covenanter rebels. However, the realization that the King was never going to legitimize him purely of his own accord, and the spectacle of the Duke of York's return to power, prompted him to begin to pay court to the Whig interest and to toy with the idea of launching a popular rebellion. His tour through the Midlands and the county of Cheshire, in September 1682, aroused the suspicion of George Jeffreys, James's Attorney General, and brought the full force of the State down upon him. Arrested and brought back to London in disgrace, he now firmly committed himself to opposition politics, hoping that Shaftesbury – who had continued to hold him at arm's length, and to view him with wry suspicion as a pure opportunist – would be the author of his revival, and gain for him a crown at James's expense.[54] However, Shaftesbury was not the power he once was and only the continuing loyalty of the City of London, and the will of a hand-picked metropolitan jury, had saved him from being convicted of treason in the winter of 1681. Furthermore, his sound political intuition and abiding sense of constitutionalism, which had always previously characterized his endeavours and had made him an uneasy and unsatisfactory partner for Monmouth, began to desert him as his misfortunes grew and multiplied. As sickness and disappointment overtook him, he joined with the young blade in advocating more brutal and immediate methods of wresting the executive away from the Duke of York.

Increasingly starved of allies from the political mainstream, Monmouth now turned to the Republican underground for support. Plans were already afoot by a group of old Commonwealth men to assassinate the King and his brother, as they returned from one of their frequent trips to the horse races at Newmarket, and Monmouth, upon hearing of the plot – which took its name from the projected spot, at Rye House, where the snipers would launch their attack – gave it his tacit support and approval. However, the outbreak of fire which swept through Newmarket in late March 1683, though disastrous for the townsfolk, proved to be highly fortunate for the King and the Duke of York. With the races abandoned and their lodgings razed to the ground, they had a complete change of plan and started back to London far sooner than had ever been imagined, thus throwing the plotters into confusion and entirely avoiding the snares which had been laid for them *en route*.[55] While Charles II had been prepared to indulge Oates's allegations and to sacrifice a number of his servants in order to appease the mob, the revelation of the Rye House Plot profoundly scared and unsettled him. He was in no doubt about the existence of a radical underground movement, which drew its support from the larger and more organized Whig party, and which had actually aimed to take his life. Consequently, he had the conspirators quickly rounded up and widened the scope of the search to include, and detain, a number of leading Whig grandees. Shaftesbury, having fled to Holland in the previous November, a tired and broken man, was now well beyond their reach. Regarded as something of an embarrassment even by his own followers, his health had been further weakened by the strain of months spent constantly on the run, hidden away in the safe-houses of his remaining friends in the capital, and, after a traumatic voyage across the Channel, death had come to claim him within barely two months of his arrival in Amsterdam. His colleagues, however, found escape a far more difficult option, and the Earl of Essex and Lord William Russell, together with the veteran Republican, Algernon Sidney, were all quickly found and taken. None of them could expect mercy from their sovereign, for Charles II, despite his late attempts to shift the blame solely on to James, was in a vengeful and unforgiving mood. In despair, Essex, who had once sat alongside the King in the Privy Council, took his own life; while Russell and Sidney, fortified by the courage of their convictions, went to their deaths with the utmost bravery and made a lasting impression upon all those who had witnessed their end.[56]

Further searches were conducted and evidence was compiled and analysed by James's new political manager, Lawrence Hyde. Too junior to have fallen with Danby and too clever to have been overly identified with James at the height of Exclusion, the Duke's brother-in-law, as a convinced Anglican and a man with a real flair for diplomacy, was one of a new breed of career politicians dedicated to the royal service, whose stars were rising at Court. He and James now determined to destroy Monmouth's influence with the King, and pressed home their advantage when the young Duke was finally persuaded to surrender himself to the authorities and was brought cowering before his father. Monmouth was in an extremely unenviable position, confronted by the arraignments of the Whig peers for treason and by the possibility that he would likewise be swiftly charged and condemned, he now had to fight for his life against the rage and hostility of the resurgent Duke of York, who had been newly restored to his place on the King's council. In the frenzied political atmosphere of the early 1680s, where violence and statecraft were beginning to appear to be insolubly linked, it looked as if it was impossible for both of the royal Dukes to continue in office at the side of the King, and that one of them had surely to go down for the last time. Yet, in a way this crisis had been brewing for many years and had been made inevitable by Charles II's desire to generate rivalry between York and Monmouth, and to play his brother and his natural son against one another, to his own narrow advantage. Even James had begun to glimpse at this and to question its wisdom, though he was ultimately unable to articulate his impressions fully or to draw lasting conclusions from them. In the summer of 1679, he had written to George Legge from his place of exile in Brussels, that 'There is one thinge troubles me very much and puts od thoughts into my head, it is that all this while his Majesty has never sayd a word nor gone about to make a good understanding bettwene me and the Duke of Monmouth, for tho it is a thing I shall never seek, yet methinks it is what his Majesty might presse.'[57]

The only hope for Monmouth was to make an appeal to his father's affections and to offer a full and frank apology to any that he might have offended, in the hope of securing their mercy. Foremost among the latter grouping was James and, in mortal terror of his uncle, the young Duke wrote to the King that he only expected to be saved 'by the intercession of the Duke [of York], whom I acknowledge to have offended', and to whom '[I] am prepared to submit myself in the humblest manner'.[58] However, while this strategy worked well with Catherine of Braganza, playing upon her sense of decency and motivating her to try to intercede with the Duke and Duchess of York on his behalf, it did little to appease James. As a huntsman he knew only too well how to attack and corner his frightened prey, and with Monmouth within his grasp he was loathe to either relinquish his prize or to allow his brother the chance to give in to his feelings of love and tenderness towards the boy. Accordingly, he made sure that Monmouth's confession of his own part in the plot and his willingness to provide evidence about the activities of his former comrades, though given on the condition that it remained strictly private intelligence, received the widest possible public exposure and dissemination. The appearance of the admission of guilt and the full details of the Rye House Plot, in the pages of consecutive editions of the government newspaper, the *Gazette*, convinced many sceptics of the truth of the conspiracy and, although Russell had already fallen under the headsman's axe, the popular outcry which resulted from these reports effectively ruled out any possibility of a pardon being obtained for Sidney. Furthermore, it also destroyed what little chance the remaining defendants, arraigned for their part in the affair, had of obtaining a fair trial and greatly benefited George Jeffrey's successful prosecution of them.[59]

For all of his bullying and bravado, Monmouth, who had been prepared to incite his friends to maim his political enemies and had once run a beadle through, though the man had only been in pursuit of his duties, had been seen to have thoroughly abased and compromised himself before the Duke and the King, and had earned nothing but the scorn of his former allies by his betrayal of them.[60] James, through sheer force and persistence had thoroughly outmanoeuvred him, through his use of carefully timed leaks and the services of the industrious Lawrence Hyde, and the ever-loyal Judge Jeffreys. In many respects, the whole affair stands as an eerie forerunner of later events after the collapse of the Western rising of 1685, but to the Duke of York in the winter of 1683–4, it was the principle of his right to succeed, rather than its actuality, which counted and had been conclusively indicated. As a discredited Monmouth fled from London and took ship for the Continent, James and his household could afford to look to the future with a renewed sense of optimism. Tickets were already being given out for a great Frost Fair to be held upon the frozen River Thames, at which the Duke of York was to be among the King's guests of honour.[61] As he responded to the cheers of the invited crowd and walked in amongst the stalls, out on the ice, James, surrounded by his Duchess, his daughter Anne, and her doughy husband, the Prince of Denmark, had every cause for satisfaction. Such a public display of family unity would have been unthinkable and highly dangerous only two years before, but with royal power more firmly concentrated than ever, the foremost Whig cities – such as London, Nottingham and York – stripped of their charters, Shaftesbury dead, Monmouth gone, and their most influential followers either broken or humbled, the Duke's undisputed right to the succession had been thoroughly reaffirmed. As his old servants began to return to office, James, in the full expectation that his brother would reign securely for many more years to come, gladly resumed his post at the Admiralty and picked up the tattered threads of an administration which he had been forced to lay down more than ten years before.

CHAPTER SEVEN

The Dominion of the Seas

I

When, in May 1660, the sails of the English battlefleet were spotted from the shores of Holland, James, Duke of York, prepared to greet both the sailors and their political masters in his guise as the Lord High Admiral of England. That he had had no formal experience of seafaring and had failed to assert his authority over the revolted fleet in 1648, mattered little. What was important was that Charles I had settled the office upon him as a child and that, following the implosion of the Commonwealth, old forms, titles and dues were quickly reasserting themselves and gaining respect at all levels of society. Moreover, James's reputation as a competent soldier and 'hard man' now became useful to Charles II. Even though the fleet had been sent across the Channel by General Monck and the new Convention Parliament, with express instructions to secure terms with the King and to facilitate his safe return to England, the loyalty of the ships' crews remained an entirely unknown quantity.

Edward Montagu, the Commander of the expedition, had served as one of Cromwell's most faithful Generals, both on land and sea, and had always been regarded as a staunch upholder of successive Republican administrations. Charles II, therefore, had good reason to be wary of his newfound friend, and acted decisively to ensure his own safety and to win the affection of the fleet. By reactivating the office of Lord High Admiral, and by formally investing James with the appointment on 16 May, he effectively superseded the existing command structure of the fleet, as laid down by the Convention Parliament. Montagu's supremacy among the flag-captains was undermined, while a new executive tier of royal control was imposed upon the Navy, allowing James to assume the official – if largely titular – command of every ship in the fleet. While Charles II paid court to former Cromwellians, wining and dining Montagu and his Captains, James undertook a bold piece of political theatre designed to underline the realities of the transference of power between the incoming and outgoing regimes. The vessels were rechristened in honour and celebration of the Stuart dynasty, removing from the fleet any explicit links with Republican forms of government, Parliament's great victories, or the Cromwell family itself. Thus, the *Speaker* became the *Mary*, the *Langport* became the *Henrietta*, the *Naseby* became the *Royal*

Charles, and the *Richard* was transformed into the *Royal James*. The oak figureheads, carved under the Commonwealth and Protectorate, were less easily removed and survived slightly longer, striking a slightly uncomfortable note as Charles II sailed home in triumph, upon a ship which bore the proud effigy of Cromwell trampling his enemies underfoot. However, once safely ashore in England, James set about remedying matters and ordered that the offending sculptures, and their accompanying coats of arms, should be removed from sight. Figureheads, which had seen service from the East and West Indies to Texel and Santa Cruz, were cut down from their bows and left to rot, half forgotten, in the royal dockyards at Chatham, Portsmouth and Harwich. A special and dramatic fate was, however, reserved for the carving of Oliver Cromwell. Despite the pleas of his clerks that the figure could be reworked and that its destruction would be a sad waste of public money, James had the image hacked from off the *Royal Charles* and ceremonially burned upon the seashore, before a crowd of cheering spectators and dockworkers.[1]

If the Duke of York had been particularly anxious to sweep away all memory of Cromwell's government, then he also made it his priority to dismantle the existing State bureaucracy which had grown up in its shadow. He attempted to reconstruct the Navy Office just as it had been in the years immediately prior to the outbreak of war in 1642. Consequently, on 4 July 1660, he dissolved both the Commission for the Admiralty, which had carried out the work of the executive power in the absence of a Lord High Admiral, and the Commission for the Navy, which had overseen the day-to-day running of the service. Henceforth, James would stand as the undisputed head of a new administration, assisted by four principal officers: the Treasurer, the Comptroller, the Surveyor and the Clerk of the Acts. These posts were – with one notable exception – filled by placemen, who had demonstrated their loyalty to the Stuarts and who had already seen service in the naval establishment of Charles I. The Duke's friend, Sir George Carteret, had served as a Vice-Admiral and Comptroller of the Navy in the 1630s, before being appointed as Treasurer. His successor in the office of Comptroller, Sir Robert Slingsby, had seen a good deal of naval service and came from a family with strong maritime connections; while Sir William Batten, the Surveyor, had already held that office from 1638 to 1642. The odd man out – who had no prior knowledge of the Navy – was one of Montagu's kinsmen, an unknown secretary by the name of Samuel Pepys, who had been appointed as Clerk of the Acts as a favour to his powerful patron, and who now moved quickly to take over the office and records of the old Commission. In time, this small nucleus of civil servants was augmented by the addition of naval specialists, who could contribute a particular expertise to the Board's deliberations. Among this number were James's old companion Sir John Berkeley of Stratton, who had seen action as a Royalist Commander in the South-West of England in the 1640s; Sir William Penn the elder, who had served as an Admiral under the Commonwealth, and Peter Pett, who had worked all his life as a shipbuilder in the yards at Chatham. Sir William Coventry, the Duke's own Secretary, was also drafted in to oversee matters, while Lord Brouncker was rewarded with a commissionership for his services at Court.[2]

However, James had to wait until 29 January 1661 before his own post was ratified by the King in Council and a patent confirming him in his offices was granted. When it came, this not only created him Lord High Admiral of England, Ireland and Wales, but also restated England's sovereignty over the Channel Islands and laid claim to the jurisdiction of waters that had last been patrolled by the English fleet during the Hundred Years War. James, so the patent boasted – without any grounding in actual fact – was also the Lord High Admiral of Normandy, Calais, Gascony and Aquitaine. A subsequent patent, dated 20 February 1662, sought to extend his sphere of influence even further and proclaimed him to be Lord High Admiral of Dunkirk – which was still in English possession at this time – and of all England's colonial domains, which stretched from New England and Jamaica in the Americas, to Tangier, 'Guinny and Binny' in Northern and Western Africa.[3] The re-establishment of the Lord High Admiralship, with all of its semi-feudal overtones, sent out a powerful message about the future direction of naval administration and reaffirmed the importance of the hereditary principle in the seeking of personal advancement.

From the outset of his tenure, James had set about stamping the service with the mark of his own royal authority, and began to fundamentally alter both its basic character and the social profile of its officer corps. During the Commonwealth and Protectorate periods, the command of warships had been entrusted to professional seamen, drawn from the ranks of warrant officers and the masters of merchant ships. However, James was determined to change this situation and was concerned that these old Captains, or 'tarpaulins' as they came to be known, might still retain a measure of loyalty to the Republican form of government that had done so much to advance their careers. He recognized that there was a need to introduce a body of dependable, propertied and strongly pro-Royalist Officers into the Navy, and soon came to realize that the distribution of newly created commissions could not only engineer this transformation, but would also provide him with an extra area of patronage which could be painlessly exploited in rewarding displays of loyalty and favours given. James further reasoned that the introduction of these 'blue blooded' Officers into the service might also have persuaded the Upper and Lower Houses to grant more money to the naval establishment, and he clearly stated his belief that 'it was the interest of an English Parliament to encourage the navy for the sake of their younger sons, who might be bred . . . to the business thereof'.[4] As a result, in 1661, the Duke began to issue royal warrants which enabled the sons of noble and gentry families to go to sea in the capacity of volunteers, establishing a precedent that was refined and expanded upon by subsequent naval administrations, and which led ultimately to the creation of the rank of midshipman. It was mainly due to James's display of royal patronage, and his subsequent willingness to promote young gentlemen rapidly through the ranks, that the levels of social prestige attached to a naval commission increased dramatically during his time as Lord High Admiral. All of a sudden, a career at sea appeared to offer a wholly respectable and potentially very lucrative form of advancement for courtiers and the younger sons of the nobility, in a way which would have been entirely unthinkable for them a generation before. Within a few years, large numbers of well-connected young Officers were rising to gain full commissions in the service, generating a climate of ruthless competition for posts, and giving rise to many bitter personal conflicts between the new breed of 'gentlemen' Officers and the older generation of 'tarpaulins'.[5] In this unequal struggle, the former grouping had the important advantage of having friends and relations at Court who could lobby on their behalf, in an appointment system which came to depend heavily on the workings of power and patronage at the very highest levels of society. In this way, the Republican administration of the Navy – though largely as the result of wartime expediency – can be seen to have aimed towards a form of meritocracy based around competency and professionalism, while James's governance had given rise to an alternative system, founded upon wealth and privilege, that was dependent upon the machinations of Court life and, most importantly, upon the person and preferences of the Lord High Admiral himself.

Thus, James saw to it that his friend, Hugh Seymour, a younger son of Sir Edward Seymour, the 3rd Baronet, was given command of his own ship. Pepys, who was busily learning his own trade, commented sourly on the whole affair, adding that the 'consequence of introducing persons of too great quality into the King's ships which R[ichard] Gibson [a clerk in the Navy Office] gives me another instance of in the late Capt. Seamour, who when but a reformado in Yarmouth, under Capt. Wager, had more observance paid him, and the officers and company more fearful of disobliging him, than of any officer in the ship'.[6] The appointment of the Duke's favourite, Jean-Baptiste Du Teil, to the command of another warship was similarly ill-starred. Du Teil was a Frenchman who had fallen under a cloud after the Four Days Fight, when his guns were said to have done far more damage to his own side than to the Dutch. However, the

Duke stuck by his friend and provoked a row with General Monck, who had dismissed Du Teil for cowardice from his own service, by rewarding him with a place in his own household and a knighthood. James's exceptional display of loyalty towards his friend is all the more remarkable in view of Du Teil's earlier conduct, while directly under the Duke's command. Writing in 1669, Pepys recorded the details of an engagement fought at the outbreak of the Second Dutch War, during which the Duke mounted a pursuit of a fleeing enemy squadron: 'Being [at] the headmost of our ships . . . his Royal Highness saw among [those that were] chased a square-sterned ship which he took (as well as the rest of the fleet) to be a man-of-war . . . (though indeed afterwards proved to be but a merchant ship come from Guinny) and put all his hopes in Du Tell taking her.' Unfortunately, thereupon the Duke's protégé 'did give over his chase and man two or three sorry flyboats, which was imputed to his cowardice'. Having seen the encounter unfold before his eyes, from start to finish, the Duke's initial amazement quickly turned to rage. He lost his temper 'with Dutel at the entering port [of his flagship] and . . . [made] ready to strike him.' However, James's anger with his servant was suddenly and unexpectedly dissipated by Du Teil's comforting words and, despite all of the evidence to the contrary, 'it seems that his highness was satisfied in the matter' and continued to find employment for his less than competent friend.[7]

Despite these setbacks, the Duke continued to consolidate his position at the top of the Admiralty structure throughout the 1660s, and was able to play off against one another the two rival camps of Officers, who had attached themselves to the interests of either General Monck or Prince Rupert. As sources of patronage and military expertise, independent of James, both figures had built upon their natural and mutually antagonistic constituencies. However, Rupert continued to regard himself as a 'Royalist' Admiral, constantly refighting in his 'blimpish' manner the battles of the Civil War; while Monck – 'That honest general . . . who is a simple hearted man' – continued in his loyalty to his old friends, who had first taken service under the Commonwealth and Protectorate.[8] Yet if James was both able to soothe and to benefit from their quarrels, then he faced an altogether more troublesome opponent in the form of Edward Montagu, who had recently been ennobled as the Earl of Sandwich. Through his undoubted military and diplomatic abilities, Sandwich was able to create a position for himself at the top of the naval administration which, during the early years of the Restoration, on occasion, came close to rivalling that of the Duke. It was only in the late 1660s that the balance of power began to dramatically shift in James's favour, as Sandwich's allies – including Pepys, his former protégé – began to desert him and as he found himself arraigned before a court martial on charges of embezzling prize money.

Although, as we shall see, the case against him, carefully orchestrated by Sir William Coventry with the Duke's full knowledge, was eventually hushed up by the King; his reputation was seriously damaged. He was never again able to recover his former influence and he was sent off on a diplomatic mission to Spain, so that he might cool his heels for a time.[9]

Thereafter James's position might have proved unassailable had it not been for his sudden conversion to Roman Catholicism, and the imposition of the provisions of the First Test Act in 1673 upon all serving officers. Under its terms on 15 June 1673, having refused to swear the oaths of Supremacy and Allegiance, which acknowledged the validity of the Anglican sacrament, James was forced to resign his post at the head of the naval administration. However, despite the formal surrender of his authority, the Duke continued to fight on behind the scenes in an attempt to retain the majority of his executive powers. The Test Act only applied to government officials working in the English establishment and, as a result, no steps were ever taken to apply its sanctions north of the border. Consequently, while James was compelled to renounce his title of Lord High Admiral of England, he retained jurisdiction over all the other territories awarded to him by his brother's patents. Most important of these was the High Admiralship of Scotland, which until 1707 had a separate Admiralty and its own administrative structure. This literal reading of his letters patent allowed James to continue to exercise a considerable degree of patronage over naval appointments and to maintain a forceful, although necessarily shadowy, presence in the war councils of King Charles throughout the mid-1670s.[10]

In order to compensate for the loss of his brother, Charles II constituted a new Navy Board under Prince Rupert for executing 'the office of the Lord Admiral of England'. However, on taking office, Rupert was horrified to discover that James had been so successful in advancing the careers of his own placemen that a large section of the officer corps continued to remain loyal to their old master, and were prepared to act as a conduit to implement his wishes. A heavy-handed attempt at purging his administration of the Duke's highly placed friends, proved both unsuccessful and divisive, and left such a feeling of rancour and ill-will in the service that morale inevitably suffered. Far more seriously still, the bitter in-fighting between Rupert and James's partisans spilled over to influence their conduct of the campaign of 1673, effectively disrupting the smooth flow of communications between the different arms of the fleet. While Rupert vainly patrolled the length of the Dutch coast, hoping to draw their navy out to give battle, he was troubled by a continual stream of contradictory orders and advice emanating from Whitehall. It soon transpired that James had been able to secure his brother's ear and had urged him to adopt an entirely different set of plans to those already agreed upon. Surprisingly, given the Duke of York's own love of battle, caution was now to be placed at a premium. Unable to maintain the confidence of the King, and with the relations with his French allies dissolving into unco-operative abuse, Rupert's ability to successfully prosecute the war was fatally compromised, while his own hold on command was reduced to little more than a cipher. In influence, if not in title, it would appear that James was still very much the Lord High Admiral.[11]

Although Rupert continued in office until May 1679, most of the important decisions about naval strategy and procurement continued to be taken by the King, acting upon the advice of James and his civil servants. Samuel Pepys even went so far as to claim that the Navy Board met only 'in cases admitting delay and requiring the formality of public debate' and, while this is almost certainly an overstatement of the facts, it does serve to demonstrate the Duke's continued presence at the heart of the decision-making process long after his official retirement had taken effect. We are further informed that 'the despatch of the general current business thereof [concerning the Commission of 1677, was] being wholly performed by the immediate direction of his Majesty (with the advice of his Royal Highness) to Mr. Pepys', and that at such 'meetings his Royal Highness did, by the King's command, always assist, until his removal out of the land in 1678 [O.S. i.e.1679] (through the malignity of the then times) his Majesty was (to the utmost ruin of his navy) bereft of his brother's further aid therein'.[12] It was only with the outbreak of the popular hysteria surrounding the Popish Plot and the onset of the Exclusion Crisis that the administration created by James suffered a near fatal blow. Shaftesbury's supporters in Parliament launched a concerted campaign to limit the monarchy's stranglehold on naval administration and set out to effectively curtail the power of the executive in that area. To this end, in the early months of 1679, Whig MPs launched a ferocious assault upon those of the Duke's friends and servants who remained in the administration. Amid allegations of corruption, disloyalty and negligence, the Navy Board, which had survived in one form or another since James had re-established it in 1660, was finally broken up. There can be little doubt that the principal target of this campaign was the Duke himself, and it is hard to see how he might have avoided impeachment at this point had he not already escaped into exile at Brussels. However, while he was afforded breathing space to reflect gloomily upon his predicament and to try to come to terms with the freefall collapse of his political fortunes, his friends at the Admiralty, for whom flight was not an option, were largely abandoned to their fates. Lord Danby, the Lord High Treasurer of the Admiralty, and Samuel Pepys, the Secretary to the Admiralty and Treasurer for Tangier, were rounded on for their support of James and were swiftly committed to the Tower, while a further purge of the Navy's 'officers Papists, and [the] D[uke] of Y[ork's] creatures' was initiated. An entirely new Admiralty Board was constituted under Sir Henry Capel and, though Pepys later sneered that its commissioners were mere 'fault-finders' with no experience, who had been chosen solely on the strength of their loyalty to Shaftesbury's party, they continued to function – and with far greater efficiency than has often been credited – up until the Tory reaction of the early 1680s.[13]

The eclipse of James's influence in the Navy was, however, far more short-lived than many would have thought possible at the time. The cases brought against his servants, such as Pepys and Will Hewer, collapsed, and he gradually began to rebuild his shattered network of power and patronage at all levels of the service. He used his time as Royal Commissioner in Edinburgh to promote his involvement with Scottish shipping, and began to publicly lay claim to the title of Lord High Admiral once again. After the collapse of the Oxford Parliament, Pepys claimed that King Charles had come 'to a sudden determination of resuming the Business of it [the Navy] into his own Hands, assisted by his Royal Brother', but the truth of the matter remained somewhat more ambiguous than this rather saturnine statement would have us believe. The Duke of York continued to remain in the shadows, and his reputation and naval career were only gradually rehabilitated. The Admiralty Board was finally overthrown in 1684 as Charles II repossessed its executive powers, Samuel Pepys returned to the Secretaryship, and James resumed his place on the Privy Council for the first time in more than a decade. By May of that year the Duke had returned to his duties at the Admiralty, and although King Charles was still obliged to sign all of the orders and warrants given under James's hand himself – in order to circumvent the provisions of the Test Act – there can be little room for doubt that, in the final months of his brother's reign, James had been fully reinstated to his position as Lord High Admiral of England.[14] His return to office in this way was helped immeasurably by the creation of a new post of Secretary of Admiralty Affairs, which carried with it sweeping administrative powers that echoed those of Louis XIV's Secretary of the Marine. Once entrusted to a safe pair of hands, in this case to those of Samuel Pepys, the appointment allowed the Duke to conduct naval policy through his own appointee, with little recourse to overt and heavy-handed tampering with the service and with the minimum of risk of offending public opinion. This arrangement proved to be so successful that Pepys was retained in this capacity even after his master became King. For his own part, James seems to have equated the control of the Navy, by the executive power, with the fundamental well-being of the nation. As Duke of York he had always jealously guarded his claim to be Lord High Admiral and had treated the Navy as his own private fiefdom, observing on his accession that 'he had also found by long experience that the places of Lord High Admiral and Lord General were fit to be exercised by the King alone', and refusing to give them up upon any grounds whatsoever.[15] Given such an uncompromising attitude towards naval affairs and having established the nature of his long tenure at the head of the administrative machine, we can now proceed towards an evaluation of the Duke's personal contribution to the long-term development of the Admiralty.

II

As we have already seen, James, as opposed to his elder brother who had learned to sail in Jersey in 1646, had precious little knowledge of the sea when Montagu's Officers received him aboard their ships and accorded him the honour of being their Admiral. Similarly, there would seem to be little in the way of truth, and much in the way of flattery, in Pepys's much quoted observation that 'it was the Rebellion and necessity' that had made a seaman out of the Duke. Apart from his brief trip to the Channel Islands in 1649, when James had advised his brother to make good his escape from a Parliamentarian flotilla before the turn of the tide, he had not been aboard ship for any significant period of time. Moreover, even Pepys himself, on becoming properly acquainted with the Duke, seems to have begun to question his earlier judgement and wrote out several little memos to remind him to enquire from his master precisely when, and where, he had begun to be taught his seamanship. However, James's relative inexperience was not so important to his subsequent career as his willingness to learn. He determined from the outset that his would not be an empty, titular appointment, but an opportunity to win fresh laurels, in the absence of land campaigns, and to carve out for himself an important new role in the largest of all the government departments. Through his own personal application and through the respect for sheer and sustained hard work, which he had acquired as an Army Officer, he could see the opportunity to mould the service in his own image and to use it as a suitable vehicle into which to channel his considerable pent-up energies and aggressions.[16]

He determined that he should learn how to sail, and had eagerly written to Edward Montagu before the Restoration 'offering to learn the seaman's trade of him'. In time, he was to become a keen yachtsman and did much to popularize the sport, which had only recently been imported from Holland. The royal brothers often took pleasure trips along the coast and raced against each other up and down the sheltered waters of the River Thames. John Evelyn recorded one such race held in October 1661, when he had 'sailed this morning with His Majesty in one of the yachts . . . on a wager betweene his other new pleasure-boat built frigate-like, and one of the Duke of York's: the wager 100 pounds; the race from Greenwich to Gravesend and back. The King lost in going, the wind being contrary, but saved stakes in returning.' On another occasion, the Reverend Gosling was invited by the King to join his party on board the *Fubbs* as they sailed around the Kent coastline. When a squall suddenly struck, the clergyman was shocked to see the royal brothers scampering among the rigging and handling the sails along with the ordinary sailors, delighting in the unexpected opportunity for exercise and excitement that the danger had afforded them.[17]

Yet if James could proudly claim in later years to have become a competent seaman by his own endeavours, his greatest claim to furthering the development of the English Navy still rests upon his record as a conscientious administrator. Samuel Pepys thought that 'no Admiral within my memory but the Duke of York . . . ever regarded more than a most superficial and stinted knowledge of one only part of the work of the Navy', while even those later historians who disparaged his intellect and motivations were forced to concede that he took his duties seriously. With more than a hint of mid-Victorian snobbery about engagement in trade and menial service, Macaulay conceded that despite all of his other faults James might have 'made a respectable clerk in the dockyard at Chatham', while in more recent times Richard Ollard, though thoroughly unimpressed with the man, attested that his 'stupidity' was at least 'hyperactive' in regard to his dealings with the Navy Office.[18] The fact remains that although Pepys, as the consummate professional, had initially chided at the Duke's habitual lateness and occasional unexplained absences from meetings, he enthusiastically reported on his ability to chair the Board's weekly discussions and his willingness to take informed advice from Coventry and Sandwich. Years later, while writing a propaganda piece in order to justify his own actions, he still held James's memory in high esteem and regarded him as having 'an immediate application to the animating and enabling its [i.e. the Navy's] officers (with suitable supplies of Money) to an industrious and effectual bestiring themselves towards the redressing' of all of the ills in the service, and that as both Duke and King he had sought to check that his orders were being carried out, being 'pleas'd to conceive from the forementioned Progress of these Works [to reform the naval establishment], confirm'd by his own frequent Visits, and Personal Inspections there into at the Yards, was such'.[19] James personally issued instructions for the disposal of decayed stores and took an interest in even the most mundane of matters, whether appointing a boatswain or a cook for his flagship, seeing to the construction of new sea defences, or enquiring as to whether or not a scheme for preserving the coastline from erosion was entirely practical. He prided himself on being an authority on shipbuilding, keeping a highly detailed pocket book in which he logged details of the naval establishment and wanted 'for his own satisfaction and use to have an account of the just rake of all the upright-stemmed ships in his royal navy, and the present seat of the step of each ship's mainmast'. Although he was naturally conservative in his tastes and cruelly scoffed at Sir William Petty for producing his innovative double-hulled ship designs, James was generally keen to preside over a period of rapid expansion in the strength of the battlefleet 'encouraging all men of that trade [shipbuilders], beginners as well as old practisers . . . foremen as well as master-builders . . . down to the very barge-maker and boat maker, to bring their draughts' to him and vouchsafing 'to administer occasion of discoursing and debating the same and the reasons apper-taining thereto. Not only to the great and universal encouragement of the men, but the improvement of their art to the benefit of the State.'[20] Pepys strongly believed that James's royal birth allowed him to push through his building projects with far greater success than would otherwise have been the case. 'We owe a great deal of the strength of our Navy', he wrote, 'to [the] D[uke of] Y[ork]'s getting ships to be begun and built in confidence that when they were begun they would not let them want finishing, who otherwise would never of themselves have spared money from lesser uses to begin to build And by this means ships have been built, though to our great shame and grief long in building.' The Duke also took care to gather intelligence reports on the new ship designs being commissioned by foreign powers. When a French squadron dropped anchor at the Spithead at Portsmouth, in 1672 and 1673, he went aboard the flagship, the *Superbe*, 'which was greatly commended' and made sure to have with him one of his shipwrights who could surreptitiously measure its dimensions, so that a copy 'as near as he could' might be ordered from the dockyard at Harwich on their return.[21]

However, before we accept all of Pepys's judgements at face value, we might do well to inject a note of caution and to temper our view of such a rapid and extraordinary naval expansion taking place as the sole result of the Duke's guiding vision. It is often believed that James's dismissal as Lord High Admiral in 1673 was nothing short of a disaster, which curtailed much enterprising work in the dockyards and threatened the very future of the Royal Navy itself. Pepys, who was instrumental in propagating this view and whose own fortunes were by this time inextricably linked to those of his royal master, lamented that: 'Only the return of the Duke of York to the Service . . . could set things right', as: 'Only under the protection of a Prince of the Blood would it be possible to withstand the powerful interests that were destroying all that was now left of the Navy.' He then chose to equate these malign forces with the new Navy Commissioners of 1679–84, who he characterized as wholly incompetent administrators, acting only out of a narrow political perspective and with complete disregard to that which was in the 'best' interests of the Navy. Yet, as J.D. Davies and S. Hornstein have convincingly demonstrated, this picture is very far from the truth. The Royal Navy did not experience a total collapse after the Duke's removal, with the greatest building plan to lay down thirty new ships in 1677, as part of an escalating 'arms race' with France, actually post-dating James's official retirement from the service.[22] Consequently, while he might have backed the plan in his private meetings with the King and made forcible representations to him on behalf of his old colleagues who still sat upon the Board, it can hardly be claimed with any degree of certainty that he was either the originator or the foremost promoter of the new plans. Moreover, the Admiralty Commissioners – far from being hopelessly inept – did actually manage to achieve a great deal between 1679 and 1683, in completing the construction of the balance of these vessels against a background of severe economic cutbacks, far greater in scope than anything that the Duke of York had had to experience during his own term of office.[23]

If James cannot then claim to have been the father of the modern battlefleet, he was undoubtedly determined to win renown as a great authority on maritime affairs and from the time of his arrival back in England, he began to assemble a large reference library for his own use and for the instruction of his civil servants. He assembled books on the fisheries, naval charts, maps showing the course taken by the Spanish Armada in 1588, and studiously filed his correspondence with his flag-captains. He also had new works on seafaring presented and dedicated to him, although they did not always meet with his wholehearted approval. When Moses Pitt presented him with a copy of his newly printed atlas in 1681, the Duke noticed that it was based upon an earlier work published in Amsterdam by Jan Janzoon and that it had 'the very Dutch words and Dutch arms not taken out of the maps, and [the] D[uke of] Y[ork]'s taking notice to Pitt . . . of the maps being of too small and close a letter, who answered, Yes, but they had a very fair margin'. A manuscript copy of Captain Charles Wylde's *Relation of a Voyage from England into the Streights or Meditteranean sea . . . bound for Constantinople*, interspersed with charts of the coastline and harbours and inscribed to James, does however seem to have met with greater favour and for the most part the Duke did seem to be genuinely flattered by the attention paid to him by professional navigators. He was reputed to have been a 'most mathematic' Admiral and could more than hold his own in a discussion with the Court scientists of Louis XIV, during his final exile. He was intrigued by new inventions to assist with sailing and sought to standardize the method of navigation used by his captains. We are told that the 'D[uke of] Y[ork] says that it is impossible for our masters to keep any good account of their sailing while they (as he says they do this day) use only the plain chart and not Mercator's [the first map on the projection of Gerardus Mercator, also known as Gerhard Kramer, had appeared in 1569 and was held to have superseded all previous charts] and seems to like very well of our masters in the West Country's judging their way not so much by the log as by their walking upon the deck, which by use he says [significantly] (in his own practice of walking) he finds may be very exact both as to way and time.'[24]

James similarly sought to standardize the conduct of his Officers and to regulate further the administration of the service. He issued his own set of instructions to the Navy Board, in 1662, and attempted to weld together a professional and centralized department of State which was capable, on occasion, of recognizing real ability. Thus, the young Samuel Pepys was quick to realize that although 'chance without merit' had gained him his position, only diligence and hard work would allow him to keep it.[25] Apart from the presence of Pepys, there is plenty of evidence to justify the view that the Duke was to assemble around him in a few short years a very able little team of clerks, who included such luminaries as Tom Hayter and Will Hewer, whose careers stretched right across the Restoration period and were characterized by good and sterling service to the Crown. It is the greatest of shames that these men did not leave similar written testaments to those of Pepys, for had they done so our understanding of the workings of the Restoration Navy would be very different to what it is now.

If James had demanded much of his Clerks, then he also expected his Officers to act in what he regarded to be the best interests of the service. To this end, he stressed 'the excellency of the naval instructions of France as they are printed in the Book of Ordinances [*Ordonnance de Louis XIV pour les Armees Navales et Arcenaux de Marine*]; France having improved on ours and the Dutch', and sought to issue his own set of *Fighting Instructions*, in 1665 and 1672–3, that all of his Captains would be obliged to follow.[26] The Duke's first book of orders, written aboard his flagship at the outset of his first campaign against the Dutch, was little more than a guide to conventional 'good practice' for fighting a successful fleet engagement. It relied heavily on the attempts of the Commonwealth's Generals-at-Sea to codify their procedures in 1653 and 1654, and simply repeated their findings with the addition of a handful of very minor alterations. The importance of the new work, therefore, clearly did not lie with its originality but rather in the fact that James had seen fit to have it published at all. It is likely that the earlier sets of instructions had fallen into disuse with the decline and fall of the Puritan Republic and that there was a pressing need to reaffirm their guiding principles, as to signalling within the fleet and battle-tactics, with the onset of a new war. In this light, James's actions in paraphrasing the texts of the existing standard works are no more than those of a conscientious Commander-in-Chief, eager to instil a sense of professionalism and discipline into his Officers after a period of relative decline and neglect.

His second set of instructions, issued at the beginning of another campaign seven years later, were, however, far more innovatory. They sought to draw lessons from the experiences of the Second Dutch War, and while they still incorporated the twenty-six original articles from the previous edition into the body of the text, the Duke had taken the time and trouble to append to them a number of important orders issued during the most recent battles. It is noticeable, however, that in compiling the new set of instructions, James was clearly working towards his own personal agenda. He forcibly reiterated his commitment to formal naval tactics and ignored all of the measures taken by Prince Rupert and the Duke of Albemarle during the Four Days Battle, in June 1666. This served to bring to the surface the serious differences in opinion held by Charles II's Admirals in respect to their fundamental practice of naval doctrine. Whereas Rupert and Albemarle exalted the freedom of their Captains to improvise and to adapt their tactics to the individual situation at hand during a battle, believing that simple initiative and the ability to fight hard would always carry the day, the Duke and his ally Sir William Penn firmly believed that discipline and the ability to follow a carefully constructed series of orders to the letter was the only sure key to victory. Helped on by the publication of the 1672–3 set of instructions, James's school of thought ultimately triumphed and, while it has received heavy censure from the biographers of later seamen such as Hawke and Nelson, there can be little doubt that its thorough implementation did much to ensure the success of King William III's fleets during the French wars at the close of the seventeenth century.[27]

Although James's adherence to the established 'rules' for action sometimes verged on the pedantic, it is worth noting that he was not entirely averse to new ideas. In his final set of instructions, which brought together all of his previous thoughts in a definitive form, he introduced for the first time rules governing an engagement when two fleets came into contact upon opposite tacks: establishing a system for stretching the length of the enemy's line and then bearing down upon it together. He also included a significant provision for cutting off a portion of the enemy fleet, to be destroyed at leisure, and then of 'containing' the rest which, although originating in the practice of Rupert and Albemarle, he was still to claim as his own idea. Finally, he emphasized once again the paramount duty of always keeping the line and made the offence of firing 'over any of our ships punishable by death'.[28]

It is noticeable, however, that the Duke's reforming zeal did not extend equally into all reaches of the service and stopped short at making any attempt to replace the system for distributing prize money among the flag-captains and their crews with a fairer method of payment, which would not be so open to abuse. It is not hard to see why James was so attached to this method of calculating the wages of naval personnel, as it provided him – in his capacity as Lord High Admiral – with roughly 15 per cent of all takings at sea and his brother, the King, with a further 10 per cent. It was simply too valuable a sinecure for either the debt-ridden Duke or Charles II to contemplate giving up out of hand. During a discussion in 1680, Samuel Pepys informed James and his colleague and friend, George Legge, 'that the King of France kept his commanders and lieutenants constantly in pay. Upon which [the] D[uke of] Y[ork] said that however, considering the benefits our captains have, our service is better to commanders than the French. Whereupon Mr. Legge and I jointly asserted, and convinced the Duke, that it was better for the King to give his commanders half-a-crown out of his purse than to suffer them to get six pence that way, they managing his service wholly in order to their coming at a good time to Cales [i.e. Cadiz, where the richest prizes could be seized on the journeys to and from the Americas], besides the disatisfaction raised in twenty commanders by the benefit which is hereby indulged with partiality to one. But then [the] D[uke of] Y[ork] observed most truly that this is never to be remedied till the gentry of England (who are the givers of money in Parliament) apply themselves more than they do to the understanding the business of the sea; for then they would encourage it . . . [the] D[uke of] Y[ork] and Legge both enlarge much upon the excellent discipline the French are arrived at in their navy, beyond what we can possibly have for want of a power to punish, arising from our want of wherewith to give a seaman a due reward, or even a subsistence, for the best of his performances.'[29] This said, James does not seem to have been overly concerned about corruption within the Navy Office, turning a blind eye to the sale of places and stores, and Pepys's own profiteering at the expense of the outlying garrison at Tangier.[30] He only sought to clamp down upon the most blatant abuses when they became public knowledge, and was particularly effective in evoking disciplinary measures only when his own interests were being directly threatened. His most effective prosecution for corruption in the service, which we have already alluded to, was brought against his rival the Earl of Sandwich and was probably motivated in the first instance by purely political considerations. Although there can be little doubt that Sandwich did order the goods from two Indiamen to be distributed among his own flag-officers, and that he did take a large share for himself without waiting for official permission from the Duke, his actions were by no means unique and he sought to justify them at his court martial as wholly practical measures designed to reward his men with an 'entertainment allowance' for their bravery and good service while on campaign. Moreover, it seems that it was his failure to attempt to disguise his actions, rather than the embezzlement itself, that so inflamed James, as he felt that it was his own authority that was being blatantly challenged.[31]

James did, however, take a far more principled stand over the question of religious toleration within the naval establishment. He expressed his bitter regret at not being able to keep several of his best Officers in employment under the provisions of the current system, before reaffirming his commitment to the principle of religious toleration as a means of allowing the ablest seamen to rise quickly in the service. He cited the case 'of Tobias, an Irishman, bred a lieutenant under Spragge [Sir Edward Spragge, one of the Duke's clients, who had commanded a Royalist privateer during the Interregnum]; that he, after the king's coming in, offered his service with no higher demand that that of being a lieutenant of a ship. But Sir William Coventry discouraged him, he went into Holland, where he was presently [i.e. immediately] entertained and had a command give him, and done them such service in the late wars as he expects a flag, and would have it, he being mightily valued by them, but that the Prince of Orange (to make his court to England) will not permit it, he being a Papist, though the States never mind the business of religion. Upon which account Tobias is resolved to remove his estate (which is said to be very considerable) and go abroad into the Spanish service.' In order to preserve the balance of his argument, James then raised the case of his friend, Sir William Jennings, who as a Protestant gentleman had 'offered his service to France, but they would not entertain him, though a very old bred seaman'.[32] This concern for the efficient running of the Navy, regardless of the religious prejudices of the times, would seem to fit well not only with our picture of James as a dedicated administrator, but also with his own conception of the practice of religion, as outlined earlier in Chapter 5. Having established something of the nature of the Duke's administrative style at the Navy Office, we can now focus our attention on to his wider direction of naval policy between 1660 and 1673.

III

James's career as Lord High Admiral was largely defined by the need to prosecute two major wars against the Dutch Republic. The beginnings of a resurgence of the national economy during the Interregnum, after a period of relative stagnation under the earlier Stuarts, allied to the belief that trade could be further stimulated if the Dutch were stripped of their role as middlemen in the transportation of England's trade in raw materials and colonial goods, had led to a growing sense of nationalism and an increasingly aggressive and belligerent attitude to her trading rivals, as England strove to achieve complete naval supremacy and mastery of the seas. These ideas, which sought to attach an enormous importance to the operation of the Navy, had originated in the works of such mercantalist writers as Thomas Mun and John Selden. They believed that the wealth of the world was finite, with nations enriching themselves at the expense of their neighbours and by the attempts of their governments to maximize their exports, while importing as little as was humanly possible. In this way, through the development of maritime power Europeans could come to dominate foreign enclaves and control the manner in which their produce was marketed. Having gained a monopoly of 'new' trade in this way, the home power was then obliged to fight to protect it tooth and claw from interlopers and trading rivals, for once lost this wealth would begin, slowly but surely, to tip the economic balance against them.[33]

The English Commonwealth, with little in the way of fraternal senti-ment for the Republican Dutch, had watched the States General's attempts to enforce their own monopolies with suspicion and had introduced the Navigation Acts of 1651 and 1652 as a means to counter them. The re-enactment of these Acts in 1660, 'for the increase of shipping and encouragement of the navigation of this nation', restricted colonial traffic to English ships and to largely English crews, prohibiting the importation of goods in third-party ships, or from countries that were not their primary producers, while a further Act of 1663 sought to confine the colonial export trade solely to English ports. The aim of all this weighty legislation was 'to turn the course of . . . trade rather than to raise any considerable revenue', and the Dutch were firmly singled out as the primary targets for these restrictive measures. Van Goens, a Commander in the forces of the Dutch East India Company, had grimly predicted that 'we are deadly hated by all nations . . . [and that] sooner or later war will be the arbiter', while the Duke of Albemarle had gruffly scoffed that 'What matters this or that reason? What we want is more of the trade the Dutch now have', and Pepys's friend Captain Cocke chose to phrase the equation with even blunter simplicity: 'The trade of the world is too little for us two, therefore one must go down.' From the scanty evidence at our disposal it seems that James fully endorsed these sentiments and espoused the mercantalist critique behind them, railing at the depredations wrought on his factories in Africa by De Ruyter's fleet and championing the 'War Party' at the meetings of the Privy Council held in the early 1660s. 'The differences and jealousies in point of trade', he confidently informed the King, 'did every day fall out and would every day increase between the English and the Dutch . . . [and] would unavoidably produce a war between them . . . the question only was, whether it were not better for us to begin it now, when they do not expect it, and we are better prepared for it . . . or to stay two or three years, in which the same jealousy would provoke them to be well provided, when probably we might not be ready.'[34]

Yet if James had chosen to espouse mercantilist policies at governmental meetings, then he held the *Mare Clausum*, the sovereignty of the English fleet over the oceans, to be a sacred trust. This view held that 'the Sea as well as the Land, is liable to the Laws of Propriety, and may be brought under the Jurisdiction and protection of particular Princes and States Contrary to the Assertion of those, who affirm, the sea to be free, and under the Dominion of no man'. It is significant that Selden's seminal work on the subject, which emphasized that the 'surrounding sea, [w]as an inseperable and perpetual Appendix of the British Empire' – Rome's true successor – was reprinted in 1663, with a new dedication to King Charles II and a sustained attack upon Dutch expansionism.[35] As late as December 1671, Charles II was to send George Downing to demand a written acknowledgement of the King's 'Dominion of the Seas', a guarantee that all Dutch ships would in future strike their topsails and lower their flags to any ship carrying English colours, 'of what rate or bigness soever', from the States General. Acceptance of this humiliating demand would have required whole Dutch fleets to defer to a single English ship whenever they passed on the high seas. James strongly believed in the enforcement of this policy and had Captain Crow court-martialled for failing to make a superior Dutch force dip their colours. After his victory at Lowestoft, in 1665, he was prepared to go further still, arrogantly informing a member of the French Embassy to London that if the French fleet sought to cross the Atlantic, then he would ensure that its ships dipped their flags in submission to his own. When the French courteously replied that in that case the English might be obliged to acknowledge the *fleur de lys* while in the Mediterranean, James snapped back that 'I mean to exact what is due to me, and I promise not to pay elsewhere what I am not bound to pay.' Furthermore, he stressed to Sandwich, in a set of orders dating from 1664, that 'the exchange of some shot' was always to be the correct response to any infringement of the regulations, although it was not the duty of any Captain to engage too closely or 'to be sunk upon such unequal terms', once the protest had been registered.[36]

However, beyond a passionate desire to preserve England's reputation for force of arms, it is doubtful if James thought deeply about the aims and objectives of wider naval policy. Clarendon thought that the Duke only espoused such arguments in order that 'his honour would be much exalted in the eye of the world' and believed that 'his nature inclined to the most difficult and dangerous enterprises, [and] was already weary of having so little to do, and too impatiently longed for *any* war, in which he could not but have the chief command'.[37] Similarly, when Samuel Pepys tried to draw him into a conversation analysing maritime strategy, he found that James approached the question in a revealing and remarkably superficial manner. Pepys had begun by 'asking [the] D[uke of] Y[ork] his opinion upon the point I have so much considered, what in truth it is that we have particularly to value ourselves upon before our neighbours in relation to the sea; he replied that in the first place we have really a more general valour in our common seamen than the French have, though their commanders and officers upon argument of honour and interest are as brave as men can be; that he believes we have more sea-men than the French. In which I seeming to differ from him, he referred me to the comparing the marine trade of France and ours, taking it for granted that ours much exceeded theirs, and seemed principally to infer our great stock of seamen from our being able to man our fleet and carry on our trade during the last [Third Dutch] war together. He added that he did not look upon the ships of France to be really so good sailers as ours.'[38] Therefore, it would seem that a narrow nationalism, a pre-deliction for the excitement of waging war, the need to protect his own financial interests from Dutch encroachment, and a vague understanding of Selden's theories were far more important to the forming of James's thought than any deep political or economic considerations.

The result of the Duke's uncritical acceptance of mercantilism and the rationale that demanded continual warfare as a means to boost foreign trade would seem, with hindsight, to have been a policy that was singularly misplaced. The Second and Third Dutch Wars only served to embroil England in protracted conflicts over very select, and relatively small, tracts of land at a time when the world market was expanding rapidly. At their close, despite a heavy cost in both human lives and national resources, James had managed to do little more than to fight the Dutch to a standstill. This was despite the English, at the outset, enjoying all of the natural advantages. They had ships of a higher tonnage and rate, as the shallow draughts of the Dutch rivers prevented the States General from laying down first-rate battleships, and possessed a marked geographical advantage. The British Isles lay squarely across the Dutch lines of communication with their colonies and primary trading partners, obliging their vessels to continually run the gauntlet of the English Channel, or else to undertake the long and hazardous voyage around the Scottish coast, in order to complete their outward and homeward journeys. As Thomas Corbett, a Secretary of the Admiralty during the eighteenth century, succinctly put it: 'It can never be the interest of the Dutch to quarrel with England. For they subsist only by Commerce . . . and the Trade they drive must pass through our Seas and under our very Nose.'[39] More importantly, neither side can be seen to have gained any real, or lasting, economic advantages from the fighting. Although James could delude himself that after 1674 the States General had been increasingly forced to accept the provisions of the Navigation Acts, which put their merchants on their honour not to trade with the English colonies during peacetime, the Dutch had to a large degree already accepted this. In a similar fashion, exactly how the English were supposed to have built their economy through the use of naval power was never explicitly stated either by James, or by any of his close colleagues. They did manage to add considerably to the merchant fleet by poaching Dutch flyboats, but apart from the seizure of New Amsterdam their colonial conquests were comparatively meagre and did not even begin to compete with the vast territories held right across the Americas by Spain and Portugal.

It would seem that the long-term reasons behind England's rise, and Holland's fall, as great commercial empires did not lie in the outcome of the wars themselves, but rather in the simple – though unglamorous – fact that those areas of influence already gained by English merchants were far more significant than those markets for spices that the Dutch had managed to hold on to. By 1661 the Dutch had already been driven out of Formosa, and had abandoned their attempt to secure major trading concessions from China, at the very moment when the Asian continent was just beginning to open up to the agents of the English East India Company. The presence of established English settlements in North America, for almost a century, served to give England a further advantage over her closest rivals, while the cultivation of tobacco and the desire for religious and economic freedoms encouraged emigration to the new colonies on a scale that was both unnecessary and utterly unsustainable by the Dutch. Finally, in terms of the European balance of power, James's vitriolic dislike of the States General – which he characterized as being packed with malignant and 'insolent republicans' – led him to ignore what were, perhaps, far more pressing foreign threats. It was France, rather than Holland, which represented England's most potent military and commercial rival during the 1660s and 1670s. Louis XIV's kingdom was internally strong and increasingly looked outwards in order to expand her colonial territories, threatening the English factories in India and the Americas, while encroaching upon the Spanish and Portuguese Empires, with which both England and Holland had close, if sometimes erratic, trading relations.[40] With the French Admiralty operating as a highly efficient and centralized organ of the State, and her dockyards producing a steady stream of new frigates – which in terms of their construction and handling, James could only marvel at and attempt to emulate – Colbert's brand of aggressive mercantilism, allied to a policy of territorial expansion on the continent of Europe, might have seemed a far more threatening development to an English Lord High Admiral than the Dutch Republic's defence of their *Mare Liberum* and outlying colonies. The explanation for James's apparently wrong-headed choice of priorities lies, however, not in primarily naval but in political consider- ations. Charles II had no great desire to tangle with his powerful cousin, whose military might dominated Europe and who, from May 1670 onwards, was effectively subsidizing his own throne. It is worth noting here that, after all his protests and posturing, the Duke was at last forced to buckle to sustained pressure from Louis XIV's government, and to abandon his demands for the statutory saluting of English shipping. A paper written by a no-doubt shamefaced James, in 1669, represented the largest single concession that Charles II ever made in this matter, ordering that no salutes were to be given or exacted beyond Cape Finisterre, in the Atlantic Ocean, or in the Mediterranean Sea.[41]

In this light, therefore, the Duke's pursuit of a violent confrontation with the Dutch may be viewed as a largely pointless exercise, offering comparatively little in the way of national gain and satisfying nothing more than James's own bloodlust. It may well be that, as Davies and Hornstein have argued in their recent works on the subject, the real triumph of the Restoration Navy did not lie in the 'heroic' endeavours of Samuel Pepys and his princely master, but in the evolution of a successful system for convoying merchantmen through the dangerous waters of the Mediterranean, a policy which was actually developed by the Duke's much maligned successors at the Admiralty during the 1670s and 1680s.[42] The freedom from the deprivations of the Barbary Corsairs, that was gained in this way for English shipping operating in the Levant trade, was a much more immediate and cheaper means of knocking out foreign competition than the costly full-blown wars conducted by the Lord High Admiral. We must, therefore, return an essentially negative view of James's conduct as a naval strategist, but this should not blind us to his worthwhile contributions to the smooth running of the service at a practical level. It does seem that the Duke was a genuinely popular Commander-in-Chief, enjoying the support of his flag-captains and civil servants alike, willing to take informed advice from his chosen panel of 'experts' and keen to keep abreast of new developments in naval science, the best of which he readily incorporated into mainstream practice. Though James could not be considered a unique or original innovator, he was an active and diligent administrator, always struggling to maintain the profile and efficiency of his department, and pushing hard for its continual expansion. His aptitude for work, even in the eyes of his detractors, marked him out as someone with all the virtues of a competent civil servant, while his love of detail, and desire to know the inner mechanisms of the large and complex organization over which he presided, fitted in well with his rigid view of the world and all its workings. Consequently, it is in this sphere that he perhaps made his most positive and durable contribution to the development of the Royal Navy. If this is indeed the case, then we may ask ourselves why it should be that the Duke of York should be so open to advice and suggestions at one period and in one area of his official life, while he could appear so very obstinate and narrow in almost all others. In the past this strange contradiction has been explained, as we have already seen, by the notion that he somehow degenerated both physically and mentally as he grew older. However, we shall now demonstrate that the answer to this riddle would seem to lie in the nature of command itself, and that the different roles assigned to James often required him to elicit wholly different responses and to display entirely different personal qualities, to those that had been expected of him as a young cavalry Officer. It was his almost total inability to shift from one mindset to another and his unpreparedness to continually relearn his trade, as new stresses and strains were placed upon him, that finally exposed him, late in life, to total defeat and ignominy. His own personal strengths and failings will come into all too sharp relief when we turn our attention to a critical examination of his effectiveness as a military leader.

CHAPTER EIGHT

A New Alexander, or the Second Nicias?

I

It never occurred to the Duke of York, or indeed to any of his modern partisans, that his military career could be viewed as anything but a glowing success, crowned by his two dramatic and hard-fought naval victories at Lowestoft and Sole Bay. The contrast, as we have already noted, between his unbroken string of successes, between 1652 and 1672, and his abject failures in 1688, 1690 and 1692, could not be stronger and has given rise to the thesis that he experienced a crisis of confidence or a collapse in his moral fibre between these two crucial and quite distinct periods in his life. However, upon a closer examination of the key developments in James's military career, and of his independent naval commands in particular, we can begin to see how these old stereotypes start to break down. In presenting a series of case studies, examining the Duke's conduct of war between 1660 and 1685, we shall venture the hypothesis that it was the changing nature of military command over the course of the seventeenth century, and not a mental or physical breakdown, that was the instrumental factor in defining James Stuart as a soldier.

While the Duke's record as a Staff Officer shows him to have been ideally suited to the following of orders to the letter and to have been physically capable of meeting the strenuous demands placed upon him in the pursuit of these duties, it can in no way inform our judgement as to his true worth as an independent General, with the responsibilty of thinking and acting for himself. Thus, it is to James's record at sea that we shall turn for our examples of his calibre as a Commander-in-Chief. In the first place, we shall look at the two great battles at which he commanded in person, then at his conduct during – and immediately after – the Dutch raid on the Medway in 1667, and finally at a related incident when his flagship, the *Gloucester*, ran aground with tragic results in 1682.

II

The age of sail, in the late seventeenth century, did not lend itself easily to grand fleet manoeuvres or to complicated battle tactics. Ships often acted as little more than lumbering gun platforms designed, once action had commenced, to be able to hurl the maximum weight of shot in a broadside on to the enemy's quarter-deck. Although they had begun to manoeuvre in squadrons, the absence of a comprehensive system of signalling meant that only very simple sets of instructions could be relayed from ship to ship throughout the fleet. As a result, large fleets increasingly came to be divided into three squadrons, each under the command of its own Admiral. They were identified by the colour of the pennant that they flew, which denoted both their seniority and their position in the line of battle. The Admiral of the Red acted as the senior commander and took his place in the centre of the fleet, while the Admiral of the White – next in seniority – commanded the vanguard, and the Admiral of the Blue brought up the rear. By hoisting their pennant in different positions in the rigging, often in a combination with another flag, the Admirals could send out simple orders – to make or to shorten sail, to chase to leeward or to windward, or to take up a specific position in the fleet – to a particular ship, or to the squadron as a whole. The importance of adhering to these rules for signalling cannot be under-estimated and often proved decisive in implementing a plan of attack, or in the successful pursuit of an enemy once he had broken. However, we must also remember that these same well-established conventions could at the same time work to severely restrict the scope for a senior Admiral, such as the Duke of York, to direct the actions of his Captains once battle had been joined. The chain of command could break down all too easily in the heat of the moment, as the line became fractured, ships became enveloped by smoke, and as chance shots tore down signal masts and rigging. In these circumstances, the individual initiative of the junior Captains assumed a new importance, as fighting became localized around separate ship-to-ship encounters, and as their personal bravery and willingness to engage at close quarters could do much to sway the ultimate balance between defeat and victory.[1]

Having long argued and pressed for a declaration of war against the Dutch Republic, it was only natural that the overall command of naval operations would be entrusted to James, as Lord High Admiral, once hostilities had commenced in earnest. Thus, in late May 1665, he led the fleet in scouring the East coast for Dutch shipping, in an attempt to draw out their squadrons and to force upon them a quick and decisive battle, which would settle the whole course of the war with a single trial of strength. Fog and poor communications initially hampered the Duke's progress and it was with some uncertainty as to the position, course and objectives of his foes that he and his flag-captains dropped anchor off the coast of Suffolk on 31 May. The following morning passed slowly, with James beginning to wonder if he had overplayed his hand and presented such an overpowering show of force that the Dutch had decided to decline his challenge altogether, and chosen to shelter in the safety of their own coastal waters. Such uncertainties were banished, when at one o'clock his scouts spotted the masts of the enemy ships upon the horizon. As the Dutch closed in, the English fleet cleared their decks and prepared for the coming battle. Morale among the English sailors was justifiably high, they were confident of their officers – Sandwich, Lawson and Penn had already beaten their enemy in the days of the Commonwealth – and were convinced that not only were their ships better built, but that their gun crews and ordnance thoroughly outmatched the Dutch. Confronted by the prospect of the battle that he had longed for, and pinned all of his hopes upon, James exuded confidence. 'All are eager to engage', wrote Sir William Coventry from aboard the Duke's flagship, 'especially the volunteers, whose beds, cabins, and even tables are down, so that there is scarce means to eat or sleep till the business is over.'[2]

The day of 2 June was spent with the two fleets carefully eyeing each other up, and with the English gradually closing in, from the point of their original anchorage, off the port of Lowestoft (see Map 1, p. 217). The Dutch kept to the windward all the time, gaining a very favourable position for themselves from which to sweep down upon the length of the opposing line, but in the end they held off from committing themselves and decided not to risk an early attack. In retrospect, this failure to seize a golden opportunity to destroy the English ships might be viewed as a decisive error, but the Dutch command was badly split. Jacob, Heer van Obdam, who in theory had been entrusted with the overall charge of the campaign, was in a totally invidious position. He had been given command not as the result of his own abilities, but because he was the least objectionable compromise candidate available to the States General. The provinces of Holland and Zeeland had both nominated their own men for the job: Cornelius van Tromp and Jan Evertsen respectively, but the subsequent bitter wranglings between these two Admirals, who hated each other intensely, had seriously damaged the structure and smooth running of the Dutch High Command. In an attempt to paper over these disagreements, and as a sop to divisive regional jealousies, the fleet had been split into not three, but seven squadrons. Each represented one of Holland's provinces and had, at its head, its own Admiral. This arrangement was obviously a recipe for disaster and made for a fundamental lack of unity, with each regional squadron seeking to operate separately from its fellows. If this were not bad enough, then Opdam had been issued with an extremely restrictive set of fighting instructions from the States General, which ignored the need to fight on the best terms possible and simply ordered him to seek an engagement with the English fleet at the first available opportunity.

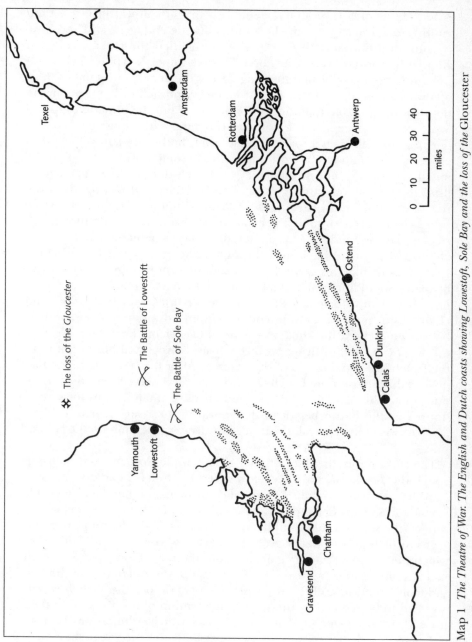

Map 1 *The Theatre of War. The English and Dutch coasts showing Lowestoft, Sole Bay and the loss of the Gloucester*

The dawn of 3 June 1665 seemed to promise nothing more than another day's inaction, but the wind suddenly changed, and the 'fine chasing' south-westerly breeze that blew in filled the Duke's sails and allowed him to go over on to the offensive. Rupert's White squadron – according to plan – formed the vanguard of the attack, with James's ships following as the central Red squadron, and Sandwich's Blue bringing up the rear. Now unable to either retire or to reclaim the initiative, Opdam was forced to accept battle and the two sides sailed past each other, opening up with their broadsides. However, both were still reluctant to close and, as Sandwich noted in his journal, 'some hurt was done' in the initial cannonade 'but not much'. The Dutch did, however, manage to draw the first blood, cutting off a straggler, the *Great Charity*, from the rest of the fleet and boarding her.[3] Prince Rupert's flagship, the *Royal James*, came under sustained fire and took a battering, but although his rigging was torn and his hull shattered in places, he immediately turned about and plunged back into the fight. The rest of the English fleet followed suit but the second pass was much more ragged, with ships breaking out of line to fall in far closer to the enemy than before. For an hour both sides slogged it out, with the air thick with ball, grape and chain shot, but neither side could gain an advantage. Then, shortly before ten o'clock, the Duke in the *Royal Charles* and Sir John Lawson in the *Royal Oak* tired of firing off inconclusive salvoes and bore right in to the Dutch line, sinking two of their vessels. After the rest of the fleet had made a third pass of the Dutch ships, Sandwich observed that 'the enemy now stood with us side by side . . . and knocked it out with us for several hours', as the battle began to degenerate into a series of individual combats with little central direction, or calls for order, imposed by either side.

The Duke was in the thick of the fighting, while close by his supporting vessel, the *Royal Oak*, was repeatedly raked by Dutch fire and was forced to withdraw. With Captain Lawson shot through the knee and mortally wounded, and his Second-in-Command lying dead, no one was left to captain the stricken ship until James was able to send Captain Jordan and a group of reinforcements over in a barge to assume command 'after which she ran in again very gallantly' into the fray.[4] Elsewhere, Sandwich had attempted to capture the enemy flagship, the *Eendracht*, but he had suddenly found himself hard pressed by a swarm of other Dutch vessels and had to be rescued by the timely intervention of the Duke, who then pressed on to engage Opdam himself. The Dutch Admiral was keen to welcome this challenge and for the next hour the two great ships were locked in a ferocious duel to the death. Repeated salvos of round and chain shot swept along both decks, decimating James's staff group and his ship's crew alike.

Indeed, the firing grew so intense that the Duke's dog fled below decks 'and sought out absolutely the very securest place in all the vessel' in which to hide, and was later discovered safely curled up in the depths of the stern.[5] Then, quite suddenly and unexpectedly, the battle between the two ships came to an end, as a stray shot from a gun on the bottom tier of the *Royal Charles* smashed into the *Eendracht's* magazine and set fire to the powder store. The explosion literally blew the Dutch flagship sky-high, scattering its timbers over a wide radius across the waters. Nearly all of her crew were lost and only five survivors were reportedly picked up from the sea, in the aftermath of the blast.

The dramatic loss of their flagship had clearly dented Dutch morale, but the decisive moment of the battle came a few short minutes later, when Sandwich, having spotted a gap that had opened up in the middle of the Dutch line, drove his ship straight through, neatly dissecting the enemy fleet. Quickly signalling, by 'putting abroad my blue flag on the mizzen peak, a sign for my squadron to follow me', Sandwich's command wrought havoc throughout the length of the Dutch line.[6] Four fireships collided with one another, setting themselves ablaze, with the result that three of them were burnt to the water line. Meanwhile, Rupert had been keeping up a steady pressure on the ships at the far end of the Dutch fleet, ensuring that they could not break off to give assistance to their stricken comrades in the centre. The explosion of the *Eendracht*, coming on top of this manoeuvre, proved to be the last straw for the remaining Dutch Captains and the fleet began to break up into its constituent parts in a frantic attempt to fight its way out to safety.

The *Groot Hollandia*, the flagship of Opdam's Second-in-Command, had been the first to fall out of line, and many of the Dutch Captains assumed that an official order had been given to take flight. This was not, however, the case. Admiral Cortenaer, unbeknown to them, had been killed in the opening stages of the battle, and it was now his junior Officers who were attempting to extricate what was left of their ship, while they still could. Unfortunately, amid all the confusion, Cortenaer's flag had been left flying and it was this which caused the misunderstanding in the Dutch ranks. Believing that they were still following their Admiral's pennant, nine Dutch ships broke away from the main fleet and were pursued out to sea by five English ships, led by Sir William Berkeley in the *Swiftsure*. Van Tromp and Evertsen both now saw their chance to assume command, each later claiming that they had been acting in the belief that the other had been killed. Van Tromp stood off with the larger part of the fleet, and attempted to run back to the safety of the Texel, while Evertson with a smaller number of ships steered a more southerly course for the harbours of Zeeland.

The action had lasted all day and had proved to be a costly affair for both sides. The English had lost no ships sunk, but had had the *Great*

Charity captured. However, casualties had been high, particularly among the Duke's closest companions. A single cannonball had scythed its way across the quarter-deck of the *Royal Charles*, striking down Lord Muskerry, who had served as one of James's Gentlemen of the Bedchamber, and decapitating Charles Berkeley, splattering the Duke, who stood beside him, with his old friend's blood and brain tissue. In the rest of the fleet losses were considerably lighter, but Rear-Admiral Sansum and Captains Kirby and Ableson had also fallen, together with the Earls of Marlborough and Portland, with a total of some 300 sailors killed and a further 500 wounded. The Dutch had lost seventeen ships sunk, and had had nine captured. Three of their Admirals – Opdam, Cortenaer and Stellingwerf – lay dead alongside many hundreds of ordinary seamen. Contemporary casualty figures may well have been exaggerated, but it seems likely that around 5,000 Dutchmen were killed, wounded, or taken prisoner, with the great majority of deaths having resulted from the explosion on the *Eendracht*.[7] From these figures alone and with the Dutch on the run, it was clear that there was a good chance of renewing the fight the next day. If they could be overhauled, then James could be confident of destroying the entire enemy fleet piecemeal and of ending the war, there and then. All that was now required to achieve such a stunning victory was an orderly and well-directed pursuit.

It took time for the Duke and his flag-captains to patch up their damaged vessels and to reimpose any sort of order upon their scattered commands; however, shortly after six o'clock in the evening the decision to mount a chase was taken and the signal was quickly relayed around the fleet. Sandwich was entrusted with leading the squadrons in their pursuit, and for a time under his energetic direction it actually looked as though the foremost English ships were gaining significant ground upon their foes. Unfortunately, after only three hours under sail, the Earl was forced to fall back astern in order to undertake vital repairs to his shattered rigging, and it fell to James, alone, to determine the course that the fleet should take overnight. At this critical moment, however, the Duke failed to issue any clear instructions to his fleet, or even to inform his immediate subordinates as to his intention to renew the fight. Exhausted by the day's events, traumatized by the death of his best friend, and confident that his victory was secure, James simply retired to his cabin and went to bed. Upon seeing this, the surviving members of his entourage naturally assumed that there was no more work to be done and that hostilities had effectively ended for the night. Consequently, the quarter-deck was practically deserted when the command for the fleet to slacken its sails was run up by Henry Brouncker, another of the Duke's Gentlemen of the Bedchamber. Such an important order would normally have had to have been checked first by Sir William Penn, who commanded the ship, but following the Duke's lead he too had gone off to bed. This left only the relatively junior figure of Captain Harman to question the wisdom of breaking off the engagement, and his furious objections were quickly overcome by the bold assertion that Brouncker's orders came directly from the Duke himself. We will probably never know why Brouncker acted as he did – contemporary gossip claimed that he had been alarmed by the scale of the killing and was acting under prior instruction from the Duchess of York, who had made him promise to ensure her husband's personal safety whenever possible – but the effect of his action was immediate.[8] Seeing the signal hoisted by their flagship, the English fleet eased off from the chase and the sailors were stood down for the night. In the darkness the Dutch made good their escape, probably unable to believe their luck, and when James emerged from his cabin the following morning, he was greeted – to his intense surprise and impotent fury – by an empty sea. By the time the rest of the fleet were notified of the misunderstanding, the Dutch ships had reached the safety of their own shores and the Duke was glumly forced to recognize that a further pursuit was, indeed, impossible. The coastal waters around Holland were simply too shallow for the deep draughts of English shipping, and the risk of running aground or of being blown ashore and marooned was just too great for James and his Captains to allow. Consequently, the chance of gaining an overwhelming victory was thrown away through a lack of care and attention to the issuing of the simplest of instructions. The Dutch fleet was allowed to refit in comparative safety, making good its losses, and the States General was able to prosecute the war for another two years – bringing it to a far more successful conclusion than might ever have been thought possible in the summer of 1665 – while James, after all of his efforts and the pursuit of a strategy that had resulted in a heavy loss of life, was forced to return home with his battered fleet and to try to put the best possible interpretation that he could upon events. The sound of rolling gunfire from the battle had shaken window frames in the town of Lowestoft and was even heard, muffled, in the courtyards of Whitehall, spreading alarm and consternation among fishermen and courtiers alike. Though a victory had been proclaimed, Chancellor Clarendon questioned its worth. Holland had not received a knock-out blow and the fighting had exposed the utter inability of the State to comprehend, or to cope, with 'a new vast charge and expense (beside the repairing the hurt ships, masts, and rigging, and fitting out new ships of war, and buying more fireships) . . . that was never foreseen or brought into any computation; which was a provision for sick and wounded men, which amounted to a great number upon all the coast, that the charge amounted in all places, notwithstanding the general charity of the people, and the convenience that many hospitals yielded, to above two thousand pounds the week for some weeks.'[9]

It is interesting to note that there was no sense of reproach or self-criticism in the Duke's own behaviour after the battle. He returned in triumph, refusing to split up his fleet or to send his ships back to their home ports to be refitted. Instead, he kept them altogether in one place, anchoring them off the Suffolk Coast for the maximum possible effect and allowing the countryfolk and day-trippers newly come out of London to marvel at his force of arms. In a moment of sheer bravado he sent his brother the tattered remnants of Opdam's banner, which had been fished out of the sea, as a bloody trophy. The news of his victory spread like wildfire, as right across England church bells rang, guns were fired in salute, and bonfires were raised in spontaneous celebration. Days of public thanksgiving were announced in London and Westminster, and a grateful Parliament voted the Duke an extra subsidy.[10] In these actions, and in the rush to publish a mountain of new ballads and broadsides to proclaim his triumph, we can see further evidence of the conscious moulding of James's image as a great General. Although it is clear that the Duke had displayed the utmost valour in engaging Opdam's flagship singlehandedly and in continuing to expose himself to danger on deck, long after those around him had fallen, there can be little doubt as to our judgment of his qualities as a Commander-in-Chief. He had issued no substantive orders, save for that to engage the enemy, and had thereafter been wholly absorbed by the reckless pursuit of physical action and the personal glory that attended it. In failing to give out explicit instructions for the pursuit of the broken enemy, and in his blind assumption that his tired and shell-shocked subordinates would be able to intuitively discern his intentions and to implement his will, he can be held to be nothing other than negligent. The protestations of his apologists that the escape of the Dutch fleet was entirely the fault of Penn and his subordinates, and the attempts of James himself to shift the blame solely upon Brouncker, simply do not stand up to close inspection.[11] On the strength of his conduct during this first independent command it would seem, therefore, that the Duke – in contrast to his meticulous record as an administrator – still thought and behaved as though he were a junior Officer, delighting in the physical danger of battle, yet having little regard for the fine details of Generalship or any perception of the wider ends of naval strategy.

These flaws in James's character will become increasingly explicit as we turn our attention to the second naval battle fought under his command: that of Sole Bay on 28 May 1672. On this occasion during the Third Dutch War, the Duke found himself leading a composite force drawn from both the French and English Navies, in a new attempt to destroy the fleets sent out by the United Provinces. The campaign started out well, with James securing for himself a strong position off the Dogger Bank. With the advantage of the tides and currents he hoped to be able to intercept all of the incoming Dutch traffic, and to effectively cut off their returning battlefleets from their home ports. Unfortunately, his own fleet – sent out prematurely and seriously underfunded, due to the insolvency of the Crown – soon found itself chronically short of both food and men, and had to abandon its blockade before its full effects could be felt. His ships sailed back through the Straits of Dover to be refitted at Sole Bay, on the Suffolk coast, and spent three days there embarking much needed men, food and ammunition.

However, this respite provided the very opportunity that De Ruyter had been waiting for, and he bore down upon the East coast in an attempt to exploit the temporary division of the allied fleet. At successive Councils of War, Sandwich had complained to James about the continual delays in the taking aboard of stores, and demanded that their ships be put out to sea again in order to rejoin the French. The Duke, however, remained sceptical and scoffed at his subordinate for being over-cautious, but on 28 May a French frigate raced in to reach them with the news that the whole of the Dutch fleet was on its tail. James had been caught napping, with his own ships strung out along the coast in no particular order and with the bulk of the French fleet far off to the South. It was only the sudden dropping of the easterly wind and the use of scores of local rowing boats, to tow the English and their allies into line, which prevented De Ruyter from immediately sailing in among them and destroying them one-by-one. No sooner had this danger been averted, and the English and French fleets had been reunited, than a second problem threatened to once again split them apart. James had sought to divide his fleet into the standard three squadrons, with himself leading twenty-five ships as the Admiral of the Red. Sandwich, as Admiral of the Blue, had charge of an equal number, while the French Admiral, Count d'Estrées, served as the Duke's Second-in-Command, and led out thirty ships in the White Squadron. However, as they sailed out to meet the Dutch and endeavoured to form line, James could only watch with horror as d'Estrées split off on a wholly divergent course to that taken by the English fleet and soon lost contact with them entirely (see Map 2, p. 224). Unphased by these peculiar manoeuvres, De Ruyter maintained contact with the French squadron, while sending Van Ghent to attack Sandwich and falling on the Duke's division himself. At this stage in the battle, the Dutch, due to the disappearance of the French, enjoyed more than a two-to-one superiority in ships and a long and bloody struggle followed, which lasted from the morning until dusk.[12]

It was a desperate battle, fought at close quarters, with the Dutch relying on their unexpected superiority in guns and fire-ships to secure

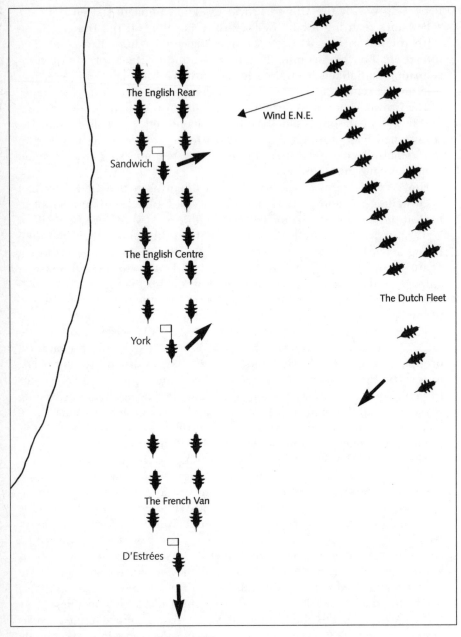

Map 2 *The Battle of Sole Bay, 7 June 1672*

them victory, against an English fleet that was still straggling out, tethered and for the moment trapped against the shore, without the advantage of the wind to help them out to sea. In the centre, De Ruyter in the *Zeven Provincien*, and Van Nes, in the *Eendracht* – a new vessel, christened after its unfortunate predecessor – led the attack on the Duke's flagship, the *Prince*, which had been exposed windward and out of line with the rest of the squadron, at the beginning of the battle. James's ship, easily distinguishable from the rest by its command pennants, was now singled out as a special prize and bore the full brunt of the attack, with other Dutch vessels converging upon the Lord High Admiral's red standard which fluttered from the foremast. The first company of the Foot Guards had been drafted aboard the *Prince* in an attempt to bolster her crew, and included several members of the Duke's household, his personal favourite John Churchill among them. Yet even their disciplined musketry could not compete with the continual strafing of the deck by Dutch cannonades and snipers. Within minutes the ship's Captain, Sir John Cox, had been killed and over 200 men – a third of the ship's total complement – had fallen dead or wounded. By eleven o'clock in the morning, with her rigging shot down and her hull holed in several places, the *Prince* was no longer tenable as a flagship and, fearing that she might be taken, James shifted his flag to the *St Michael*. However, once he had clambered aboard the *St Michael* it was very difficult for the Duke's subordinates, or for that matter the Dutch themselves, to locate him and since the lack of a strong wind had combined with the billowing smoke to obscure his standard from sight, his further communication with his Captains was now made almost impossible. The *St Michael*, too, soon came under a sustained attack and at one point almost ran aground on the shoals off Lowestoft, only being saved by the timely advice to tack and turn southwards that was given to James by his Chief Pilot. By early evening, the ship had lost its masts and, like the *Prince* before it, was taken out of action. James, once again, chose to move to safety and this time raised his flag aboard the *London*, which had been comparatively untouched by the fighting.

Perhaps the most serious confrontation of the day had developed as a small Dutch vessel had managed to swing round under the bowsprit of Sandwich's flagship, the *Royal James*, and had wedged itself there. Thus completely immobilized, the *James* fell prey to a swarm of fireships which, despite the best efforts of its gunnery Officers, repeatedly rammed its hull causing it to catch light. As the flames grew, Sandwich was eventually driven overboard where he drowned. Both sides then edged away, waiting for the stricken ship's magazine to catch fire and explode, but the blast never came as the last of the *James's* ammunition had already been expended before she sank beneath the waves. Desultory firing continued until seven o'clock in the evening, and only sunset and the fear that the French fleet might return brought the fighting to a close, as the Dutch withdrew to take stock of the situation and to reform their ranks. By nightfall, both the two English squadrons and the Dutch fleet were more or less reunited, with the rival fleets steering the same south-easterly course, but with the Dutch far ahead and with the advantage of the wind gauge. The French were still some distance away and did not rejoin the English until the next morning, by which time fog and high winds had made it impossible for James to renew the action.[13]

De Ruyter, a seasoned veteran of some thirty-two engagements, was later to describe the battle as the hardest-fought action that he had ever experienced. Although both sides were to claim a victory, it would seem that honours had been equally shared. The allied forces had lost Admiral Sandwich and 737 other seamen killed, with most of the losses occurring when the *Royal James* sank. There were also an unspecified number of English prisoners taken, including the Duke's companion Richard Talbot, while the *Westergo* burned to the waterline due to an accident that night. On the Dutch side, Admiral van Ghent had been killed along with 600 other sailors and 1,200 wounded. The *Stavoren* and the *Josua* had both been lost in the fighting, but they were of a much smaller rate than the English losses; accounting for 48 and 54 guns respectively, when set against the 100 guns of the *Royal James* and the 56 of the *Westergo*.[14] In view of the long-term objectives held by both sides, it could be argued that the Dutch had again come out of the encounter rather better than they might have expected. With a far smaller force at their disposal, they had effectively crippled both of the allied Navies for several weeks and prevented them from launching raids up and down the Dutch coast in support of the armies of Louis XIV, which had been intent on driving deep into Holland. De Ruyter had, therefore, been able to gain a much-needed respite for his country and had put an end to the offensive capability of the allied fleets for the rest of the campaigning season. All that the English and French Commanders were left with was a sense that they had been cheated out of a victory that had been theirs by right, and with their pride hurt they soon fell victim to bitter recriminations. Haddock and the Officers of the Blue Squadron reprimanded Captain Jordan for his failure to come to Sandwich's assistance in time to save him, while all of the English seamen joined together to voice a chorus of opprobrium, which identified the French as being the root cause of their woes. For his part, d'Estrées held his subordinate Du Quesne to blame, claiming that he had kept too far from the enemy guns. However, given that Officer's otherwise unblemished reputation and his later career, spent in clearing out the Barbary Corsairs and reforming the structure of the French Navy, this might not seem to have been the case.[15]

It is obvious that the splitting of the allied fleets was the decisive factor upon which the course of the battle hung. James's biographers have always sought to acquit him of any responsibility for this disastrous manoeuvre, and have consistently blamed the French for their seemingly treacherous conduct.[16] However this is not entirely the case, and James was always careful to hush up the incident as much as was possible, assuring d'Estrées that he – for one – did not in any way impugn his courage.[17] When the Dutch had first sailed into view, it is clear that d'Estrées had been leading the fleet as the Admiral of the White. He had under his command those ships which had already been designated as the vanguard squadron, and in the absence of any orders to the contrary he would have naturally expected to have led these vessels out of the Bay and into battle, with the rest of the fleet following on behind. However, just as he was beginning to execute this complicated manoeuvre, his Commander-in-Chief was struck by an idea that would radically upset the existing battle plan. James had suddenly come to the conclusion that an initial attack could be pressed home far more successfully if it came from a northerly, rather than from a southerly, direction. This may well have been the case, and the Duke's intention to change course was immediately understood by Sandwich at the rear of the line, but unfortunately d'Estrées – at the head of his squadron – had already committed himself to the action and could not possibly have seen what was happening behind him. To make matters worse, while James had thought to signal to his own Rear-Admiral, Harman, to 'lead the van of his own squadron and keep next to the Blue' – thus confirming his intention to completely reverse the agreed order of battle – he completely forgot to make any signal at all to his allies.[18] As a result, the French fleet drifted off far to the south – still obeying their last verbal command to keep close to the wind – and soon lost contact altogether, while Sandwich's Captains jostled each other for position, in an attempt to make some sense of the confusing situation in which they now found themselves. In charging after the enemy, as though he was still a young cavalryman or else a huntsman in pursuit of a fox, James had shown a total disregard for his own responsibilities as the Commander-in-Chief of a large allied fleet. He had not only forgotten the provisions of his own *Fighting Instructions*, which had forbidden rash individual actions, but had also completely failed to co-ordinate the activities of his flag-captains, in communicating clear and precise sets of orders to them at all times. As at Lowestoft, he had assumed that his subordinates would immediately understand his will and would implicitly act to obey it. His over-confidence in his own abilities and his failure to understand the problems of others, negated his personal bravery and the advantage of the superior naval forces at his disposal, denying him an outright victory in both cases, and ensuring that the engagements at Lowestoft and Sole Bay would be as indecisive as they were bloody. However, if we have demonstrated that James's record as a fleet-Commander was not so glorious as the pages of the *Life* would suggest, then his conduct at the head of the service must be further questioned when we come to consider his role during the Dutch raid on the Medway and in the loss of the *Gloucester*.[19]

III

One unexpected side-effect of James's propaganda offensive after the Battle of Lowestoft and his continual 'talking-up' of his pyrrhic victory, was that the political nation began to assume that the Dutch naval threat had been effectively neutralized, and that their government – the States General – would therefore rush to conclude a peace treaty as soon as was humanly possible. England's triumphant emergence from the war was thought to be have been already guaranteed and a steady stream of sanguine intelligence reports, issued under the orders of the Earl of Arlington, only served to further underline this point. Consequently, before 1666 was out, the Privy Council sat down to discuss the possibility of laying up the battlefleet during the next summer. James was resolutely against this plan, and fought as hard as he possibly could to stop the implementation of its provisions. To this end, he made common cause with the Archbishop of Canterbury, and even managed to bury his past differences with Prince Rupert and the Duke of Albemarle, in order to present a united front to the King. Unfortunately the rest of the Privy Council were war-weary, and had been swayed by the persuasive arguments put forward by Sir William Coventry as to the enormous costs of fitting out a new fleet and the advantages inherent in laying up the old one. Although Coventry was the Duke's own servant, he had become tired of making fruitless demands on the Treasury for money that was simply not there. He knew that, with the State verging on bankruptcy and with the Navy's debts totalling over a million pounds, central government could not realistically hope to finance such a costly and protracted war. With no one else on the Privy Council prepared to present a similarly detailed opposing plan – showing how the £526,000, that he had estimated it would cost just to send out the fleet again, might be raised – Coventry's scheme was duly passed before those assembled and approved by the King.[20]

While James had reason to feel betrayed, and began to withdraw his favour from his old servant – leading to Coventry's eventual dismissal from the Navy Office – Charles II was delighted with the measure, which sought to curtail the expenditure of the Crown without infringing upon any of his own pleasures. As a result, in March 1667, it was decided that the fleet should be effectively mothballed, laid up 'in ordinary' in the

Royal Dockyards, rather than being deployed again. At the same time, no doubt as a sop to James and his fellow Admirals, cosmetic measures were also announced in order to preserve the illusion that the war was still going to be prosecuted with vigour, until the very end. The coastal defences were to be strengthened in case of a surprise attack and a handful of flying squadrons, drawn from ports in the North and West, were to resume patrolling the trade routes and harrying the remaining Dutch convoys.[21]

James was all too well aware that the Royal Dockyards were vulnerable to attack and that their defences, ranged along the banks of the Thames and Medway, were either non-existent or in a sorry state of disrepair. He had already issued a series of instructions aimed at remedying the situation, and had ordered that a new twelve-gun battery was to be built at Sheerness Point, that a boom was to be laid across the mouth of the estuary closing the Medway off to any possible Dutch attack, and that those ships stationed higher up the river were to be rearmed and issued with grapnels. However, no measures were taken to supervise either the quality of the work or the pace at which it progressed and so, when six months later the Dutch did sail up the Medway, the boom was found to be too weak to hold and had not been properly fastened to the shore, while the battery was still only half-finished and the handful of guns that it did manage to bring to bear on De Ruyter's ships were quickly silenced.

During the time that the Duke was supposedly refortifying the approaches, Cornelius De Witt had been carefully amassing a series of detailed intelligence reports from Ghijsen, his spy, plotting the positions of the English defences and charting the draught of the Medway at Chatham.[22] The decision of Charles II not to send out his fleet again, therefore, came as an unexpected piece of good news and made a pre-emptive strike against the dockyards possible. A force of over 70 warships, 25 fireships, and 3–4,000 men was assembled under De Ruyter and was given strict instructions to attack and seize any English ships found in the Thames and Medway. However, it was the dockyard at Chatham which was designated as the primary target of the raid, and landing parties were allocated to seize nearby installations and to burn stores and equipment.

On arriving off the English coast, De Ruyter's scouts reported that although there seemed to be a large number of merchantmen in the Thames, they were anchored far up the river and would be difficult to attack. Consequently, the Dutch reluctantly decided to abandon any attempt on them and to concentrate the force of their attack solely upon the traffic in the lower reaches of the river and upon the Royal Dockyards situated along the banks of its tributary, the Medway (see Map 3, p. 231). News of the approach of the Dutch fleet was not slow to reach the English government, but in spite of the alarm which was spreading rapidly through London and the Home Counties, the King and his ministers seemed reluctant to act. Convinced that the incursion was little more than a feint, designed to improve their enemy's bargaining position at the peace talks, and confident that they had already won the diplomatic battle at Breda, they undertook no decisive action. Charles II did, at the last minute, order two of his best Generals, Prince Rupert and the Duke of Albemarle, to take charge of the defence of the arsenals at Woolwich and Chatham, respectively, but by this time it was simply a case of too little, too late.[23] Panic had already gripped the English fleet, with ships abandoned or scuttled as their skeleton crews rushed to desert, while at the mouth of the Medway, the garrison of Sheerness Fort, who had not been paid for weeks, turned tail and fled before the Dutch landing parties. The almost total absence of steady, professional troops who could be used to try to reimpose some semblance of order upon the rapidly deteriorating situation, and to limit the scale of destruction wrought by enemy action, now became the single biggest problem to confront the remaining English Officers. This failure to ensure the presence of an adequate reserve was due in part to the Duke's own prior dispositions. James seems to have believed that if a Dutch raid did materialize, then it would be directed against the port of Harwich, rather than against the Royal Dockyards which lined the Medway and Thames.[24] As a result, he had already drafted several companies of his own Maritime Regiment into that town and had reinforced the little fort at Landguard, which protected its harbour from a neighbouring headland. While these men, under Captain Nathaniel Darell and the Duke's friends Colonel George Legge and Sir Charles Littleton, were to prove invaluable in thwarting another Dutch raid a month later, their absence from the mouth of the Thames severely hampered the defence of the river. In a desperate attempt to get more men under arms, in case of a full-blown invasion, the King was forced to send the Earl of Oxford down to Essex 'to raise the country there', while Lord Berkeley of Stratton was hurriedly appointed Lieutenant-General of the militia in Suffolk, Cambridge and the Isle of Ely. He left the Court accompanied by 'a great many young hectors', the younger sons of the nobility and gentry, who had attached themselves to his train in the high hopes of beating back a Dutch Army. Unfortunately, once outside the City limits, Lord Berkeley quickly discovered that he could only raise a handful of militiamen, who could do little more than mount isolated patrols along the coastline, while his gentlemen volunteers served 'but to little purpose', managing only 'to debauch the country women thereabouts'.[25]

Ships were seized and promptly sunk at Woolwich and Blackwall in an attempt to hinder the progress of the Dutch fleet any further up the Thames, but it soon transpired that they had been the wrong vessels.

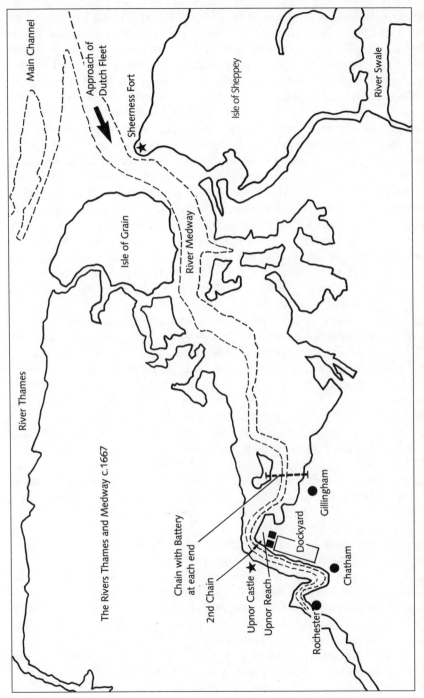

Map 3 *The Dutch raid upon the Rivers Thames and Medway, 1667*

Main Channel

Approach of
Dutch Fleet

Sheerness Fort

River Thames

Isle of Grain

River Medway

Isle of Sheppey

River Swale

The Rivers Thames and Medway c.1667

Chain with Battery
at each end

2nd Chain

Upnor Castle

Upnor Reach

Dockyard

Gillingham

Chatham

Rochester

Rather than the empty transports and hulks that littered the quaysides, they had chosen to scuttle naval supply boats which contained much-needed provisions and munitions. It was left to the guns sited at Upnor Castle to mount a far more vigorous defence, throwing a wall of shot against the Dutch vessels and finally deterring them from pressing any further upriver. However, while the movements of the Dutch fleet remained obvious to all during these crucial days and hours, those of James himself are far harder to trace, especially as he neglected to make any reference to them in the pages of his own memoirs.[26] The Earl of Castlemaine, for one, had no idea of James's whereabouts at the height of the fighting and, when he heard the news of the capture of the *Royal Charles*, feared that the Duke had been taken along with his one-time flagship.[27] What is certain is that, although James issued a number of instructions throughout the week to his Commanders, advising them as to the best disposition of their ships, he was not where the fighting was at it thickest and exercised little in the way of executive control, preferring for the most part to rely upon the individual initiatives of Rupert and Albemarle to see to the defence of the dockyards as best they could. His only direct contribution to the outcome of the crisis stemmed from the steadying influence of his own physical presence at Whitehall, at a time when the wholesale evacuation of the capital was being seriously suggested.

Despite the attempts of generations of British naval historians to downplay the significance of the action and of James himself, who chose to almost entirely ignore the event in his personal writings, the raid on the Medway constituted the most humiliating defeat ever inflicted upon the English Navy. At the end of the action, the Dutch fleet was able to sail majestically out of the mouth of the Thames and into the Channel, towing their prizes behind them, while for days to come the floodtide would wash up the remains of sheep carcasses, butchered on the Isle of Sheppy in order to feed their raiding soldiers. John Evelyn thought that the affair was 'A dreadful spectacle as ever Englishmen saw and a dishonour never to be wiped off!'[28] Suddenly, any notion of the Dutch making major concessions at the talks at Breda was abandoned, and Charles II was forced to conclude a swift peace treaty which would preserve the status quo. The English were to retain control of New York, but the Dutch were to be confirmed in their conquest of Surinam. Pett, as Navy Commissioner, was made the official scapegoat for the disaster and stripped of his offices. Arlington commented dryly that in the world of *realpolitik* 'If he [Pett] deserved hanging, as most thinke he does, and have it, much of the staine will be wip'd off of the Government which lyes heavily upon it.'[29] In the event, the unfortunate civil servant was placed under arrest and threatened with impeachment, but in the end was allowed to retire quietly into private life. James himself was quick to blame the disloyalty of the dockyard workers for much of the damage inflicted by the Dutch, even though a great deal of the blame and disgrace for the defeat must rest squarely upon his own shoulders. He was the Lord High Admiral, the Chief Officer of the Navy, whose administration had presided over the debacle. He had not properly supervised the rebuilding of Sheerness Fort and had failed to see that it was adequately garrisoned 'to which neglect' Prince Rupert had reported to the Commons, 'we may justly ascribe the burning of the ships at Chatham and the dishonour that attended it'.[30] Similarly, although he was to claim that he had ordered Pett to convey all of the larger men-of-war higher up the Thames, he once again neglected to check that his orders had been carried out. When the Dutch broke through the boom at Gillingham, both he and his civil servants seemed unable to act, paralysed by uncertainty, and spent several days wandering in and out of the Admiralty buildings asking each other what should be done. Moreover, as we witnessed earlier in the case of Sir Thomas Povey, there was an unhealthy climate of denial at the heart of the Duke's service. James liked to be told what he wanted to hear and surrounded himself with people who were only too happy to oblige him. Coventry was in continual fear for his own position, and was quoted as saying that he would no longer speak his mind in front of the Princes in case it displeased them. He and Pepys, the Duke's closest and most important servants in the Navy Office, were the very officials who had chosen to ignore the dire warnings predicting a surprise attack simply because they had emanated from their political rivals, the Duke of Albemarle and Sir Robert Holmes.[31] Significantly, James himself never showed the slightest remorse for his own part in the disaster and never once questioned his actions, or considered relinquishing his position as Lord High Admiral. This inability to learn from past mistakes, or to feel any guilt for them, is admirably demonstrated by his behaviour during, and immediately after, the sinking of the *Gloucester* in 1682.

The Duke's voyage back to Scotland, in May 1682, was intended to be a stately progress which would confirm a new political order upon the nation and mark the resurgence of James's own fortunes.[32] To this end, the convoy of naval frigates that departed from Erith was swelled by a flotilla of private yachts, containing the cream of Scotland's new governing elite: the Marquis of Montrose, the Earls of Roxburgh and Perth, Lord Hopetoun and the Lord Provost of Edinburgh. There was a holiday atmosphere on board the Duke's flagship, the *Gloucester*, as he lined the decks with his own musicians and chose to announce the unfurling of the Royal Standard with the sound of a full broadside. However, within less than forty-eight hours, this most routine of journeys was to turn into an unmitigated disaster which has divided opinion, ever since, over James's fitness to command.

The Duke had gathered a very experienced crew about him for the short voyage up the coast. The *Gloucester's* Captain was Sir John Berry, a veteran seaman who had commanded ships for the last seventeen years without a single mishap; her Master was Benjamin Holmes who had distinguished himself in that capacity for almost a decade and who had had charge of the *Royal William*, the largest and most prestigious first-rate of her day; while her pilot was James Aire, another veteran of the Dutch wars who had risen largely through his own merits and was acknowledged to be the most skilled navigator available to guide them through the waters north of the Thames. Sailing close by, Christopher Gunman, 'a sober, frugal, cheerful and temperate man', commanded the yacht the *Mary* as it cut its path through the waves.[33] Unfortunately, from the very outset things did not go as planned. On the first evening at sea the wind shifted to the north and the weather changed for the worse. The squadron became fogbound as night fell, and all the next day battled a fresh easterly gale off the East Anglian coast. Then as night fell on the second day, the lights of the town of Lowestoft became visible and the ships stood off out to sea in order to avoid the Yarmouth Sands. It was then that a furious argument took place aboard the Duke's flagship about the best course of action to take in order to safely navigate the treacherous reaches. Although the area was well charted and should have posed no great danger for such professional seamen, it still required care and thought to find the right channel through the sandbanks, as Lord Sandwich's fleet had discovered to its cost several years before.[34]

It seems likely, on the evidence given by Sir John Berry to Lord Hyde, that the Duke – acting upon the advice of Captain Gunman and Captain Sanderson – had decided to take the navigation of the ship out of the hands of the pilot on the evening of the 5 May. Aire was understandably annoyed at having his judgement brought into question so publicly, at the subsequent meeting of the Duke's staff, and thereafter became sulky and unco-operative. With James in full command, the *Gloucester* was then steered away from the coastal waters which Aire knew well, and out towards the open sea, of which he had little knowledge. Unwilling to lose his position and afraid of further angering his royal master, Aire did not, however, resign his warrant on the spot but simply returned to his duties about the ship. It was at this point that he was forced into venturing an opinion upon a crucial subject of which he had little or no knowledge. Benjamin Holmes, the Master, wanted to stand south-east till after midnight in an attempt to clear the sands, but at 8 o'clock in the evening Aire was asked to give his own view and suggested that they hold a northerly course in order to make the passage along a route that he knew. After further discussion, it was James himself who two hours later made the decision to take the disastrous middle course through the sandbanks. Having seen to it that the course was altered, the Duke then promptly turned in for the night. Taking their cue from his actions, Aire and the other Officers – including the Captains of the yachts sailing on ahead of the convoy – followed suit, accompanied by the majority of the members of the Duke's large entourage. Pepys was later to claim that within an hour and a half, only one of the Captains, Wyborne of the *Happy Return*, was still awake and up on deck.[35]

Early in the morning of 6 May 1682, the *Gloucester* ran aground on a sandbank and, propelled by a strong easterly breeze, smashed against it again and again, taking a hard pounding before the rudder and a shard of the planking were torn off by the jarring of the motion. 'In a moment', we are told by Captain Berry, the hold was filled with up to 8 ft of water. Attempts at pumping were soon abandoned and, rudderless and waterlogged, the *Gloucester* finally slipped off into deeper water and began slowly to sink. Bishop Burnet in his later writings was to paint a very graphic picture of the ensuing chaos, as every man fought for his own survival and as James, gripped by terror, was rendered insensible. It was alleged that he thought only of saving himself, his dogs and his priests, but this would seem to be far from the truth and a view that was coloured by Anglican bigotry, as no eye-witness account or inventory records the presence of Catholic clergy aboard.[36] Rather, it would seem that James when confronted by disaster simply obeyed the conventions of the times, staying aboard the stricken vessel and directing affairs until all hope of saving her was lost. He delayed having his barge hoisted until almost the last moment and even then, according to Dartmouth's son, only left reluctantly 'out of the large window of the cabin where his little boat was ordered quietly to attend him lest the passengers and seamen should have thronged so in upon him as to overset his boat'. After holding off the press of men at sword point, John Churchill accompanied the Duke, the Earl of Winton and Sir David Falconer into the boat, while a handful of desperate sailors and some of James's servants attempted to fling themselves into it, after them. James tried to encourage the dithering Marquis of Montrose to jump to safety, but he fell short of his target and had to be hauled in by the Duke's bargemen.[37]

The Duke's escape was the signal for general panic: 'The government of the ship being lost and everyone crying for help . . .', and if dawn had not already been breaking on the horizon then the whole of the ship's company would have surely been lost. As it was, the little yachts scuttled to and fro in an attempt to pick up survivors until the waters reached more than 3 ft above the gundeck. Sir Charles Scarborough was picked up from the waters, half dead from the cold, after having fought for the possession of a plank with the Duke's dog 'Mumper', who had evidently not been rushed to safety as Bishop Burnet had suggested. Colonel Legge and Sir John Berry, who was reported to have been the last man of quality to leave the sinking ship, were both saved but more than 130 sailors were drowned, together with many of the Duke's servants, including Hollis, his equerry. Great care had been taken to preserve the lives of the noblemen on board, but the disaster had overtaken the ship so suddenly that some lives were lost even among their number. The Earl of Roxburgh, Lord O'Brien, Lord Hopetoun, Sir Joseph Douglas and James Hyde, the Duke's young brother-in-law, were all drowned after being forgotten amid the 'general disorder' and confusion.[38]

The loss of any royal ship, whether by accident or in action, demanded a court martial of those responsible, and Pepys, who had witnessed the disaster unfold from a nearby yacht, wrote a stinging attack on Aire demanding that he should be hanged like a common criminal in the tollbooth at Edinburgh. More sinister rumours circulated as to the cause of the shipwreck, and a Londoner by the name of Mr Ridley wrote to a friend in the country that 'I must inform you that the pilot is a known Republican, but his Royal Highness having a particular knowledge of his ability trusted him . . . but it is not only suspicion but evident he designed his ruin with the whole ship, having made provision for his own escape.'[39] Aire was brought to trial on 6 June 1682 and, although no records of the proceedings of the court martial have survived, it seems that he was convicted of negligence and served a short term of imprisonment in order to appease an outraged public opinion. He was not, however, arraigned on the charge of high treason and no allegations were ever brought against him for deliberately seeking to wreck the *Gloucester*. A subsequent court martial also found against Captain Gunman for neglecting his duty and failing to sound a warning shot when the frigate had first struck the sands. Yet the Duke stuck rigidly by his friend, and even allowed him to take command of one of his ships on a later journey back down to London.[40] The remits of both enquiries did not extend as far as an examination of James's own culpability in the loss, and for once he appears to have been remarkably reticent about attributing blame to anyone other than the unfortunate Aire. His own writings recorded only that he had been touched by the loyalty of his crew, who had raised one last great cheer as they saw him carried to safety, while the *Gloucester* sank beneath the waves. This particular insight into the tragedy provides us with another clear example of James's overriding self-obsession. He was more concerned with professions of loyalty than with the human loss, and was moved only by the thought that the sailors' last concerns were for him, never considering for a moment that the loss of life had been wholly avoidable or that he might in some way have been responsible for it. It was with this particular interpretation of events, seen solely from James's point of view, that the Duke's image-makers soon got to work, producing a series of propaganda materials which celebrated his miraculous delivery in painting, print and die-cast metal (see Plate 11).[41]

Yet James cannot be so easily exonerated from blame. Although he was familiar with the waters around the Yarmouth Sands from his earlier naval battles, which had taken place only a few miles away, he consistently underestimated the dangers that they posed. He assumed and then delegated command of his vessel almost at will, and then finally retired to bed at an inopportune moment, just as he had done years before at the Battle of Lowestoft. It would seem, therefore, that at all levels of his naval career the Duke had shown himself to be unequal to the tasks at hand. Over the seventeen-year period that we have charted, he repeated the same sort of fundamental mistakes time and again. The pattern that emerges is not one of a tragic decline into premature old age, but of a consistent failure to take responsibility for his actions, and a willingness to hide behind his privileged position and to scapegoat others when things went badly wrong. While his personal bravery and ability to act effectively under close supervision cannot be doubted, his talents lay as a capable subordinate in charge of relatively modest forces, rather than as a Commander-in-Chief entrusted with both planning and executing a complicated campaign. If we have sought to remove the thesis of James's degeneration from the balance sheet, then his failures as a military leader can be satisfactorily explained through more conventional means. In his ground-breaking study of military incompetence, N.F. Dixon defined those characteristics which he felt to be potentially disastrous for any senior office. His careful description of the authoritarian, or 'con-vergent', General, who is unimaginative, rigid, destructive and overly obsessed with the idea of strength and 'toughness', corresponds closely to what we already know of the Duke of York. Thus, his failures were not the product of illness or outside agencies, but resulted primarily from his unsuitability for high command and his personal, and intellectual, inadequacies.[42] Although his apologists might have continued to champion him as a second Alexander, in the light of his wasted and unspectacular victories, his humiliating defeat on the Medway and his unforgivable casting away of the *Gloucester*, it is perhaps more fitting to think of James as a second Nicias – impotently chafing before the gates of Syracuse.

CHAPTER NINE

Merchants and Monopolies

I

If James Stuart was a soldier and a statesman, then he was also a very considerable shareholder in the new joint-stock companies that proliferated in the City of London throughout the Restoration period. It would seem that he was interested in business from the very first, assiduously adding to his portfolio at every opportunity, from the time of his brother's return to England right up to – and beyond – his own accession to the throne in 1685. His involvement with trade appeared to be deep and all-embracing, as his investments spanned the globe: from the East Indies to the shores of Africa and from the Americas to the Northern Fisheries. He sat as Governor on the boards of three major trading companies – the Royal Fishery Company, the Royal African Company and the Hudson's Bay Company – directing their business and overseeing their development from his own suite of offices in Whitehall. On a more personal level, the Duke always claimed that he was a great patron of trade, attributing to himself the most high-minded of motives for his participation in such potentially hazardous overseas ventures. He argued that he acted only out of a desire to enrich the English people, investing his money wisely in order to stimulate the national economy, and congratulated himself on his own particular insight into the link between wealth creation and sea-power.[1] These arguments were advanced so persistently, and so persuasively, that some later historians even began to think that his involvement in commerce was part of a greater scheme, and credited him as being the father of the British Empire: a visionary imperialist and man of business who understood the fledgling world of commerce and promoted it at every opportunity as an expression of his own nationalism.[2]

However, over the course of this chapter we shall demonstrate that this model is very far from being the truth, and that James's interest in trade was not as sustained, evenly applied, or as homogeneous as has previously been thought. Moreover, given the changing attitudes of historians – and of society at large – towards the exploitation of indigenous peoples, raw materials and the natural environment, the shadow cast by the activities of this Prince can be viewed in a much more malign and revealing light than was once the case. The Duke's motivations for investing in business, his style and manner of work, and his long-term objectives in the cultivation of strong links with the City's mercantile community, will be primarily explored through a detailed examination of the formation and growth of the Royal African Company, under his patronage. No other commercial body came to be so closely associated with the political fortunes of its governor during our period, as for more than twenty years James was to preside, though with varying degrees of success, over every aspect of its development and ultimate expansion. His enduring presence served to guarantee the maintenance of its monopoly of trade with the West Coast of Africa, and when he finally fell from power in the winter of 1688 the Company was dealt a terrible blow from which it was never fully able to recover.[3]

By the mid-seventeenth century, all of the European colonial powers had come to hold the West Coast of Africa in the very highest esteem. Stories of the fabulous wealth to be had there had become common-place, and when Prince Rupert returned to Whitehall in 1660 he found a ready audience among a new generation of courtiers for tales of his adventures along the Gambia River. His battered fleet had sought refuge there in 1652 after outrunning a Commonwealth squadron and, while he was conducting repairs, word was brought to him by the local inhabitants of rich goldmines located close by. He already knew that the tribesmen regularly brought down supplies of gold from the interior in order to trade with the handful of Dutch merchants stationed along the coast, and came to believe that the source of this supply lay close to the path of the river.[4] Although he had no time to test his theory, he remained keen to mount a fresh exploratory mission to the region at the first available opportunity. The return of the monarchy made such a scheme possible, and he quickly began to solicit backers for a new voyage, finding in the Duke of York an early and enthusiastic convert. A plan was formulated with a view to prospecting for gold along the banks of the Gambia, and for sinking deep shafts in order to mine the ore once it had been discovered. Starting capital was raised from a galaxy of wealthy sponsors, and the initial projections seemed very promising indeed when Colonel Vermuyden returned from his reconnaissance of the area with news of the discovery of a 'vast Proportion of Gold'.[5]

However, from the very beginning, doubts were raised in some quarters about the viability of the project. The Earl of Sandwich, who knew something about the geography of Africa from his own voyages, did not share the optimism of Rupert and James and confided darkly to his cousin that he did not like the scheme at all. Nevertheless, money continued to roll in to fund a further expedition in September 1662 and for James, who was already beginning to find difficulties in living within his income, the chance of claiming a stake in the riches of Africa was just too good an offer to be passed up. Despite the generous funds made available to him by

Parliament, cash was still a difficult thing to come by – as his account books readily testify – and the opportunity of securing a regular and independent source of income must have appeared extremely attractive to him.[6] He was clearly not the only leading courtier to think in this way, as a form of 'gold fever' seemed to grip the Palace of Whitehall. Indeed, the single most significant fact about the list of the early subscribers to the Company of Royal Adventurers Trading Into Africa was the importance of their stations at Court: more than half of the shareholders were either peers or members of the royal family. They ranged in status from Stuart Princesses such as Henrietta of Orléans and Mary of Orange, to old Royalists such as Lord Craven and Lord Berkeley of Stratton, and to an aggressive new breed of young courtiers eager to secure their place in the world; such as Henry Jermyn and George Villiers, the Duke of Buckingham. However, as yet this select band included precious few representatives from among the mercantile classes; the Company of 'Royal' Adventurers Trading into Africa intended to remain precisely that.[7]

James was not slow to stamp his own authority upon the young company, which clearly interested him in a way that no other trading venture did. In marked contrast to the Hudson's Bay Company, which he was quite happy to allow to develop under the auspices of Prince Rupert, he moved quickly to eclipse his cousin's influence at the heart of the Royal Adventurers. The Duke's name was used liberally to advertise the benefits of investing in African stock, and by the autumn of 1662 he had already consolidated his position as the Company's largest single shareholder. He pledged an investment of some £3,600, which can be set against £800 each from Rupert, the King and the Duke of Buckingham, and for once he seems to have promptly paid out the money that he owed.[8] He regularly attended the weekly meetings of the Courts of Assistants and made sure that they were held in his own apartments at Whitehall. In this atmosphere, it is no surprise that the conduct of business began to take on the aspect of a social gathering at a 'gentle-man's club', as a large number of James's friends and clients took out share portfolios, and that by the following year the Company had come to be considered as being 'under the special management of the Duke of York'. His appointment as Governor, in July 1664, offered the City merchants a powerful friend at Court, who had the ear of the King at all times, and held the vitally important position of Lord High Admiral. It was widely recognized that if English traders were ever to seize the African trade for themseves, and then hold on to it for any length of time, they needed first to control the sea lanes. This knowledge was decisive in guaranteeing the Duke's election to office, and it is noticeable that one of his most significant actions as Governor was to release Royal Navy ships for an expedition to the Continent.[9]

James had secured for himself what he believed to be a lucrative prize, but already the assumptions on which the Company had been founded were being called into question and the Duke and his advisers needed to find fresh sources of revenue if they were not to experience an almost immediate, and humiliating, collapse in their investment. The Company had outlined its original objectives in its first Charter, granted in December 1660, and had announced that it aimed towards 'the setting forward and furthering of the trade intended in the parts aforesaid [which were stipulated as redwood, hides and elephants' teeth] and the encouragement of the undertakers in discovering the golden mines and setting of plantations there'. In return, King Charles II was to 'have, take and receive two third parts of all the gold mines which shall be seized, possessed and wrought . . . paying and bearing two third parts of all the charges incident to the working and transporting of the said gold', while the Company was to take the other third of the profits and to bear the remainder of the expenses itself.[10] So confident was Charles II of securing new gold reserves in this way that he declared that all of the gold imported by the Company from Africa should be minted into coins bearing an elephant on one side, clearly distinguishing them from all previous issues of high value. These 'guineas' were intended to raise the profile of the Royal Adventurers, and to have borne witness to the Company's ever-increasing wealth and prestige.

Unfortunately, against all expectations the promised gold was not forthcoming, and the Duke's agents were henceforth obliged to scour the coast in a largely futile search for deposits of the precious metal. The Governor of Cacheo observed that the Africans themselves traded chiefly in ivory, wax and animal hides, while Captain Thurloe thought that a 'good store [of these commodities] may be had and at cheape rates' along the banks of the Rio Grande, although he added rather ominously, that for his own part, he had never traded directly with these remote regions. This lack of any sort of concrete intelligence about the interior, and the precise location of such highly prized raw materials, was to seriously hamper all of James's commercial ventures on the continent of Africa. The result was that, while small amounts of copper were eventually obtained, gold in significant quantities was never extracted and the secret whereabouts of the existing mines, deep in the hinterland, was kept a closely guarded secret by the indigenous peoples who worked them.[11] As a consequence, the Company's own much-touted mining project was never seriously pursued, and was quietly dropped after the excitement of the early 1660s had died down. After this disappointment, the Company's agents began to trade, instead, for small deposits of precious metals brought in by African merchants from Bambuk and Bure, or to conscript local villagers to pan the river estuaries along the length of the Gold Coast for trace elements. There is some evidence of silks and other precious items being taken out as gifts for important chieftains and kings in the expectation of fabulous returns in the way of gold and ivories, but these pipe-dreams were destined to go largely unfulfilled. When some years later an inventory was taken at Jamaica of the goods left on board the *Martha*, a ship that had just arrived from the English factories in Africa, the Duke's agents sadly recorded that 'some of the riches of the outward cargo' still remained untouched, below decks. Try as they might, there had simply been no raw materials worth trading these items for.[12] In order to recoup their losses, some English merchants bought camwood, a hard timber, which could be easily cut and then processed in the manufacture of red dye. Others were able to assemble large one-off cargoes of ivory, culled from the dwindling numbers of elephants left alive on Sherbro Island, but most turned to the only other traffic that remained available to them: slaves.

In the early documents issued by the Royal Adventurers no mention had been made of the slave trade. However, as the prospect of exploiting the vast natural resources of an African 'El Dorado' had faded away to nothing, the opportunities afforded by the seizure of the existing networks for the supply of human cargoes – which up until that time had been the preserve of Arab traders, together with the Spanish, Portuguese and the Dutch – became ever more attractive. Although the Duke of York was not solely responsible for this shift away from trade goods and into slaves, the Company's African agents had already begun to effect this gradual change in all of their day-to-day transactions along the coast and he was undoubtedly a prime mover in this transition. His appointment as Governor coincided with his award by Charles II of a grant for the personal and exclusive rights for the trading of slaves along the entire West Coast of Africa, from Morocco right down to the Cape of Good Hope, and with the issuing of a second Charter to the Company of Royal Adventurers which now made explicit reference to the desirability of procuring slaves from the lands under their control.[13] Thereafter, the Duke's personal fortune became increasingly tied to the success or failure of the slave trade, and he did everything in his power to foster its growth in his own colonial fiefdoms. Consequently, while his claims to be the founder of the British Empire can be seen to be built on decidedly shaky ground, there is solid reason to credit him with the formal establishment of the British slave trade.

At the accession of Charles II few English merchantmen trafficked in slaves, and only a handful of Black Africans were transported to the colonies in the West Indies. Even then, the overwhelming majority of the trade was conducted by the Dutch West India Company. However, the imposition of the Navigation Act of 1660 served to restrict the planters' freedom of trade and to lessen the hold of the Dutch on their traditional market, effectively seeking to make all commerce between the West Indies and the West Coast of Africa flow through the hands of the Royal Adventurers. At the same time, the rapid expansion in the growing of sugar cane and indigo had opened up enormous opportunities for the plantation owners, but the supply of labour provided by indentured servants was never enough to meet their needs. Furthermore, they remained extremely wary of shipping over English servants, who at the end of their seven years' service would go free and might attempt to involve themselves in the politics of the islands. The importation of large numbers of Africans appeared to offer the perfect solution to this thorny problem, providing the planters with cheap and utterly disenfranchised workers, while allowing the Company access to the sugar and other plantation products which they could then carry back to England on the return leg of their journey. As a slightly later pamphlet sought to point out: 'By the Negro Trade the Company yearly at very reasonable rates, furnish with vast Numbers of servants all his Majesties American plantations . . . by which all the Plantations do flourish more than formerly. A great increase is made to his Majesties Revenue, and to the wealth of this Nation. So that the riches of that part of the world, (being the result and product of Industry and labour) is in good measure owing to the . . . Company. Besides that, it hinders the exhausting this Nation of its natural born subjects.'[14] Thus, from the mid-1660s onwards, the Company's agents and those of its successor, the Royal African Company, who were to all intents and purposes the self-same individuals, began to collect slaves from places such as Sekondi and Kormantse and to make dramatic inroads into the western half of the Gold Coast, as the demand for labour in the West Indies continued to spiral. Cape Coast Castle became the centre for slaving operations, while the islands of Barbados, Nevis, Antigua and Monserrat became the primary entrepots into the New World for the cargoes carried out to them by the Duke's ships. It is clear from the extant records that, by 1678, the slave trade had assumed a predominant position in England's trade with Africa and the Caribbean.[15] Despite a high mortality rate – the result of suicide, insanitary living conditions and the ravages of pleurisy and smallpox – on the voyage across the Atlantic, as many as 5,000 slaves a year were being transported to serve in the sugar plantations of the West Indies.[16]

As the trade became formalized, so too did the rationale behind it. In the early years of the Royal Adventurers the pretence that African slaves were 'servants', in the same way as indentured Englishmen or domestic day-labour, was perpetuated in the accounts' books and official literature issued by James and his board of share-holders. However, with the re-establishment of the trade in 1672 and the creation of the Royal African

Company, the language changed significantly. The Charter re-affirming the Duke of York's rights now sought to adopt the terminology previously used by the Portuguese and Dutch, which regarded the slave as a 'piece' measurable in exactly the same manner as any other inanimate commodity. African men and women were, therefore, effectively dehumanized and were henceforth to be bracketed together with gold, ivory and beeswax, as the Company's African exports.[17] If James Stuart conceived of slaves at all, then it was primarily in the context of their being entries on a list of financial transactions. His personal contact with captured Africans was limited to the handful of 'exotic' *Blackamoor* servants whom he sold to his friends at Court, upon their becoming fashionable on the London scene. While his conscience remained untroubled by the slaving expeditions carried out in his name and the untold human suffering that they had caused, he came to worry increasingly about the state of the slaves' souls and urged 'That the Negros in all the Plantations should be Baptized, exceedingly declaiming against that impiety, of their masters prohibiting it, out of a mistake[n] opinion, that they were [thence] *ipso facto* free.' He stood as the sponsor to his own personal slave, who he had christened as 'Mr. James York', but was subsequently scandalized by his amorous affairs with the ladies of the Court and by his sudden, though thoroughly understandable decision, to flee back to Africa at the first available opportunity.[18]

The move into slaves was, thus, not entirely without risk and its fair share of wholly unforeseen consequences. When the Duke of York had accepted the Governorship he had also assumed responsibility for 'the propriety and government of all the said regions, territories, countries, dominions, continents, coasts and places, in trust for the Company'. These African lands, unlike James's American dominions or Charles II's beleaguered colony of Tangier, were never intended to constitute themselves as part of an 'empire' and no firm plans for their colonization were ever advanced. Instead, they were to be first and foremost commercial concerns, trading posts, centering around the acquisition of raw materials and slaves and their shipment abroad. They often operated on a shoestring, underfunded and undermanned, with their agents continually complaining that basic administrative tasks and the auditing of accounts were increasingly becoming beyond the range of their abilities.[19] However, their biggest worry was the enduring problem of how best to defend their outlying posts.

Despite confident reports of the walls of Cape Coast Castle being 'much enlarged', a combination of humidity, torrential rains and fierce heat served to rot its fabric within the space of a few short years. One later commentator marvelled that ''Tis something strange our several forts should need so frequent and great repairs; we doubt either skill or due care has been wanting', and by the early 1680s it was observed that Cape Castle had fallen into ruins, wanting timber, planks and the necessary tradesmen to complete the repairs before a new series of rain storms washed it away entirely. Part of its tower had already fallen down and the rest of the structure was 'in a very dangerous condition'. With the roofs torn off the neighbouring buildings, the garrison was reduced to a pitiful state, washed out and unable to replace the tiles because 'Both our Plummers are dead so that wee know not how to dispose of your lead till your Honours send two others in their stead.'[20] Mortality rates among the Company's officials continued to be high, with the hazardous sea journey to and from the enclave accounting for some deaths – as in the case of John Allen who was drowned and washed up 'on the Coast of Guiny before he came to [the] Factoryes' – and the heat, disease and the poor state of the water supply, even more. The authorities at the Cape sent out repeated appeals for 'a constant supply [of soldiers] in the Room of those that dye weekly, we do likewise stand in need of some able men for factors having but few left a live upon the Coast'.[21] Those officials that remained formed a hardened and extremely close-knit fraternity, resenting all outside interference, and often becoming a law unto themselves, refusing to recognize the authority of newly appointed agents and attempting to cut their own deals with private traders.[22]

The change in the business, of both the Royal Adventurers and the Royal African Company, over to the capture, purchase and sale of slaves undoubtedly multiplied these problems. Fears of a major rising among their captives were never too far from the thoughts of the Duke's employees. The factory at Accra was troubled by continual outbreaks of violence in 1678, and a slaver by the name of Captain Brooks refused to go out on another raid, citing both 'the mortality of his men' and his fear of another insurrection taking place in his absence. Perhaps more dangerous still was the hostility of the local population, a 'Barbarous and Infidel people (with whom his Majesty hath no Articles of Peace and Commerce)', and the sudden lightning raids despatched by their rulers.[23] James's own response to this situation was as ingenious as it was bizarre. He recognized that a major stumbling block to peace in the region was the large number of kings and petty chieftains with whom English merchants had to conclude separate treaties, and that despite their frequent claims to the contrary, the authority of none of these individuals stretched for any great distance. Consequently, he decided to intervene in his capacity as a member of the English royal family, for 'Alyances and confederations [with these rulers could] . . . be made only by Princes themselves, or by Powers derived from them', imposing his own sovereignty from above in an attempt to broker a primitive form of the *Pax Britannica*. To this end, in the summer of 1664, he attempted to pay

court to such men as the 'Great King of Ardra' – presenting them with
high-flown letters of introduction – and suggesting to them that the
speedy acceptance of European slavers into their lands provided them
with the surest way of enlarging upon their own domains, and of
guaranteeing their people's long-term prosperity. James intended to
speak to them as one prince did to another, confirming their 'legitimacy'
and bringing their monarchies into line with those already well
established in Western Europe. This was precisely what he sought to
achieve when he enclosed a little copper crown in with his address to the
King of Ardra, confiding to him that: 'Wee have so great a Value for your
Person and Dignity that we have sent You . . . a Crowne which is the
Badge of the highest Authority . . . in these Parts.'[24] Unfortunately, we
shall never know quite what the 'Great King' would have made of his
present, or of the prospect of becoming a client of Charles II, for James's
overture was never fated to reach its destination and was instead
intercepted *en route* by De Ruyter, and spirited back to Holland as a
trophy.[25] It seems likely that, even in the absence of Dutch intervention,
this diplomatic offensive was always going to be doomed to failure. The
vast distances that obstructed easy negotiation, the clash of vastly
conflicting cultures and the simple fact that James's declaration was
inscribed in English – with no thought ever being made to translate it
into the regional dialect – all conspired against it.

Given this failure, military considerations once again began to weigh
heavily upon the Company's agents, ensconced behind their walls in
Cape Castle and yet still charged with ensuring the steady flow of ivory
and slaves from out of the interior. The continuing reluctance of the
indigenous peoples to 'be obliged by Treaties', had necessitated the
presence of 'a continuing and permanent force' of soldiers and sailors
that was eventually estimated to have cost the Company as much as
£20,000 'a year in time of peace, and . . . much more in time of Warre'.[26]
Having been unable to displace the African kings or to extend their
influence too far from their original coastal bridgeheads, the Duke of
York and his friends now hit upon another, and ultimately far more
damaging, expedient in order to defray their costs: they would attempt to
gain an unchallengeable monopoly of the continent's trade by seizing the
territory and assets of their Dutch rivals.

The representatives of many different European nations jostled each
other for control of the narrow Atlantic coastline, with the developments
of their forts and factories often leapfrogging over one another in their
rush to gain a short-term advantage, in the way of a safe harbour or an
easily defensible promontory (see Map 4, p. 249). The early voyages
sponsored by the Royal Adventurers had managed to establish a
significant English presence in the region, the Island of St André had

been taken from the Duke of Courland and settlements were quickly constructed on two rocky outcrops that lay nearby. These twin islands, which were hastily christened after the Company's royal sponsors, Charles and James, were thought to be ideally situated for both trade and defence, and the latter soon evolved into the main English stronghold in that part of Africa. However, once the expeditionary fleets had sailed for home, the balance of power between the garrisons left behind by the Royal Adventurers, and those of the Dutch West India Company, were found to be so evenly poised that neither side could make any further inroads into the territories held by the other. In order to break this stalemate, both sides sought to hire auxiliaries from among the local warriors, and funded tribal wars which they hoped to direct against the property of their foes. Although these conflicts were to prove bloody and spectacular, they ultimately did nothing to expand upon the Duke of York's patrimony and he threw all of his energies into organizing a fresh naval expedition which would settle the matter once and for all.[27]

Even though he was officially acting only in his capacity as the Governor of a private trading company, James had no hesitation about using his position as Lord High Admiral to promote what was little more than an act of piracy. He detached a Royal Navy frigate, the *Jersey*, in November 1664 and put her under the command of Sir Robert Holmes, with explicit orders to protect and promote 'the Interests of the R[oyal] Company, which is the sole end of your present voyage'.[28] Unfortunately, James's instructions did not go on to explain how this was to be achieved, with the result that Holmes was given virtual *carte blanche* to wage war against the Dutch, wherever he found them 'to kill, take, sink or destroy such as shall oppose you and to send home such shipps as you shall soe take'. To begin with all went well, Holmes swept down the coasts of Gambia and Sierra Leone, effecting a successful rendezvous with ships owned by the Company and taking a number of prizes, before falling upon the Dutch settlements clustered around the Cape. The rival forts and factories from Goree in the north, to Anta and Anambo in the south, fell to him one after another with only Elmina stubbornly holding out against his guns. However, the campaign was marred by the failure of Holmes to control his African mercenaries after the surrender of the Dutch garrison at Aga. They fell upon the prisoners, massacring all of those that they could find, and took the heads of some for gruesome trophies. This clear contravention of the established rules of war handed to the Dutch a powerful and emotive image with which to rally their own people and to berate their foes.[29] Thereafter, it would impossible for Johan De Witt not to authorize some strong retaliatory strike against England's African interests.

The Duke of York had fully anticipated such a counter-attack, but in the euphoria which greeted the news of Holmes's triumphant progress he allowed himself to be wrong-footed by De Witt. He had ordered the English fleet out into the Channel, hoping to catch the Dutch as they sallied out of the Hook of Holland and so provoke a full-scale war. This stratagem had worked well for the Commonwealth in 1652, but unfortunately for James, De Witt was well aware of past history and refused to rise to the bait. Consequently, while the English fleet continued to wait patiently at their station, a set of instructions from the States General authorizing retaliation slipped past them and reached Admiral De Ruyter, who was patrolling the Mediterranean with his own squadron of 'eleven great . . . Ships of War'. His subsequent descent upon the English factories in West Africa was, if anything, far more clinical and devastating than anything Holmes could have possibly achieved. With the exception of Cape Coast Castle, all of the Company's possessions and the greater part of her merchant fleet were taken within the space of a few short weeks. On his return home in December 1664, Captain Holmes was surprised to find that all of his work had been undone, while Samuel Pepys – after seeing the reports of fresh losses that had come into the Admiralty on an almost daily basis – confided sadly that, after all their 'mischief', the English had been 'beaten to dirt at Guinny'.[30]

National pride apart, the real loser to emerge from the Duke of York's private war was the Company of Royal Adventurers itself. Its assets were effectively wiped out by the actions of the Dutch, and the outbreak of full-scale conflict between King Charles and the States General, in the following year, only served to make matters much worse. The Company depended upon naval superiority in the Atlantic Ocean for its survival and, when this was successfully challenged by the Dutch from 1665 to 1667, they were faced with utter ruin. Commercial confidence was severely dented, and one anonymous pamphleteer expressed his fears that 'the whole Trade was in Eminent danger to be lost to this Nation'.[31] With the returns from new voyages falling far below the figures projected, the Company became increasingly moribund. An attempt was made to save the situation in late 1664, but although the Duke and his friends led the way in adding to their existing share portfolios, the City financiers remained wary and only a further £18,200 was pledged. Faced with mounting debts, James tried one last time to reinvigorate the Adventurers' flagging fortunes, by using what little money he had at hand to pay off their creditors and to try to reduce their ever-increasing arrears of interest. A half-hearted attempt was made at the end of the Dutch war to reactivate the Company, but by then its assets and infrastructure had become so eroded that many of its own members had begun to trade with Africa as private individuals. As the privileges granted to them in their Charter were hived off, one by one, to other cartels – such as the Gambia Adventurers, who agreed to pay £1,000 a year for the trading rights to

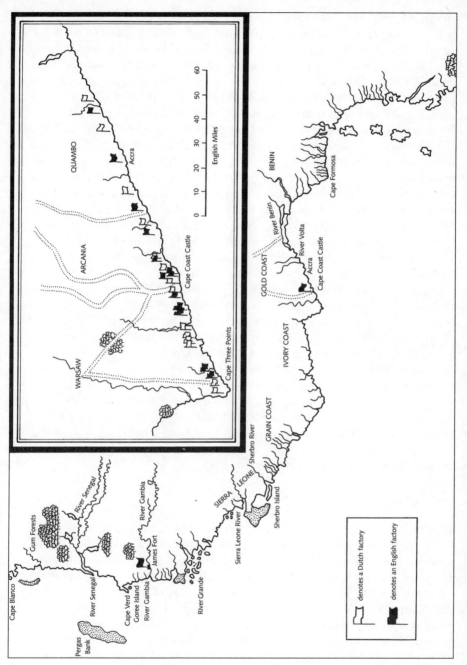

Map 4 *The East Coast of Africa, c. 1670s (after M. Postlethwayt)*

Cape Blanco

Pergas
Bank

River Senegal

Gum Forests

River Senegal

Cape Verd
Goree Island
River Gambia

River Gambia

James Fort

River Grande

SIERRA LEONE

Sierra Leone River

Sherbro River

Sherbro Island

GRAIN COAST

IVORY COAST

QUAMBO

Accra

ARCANIA

Cape Coast Castle

WARSAW

Cape Three Points

English Miles

0 10 20 30 40 50 60

GOLD COAST

River Benin

River Volta

Accra

Cape Coast Castle

BENIN

Cape Formosa

denotes a Dutch factory

denotes an English factory

North Africa – the hold of the Royal Adventurers on the African trade had become so slight by the late 1660s that, at the suggestion of the King, Lord Arlington had caustically asked James and his board if they intended to continue in the business at all. The complete collapse of the Company was only a short way off, but it is interesting to note at this point just how spectacularly misplaced James's equation of economics with warfare and territorial expansion had been.[32] Though he had set his heart upon a war with the Dutch and 'loved to speak of it, and the benefits which would attend it', he had never for one second countenanced the possibility of defeat, or the havoc which a policy of fire and sword could wreak among his business ventures. Furthermore, the recourse to armed struggle in an attempt to grab existing markets from the other European powers smacked of nothing, if not of desperation. 'The truth was', as Clarendon observed, that 'the Dutch were there some time before us, and the Dane before either: and the Dutch, which was the true grievance, had planted themselves more advantageously . . . than we had done, and by the erection of more forts were more strongly seated, and done a much greater trade, which they did not believe they would be persuaded to quit'.[33] It would seem that what the Duke of York desired from the Company was quick profits, and that he was unwilling to build from a low base or to attempt to wrest the African trade from the Dutch through purely commercial means. The workings of the maritime trade remained the overwhelming preserve of the merchant classes and, therefore, appeared to be largely unfamiliar and uninviting to him. Rather than demonstrating his flair for, and his understanding of, business, the Duke's willingness to fall back upon tried and tested military expedients, once the expected profits had failed to materialize, spoke eloquently of his failure to adapt to new circumstances and to master the politics and mechanisms of trade.

II

Despite the failure of their first venture into Africa, the allure of ivory and slaves still held a great deal of attraction for James and a significant body of London financiers. Moreover, in his capacity as a privy councillor and confidant to the King, the Duke of York had learned in advance of the provisions of the Secret Treaty of Dover, rumours of a new Dutch war and an alliance with France. He was well aware that if these developments went ahead as planned, and the Dutch fleet – which represented the major threat to his holdings – could be neutralized, then there would be rich pickings to be had for English merchants from the factories established all along the Gold Coast. Consequently, fresh plans were put forward in the winter of 1671 for the resumption of large-scale trade with the African continent. Outstanding debts precluded the use of the old corporate name, and so it was as the Royal African Company that the new project was launched in the following spring. In the past, joint-stock companies had had great difficulties in recruiting initial subscribers, and in collecting outstanding monies from them thereafter. However, this was not to be the case with the African Company and within a comparatively short period of time over two hundred individuals were found to underwrite a stock of some £111,600.[34] The success of this flotation was due in large measure to the radically different nature of the re-established Company from its predecessor. From the outset its prospectuses stressed that it would deal primarily in the sale of slaves, a commodity which the City and the plantation owners in Barbados – who now pledged monies in the hope of influencing the flow of labour to the West Indies – considered to be extremely desirable. Furthermore, in marked contrast to the relatively aristocratic composition of the Royal Adventurers, the Royal African Company came increasingly to be the preserve of the mercantile community who dominated its business, in both the provision of capital and in the close direction of its affairs. The illustrious names, which had been so closely associated with the formation of the original company, were now largely absent from the new list of subscribers. Prince Rupert, the Earl of Bath, Lord Hawley and Sir William Coventry all withdrew from the project before their shares had been fully paid up while, besides James, only Lord Craven and Lord Powis were actively involved throughout.[35] Those of the Duke's friends who did make investments – men such as Lawrence Dupuy, Matthew Wren and Sir Edmund Andros – had ventured only nominal sums, doubtless out of courtesy towards their patron and a desire to be further associated with his interests. By way of contrast, three-quarters of the accumulated capital was now found to have been staked by businessmen, the majority of whom were already engaged in overseas trade with the West Indies, the Levant and the Baltic. Bankers and revenue farmers also constituted an important group, while a small number of widows and country gentlemen made up the remnant. Despite this marked change in the social complexion of the Company, by 1675 only fourteen shareholders owned more than £1,000 in stocks, leaving James with his investment of £3,000, and Lord Shaftesbury – who had come late to the venture – with a stake of £2,000, as representing very considerable forces in the boardroom indeed.[36]

This new balance of power was duly reflected in the first elections of the Company's directors in January 1672. James, who had proved his worth once again in successfully expediting the granting of a new Charter from the King, was returned to office as Governor, while Shaftesbury was elected as his Sub-Governor, and John Buckworth filled the position of Deputy Governor, a post which had been created especially for a City merchant.[37] To begin with, all went well for the new African Company. Buckworth took executive control of all its day-to-day business interests, while the continued presence of the Duke and Shaftesbury, as nominal chief executives, seemed to attest to its reputation for financial acumen and fiscal probity. The Company pursued an ambitious and strident policy, seeking to monopolize the whole of the African slave trade, and soon proved itself to be a far more effective organization in eliminating foreign competition than its unfortunate predecessor. It was helped in this by the simple fact that the Third Dutch War was predominantly fought out in the Northern Hemisphere, and left the African continent virtually unscathed. Moreover, in the years from 1674 to 1678, the African Company took advantage of England's political neutrality as her chief rivals – France and Holland – fought each other to a standstill, and expanded and consolidated its interests on either side of the Atlantic. Thus, it was through peaceful commerce rather than through the pursuit of all-out war, as had been advocated by the Duke, that the Company edged towards solvency. With the restoration of English naval superiority and the bankruptcy of the Dutch West India Company, James and his fellow Directors were able to impose their monopoly with increasing effectiveness and for a brief period of time it looked as if their hold on the region would become unchallengeable.

However, the African Company's grip on the slave trade was coming to be increasingly resented by the plantation owners in the West Indies over the course of the 1670s. They chafed at the low numbers and high prices of the slaves that were allegedly being foisted upon them, and complained continuously about the 'foul monopoly' exercised by the Company's agents. It was alleged that this potentially lucrative trade had become a preserve for the special interest groups which coalesced around the Duke of York, and that its original expansionary impetus had now become dissipated, leaving behind no more than a series of cosy financial arrangements which benefited no one apart from the colonial governors and the boardrooms back in London.[38] There were certainly some grounds for these suspicions: men like Henry Drax, Christopher Codrington and John Hallet – who eventually ended up commissioning their own slave-trading voyages in order to smash the monopoly – could see that although the Company often lost money on its expeditions, some of its employees who sold their captives to themselves or on to their friends were actually making large personal fortunes. James, in particular, did not appear to lose out from his investment and continued to make an annual return of 12 per cent on his money throughout this period, even though the market price of shares continued to fluctuate wildly.[39]

It was not long before criticism of the Company's agents in the West Indies began to be voiced in England as well, but it took a serious split within the boards' own ranks before matters finally came to a head. Lord Shaftesbury had been happy enough to accept his share of the dividends while in office, but he increasingly began to question the legality of the monopoly with his gradual slide into opposition politics. His position within the African Company had become increasingly isolated. He had few friends and natural allies on a board dominated by such ultra-royalists as the Earl of Craven, Sir George Carteret and Sir Peter Colleton; with the influence of Prince Rupert dwindling it was not difficult for his arch-rival, James, to exert his own influence against him almost at will. With many of his supporters being eased out of their positions of authority by the Duke's placemen, he finally decided to 'sell as much of my Guinea stocks as will sell for thirty per cent profit or better' in August 1676, and his departure from the Company in the following April effectively spelled the end of any Whiggish influence in its councils. Thereafter, the Royal African Company came to be seen primarily as an instrument of Tory power, closely associated by its critics with the Court party and the abuses of the royal prerogative.[40] Although all of the companies chartered during the Restoration era were to some extent identified with the exercise of royal power, the African Company represented an exceptional and high-profile case. Its status and power were derived solely from the gift of the monarch and its future prospects were inexorably tied to the fortunes of the House of Stuart, as even its motto '*Regio floret patricino commercium, commercioque regnum* [The Kingdom and King flourish alike through the encouragement of trade]' sought to emphasize. It had gained, under James, an unprecedented degree of royal support, with its interests becoming synonymous with those of the Crown, and its demands and protests being always assured a favourable hearing before the State Council, and its myriad of committees and offshoots. Company merchants eventually came to dominate the City Corporation, and extended their influence into the government of many of its local parishes. However, the presence of the Duke of York as both Governor and as the largest single shareholder ultimately proved to be a liability, bringing the nature of its operations under a closer and more hostile scrutiny at the time of the Exclusion Crisis than would otherwise have been the case.[41]

On 28 April 1679, during the second day of business conducted by the Exclusion Parliament, alongside the measures for combating 'Popery' and debarring the Catholic heir to the throne, a committee was set up to examine affairs of the Royal African Company and the 'miscarriages relating to his Majesty's Navy . . . and likewise the information that hath been given in touching the Ship called the *Hunter*'. The *Hunter* was a small Dutch frigate which had been taken in action by the Royal Navy in 1672, and incorporated into the English fleet after a sitting of the prize-board, which was dominated by the Duke of York and his friends. Despite being the property of the State, the vessel was soon trading in the interests of James's own private company and in 1676 was hired out to them for a slaving voyage to West Africa, under the command of Captain Dickinson. Once off the African coast the ship had engaged with two interlopers and, after a brief struggle, had succeeded in taking both of them together with their lucrative cargoes. The profits from the action, amounting to some £2,800, were then divided up according to the provisions of the Company's Charter, with half of the money going straight to the King and the remainder being distributed to James and his fellow shareholders. This division of the spoils was, however, to provoke howls of outrage not only among the proprietors of the vessels themselves, who had seen their most valuable assets wiped out at a stroke, but also among the West Indian plantation owners in whose interests they had been ultimately operating. Although the practice of hiring out warships as letters of marque to private individuals and consortiums was a well-established custom, the seizure of English – rather than foreign – ships who had acted in the name of free trade, and whose only crime appeared to be the attempt to break an unfair and unjust monopoly, ensured that this case would rapidly become something of a *cause célèbre*. The Duke of York's actions were viewed as being little short of piratical and the Parliamentary committee, in exposing them, aimed to strike at the heart of his interests as both Lord High Admiral and commercial proprietor.[42]

While the committee busied itself, demanding copies of the sets of instructions given out to the Captains of the *Hunter* and the *Constant Warwick*, another Royal Navy ship that had been similarly employed by the Company, James and his board began to hastily improvise their defences. They set up a special working party, consisting of influential shareholders and representatives of the mercantile community, in order to co-ordinate their actions, and embarked upon the task of lobbying MPs and obtaining signatures for a grand petition in support of the continuation of their monopoly. The Company was well aware that, if it was to survive a protracted onslaught from the Commons committee, it had to effectively distance itself from the political activities of its patron and consequently appealed across the floor of the House, to be heard in its own defence. However, only hours after the petition was read to the Commons on 27th May 1679, King Charles prorogued the Parliament as a prelude to having it dissolved. As a result the committee was disbanded, and nothing further came of its allegations. The Company was not slow to express its relief at such an unexpected delivery and sent its thanks to those MPs who had actively supported it, while leaving its Sub-Governor to 'dispose of fifty pounds for the Companyes service as he sees fitt', monies which had presumably already been allotted as bribes.[43]

Although the immediate danger had passed, the activities of the West Indian planters – who had formed themselves into a very effective pressure group, that was adept at sponsoring lawsuits and retaliatory motions in the colonial legislatures – continued to represent a thorn in the side of the African Company. The incursions of private merchantmen continued largely unabated, with the look-outs at Cape Castle reporting that their vessels infested the seas for miles around. Even when they were caught, as in the case of Captain Daniell, whose ship was impounded after docking in Jamaica in January 1680, effective action was not always possible, as the cargo of slaves had already been whisked away and sold on, even before the authorities had a chance to arrive. Worse was to come a few months later, when two interlopers caught off the coast of Sierra Leone did not even try to hide their guilt, and 'made great braggs of assistance that they expect from Parliament', adding that their friends in the Commons had given them 'permission' to overturn the royal prerogative 'to goe trade at Guynia'.[44] For its part, the Company repeatedly tried to get the cases of those ships caught trespassing heard in the Admiralty Courts, which still fell under the sway of the Duke's influence, rather than in the ordinary courts of law, where they would be far less sure of gaining the result that they desired. They also attempted to deflect many of the criticisms of the monopoly advanced so forcibly by the planters and their Whig friends in the City by courting public opinion with the publication of such pamphlets as the *Certain Considerations Relating to the Royal African Company of England*. Published anonymously in London, in 1680, this work sought to demonstrate 'the Growth, and National Advantages of the Guineay Trade . . . [and] also that the same Trade cannot be carried on, but by a Company and Joint-Stock'. Moreover, in an attack on the damage inflicted upon the established order by the calls for Exclusion, the pamphlet explicitly concluded that 'trade and commerce cannot be maintained or increased without Government, Order, and regular discipline; for in all confused Traffique it must necessarily happen, that while every single person pursues his own particular interest, the publique is deserted by all, and consequently must fall to ruine. For which reason, the Crown hath erected and established fraternities or companies of Merchants, with Grant of priviledges exclusive to all others . . . that by such undertakings, navigation was increased, and the publique good of the whole Kingdom very much advanced.'[45] Although James's name is not mentioned anywhere within the text, out of a desire not to further enrage anti-Catholic sentiment or to overtly identify the Company with his cause, its aim, together with that of the board of Directors, who despite their protestations stood or fell with his person, was to strengthen the Duke's position.

255

The African Company soon had cause to be grateful that they had continued in their support for James, when he directly intervened in a parallel court case which threatened to destroy the monopolies of all the Chartered companies. The danger had arisen after an interloper in the East India trade, by the name of Thomas Sandys, was apprehended and brought to trial in 1683. His defence council was the noted Whig, William Williams, who cast doubts as to the legality of the Charter under which the East India Company operated and suggested that in future Parliament should 'help' the King to regulate the nation's trade. James – who was also a keen supporter of the Honourable Company, and had seen good returns from his investment of some £3,000 in its stock – now realized that it was not just the fate of one individual that was being decided in the law courts, but that of the whole future of the monopoly trades.[46] He therefore suggested that his own Solicitor General, Sir George Jeffreys, should try the case, and the speedy acceptance of his candidate did much to predetermine the outcome of the suit before it had even begun. In the event, Jeffreys did not disappoint either his patron or the vested interests that had backed him, and within a few days of the opening hearings Sir Josiah Child, a Director of the East India Company and friend to the Duke, was publicly celebrating his victory. Jeffreys' final summing up, a year later, not only confirmed the legality of the Charter and the desirability of monopoly trade – confirming that 'The East India Company have solely run the hazard and been at great expenses in discovering places, erecting forts and . . . settling factories . . . [that it] would be against natural justice and equity . . . (which no municipal law can take away) for others to reap the benefit and advantage of all this' – but also provided a ringing endorsement of the royal prerogative. 'God be praised', declared the Judge, that 'it is in the King's power to call and dissolve Parliaments, when and how he pleases; and he is the only judge of these *ardua regni* [problems of State], that he should think fit to consult with the Parliament about', and he chose to end with a threat equating the pursuit of free trade, so soon after the Rye House Plot, with treason. 'Mr. Williams', he concluded, 'would do well to save himself the trouble of advising the King what things are fit for him to consult with his parliament about, until such time as he is thereunto called.' Charles II was so pleased by this reaffirmation of his rights that he rewarded Jeffreys with the gift of a diamond ring, while James continued to hold him in the very greatest esteem, creating him Baronet and Lord Chancellor upon his accession only a few months later.[47] With the resolution of this test case the future of both the Africa and East India Companies seemed assured and, with the storm clouds of 1688–9 still far on the horizon, the Duke of York and his shareholders were in a potentially stronger legal and financial position than at any time since

1660. Though interlopers would continue to erode a substantial portion of the African Company's profits, they were no longer in any sort of position to challenge its commercial dominance. The teething troubles of the Company's early years were behind it, and the gradual adoption of the slave trade over the procurement and transportation of raw materials had at last begun to pay regular dividends.[48] It is little wonder therefore that, on his brother's death, James Stuart should seek to retain his full and perpetual title as Governor of his African holdings, or that he should embark upon a fresh round of speculative investments in the City of London, using his past experience of tried and tested economic orthodoxies and expedients to pave the way for his apparently bright future as King.

III

We have so far looked at a single case study, highlighting James's involvement in one specific commercial endeavour. However, we now need to broaden our picture in order to assess his overall impact as a man of business. It would seem from the evidence that has already been presented that, despite political and logistical difficulties, the influence of the Duke of York could be a decisive factor in the formation of a new company's overall character and direction. If these findings were to be repeated across the broad spectrum of joint-stock companies with which he had dealings, then James would have a very strong claim to be an important figure in the rise of English maritime trade and in the development of the stock market. However, it would seem from the extant record books of the Royal Fishery and Hudson's Bay Companies, both of which he was to lead as Governor, that this is not to be the case and that his record as an administrator outside of the African Company is at best patchy, if revealing.

The Royal Fishery Corporation had been established in March 1664 as a means of stimulating the English fishing industry in the face of very significant Dutch successes. Great fleets of herring boats, or busses as they were known to their contemporaries, were despatched every year from Holland and Zeeland, to fish the waters of the North Sea. With the Orkneys and the Shetland Islands reduced to being little more than colonies, existing to service these foreign vessels, and the knowledge that English fishermen had already achieved significant successes in harvesting catches from the North Atlantic, Charles II's government determined to create a new herring fleet in order to displace the Dutch from their traditional markets.[49] Given his expertise as a seaman, James once again appeared to be the natural choice for Governor, while a large number of courtiers such as Lord Craven and the Earl of Pembroke, who were already heavily involved with the Company of Royal Adventurers, also lent their support to the project. However, the similarities between these two companies did not end with their shared social composition, as the Corporation struggled from the outset over the issues of finance and commercial policy. To make matters worse, the Royal Fishery was established at a singularly inauspicious time, in the midst of a severe economic downturn and with the outbreak of the Second Dutch War – which was to put an end to any attempt at deep-sea fishing – less than a year away. More damaging still, in the long term, was the almost total apathy with which the City merchants greeted almost all of its endeavours. It was seriously under-funded throughout its short history and ambitious plans for the construction of an English herring fleet were either shelved, or contracted out to Dutch shipyards for their completion. Although King Charles II had granted the Corporation 'a very large and a very serious charter', this had actually proved to be far more of a hindrance than a help, raising impossible expectations of a rapid and highly lucrative expansion in the maritime sector, while placing an intolerable great strain upon a board who were ill-equipped to deliver upon these promises. Its members were 'generally so ill-fitted for so serious a work', that Samuel Pepys did 'much fear [that] it will come to little'. After an initial burst of enthusiasm, the Duke and his friends stayed resolutely away from its meetings and showed no further interest in the advancement of plans for the training of Yarmouth fishermen, in the catching and preservation of herrings.[50] Yet if the growth of the fisheries did little to excite the passions of this Stuart Prince, then the manner by which they might come to be funded certainly did. It was clear that private enterprise was incapable of bearing the enormous costs inherent in building a new merchant fleet from scratch, and that the central government was in no position to increase direct taxation in order to pay for it. Another source of income, therefore, had to be found, and the idea of granting a monopoly of national lottery licences to the board seemed to present the perfect answer. Then, as now, the granting of such a privilege was seen to be a virtual license to print money. Captain Poyntz, who owned a gaming house, was brought in to advise James and his fellow directors about the best way to organize such a scheme, but within a matter of a few short weeks their plans had collapsed amid confusion and allegations of utter financial incompetence and wrong-doing. Pepys saw fit to conclude that 'the lose and base manner that monies so collected are disposed of in, would make a man never part with a penny in that manner', and the whole sorry affair does not sit well with James's reputation for business acumen, financial probity and utter devotion to the national interest.[51]

The shadow cast over the Corporation's affairs by the scandal may have caused Charles II to have been extremely wary of backing subsequent similar schemes for the recouping of their losses. Plans to grant the company the sole rights to mint farthings – and to keep back 5s in every pound in order to reinvigorate its finances – were presented before the King in both 1667 and 1668, and were rejected out of hand on both occasions. In the absence of new City backers and with their last chance of obtaining a secure source of investment denied to them, the company's voyages practically ceased. The resumption of hostilities with the Dutch Republic, in 1672, saw the abandonment of its remaining vessels, which were allowed to rot at their moorings and soon deteriorated into useless hulks. A brief attempt was made to re-establish the Corporation in 1676, with James again as Governor, but although the problem of finance seemed to have been provided for this time – in the shape of a direct government subsidy of £20 a year for every ship they employed in the industry – war, once again, disrupted their plans.[52] Rather than building their own ships, the board had taken the decision to purchase a little fleet of busses built and crewed by Dutchmen. This would have secured an initial return from their catches, and guaranteed their subsidy, at very little cost in the way of an initial outlay. Unfortunately while England remained at peace, France and Holland were locked in conflict and six of the seven ships commissioned were immediately seized as prizes. The French men-of-war claimed that as they were Dutch, rather than English, vessels they had acted well within their rights in taking them. In these circumstances, with Charles II and the Duke unwilling and unable to press the matter with King Louis, the issue was quietly dropped and the Royal Fishery was finally condemned to bankruptcy.[53]

If James had been a powerful force behind the inception of the African and Fishery Companies, then he came late to the development of the Hudson's Bay Company. From the time of Pierre Radisson's arrival in England in 1662, that Company had come to be regarded as the foremost preserve of Prince Rupert, who had promoted its cause at every possible opportunity and had been duly rewarded with election to the post of its first Governor. By way of contrast, the Duke of York had only taken a nominal £300 share in its stock in 1672, and even then had not actually seen fit to pay for it.[54] While he willingly attended the noisy scrummage that marked the first sale of the Company's furs in England, he only grudgingly released a Royal Navy ketch for an exploratory survey of Canada's Northern shores, after turning down an earlier request for the use of a far bigger vessel. Given these circumstances, it would seem safe to assume that James remained completely unmoved by both the mode of operation and the general commercial prospects of the Hudson's Bay Company, until at least the early 1680s.[55] This profound lack of interest may have been the result of a genuine unwillingness to intrude too far into his cousin's private domain, or – as is more likely – might have stemmed from a reluctance to associate himself too closely with an unglamorous venture that was almost entirely the preserve of merchants.

The replacement of courtiers such as Sir George Carteret, Lord Shaftesbury and the Earl of Arlington, as investors, with businessmen such as Sir James Hayes, Sir Robert Vyner and William Pretyman, had occurred far earlier and far more completely in the Hudson's Bay Company, than in any of the other joint-stocks with which James was involved. Consequently, by 1679 the Company's decision-making process resided almost entirely in the hands of Sir James Hayes, as the Deputy Governor, and with the two great banking houses of Thomas Cook and Stephen Evans.[56] Furthermore, the original grand schemes for the colonization and settlement of the Bay and 'Rupert Land' had been abandoned as being wholly impractical, given the region's harsh arctic climate. Business was now solely directed towards the establishment of a monopoly market for their furs in England, America and mainland Europe, while the administration of the Company itself was becoming ever more centralized under the control of a secretary-husband, a series of bankers and a treasury team drawn from among the ranks of the board. Although the ordinary shareholders still had the right to attend board meetings, they were not allowed to see the papers under discussion and the actual conduct of affairs remained the preserve of a chosen few.[57] It was at this point in the Company's history that James was chosen as an unlikely second Governor.

Prince Rupert's failing health had increasingly relegated his position to that of a titular head, but at the time of his death from pleurisy, in November 1682, there was no natural successor of sufficient status within the Company to take over his role. It took six meetings, and a great deal of deliberation, before James was finally elected as the new Governor in January of the following year. The unanimous vote recorded for his candidature reflects more, however, upon the power and influence of Sir James Hayes, who had campaigned vigorously on his behalf, than upon the Duke's own standing with individual shareholders.[58] Hayes, as a Tory and a bitter opponent of Lord Shaftesbury, had perceived James to be a useful ally in his attempts to enforce and expand the remit of the Company's existing charter; to begin with it looked as if he had chosen well. The Duke immediately called for the document so that he could study its provisions for himself, and seemed to be flattered when the River Chichewan was renamed as Albany, in his honour. However, relations soon turned sour as Hayes and a small deputation of board members paid a call upon James, to ask him if he would sign a set of the Company's annual instructions to its chief officers. This should have been no more than a mere formality, as there was nothing that was either complicated or controversial contained within them, but the Duke waved his Deputy away and, angered by the presumption of the merchants, told them 'that he did never signe any Orders or papers of any Company he was Governor of'.[59]

Thereafter, James proved himself to be a far more distant and less partisan chief executive than had been hoped, refusing point-blank to embroil himself in any of the Company's affairs. This might seem strange in a man who had claimed to be fascinated by all aspects of navigation and yet showed no interest in sponsoring the search for the North-west Passage, and whose American proprietories stood to benefit from any increase in the trade in beaver skins, but it should be remembered that the main threat to the Company's monopoly at this time came from the activities of French Canadian settlers who were also trying to stake their claim to the territories along the Hudson River. James, as heir pre-sumptive and the brother of the major recipient of Louis XIV's subsidies, had no wish to anger the French King or to provoke a fresh trade war that he stood precious little chance of winning. He consequently pre-ferred to urge caution to the more militant members of his board, who called for a rapid expansion into the disputed lands, and chose to ignore altogether the stream of complaints levied against the missionary zeal of the French Jesuits who operated out of Quebec.[60] With only one modest dividend paid so far on the Company's shares, James appeared to be in doubt as to its long-term financial prospects, and was only too glad to try to divest himself of his potentially embarrassing governorship at the first available opportunity. This came with his accession to the throne when, after Hayes's polite enquiry as to whether he could still legally continue in office, 'seeing our Governour is now our Sovereigne Lord the King', he chose to resign his post, conferring it upon John Churchill as a man he believed he could trust.[61]

It is interesting to note that, while the Duke's interest in trade fluctuated wildly during our period, and depended largely upon individual circumstance, his rather aloof, if somewhat predatory, conduct of financial affairs did not significantly alter. If he had been experiencing health problems, a crisis of confidence or a gradual breaking down of resolve, these matters might have found some expression in the course of his relationships with his Company directors. This, however, was not the case, and James was able to maintain his involvement with the African companies for more than a quarter of a century, never once deviating from established policy as his brother's reign progressed. Moreover, while Prince Rupert's faltering spirit and gradual retreat from business affairs is hinted at in the records of the Hudson's Bay Company, we are offered no such insights into James's physical or mental condition by Company executives beyond a general sense of disappointment that their patron had chosen to devote his attention to other, more princely, matters.[62]

Given James's apparent indifference to the fortunes of the Hudson's Bay Company, we might well seek to ask ourselves why he should have sought to involve himself in their affairs in the first place. The answer would seem to lie in the fact that he accepted the governorship at a time when royal control of the square mile hung precariously in the balance, and the City Charter was about to be suspended. Control over an additional and high-profile corporate body would have allowed the Duke to gain another political foothold in the capital, and would have considerably extended his opportunities for dispensing patronage.[63] Once again we can see James, as the royal entrepreneur, continually reacting to events rather than shaping them, and there is a strong case to be made for expediency, rather than a sense of an overarching ambition, to be established as the key factor in any attempt to understand or account for his own particular interest in trade.

James's bitter experience of youthful exile which had deprived him of a luxurious and pampered lifestyle, the greater reliance of the Crown upon Parliamentary grants, and his own impecunity after the mid-1660s, had all combined to raise his awareness of the relationship between money and power. It was this insight into his dependency upon an unstable source of personal income, and the havoc its sudden withdrawal could inflict upon his political standing, that first prompted him to make his investments in stocks and shares. We have no way of estimating the Duke's overall effectiveness as a businessman, but should not be too surprised to discover that, in the absence of a formal civil service, he chose not to work a regular 9 to 5 day on the behalf of his shareholders. His attendances at board meetings outside of the African Company were sparse, and even then he was not involved in the day-to-day running of the mercantile administration. His status as a Prince, as the Directors of the Hudson's Bay Company had found out to their cost, when combined with the opportunities for amusement and self-gratification offered by life at the Court, effectively precluded any closer involvement.[64] His value, therefore, lay as a behind-the-scenes manipulator of political patronage and sea-power, and in the scope and breadth of his personal connections and financial concerns. The major significance of his actions was that he was involved with these companies at all, and that he was one of a small band of Restoration courtiers, including Arlington, Rupert, Shaftesbury and Sandwich, who showed an interest – however fleeting – in trade: choosing to involve themselves and their capital in new and speculative investments, and being prepared to align their own aristocratic interests with those of the aspiring merchant class.

James's commercial legacy remains at best ambiguous, and at worst malevolent. His central role in the creation and management of the British slave trade must surely weigh heavily against him, and there can be little room for doubt that private profit, as opposed to the national good, remained as the primary motivation behind all of his trading schemes. He was often involved in pure speculation for very limited and short-term gains, and he did not show himself to be adverse to blatant asset-stripping if the opportunity presented itself.[65] Similarly, his position at the heart of the establishment, which had ensured that he was able to get access to highly confidential and privileged government information, was used to further his own personal interests, as happened in late 1671 when he stole a march on his competitors in Africa. In terms of his understanding of trade and its relation to commercial policy, his activities would seem to present us with yet another record of his dismal failure. He never seems to have deviated from his central premise, that the commercial privileges of Englishmen in foreign parts could only be protected by the exercise of overwhelming military force. Even though the destruction of his African factories and his fleet of herring boats in the North Sea seemed to argue a contrary view, James continued to maintain that the waging of war was the single most important factor in the growth of trade.[66] His stubborn defence of the rights of the Chartered Companies was built upon much firmer ground: the enforcement of a monopoly could effectively surmount the logistical difficulties and enormous initial costs entailed in trying to run an overseas operation from a distance of several thousand miles. However, the centralized and often authoritarian hold on business that this policy required may well have appeared attractive enough to the Duke on its own terms, fitting in well with his established view of the world and the necessity for social order. It seems safe to conclude, therefore, that James's reputation as the champion and protector of English trade was not built upon very solid foundations, and that beyond his frequent repetition of a few commonplace words and phrases – which simply suggested that plentiful trade was rather better than no trade at all – he cannot realistically be credited with any particular insight, or with a superior understanding of the workings of mercantile expansion and finance.[67]

CHAPTER TEN

The Imperial Vision

I

If we are looking for the style of government most favoured by the Duke of York, or for further evidence of his deterioration into authoritarianism and narrow absolutism, then we should look to draw our examples from his administrations in North America and Scotland. In both cases he wielded strong executive powers, freed from the constraints of an English Parliament, and was able to conduct policy in the name of King Charles II, as a virtually autonomous ruler. His tenure as the colonial proprietor of New York, from 1664 onwards, with only the shortest of breaks in the early 1670s, will enable us to chart both the evolution and long-term development of his system of government, while his brief service as the Viceroy of Scotland, from 1679 to 1682, will provide us with a sharply focused insight into his political beliefs at a critical juncture: the time which has often been thought to signify the beginning of his personal decline, and the moment when his cruelty and absolutism first asserted themselves.[1] We shall turn our attention in the first place to a study of James's impact upon his American possessions.

The presence of the Dutch enclave of New Amsterdam, situated at the mouth of the Hudson River, had proved to be a constant source of irritation for the colonial legislatures of New England and for the central government of Charles II alike. To them it represented no more than a stubborn anomaly, a little outpost of the Dutch Republic set adrift amid a great sea of English lands, disrupting the pattern of trade from North to South and driving a wedge between the colonies of Connecticut and Maryland. Its sheltered harbour guaranteed the city its wealth and position as the region's foremost trading centre, while providing a valuable entrepôt for goods brought in by the Dutch West India Company, and effectively frustrating English attempts to enforce the Navigation Acts, or the collection of customs duties, along the length of the Atlantic seaboard. The presence of a significant, and vocal, minority of English settlers who had chosen to live among the burghers of Long Island only served to heighten tensions and, when taken together, these factors seemed to present a compelling argument for the complete removal of Dutch interests from the area. This desire to unite England's possessions in North America, and to gain sovereignty over both the continent and the Atlantic Ocean, fitted in well with the stated foreign policy objectives of James Stuart, who had been actively pressing for a declaration of war against the States General for more than two years.[2] Moreover, Charles II was only too aware that time weighed heavily upon his brother's hands, and that the creation of a new Imperial patrimony for his benefit would not only confer upon him an increased source of personal authority, but might also open up access to the natural resources of the Mohawk and Hudson valleys, stimulate English maritime trade in general, and settle a fitting revenue upon James that would solve his financial worries, once and for all, without the recourse to additional taxation.

To this end, in the early weeks of 1664, he took the decision to authorize an expedition against New Amsterdam and the surrounding territories of the New Netherlands. However, the problem remained of how to justify such a pre-emptive strike, against a power with which he was not yet formally at war. An obvious pretext was not forthcoming, as the Dutch had been settled in their territories for more than a generation and, despite the occasional complaints of English colonists that they were forced to endure the arbitary government of a foreign power, the burghers of the New Netherlands had for the most part treated them with great tolerance, and had sought to live peaceably with their neighbours in the provinces of New England. Consequently, the Council of Foreign Plantations, a body which at that time was under the firm influence of the Crown, began to propagate stories of Dutch cruelty and double-dealing. It was claimed that all of the lands from Long Island to the Delaware had been originally discovered by an English subject, Henry Hudson, who had taken possession of them in the name of the King. According to this version of events, the Dutch had appeared on the scene much later and were no more than 'monstrous and bold usurpers', stealing lands that did not rightfully belong to them and perpetrating a series of atrocities on the unsuspecting English settlers. Hudson, it was alleged, had been brutally assaulted and cast far out to sea in an open boat, while a trader by the name of Daniel How had been 'cruelly murdered and staked alive'.[3] In the light of such serious and disturbing 'evidence', the Council rejected the Dutch claims to sovereignty and voted to have them expelled from their lands at the first available opportunity. In order to bring this about, they established a committee packed with the Duke's closest friends and confidants – including Lord John Berkeley of Stratton, Sir George Carteret and Sir William Coventry – to work on a plan for the successful conquest of New Amsterdam. From the intelligence reports that they were able to gather from merchants and traders to the colony, they estimated that the Dutch garrison was not particularly strong and that their defences could be quickly breached if the King were to authorize the release of four small ships and three companies of veteran soldiers for the expedition. This scratch force, drawn predominantly from the Lord High Admiral's Regiment, was quickly assembled, with James being allowed to nominate his own Officers and Commissioners to lead it. He chose men from among his own inner circle, hardened military men like Sir Robert Carr and Sir George Cartwright, and entrusted overall command to Sir Richard Nicolls, an old friend from his days in exile and a Groom to his Bedchamber. However, he also appointed a merchant, Samuel Maverick, as Commissioner, who was known to be a loyal up-holder of the rights of the Crown in the colonies and whose actions had already brought him into conflict with his neighbours in Massachusetts. It was his job to report back to the Duke on the economic prospects offered by the New Netherlands, and to oversee their subsequent growth in trade and profitability.[4]

The legal instruments formalizing the transition of the Dutch colony to the ownership of the Duke of York were completed in March 1664, when a patent was issued granting him claim to all of the lands in America from St Croix to Long Island, and a set of detailed instructions were despatched post-haste from the King to Colonel Nicolls, outlining the objectives of his mission. He was to strike decisively at Dutch interests on the mainland, 'possessing Long Island, and reduceing that people to an entyre submission and obedience to us & our government, now vested by our grant and Commission in our Brother the Duke of York, and by rais-ing forts or any other way you shall judge most convenient or necessary soe to secure the whole trade to our subjects, that the Dutch maye noe longer ingrosse and exercise that trade which they have wrongfully possessed themselves of'.[5] Significantly, however, for the future of both the new colony and for the existing territories of New England, James's Officers were required to pursue a secondary, and far longer-term, objective. They were to ensure 'that the Act of Navigation be punctually observed' throughout North America, clamping down on infringements made by the local legislatures and obtaining the largest return of revenue possible for the Crown. The deployment of regular troops on the con-tinent was intended to demonstrate the range and power exerted by central government under Charles II, and in this light can be seen to have been aimed as much against Governor Winthrop and the Puritan merchants of Massachusetts Bay, as it was against Governor Stuyvesant and the Dutch Republic.[6]

However, before these schemes could be turned into reality, there remained the small matter of actually seizing the New Netherlands and of dispossessing their current owners. Fortunately for James, he had chosen the right Commander for the task at hand and Nicoll's descent upon the Dutch colony, in August 1664, proved to be a textbook operation, executed with good sense, timing and a certain amount of flair. On his arrival in the Americas, Nicolls had secured additional troops from Governor Winthrop before regrouping his little squadron for a final push on New Amsterdam. He dropped anchor in a sheltered bay off Coney Island and trained his guns on the City walls, summoning the garrison to surrender within forty-eight hours upon the most generous of terms. Governor Stuyvesant was determined to fight to the last, but his soldiers hesitated, concerned that their supplies of powder and grain would not last more than a few days. While the soldiers debated what they should do, it was the civilian population who now took the decisive action. They had initially been terrified by the unexpected appearance of hostile warships and had feared for their lives and property. However, the reassurances offered by Nicolls – that they would not be harmed in any way, and that their liberty of conscience, rights to free trade with Holland, and inheritance laws would all be respected – convinced them that nothing could be gained by bloodshed, and that the only course of action left open to them was that of an honourable surrender. A reluctant Stuyvesant was forced into agreeing to the terms and, as English soldiers replaced the garrison of Fort Amsterdam, Nicolls sent word of his victory back to Massachusetts, rechristening both City and colony as 'New Yorke' in honour of his illustrious patron.[7]

The rest of the New Netherlands capitulated quickly, with the Swedish settlers on the Delaware broadly welcoming the English occupation, and the forts at New Amstel and Casimir falling after a brief, if bloody, confrontation.[8] However, even before these outposts had been taken, and the flag of the States General had been lowered from Stuyvesant's walls, James had made a decision which would have an enormous effect on the future of his new possessions. Although an ocean away, he was supremely confident of victory and began to parcel up his newly granted territory even before it had been won, hiving off great swathes of land between the Atlantic Ocean and the Delaware River to be distributed as gifts for his closest friends (see Map 5, p. 269). Sir George Carteret and Lord John Berkeley, who had been instrumental in planning the campaign against the Dutch, benefited in this way from the creation of a new province to be known as Nova Caesarea, or more popularly as East and West New Jersey.[9] From the Duke's point of view, this was a simple and relatively painless expedient, rewarding outstanding service in a way that, although generous, did not cost him too dearly in terms of capital expenditure from his Parliamentary grant, or eat into the acreage of his existing English estates. Moreover, as a Prince and the sole proprietor of New York, James was perfectly within his rights to treat the colony as though it were a piece of his own private property, buying, selling or dividing it as he would with any other commodity. Unfortunately, while this rather high-handed behaviour might have made sense within the confines and constraints of the Palace of Whitehall, the Duke was to remain blissfully unaware of the adminstrative havoc that such an artificial separation would wreak on the territories concerned.

James had never planned to relinquish his political authority over New Jersey, and believed that his gift of the territories had conveyed a private rather than a political ownership to Carteret and Berkeley. They, however, did not choose to see things in this way and Carteret promptly created his cousin, Philip, Governor of the new province. This was a significant appointment, confirming the break-up of the political unit that had been the New Netherlands and ensuring that henceforth New Jersey and New York would be ruled by two entirely different administrations. Moreover, the subdivision of land and the powers of government that had begun with James's original grant did not stop there and within a decade New Jersey had become virtually ungovernable, with scores of shareholders, scattered throughout England and the Americas, seeking to contest the sovereignty of the region with the Duke's agents at every opportunity.[10] As a result of the creation of so many special interest groups, the system of proprietorial government that had evolved there was particularly fragile and ill-suited to achieving a lasting stability. Given such a volatile climate, family disputes could loom large and political opportunism flourished. In this way, an adventurer like Captain James Carteret could rally opposition against his father, Philip, and depose him as Governor, ruling in his place as the 'President' of New Jersey in 1672, until the Duke of York was finally persuaded to intervene against him, stripping him of his offices and sending him home in disgrace.[11]

If the political damage inflicted upon New York by the creation of a rival province had gone unforeseen by James, then the economic consequences of the land division were clearly pointed out to him by Sir Richard Nicolls. The Duke had waited until 29 November 1664, a full three months after the invasion, to inform Nicolls, whom he had appointed Governor of New York, that he intended to grant New Jersey away to his favourites. Nicolls was horrified and wrote back at once to protest, urging that the scheme should be dropped and that the courtiers could be better compensated with a grant of some 100,000 acres on the lower Delaware, which would not serve to limit the subsequent expansion of the colony to the West. James, however, showed a marked reluctance to listen to his informed advice and did not even bother to reply to his increasingly urgent pleas.[12] In consequence, both the City and colony of New York were saddled with a number of intractable, yet wholly avoidable, problems which would mar their future commercial developments and frustrate the original plans for their development. In creating New Jersey, James had ceded away a far richer and more extensive territory than that which he had retained for himself; the soil on Long Island was

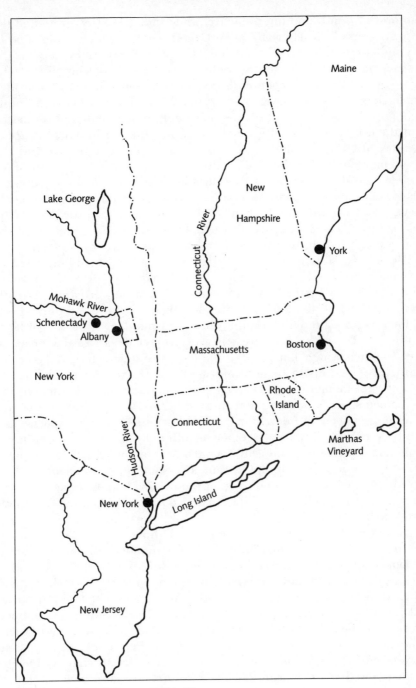

Map 5 *New York Colony, c. 1664–85*

notoriously sandy and unproductive, while Indian activity prohibited the opening up of the Hudson Valley. Colonists felt themselves hemmed in by the encroachments of Connecticut on one hand, and chafed at the infringements of their customs rights by the Jerseys, on the other.[13] The presence of a new entrepôt on the western borders of New York provided smugglers with a safe haven and offered them a means of circumventing the port duties, rents and surveys that would otherwise have been levied on them by the colonial government. The Duke's spontaneous act of generosity, uninformed by a knowledge of the geography and the economic climate of the region, thus served to stifle the growth of his colony and denied its adminstration a much-needed source of revenue. This failure to tax effectively imposed a severe restraint on the actions of successive Governors, while their inability to enforce the provisions of the Navigation Acts struck directly at that very body of legislation which James had originally intervened in the Americas in order to defend.[14]

Denied its full potential, New York did not, as the Dutch burghers had originally promised James, 'bloom and grow like the Cedars of Lebanon', but developed instead into an imperial frontier province. Nicolls reported back to the Earl of Clarendon that he had found only fifteen poor villages scattered along the whole 120-mile length of Long Island, while the Duke's own interest in the project began to waiver as he became increasingly impatient at the length of time it took for even his initial instructions to be accomplished.[15] With New Jersey competing strongly for immigrants and capital investment, returns from the outlying settlements, which had been encouraged by the Dutch to trade for beaver furs at the expense of developing their agriculture, were not spectacular. Only New York City itself seemed to offer the promise of yielding a substantial increase on the Duke's initial investment and, as the result of its success as a seaport, it rapidly came to assume a predominant position in the political and economic life of the colony. Nicolls thought that in time its wealth might even eclipse that of Boston, and boasted that it was likely to become the 'best of all his majesty's townes in America'.[16]

However, the problem remained that its hold on trade relied upon business networks that had built up over generations of Dutch control. Export goods such as furs and hides sent down from Albany, and tobacco grown in Maryland and Virginia, were shipped directly to Holland, and then dispersed throughout mainland Europe. Ties with the Caribbean island of Curaçao and the South American enclave of Surinam continued to provide the merchants of New York with regular consignments of sugar and dyed fabrics, while the vast majority of their staple supplies and manufactured goods came out to them on ships directly chartered by the Dutch West India Company. Nicolls was quick to realize that the future prosperity of the colony, and the political stability of his own administration, depended in the first case upon the support of the leading members of the existing Dutch business community. He came to equate their interests in furthering the trade with Holland with his own, in establishing the firm foundations of English rule and securing new financial resources for his royal master. The one thing he sought above all to avoid was the mass exodus of the colony's inhabitants, as had happened after the English occupation of Tangier, and assiduously began to pay court to the Dutch, promising them that he would do nothing to jeopardize their free trade with Holland.[17]

It would take a long time before alternative patterns of trade with the English colonies in the West Indies could be fully developed, and in the meantime the dominance of the Dutch merchants could only be successfully challenged in one major sphere. As new English, French and Dutch settlers combined to swell the city's population, they increased the market for slaves, the one commodity which the young colony's proprietor was quite willing and able to supply to them, in his capacity as Governor of the African companies. In marked contrast to the Dutch West India Company, which had used slavery to implement its colonial policy, James sought only private financial gain and was quite prepared to use New York in order to foster slavery for its own sake. His patronage ensured that the slave trade became an integral part of this emerging colonial society, and ensured that by the end of the century the trade in human lives had become a staple of the provincal economy.[18] With the establishment of a new market for his own goods, and with Nicolls' success in guaranteeing the continued presence and co-operation of the Dutch mercantile community, James had reasonable grounds for feeling pleased at the opportunities afforded him by his American conquests. However, if the financial prospects of New York City seemed to have been assured, then the political future of his colony, as a whole, was to remain troubled and would not be so easily resolved.

II

The Charter which Charles II had given to his brother in March 1664, had attempted to set out a blueprint for the Duke's government in the colonies. Unfortunately, the speed at which the expedition to the New Netherlands had been mounted – which was vital for its military success – had also meant that the document itself had to be prepared in great haste, without due deliberation or a careful consideration of the full implications of vesting such enormous sovereign powers in the hands of a single individual. The Duke was confirmed as the single proprietor of the new territories, answerable only to the King, with the right to appoint his own officials, make his own laws and ordinances, and sit in judgment on legal cases, both civil and criminal. He had complete control over the regulation of trade, taxation and land disputes, and reserved the right to oversee the colony's defences in times of war.[19] In stark contrast to the provisions of the other colonial charters granted in the 1660s, no mention was ever made of establishing a representative assembly and New York's inhabitants were henceforth to be denied any sort of say in the formulation of the laws under which they were to be governed. This authoritarian style of government reflected less upon James's own prejudices than upon the colony's own unique status as a conquered territory with a population who were overwhelmingly Dutch, and hostile to their new position as a subject people.[20] The problem remained, however, that while the Charter had fulfilled its primary purpose in creating a substantial patrimony for the Duke and in confirming his executive powers therein, it had made absolutely no provision for the establishment and conduct of local government in the region. Moreover, it remained decidedly ambiguous as to how James's authority should actually be exercised. If there was never any intention for him to visit the colony which now bore his name, or to administer its welfare directly from Whitehall – a task which was probably logistically impossible, anyway, given the barrier to communication represented by the Atlantic Ocean – then arrangements for the day-to-day running of his administration would have to devolve upon successive governors.

It fell, therefore, to Nicolls to try to evolve a system of government which would reconcile the preconditions for English rule set out in the Charter, with the practical requirements of a new Anglo-Dutch frontier society. He began by stamping his master's authority across the map of his new territories, anglicizing the names of a series of Dutch settlements, before issuing a fresh compendium of *Lawes for New York*, which came to be popularly known as the Duke's code. This great raft of legislation – first ratified in March 1665 and subsequently added to in 1666, 1672 and 1675 – sought to combine the best practice of existing English, Dutch and New England codes, and covered everything from the registration of births and deaths, to the regulation of the local militia, Indian relations and the hunting of wolves.[21] The Dutch tradition of religious toleration was respected, provided that 'the Minister of every Parish shall Preach constantly every Sunday, and shall also pray for the Kinge, Queene, Duke of Yorke, and the Royal family', allowing for 'religions of all sorts' to flourish, with Calvinists, Independents, Anabaptists, Quakers and Jews continuing to live and worship side by side. Other Dutch precedents, such as those governing the double nomination of local officials and the partial retirement from work in old age, were also adhered to, but some of the fundamental principles of legislation in the New England colonies were not included among these final provisions. No mention was made of the importance of town meetings in the governing of small communities, and any suggestion of an assembly was once again firmly ruled out. These omissions were crucial for the development of New York, ensuring – as Nicolls acutely observed to the Lord Chancellor – that 'Our new Lawes are not contrived soe Democratically as the rest', and serving to reinforce both the position of the Duke of York as proprietor and 'the Authority of his Majesties Letters patents'.[22] In this atmosphere, Nicolls was able to create around him a highly centralized form of government, consisting of an advisory council, which he himself appointed in his capacity as Governor, and a series of local magistrates whose job it was to enforce the letter of the law. More controversially still, he introduced a series of measures which owed little to either English or Dutch cultures, but a great deal to the pressing need to raise revenue, and set about ordering the compulsory renewal of all the former deeds and patents to land and property. By invalidating all of the old grants awarded during the Dutch occupation, Nicolls committed the sitting tenants to undertaking new surveys upon their holdings and forced them to pay an additional fee in order to re-register their patents of ownership. This indirect source of property tax, unsurprisingly, became the first of many issues around which opposition and discontent with the Duke's regime began to crystallize.

Ironically, it was initially among the English-speaking towns of Long Island that organized resistance to James's provincial administration was at its strongest. Many of their citizens objected to taking the oaths of allegiance required by their new proprietor, and to the failure of his Governor to grant them rights equal to those already enjoyed by their neighbours in Connecticut. Nicolls was caught in a dilemma: his instructions from the Duke strictly forbade him from conceding to an elected assembly, but at the same time he could not risk alienating the minority of English settlers, whose continued support and approval were vital for the survival of his government, in the face of a disaffected Dutch majority. More seriously still, his ability to quell dissent and to stifle calls for reform was seriously challenged by the outbreak of war with the States General, in March 1665. The maritime trade, upon which the colony's prosperity depended, was effectively curtailed by the depredations of the rival fleets, and Nicolls was forced to beg his patron to despatch cargoes of English goods to New York in order to replace those that were no longer available from Holland. James consulted with Thomas Povey and his acquaintances among London's merchant community, as to the viability of such a scheme, but took no further action. Instead, he wrote back to his Governor simply entrusting him with the task of raising the morale of his garrison and of securing the loyalty and devotion of his subjects to his cause. It became increasingly clear that the Duke was only interested in deriving a steady income from his new lands, and that once the 'great revenues' from trade he had been promised failed to materialize, he had little further appetite for subsidizing the struggling colonial administration carried out in his name.[23] As he continued to turn a deaf ear to Nicoll's increasingly desperate pleas for help, the colony's soldiers and officials went unpaid. Only the arrival of occasional Dutch supply ships prevented the wholesale exodus of New York's merchants, while the sudden outbreak of rioting which engulfed the Long Island villages of Southampton, Southwold and Easthampton in the spring of 1668 caused the Governor to seriously reconsider his position. Having run up private debts of over £8,000 in a desperate attempt to bolster the local economy, Nicolls now appealed to his master to be relieved of his duties and sailed for home in the August of that year. The inability of the Duke and the English merchant fleet to service the needs of the colony was brought graphically home, as the 'conqueror' of New Amsterdam was forced to seek passage back to England on board a Dutch merchantman, as the only available form of transportation to hand.[24]

The Duke chose another soldier, Francis Lovelace, as Nicolls' replacement, in the hope that he might be better able to see to the colony's defences and to rebuild its shattered economic base. However, he was soon to be sorely disappointed on both counts. Lovelace had decided, even before he arrived in New York, to use his tenure as Governor in order to enrich himself and his family. In order to fulfil his purpose, he was accompanied by his brother, Thomas, a land speculator, who masqueraded as the colony's 'Commercial Advisor'. While Francis used his authority to try to encourage immigrants from Bermuda to settle in the colony, Thomas began to buy up cheap land on Staten Island, the banks of the Delaware River, and in New York City itself, which had already been secretly set aside in order to house the new arrivals. Having achieved a modicum of success with this venture, the Lovelaces then sought to extend their influence into the trade with Holland, forging links with the money markets in Amsterdam through the intercession of the colony's Dutch merchants. Furthermore, in an attempt to broaden the basis upon which his administration and personal finances were built, Governor Lovelace began to co-opt some of the members of New York's leading Dutch families on to his council and started to enforce a far tighter control on the collection of customs duties from the trade with Connecticut, Massachusetts and Rhode Island.[25] Although this latter measure might well have been calculated to curry favour with James, it did nothing to restore the fortunes of his colony, and the Duke's administration continued to be plagued by mounting debts. The privileged position enjoyed by New York City was a source of continual resentment for all the other settlements in the province, and some of the eastern towns even tried to secede, attempting to reconstitute themselves as independent corporations or applying to be incorporated into Connecticut.[26] It was at this point that the Governor's entrepreneurial schemes were brought to a sudden and entirely unforeseen end, by the arrival of a Dutch invasion fleet.

Despite Charles II's declaration of a Third Dutch War in March 1672, there was little outward sign of a change in the life of the colony for more than a year. Dutch merchantmen continued to ply their trade along its coasts, offloading their cargoes on to the city's waterfront and filling its warehouses with the raw materials and consumer goods that ensured its survival. With both sides in the conflict showing a marked reluctance to disrupt a trade that was mutually beneficial, the colony's supply lines across the Atlantic remained open to business, while its shipping escaped relatively unscathed from the fighting. New York itself remained quiet and Governor Lovelace, discounting sightings of a Dutch fleet off the coast of Virginia as mere scaremongering, chose to leave his command in the hands of a junior Officer, Captain John Manning, and pay a visit to Governor Winthrop of Massachusetts.[27] His departure could not have been more badly timed, as within a matter of days a squadron of eight Dutch men-of-war, under Cornelius Evertson, sailed into view of Staten Island and promptly summoned the garrison of New York to surrender. Manning tried to play for time, demanding to know by what right they came 'into the river that belongs to the Duke of York?', and hoping to prolong negotiations for long enough that Lovelace might return from Connecticut with a relief force.[28] However, he knew that he was in a desperate situation. He had a mere eighty soldiers with which to defend the entire circuit of the city walls, the Long Island militia had stubbornly refused to obey his summonses, and the foundations of Fort James – his only strong point – were crumbling beneath him. The Duke had entrusted Lovelace with the rebuilding and restocking of the fort, but sufficient money had never been found, as the colonists had always protested that it was of no use to them, and that the high prices charged by the Dutch merchants prevented them from paying additional taxes for its upkeep. Furthermore, James's refusal to grant an assembly, and Lovelace's policy of favouring New York City at the expense of the other towns, now caused the support for the Duke's government to haemorrhage away. The English settlers remained neutral, while the Dutch rushed to congratulate Evertson and to hail him as a liberator. As Dutch landing parties swarmed ashore, Manning offered the best resistance he could and kept up an artillery barrage for four hours, before finally bowing to the inevitable and suing for terms.[29] His subsequent evacuation of the city, and the suddenness with which James's administration had collapsed, sparked a brief renaissance in Dutch colonial affairs, as old governmental titles and institutions reasserted themselves, and revealed just how fragile and superficial had been the English hold on power.[30]

While the legislatures in Connecticut and Massachusetts continued to pass resolutions condemning the Dutch attack, and appealing for military action in order to retake the province, the Duke and his advisers remained powerless to act. However much of a heavy blow the loss of New York had delivered to James's prestige, the passing of the First Test Act and the prosecution of the war closer to home – in the North Sea and the Channel – figured far more prominently in his thoughts than any consideration of the fate of his own stricken colony. Fortunately for the English settlers on Long Island, the States General were no more interested in the fate of the region than its ex-proprietor. They saw the colony as being unproductive, surrounded on all sides by hostile territories, and representing a constant drain on their resources. In their eyes, Evertson's victory came to be viewed as a mere 'windfall' conquest, which could eventually be bargained away, to a greater and more lasting advantage, at subsequent peace talks. Consequently, the Dutch government was prepared to return the colony to English rule at the first available opportunity, in order to demonstrate their goodwill, and to secure their hold over their more profitable possessions in Surinam. At the Treaty of Westminster, in February 1674, they signed away their rights to New York in perpetuity, and enabled James to take control of the territories once again.[31]

The Duke now moved quickly to reassert his position. He despatched a new Governor in the person of Sir Edmund Andros to take over from Lovelace, who in the meantime had been imprisoned in the Tower for debt, and strove to regulate the affairs of the colony much more closely than had hitherto been the case.[32] James seems to have reached the conclusion that the failure of New York to return the large profits expected of it could only be explained through the practice of large-scale fraud. In order to make sure that all of the monies due to him reached their destination, he now appointed John Lewin as his personal auditor and agent in the colonies, to investigate and report back to him on the economic development of his proprietory. Moreover, he entrusted the collection of taxation and the conveyancing of land to his own household officers, Sir Alan Apsley and Sir John Werden, who operated out of his own apartments in Whitehall and St James's.[33]

Andros's instructions from the Duke urged him not to levy additional taxation upon the colonists, but to rely instead for the growth in his revenue from an expansion in customs and harbour duties. This injunction, to use every means at his disposal to increase the volume of trade flowing through the colony, meant that – like Lovelace before him – he was forced back on to an uneasy alliance with the Dutch traders in the provincial capital, and was obliged to fight to defend the rights of the shipping magnates operating out of Holland. Thus, while political expediency and the concern for defence demanded that he exclude Dutch advisers from his original councils, financial necessity and Lewin's expectation of increased profits eventually compelled him to readmit them. By concentrating wealth and power in the hands of a narrow urban elite, Andros was able to rule authoritatively without the recourse to an elected assembly.[34] However, this style of government, although well suited to the authoritarian personalities of both Governor and proprietor alike, frustrated attempts by the settlers of Long Island and the Hudson and Delaware Valleys, to share in the social and economic benefits enjoyed by their neighbours in the city. If he was not to permanently alienate these powerful interest groups from his administration, Andros realized that he would have to meet their own desire for territorial and commercial expansion through the opening up of new markets in the interior. The only way to accomplish this task was to break free of the colony's existing geographical constraints, and to annexe significant tracts of New Jersey and Western Connecticut from their current owners. Unfortunately, James would still not commit himself on the matter, and attempts to dispute Philip Carteret's right to govern in the Jerseys foundered on legal technicalities, while Andros's own opportunistic raid on Connecticut, in the midst of an Indian war, was quickly rebuffed by the deployment of the colonial militias.[35] The failure of these measures condemned Andros to an unsatisfactory dependency upon metropolitan support, confirmed the existing division of the Duke's original patrimony, and effectively limited the room for manoeuvre of all future colonial governors.

Andros's reliance upon Dutch merchants came to be increasingly frowned upon by the City of London, as it attempted to encroach upon the established patterns of trade with Holland, and as a new generation of English entrepreneurs began to set up business in the colonies. These trends were clearly at odds with the complete indifference with which New York had been previously regarded by the London money markets, and it may well be that the provisions of the Treaty of Westminster, which had removed any threat of a further change in the colony's sovereignty, had served to reassure English merchants that their future investments in the region would be safeguarded. Andros, however, did not seek to welcome the activities of his fellow countrymen and moved to prosecute a number of the major English trading houses for infringements of his monopoly.[36] Such high-handed and unpatriotic behaviour provoked howls of rage from the City of London, and a group of its foremost merchants now began an intensive lobbying campaign to persuade the Duke to remove his servant from office. To their surprise, they found that

James was predisposed to listen to them. The low yield of returns from his American colony still troubled him and, as he was unable to accept that the root cause of the problem lay with his own gift to Carteret and Berkeley, he clung to the belief that he was being defrauded on a massive scale. As a result, the allegations that Andros was allowing an illegal trade with the Netherlands to go unpunished, while permitting his friends to circumvent the Navigation Acts and to bring in their own cargoes duty-free, struck a deep chord with the Duke. He wrote to demand Andros's immediate return, in May 1680, and sent out John Lewin to fully investigate any hint of financial irregularities in the colony.[37]

Even though no specific charges had as yet been levelled against him, Andros was well aware that they were imminent and hurriedly left for London in an attempt to forestall the inquiry, and clear his name. Rather than overseeing the smooth transition to a new Governor, he virtually abrogated all responsibility for his post, transferring power to Captain Brockholls – as an inexperienced caretaker – and neglecting to furnish him with a sufficiently detailed set of instructions, which might have enabled him to administer the government of the colony more effectively in his absence. Consequently, although the fact of his departure did nothing to upset the political balance of the colony, the manner of his leaving served to plunge his entire administration into chaos and created a power vacuum at the heart of the government. This soon became apparent when the customs duties – which should have been renewed every three years, under the provisions of James's own legislation – expired in November 1680, and neither the Duke, Brockhalls nor William Dyre, his tax collector, appeared to notice. Under normal circumstances this oversight might not have aroused much adverse comment, but the spectacle of Brockholls and Dyre continuing to collect taxes, to which they were not legally entitled, enflamed passions and sparked off a major customs strike throughout the colony.[38] With Brockholls' council both unwilling and unable to take any firm action in order to protect their officials, Dyre found himself arraigned for high treason, after trying to collect customs duties from the English merchantmen who had docked in New York harbour. His spirited defence of his actions at the Court of Assize and appeal to the authority of his royal patent, did enough, however, to wrong-foot his prosecutors and to convince them that he could be better dealt with back in England.[39]

While the evidence against Dyre was being collected, John Lewin was already compiling his own dossier on the activities of Governor Andros. As a businessman with extensive holdings in the City of London, Lewin was hardly likely to be an impartial judge of the record of the now discredited Governor, and filed a damning report, that was critical of almost every aspect of his administration. His findings revealed that the colony was ruled by a narrow and corrupt clique, loyal to Andros, who not only sought to cheat their proprietor out of his revenues, but also practised the most arbitary and self-serving form of government imaginable.[40] Having cast serious doubts as to the probity of his principal Officers and initiated a process by which they might be replaced, James had raised expectations of reform and had – quite unwittingly – almost succeeded in bringing his colony to the brink of a full-scale revolt. In these circumstances it might have been thought that he would have pressed hard for the speedy conviction of the wrong-doers, but at this crucial moment he seems to have lost all interest in the enterprise. The case against Dyre was quietly dropped, while after a protracted and often furious courtroom battle between Lewin and Andros, James directed John Churchill, as his Solicitor General, to acquit the defendant.[41] Although he was not immediately restored to his post as Governor, Andros managed to regain the Duke's favour and continued in his service. This amazing turn of events would have appeared to have been inexplicable and nothing short of the miraculous, if it were not in keeping with what we have already established about the pattern of James's vascillating behaviour, as demonstrated by his conduct during his naval battles, the sinking of the *Gloucester*, and by his later debacle upon Salisbury Plain.

During the court hearings, tax collection across the colony had been suspended and Albany and Long Island had become virtually autonomous regions, paying little heed to the diktats of central government. With the Brockholls administration facing bankruptcy and the power of the Crown in the colonies seriously weakened by the effects of the Exclusion Crisis, calls for the granting of an assembly for New York could no longer go entirely unheeded by the Duke. James had always tried to constrain his Governors to a fairly narrow set of objectives, and had wanted, above all, peace and quiet from his troublesome colony. The granting of a colonial Parliament, which would have been filled by an explosive mixture of English puritans and Dutch Calvinists, had always seemed to offer nothing but trouble and James had raised fundamental doubts as to the loyalty of any such assembly.[42] However, given the erosion of his authority in the colony and the insolvency of his administration, the Duke was forced to offer the colonists a more representative form of government in the early months of 1682. After almost twenty years of bitter opposition to any such suggestion, it might seem strange that James should so suddenly have embraced the very system which had previously been anathema to him. Moreover, if the Duke had been experiencing a marked degeneration in his character as his brother's reign progressed, we might expect to have found rather more evidence for his political acumen and receptiveness to change in the 1660s, and altogether less for his pragmatism and adaptability in the early 1680s. The key to his fundamental change in tactics would seem to lie with his own shifting circumstances, rather than with any mysterious medical complaint. Governor Andros had suggested calling an assembly in 1675, as a means of solving their financial problems, only to be rejected out of hand. The difference in February 1682 was that James was in a far weaker political position, far removed in Scotland from the councils of the King in Whitehall, and anxious not to squander his own personal fortune in propping up an ailing and distant regime.[43] In addition, the conclusions of John Lewin's final report, which told him in no uncertain terms that the economy of New York was wholly unsustainable in its present form, may well have proved decisive in forcing his hand.

The new Parliament, which was elected in September 1683 by the freeholders, comprised of eighteen deputies drawn from throughout the colony. They were granted the right to debate freely and set about drafting a new Charter of Liberties which would have substantially amended the Duke's Laws. While reaffirming the principle of religious toleration and the predominance of the Dutch merchants in the commercial life of the colony, it also sought the right to levy taxes, and to strengthen the authority of the members of the assembly; giving them powers commensurate with those of English MPs. The Duke's position as proprietor was not directly challenged, but in future he and his council would have to work in tandem with the settlers' elected representatives. James, however, had retained his control over public appointments, the militia and the distribution of new land grants. More importantly, he still retained his right, as the proprietor of the colony, to have the final say in the passing of any legislation formulated by the assembly. Consequently, he was able to wave through a massive 100 per cent increase in customs duties, which could be used to benefit his own subsequent administrations, while retarding the progress of the Charter, through its final stages, as Charles II's imperial policy dramatically changed its direction. The crushing of the Oxford Parliament and the revival of Tory fortunes at home, greatly strengthened the power of the executive and allowed the administration of the colonies to be brought under a much firmer and far more centralized method of control. With the gradual reassertion of the prerogative across the colonial legislatures and the knowledge that, after the plantation of the Carolinas and the recovery of New York, the English colonies on the Atlantic seaboard now formed an unbroken geographical unit, it was at last possible to implement a common administrative system throughout the region.[44] Having secured his revenues from the assembly, James could now afford to follow the example of his brother far more closely. Although he had granted his preliminary approval to the Charter of Liberties in October 1684, the Duke now temporized and failed to give his final assent to Sir John

Werden, despite the continued promptings of the legislature. The death of Charles II, just four months later, threw the future of New York into the melting pot, as James now chose to reject the Charter and allowed the assembly itself to lapse. All talk of representative government was forgotten, and the colony was reforged as both a royal province and a constituent element in a new and unified 'Dominion of New England'.[45]

James's record as a colonial administrator does not, therefore, sit well with his reputation as a strong advocate of Empire and a stern practitioner of effective public finance. While he certainly enjoyed the trappings of power which his American colony bestowed upon him, it is doubtful whether he had anything more than the most superficial knowledge of, and interest in, the problems facing the settlers of New York. Although he certainly wanted to govern his province authoritatively, the evidence provided by his granting away of New Jersey, the collapse of his public finances and his administrative dilettantism, would seem to indicate that he was entirely lacking in both the application and the resources to do so. Furthermore, given the weakness of the State apparatus at his disposal, his continued commitment to the maintenance of a highly expensive and autocratic system of government, over a vast and socially diverse colony, could only serve to drive a wedge between the Duke and his subject peoples, and represented a strategy that was as divisive as it was inappropriate.[46] The fact that James despatched a garrison to his proprietary, or that his Governors came from predominantly military backgrounds, can be seen as reflecting New York's special status as a conquered frontier territory, which was vulnerable to both Dutch and Indian attacks, rather than a more sinister imperialist philosophy.[47] The military usefulness of his soldiers was more than negated by the extraordinarily high costs of their upkeep, and it is doubtful whether James was ever possessed by a grand imperial vision. His actions in eventually bowing to the inevitable, and granting a colonial assembly with a minimum of fuss, would appear to argue that he was not too strongly bound to any particular ideological constraints, and that he was quite capable of pursuing purely pragmatic policies when he was afforded no other choice. As he did not set down his thoughts on Empire for posterity, it is extremely difficult to attribute to him such an ambitious and original concept. Moreover, his sparse attendance on the Committees for Tangier, and Trade and Plantations, which might be thought to have been the powerhouses for formulating imperial policy, would seem to suggest that the Duke's interest was far more limited than has previously been thought. When he was called upon for his specialist opinion, as in the cases of Bacon's Revolt in 1676 and the evacuation of Tangier in 1683, it was always primarily as a soldier rather than as a 'mature' empire builder.[48] His distrust of representative bodies and any expression of dissent is implicit in all his public actions and utterances, but his world view was essentially limited, if not actually parochial.

James saw himself as being an essentially European Prince, with his possessions in the colonies adding no more to him than an additional lustre (see Map 6, p. 283). Despite occasional visits to France and his unwelcome exiles in Scotland and Brussels, he rarely moved far from London in the quarter of a century after 1660. He learnt of Africa and the New World only through his naval and mercantile contacts, and from discussions held in the Admiralty Office, his Whitehall apartments and in boardrooms of the joint-stock companies with which he was involved. His conception of these territories, their indigenous peoples and their physical geographies, were therefore often quite limited, and heavily influenced by the intellectual and artistic models that had evolved under the Roman Empire and Medieval Europe. Consequently, in the same way that his imperial portraiture had showed him to be a classical warrior, he now fell back upon the familiar symbols of European culture in order to enforce his authority upon far-flung continents. This not only explains his gift of a consignment of coronets to the kings of Africa, but also accounts for his bizarre attempt to erect posts bearing his ducal coat of arms in the villages of the Iroquois confederacy.[49]

With his knowledge of the colonies severely restricted in this manner, James's philosophy of Empire remained essentially emotional and undeveloped. Although he did not doubt for a moment that a nation, or an individual, could become more wealthy through the acquisition of new territories, he had little idea of how to gain revenue from New York once the conquest of the territories had been achieved. Proprietorial government, without the recourse to an elected tax-raising assembly, could only flourish given the careful attention of its master and vast injections of money from his own private purse. Unfortunately, James was prepared to invest neither, and desiring no more than quick profits and a pliant colonial population, he created a system of government for New York which was old-fashioned, autocratic and ultimately spectacularly unsuccessful.[50] If his administration in the Americas had little to recommend it, we should now turn our attention to his governance of Scotland which has often been seen as signifying the turning point of his entire political career.[51]

III

James was to spend just under two years as High Commissioner in Scotland, acting as his brother's most senior representative in the northern kingdom from November 1679 to February 1680, and again from October 1680 to March 1682. In that time, he attempted to restore law and order to a land shattered by rebellion, and to remodel the

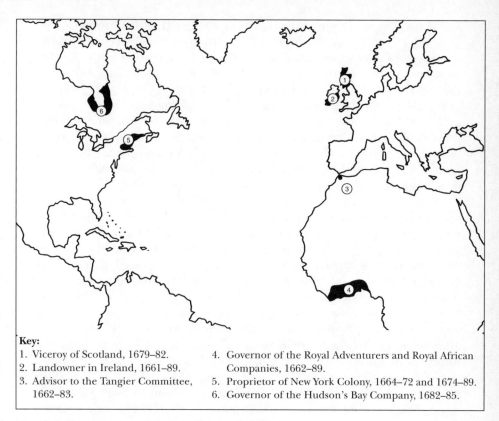

Key:

1. Viceroy of Scotland, 1679–82.
2. Landowner in Ireland, 1661–89.
3. Advisor to the Tangier Committee, 1662–83.
4. Governor of the Royal Adventurers and Royal African Companies, 1662–89.
5. Proprietor of New York Colony, 1664–72 and 1674–89.
6. Governor of the Hudson's Bay Company, 1682–85.

Map 6 *A World Empire. The global influence of James Stuart*

faltering administration bequeathed to him by the Duke of Lauderdale. The Duke had, however, shown little initial desire to take up this most difficult of postings, preferring instead the company of his friends at Whitehall, and going to the extent of feigning an illness for his wife in order to delay the date of his departure. Despite an emotional intervention by John Churchill and the offer of a compromise solution, by which the young Duchess might remain behind in London to convalesce, Charles II remained firm in his resolve that James should travel North at the first available opportunity, and let it be known that he would not entertain any further discussion of the matter. The reality of the situation was that the King simply could not afford to be seen with the Duke at his side. With political temperatures running high, the continued strength of Exclusionist sentiment in the capital, and indeed throughout the country at large, had succeeded in transforming James into a hate figure for a significant proportion of the Protestant nation and it had become abundantly clear to Charles II that his brother could no longer remain safe in England for any prolonged period of time. However, if James represented an enormous liability to political stability South of the border, then it occurred to the King that in the absence of the Duke of Monmouth, his talents as a soldier might be put to good use in Scotland, where a long-running rebellion still smouldered and offered a potent challenge to the authority of the Crown.[52] Furthermore, while Edinburgh was sufficiently remote from London to allow the Duke of York to lay low for a time, and to remain out of sight of Shaftesbury's partisans, it was still near enough for him to lead a Scottish Army South, if the position of the monarchy were to deteriorate rapidly.

Although James's journey North took on the appearance of a royal progress, with his cavalcade travelling at a leisurely pace, and the Duke taking every opportunity to pause *en route* in order to pay court to the local Tory gentry, he had no real idea of the situation that would face him once he reached Scotland.[53] The western counties of Lanark and Galloway had been in open rebellion since the start of the summer and, despite a heavy defeat at Bothwell Bridge, the spirit of the Field Conventicles – those Presbyterians who had refused to accept the reimposition of episcopacy, and had chosen to preach in the countryside after being ejected from their ministries – remained largely unbroken. Reprisals by government forces had been brutal but not decisive, and there can be little doubt that James reached Berwick with a certain amount of trepidation, unsure whether he was about to wage a full-scale war against the remnants of a rebel army, or to simply conduct a policing action against those Covenanters who were still under arms, though scattered in the hills. After the cold reception he had been accorded by the City and Corporation of York, and the virtual indifference of the northern gentry to his cause, his tumultuous welcome at the gates of Berwick-upon-Tweed must have done much to have allayed his fears. The whole of the Scottish Privy Council had ridden out to greet him, along with almost 2,000 'other nobility and gentry of several shires', and the King's troop of horse, which now formed his escort.[54] After a triumphant entry into Edinburgh, James took up residence at Holyrood House and began to gather up the reins of government.

Unfortunately, he still lacked an official position. Since his childhood he had held the title of Privy Councillor of Scotland, but this had always been a purely honorary position and had carried with it no actual responsibility or power. Consequently, when he tried to take his seat on the Council, the problem arose over his swearing of the necessary oaths of allegiance. As the Scottish formula had been drafted in accordance with the English Test Acts, James should have theoretically been debarred. However, the Council was far more concerned about the activities of the Protestant rebels than about the Duke's own profession of faith, and was prepared to appeal to the King to provide them with a swift resolution to their dilemma. Charles II wrote back, confirming his brother in office by use of the royal prerogative and stating that it was by his own 'pleasure that he continue to act as a Privy Councillour, in that our ancient Kingdome, without taking any oath'.[55] Having secured this powerful endorsement, James finally took his place at the head of the Privy Council on 4 December 1679, and immediately began to impose his authority on that body, pressing for effective measures to restore order throughout the kingdom. In marked contrast to the attitude he displayed towards the board of the Hudson's Bay Company and the Committee for Trade and Plantations, the Duke showed an enormous amount of interest in the proceedings of the Council, attending thirty-one of its meetings in the space of little more than four months.[56] Later generations of Lowland Scottish writers, from Robert Wodrow in his seminal *History of the Sufferings of the Church in Scotland* to Walter Scott in his *Tales of a Grandfather*, would come to see this first period of James's rule in the North as marking a revitalization of the Privy Council, and ushering in a new era of cruel and extraordinary repression for their people.[57] However, there is little evidence to suggest that, during his first stay, James did anything more than adhere to the existing policies of central government, as laid down in both London and Edinburgh. He approved the legislation that was already in place for prosecuting the Covenanters, drilled his soldiers and authorized new raids by his dragoons against the rebels, but in general seems to have held himself aloof from the struggles in Council fought out by the various shifting aristocratic factions. More concerned about the political developments taking place in England, he wrote to George Legge, in December 1679, in order to outline his own objectives: 'I live here as cautiously as I can, and am very careful to give offence to none and to have no partialities, and preach to them laying aside all private animosities and securing the King his own way. None shall have reason to complain of me, and though some of either party here might have hoped I should have showed my partiality for them, and some of my friends have been of [the] opinion it had been best for me to have done so, and by it have secured one side to me, yet I am convinced it was not fit for me to do it, it being no way good for His Majesty's service.'[58] For once, it seems, James was content to act prudently and to accept his own limitations, strengthening the power of the Crown through mediation between the great noble families and by uniting all of those who wished for peace and social stability, in common cause, against the western rebels. As a result, he was a great success, and his attempts to recreate a Court society around his residence at Holyrood House, coupled with his willingness to spend lavishly on entertainments and civic improvements, ensured that he won himself many friends within the Scottish establishment. His departure back to England, in March 1680, was accompanied by expressions of genuine – if conventional – sorrow, and he and his inner circle of English advisers, including John Werden and John Churchill, were honoured with the distinction of being created burgesses and guild brothers of the City of Edinburgh.[59]

Although James had hoped that his recall from Scotland would be a permanent measure, and his Duchess certainly made no attempt to disguise her delight in leaving, his failure to wring the promise of unconditional protection from the King in the event of his impeachment, and the overwhelming hostility of the new Parliament, called in August 1680, compelled him to seek sanctuary in the North for a second time. On this occasion, however, the Duke returned with greatly enhanced powers and an explicit brief from his brother to ensure 'the generall setlement of the peace and quiet of that our ancient Kingdome', through the creation of a 'new model of the militia', which would amount to a virtual standing army.[60] The fall of the Duke of Lauderdale, who had dominated the political life of Scotland for more than twenty years, neatly coincided with James's arrival in October 1680, and did much to increase his freedom of action. The two men had at one time worked closely together, but James had shown no wish to associate himself with the Duke's failures during his first visit to Scotland, and had done nothing thereafter to shore up the crumbling personal support of an old and increasingly sick man. Relations had deteriorated to the point where it was not expected that the two men could have been brought to sit together on the same councils. However, Lauderdale's resignation as Chancellor, followed so closely by the death of his successor the Duke of Rothes, made the transition of power to James, as the *de facto* Head of State, a much smoother process than might otherwise have been the case, while ensuring that the Duke inherited a position of authority that was almost unassailable.[61]

James continued his rule where he had been forced to break off, six months earlier, firmly establishing his habit of attending the meetings of the Privy Council at every available opportunity, and throwing himself into a vigorous attempt to reform the Scottish military. He issued a stream of orders aimed at standardizing his soldiers' equipment and at bringing them into line with the practice of the English regular army, and decreed that the Scots should in future abandon their traditional hodden grey – which his advisers thought gave them the appearance of: 'skulking and vagrant persons' – in favour of English redcoats.[62] The wastage of large amounts of gunpowder, in the firing of ceremonial salutes, also seems to have provoked his displeasure, although his instructions to limit such displays in his honour came too late to prevent Mons Meg, a medieval cannon which had remained on the walls of Edinburgh Castle for more than three centuries, from splitting its barrel and blowing itself up. More significantly, James also commissioned a small team of experts to survey the castles and strongholds along the border region, and to report back to him detailing their state of repair. The Duke aimed eventually to have them strengthened and rebuilt, and it is interesting to note that several years later, after his accession to the throne, he had plans to build a great royal 'pallace' at Berwick-upon-Tweed, a town whose strategic value he seems to have noted on his way North.[63]

Although the threat from the Covenanters gradually diminished over the next eighteen months, as one of their most prominent, uncompromising and charismatic leaders, Richard Cameron, fell in a skirmish with government soldiers, and another, Donald Cargill, was brought to trial and hanged for his part in the rebellion, James seems to have been remarkably reluctant to have delivered the *coup de grâce* to the rebels in person. While large-scale, formal battles continued to hold his attention, he had little interest in involving himself in the less glorious, but infinitely more confused, cycle of ambushes and retaliatory raids which now characterized the war in the South-West. He looked instead to preserve his own safety from snipers and assassins, exercising the executive control of operations from his stronghold in Edinburgh, and seldom venturing far from his capital, save for isolated visits to Stirling Castle and the City of Glasgow.[64] This reluctance to travel led to the Duke developing a rather insular view of both Scotland and its people. He never witnessed the ravages inflicted by the fighting in Galloway, Ayr and Lanarkshire, and never saw the conditions under which the Highland clansmen lived to the North.

While James can be said to have done no more than conform to the established pattern of English rule throughout the seventeenth century, pandering to the prejudices of the Scottish ruling class and attempting at every turn to maintain law and order for the executive in London, he failed to gain a wider perspective on either the nature of the conflict with the western rebels, or the marked division that existed in society as a whole, between the attitudes and aspirations of the Highland and Lowland Scots. Worse still, his decision to remain aloof from those that he ruled, while in keeping with his princely station, effectively prevented him from achieving any deep understanding of his enemies' viewpoint or motivation. Consequently, it was not a sense of calculating and stony-hearted cruelty which denoted James's treatment of those who were brought before him, but rather an attitude of intense frustration, at the wilfulness and persistence of those who sought a recourse to arms, and of disbelief at their total preparedness to suffer martyrdom for their cause. His attempts to show mercy were, therefore, often entirely mistimed or else curiously hamfisted. When a group of young men were brought before him on charges of high treason, the Duke offered to save their lives and to pardon them, if they would enlist in his regiment and go to fight in

Flanders. He was convinced that they could not possibly refuse such generous and reasonable terms, especially when all they were required to do in return was to shout: 'God save the King!'. However he was in for an unpleasant surprise, as each in turn refused to do so on the grounds of their conscience, which allowed them to accept no authority other than that of God, and chose to couch their replies in such coarse and seditious language that the Duke and his officials could scarcely believe their ears. James seems to have signed their death warrants with a sense of weary resignation, and did not try to strike a similar bargain again, having already confided on another occasion that the rebels 'deserved a bedlam rather than a gallows'.[65] More than anything else, the episode shows that while James was prepared to hold fast to his own beliefs regardless of the consequences, he was totally unable to acknowledge that similar, dearly held principles motivated the actions of others. For him, religious and secular authority were insolubly intertwined and could neither be challenged, nor broken, with good will or reason. Having come to accept the central role of both the apostolic and monarchical succession in the preservation of social order, Cameron's followers who spoke ecstatically of the establishment of an egalitarian theocracy in the Lowlands, which would rival both Geneva and Jerusalem, could not help but appear to James as the most vile, dangerous and thoroughly incomprehensible men imaginable. The very notion that a whole nation, rather than a chosen individual, might attempt to secure a relationship with God, and to covenant themselves to Him to the detriment of their temporal rulers, was clearly abhorrent to the Duke. Furthermore, if they were prepared to continue in their errors and in their disobedience to the Crown, then, James reasoned, any measures to bring them back under the control of the civil authorities were fully justified. However, in equating all Lowland Presbyterians with the activities of Cameron and his small band of adherents, James followed in the mistaken and highly repressive path pioneered by Lauderdale and Rothes, and authorized the free-quartering of troops upon communities which, though hating the episcopacy, were still ostensibly loyal and had little sympathy for the remaining insurgents.[66]

If, however, the prosecution of the war in the Lowlands was not already enough, then James's desire to extend the rule of law and the jurisdiction of the Crown into every corner of Scotland soon brought him into a second area of conflict and controversy: this time with the Highland chiefs themselves. He saw the clan system, with its blood feuds, cattle raids and private armies; as representing an unacceptable challenge to his brother's authority, for in the absence of public order 'he conceaved, the King is not entirely the King of the Whole Kingdome'. The inability of central government to extend its influence much beyond the walls of Stirling Castle clearly infuriated him and, as the chairman of the Commission for

Pacifying the Highlands, he drew up a new series of measures aimed at curtailing the 'incursions, depredations and the barberous cruelty of thieves . . . and broken men' in those regions. Professional soldiers were to be stationed throughout the Highlands and Islands, and were to be provisioned by the cattle and corn confiscated from disaffected clansmen. Existing strongholds were to be refortified, and two new companies of Lowland foot were to be raised from among 'neutrall and disinterested persons', who would be prepared to give 'more universal obedience . . . and be more terrible to all of them [i.e. the clans] than any of the natives can be'.[67] James simply did not trust the Highland troops already posted to the region, and decreed that they should be disbanded in order to pay for their southern replacements. Moreover, with an eye to the situation in England, he made it plain that his Lowlanders were not to be restricted in their service, and could be employed 'upon all occasions' wherever, and whenever, he thought fit. Local government, in the form of the baillies, together with the landowners and the clan chiefs, would all, henceforth, be held directly accountable for the behaviour of their neighbours, tenants and servants.[68]

Lists were to be drawn up 'of all males within their bounds above the age of sixteen', and the Highland nobility were obliged to travel to Edinburgh in order to appear before James in person, and to sign a pledge to 'produce before His Majesty's Privy Council . . . any of my men . . . or any person of my name, descended of my family who shall commit murder, deforcement of messengers, reif, theft, depredations, open and avowed fire-raisings upon deadly feuds, or any other deeds contrary to the Acts of Parliament'. Unfortunately, the Duke had absolutely no way of enforcing such attendance and the appointed day for the Highland muster came and went, in July 1681, with only a handful of the great chieftains turning out. Those who did sign the bond did so under duress, having already been apprehended in the capital while they were about other business.[69] The simple truth remained that James's authority in the Highlands was directly proportional to the strength of his troops on the ground. While his plans for the new Lowland companies ran into a barrage of criticism, his isolated garrisons provided soft targets for raiding parties of MacDonald and Cameron clansmen, who were conducting their own private wars, virtually unchecked. In this way, a small detachment of government soldiers became cut off at Inverlochy, in early 1682, by a force of between 3–400 Highlanders under the command of the clan chief, Ewen Cameron of Lochiel. After a short fight, the soldiers were disarmed before being 'cruelly beaten, wounded and robbed of their clothes . . . hardly escaping with their lives, and brought to the extremity of starving in their wounds before they could get any relief'.[70]

Although there is no evidence to suggest that James's antipathy towards the Highlanders ever lessened during his time in Scotland, but if anything grew stronger with the passing months, it is worth reflecting here that, had he been successful in breaking the power of the hereditary chieftains and in smashing the basis upon which the clan system was built, he would have destroyed a vital reservoir of future support for his cause, which not only sustained the armies of Claverhouse and the Pretenders, but also fed the creation and potency of the Jacobite Highland myth.[71] Given the intractable nature of the struggle for the control of the Highlands, James came to realize that the surest way to command obedience in the North was to persevere with the remodelling of the Scottish Army. Unfortunately, in order to accomplish this task effectively he and his brother needed to raise money, which could only come from a reconvened Scottish Parliament.

IV

With King Charles II's Oxford Parliament newly dissolved, the calling of a fresh legislature North of the border, in July 1681, was calculated to further emphasize the resurgence of the monarchy and the strengthening of the royal prerogative. James provided a glittering spectacle for the opening session on 28 July, with the traditional 'Riding' of the Scottish nobility along the length of the Royal Mile. This ceremony was calculated to underline the place of the aristocracy in a rigid social hierarchy and drew a clear distinction between each rank of the peerage: with a duke being allowed eight attendants, a marquess six, an earl four and a viscount three; although in practice the orderly procession soon broke up as the riders jostled for position beside the Duke of York. The tone of the proceedings was set from the very beginning by the reading of a letter from Charles II, which exhorted those present to 'adhere unto it [the government and royal family] with unshaken loyalty as much as ever; . . . [for] This being once effectively done, we may reasonably hope that our government in Church and State, as by Law presently established, shall recieve its due reverence and obedience, and that all our good subjects shall be preserved in peace, tranquility and happiness.'[72] The King then went on to confirm James in his vice-regal powers, as the High Commissioner of the Parliament, 'since his interest is so unseperable from ours, we shall not doubt of your ready and cheerful concurrence to render his endeavours amongst you successful for securing our government'. Although both royal brothers in their initial addresses had left it in no doubt that the Parliament had been summoned in order 'to fall upon effectual courses, for supressing those seditious and rebellious Coventicles, from whence proceed all disorder and confusion', and to raise money to combat the lawlessness in the Highlands, their central objectives were formed with the English political situation very much in mind. Shaftesbury's supporters, despite raising occasional bonfires and cries of 'no popery', had made little impact upon the streets of Edinburgh, and the dissent of the propertied classes had been virtually silenced by their fears of a return to Covenanter violence, and the destruction that would inevitably accompany any such outbreak.[73] This failure of the opposition North of the border did much to guarantee the loyalty of the Scottish Parliament, and enabled Charles II, through the actions of his brother, to test out legislation aimed at increasing the power of the royal prerogative, which could then be introduced on to the English statute books at a later, and more convenient, date.

After settling a generous revenue grant upon the Duke of York, advancing subsidies for the provision of a new army, and introducing measures aimed at strengthening the Church of Scotland, much of the available Parliamentary time was taken up with the discussion of relatively uncontroversial measures. James was particularly interested in the promotion of a bill for the encouragement of home-grown trade and manufactures. He had remarked on the poverty of Scotland soon after his return, and had tried to reinvigorate the previously moribund Council of Trade, taking depositions from merchants 'to give their advyce anent [concerning] the causes of the decay of trade and what they would propose for the remeid [remedy] thereof', and welcoming suggestions for the establishment of new plantations in America. Plans to develop the economy, and to implement a form of protectionism in order to restore 'a dew balance betwixt export and import', were passed by the Parliament in September, and the production of cloth and stockings was begun at Newmills shortly afterwards, with the Privy Council acting to prohibit the importation of all rival English cloths at the same time.[74] However, when it came time for James and his council to order the new uniforms for their troops, from the monies Parliament had granted, they waived aside the samples offered to them from the factories at Newmills, ignored their own ban and bought English cloth instead. Moreover, although James's interest in Scottish trade has often been commended, his own advice on how it might best be increased was only rarely recorded, and even then amounted to no more than a simple observation on the value of thrift and displayed a lack of understanding of local customs. The Duke, we are told, 'had taken notice of the great extravagance and expenses used and bestowed upon burialls, mareages, and christnings [*sic*], contrair to the custome of all well governed kingdoms, to the great impoverishment of the nobility, gentry, and burrows', and gave strict instructions to the Council of Trade to rectify the 'said abuse' at once.[75]

If James's initiatives to help boost the economy were to prove ineffectual, then his continued clampdown on the Covenanters yielded immediate results. The Parliament introduced a whole raft of legislation aimed at breaking resistance in the South-West. Intelligence reports had suggested that schoolmasters in the towns, and chapmen who travelled widely throughout the countryside, had helped to spread dissent and the news of fresh risings. Consequently, laws were passed to strip would-be rebels of their livelihoods, while heavy fines were imposed on anyone who let their land, or even that of their tenants, be used for the purpose of holding a Field Conventicle.[76] Yet the impact of these measures, whose scope was limited by the need to make the Scottish government operate more efficiently and to safeguard against rebellion, was nothing when compared with the far-reaching implications for the British Isles contained in the two central enactments pushed through the Parliament by James. The first of these was an Act of Succession, which sought to firmly regulate the descent of the Scottish Crown, establishing a precedent which could not be tampered with, or disregarded, by subsequent administrations or by the actions of any of the monarch's subjects. There was to be no doubt that the succession to the throne was to be the concern of no one save God and the King, and that the hereditary principle of the royal bloodline, and the political primacy of the ruling house were to be held sacrosanct. The Crown was to be 'transmitted and devolved by a lineal succession, according to the proximity of blood', while it was clearly stipulated that 'no difference of religion, nor no law nor Act of Parliament, made or to be made, can alter or divert the right of succession'. Thus, James as a Roman Catholic could not be legally debarred from becoming King and any attempt to obstruct his accession, or to question his birthright, would in future be classed as high treason.[77] Although the Act served to confirm the rout of the English Exclusionists after their defeat in Oxford, and aroused a great deal of consternation and bitter criticism from among Scotland's Presbyterian and Episcopalian majority, its immediate significance was less disturbing to them than the passing of a new Test for the holders of public office. Charles II still seemed to be in the prime of life, and the chances of James, who was only slightly younger and whose constitution did not appear so robust, sitting upon the throne for any length of time, remained only a distant possibility. However, the threat to existing placemen and administrators represented by the imposition of a reworked Test Act could be seen to be both real and imminent.

Even though the Duke himself, as 'the King's lawful brother', and his heirs were exempted from swearing the oath, every other public servant – from the bishops and their clergy, to the soldiers and lawyers, and right down to borough clerks and schoolteachers – were required to take the Test, or else risk being stripped of their offices.[78] In theory, the aim of the legislation was to curb dissent and division, and to promote social cohesion and a sense of loyalty to the State. In practice, however, the achievement of these criteria was anything but simple, as the Act had been rushed through without the sufficient debate, or necessary pause for thought, which might have done much to iron out the ambiguities and inconsistencies that bedevilled its operation. The main problem with the Test was that it was enormously long and complicated, as the result of having been stitched together from two entirely different affirmations. The first and less controversial of these was a simple, and surprisingly loose, Confession of Faith, which had originally been introduced during the reign of King James VI, and did little more than commit the individual to an acceptance of 'the true Protestant religion . . . founded on and agreeable to the written word of God', and a rejection of 'popish' and 'Phanaticall' practices.[79] The second clause, however, represented a quite different and innovatory addition to the statute, which demanded an Oath of Allegiance to the sovereign that was in keeping with the Act of Succession. The subject was now expected to pledge loyalty to 'the King's Majesty, his heirs and lawful successors', and to undertake no action that might undermine, change or alter, the structure of the government.[80] Unfortunately, several of the statements contained in these two testaments flatly contradicted one another, as in the case of the status of Jesus as being the sole head of the Church, which was upheld according to the provisions of the first, but totally rejected under those of the second. Given the presence of so many grey areas, where the implications of the Test went wholly unexplained, it was not surprising, therefore, to find that it was open to radically different interpretations by those that came to take it. In these circumstances it was the operation, and enforcement, of the Test which assumed a decisive importance, rather than its actual institution. If it was decided that a general affirmation to its guiding spirit would suffice, then few public servants would be unduly troubled by it. However, if a more severe and legalistic approach to each and every one of its provisions were to be adopted, then it might well have been the signal for a wholesale purge of Crown officials.

In the event, James chose to apply the rigour of the Test selectively. He, and perhaps more importantly his advisers, had no great wish to dismantle their own administrative framework, and push scores of clergymen and civil servants through the courts, and into the arms of their opponents. Instead, they issued sets of supplementary instructions to their officials and bishops, quietening the storm of protest, and making it clear that the swearing of the oaths did not have to represent a definitive statement of faith, but could be best regarded as a more general guideline for the shaping of their future behaviour.[81] If James was prepared to show leniency, and a certain amount of common sense, in drawing back from a confrontation with the vast majority of Scotland's elite, then he showed no similar compunction in the treatment of legitimate dissent within his own Privy Council. He had long been wary of the influence exerted by the Dukes of Monmouth and Hamilton, and by the Earl of Argyll, and now took steps to remedy the situation once and for all, using the Test Act as a convenient pretext for their removal. Monmouth, who had won a reputation for valour and humanity during his command in Scotland, was James's most serious rival for the throne, while Hamilton had consistently opposed Lauderdale's government and was suspected of turning a blind eye to the meetings of Coventicles on his Lanarkshire estates. Archibald Campbell, the taciturn ninth Earl of Argyll, perhaps represented the most serious and effective challenge to the Duke of York's authority both on the Council and in the Highlands of Scotland, where he held vast lands and wielded enormous power as a clan chief.[82] It was, therefore, with these three prominent individuals in mind that James convened a meeting of the Privy Council, on 20 September 1681, just three days after the Parliament had been adjourned, in order that they might collectively subscribe to the provisions of the Test.

Monmouth was not present, but his uncle wrote to the Earl of Moray, as the representative of the Scottish government in London, to instruct him to present his nephew with the Test Act and to oblige him to sign it forthwith. Monmouth stubbornly refused to sign, adding caustically that although he was 'so great a lover of Parliaments that he would not be the first to break one of its Acts', he was only empowered as a Privy Councillor while he was actually residing in Scotland. As he was now South of the border he had no jurisdiction and there was no need for him to give his assent. His flippant reply was hardly calculated to appease James, who now had his Council draft a second and far grimmer letter to Moray, in which the Earl was directed to contact Monmouth again. This time, Moray was to inform him that despite his extremely privileged position, he would not be exempt from the full force of the Act and that unless he complied with its regulations before 1 January 1682, he would forfeit all of his offices and sinecures in the North. Monmouth's 'ill example' was reported to the King, but despite the Duke of York's warnings that it was necessary 'for his Majesties Gov[ernmen]t to see the acts of that loyall and judicious Parliament obeyed with firmness and steddiness', Charles II was still inclined to be indulgent towards his son. He rejected York's suggestion that Monmouth should be replaced on the Privy Council, and concluded that any action against him would be unfair and unnecessary at the present time.[83] While Monmouth had escaped the net, the Duke of Hamilton simply played for time. He had initially refused to sign the Act, but realizing James's deadly seriousness in prosecuting him for his actions, he had sent his son to plead his cause before the entire Council. When this stratagem failed, and he began to be stripped of his titles one by one, he decided to save himself and finally capitulated, taking the Test without reservation in March 1682.[84]

The Earl of Argyll, however, was not so lucky. He, too, had refused to swear the oaths and to put his signature to the legislation, claiming that he was not acting out of disloyalty to the Crown, but was merely seeking a clarification of the wording of the Test. James refused to compromise, knowing that the Earl had already declined to send his Highlanders to fight the Covenanters and that he had openly questioned the right of the royal family to escape taking the oaths of Faith and Allegiance. Argyll's increasingly desperate overtures of friendship were rejected and his attempt to mumble his way through the Test, obscuring those statements with which he did not agree, was declared unsatisfactory and disqualified by the Duke. James sent for him the very next day, on 4 November 1681, and demanded that he should account for his actions, and the manner in which he had chosen to swear his loyalty. Argyll mounted a skilful defence, using exactly the same arguments that had already been advanced by the Privy Council itself in order to explain away the contradictions of the text to the citizens of Edinburgh. He maintained that he was not questioning the Duke's authority to rule, and was prepared to take the oaths in as much as they stayed true to themselves and to the integrity of the Protestant religion, but begged for several days leave from the Council in order to seek a legal opinion upon the matter. This was denied by James, who within less than a week had signed an arrest warrant for him and consigned him under guard to Edinburgh Castle. Although James's apologists have often tried to downplay the significance of his arraignment of the Earl on charges of high treason, and despite the Duke's own assurances on the matter to William of Orange, Argyll's subsequent trial can hardly be viewed as a triumph for British justice.[85] Many of the nobles who sat on the Privy Council envied his estates and, safe in the knowledge that they would be redistributed if he were found guilty of treason, they hardened their resolve to see him convicted. Moreover, James refused to grant him the services of Sir George Lockhart as his first choice of defence council, although he did point out to the Earl that he would give his full consideration to approving the names of any other lawyers that he might suggest. In these circumstances, his swift trial and sentencing was a foregone conclusion. He was found guilty of treason, perjury and of attempting to seize legislative power. Despite the claims of James and his Council that Argyll had brought the relationship between the King, his Scottish Parliament and his people into disrepute, and that he had fallen because of his impertinence in 'reproaching your [Charles II's] laws and acts of Parliament', back in London the Marquis Halifax could sniff – with more than a hint of chauvinism – that in England a dog would not have been hanged on such flimsy evidence.[86] The death sentence, though approved, could not, however, immediately be carried out, as shortly after his conviction Argyll had mounted a daring escape from his jail cell. Disguised in his stepdaughter's dress, he had slipped out of the gates of Edinburgh Castle and was taken first to London, and then to safety in Holland. Writing to William of Orange, shortly after the event, James went to great trouble to laugh the whole incident off, belittling its importance to either himself or to his intended victim, and explaining that 'It was easy for him to do it since he was not kept a close prisoner . . . his life was in no danger, which he and his friends knew very well.' This statement has often been used as conclusive proof that the Duke of York wanted to do little more than clip Argyll's wings, and deprive him of some of his feudal dues. However, it does not seem to fit with James's subsequent interrogation of the Earl's gaolers, with a view to establishing whether or not they were complicit in their prisoner's escape, his annoyance when Charles II turned down his appeal to strip Argyll's son of his lands and title, and his decision to execute the Earl four years later, after an abortive Highland rising, on precisely the same evidence that was presented at his original trial.[87] After raising the political stakes and drawing criticism of his heavy-handed tactics from many of his own supporters and Privy Councillors, including the unlikely figure of the now decrepit Lauderdale, he had shown himself willing to enter into a new period of protracted conflict, and possibly even of social upheaval in the Highlands, in order to gain a single conviction. Furthermore, having gone to such great lengths he threw away his final victory, much as he had by his inattention to detail at the Battles of Lowestoft and Sole Bay, by failing to make sure that a sufficient number of guards were posted to watch over the captive Earl.

Barely three months after Argyll's fall, James was permanently recalled to England and took ship along with members of his new Scottish administration, men such as the Earls of Middleton and Perth and the Marquis of Montrose, who were keen to have their appointments ratified by the King, and their final triumph over Lauderdale's faction confirmed. James himself may well have felt that he had good reason to feel pleased with his record of independent rule, as his brother's viceroy in the North. He had successfully prosecuted the war against the Covenanters, and overseen the destruction of the last organized pockets of resistance to royal authority in the Lowlands. He had laid the foundations of a professional Scottish army, and had demonstrated some administrative ability in ensuring that his troops had been quartered and provisioned with the minimum of trouble and criticism from the civilian population. Under his guidance, the Scots Parliament had charted through some difficult legislation, and done much to bolster the rights of both the Crown and the prerogative, demonstrating that the tide of Exclusionist sentiment was not ultimately irreversible. Arygll's influence in the government of the kingdom had been effectively neutralized, and in so doing the loyalty of the clans of the Great Glen had been decisively secured for the House of Stuart.

Although his short tenure as Viceroy, and the intractable nature of many of the vested interests which confronted him, had severely limited his room for manoeuvre and had similarly defeated Lauderdale's earlier regime, it is still fair to conclude, that with the benefit of hindsight, James's government of Scotland had done little to remedy the nation's fundamental problems. The Duke had been powerless to impose the rule of law upon the Highlands and his policing actions, while brutally effective in the short term, had managed to alienate influential sections of both Highland and Lowland society even further from his administration. He did nothing to reconcile the cultural and political differences between the North and the South of Scotland, and indeed may well have aggravated their deep mutual distrust, by his policy of playing one group off against the other. The show trial of the Earl of Argyll did not in the end yield him the benefits of land and additional resources that he had orginally hoped for, and served only to drive an influential magnate – who had always maintained a show of loyalty, and who posed no immediate threat – into a career of opposition, and ultimately revolutionary, politics. Furthermore, James's sporadic attempts to enforce a trading monopoly, and to reform and stimulate the national economy, were characterized by far more show than substance. The concerns of the High Church and the Kirk alike seem to have eluded him, while his failure to understand the virulent passions that the Protestant religion could arouse condemned his own endeavours to encourage the hopes of the urban Roman Catholic minority to be entirely misconstrued and to become the objects of widespread loathing.[88] Consequently, although his departure from Leith was accompanied by all the customary professions of affection and devotion, there were doubtless many Scots – both Highland and Lowland, Catholic and Protestant – who had good reason to breathe a sigh of relief at his passing.

The Impolitic Prince –
A Study in Consistency

I

On the morning of Monday 2 February 1685, the Duke of York was rudely awakened by his servants with the news that his brother, the King, had suddenly been taken ill in the night. This came as a great surprise, as Charles II's good health had always been taken for granted, and his illnesses of 1679 and 1680 had faded to no more than a distant memory. Indeed, the King had been reported to be in high spirits on the previous evening, entertaining his friends at supper and even paying a call upon his mistress, the Duchess of Portsmouth.[1] The arrival of Lord Ailesbury at the Duke's apartments in St James's could not, therefore, have been calculated to have thrown the heir apparent into greater confusion. He left James in no doubt that his brother – having already been bled and scalded – was dying, and that he should return with him immediately to the King's bedside. In his haste, James left the palace, throwing off his dressing-gown and pulling on his wig as he went. However, on his arrival at the Privy Chamber, it was noted by the courtiers already present that, although he had remembered to pull one shoe on, his other foot was still in a slipper.[2] On the fourth day of the King's illness, Barrillon, the French Ambassador, observed that James still acted as though he were in a dream, and it was only when it was suggested that he should hurry to fetch a Roman Catholic priest to administer the last rites that he finally roused himself from his private thoughts.[3] The strain of events, and the burden of his personal grief, clearly manifested themselves in his letter to William of Orange, written just hours after Charles II's death. James departed from all the conventional forms and impersonal addresses of an official diplomatic communication, to scrawl only the briefest and most hurried of notes to inform his son-in-law 'that it has pleased God Almighty, to take out of this world, the King my Brother', and to add with an unconscious irony that after 'all the usual ceremonys were performed . . . you shall find me as kind to you as [you] can expect'.[4]

II

Far from being an aberration, or the beginning of a descent into defeat and disillusionment, the Duke's panicked conduct on learning of his imminent succession to the throne would seem to be perfectly in keeping with what we have shown to be his record, in both public and private life, over the previous quarter of a century. This stress upon the consistency of James's behaviour, throughout his long apprenticeship to politics, would seem to be wholly at odds with the received wisdom about the course of his early career, as outlined in the pages of such eminent historians as Turner, Ashley and Miller. Consequently, in the first, third and fifth chapters, there was a need to stress the seminal role played by James's personal writings and use of imagery in establishing an attractive, and plausible, account of his endeavours and achievements as Duke of York. In particular, attention was drawn to the strengths and weaknesses of the palimpsest copy of James's voluminous memoirs, and it was suggested that although it has provided generations of historians with an invaluable source from which to work, it has not always been read with sufficient caution when dealing with the years prior to his accession. In this light, the discovery that the officially sanctioned *Life* reveals to us no more than a glowing portrait of the Duke of York, and his varied exploits, should come as no great surprise.

What, however, is extraordinary about these memoirs is the fact that they were written at all. They reveal that James possessed a remarkable degree of self-awareness, and an unflinching belief that his own exploits – and especially those which had taken place on the battlefield – should be recorded for the benefit of posterity. Moreover, it is significant that he began to chronicle his service in France and Flanders almost immediately after his return to England in 1660. At the very time when he had been restored to his offices and estates, and could reasonably have been expected to have entered into the most rewarding and fulfilling period of his life, free from the trials and dangers of civil war and exile, he consciously took the decision to look back upon his days campaigning with Marshal Turenne, and to base all of his subsequent claims to greatness around them. Though the evidence of James's physical bravery contained in these accounts is indisputable and worthy of acclaim, it is remarkable that a man barely in his thirties should be so concerned with reliving the events of his first military career, a set of experiences which were effectively over by the time of his twenty-fifth birthday. Furthermore, they continued to act as the measure by which all of his subsequent achievements were judged.

Sir William Coventry was familiar with the tales of his skirmishes on the Continent by the early 1660s, and in moments of leisure James would regale his Admiralty clerks with stories of his martial prowess throughout that decade.[5] In time, his accounts of the Battles of Lowestoft and Sole Bay would take their place beside those of his earlier exploits, and it is no understatement to suggest that over the next forty years these same narratives would be honed, retold and reproduced for countless new audiences. Eventually, in the light of his failures as King of England and as a General at the Boyne and La Hogue, the constant reiteration of his past glories would begin to tire the patience of the courtiers of Versailles and St Germain, but for later generations of historians his spirited accounts of battles and forced marches served to retain something of their freshness and fascination.[6]

Given the lack of corroborative evidence from within James's own household – Jermyn, Talbot and Churchill left precious little in the way of reflective works – and the highly partisan, and frequently inaccurate, sketches of him penned by the Earl of Shaftesbury's partisans, it is easy to see how the *Life* became so firmly established as the central authority for any consideration of the Duke's impact upon English politics between 1660 and 1685. However, the problem remains that this source was always intended to be a propaganda piece and, therefore, constantly needs to be read alongside corroborative evidence – whether official documentation from the Naval Office and trading companies, or the work of other contemporary commentators, most notably Pepys, Evelyn and Reresby – in order to judge its veracity. It is the central contention of this book that historians in the past have been guided, both consciously and unconsciously, by the structure and emphasis of the *Life* itself into accepting its own narrow guidelines for the study of James as Duke of York, and into taking for granted its implicit value system, with its high premium set on honour and dignity, and the simple equation of might with right.

Consequently, the carefully nurtured image of the Duke created by James himself and his partisans has filtered down, virtually unaltered, through the writings of successive generations of Tory apologists. For the most part, they have sought to produce a critique of his actions that is based primarily upon emotional sentiment, a romantic attachment to the lost Stuart cause, and the echoes of a chivalric ideal to be distantly found in James's own personal imagery. This is not to say that the Whig tradition of history, which so dominated the terms of debate throughout the nineteenth and early twentieth centuries, does not need a substantial qualification. Macaulay, Trevelyan and even, ironically, Winston Churchill, who in many respects followed in their interpretative footsteps, were perhaps a little too eager to blacken James's character in every respect. In seeking to thoroughly legitimize the events of 1688–9, denuding them of their truly revolutionary and popular appeal, they overemphasized the lengths to which James would go in order to achieve his objectives and to destabilize the already existing 'constitution'. Ignoring his genuine and deeply felt sense of English nationalism, they produced a harsh caricature of the profession and practice of his religion, and miscast him as a total quisling and dependant of France. In a similar fashion, they discredited much that was valid in their evaluation of his rule in Scotland by concentrating disproportionately on the wilder allegations of his being present at, and taking voyeuristic delight in, the interrogation and torture of Covenanter prisoners.[7] However, if we would seek to totally dismantle the Whig consensus, we should also attempt to put something that is concrete in its place. Given that the existing Tory historiography has sought overwhelmingly to address the problems and uncertainties of the present, to the exclusion of those of the seventeenth-century past, and in the absence of a fully developed Marxist model with which to account for the successes of the Restoration monarchy, we are forced back to accept the validity of much, though by no means all, of the findings of the early Whig school as typified, at its best, by Charles James Fox.

Having taken this critique of the established literature as our central premise, our thorough re-examination of James's claims to greatness – in those fields of domestic politics, naval reform, high military command, trade and overseas empire by which he set such high store – has clearly diverged dramatically from the glowing testament to the Duke's foresight and energy, which was enshrined within the pages of the *Life* and in the works of his subsequent defenders. Rather than confirming the established picture of the tragic warrior prince cut down by a prolonged mental and physical deterioration, we have uncovered an altogether more complicated version of events, centering around both the social limitations placed upon a prince of the blood and James's own desire for an active role at the very heart of the State apparatus. Herein lies the great paradox of the Duke's career. From his conversion in 1669 up until his accession in 1685, he consistently sought to publicly profess his own unshakeable adherence to the Roman Catholic faith, while at the same time maintaining his status as the heir apparent, the most vigorous up-holder of the rights of the royal prerogative, and as the single most important manipulator of military patronage on both land and sea. It was these mutually exclusive objectives when taken together, rather than when seen in their constituent parts, which made James fall victim to the prejudices and fears of so many of his brother's subjects, and which ultimately frustrated his ambition to pursue a military campaign to fruition.

However, if his hopes for securing a truly independent command were to be frustrated after the passing of the Test Acts, then the sheer sweep and scale of the Duke's commitments in the administration of the Navy, trade and Empire remained nothing short of breathtaking. There can be little doubt that he was a powerful advocate of sea-power, who sought to enhance the size and prestige of the Navy at every available opportunity, and who attempted to professionalize and standardize the conduct of all those government departments with which he had prolonged contact. Similarly, the very fact of his interest in naval affairs and his sustained patronage of the service cannot but have helped in the raising of morale and in the securing of new Parliamentary grants. Those reforms carried out in his name attest to the truth of his claims to have had more than a passing interest in achieving an established code of 'best practice' amongst his flag-captains, yet it must be firmly borne in mind that had he never existed the maritime power of Great Britain would probably have continued to expand in much the same fashion: the Algerine pirates would still have been successfully combated in the Mediterranean, and the Admiralty Commission of 1679 would still have pursued their work with a vigour and integrity far removed from his own influence, or that of his servants.

In terms of his trading concerns, James's record of direct involvement was far more ambiguous. Although he was an active participant in the affairs of the African companies, his behaviour was that of a speculator when it came to the awarding of lottery concessions to the Royal Fisheries, and he acted as no more than a sleeping partner throughout the development of the Hudson's Bay Company. The available evidence does not seem to bear out his lofty claims to financial prudence and selfless commercial acumen. Rather than consistently striving to ensure the national good and England's continuing mercantile prosperity, it would seem that his interest in the new joint-stock companies was attributable to far more limited and short-term concerns. He wished to obtain a personal income that was independent of Parliamentary scrutiny and interference, and hoped that the rapidly expanding commercial sector might provide him with an additional area in which to exert his considerable reservoir of patronage. In playing court to his new allies within the City of London, James could hope to effectively limit the growth of Shaftesbury's power-base in the capital. In a similar vein, his proprietorship of New York Colony was primarily driven by the need for an additional source of revenue and by the opportunity it presented to enhance his own prestige.

It is the constant search for *gloire* that is important for this Prince of the Restoration, driving him onwards and informing both his choice of imagery and practice of the art of politics, to the detriment of other, more pressing, considerations. Consequently, the fact that his naval battles had been won at an unnecessarily high cost, or that the advantages they should have bestowed were needlessly squandered, did not unduly trouble him. Moreover, it should be remembered that throughout this period, while James gained invaluable administrative experience as the head of the Navy Office, he was allowed little direct input into the governance of England. Although he was capable of marshalling and deploying his supporters to good effect in the Houses of Parliament, as demonstrated by the Roos divorce case, he was used selectively by his brother, and had continued to lack both an interest in – and experience of – sustained Parliamentary business right up to his succession. Furthermore, due to his forced removal from English politics at the height of the Exclusion Crisis, there are comparatively few examples with which to judge James's political acumen before 1685. On the two occasions when he was called to display statecraft, during his governorships of Scotland and New York, he proved himself to be an often remote, uninformed and even divisive figure, who seldom grasped the fundamental problems faced by his subordinates. Therefore, it should be argued that the change in perceptions of James's abilities owes far more to the differences in those roles assigned to him, and the expectations placed upon him, throughout the Restoration period, than to an illusive degenerative disease. In this way, it is quite possible for a brave and loyal subordinate, who had served with great competence as a junior Officer and administrator, to suddenly find himself completely out of his depth when confronted by the strains and responsibilities of high command, and the pressures of rapid decision-taking. The Duke's desire to recapture his 'halycon' days under Turenne might, therefore, have reflected no more than his growing uncertainty about his position within the restored monarchy, and his inability to confront the complex series of challenges and uncertainties which faced him after his return to England. It would appear, on the balance of evidence, that this is precisely what happened to James, and that his admirable qualities – his bravery, loyalty and the integrity with which he clung to his religious convictions – were swamped by his inability to respond to rapidly changing circumstances, his limited intellectual abilities and his supreme self-obsession, which increasingly led him to distance himself from the consequences of his own actions.

The rejection of the thesis of James's degeneration stems not only from our interpretation of the sources other than the *Life* and our case studies, but also from the failure of successive historians to attribute a definite timescale to the change in his personality. Only Winston Churchill provided a definite clue, suggesting that – although the Duke had always been potentially tyrannical – he only gradually revealed his nature to those around him, through his rule in Scotland and conduct on board the stricken *Gloucester*. If we are to discard the notion that James was always entirely malevolent, and with it the scurrilous Whig notion that exposure to Catholicism was solely responsible for his decline, then there are only two possible explanations for the contrast between the heroic young Prince and the cruel, and by turns cowardly, King. The first – as we have already seen – is an extremely personal view of the individual within history, which seeks to stress the physical and mental failings of the Duke at the expense of external political and social factors. Unfortunately, without an explicit statement outlining just when, and where, James first fell ill, it is impossible to examine these claims in any great depth. What is clear is that the stories concerning the Duke's contraction of a venereal disease have their basis in Pepys' diary entries for March 1665 and April 1668.[8] If this were so and illness had begun to grip him, one might well assume that its effects would certainly have been taking their toll upon James by the time of his victories at Lowestoft and Sole Bay. Yet this is precisely the period, from 1665 until 1672, to which have been ascribed his greatest successes.[9] Moreover, given the virulency of syphilis in its seventeenth-century strain, the survival of many of his children into adulthood, and the evidence from the *ad hoc* autopsy carried out on his body at the time of the French Revolution, it would seem safe to rule out this hypothesis entirely.[10] Given the elusive nature of James's apparent degeneration, we can, therefore, return to our own counter-argument which lays a greater stress upon the empirical evidence for his close involvement with sea-borne trade and Empire, and has sought to emphasize the opportunities and constraints which did so much to shape the course of his career.

Where previously a gulf was thought to exist, separating two starkly contrasting views of James's conduct as King and as Duke of York, our findings have led us to present a completely different version of events: in which the consistency of his character is stressed, rather than its sudden divergence. In conclusion, there would seem to be a large body of evidence to suggest that James's failings had manifested themselves, even without the benefit of hindsight, in the years prior to his accession. By the time of his brother's death, James had already proven himself to be ill-equipped to occupy such a high public office. He desired to be an active political figure, with a position at the heart of Restoration government, and savoured the status and glory which his appointments could offer him. However, while he was prepared to guard his own position jealously, he appears at times to have enjoyed power only for its own sake.[11] His interest in administration was at best patchy and uneven, and although he was certainly capable of sustained and conscientious effort – as attested to by his conduct of business at the Admiralty and the Scottish Privy Council – his energies were easily diverted by his impetuosity, lack of forethought and his need for immediate personal gratification. These traits can be clearly discerned in his obsessive love of hunting, his inattention to detail during the pursuit of the enemy fleet after

Lowestoft, and in his reckless dismemberment of New York Colony, in order to create a suitable gift for his friends.

Moreover, his long-term objectives were often frustrated by his tactlessness and his almost total inability to tolerate – or even to understand – any form of dissent, however mildly it might be expressed. As a result, he showed a preference for confronting problems head-on and for the use of force, where a combination of guile and conciliation would have yielded far more effective and durable results. Despite his personal bravery, his military capabilities were severely flawed and his temperament rendered him unsuitable for the highest echelons of command. Similarly his direction of policy, whether at the Admiralty – where he pursued an uncompromising pro-war platform against the Dutch Republic – or in the boardroom, where he attempted to make good a personal fortune which he had squandered on lavish entertainments, was often counter-productive and bedevilled by his inability to forge and maintain close political alliances. In the face of adversity, his Roman Catholic faith and deep spiritual convictions were, however, upheld with a great deal of dignity and would have done much to salvage his posthumous reputation had they not been so closely allied to his overt sense of militarism.[12]

Behind the carefully constructed public façade, of the brave soldier and the diligent administrator, there clearly emerges through the course of our study a much more forceful vision of a flawed Commander, a quixotic and curiously out-dated politician, a prime mover in the establishment of English slavery, and of a ruthless profiteer from the trade in human lives. Rather than expressing surprise at the rapidity with which his regime collapsed in the winter of 1688–9, we should view it as conforming to an already well-established pattern of personal and political failure. The enormous gains won by Charles II for the Stuart monarchy, in the last years of his reign, and the crushing of internal opposition after the dissolution of the Oxford Parliament, had ensured that James would succeed peacefully to the throne on St George's Day 1685. Yet even at the zenith of his career, as the crowds lining the nave of Westminster Abbey fell silent and the imperial crown was settled upon his brow, much was still left to be decided, and for this 'impolitic' Prince, it would seem that the seeds of his own destruction were there from the very first.

Notes

CHAPTER ONE

1. J.G. Alger, 'The Posthumous Vicissitudes of James the Second', *Nineteenth Century and After*, vol. XXV (1889), pp. 104–9; W.S. Churchill, *Marlborough. His Life and Times*, vol. I (4 vols, London, 1933, rpt 1967), p. 302; A. Fea, *James II and his Wives* (London, 1908), pp. 288–9, 291–7; P. Jones, 'James the Second, His Remains', *Notes and Queries*, 1st series, vol. II, no. 46 (14 September 1850), pp. 243–4; *Life*, vol. I, pp. v–vii, ix, xii and xxvi.

2. M. Ashley, *James II* (London, 1977), p. 300; Churchill, *Marlborough*, vol. I, pp. 302–3; *Life*, vol. I, pp. xvi–xviii.

3. G. Davies (ed.), *Papers of Devotion of James II* (Oxford, 1925), p. 17. Hereafter styled simply as *Devotions*.

4. *Burnet*, vol. I, p. 304 (Book II, pp. 168–9); G. Burnet, *Supplement to the History of My Own Time*, ed. H.C. Foxcroft (Oxford, 1902), p. 50; Cardinal Bouillon quoted in A.L. Sells (ed.), *The Memoirs of James II* (London, 1962), p. 52.

5. There is much confusion surrounding the number and identity of the editors who worked on James's papers while he was still alive. Although there were undoubtedly others, I have cited Anne Hyde and Charles Dryden alone here, as they are the only ones positively attested to by contemporary sources. It seems likely that James dictated a large amount of his memoirs to his secretaries. This is certainly the way Charles II worked when setting down his reminiscences, at the prompting of James.
   Burnet, vol. I, p. 307 (Book II, p. 170) and vol. II, p. 28 (Book III, pp. 629–30); Burnet, *Supplement*, p. 50; *Life*, vol. II, pp. 5, 7, 9; W. Mathews (ed.), *Charles II's Escape from Worcester* (Berkeley and Los Angeles, 1966), p. 98.

6. Ashley, *James II*, p. 290; *Life*, vol. II, pp. 242–3.

7. M. Kroll (ed.), *Letters from Liselotte. Elizabeth Charlotte, Princess Palatine and Duchess of Orléans, 'Madame', 1652–1722* (London, 1970), pp. 57, 59–60, 93; A.M. Ramsay, *Histoire du Vicomte Turenne*, vol. I (2 vols, Paris, 1735), pp. x–xi; Ramsay's work also appeared in an English edition as: A.M. Ramsay, *The History of Henri de la Tour d'Auvergne*, vol. I (2 vols, London, 1740), p. v; Sells (ed.), *Memoirs of James II*, pp. 13–15, 37, 39–44, 52–3.

8. Ramsay, *Histoire du Vicomte Turenne*, vol. II, pp. iii–cl; Ramsay, *History of Henri de la Tour d'Auvergne*, vol. II, pp. 340–516; Sells (ed.), *Memoirs of James II*, pp. 57–292.

9. Although several names have been put forward as being the editors of the manuscript acquired by the Prince Regent – and Clarke, himself, believed that it was John Caryll Secretary of State to the exiled Jacobite Court – modern opinion is united in attributing the work to William Dicconson. This is confirmed in a letter to Thomas Carte from James Edgar, the Secretary to the Old Pretender, dated 10 January 1741: 'The King is pleased . . . to give you perusal at the Scots College at Paris of the

complete Life of the late King his father, writ by Mr. Dicconson in consequence of royal orders, all taken out of, and supported by the late King's MSS'.

Ashley, *James II*, p. 290; Churchill, *Marlborough*, vol. I, p. 304; J. Gillow, *Bibliographical Dictionary of the English Catholics*, vol. II (London, 1855), pp. 60–2; J. Miller, *James II. A Study in Kingship* (London, 1978), pp. 243–5; L. von Ranke, *A History of England, Principally in the Seventeenth Century*, vol. VI (6 vols, Oxford, 1875), p. 30; Sells (ed.), *Memoirs of James II*, p. 28.

10. According to Clarke and Fox, housed in the library of the Scots College were four folio volumes and six quarto volumes of James's memoirs beginning from the time he was sixteen, two thin quarto volumes of correspondence from the Privy Council to James in exile in Brussels and Scotland, and two thin quarto volumes of letters from Charles II to James.

    Unfortunately, Fox did not record where the memoirs in James's own hand finished. It seems more than likely that the volumes of correspondence, that he mentioned, formed the basis of Dicconson's account of James's exile and rule in Scotland, from 1679–83. Clarke's transcription of Dicconson certainly relies heavily upon extracts from the Duke's letters for these years.

    C.J. Fox, *A History of the Early Part of the Reign of James the Second* (London, 1808), pp. xviii–xxv; *Life*, vol. I, p. xiv and vol. II, pp. 702–7.

11. Bodleian Library, Oxford, MS Carte, 198; J. Macpherson (ed.), *Original Papers Containing the Secret History of Britain* (2 vols, London, 1775).

12. Although Macpherson's book has often been discussed as though it were a biography of James, this is far from being the case and has led to it being misread. Macpherson sought to write a general history running from 1660–1725, and may well have modelled his popular, and sometimes salacious, *Secret History* on Procopious's similarly titled work on the Byzantine Court. James and his memoirs are only dealt with in part of the first volume, and account for just 247 out of its 711 pages. All Macpherson does is to give an abridged précis of James's memoirs and Carte's notes, leaving out the longer and more descriptive passages. He reproduces little more than generalized headings and extracts from the original.

    G. Davies, 'Macpherson and the Nairne Papers', *English History Review*, vol. XXXV (1920), pp. 367–76; J. Macpherson, *Fingal* (London, 1762); J. Macpherson, *Temora* (London, 1763); A. Parnell, 'James Macpherson and the Nairne Papers', *English History Review*, vol. XII (1897), pp. 254–84.

13. The copy of Dicconson bought by the Prince Regent had originally belonged to the Young Pretender. He had bequeathed it to his natural daughter, Charlotte Duchess of Albany, and on her death in 1789 it was deposited with the Order of English Benedictines for safekeeping. It escaped the fate of King James's original memoirs and was successfully returned to England, from Italy, at the time of the French Revolutionary Wars.

    J.S. Clarke and J. M'Arthur, *The Life of Lord Nelson* (2 vols, London, 1809); D. Daiches, *Charles Edward Stuart. The Life and Times of Bonny Prince Charlie* (London, 1973), pp. 289, 321–2; *Life*, vol. I, pp. xiii, xxvi–xxvii and xxix.

    For a guide to the other papers of the fallen Stuarts held at Windsor, see: M.F. Gain, 'The Stuart Papers at Windsor', *Royal Stuart Society*, Occasional Paper No. XVII (1981); A. and H. Tayler (eds), *The Stuart Papers at Windsor* (London, 1939). Unfortunately, the vast majority of the material collected there dates from after 1719.

14. C.H. Firth, *A Commentary on Macaulay's History of England* (London, 1964), pp. 277–303; J. Haswell, *James II. Soldier and Sailor* (London, 1972), pp. xi–xii, 59–128; M.V. Hay, *The Enigma of James II* (London, 1938), pp. xi–xii; T. Longueville, *The Adventures of King James II of England* (London, 1904), p. xvii; M. Trevor, *The Shadow of a Crown, The Life Story of James II of England and VII of Scotland* (London, 1988), pp. 15–24, 300.

15. J. Dryden, *All for Love* (London, 1678); G. Etherege, *The Man of Mode* (London, 1676); A. Hamilton, *Memoirs of the Count de Grammont*, trans. and ed. H. Walpole (London, n.d., *c.* 1900); L. Magalotti, *Lorenzo Magalotti at the Court of Charles II. His Relazione d'Inghilterra of 1668*, ed. W.E.K. Middleton (Waterloo, Canada, 1980); W. Wycherley, *The Country Wife* (London, 1675).

16. C.B. Macpherson, *The Political Theory of Possessive Individualism, Hobbes to Locke* (Oxford, 1962); C. Mooers, *The Making of Bourgeois Europe. Absolutism, Revolution, and the Rise of Capitalism in England, France and Germany* (London and New York, 1991); I. Morley, *A Thousand Lives. An Account of the English Revolutionary Movement of 1660–1685* (London, 1954); A.L. Morton, C. Hill and W. Thompson, '1688. How Glorious was the Revolution?', *Our History*, No. 79 (1988); W. Thompson, 'Samuel Pepys and the Emergent Bourgeoisie', *Socialist History*, vol. I (1993), pp. 36–48.

17. A. Fletcher, *The Outbreak of the English Civil War* (London, 1981); C. Hill, *The Century of Revolution, 1603–1714* (Edinburgh, 1961); H.J. Kaye, *The British Marxist Historians* (London, 1984, rpt 1995), pp. 99–130; J.S. Morrill, *The Nature of the English Revolution* (London, 1993).

18. T.B. Macaulay, *The History of England*, ed. C.H. Firth, vol. I (London, 1913), p. 260.

19. The government-backed celebrations to mark the 300th anniversary of the Glorious Revolution in 1988 singularly failed to capture the public imagination, despite the generous funding of re-enactments and elaborate museum exhibitions.
Anon., *Parliament and the Glorious Revolution. An Exhibition to Commemorate the Three Hundredth Anniversary* (London, 1988); K.M. Chacksfield, *Glorious Revolution, 1688* (Wincanton, Somerset, 1988), p. 5; D. Szechi, 'Mythistory versus History: the Fading of the Revolution of 1688', *Historical Journal*, vol. 33 (1990), pp. 143–53.

20. Macaulay, *History of England*, vol. I, p. 151.

21. We can compare their characterizations of James with those made by Macaulay, who declared that 'His understanding was singularly slow and narrow, and his temper obstinate, harsh, and unforgiving.' According to Chandler, James exhibited 'inflexibility and obstinacy'. Churchill thought his 'obstinacy, his stern religious faith . . . combined to lead him to disaster' and that James remained 'a stubborn anomaly upon a Protestant throne'. Webb saw him as being bound by 'bigotry, inflexibility, credulity, and irrationality', while Bryant thought 'James was obtuse, obstinate and morose . . . he could never understand the motives or anticipate the actions of others.'
A. Bryant, *Samuel Pepys. The Years of Peril* (Cambridge, 1935), p. 9; D. Chandler, *Sedgemoor, 1685* (Staplehurst, 1995), p. 13; Churchill, *Marlborough*, vol. I, p. 264; Macaulay, *History of England*, vol. I, p. 151; S.S. Webb, *1676. The End of American Independence* (New York, 1984), p. 196 i–ii.

22. Fox, *Early Part of the Reign of James II*, p. 47.

23. Fox, *Early Part of the Reign of James II*, pp. 132–3.

24. Fox had started work on the project in 1797 but had only completed three chapters by the time of his death in 1806. These passages charted developments over the course of

the last years of Charles II's reign and James's accession, through to the Battle of Sedgemoor and the executions of Monmouth and Argyll. They were published together with Fox's fragmentary notes for a fourth chapter and a selection of primary documents, which he had assembled in order to assist with his researches.

25. J. Lingard, *A History of England*, vol. X (London, 1855), pp. 63, 66, 115–16, 122–3. See also: W. Cobbett, *A History of the Protestant Reformation*, ed. H. Arnold (London, 1994); H. Howard, *Remarks on the Erroneous Opinions Entertained respecting the Catholic Religion* (Carlisle, 1825); A. Strickland, *Lives of the Queens of England* (16 vols, London, 1840–1848).

26. Lingard, *History of England*, vol. IX, pp. 48–9.

27. H. Ainsworth, *James the Second; or the Revolution of 1688. An Historical Romance* (3 vols in a single edition, London, 1848); W. Scott, *Redgauntlet* (Edinburgh and London, 1824); W. Scott, *Rob Roy* (Edinburgh and London, 1817); W. Scott, *Waverley* (Edinburgh and London, 1814); R.L. Stevenson, *Catriona* (London, 1893); R.L. Stevenson, *Kidnapped* (London, 1886); R.L. Stevenson, *The Master of Ballantrae* (London, 1889).
The influence of these works of popular fiction is clearly detectable in: J. Lane, *King James the Last* (London, 1942); T. Longueville, *The Adventures of James II of England* (London, 1904).

28. H. Belloc, *James the Second* (London, 1928), pp. 27–9, 83–109.

29. Belloc, *James the Second*, pp. xi–xii, 14, 17, 59, 118, 153, 187, 196, 219, 226–8, 282–3; H. Belloc, *The Last Rally* (London, 1940), pp. 3–4; M.V. Hay, *The Enigma of James II* (London, 1938), pp. 34, 41, 57, 59, 61, 125–6, 130–1, 140, 147, 201–3, 216–17; M.V. Hay, *Winston Churchill and James II of England* (London, 1934), pp. 19, 44, 55, 60–1; C. Petrie, *The Jacobite Movement. The First Phase, 1688–1716* (London, 1948), pp. 30, 50, 61–2, 66–7; C. Petrie, 'James the Second. A Revaluation', *Nineteenth Century*, vol. 114 (1933), pp. 475, 477, 479–81, 483–4; C. Petrie, *The Marshal Duke of Berwick* (London, 1953), pp. 15–17, 26–7, 41, 47–48; A.N. Wilson, *Hilaire Belloc* (London, 1984), pp. 307–8.

30. Belloc, *James the Second*, pp. 21, 83, 47–9, 192–3, 252, 281; R.F.J. Parsons, 'The Role of Jacobitism in the Modern World', *Royal Stuart Society*, Occasional Paper No. XXVIII (1986), pp. 16, 18, 33, 35–39; Petrie, 'James the Second', p. 479; Wilson, *Hilaire Belloc*, pp. 253–4, 289–92, 342–3, 346, 356–7.

31. Churchill, *Marlborough*, vol. I, pp. 217, 220–1; J. Miller, *The Glorious Revolution* (London and New York, 1983), p. vi; D. Ogg, *England in the Reigns of James II and William III* (Oxford, 1955), p. 221; D. Ogg, *William III* (London, 1956), p. 33; S.S. Webb, *Lord Churchill's Coup. The Anglo-American Empire and the Glorious Revolution Reconsidered* (New York, 1995), p. 3.

32. Churchill, *Marlborough*, vol. I, pp. 147, 153–4, 263.

33. Churchill's first volume, in its 1967 reprinting, ran to almost 500 pages. Of these, roughly 150 dealt specifically with James's life and reign. Hay took issue with only a fraction of the conclusions made therein, and centred his arguments primarily around only fifteen pages.
Churchill, *Marlborough*, vol. I, pp. 140–54; Hay, *Enigma of James II*, pp. 1–33; Hay, *Winston Churchill and James II of England*, pp. 8–9, 19, 31–2, 34, 40–1, 44, 54–5, 60–1; Macaulay, *History of England*, vol. I, pp. 260–2.

34. J. Haswell, *James II. Soldier and Sailor* (London, 1972), pp. xi–xii, 3, 65–7, 115–20, 158–64, 185–91, 236, 258, 272, 277–80, 309–10; F.M.G. Higham, *King James the Second* (London, 1934), pp. 35–49, 100–4, 131–2, 239–41, 244–7, 255–8, 277, 280.

35. Belloc, *James the Second*, pp. ix–x, 111, 121; Haswell, *James II*, pp. 150–1; Hay *Enigma of James II*, pp. xi–xii; Higham, *King James the Second*, pp. 90–1; Petrie, 'James the Second', p. 483.

36. E.S. De Beer, 'Members of the Court Party in the House of Commons, 1670–1678', *Bulletin of the Institute of Historical Research*, vol. 11 (1933), pp. 1–23; K. Feiling, *A History of the Tory Party, 1640–1714* (Oxford, 1924); D. Ogg, *England in the Reign of Charles II* (2 vols, London, 1948).

37. F.C. Turner, *James II* (London, 1948), pp. 39–42, 55, 71–4, 77–81, 103–4.

38. A. Bryant, *Samuel Pepys. The Man in the Making* (London, 1933); A. Bryant, *Samuel Pepys. The Saviour of the Navy* (London, 1938); A. Bryant, *Samuel Pepys. The Years of Peril* (London, 1935).

39. Turner, *James II*, pp. 82–3.

40. F.M.G. Higham, 'Review of Turner's "James II"', *History*, new series, vol. XXXV (1950), p. 129. Higham's criticisms of Turner's work beg the question – why, then, did she not attempt to examine the areas of trade and empire in her own biography of James?

41. Turner, *James II*, pp. 234, 456–9.

42. Charles James Fox, as a firm advocate of religious toleration, was the exception to this trend. He rejected the view held by Whig and Tory writers, alike, that Roman Catholicism had destroyed James's political judgement and pointed to the long list of Protestant lords who had willingly assisted him in his Scottish campaigns. Fox's ideas were later to find an echo in the writings of Armand Carrel, a young French liberal.
   Burnet, vol. I, p. 304 (Book II, pp. 168–9); A. Carrel, *History of the Counter-Revolution in England for the Re-establishment of Popery under Charles II and James II* (London, 1846), pp. 97, 144, 346–8; Fox *Early Part of the Reign of James II*, pp. 108–10, 132–3; H.M. Gwatkin, *Church and State in England to the Death of Queen Anne* (London, 1917), p. 367; Macaulay, *History of England*, vol. I, pp. 151, 168, 190, 195, 462, 465, 468, 505–6, vol. II, pp. 708–9; T. Smollett, *History of England*, vol. III (London, 1804), p. 273.

43. Ashley, *James II*, pp. 9–14, 295; J.R. Jones, *The Revolution of 1688 in England* (London, 1972, rpt 1988), p. 53; D. Middleton, *The Life of Charles, 2nd Earl of Middleton* (London, 1957), pp. 74–5; M. Mullett, *James II and English Politics, 1678–1688* (London and New York, 1994), p. 1; W.A. Speck, *Reluctant Revolutionaries* (Oxford and New York, 1988), pp. 119–20; H. and B. van der Zee, *William and Mary* (London, 1973), pp. 58–9.

44. *Burnet*, vol. I, pp. 416–19 (Book II, pp. 227–8); A. Hamilton, *Memoirs of the Count de Grammont*, ed. and trans. H. Walpole (London, n.d., *c.* 1900), pp. 192–3; L. Magalotti, *Lorenzo Magalotti at the Court of Charles II. His Relazione d'Inghilterra of 1668*, ed. W.E.K. Middleton (Waterloo, Canada, 1980), p. 78; *Pepys Diary* (19 March 1665), vol. VI, p. 60 and (6 April 1668), vol. IX, pp. 154–5.

45. Anon. (ed.), *Memoirs of the Chevalier de St George: With some Private Passages of the Life of the Late James II, Never before published* (London, 1712), pp. 7–8; H.W. Chapman, *Mary II, Queen of England* (London, 1953), pp. 249–54; H.W. Chapman, *Queen Anne's Son. A Memoir of William Henry, Duke of Gloucester, 1689–1700* (London, 1954), pp. 21–3, 137–40; *Devotions*, p. 107; J. Fitz-James, *The Memoirs of the Marshal Duke of Berwick. Written by Himself*, ed. C.L. Montesquieu, vol. I (2 vols, London, 1779), pp. 1–3; A.L. Rowse, *The Early Churchills* (Harmondsworth, Middlesex, 1956, rpt 1969), p. 138; Tayler, *Stuart Papers at Windsor*, p. 113.

46. Alger, 'Posthumous Vicissitudes', p. 106; Fea, *James II and his Wives*, p. 294; Jones, 'James the Second, His Remains', p. 244.

47. M. Ashley, 'Is there a Case for James II?', *History Today*, vol. 13 (1963), pp. 347–8, 351–2; Ashley, *James II*, pp. 9–14, 34–9, 41–6, 51, 55–64, 67, 74–84, 96–7, 105–7, 109–11, 155, 264, 290–5, 302–5; M. Kishlansky, *A Monarchy Transformed, Britain 1603–1714* (London, 1996), p. 267.

48. J. Miller, *James II. A Study in Kingship* (London, 1978), pp. 42–3, 168.

49. Miller, *James II*, pp. 46, 234–5, 237.

50. Chapman, *Queen Anne's Son . . . William Henry, Duke of Gloucester*; R. Strong, *Henry Prince of Wales and England's Lost Renaissance* (New York, 1986).

51. Bouillon MS (1696), ff. 1–290; *Life*, vol. I, pp. 1–384; Ramsay, *Histoire du Vicomte Turenne*, vol. II, pp. iii–cl; Sells (ed.), *Memoirs of James II*, pp. 57–292.

52. Sells (ed.), *Memoirs of James II*, pp. 82–96, 123–4, 143–53, 157–90, 259–74; *Life*, vol. I, pp. 9–18.

53. This preoccupation with James's military career at the expense of his other endeavours as Duke of York can be seen in its more extreme forms in Belloc, Haswell, Higham and Trevor. Their accounts of the acquisition of New York colony and the Duke's African possessions tally almost exactly with those already given in the *Life*.
Belloc, *Last Rally*, pp. 11, 57, 139–40; Haswell, *James II*, pp. 150–1; Higham, *King James the Second*, p. 90; *Life*, vol. I, pp. 400–1; M. Trevor, *The Shadow of a Crown. The Life Story of James II of England and VII of Scotland* (London, 1988), p. 36.
    Similarly, the structure of the *Life* does much to shape Ashley's treatment of the Duke. Compare his account of the Battles of Lowestoft and Sole Bay with those contained in the *Life*: Ashley, *James II*, pp. 82–3, 105–7; *Life*, vol. I, pp. 410–15, 464–74.

54. *Life*, vol. I, pp. 410–15, 464–74.

55. *Life*, vol. I, p. 400.

56. *Life*, vol. I, pp. 243–4, 400–1; *Life*, vol. II, pp. 609, 611–12, 633–4.

57. The *Devotional Papers* were preserved by James's grandson, Cardinal Henry Stuart. After his death in 1807 the contents of his villa were sold off. The papers were handed down through the family of the Maquis Malatesta, before being purchased in 1842 by Father B.T. Balfour, a parish priest from Drogheda. *Papers of Devotions*, pp. xi–xii; Trinity College, Dublin, MS 3529.

58. *Life*, vol. II, pp. 5, 7, 9, 582–5.

59. *Life*, vol. II, pp. 634, 609, respectively.

60. Anon., *The Life of King James II. Late King of England – Containing Accounts of his . . . Enterprises both Home and Abroad – In Peace and War* (London, 1702), pp. ii, 5–12, 412–13; Anon., *Memoirs of the English Affairs, chiefly Naval, From the Year 1660 to 1673* (London, 1729), pp. ix–x; Anon., *The Memoirs of King James II – Containing an Account of the Transactions of the Last Twelve Years of his Life: with the Circumstances of his Death* (London, 1702); Anon., *Memoirs of the Chevalier de St George*, pp. 1–7, 36–41. Haswell, for instance, transcribes James's own account of his work in setting up the Royal African Company word for word: Haswell, *James II*, p. 150; Higham, *King James the Second*, pp. 190–1; *Life*, vol. I, p. 400; Trevor, *Shadow of a Crown*, p. 36.

61. J.P. Cooper and J. Thirsk (eds), *17th Century Economic Documents* (Oxford, 1972), pp. 708–12, 788–9, 790–811; R. Davis, 'A Commercial Revolution', *Historical Association*, pamphlet no. 64 (1967), pp. 9–10, 15–18; *Life*, vol. II, pp. 633–4; S. Pepys, *Memories*

Relating to the State of the Royal Navy of England (London, 1690), pp. 1, 12, 22–3, 103, 127–8, 213–14.

62. Carrel, *History of the Counter-Revolution*, p. 334; *Life*, vol. II, pp. 617–42; Louis XIV, *Memoires for the Instruction of the Dauphin*, trans. and ed. P. Sonnino (New York and London, 1970), pp. 5, 7; J.B. Wolf, *Louis XIV* (London, 1968), pp. 112–13.

63. Anon., *Dux Redux: or, London's Thanksgiving* (London, 1672); Anon., *Memoirs of the English Affairs*; Anon., *A New Ballad of Jocky's Journey into England, in the Year, 1681* (London, 1681); Anon., *Old Jemmy. An Excellent New Ballad* (London, 1681); Anon., *On the Arrival of His Royal Highness, the Duke into England. A Congratulatory Poem* (London, 1679); Anon., *Pereat Papa: or, Reasons why a Presumptive Heir, or Popish Successor should not Inherit the Crown* (London, *c.* 1681); Anon., *A Poem on the Happy Return of His Royal Highness from Scotland* (London, 1680); Anon., *The Several Declarations of the Company of Royal Adventurers of England Trading into Africa* (London, 1669); Anon., *The Swans Welcome to His Royal Highness the Duke* (London, 1679); Anon., *To His Royal Highness the Duke of York, Upon his Victory over the Dutch, May 28. 1672* (London, 1672).

64. Historical Manuscripts Commission, *The Manuscripts of the Right Honourable F.J. Savile Foljambe of Osberton* (London, 1897), pp. 123–40; Public Record Office, Kew, S.P.8. 3., ff. 1–228, The King's Chest. Letters from the Duke of York to William Prince of Orange, written from Whitehall, February 1674–February 1685. Another selection of these letters can be found in: G. van Prinsterer, *Archives de la Maison d'Orange-Nassau*, 2nd series (5 vols, The Hague, 1858–61). James's correspondence with William after his accession to the throne are to be found in the: PRO, S.P.8. 4. Unfortunately, through accident or design, William's letters to James have not survived.

65. Bodleian Library, MS. Rawl. Letters, 108, f. 2; Bodl. Lib., MS. Rawl. Letters, 115, f. 120; Bodl. Lib., MS. Pigott, d.10; British Library, Add. MS. 12,093.

66. Kenyon is extremely dismissive of James's letters, citing them as 'brief, clumsy, replete with schoolboy platitudes, stock phrases, even recurrent stock sentences, untouched by any emotion save anger, and innocent of any intellectual concept'. This damning verdict is, perhaps, a little unjustified. James was constrained by both the formality of his situation, in addressing a fellow Prince, and by the haste and secrecy with which his messages often had to be delivered. Verbal briefings, which contained the most sensitive information, were also very important. In June 1677, he informed his nephew that his courier would 'inform you of all I have charged him to say to you, which is to[o] long for a letter'. While in March 1677, he hurriedly finished writing as 'it is late and the post [is] ready to go'.

J.P. Kenyon, *The Stuarts*, 2nd edn (Glasgow, 1970), p. 144; PRO, S.P.8. 3., ff. 11, 33, 47, 49.

67. Bodl. Lib., MS. Rawl. Letters, 108 f. 2; PRO, S.P.8. 3., ff. 26, 30, 33, 35, 43, 45, 47, 53.

68. Bodl. Lib., MS. Bodl., 891; BL, Add. MS., 18,958; BL, Add. MS., 38,863; Cambridge University Library, Add. MS., 7091; John Rylands Library, Manchester, ENG. MS., 294 ff. 1–17.

69. John Churchill's literary remains are vast. His correpondence from 1678–1722 is preserved in: BL, Add. MSS., 61101–61413.

Sir William Coventry's naval and miscellaneous papers are held at: BL, Add. MS., 32094, while five of his letters to Sir William Penn, the elder, are preserved at: National

Maritime Museum, Greenwich, WYN / 14. Henry Jermyn's writings, perhaps unsurprisingly, have not survived in anything like the same quantity or quality, but his account books and rent rolls from 1662–3, 1676 are held at: BL, Add. MSS., 22062–22063.

George Legge, Earl of Dartmouth, left accounts of James's naval battles and copies of the Duke's sailing and fighting instructions which are held at: NMM, DAR / 9 / 13 / 14 / 24. His personal papers and correspondence with James was republished as: Historical Manuscripts Commission, *The Manuscripts of the Earl of Dartmouth*, 11th Report, Appendix, Part V, vol. I (London, 1887).

Sir Charles Littleton's letters on the composition of the Duke's household and keen interest in military affairs were reprinted, by the Camden Society, as: E.M. Thompson (ed.), *Correspondence of the Family of Hatton*, vol. I (London, 1878).

112 of Richard Talbot, the future Duke of Tyrconnel's, letters are to be found at: Bodl. Lib., MSS. Talbot. Although most of these papers relate to his career from 1685 onwards, they do contain some items relating to his land-holding at the time of the Restoration.

70. Anne Hyde left behind her: Bodl. Lib., MS. Rawl. Letters, 107 f. 16; A. Hyde, *A Copy of a Paper Written by the Late Dutchess* [sic] *of York* (London, 1670, rpt Dublin, *c*. 1685–8). Mary of Modena's papers, again mostly dating from post-1685, are preserved at: Bodl. Lib., MSS. Add. C., 106–7. Princess Mary's early letters are reprinted in: B. Bathurst (ed.), *Letters of Two Queens* (London, 1924); M. Bentinck (ed.), *Lettres et Memoires de Marie II* (The Hague, 1880).

James Fitz-James, the Duke of Berwick, comprehensive memoirs were published after his death in battle: Fitz-James, *Memoirs of the Marshal Duke of Berwick*. Clarendon's prolific writings are represented here by: Bodl. Lib., Eng. Hist., c. 44 f. 12; E. Hyde, Earl of Clarendon, *The History of the Rebellion and Civil Wars in England, Begun in the Year 1641*, ed. W.D. Macray (6 vols, Oxford, 1888); E. Hyde, Earl of Clarendon, *The Life of Edward Earl of Clarendon* (3 vols, Oxford, 1827)

71. Bodl. Lib., Add. MS., 39822, Pepys's handwritten draft of the *Memorial on the Navy, 1685–95*; C.H. Hull (ed.), *The Economic Writings of Sir William Petty* (Cambridge, 1899); Marquis of Lansdowne (ed.), *The Petty Papers* (London, 1927); Marquis of Lansdowne (ed.), *The Petty-Southwell Correspondence, 1676–1687* (New York, 1967); R. Latham (ed.), *Samuel Pepys and the Second Dutch War. Samuel Pepys's Navy White Book and Brooke House Papers* (Aldershot and Vermont, USA, 1995); *Naval Minutes*; *Pepys Diary*, 10 vols; J.R. Tanner (ed.), *A Descriptive Catalogue of the Naval Manuscripts in the Pepysian Library* (4 vols, London, 1903–23).

72. *Burnet*, 6 vols; *Evelyn Diary*; H.C. Foxcroft, *A Supplement to Burnet's History of My Own Times* (London, 1902); Magalotti, *Lorenzo Magalotti at the Court of Charles II*; J. Reresby, *The Memoirs of Sir John Reresby, 1634–1689*, ed. J.A. Cartwright (London, 1875).

73. *CSPC, CSPD, CSPI* and *RPCS, passim*. NMM, DAR / 9 / 10.

74. R.C. Anderson (ed.), *Journals and Narratives of the Third Dutch War* (London, 1946); E.E. Rich (ed.), *Copy-Book of Letters Outward of the Hudson's Bay Company, 1679–1684* (London, 1948); E.E. Rich (ed.), *Minutes of the Hudson's Bay Company, 1679–1684*, First Part 1679–1682 (London, 1945).

75. Anon., *Certain Considerations Relating to the Royal African Company of England* (London, 1680); PRO, T. 70, Africa Company Records; *The Several Declarations*.

The records of the Hudson's Bay Company were moved to Canada in the 1970s, but a microfilm copy of them is retained at the PRO, as BH1. A series of records for the East India Company are also held at the PRO, as FO 677, but unfortunately are only of limited use for our period and purposes.

The records of the African Companies are vast. Most useful to us are the Abstracts from the Committees of Correspondence, 1678–82, (PRO, T. 70 / 20), 1683–98, (PRO, T. 70 / 11), the Abstracts from the Committee of Goods, 1678–81, (PRO, T. 70 / 20), the records of the Court of Assistants from 1678–87, (PRO, T. 70 / 78–81), and the Petitions received by the Company from 1681–96, (PRO, T. 70 / 169).

CHAPTER TWO

1. *CSPD* (1633–4), pp. 246, 251, 264, 298; C. Oman, *Henrietta Maria* (London, Sydney and Toronto, 1936, rpt 1951), p. 70.
2. *CSPD* (1633–4), p. 297.
3. *CSPD* (1635), pp. 43, 80, 138, 550; *CSPD* (1635–6), pp. 191, 429; *CSPD* (1636–7), p. 48; R. Hutton, *Charles II. King of England, Scotland and Ireland* (Oxford, 1989), pp. 1–2; P. Morrah, *A Royal Family* (London, 1982), pp. 4, 36–7.
4. Quoted in: O. Millar, *Van Dyck in England* (London, 1982), pp. 60–1, 109.
5. Millar, *Van Dyck*, pp. 60–1, 71–2.
6. Anon., *A Short View of the Life and Actions of the Most Illustrious James Duke of York, Together with His Character* (London, 1660), p. 3. Copies of the prints by Mesians and Hollar are to be found at the Ashmolean Museum, Oxford and the National Army Museum, Chelsea, respectively. Johnson's portraits are held by the National Portrait Gallery, London.
7. *CSPD* (1637–8), pp. 321, 351, 445; *CSPD* (1640–41), p. 378; W.G. Perrin, 'The Lord High Admiral and the Board of Admiralty', *Marriners Mirror*, vol. XIV (1926), pp. 117–18, 124–33.
8. *CSPD* (1637–8), p. 351; Perrin, 'Lord High Admiral', p. 133.
9. *Burnet*, vol. III, p. 3 (Book IV, p. 618); *CSPD* (1636–37), p. 474; *CSPD* (1637), p. 63; *CSPD* (1638–9), pp. 426, 485; *CSPD* (1641–3), p. 493; C. Carlton, *Charles I. The Personal Monarch*, 2nd edn (London and New York, 1995), p. 133.
10. T.T. Carter (ed.), *Nicholas Ferrar* (London and New York, 1892), pp. 283–4; N. Ferrar, *Two Lives*, ed. J.E.B. Major (Cambridge, 1885), pp. 126–37.
11. Earl of Clarendon, *The History of the Rebellion and Civil Wars in England, Begun in the Year 1641*, ed. W.D. Macray, vol. I (6 vols, Oxford, 1888), pp. 482–5 (Book IV, pp. 152–4, 156); W.H. Coates, A.S. Young and V.F. Snow (eds), *The Private Journals of the Long Parliament, 3 January to 5 March 1642*, vol. I (New Haven and London, 1982), pp. 7–17; *Life*, vol. I, p. 1; E. Ludlow, *The Memoirs of Edmund Ludlow*, ed. C.H. Firth, vol. I (2 vols, Oxford, 1894), pp. 24–7.
12. *CSPD* (1641–3), p. 312; Ludlow, *Memoirs*, vol. I, p. 27.
13. *CSPD* (1641–3), pp. 307, 312, 315; *Life*, vol. I, p. 2.
14. *CSPD* (1641–3), pp. 253, 264, 311, 314, 355; Clarendon, *History of the Rebellion*, vol. II, p. 45–9 (Book V, pp. 88–91); L. Hutchinson, *Memoirs of the Life of Colonel Hutchinson* (London, 1914), p. 110; J.R. Powell and E.K. Timings (eds), *Documents Relating to the Civil War, 1642–1648* (London and Colchester, 1963), pp. 2, 10–11.

15. *CSPD* (1641–3), pp. 315–17, 324; Clarendon, *History of the Rebellion*, vol. II, p. 46 n. 1, pp. 47–8 n. 1, pp. 49–50 (Book V, p. 91); *Life*, vol. I, pp. 2–5.

16. *Life*, vol. I, pp. 2–5.

17. *Life*, vol. I, pp. 3, 5–6; *Life*, vol. II, pp. 649–52.

18. *CSPD* (1641–3), pp. 316, 336, 344; Clarendon, *History of the Rebellion*, vol. II, p. 50 (Book V, p. 91); *Life*, vol. I, pp. 10–12; P. Young, *Edgehill, 1642. The Campaign and the Battle* (Kineton, 1967), pp. 50–5, 73, 75, 77–9.

19. *Life*, vol. I, pp. 12, 16. See also: Clarendon, *History of the Rebellion*, pp. 358, 361–4 (Book VI, pp. 82, 85–9); *Life*, vol. I, pp. 10–17.

20. *Evelyn Diary* (12 Nov. 1642), p. 39; R. Fasnacht, *A History of the City of Oxford* (Oxford, 1954), pp. 111, 113–17, 119–20, 122; R. Hutton, *The Royalist War Effort, 1642–1646* (London and New York, 1982), p. 96; Ludlow, *Memoirs*, vol. I, pp. 45–8; M. Toynbee and P. Young, *Strangers in Oxford* (London and Chichester, 1973), p. 31; A. Wood, *The Life and Times of Anthony Wood, Antiquary of Oxford*, ed. A. Clark, vol. I (5 vols, Oxford, 1891), pp. 82–3, 91, 93.

21. Anon., *A Short View of the Life and Actions of . . . James Duke of York*, p. 3; Anon., *Some Historical Memoires of the Life and Actions of His Royal Highness, The Renowned and most Illustrious Prince, James Duke of York* (London, 1683), p. 10; M.W. Brownley, *Clarendon and the Rhetoric of Historical Form* (Philadelphia, 1985), p. 137; Turner, *James II*, p. 13.

22. Anon., *Some Historical Memoires of the Life and Actions of . . . James Duke of York*, p. 10; G.F. Warner (ed.), *The Nicholas Papers*, vol. I (4 vols, London, 1886–1920), p. 76.

23. Clarendon, *History of the Rebellion*, vol. III, pp. 132–3 (Book VII, pp. 160–2); J. Washbourn, *Bibliotheca Gloucesterensis*, vol. II (London, 1825), pp. 209–12.

24. H.W. Chapman, *The Tragedy of Charles II* (London, 1964), p. 68; S.R. Gardiner, *History of the Great Civil War*, vol. I (4 vols, London, 1893, rpt 1987), pp. 198–9; *Life*, vol. I, p. 20.

25. *CSPD* (1644), p. 138; Gardiner, *History of the Great Civil War*, vol. I, p. 206; *Life*, vol. I, p. 20.

26. C.H. Firth, *The House of Lords During the Civil War* (London, New York, Bombay and Calcutta, 1910), p. 130; M.P. Schoenfeld, *The Restored House of Lords* (The Hague and Paris, 1967), pp. 22–4; B.H.G. Wormald, *Clarendon. Politics, history and religion, 1640–1660* (Cambridge, 1951, rpt 1989), pp. 133–43, 157–8.

27. *CSPD* (1644–5), p. 464; *CSPD* (1645–7), p. 51; Ludlow, *Memoirs*, vol. I, p. 129; C. Petrie (ed.), *King Charles, Prince Rupert, and the Civil War from Original Letters* (London, 1974), pp. 17–18; S. Reid, *Officers and Regiments of the Royalist Army*, vol. IV (4 vols, Leigh-on-Sea, n.d., *c.* 1980s), pp. 154–5, 197; J. Sprigge, *Anglia Rediviva* (London, 1647), p. 40; Toynbee and Young, *Strangers in Oxford*, p. 27.

28. J. Bruce (ed.), *Charles I in 1646. Letters of King Charles I to Henrietta Maria* (London, 1856), pp. 20–1, 40–1, 44, 54; *Burnet*, vol. I, pp. 93–5 (Book I, pp. 50–1); C. Oman, *Mary of Modena* (London, 1962), p. 62.

29. Bruce (ed.), *Charles I in 1646*, pp. 2, 37–8; *CSPD* (1644–5), pp. 429, 449, 470; *CSPD* (1645–7), pp. 433, 435; Hutchinson, *Memoirs of Colonel Hutchinson*, p. 291; Hutton, *Royalist War Effort*, pp. 196–7; *Life*, vol. I, p. 27; Ludlow, *Memoirs*, vol. I, pp. 137–8; Petrie (ed.), *King Charles . . . from Original Letters*, pp. 49–50.

30. Bruce (ed.), *Charles I in 1646*, p. 53; *CSPD* (1645–7), p. 224; *Life*, vol. I, p. 29; C.V. Wedgwood, *The King's War, 1641–1647* (London, 1958), p. 564; J. Wilson, *Fairfax, General of Parliament's forces in the English Civil War* (New York, 1985), p. 92.

31. Clarendon, *History of the Rebellion*, pp. 209, 237 (Book X, pp. 62, 103); *Life*, vol. I, pp. 28–30; Ludlow, *Memoirs*, vol. I, pp. 139–40; Wilson, *Fairfax*, pp. 92–3.

32. J. Bampfield, *Colonel Joseph Bampfield's Apology*, ed. J. Loftis and P.H. Hardacre (London and Toronto, 1993), p. 125; *Burnet*, vol. III, p. 3 (Book IV, p. 618); Gardiner, *History of the Great Civil War*, vol. IV, pp. 101–2; Kishlansky, *Monarchy Transformed*, p. 178.

33. Turner, *James II*, pp. 14–15.

34. J. Adamson, 'Of armies and architecture: the employments of Robert Scawen', in I. Gentles, J. Morrill and B. Worden (eds), *Soldiers, Writers and Statesmen of the English Revolution* (Cambridge, 1998), pp. 40, 43–5, 49 56–8, 62–3; *Life*, vol. I, pp. 30–1.

35. Clarendon, *History of the Rebellion*, vol. IV, pp. 250–3 (Book X, pp. 115–18); Millar, *Lely*, pp. 37–9.

36. Anon., *Eikon Basilike. The Portraiture of His Sacred Majesty in His Solitudes and Sufferings*, ed. P.A. Knachel (1649, rpt Ithaca, New York, USA, 1966), pp. 158–71, 192–4; Clarendon, *History of the Rebellion*, vol. IV, pp. 236–8, 250–3 (Book X, pp. 103, 115–19).

37. Anon., *Eikon Basilike*, pp. 70–4, 94–111, 171–87; Anon., *A Short View of the Life and Actions of . . . James Duke of York*, p. 3; Anon., *Some Historical Memoires of the Life and Actions of . . . James Duke of York*, pp. 10–11; J. Bruce (ed.), *Charles I in 1646. Letters of King Charles I to Queen Henrietta Maria* (London and New York, 1856, rpt 1968), p. 61 and fn; *Burnet*, vol. III, p. 3 (Book IV, p. 618); Earl of Clarendon, *The Life of Edward Earl of Clarendon: in which is included a continuation of his History of the Grand Rebellion*, vol. I (3 vols, Oxford, 1827), p. 285; *Devotions*, pp. 1–2, 23–4; *Life*, vol. I, pp. 539–40.

38. Bampfield, *Apology*, p. 69; *Burnet*, vol. III, p. 3 (Book IV, p. 618); *CSPD* (1648–9), pp. 19, 38–9; *Life*, vol. I, pp. 32–3.

39. *CSPD* (1648–9), pp. 38–9; *Life*, vol. I, pp. 5–6, 32–3.

40. Anon., *A Plain Authentick and Faithful Narrative of Several Passages of the Young Chevalier from the Battle of Culloden to his Embarkation for France* (London, 1765); D. Chandler, *Sedgemoor, 1685. From Monmouth's Invasion to the Bloody Assizes* (Staplehurst, 1995), pp. 76–7; Matthews (ed.), *Charles II's Escape from Worcester*, pp. 34–162.

41. Bampfield, *Apology*, pp. 69, 126; Bruce (ed.), *Charles I in 1646*, pp. 67–8, 72; *Burnet*, vol. I, p. 3 (Book IV, p. 168); *Life*, vol. I, pp. 33–7; J. Loftis (ed.), *The Memoirs of Anne, Lady Halkett and Ann, Lady Fanshawe* (Oxford, 1979), pp. 23, 25–6.

42. Anon., *A Short View of the Life and Actions of . . . James Duke of York*, p. 9; Bampfield, *Apology*, pp. 69–70; *CSPD* (1648–9), p. 19; *Life*, vol. I, pp. 34–5, 37; Loftis (ed.), *Memoirs of Lady Halkett and Lady Fanshawe*, pp. 24–5.

CHAPTER THREE

1. Bampfield, *Apology*, pp. 70, 241; Loftis (ed.), *Memoirs of Lady Halkett and Lady Fanshawe*, pp. 25–6, 29; Powell and Timmings (eds), *Documents Relating to the Civil War*, p. 324.

2. Bampfield, *Apology*, pp. 18, 22–3, 27, 78, 80, 134–8, 144, 175, 186, 239, 241; Bruce (ed.), *Charles I in 1646*, p. 67; Clarendon, *History of the Rebellion*, vol. IV, p. 328 (Book XI, p. 21); Loftis (ed.), *Memoirs of Lady Halkett and Lady Fanshawe*, pp. 24–6; Hutton, *Charles II*, pp. 34–5, 40–3; R. Ollard, *Clarendon and his Friends* (New York, 1988), pp. 84, 91, 94; Schoenfeld, *The Restored House of Lords*, pp. 30–1; E. Scott, *The King in Exile. The*

Wanderings of Charles II from June 1646 to July 1654 (London, 1905), pp. 444–5;
Wormald, *Clarendon*, pp. 155–6, 160–2.

3. B. Capp, *Cromwell's Navy: The Fleet and the English Revolution, 1648–1660* (Oxford, 1989),
pp. 15–17, 43–6; *CSPD* (1648–9), pp. 361–2; Gardiner, *History of the Great Civil War*, vol.
I, p. 306, vol. II, p. 190, vol. IV, pp. 135, 146; Perrin, 'Lord High Admiral', pp. 133–6;
Powell and Timings (eds), *Documents Relating to the Civil War*, pp. 7, 15–19, 21, 37,
310–11.

4. Powell and Timings (eds), *Documents Relating to the Civil War*, pp. 194–5, 301–5, 311,
332–4, 337–42, 353–5; Scott, *The King in Exile*, pp. 46–8.

5. Earl of Clarendon, *Clarendon's Four Portraits*, (ed.) R. Ollard (London, 1989), p. 117;
Clarendon, *History of the Rebellion*, vol. IV, pp. 416–17 (Book IX, p. 141); *Life*, vol. I, pp.
40–4; Powell and Timings (eds), *Documents Relating to the Civil War*, p. 392.

6. Clarendon, *History of the Rebellion*, vol. IV, pp. 417–18 (Book IX, p. 142); *Life*, vol. I, pp.
40, 44, 48; Powell and Timmings (eds), *Documents Relating to the Civil War*, p. 392.

7. Bampfield, *Apology*, pp. 71–3; Clarendon, *History of the Rebellion*, vol. IV, pp. 417–21,
423–6 (Book XI, pp. 142, 145–7, 149–52); Scott, *The King in Exile*, pp. 65–7.

8. Bampfield, *Apology*, p. 150; Clarendon, *History of the Rebellion*, vol. IV, pp. 407, 417
(Book IX, pp. 127, 141); *Life*, vol. I, pp. 43–4; Sells (ed.), *The Memoirs of James II*, p. 292.

9. Anon., *Eikon Basilike*, pp. xiii–xix, 140–52, 158–82; Burnet, vol. I, pp. 93–5 (Book I, pp.
50–1); *Life*, vol. I, p. 46; C.V. Wedgwood, *Montrose* (London and Glasgow, 1952), pp.
125–6; C.V. Wedgwood, *Trial of Charles I* (London, 1964), pp. 198–9.

10. Clarendon, E. Hyde, Earl of, *The Life of Edward Earl of Clarendon*, vol. I (Oxford, 1827),
p. 284; R. Grassby, *The English Gentleman in Trade. The Life and Works of Sir Dudley North,
1641–1691* (Oxford, 1994), pp. 149–50; *Life*, vol. I, pp. 1–5, 426.

11. Historical Manuscripts Commission, *The Manuscripts of the Earl of Dartmouth*, 11th
Report, Appendix, Part V, vol. I (London, 1887), p. 41; *Life*, vol. I, pp. 422, 426, 431,
437, 448–9, 746.

12. V. Barbour, *Henry Bennet, Earl of Arlington, Secretary of State to Charles II* (London and
Washington, 1914), p. 16; Clarendon, *History of the Rebellion*, vol. V, pp. 66, 104–6 (Book
XII, pp. 77, 119–21); J.D. Davies, 'A Love of the Sea and Skillful in Shipping: King
Charles and his Navy', *Royal Stuart Society*, Occasional Paper No. XLII (1992), p. 1; *Life*,
vol. I, p. 47; Turner, *James II*, pp. 24–7.

13. Barbour, *Henry Bennet, Earl of Arlington*, pp. 14–16; Clarendon, *History of the Great
Rebellion*, vol. V, pp. 45–6 (Book XII, p. 50); Clarendon, *Life of Clarendon*, vol. I, pp.
284–7; C.H. Hartmann, *The King's Friend. A Life of Charles Berkeley, Viscount Fitzhardinge,
Earl of Falmouth* (London, 1951), p. 7.

14. Barbour, *Henry Bennet, Earl of Arlington*, pp. 16–17; Clarendon, *History of the Great
Rebellion*, vol. V, pp. 162–5 (Book XIII, pp. 38, 41–2); Clarendon, *Life of Clarendon*, vol. I,
pp. 287–90; *Life*, vol. I, pp. 49–50; Scott, *The King in Exile*, pp. 303–4, 314; G. Treasure,
Mazarin. The Crisis of Absolutism in France (London and New York, 1995), pp. 142, 250.

15. Clarendon, *Life of Clarendon*, vol. I, p. 290; *Life*, vol. I, p. 51.

16. Quoted in Turner, *James II*, p. 31.

17. Clarendon, *History of the Rebellion*, vol. V, pp. 168–9 (Book XIII, p. 46).

18. Chapman, *Tragedy of Charles II*, pp. 223, 233; Clarendon, *History of the Rebellion*, vol. V, p.
232 (Book XIII, p. 129); *Life*, vol. I, pp. 51–4; Scott, *The King in Exile*, pp. 279–80, 284;
Turner, *James II*, p. 37.

19. Clarendon, *History of the Rebellion*, vol. V, pp. 224–6, 230–1 (Book XIII, pp. 122–3, 128); Sells (ed.), *Memoirs of James II*, pp. 57, 59–60.

20. Clarendon, *Four Portraits*, p. 118; *Life*, vol. I, pp. 54–5; Sells (ed.), *Memoirs of James II*, pp. 57–8.

21. Sells (ed.), *Memoirs of James II*, p. 58.

22. J.W. Fortesque, *A History of the British Army*, vol. I (London, 1899), p. 298; D. Middleton, *The Life of Charles, 2nd Earl of Middleton* (London, 1957), pp. 74–5. See also: Ashley, *James II*, pp. 251–6, 275–6; D. Chandler, *Marlborough as Military Commander* (London, 1973), pp. 11, 22–5; Churchill, *Marlborough*, vol. I, pp. 153–4, 192–3, 226, 249–64; Miller, *James II*, pp. 200–5, 223–33; Speck, *Reluctant Revolutionaries*, pp. 118–24; Turner, *James II*, p. 215.

23. A.M. Ramsay, *The History of Henri de la Tour d'Auvergne*, vol. I (2 vols, London, 1740), p. 213; Sells (ed.), *Memoirs of James II*, pp. 53, 64, 74–5, 99, 104, 166–7, 171, 222.

24. Anon., *A Faithful Compendium, of the Birth, Education, Heroick Exploits and Victories of his Royal Highness, The Illustrious Prince James, Duke of York* (London, 1679), pp. 2–3; Anon., *A Short View of the Life and Actions of the Most Illustrious James Duke of York, Together with His Character* (London, 1660), pp. 15–22, 24–5; Anon., *Some Historical Memoires of the Life and Actions of His Royal Highness, The Renowned and most Illustrious Prince, James Duke of York and Albany* (London, 1683), pp. iv, 22; Ashley, *James II*, pp. 9–10, 13, 34, 38–9, 44, 62–3; Belloc, *James the Second*, pp. 73–8; Haswell, *James II*, pp. 65–6, 98, 101; Higham, *King James the Second*, pp. 35–47; Sells (ed.), pp. 53, 104, 162–3, 178–85, 228–33, 241–2, 255–75, 287–9; Trevor, *Shadow of a Crown*, pp. 14–24.

25. *Life*, vol. I, pp. 107, 122; Ramsay, *History of Henri de la Tour d'Auvergne*, vol. II, pp. 128–9, 131; Sells (ed.), *Memoirs of James II*, p. 104.

26. Clarendon, *History of the Rebellion*, vol. V, p. 231 (Book XIII, p. 128); T. Longueville, *Marshal Turenne* (London, 1907), p. 174; Ramsay, *History of Henri de la Tour d'Auvergne*, vol. I, p. 213; Sells (ed.), *Memoirs of James II*, p. 80; M. Weygrand, *Turenne, Marshal of France* (London, 1930), p. 53.

27. J. Berenger, *Turenne* (Paris, 1987), pp. 305–8, 429–41; Ramsay, *History of Henri de la Tour d'Auvergne*, vol. I, pp. 284, 489–94; O. Ranum, *The Fronde. A French Revolution* (New York and London, 1993), pp. 314–15; Sells (ed.), *Memoirs of James II*, p. 142; Weygrand, *Turenne*, pp. 53–4, 133–4, 137–41.

28. D.C. Baxter, *Servants of the Sword, French Intendants of the Army, 1630–70* (Urbana, Chicago and London, 1976), pp. 86, 117–38; J.A. Lynn, *Giant of the Grand Siècle. The French Army, 1610–1715* (Cambridge, 1997), pp. 59–61, 79–92, 463; R. Martin, 'The Army of Louis XIV' in P. Sonnino (ed.), *The Reign of Louis XIV* (New Jersey and London, 1990), pp. 111–25; Sells (ed.), *Memoirs of James II*, pp. 168–70.

29. Longueville, *Marshal Turenne*, p. 216; Sells (ed.), *Memoirs of James II*, pp. 89, 123, 167–8.

30. *Pepys Diary* (4 June 1664), vol. V, pp. 170–1; Sells (ed.), *Memoirs of James II*, pp. 53, 168.

31. *Burnet*, vol. I, p. 304 (Book II) and vol. III, pp. 4–5 (Book IV, p. 619).

32. Sells (ed.), pp. 104, 148, 222, 287.

33. Ashley, *James II*, p. 10; *Life*, vol. I, pp. 279, 282–4; Sells (ed.), *Memoirs of James II*, p. 157; Turner, *James II*, pp. 40–1.

34. Anon., *Some Historical Memoires of the Life and Actions of . . . James Duke of York*, p. 22; Berenger, *Turenne*, pp. 332–3; A. Bryant (ed.), *The Letters, Speeches and Declarations of King Charles II* (London, Toronto, Melbourne and Sydney, 1935), pp. 44–5; Clarendon,

History of the Rebellion, vol. VI, pp. 47–8 (Book XV, p. 76); Clarendon, *Four Portraits*, p. 86; *Life*, vol. I, pp. 264–6; Louis XIV, *Memoires*, pp. 90–1; Sells (ed.), *Memoirs of James II*, pp. 218–19; Treasure, *Mazarin*, pp. 252–3.

35. Hutton, *Charles II*, p. 103; Scott, *The Travels of the King*, pp. 127–9; Sells (ed.), *Memoirs of James II*, p. 222; Turner, *James II*, pp. 45–6.

36. Barbour, *Henry Bennet, Earl of Arlington*, pp. 20–2; Hartmann, *The King's Friend*, pp. 17–19; Scott, *The Travels of the King*, pp. 277, 285.

37. Barbour, *Henry Bennet, Earl of Arlington*, pp. 22–5; Clarendon, *Four Portraits*, pp. 115–21; Hutton, *Charles II*, p. 104; *Life*, vol. I, pp. 276–7; Scott, *The Travels of the King*, p. 276; Sells (ed.), *Memoirs of James II*, pp. 223–5.

38. Barbour, *Henry Bennet, Earl of Arlington*, pp. 25–6; Chapman, *The Tragedy of Charles II*, p. 321; Scott, *The Travels of the King*, pp. 278–80.

39. Clarendon, *Four Portraits*, pp. 119–20; Hartmann, *The King's Friend*, pp. 23–6; Scott, *The Travels of the King*, pp. 280–4, 286.

40. Scott, *The Travels of the King*, p. 285; Turner, *James II*, p. 53.

41. Barbour, *Henry Bennet, Earl of Arlington*, pp. 27–8; Clarendon, *Four Portraits*, p. 120; *Pepys Diary* (20 Dec. 1668), vol. IX, p. 396; Ramsay, *History of Henri de la Tour d'Auvergne*, vol. I, pp. 283–5; Sells (ed.), *Memoirs of James II*, pp. 223, 227, 229, 231, 234–5, 275; Turner, *James II*, p. 41.

42. Ramsay, *History of Henri de la Tour d'Auvergne*, vol. II, pp. 166–7; Scott, *The Travels of the King*, p. 306; Sells (ed.), *Memoirs of James II*, pp. 231–3, 239–40.

43. *Evelyn Diary* (3–15 Aug. 1690), p. 542; T. Gray, *No Surrender! The Siege of Londonderry, 1689* (London, 1975), pp. 79–81; J. Kinross, *The Boyne and Aughrim* (Moreton-in-Marsh, Gloucestershire, 1997), pp. 42, 45–50; Kroll (ed.), *Letters from Liselotte*, pp. 57, 59–60, 93; *Pepys Diary* (24 March 1667), vol. VIII, p. 127 and (20 Dec. 1668), vol. IX, pp. 396–7; N. Plunket, *Derry and the Boyne*, ed. B. Clifford (Belfast, 1990), pp. 119, 123–8; Sells (ed.), *Memoirs of James II*, pp. 15, 52–3, 64, 98–9, 131–2, 167–8, 171, 240.

44. Sells (ed.), *Memoirs of James II*, p. 240.

45. Sells (ed.), *Memoirs of James II*, pp. 231, 234–7, 256, 265, 276, 278, 280, 290–2.

46. Berenger, *Turenne*, pp. 329–31; BL, Add. MS. 14,007, f. 337; Longueville, *Marshal Turenne*, pp. 246–9, 251; R.A. Stradling, *Philip IV and the Government of Spain, 1621–1665* (Cambridge, 1988), pp. 288–90, 292–4; Weygrand, *Turenne*, pp. 77–8.

47. Clarendon, *History of the Rebellion*, vol. VI, p. 83 (Book XV, p. 136); Scott, *The Travels of the King*, pp. 305–6; Sells (ed.), *The Memoirs of James II*, pp. 231, 234, 241–2, 260.

48. E. Godley, *The Great Condé* (London, 1915), pp. 491–2, 495–6; Longueville, *Marshal Turenne*, p. 258; T. Morgan, 'A True and Just Relation of Major-General Sir Thomas Morgan's Progress in France and Flanders . . . in the years 1657 and 1658, at the taking of Dunkirk' (London, 1699), reprinted in C.H. Firth (ed.), *An English Garner. Stuart Tracts, 1603–1693* (Edinburgh, 1903), pp. 406–7, 410; Sells (ed.), *The Memoirs of James II*, pp. 253–9; O.L. Spaulding, H. Nickerson and J.W. Wright, *Warfare. A Study of Military Methods from the Earliest Times* (London, Calcutta and Sydney, 1924), p. 501; R.A. Stradling, *The Armada of Flanders* (Cambridge, 1992), pp. 149–50.

49. *CSPD* (1658–9), pp. 50–1; Godley, *Condé*, pp. 494, 496; Morgan in Firth (ed.), *Stuart Tracts*, pp. 410, 413; Sells (ed.), *Memoirs of James II*, pp. 258–9.

50. Anon., *A Short View of the Life and Actions of . . . James Duke of York*, p. 22; Clarendon, *History of the Rebellion*, vol. VI, p. 84 (Book XV, p. 137); Du Buisson, *Vicomte Turenne*, pp.

298–9; *CSPD* (1658–9), pp. 49–50; Morgan in Firth (ed.), *Stuart Tracts*, p. 411; Sells (ed.), *Memoirs of James II*, p. 264.

51. Morgan in Firth (ed.), *Stuart Tracts*, pp. 411–14; Sells (ed.), *Memoirs of James II*, pp. 265–6.

52. Anon., *A Short View of the Life and Actions of . . . James Duke of York*, p. 22; Berenger, *Turenne*, p. 335; Clarendon, *History of the Rebellion*, vol. VI, p. 85 (Book XV, p. 138); Godley, *Condé*, p. 500; Morgan in Firth (ed.), *Stuart Tracts*, p. 414; Sells (ed.), *Memoirs of James II*, pp. 265–71; Weygrand, *Turenne*, p. 87.

53. *CSPD* (1658–9), pp. 49–50, 178; Godley, *Condé*, pp. 499–501; Morgan in Firth (ed.), *Stuart Tracts*, pp. 414–15; Sells (ed.), *The Memoirs of James II*, pp. 265–6, 275–6; Spaulding et al., *Warfare*, p. 505.

54. Berenger, *Turenne*, pp. 335–6; Du Buisson, *Vicomte Turenne*, p. 300; Clarendon, *History of the Rebellion*, vol. VI, pp. 84–5 (Book XV, pp. 137–8); Longueville, *Marshal Turenne*, p. 265; Morgan in Firth (ed.), *Stuart Tracts*, pp. 415–23; Ramsay, *History de la Henri de la Tour d'Auvergne*, vol. II, pp. 185–8; Sells (ed.), *The Memoirs of James II*, pp. 274, 276; Stradling, *Philip IV*, p. 294; Weygrand, *Turenne*, pp. 87–8.

55. Ramsay, *History of Henri de la Tour d'Auvergne*, vol. II, p. 188.

56. Sells (ed.), *The Memoirs of James II*, pp. 273–4

57. Ramsay, *History of Henri de la Tour d'Auvergne*, vol. II, p. 193; Sells (ed.), *The Memoirs of James II*, pp. 278–81.

58. Berenger, *Turenne*, p. 328; Longueville, *Marshal Turenne*, pp. 271–2; Ramsay, *History of Henri de la Tour d'Auvergne*, vol. II, pp. 263, 264; Schoenfeld, *Restored House of Lords*, p. 30; Sells (ed.), *The Memoirs of James II*, pp. 287–8.

59. Clarendon, *History of the Rebellion*, vol. VI, p. 122 (Book XVI, p. 45); R. Hutton, *The Restoration. A Political and Religious History of England and Wales, 1658–1667* (Oxford and New York, 1985), pp. 57–9; Ramsay, *History of Henri de la Tour d'Auvergne*, vol. II, pp. 262–3; Sells (ed.), *The Memoirs of James II*, p. 287; Weygrand, *Turenne*, p. 102.

60. Sells (ed.), *The Memoirs of James II*, pp. 288–9.

61. Clarendon, *History of the Rebellion*, vol. VI, pp. 122–3 (Book XVI, p. 46); Longueville, *Marshal Turenne*, pp. 271–2; Scott, *The Travels of the King*, pp. 441–2, 448; Sells (ed.), *The Memoirs of James II*, pp. 289–90.

62. Berenger, *Turenne*, p. 336; Godley, *Condé*, pp. 503–11; Treasure, *Mazarin*, pp. 254–60.

63. Schoenfeld, *Restored House of Lords*, p. 30; Sells (ed.), pp. 290–1.

64. M. Nedham, *News from Brussels. In a Letter from a neer Attendant on His Majesties Person* (Brussels, 1660), p. 8; Schoenfeld, *Restored House of Lords*, pp. 30–1.

CHAPTER FOUR

1. *Life*, vol. I, p. 381; G. Parker, *The Thirty Years' War* (London and New York, 1984), pp. 63, 66–7, 126–7, 129, 131, 141, 143, 145–6, 162, 167, 181; Sells (ed.), *Memoirs of James II*, p. 291.

2. *Life*, vol. I, p. 381; Scott, *Travels of the King*, pp. 433–4, 464; Sells (ed.), *Memoirs of James II*, p. 291; Stradling, *The Armada of Flanders*, p. 233.

3. Anon., *England's Joy, or a Relation of the Most Remarkable passages, from his Majesty's Arrival at Dover, to His entrance at Whitehall* (London, 1660), reprinted in C.H. Firth (ed.),

Notes

Stuart Tracts, pp. 427–30; Hutton, *The Restoration*, pp. 105–8, 111–14, 117–19, 126–7; P. Seaward, *The Cavalier Parliament and the Reconstruction of the Old Regime, 1661–1667* (Cambridge, 1989), pp. 11, 25–8, 31, 35–70; J.M. Sosin, *English America and the Restoration Monarchy of Charles II. Transatlantic Politics, Commerce, and Kinship* (Lincoln, USA and London, 1980), pp. 24–8.

4. P. Morrah, *Prince Rupert of the Rhine* (London, 1976), pp. 28, 218–19, 224, 278, 426; Sells (ed.), *Memoirs of James II*, pp. 75, 104, 178–85, 232–3, 242, 255–75.

5. C.R. Boxer, 'Three Sights To Be Seen: Bombay, Tangier and a Barren Queen, 1661–1684', *Portuguese Studies*, vol. III (1987), pp. 77–83; *CSPD* (1665–6), p. 232; C.H. Hartman, *The King My Brother* (London, 1954), pp. 216–17, 266; T. Palmer, *Charles II. Portrait of an Age* (London, 1979), p. 297; *Pepys Diary* (14 June 1667), vol. VIII, p. 269 and (9 May 1668), vol. IX, p. 191.

6. Clarendon, *Life of Clarendon*, vol. I, pp. 302–5; A. Hamilton, *Memoirs of the Count Grammont, Containing the History of the English Court under Charles II*, trans. and ed. W. Scott and Mrs. Jameson (London, n.d., *c.* 1900), pp. 114–15; R. Josselin, *The Diary of Ralph Josselin, 1616–1683*, ed. A.Macfarlane (London, 1976) (27 Oct. 1660), p. 471; *Life*, vol. I, p. 387; Magalotti, *Lorenzo Magalotti at the Court of Charles II*, pp. 36, 78; *Pepys Diary* (Initial entry), vol. II, p. 1; Sells (ed.), *Memoirs of James II*, p. 219.

7. Clarendon, *Life of Clarendon*, vol. I, p. 377.

8. Clarendon, *Life of Clarendon*, vol. I, pp. 373–6, 378; *Evelyn Diary* (7 Oct. 1660), p. 268; Hamilton, *Memoirs of the Count Grammont*, pp. 186–9; Hartmann, *The King's Friend*, pp. 36–7, 48–9, 54; *Pepys Diary* (10 Dec. 1660), vol. I, p. 315.

9. *CSPD* (1660–1), p. 412; *Evelyn Diary* (22 Dec. 1660), p. 270; *Life*, vol. I, pp. 387–8; Hamilton, *Memoirs of the Count Grammont*, pp. 189–90; Hartmann, *The King's Friend*, p. 39; *Pepys Diary* (21 Dec. 1660), vol. I, p. 319 and (23 Feb. 1661), vol. II, pp. 40–1.

10. *Devotions*, pp. xxiv, 1–2, 4, 61, 85, 92–3, 96–9, 144–5; *Life*, vol. I, p. 585.

11. Clarendon, *Life of Clarendon*, vol. I, p. 382; Magalotti, *Lorenzo Magalotti at the Court of Charles II*, p. 36.

12. Oman, *Mary of Modena*, pp. 1–12, 19; J. Southorn, 'Mary of Modena, Queen Consort of James II and VII', *Royal Stuart Society*, Occasional Papers No. XL (1992), pp. 2–4.

13. *Life*, vol. I, p. 485; Oman, *Mary of Modena*, pp. 30–1.

14. *Evelyn Diary* (5 Nov. 1673), p. 377; James VI and I, *The Basilicon Doron*, ed. J. Craige, vol. I (Edinburgh and London, 1944), p. 163; Josselin, *Diary* (11 Feb. 1673), p. 656; Southorn, 'Mary of Modena', p. 5.

15. *Burnet*, vol. I, pp. 308–9 (Book II, pp. 170–1); *Devotions*, p. 107; *Evelyn Diary* (13 Sept. 1660), p. 268; A. Fraser, *King Charles II* (London, 1979), p. 201; Hartmann, *The King My Brother*, p. 19.

16. Ashley, *James II*, pp. 48–9; Bodleian Library, Oxford, MS. Rawl. Letters 115, f. 132 ff; Chapman, *Tragedy of Charles II*, pp. 272–82; A. Fraser, *Charles II. His Life and Times* (London, 1993), plate on p. 90 and p. 264; Reresby, *Memoirs*, p. 49; Sells (ed.), *Memoirs of James II*, pp. 34, 242, 266, 290; Scott, *Travels of the King*, pp. 41, 43, 45, 47.

17. *Pepys Diary* (3 June 1664), vol. V, p. 167; Magalotti, *Lorenzo Magalotti at the Court of Charles II*, p. 39; G. Martin, 'Prince Rupert and the Surgeons', *History Today*, vol. 40 (1990), pp. 38–43.

18. Fraser, *Charles II* (1979), p. 201.

19. *CSPD* (1666–7), p. 228; *CSPD* (1667), p. 497; *Pepys Diary* (14 May 1667), vol. VIII, p. 214 and (14 June 1667), vol. VIII, p. 269, n. 2.

20. *CSPD* (1666–7), p. 315.

21. Quoted in Trevor, *Shadow of a Crown*, p. 46.

22. Anon. (ed.), *Memoirs of the Chevalier de St George. With some Private Passages of the Life of the Late James II, Never before Published* (London, 1712), pp. 7–8; Haswell, *James II*, p. 135.

23. *CSPD* (1663–4), p. 646; *CSPD* (Nov. 1673–Feb. 1675), pp. 131–2; *CSPD* (March 1676 to February 1677), p. 255; Gardiner, *History of the Great Civil War*, vol. IV, pp. 101–2; Kroll (ed.), *Letters from Liselotte*, pp. 12–13, 52, 72, 76, 96, 99; Scott, *Travels of the King*, pp. 232–3, 383–4; Treasure, *Mazarin*, p. 263; Wolf, *Louis XIV*, pp. 731–2.

24. *CSPD* (1660–1), pp. 142, 312; *CSPD* (1663–4), pp. 157, 285, 424–6, 435, 458, 578, 629, 676; *CSPD* (1667), pp. 76, 91; J. Childs, *The Army of Charles II* (London, 1976), pp. 32–3, 36–7, 180–1; C.D. Ellestad, 'The Mutinies of 1689', *JSAHR*, vol. LIII (1975), pp. 4–5, 9–11, 20; C.C.P. Lawson, *A History of the Uniforms of the British Army*, vol. I (London, 1940), p. 54; John Rylands Library, Manchester, ENG. MS. 294, f. 1; R.E. Scouller, 'The Mutiny Acts', *JSAHR*, vol. L (1972), pp. 42–4.

25. J. Childs, *The Army, James II and the Glorious Revolution* (Manchester, 1980), pp. 40–1; Childs, *Army of Charles II*, pp. 7–11, 13–14, 91, 93–5; Fortescue, *History of the British Army*, vol. I, pp. 298–9; A.J. Guy and J. Spencer-Smith (eds), *1688 – Glorious Revolution? The Fall and Rise of the British Army, 1660–1704* (London, 1988), pp. 8–9; Magalotti, *Lorenzo Magalotti at the Court of Charles II*, p. 42; *Pepys Diary* (2 Jan. 1660), vol. I, p. 4, (4 Jan. 1660), vol. I, p. 7, (24 April 1660), vol. I, pp. 114–15 and (4 June 1664), vol. V, pp. 170–1; Public Record Office, Kew, S.P.8. 3., ff. 26, 30, 33, 35, 43, 47, 53; J.R. Tanner, *Samuel Pepys and the Royal Navy* (Cambridge, 1920), p. 34; A. Woolrych, *Battles of the English Civil War* (London, 1961), pp. 183–7.

26. *CSPD* (1660–1), pp. 470–1; Childs, *Army of Charles II*, pp. 15–17; R.L. Greaves, *Enemies Under His Feet* (Stanford, California, 1990), p. 2; *Life*, vol. I, pp. 388–90; D. Ogg, *England in the Reign of Charles II*, vol. I (2nd edn, Oxford, 1966), pp. 208–9; Palmer, *Charles II*, p. 46; *Pepys Diary* (7 Jan.–10 Jan. 1661), vol. II, pp. 7–11.

27. Bodl. Lib., MS. Rawl. Letters 107, f. 16; Bodl. Lib., MS. Rawl. Letters 108, f. 16; A. Browning, *Thomas Osborne, Earl of Danby and Duke of Leeds, 1632–1712*, vol. I (Glasgow, 1951), pp. 36–8; *Life*, vol. I, pp. 421–2; *Pepys Diary* (6 Sept. 1664), vol. V, p. 264; Turner, *James II*, p. 76.

28. Coventry quoted in Higham, *King James the Second*, p. 106. See also: Reresby, *Memoirs*, p. 65; Turner, *James II*, pp. 84–5.

29. *CSPD* (1666–7), pp. 576–7, 581; *CSPD* (1667), pp. 8, 38, 41, 44; *CSPD* (1667–8), pp. 582–3; T. Delaune, *Angliae Metropolis: Or, The Present State of London* (London, 1690), p. 282; G. Parnell, 'The Re-fortification of the Tower of London, 1679–1686', *Antiquaries Journal*, vol. LXIII (1983), pp. 337–52; G.A. Raikes, *The History of the Honourable Artillery Company*, vol. I (London, 1878), pp. xxxii, 101, 166–70; H. Tomlinson, 'The Ordinance Office and the King's Forts, 1660–1714', *Architectural History*, vol. XVI (1973), pp. 5–25; P.M. Wilkinson, 'Excavations at Tilbury Fort, Essex', *Post-Medieval Archaeology*, vol. XVII (1983), pp. 111–62.

30. D. Allen, 'The Role of the London Trained Bands in the Exclusion Crisis, 1678–1681', *English Historical Review*, vol. LXXXVII (1972), pp. 293–4; *CSPD* (1682), pp. 173–4; Raikes, *Honourable Artillery Company*, pp. 168, 171–9, 198.

31. Allen, 'Role of the London Trained Bands', pp. 294; Raikes, *Honourable Artillery Company*, pp. 195–6, 198–9.
32. BL, Add. MS. 14,007, f. 337; *CSPC* (1675–6), nos 1024–5; *CSPD* (1660–1), pp. 313, 443–4, 489, 570; *CSPD* (1661–2), pp. 21, 105, 249, 261, 287, 312, 373, 409, 469, 492, 544–5, 586, 608, 632; *CSPD* (1663–4), pp. 157, 285, 424–6, 435, 578, 629, 676; *CSPD* (March 1675–Feb. 1676), p. 355; PRO, S.P.8. 3., ff. 26, 30, 33, 35, 43, 47, 53.
33. W.B.T. Abbey, *Tangier under British Rule* (London, 1940), pp. 48–51; Childs, *Army of Charles II*, pp. 40, 48–53, 91; J. Childs, *Nobles, Gentlemen and the Profession of Arms in England* (London, 1987), pp. 7, 9, 17, 21, 26, 31–2, 75, 89–90, 96; Churchill, *Marlborough*, vol. I, pp. 50–1; C. Dalton (ed.), *English Army Lists and Commission Registers, 1661–1714*, vol. I (London, 1892), p. 42; *Life*, vol. I, p. 443; *Naval Minutes*, p. 41; *Pepys Diary*, vol. X, pp. 9–10, 85, 210, 230, 407, 473; S.S. Webb, 'Brave Men and Servants to His Royal Highness. The Household of James Stuart', *Perspectives on American History*, vol. VIII (1974), pp. 57, 65–9, 75–6; S.S. Webb, *The Governors-General. The English Army and the Definition of Empire* (Chapel Hill, North Carolina, 1979), pp. 96, 478–9, 498, 508.
34. *CSPD* (Oct. 1672–Feb. 1673), p. 184; Lawson, *History of the Uniforms of the British Army*, vol. I, p. 54; *Naval Minutes*, p. 41; Webb, *Governors-General*, p. 508.
35. PRO, S.P.8. 3., ff. 26, 35, 45, 53; Turner, *James II*, p. 137.
36. B. Bevan, *James Duke of Monmouth* (London, 1973), p. 91; Childs, *Army of Charles II*, p. 186; J.N.P. Watson, *Captain-General and Rebel Chief. The Life of James, Duke of Monmouth* (London, 1979), p. 82; PRO, S.P.8. 3., f. 47.
37. Charles II to Barrillon, quoted in Turner, *James II*, p. 136.
38. PRO, S.P.8. 3., ff. 33, 35, 53.
39. BL, Add. MS. 14,007, f. 337. 'Disadvantages of Appointing James, Duke of York, as Governor of Flanders [1678]'.
40. Childs, *Army of Charles II*, pp. 188, 191–3; J. Childs, 'Monmouth and the Army in Flanders', *JSAHR*, vol. LII (1974), pp. 3–12; R. Clifton, *The Last Popular Rebellion. The Western Rising of 1685* (London, 1984), p. 99.
41. Davies, 'Charles II in 1660', pp. 257–8; K. Gibson, 'The Cult of Charles II', *Royal Stuart Society*, Occasional Paper No. XLVII (n.d.), pp. 1, 5–7; Hutton, *The Restoration*, pp. 125–6; R. Hutton, *The Rise and Fall of Merry England* (Oxford, 1994), pp. 213–14, 221, 246, 249–51; J. Morrill (ed.), *Revolution and Restoration. England in the 1650s* (London, 1992), pp. 110–11; *Pepys Diary* (1 May 1660), vol. I, p. 121; R. Sherwood, *Oliver Cromwell. King in all but name* (Stroud, Gloucestershire,1997), pp. 20–1, 26–31, 33–46, 48–56, 80–107.
42. Bodl. Lib., Ms. Bodl. 891, f. 2; *CSPD* (1660–1), pp. 18, 24–5, 30, 77, 91, 159, 235–6, 240, 249, 276, 292, 332, 347, 379, 386, 393, 502, 521; *CSPD* (1661–2), pp. 260–1; *CSPD* (1663–4), p. 581; Magalotti, *Lorenzo Magalotti at the Court of Charles II*, p. 110; Miller, *James II*, p. 42; Reresby, *Memoirs*, p. 48.
43. Bodl. Lib., MS. Bodl. 891, ff. 9, 13–15; BL, Ad. MS. 18,958, f. 6; BL, Ad. MS. 38,863, ff. 5, 9. *CSPD* (1660–1), p. 393; *CSPD* (1663–4), pp. 161, 581; H.M. Colvin (ed.), *The History of the King's Works*, vol. V (London, 1976), pp. 153, 217; E. Hawkins, *Medallic Illustrations of the History of Great Britain and Ireland*, vol. I (Portsmouth, 1885), pp. 538–9; John Rylands Library, ENG. MS. 294, ff. 3, 5–6.
44. J.P. Kenyon, *The Popish Plot* (London, 1972), p. 33.

45. BL, Add. MS. 18,958, ff. 1–3, 5; BL, Add. MS. 38,863, ff. 3–6, 8; *Pepys Diary* (24 June 1663), vol. IV, p. 194 and (8 Sept. 1667), vol. VIII, p. 424.

46. Anon. (ed.), *Memoirs of the Chevalier de St George*, pp. 7–8; Bodl. Lib., MS. Bodl. 891, ff. 21–2; BL, Add. MS. 18,958, ff. 1–2, 4–5, 7–9; BL, Add. MS. 38,863, ff. 3–4, 6, 8, 10–11, 14, 16; *CSPD* (1660–1), pp. 240, 521; Churchill, *Marlborough*, vol. I, pp. 35, 46–7, 50–1, 126, 142–3; J. Fitz-James, *The Memoirs of the Marshal Duke of Berwick. Written by Himself*, ed. C.L. Montesquieu, vol. I (2 vols, London, 1779), pp. 1–2; *Pepys Diary* (24 Sept. 1664), vol. V, p. 279, (13 June 1666), vol. VII, p. 163, (5 Aug. 1667), vol. VIII, p. 374 and vol. X (Companion), pp. 27–8; A.L. Rowse, *The Early Churchills* (London, 1956), pp. 60–2; John Rylands Library, ENG. MS. 294, ff. 1–9.

47. Bodl. Lib., MS. Bodl. 891, ff. 9, 16; BL, Add. MS. 18,958, ff. 11–12; BL, Add. MS. 38,863, ff. 14–16; E. Gregg, *Queen Anne* (London, 1980, rpt 1984), pp. 11–13; *Pepys Diary* (29 April 1667), vol. VIII, p. 190 and (4 March 1669), vol. IX, p. 468.

48. BL, Add. MS. 18,958, ff. 4, 6; BL, Add. MS. 38,863, ff. 7, 9; *CSPV* (1661–4), p. 28; *Life*, vol. I, p. 445; John Rylands Library, ENG. MS. 294, f. 3.

49. BL, Add. MS. 18,958, f. 4; BL, Add. MS. 38,863, f. 7; *CSPC* (1675–76), no. 1166; Magalotti, *Lorenzo Magalotti at the Court of Charles II*, pp. 36–7; *Pepys Diary* (9 Nov. 1663), vol. IV, p. 192 and (22 June 1663), vol. IV, p. 192 and (8 Aug. 1666), vol. VII, p. 239.

50. BL, Add. MS. 18,958, ff. 6, 23–5; BL, Add. MS. 38,863, ff. 7, 9; *Evelyn Diary* (17 Dec. 1684), p. 461; John Rylands Library, ENG. MS. 294, ff. 5–6.

51. *CSPD* (1661–2), p. 122; *Pepys Diary* (24 June 1667), vol. VIII, p. 286; John Rylands Library, ENG. MS. 294, ff. 3–4.

52. *CSPD* (1660–1), pp. 72, 137, 239–40, 248–9, 470, 559; *CSPD* (1661–2), pp. 147, 241, 292; *CSPD* (1663–4), pp. 227, 514; John Rylands Library, ENG. MS. 294, f. 3.

53. R. Bagwell, *Ireland under the Stuarts*, vol. III (London, 1916), pp. 25–6; *CSPI* (1660–2), pp. 322, 490–1, 668, 688; *CSPI* (1663–5), pp. 9, 96–7, 199, 205, 343, 370–1, 388, 562; *CSPI* (1666–9), pp. 34, 96–7, 111, 199, 243–4, 257–8, 343–4, 494–8, 527–30; *CSPI* (1669–70), pp. 5, 108.

54. *CSPC* (1661–8), nos 446, 1199; *CSPD* (1661–2), pp. 129, 165, 170, 245; *CSPD* (1663–4), pp. 187, 222, 242, 401, 451, 459, 485, 518, 598; *CSPD* (1664–5), p. 405; C.D. Chandaman, *The English Public Revenue 1660–1688* (Oxford, 1975), p. 117; Miller, *James II*, p. 42; *Pepys Diary* (25 March 1668), vol. IX, p. 132; John Rylands Library, ENG. MS. 294, f. 3.

55. *CSPD* (1660–1), pp. 165, 502, 522; *CSPD* (1661–2), pp. 93, 203; *CSPD* (1663–4), p. 581; *Life*, vol. I, p. 422; Miller, *James II*, p. 42; *Pepys Diary* (16 Oct. 1665), vol. VI, p. 267 and (28 Oct. 1665), vol. VI, p. 281; John Rylands Library, ENG. MS. 294, ff. 3–4.

56. John Rylands Library, ENG. MS. 294, ff. 1–2.

57. Miller, *James II*, p. 42; *Pepys Diary* (24 June 1667), vol. VIII, pp. 286–7; R.C. Ritchie, 'The Duke of York's Commission of Revenue', *New York Historical Society Quarterly*, vol. LVIII (1974), p. 177; John Rylands Library, ENG. MS. 294, ff. 3–4.

58. *CSPD* (1663–4), pp. 255, 264; *Pepys Diary* (24 June 1667), vol. VIII, pp. 286–7 and (11 Sept. 1667), vol. VIII, p. 434; Ritchie, 'Duke of York's Commission', p. 177; John Rylands Library, ENG. MS. 294, f. 4.

59. Bodl. Lib., MS. Bodl. 891, f. 17; *Pepys Diary* (6 Oct. 1662), vol. III, p. 214 and (13 April 1664), vol. V, p. 120; V. Vale, 'Clarendon, Coventry, and the Sale of Naval Offices, 1660–1668', *The Cambridge Historical Journal*, vol. XII (1956), pp. 107–25.

60. *Pepys Diary* (3 July 1666), vol. VII, pp. 191–2; John Rylands Library, ENG. MS. 294, ff. 3–14, 16–17.
61. *Pepys Diary* (24 June 1667), vol. VIII, pp. 286–7; John Rylands Library, ENG. MS. 294, f. 4.
62. Magalotti, *Lorenzo Magalotti at the Court of Charles II*, p. 37; *Pepys Diary* (24 June 1667), vol. VIII, pp. 286–7, (22 Aug. 1667), vol. VIII, pp. 394–5, (30 Oct. 1668), vol. IX, pp. 341–2, (27 Jan. 1669), vol. IX, p. 38 and (Companion) vol. X, pp. 9–10, 344–5; Rowse, *Early Churchills*, pp. 88–9.
63. *Burnet*, vol. I, pp. 307–8 (Book II, p. 170); *Pepys Diary* (30 July 1667), vol. VIII, p. 368 and n. 2.
64. *Evelyn Diary* (6 Jan. 1662), pp. 281–2 and (12 March 1672), p. 363; Hartmann, *The King My Brother*, p. 13; *Pepys Diary* (13 April 1664), vol. V, p. 120, (24 June 1667), vol. VIII, pp. 286–7 and (12 July 1667), vol. VIII, p. 331.
65. *Pepys Diary* (7 Sept. 1665), vol. VI, p. 215, (26 Dec. 1667), vol. VIII, pp. 591–2 and (27 Aug. 1668), vol. IX, p. 290; Ritchie, 'The Duke of York's Commission', pp. 178–9.
66. *Pepys Diary* (27 Jan. 1668), vol. IX, p. 38 and n. 2; John Rylands Library, ENG. MS. 294, ff. 15–16.
67. BL, Add. MS. 18,958; BL, Add. MS. 38,863; *CSPD* (1663–4), p. 264; *CSPD* (1682), p. 561; Chandaman, *English Public Revenue*, pp. 117, 120, 132; Miller, *James II*, p. 41; *Pepys Diary* (22 Aug. 1667), vol. VIII, pp. 394–5 and (27 Aug. 1668), vol. IX, p. 290; Ritchie, 'The Duke of York's Commission', pp. 177–9; John Rylands Library, ENG. MS. 294, ff. 3, 9–10, 14.

CHAPTER FIVE

1. Dugdale, *Whitehall through the Centuries*, p. 76; D. Green, *Grinling Gibbons. His Work as a Carver and Statuary, 1648–1721* (Guildford and London, 1964), pp. 52–3, 56–7, 59–60, 65 and plates 60–7; M. Jones, *Michael Foot* (London, 1994), p. 399; A. Mourby, 'To Play a King', *The Guardian*, 18 March 1995; Palace Green Library, University of Durham, Elephant Case + 913.42; D. Thomson and R.K. Marshal et al., *Dynasty: the Royal House of Stewart* (Edinburgh, 1990), p. 84; J.H. Wilson, *A Rake and His Times. George Villiers, 2nd Duke of Buckingham* (London, 1954), p. 17.
2. Anon., *A Short View of the Life and Actions of the Most Illustrious James Duke of York, Together with His Character* (London, 1660), pp. 15, 24–5; Magalotti, *Lorenzo Magalotti at the Court of Charles II*, pp. 27, 37; Scott, *Travels of the King*, pp. 228–9, 232–3, 360; Sells (ed.), *Memoirs of James II*, pp. 57–8, 77–8, 178–85, 244–6, 248–9, 255, 289; Webb, *1676*, pp. 196–7.
3. Bodl. Lib., MS. Bodl., 891. f. 17; *CSPD* (1661–2), pp. 213, 445, 577; *Evelyn Diary* (1 Oct. 1661), p. 278 and (4 Dec. 1661), p. 281; Hay, *Winston Churchill and James II*, pp. 31–2; Lamb, *So Idle a Rogue*, pp. 33–4, 36–7, 45; *Life*, vol. II, p. 604; D. McKie, 'James Duke of York, F.R.S.', *Notes and Records of the Royal Society, London*, vol. XIII (1958), pp. 8–15; Magalotti, *Lorenzo Magalotti at the Court of Charles II*, pp. 35, 37; Oman, *Mary of Modena*, p. 45; *Pepys Diary* (29 Feb. 1664), vol. V, pp. 70–1, (7 Dec. 1664), vol. V, p. 339 and (5 Aug. 1667), vol. VIII, p. 374; C.R. Weld, *A History of the Royal Society, with Memoirs of the Presidents*, vol. I (London, 1848), pp. 306–7.

4. Anon., *The Duke on his Return* (London, 1682), p. 2; Anon., *A Faithful Compendium*, p. 2; Anon., *The Life and Actions of the Most Illustrious James Duke of York*, pp. 17–24; Anon., *Some Historical Memoires of the Life and Actions of His Royal Highness, the Renowned and Most Illustrious Prince James Duke of York and Albany* (London, 1683), pp. iii, 22, 51, 67–8, 75; Anon., *The Swans Welcome To His Royal Highness The Duke* (London, 1679), p. 4; P. Aubrey, *The Defeat of James Stuart's Armada, 1692* (Leicester, 1979), p. 121; *Life*, vol. I, pp. 9–18; Sells (ed.), *Memoirs of James II*, pp. 263–4.

5. Bodl. Lib., MS. Bodl., 891 f. 1; K. Gibson, 'The Cult of Charles II', *The Royal Stuart Society*, Occasional Paper No. XLVII (n.d.), pp. 7–8; O. Millar, *Sir Peter Lely, 1618–1680: Exhibition in London* (London, 1978), pp. 58–60; *Pepys Diary* (4 July 1663), vol. IV, p. 217, (18 April 1666), vol. VII, p. 102 and (18 July 1666), vol. VII, p. 209; A. Wace, *The Marlborough Tapestries* (London and New York (1968), pp. 24–5.

6. BL, Add. MS., 18,958 f. 25; BL, Add. MS., 38,863 f. 7; G. Grose, *Military Antiquities respecting a History of the English Army*, vol. II (London, 1801), pp. 140–1; John Rylands Library, Manchester, ENG. MS., 294 ff. 3, 6; Lawson, *History of the Uniforms of the British Army*, vol. I, p. 129.

7. Dugdale, *Whitehall through the Centuries*, pp. 84–5; Gibson, 'Cult of Charles II', pp. 5–7, 9; Green, *Grinling Gibbons*, plate 39; Lamb, *So Idle a Rogue*, pp. 160–1; H.W. Rendall, 'The Rise and Fall of a Martyrology: Sermons on Charles I', *Huntington Library Quarterly*, vol. X (1947), pp. 135–6, 144–54; Royal Academy, *The Age of Charles II* (London, 1960), p. 21.

8. C.H.C. Baker, *Lely and Kneller* (London, 1922), pp. 73, 80; R.B. Beckett, *Lely* (London, 1951), pp. 48–9; D. Foskett, *Samuel Cooper and his Contemporaries* (London, 1974), p. 47; Higham, *James II*, p. 96; Royal Academy, *Age of Charles II*, pp. 18, 135, 154; Trevor, *Shadow of a Crown*, pp. x, 148–9.

9. Clarendon, *Life of Clarendon*, vol. I, pp. 373–89; Clarendon, *Life of Clarendon*, vol. II, pp. 232–40; *Life*, vol. I, pp. 399–401; Oman, *Mary of Modena*, p. vii; Thomson and Marshal, *Dynasty: the Royal House of Stewart*, p. 83.

10. *Pepys Diary* (6 March 1665), vol. VI, p. 51. See also: Beckett, *Lely* p. 66; C.J. Ffoulkes, *Inventory and Survey of the Armouries of the Tower of London*, vol. I, Class II (London, 1915), no. 123, p. 138 and Plate XIX; Foskett, *Samuel Cooper*, p. 47; Lawson, *History of the Uniforms of the British Army*, vol. I, pp. 180–1; Millar, *Sir Peter Lely*, p. 54; National Army Museum, Chelsea, Cat. no. 8701–1; M. Rogers, *William Dobson, 1611–1646* (London, 1983), pp. 16–18, 36, 38, 40, 58–60; Royal Academy, *Age of Charles II*, p. 18; Tower of London, piece II.123.

11. *Pepys Diary* (2 Nov. 1663), vol. IV, p. 360 and (15 Feb. 1664), vol. V, p. 49.

12. Anon., *The Life of James II. Late King of England* (London, 1702), pp. 1, 13–14, 20, 82; Bowen, *William, Prince of Orange*, pp. 316–8; P. Burke, *The Fabrication of Louis XIV* (New Haven and London, 1992), pp. 16, 26, 62–3, 110–13; E. Hawkins, *Medallic Inscriptions of the History of Great Britain and Ireland*, vol. I (Portsmouth, 1885), pp. 504–5, 581, 586, 589.

It is worth noting that even James's use of medallic representations could be stark, brutal and even somewhat counter-productive. One piece, struck immediately after the failure of the Monmouth rebellion, depicted James resplendent as a Roman Emperor on its obverse. He is surrounded by his battlefleet, while Neptune rides across the waves in his chariot in order to salute, and to confer honours upon, him. However, on the reverse side, the figure of Justice – brandishing her sword and scales – stands over the decapitated bodies of Monmouth and Argyll. Their skulls are perched on two nearby altars, while a serpent is trampled underfoot and their armies are scattered in the background. Neptune again looks on approvingly, denoting James's office as Lord High Admiral, as other skulls of traitors are spiked on the city walls. The motto '*Ambitio Malesuada Ruit* [Malevolent Ambition leads to Ruin]' runs around the rim. This rather gory depiction of divine retribution – rather than signifying power and self-confidence, as was intended – actually only serves to exude a sense of the monarch's insecurity and terror in his dealings with his subjects.

Anon., *The Life of James II. Late King of England*, p. 119; Hawkins, *Medallic Inscriptions*, vol. II, pp. 615–16.

13. Anon., *The Life of James II. Late King of England*, p. 13; C. Blair, *European Armour* (London, 1958), pp. 135–6; C.M. Gavin, *Royal Yachts* (London, 1932), pp. 58, 231; Hawkins, *Medallic Inscriptions*, vol. I, p. 504; *Life*, vol. I, pp. 477–8; Letter from Lindsey Macfarlane, Curator of the Picture Library, National Maritime Museum, Greenwich, to the author, 31/10/1996; National Maritime Museum, Greenwich, BHC. 2797.

14. H. Bourne, *The History of Newcastle-Upon-Tyne* (Newcastle-Upon-Tyne, 1736), p. 126; Burke, *Fabrication of Louis XIV*, pp. 78, 80, 87–8; E. Mackenzie, *A Descriptive and Historical Account of the Town and County of Newcastle-Upon-Tyne*, vol. I (Newcastle-Upon-Tyne, 1827), pp. 48, 160; Palace Green Library, University of Durham, Elephant Case + 913.42; D. Piper (ed.), *Catalogue of Seventeenth-Century Portraits in the National Portrait Gallery, 1625–1714* (Cambridge, 1963), pp. 176–7; E. Waterhouse, *Painting in Britain, 1530 to 1790*, 2nd edn (Harmondsworth, Middlesex, 1962), pp. 65–6.

15. *Evelyn Diary* (6 August 1674), p. 380.

16. Charles II's change of imagery was so radical, and so thorough-going in its appropriation of forms which had to date been the preserve of James, that some later commentators managed to confuse the portraiture of the two royal brothers during this later period.

B. Ford, *The Cambridge Guide to the Arts in Britain*, vol. IV (Cambridge, 1989), pp. 238, 242; Gibson, 'Cult of Charles II', pp. 9–12; Haswell, *James II*, p. viii and plates pp. 260–1; R. Strong, *Henry, Prince of Wales and England's Lost Renaissance* (The German Democratic Republic, 1986), *passim* and plates 38–9.

17. *Life*, vol. I, p. 487.

18. Belloc, *James the Second*, p. 123.

19. J. Foxe, *Acts and Monuments of these latter and perilous days*, ed. S.R. Cattley, 8 vols (London, 1841); C. Hill, *The English Revolution, 1640* (London, 1940), pp. 16–17; R. Hutton, *The Stations of the Sun. A History of the Ritual Year in Britain* (Oxford and New York, 1996), pp. 393–6; A. Marvell, *An Account of the Growth of Popery and Arbitrary Government in England* (Amsterdam, 1677), p. 6; J. Miller, *Popery and Politics in England, 1660–1688* (Cambridge, 1973), pp. 72–5, 121.

20. A.C.F. Beales, *Education under Penalty. English Catholic Education from the Reformation to the Fall of James II* (London, 1963), p. 4; J. Bossy, *The English Catholic Community, 1570–1850* (London, 1975), pp. 186–94; *Evelyn Diary* (3 July 1662), p. 286, (4 April 1672), p. 365, (5 Nov. 1673), p. 377 and (5 March 1685), p. 469; J.P. Kenyon, *The Popish Plot* (London, 1972), pp. 11, 28–32, 34, 62–7, 75, 110–11, 235–40; J. Lane, *Titus Oates*

(London, 1949), pp. 41, 75; Miller, *Popery and Politics*, pp. 9–12; J. Spurr, *The Restoration Church of England, 1646–1689* (New Haven and London, 1991), pp. 64–5, 75–8, 100, 110–11, 266–7; A. Woodrow, *The Jesuits* (London, 1995), pp. 105–11.

21. Bampfield, *Apology*, pp. 23–5, 50, 69–70, 88, 90, 118, 129–32, 159–60; Beckett, *Lely*, p. 39; *Burnet*, vol. I, pp. 82, 93 (Book I, pp. 47, 50); Clarendon, *Life of Clarendon*, vol. I, p. 382; *Devotions*, p. 2; Millar, *Sir Peter Lely*, pp. 37–8; Miller, *James II*, pp. 54–5; Royal Academy, *Age of Charles II*, p. 4; Sells (ed.), *Memoirs of James II*, pp. 173–4, 222–3, 284, 286; Turner, *James II*, p. 96; Weygrand, *Turenne*, pp. 3–4, 9, 34, 166–8.

22. Bodl. Lib., Eng. Hist., c. 44 ff. 11–12; *Devotions*, pp. 1–5, 23–7; A. Hyde, *A Copy of a Paper Written by the Late Duchess of York* (London, 1670, rpt Dublin, *c.* 1685–8), pp. 1–2; *Life*, vol. I, pp. 440–2; Magalotti, *Lorenzo Magalotti at the Court of Charles II*, p. 36.

23. *Devotions*, pp. 1–2. See also: *Devotions*, xviii–xix, 3–26.

24. *Burnet*, vol. I, pp. 136, 304–6 (Book I, p. 74 and Book II, pp. 169–70); G. Burnet, *Supplement to the History of My Own Time*, ed. H.C. Foxcroft (Oxford, 1902), pp. 51–2; H. Foley (ed.), *The Records of the English Province of the Society of Jesus*, vol. V (8 vols, London, 1877–83), p. 5 n; *Life*, vol. I, p. 630.

25. BL, Add. MS., 12,093; C.L. Grose, 'The Dunkirk Money, 1662', *Journal of Modern History*, vol. V (1933), p. 2 n. 2, p. 8; Louis XIV, *Memoires*, pp. 94–5; *Pepys Diary* (20 Dec. 1668), vol. IX, p. 397; Voltaire, *Siecle de Louis XIV*, vol. I (Paris, 1751), pp. 186–7; Weygrand, *Turenne*, pp. 94–5, 126–7, 173.

26. Berenger, *Turenne*, pp. 458–70; Du Buisson, *Vicomte Turenne*, pp. 315–16; *Devotions*, pp. 3, 96–101, 107–8, 111–13, 162; Longueville, *Marshal Turenne*, pp. 283–91; Ramsay, *History of Henri de la Tour d'Auvergne*, vol. I, pp. 328–9, vol. II, pp. 265–6, 354–6; Weygrand, *Turenne*, pp. 166–71.

27. *Burnet*, vol. I, p. 307 (Book II, p. 170); Hyde, *Paper Written by the Late Duchess of York*, pp. 1–2; J.R. Henslowe, *Anne Hyde* (London, 1915), p. 249.

28. *Burnet*, vol. I, pp. 305–6 (Book II, p. 169); *Devotions*, pp. 23–5; R. Hooker, *Of the Lawes of Ecclesiastical Politie* (London, 1594).

29. Hyde, *Paper Written by the Late Duchess of York*, p. 1. See also: *Burnet*, vol. II, p. 24 (Book III, p. 357); *Devotions*, p. 26; P. Heylin, *Ecclesia Restaurata; or the History of the Reformation of the Church of England* (London, 1661); H. Trevor-Roper, *From Counter-Reformation to Glorious Revolution* (London, 1992), pp. 181, 187.

30. M. Bentick (ed.), *Lettres et Memoires de Marie, Reine d'Angleterre* (The Hague, 1880), pp. 7–8; *Burnet*, vol. II, pp. 22–3 (Book III, p. 356); *Devotions*, pp. 24–5.

31. *Devotions*, p. 23.

32. Bodl. Lib., Eng. Hist., c. 44. f. 12; *Devotions*, pp. 23, 25–6; Foley (ed.), *Records of the English Province*, vol. I, pp. 272–3 n. and vol. VII, Part I, pp. 463–4; P. Guilday, *The English Catholic Refugees on the Continent, 1558–1795* (London, 1914), p. 392; *Life*, vol. I, p. 440.

33. Woodrow, *The Jesuits*, p. 104.

34. M. Blundell (ed.), *Cavalier. Letters of William Blundell to his friends, 1620–1698* (London and New York, 1933); B.C. O'Carm, 'The Cardinal of Norfolk, Philip Howard OP', *Royal Stuart Society*, Occasional Paper No. XV (1980), pp. 1–2, 6–9, 14–16; W. Doran, 'Bishop Thomas Nicolson: First Vicar-Apostolic, 1695–1718', *Innes Review*, vol. II (1988), pp. 109–11; *Pepys Diary* (23 Jan. 1667), vol. VIII, p. 25.

35. *Evelyn Diary* (16 Sept. 1685), p. 485; Gwatkin, *Church and State in England*, p. 367.

36. E. Corp, 'James II and Toleration: The Years in Exile at Saint-Germain-en-Laye', *Royal Stuart Society*, Occasional Paper No. LI (1997), pp. 3–4; *Devotions*, pp. 2–3, 18–21; *Life*, vol. II, p. 609.

37. V. Buranelli, 'William Penn and James II', *Proceedings of the American Philosophical Society*, vol. CIV (1960), pp. 35–7, 48–51; Corp, 'James II and Toleration', p. 7; C. Evans, *Friends in the Seventeenth Century* (Philadelphia, USA, 1875), p. 346; R.D. Gwynn, 'James II in the Light of his Treatment of Huguenot Refugees in England, 1685', *English Historical Review*, vol. XCII (1977), p. 820–33; T. Hodgkin, 'Ruillick-Ny-Quakeryn. Notes on the History of Friends in the Isle of Man', *Friends Quarterly Examiner* (Oct. 1908), pp. 486–7; *Life*, vol. II, pp. 609, 611; J.E. Pomfret, 'Robert Barclay and James II: Barclay's "Vindication" 1689', *Bulletin of the Friends Historical Association*, vol. XLII (1953), pp. 33–40; Reresby, *Memoirs*, p. 81; Spurr, *Restoration Church of England*, p. 67; R.H. Whitworth, '1685 – James II, the Army and the Huguenots', *JSAHR*, vol. LXIII (1985), pp. 130–7.

38. Lord Acton (ed.), 'Letters from the King of England to the Dominican Father Armand Jean Abbe of La Trappe, 8th December 1690–20th September 1700', *Miscellanies of the Philobiblon Society*, vol. XIV (1872–6), pp. vii–xv; A. Clark (ed.), *The Life and Times of Anthony Wood*, vol. III (London, 1894), pp. 236–7; Childs, *Nobles, Gentlemen and the Profession of Arms*, p. 48; *Devotions*, pp. 3, 96–101, 108, 111–13, 162; Hyde, *Paper Written by the Late Duchess of York*, pp. 1–2; *Life*, vol. I, pp. 440–2, 487; *Life*, vol. II, pp. 585–7; Royal Academy, *Age of Charles II*, pp. 106–7.

39. Foley (ed.), *Records of the English Province*, pp. 272–3n; Guilday, *English Catholic Refugees*, p. 157; Henslowe, *Anne Hyde*, p. 249; *Life*, vol. I, p. 441.

40. *Evelyn Diary* (30 March 1673), p. 372; *Life*, vol. I, pp. 441–2.

41. Bodl. Lib., Eng. Hist., c 44 f. 11; Burnet, vol. I, pp. 93–4 (Book I, pp. 50–1); *Devotions*, pp. 88–9, 97–8, 106, 112, 162; J.P. Kenyon, *The Stuarts* (Glasgow, 1958), p. 144; *Life*, vol. II, pp. 585–6, 592–601; P. Verax, *A Letter to His Royal Highness the Duke of York touching his Revolt from, or Return to the Protestant Religion* (London, 1681), p. 3.

42. Bodl. Lib., Eng. Hist., c. 44 f. 11.

43. Anon., *An Elegy on the Lamented Death of the most Illustrious Princess, Anne Dutchess* [sic] *of York* (London, 1671); Burnet, vol. I, p. 568 (Book II, p. 309); Henslowe, *Anne Hyde*, p. 298; *Life*, vol. I, p. 452.

44. Anon., *Pereat Papa: or Reasons why a Presumptive Heir, or Popish Successor should not inherit the Crown* (London, *c.* 1681), pp. 1, 3; S. Johnson, *Julian the Apostate: Being a Short Account of his Life; The sense of the Primitive Christians about his Succession; and their behaviour towards him. Together with a Comparison of Popery and Paganism* (London, 1682), *passim.* See also: BL, Add. MS., 18,958 f. 3; BL, Add. MS., 38,863 f. 5; Burnet, vol. I, p. 565 (Book II, p. 308); *Devotions*, pp. xxi and p. 3; *Evelyn Diary* (30 March 1676), p. 389; *Life*, vol. I, pp. 482–3, 631.

45. Anon., *Pereat Papa*, pp. 1–3; Verax, *Letter to His Royal Highness*, pp. 4, 6.

46. Anon., *Remarkable Enterprises*, pp. 1–6, 7–12, respectively for and against James. The quotation is taken from p. 7.

47. Verax, *Letter to His Royal Highness*, pp. 1- 2. See also: Bodl. Lib., MS. Jones, 24.

48. Burnet, vol. II, p. 25 (Book III, pp. 357–8); Historical Manuscripts Commission, *The Manuscripts of the Earl of Dartmouth*, 11th Report, Appendix, Part V, vol. I (London, 1887), p. 36; G. D'Oyly, *Life of Archbishop Sancroft* (London, 1821), p. 176.

49. Anon., *A Congratulatory Poem on His Royal Highnesses Restauration* [sic] *to the Dignity of Lord High Admiral of England* (London, 1684); Anon., *A New Ballad of Jocky's Journey into England, in the Year, 1681* (London, 1681); Anon., *Old Jemmy: An Excellent New Ballad* (London, 1681); Anon., *On the Arrival of His Royal Highness, the Duke into England. A Congratulatory Poem* (London, 1680); Anon., *A Panegyrick to His Royal Highness. Upon His Majesties late Declaration* (London, 1680); Anon., *A Poem on the Happy Return of His Royal Highness from Scotland* (London, 1680). See also: Verax, *Letter to His Royal Highness*, pp. 1–2.

50. Anon., *A Faithful Compendium*, pp. 2–3.

51. *CSPD* (1682), pp. 79, 334, 349, 540; Jones, *Revolution of 1688*, pp. 88–9; Magalotti, *Lorenzo Magalotti at the Court of Charles II*, p. 35; Raikes, *History of the Honourable Artillery Company*, vol. I, p. 201; Verax, *Letter to His Royal Highness*, p. 5.

CHAPTER SIX

1. R. Hutton, *Charles II. King of England, Scotland, and Ireland* (Oxford, 1989), p. 165; *Pepys Diary* (23 April 1661), vol. II, pp. 83–7.

2. A. Browning, *Thomas Osborne, Earl of Danby and Leeds, 1632–1712*, vol. III (3 vols, Glasgow, 1951), pp. 36–8; *CSPD* (1660–1), pp. 142, 224, 314; *CSPD* (1663–4), pp. 458, 557; *CSPD* (March 1675–Feb. 1676), p. 542; Historical Manuscripts Commission, *The Manuscripts of the Earl of Dartmouth*, 11th Report, Appendix, Part V, vol. I (London, 1887), pp. 26–7; *Pepys Diary* (21 Oct. 1666), vol. VII, p. 337, (29 May 1667), vol. VIII, p. 241 and (3 June 1667), vol. VIII, pp. 247–8; Reresby, *Memoirs*, p. 81; J. Spurr, *The Restoration Church of England, 1646–1689* (New Haven and London, 1991), p. 74.

3. *Pepys Diary* (21 Oct. 1666), vol. VII, p. 337 and (Companion) vol. X, p. 242.

4. Clarendon, *Life of Clarendon*, vol. I, p. 382; R. Ollard, *Clarendon and his Friends* (New York, 1988), pp. 286–7; *Pepys Diary* (14 May 1667), vol. VIII, p. 214.

5. *Burnet*, vol. I, p. 455 (Book II, p. 248–9); *Pepys Diary* (30 Oct. 1668), vol. IX, pp. 341–2; C. Roberts, 'The Impeachment of the Earl of Clarendon', *The Cambridge Historical Journal*, vol. XIII (1957), pp. 1–2, 4–5.

6. Anon., *The Proceedings in the House of Commons, Touching the Impeachment of Edward Late Earl of Clarendon, Lord High Chancellor of England* (London, 1700), p. iii; Boxer, 'Three Sights to be Seen', pp. 77–9; *Burnet*, vol. I, pp. 455–7 (Book II, p. 249); Clarendon, *Life of Clarendon*, vol. III, p. 265; Grose, 'The Dunkirk Money, 1662', pp. 8, 15–16; V. Vale, 'Clarendon, Coventry, and the Sale of Naval Offices, 1660–8', *The Cambridge Historical Journal*, vol. XII (1956), pp. 108–10, 112–13, 123–5.

7. Anon., *Proceedings . . . Touching the Impeachment . . . of Clarendon*, p. 45; *Burnet*, vol. I, pp. 457–8 (Book II, p. 250); Clarendon, *Life of Clarendon*, vol. III, pp. 265–7; *Life*, vol. I, p. 431; Roberts, 'Impeachment of the Earl of Clarendon', pp. 4–5.

8. *Life*, vol. I, pp. 432–3.

9. Anon., *Proceedings . . . Touching the Impeachment . . . of Clarendon*, pp. 101–14; Clarendon, *Life of Clarendon*, vol. III, pp. 282–5, 292–4; *Life*, vol. I, pp. 427–9; *Pepys Diary* (2 Sept. 1667), vol. VIII, p. 414 and (8 Sept. 1667), vol. VIII, p. 424.

10. Anon., *Proceedings . . . Touching the Impeachment . . . of Clarendon*, pp. 13–17, 49, 83, 135; *Burnet*, vol. I, pp. 467–71 (Book II, pp. 254–7); Clarendon, *Life of Clarendon*, vol. III, pp.

277–8, 292–4, 296–7, 300–1, 304–7, 308–9, 318–21, 332–3; *Evelyn Diary* (9 Dec. 1667), p. 335; *Life*, vol. I, pp. 431–2; Roberts, 'Impeachment of Clarendon', pp. 6–15.

11. Hutton, *Charles II*, p. 253; *Pepys Diary* (16 Nov. 1667), vol. VIII, pp. 532–4; M. Girouard, *Life in the English Country House. A Social and Architectural History*, (New Haven and London, 1978), p. 127.

12. P.H. Hardacre, 'Clarendon and the University of Oxford, 1660–1667', *British Journal of Educational Studies*, vol. IX (1960–1), pp. 129–31; *Life*, vol. I, p. 431; *Pepys Diary* (29 Aug. 1667), vol. VIII, p. 406, (2 Sept. 1667), vol. VIII, p. 416, (23 Sept. 1667), vol. VIII, p. 447, (23 Oct. 1668), vol. IX, p. 336 and (30 Oct. 1668), vol. IX, p. 342; Roberts, 'Impeachment of the Earl of Clarendon', pp. 5–6; Spurr, *Restoration Church of England*, pp. 41–2.

13. R. Clifton, *The Last Popular Rebellion. The Western Rising of 1685* (London and New York, 1984), pp. 84–8; *Life*, vol. I, pp. 433–4; *Pepys Diary* (24 Dec. 1662), vol. III, p. 290, (20 Jan. 1664), vol. V, p. 21, (30 Dec. 1667), vol. VIII, p. 596 and (23 Nov. 1668), vol. IX, p. 373; Roberts, 'Impeachment of the Earl of Clarendon', p. 17.

14. Anon., *Proceedings . . . Touching the Impeachment . . . of Clarendon*, p. 114; *Life*, vol. I, p. 436; H.M. Margoliouth (ed.), *The Poems and Letters of Andrew Marvell*, vol. II (Oxford, 1927), pp. 301–2; *Pepys Diary* (29 Oct. 1668), vol. IX, pp. 340–1, (13 Nov. 1668), vol. IX, p. 361, (23 Nov. 1668), vol. IX, p. 373, (6 March 1669), vol. IX, p. 472 and (10 May 1669), vol. IX, pp. 550–1.

15. Boxer, 'Three Sights to be Seen', pp. 77–8; *Burnet*, vol. I, pp. 481–2 (Book II, pp. 261–2); *Evelyn Diary* (22 March 1670), pp. 344–5; J. Miller, *Charles II* (London, 1991), p. 171; *Pepys Diary* (14 June 1667), vol. VIII, p. 269; J.H. Wilson, *A Rake and His Times. George Villiers, 2nd Duke of Buckingham* (London, 1954), pp. 53–5.

16. *Burnet*, vol. I, pp. 464–5 (Book II, p. 253); *Life*, vol. I, pp. 437–9; D. Lindley, *The Trials of Frances Howard. Fact and Fiction at the Court of King James* (London and New York, 1993), pp. 57, 67, 81, 94–8, 116–17, 135, 139, 166; Miller, *Charles II*, p. 171; B.J. Shapiro, *John Wilkins, 1614–1672* (Berkeley and Los Angeles, 1969), pp. 219, 288; A. Somerset, *Unnatural Murder. Poison at the Court of James I* (London, 1997), pp. 98–100; Surtees Society, *The Correspondence of John Cosin, D.D., Lord Bishop of Durham*, vol. II (Durham, London and Edinburgh, 1869), pp. 232–3, p. 233, n.

17. *Pepys Diary* (6 April 1668), vol. IX, pp. 153–4 and (16 January 1669), p. 417; Miller, *James II*, p. 56.

18. *CSPI* (1669–70), pp. 88–9; Feiling, *History of the Tory Party*, p. 137; K.H.D. Haley, *The First Earl of Shaftesbury*, (Oxford, 1968), pp. 278–80; *Life*, vol. I, pp. 437–9; Macpherson, *Original Papers*, vol. I, p. 53; Miller, *Charles II*, p. 207; Reresby, *Memoirs*, p. 82; Rowse, *Early Churchills*, p. 98; Schoenfeld, *Restored House of Lords*, p. 134.

19. *CSPI* (Jan.–Dec. 1671), p. 71; Hamilton, *Memoirs of Count Grammont*, p. 138; *Pepys Diary* (19 Aug. 1662), vol. III, pp. 170–1, (22 July 1667), vol. VIII, p. 348 and n. 1, (17 Jan. 1668), vol. IX, pp. 26–7 and (19 May 1669), vol. IX, pp. 557–8; E.M. Thompson (ed.), *The Correspondence of the Family of Hatton, 1601–1704*, vol. I (London, 1878), p. 66.

20. R. Bagwell, *Ireland under the Stuarts*, vol. III (London, 1916), pp. 25–6; *CSPI* (1660–2), p. xxxix; *CSPI* (1666–9), pp. 243–4, 427–8, 574; Churchill, *Marlborough*, vol. I, pp. 43–4; Rowse, *Early Churchills*, pp. 60–2, 86–7, 91.

21. J. Bramston, *The Autobiography of Sir John Bramston, K.B.* (London, 1845), pp. 128–9; Reresby, *Memoirs*, p. 180.

22. R.R. Johnson, 'The Imperial Webb: The Thesis of Garrison Government in Early America Considered', *W&MQ*, 3rd series, vol. XLIII (1986), pp. 415–25, 429–30; S.S. Webb, 'Brave Men and Servants to his Royal Highness. The Household of James Stuart in the Evolution of English Imperialism', *Perspectives in American History*, vol. II (1974), pp. 56–61; S.S. Webb, *The Governor-General. The English Army and the Definition of the Empire, 1569–1681* (Chapel Hill, North Carolina, 1979), pp. 31–3, 39, 42–3, 96, 213, 218–19, 478, 497–8.

23. Magalotti, *Lorenzo Magalotti at the Court of Charles II*, p. 36.

24. Thompson (ed.), *Hatton Correspondence*, vol. I, p. 233.

25. *Life*, vol. II, p. 607.

26. *Burnet*, vol. II, p. 149 (Book III, p. 425); J.P. Kenyon, *The Popish Plot* (London, 1972), pp. 51–2; J. Lane, *Titus Oates* (London, 1949), pp. 76–7.

27. Anon. (S.N.D.), *Sir William Howard, Viscount Stafford, 1612–1680* (London, 1929), pp. 92–3; *Burnet*, vol. II, pp. 147–9 (Book III, pp. 424–5); *CSPD* (1678), pp. 422, 425, 433, 453; *Evelyn Diary* (1 Oct. 1678), p. 405; Kenyon, *Popish Plot*, pp. 45–9; Lane, *Titus Oates*, pp. 22–4, 29–31, 48, 50, 56, 62; *Life*, vol. I, p. 514.

28. Anon., *Sir William Howard*, pp. 138–49, 208–19; Barbour, *Henry Bennet, Earl of Arlington*, pp. 154–62; *CSPD* (1678), pp. 426, 431–3, 451, 453, 519; C.H. Hartmann, *Clifford of the Cabal* (London, 1937), pp. 136–45; Kenyon, *Popish Plot*, p. 44; J. Miller, *Popery and Politics in England, 1660–1688* (Cambridge, 1973), pp. 108–11, 114–16, 119–20, 123; Verax, *Letter to His Royal Highness*, p. 5.

29. Bramston, *Autobiography*, p. 180; *CSPD* (1678), pp. 427, 448, 459, 462, 482; Historical Manuscripts Commission, *The Manuscripts of the House of Lords, 1678–1688*, 11th Report, Appendix, Part II (London, 1887), pp. 4, 6.

30. HMC, *House of Lords*, p. 44; Kenyon, *Popish Plot*, pp. 34–8; Mullett, *James II*, p. 6; Oman, *Mary of Modena*, pp. 41, 50.

31. *CSPD* (1678), pp. 466, 472, 506, 517, 522, 545, 551–2, 589, 622; *Evelyn Diary* (21 Oct. 1678), p. 405; Kenyon, *Popish Plot*, pp. 264–70; S. Knight, *The Killing of Justice Godfrey* (London and New York, 1984), pp. 82–7, 94–104; *Life*, vol. I, p. 533; A. Marshall, *The Strange Death of Edmund Godfrey. Plots and Politics in Restoration London* (Stroud, Gloucestershire, 1999), pp. 180–5; Oman, *Mary of Modena*, p. 59.

32. *CSPD* (1682), pp. 4–5, 504; Knight, *Killing of Justice Godfrey*, p. 109; Magalotti, *Lorenzo Magalotti at the Court of Charles II*, p. 35; Marshall, *Strange Death of Edmund Godfrey*, pp. 115–16, 119–20; Miller, *James II*, p. 100; Mullett, *James II*, p. 20; N. Thompson, *A True and Perfect Narrative of the Late . . . Bloody Murther of Sir E[dmund] G [odfrey]* (London, 1678); N. Thompson, *Sir Edmundbury Godfrey's Ghost* (London, 1682).

33. R.M. Bliss, *Revolution and Empire. English Politics and the American Colonies in the Seventeenth Century* (Manchester and New York, 1990), p. 200.

34. J.R. Jones, *The First Whigs. The Politics of the Exclusion Crisis, 1678–1683* (London, 1961), pp. 10–19; *Life*, vol. I, pp. 488–9.

35. M.A. Elder, *The Highland Host of 1678* (Glasgow, 1914), pp. 16–50; W.C. Mackenzie, *The Life and Times of John Maitland, Duke of Lauderdale, 1616–1682* (London and New York, 1923), pp. 404–5, 409–11.

36. *CSPD* (1679–80), p. 296; P. Fraser, *The Intelligence of the Secretaries of State and their Monopoly of Licensed News, 1660–1688* (Cambridge, 1956), pp. 114–15, 119–22, 127, 129–31; A. Marvell, *An Account of the Growth of Popery and Arbitary Government in England*

(Amsterdam, 1677); A. Sidney, *A Just and Modest Vindication of the Proceedings of the Two Last Parliaments* (London?, 1681).

37. D.C. Douglas (ed.), *English Historical Documents*, vol. VIII, 1660–1714 (London, 1966), pp. 391–4; HMC, *House of Lords*, p. 61.

38. C.A. Edie, 'Succession and Monarchy: The Controversy of 1679–1681', *American Historical Review*, vol. 70 (1965), pp. 353–4; Her Majesty's Stationary Office, *The Manuscripts of the Right Honourable F.J. Savile Foljambe of Osberton* (London, 1897), p. 330.

39. *Burnet*, vol. II, pp. 175–8 (Book III, pp. 440–1); A.M. Evans, 'The Imprisonment of Lord Danby in the Tower, 1679–1684', *TRHS*, 4th series, vol. XII (1929), pp. 105–7; J.P. Kenyon, 'The Exclusion Crisis', Part One, *History Today*, vol. 14 (1964), p. 256.

40. Bliss, *Revolution and Empire*, pp. 177–8; Browning, *Thomas Osborne, Earl of Danby*, vol. I, pp. 218–19, 270; *Burnet*, vol. II, pp. 179–80 (Book III, p. 442); Feiling, *History of the Tory Party, 1640–1714*, pp. 156–7, 162; G. Holmes, *The Making of a Great Power* (London and New York, 1993), pp. 115–18; PRO S.P.8. 3., ff. 33, 35, 47, 53; *Life*, vol. I, p. 498.

41. W.D. Christie, *A Life of Anthony Ashley Cooper, First Earl of Shaftesbury*, vol. II (London, 1871), p. 314; Verax, *Letter to His Royal Highness*, pp. 1–2.

42. *CSPD* (1682), p. 603; Edie, 'Succession and Monarchy', pp. 350, 354, 362, 367, 369–70; HMC, *House of Lords*, pp. 195–7, 220–1.

43. B. Behrens, 'The Whig Theory of the Constitution in the Reign of Charles II', *Cambridge Historical Journal*, vol. VII (1941), pp. 45–71; Evans, 'Imprisonment of Lord Danby', pp. 107–9; Haley, *Shaftesbury*, p. 359; A. Sidney, *A Just and Modest Vindication of the Proceedings of the Two Last Parliaments* (London?, *c.* 1681), pp. 1–3, 28–31; T.P. Slaughter, '"Abdicate" and "Contract" in the Glorious Revolution', *The Historical Journal*, vol. XXIV (1981), pp. 329–36.

44. HMC, *Dartmouth*, p. 36; Josselin, *Diary* (7–8 March and 18 April 1679), p. 620; *Life*, vol. I, pp. 537–40, 547.

45. HMC, *Dartmouth*, pp. 31, 36; HMC, *House of Lords*, pp. 209–10; *Life*, vol. I, p. 542.

46. Higham, *King James II*, pp. 185–6; Oman, *Mary of Modena*, p. 60.

47. HMC, *Dartmouth*, pp. 30–7; HMC, *House of Lords*, pp. 199, 268.

48. Anon., *The Debates in the House of Commons Assembled at Oxford, March the 21st 1680 [/81]* (London, 1681), pp. 27–8; Anon., *His Majesties Declaration To all His Loving Subjects, Touching the Cause and Reasons that moved Him to Dissolve the two last Parliaments* (Dublin, 1681), pp. 2, 5–8; Anon., *His Majesties Most Gracious Speech To both Houses of Parliament, At the Opening of the Parliament at Oxford, Monday the 21st of March 1680/81* (London, 1681), pp. 1–4; Anon., *Votes of the House of Commons at Oxford* (London, 1681), p. 12; *CSPD* (1679–80), pp. 176, 260, 597; Sidney, *Just and Modest Vindication*, p. 31; E.R. Turner, 'The Privy Council of 1679', *English Historical Review*, vol. XXX (1915), pp. 251–70.

49. *CSPD* (1682), pp. 4, 15, 18, 201–3, 245–6, 492–3, 504–7, 575–7; Jones, *First Whigs*, pp. 180–1, 211, 213–14, 216; *Life*, vol. I, p. 547; J.H. Plumb, 'The First Earl of Shaftesbury', *History Today*, vol. 3 (1953), pp. 268–9; R.G. Schafer, 'The Making of a Tory', *Huntington Library Quarterly*, vol. XXIII (1960), pp. 123, 125–7, 131, 133.

50. Anon., *Lachrymae Anglicanae, or England's Tears for the Dissolution of the Parliament, At Oxford, Monday 28. 1681* (London?, 1681), pp. 1–2; HMC, *Dartmouth*, p. 45; J. Walker, 'The Censorship of the Press in the Reign of Charles II', *History*, vol. XXXV (1950), pp. 231, 235–8.

51. R. Beddard, 'The Commission for Ecclesiastical Promotions, 1681–84: An Instrument of Tory Reaction', *The Historical Journal*, vol. X (1967), pp. 14–18, 25–6, 28–32, 40; Bliss, *Revolution and Empire*, p. 234; H.C. Foxcroft, *The Life and Letters of Sir George Savile, Bart., First Marquis of Halifax*, vol. I (2 vols, London, New York and Bombay, 1898), pp. 300–1, 326, 357–8; Haley, *Shaftesbury*, pp. 688, 690, 698–700; Hutton, *Charles II*, pp. 394–403, 454, 457; Jones, *First Whigs*, pp. 200–6; Miller, *Charles II*, pp. 335–6, 341, 347, 349–51, 355, 368–72.

52. Anon., *Some Historical Memoires of the Life and Actions of His Royal Highness, The Renowned and Most Illustrious Prince James Duke of York and Albany* (London, 1683), p. 76; Josselin, *Diary* (12 March 1682), p. 637.

53. M. Bowen, *William Prince of Orange*, (London and New York, 1928), pp. 285–91; Gregg, *Queen Anne*, pp. 6–7, 11, 32–3; Haley, *Shaftesbury*, pp. 332–3, 627–8; Jones, *First Whigs*, pp. 136–7, 207–10; L.C. O'Malley, 'The Whig Prince: Prince Rupert and the Court vs. Country factions during the Reign of Charles II', *Albion*, vol. VIII (1976), pp. 336–46; J. Miller, *William and Mary* (London, 1974), pp. 49, 52–3, 61, 64–5; D. Ogg, *William III* (London, 1956), pp. 18, 21–2.

54. Cheshire Record Office, Chester, DDX7, Acc. 23.

55. Anon., *A Brief Account of the Designs which the Papists have had against the Earl of Shaftesbury, occasioned by his commitment, July 2 1681* (London, 1681), pp. 1–4; Anon., *A Particular Account of the Proceedings at the Old Bayly . . . with Relation to the Earl of Shaftesbury* (London, 1681), p. 1; Anon., *The Proceedings at the Sessions-House in the Old Baily, London . . . upon the Bill of Indictment for High-Treason Against Anthony Earl of Shaftesbury* (Dublin, 1681), *passim*; Anon., *The Earl of Shaftsbury's Grand-Jury Vindicated* (London, 1682), pp. 1–2; M. Ashley, *John Wildman, Plotter and Postmaster* (London, 1947), pp. 238–41; *CSPD* (1682), p. 82; Marshall, *Intelligence and Espionage in the Reign of Charles II*, pp. 74–7.

56. Anon., *The Abdicated Prince* (London, 1690), pp. 49–53; Ashley, *John Wildman*, pp. 244–8; *CSPD* (1682), pp. 455, 463, 581; A.C. Houston, *Algernon Sidney and the Republican Heritage in England and America* (Princeton, New Jersey, 1991), pp. 58–66; J. Scott, *Algernon Sidney and the Restoration Crisis, 1677–1683* (Cambridge, 1991), pp. 267, 346–7; Walker, 'Censorship of the Press', pp. 227, 229.

57. HMC, *Dartmouth*, p. 36.

58. J.P. Watson, *Captain-General and Rebel Chief, The Life of James, Duke of Monmouth* (London, Boston and Sydney, 1979), p. 173.

59. E. D'Oyley, *James, Duke of Monmouth* (London,1938, rpt Bath, 1967), pp. 244–7; Watson, *Captain-General*, pp. 173–8.

60. I. Morley, *A Thousand Lives. An Account of the English Revolutionary Movement of 1660–1685* (London, 1954), pp. 154–5; D'Oyly, *Monmouth*, pp. 247–9; Watson, *Captain-General*, pp. 176–8.

61. Clifton, *Last Popular Rebellion*, pp. 227–8; *Life*, vol. I, p. 746; M. Strigley, 'The Great Frost Fair of 1683–4', *History Today*, vol. 10 (1960), pp. 848–55.

CHAPTER SEVEN

1. Ollard, *Cromwell's Earl*, pp. 84–5; *Pepys Diary* (21–22 May 1660), vol. I, p. 152, (23 May 1660), vol. I, p. 154 and (14 Dec. 1663), vol. IV, p. 418; Perrin, 'Lord High Admiral

Notes

and the Board of Admiralty', p. 137; J.R. Tanner, 'The Administration of the Navy from the Restoration to the Revolution', Part One, *English History Review*, vol. XII (1897), p. 21.

2. *CSPD* (1660–1), p. 16; J.B. Hattendorf, R.J.B. Knight et.al. (eds), *British Naval Documents, 1204–1960* (Aldershot and Vermont, USA, 1993), pp. 237–8; *Life*, vol. I, p. 399. *Naval Minutes*, p. 32; *Pepys Diary* (Companion), vol. X, pp. 21–2, 27–8, 53–4, 291–8, 312–13, 325, 398–9; Perrin, 'Lord High Admiral and the Board of Admiralty', pp. 136–7; Tanner, 'Administration of the Navy', pp. 21–5; J.R. Tanner, *Samuel Pepys and the Royal Navy* (Cambridge, 1920), pp. 18–20, 22–3; A.W. Tedder, *The Navy of the Restoration* (London, 1919), pp. 42–4; L.A. Wilcox, *Mr. Pepys' Navy* (London, 1966), p. 19.

3. *CSPC* (1661–8), nos 245, 910; *CSPD* (1661–2), pp. 43, 53, 255, 279, 364, 498; G. de Ford, *Poems on Affairs of State, Augustan Satirical Verse, 1660–1714*, vol. I 1660–78 (New Haven and London, 1963), pp. 23–4; Hattendorf (ed.), *British Naval Documents*, pp. 242–4; *Life*, vol. I, p. 399; Perrin, 'Lord High Admiral and the Board of Admiralty', pp. 137–8; Tanner, 'Administration of the Navy', p. 24; Tanner, *Samuel Pepys and the Royal Navy*, pp. 18, 25, 33.

4. *Naval Minutes*, p. 34. See also: *Burnet*, vol. I, pp. 306–7 (Book II, p. 170); Hattendorf (ed.), *British Naval Documents*, pp. 283, 300; *Naval Minutes*, p. 62.

5. E. Chappell (ed.), *The Tangier Papers of Samuel Pepys* (London, 1935), pp. 106, 122, 206–7, 212–13, 229; J.D. Davies, *Gentlemen and Tarpaulins: The Officers and Men of the Restoration Navy* (Oxford, 1991), pp. 32, 161; J.R. Jones, *The Anglo-Dutch Wars of the Seventeenth Century* (London and New York, 1996), pp. 53–6; M.A. Lewis, *England's Sea-Officers* (London, 1939), p. 195; *Naval Minutes*, pp. 53–4, 64, 83, 119, 194, 230, 267, 315, 426; *Pepys Diary* (4 June 1661), vol. II, p. 114, (10 Jan. 1666), vol. VII, pp. 10–11, (16 Dec. 1666), vol. VII, pp. 409–10, (29 June 1667), vol. VIII, p. 304, (8 Dec. 1667), vol. VII, p. 571 and (28 Jan. 1668), vol. IX, pp. 39–40.

6. R. Latham (ed.), *Samuel Pepys and the Second Dutch War. Pepy's White Book and Brooke House Papers* (Aldershot and Vermont, USA, 1995), p. 232.

7. Latham (ed.), *Samuel Pepys and the Second Dutch War*, p. 239; *Pepys Diary* (13 June 1666), vol. VII, p. 163, (27 July 1666), vol. VII, pp. 222–3, (4 April 1667), vol. VIII, p. 147 and (Companion) vol. X, pp. 429–30.

8. Quoted in P. Young (ed.), *Leaders of the Civil Wars* (Kineton, Warwickshire, 1977), p. 1. See also: Davies, *Gentlemen and Tarpaulins*, pp. 146–58, 162–63; B. Fergusson, *Rupert of the Rhine* (London, 1952), p. 133; Jones, *Anglo-Dutch Wars*, pp. 54–5, 157; *Life*, vol. I, p. 445; Ollard, *Man of War*, pp. 136–7, 141–2, 163; Ollard, *Cromwell's Earl*, pp. 91–2; *Pepys Diary* (5 July 1665), vol. VI, p. 148, (25 Oct. 1665), vol. VI, p. 276, (6 Nov. 1665), vol. VI, p. 291, (8 Oct. 1666), vol. VII, pp. 314–15, (15 Oct. 1666), vol. VII, pp. 323–5, (20 Oct. 1666), vol. VII, p. 333, (24 Oct. 1666), vol. VII, p. 340, (28 Jan. 1668), vol. IX, pp. 39–40 and (18 Feb. 1668), vol. IX, p. 76; E. Scott, *Rupert Prince Palatine* (London, 1899), pp. 303, 314, 317–18, 325–7; R.J.A. Shelley, 'The Division of the English Fleet in 1666', *Marriners Mirror*, vol. XXVII (1939), pp. 179–82.

9. R.C. Anderson, *The Journal of Edward Mountagu, First Earl of Sandwich* (London, 1929), pp. lx and lxix; *Evelyn Diary* (31 May 1672), pp. 367–8; Ford (ed.), *Poems on Affairs of State*, p. xl; Ollard, *Cromwell's Earl*, pp. 91–4, 113–14, 139–42, 145–51; *Pepys Diary* (6 June 1660), vol. I, p. 170, (30 July 1662), vol. III, p. 149, (10 Sept. 1665), vol. VI, p.

219, (23 Sept. 1665), vol. VI, pp. 238–9, (12 Oct. 1665), vol. VI, pp. 263–4, (3 Nov. 1665), vol. VI, p. 287, (6 Nov. 1665), vol. VI, p. 291, (17 Nov. 1665), vol. VI, p. 302, (6–7 Dec. 1665), vol. VI, pp. 320–3, (10 Jan. 1666), vol. VII, p. 10 and (23 Feb. 1668), vol. IX, p. 87.

10. *CSPD* (March–Oct. 1673), pp. 374, 377; Davies, *Gentlemen and Tarpaulins*, p. 5; Marquis of Landsdowne (ed.), *The Petty-Southwell Correspondence, 1676–1687* (London, 1928), pp. 37–9, 51, 225; *Life*, vol. I, pp. 445, 487; *Naval Minutes*, p. 41; Perrin, 'Lord High Admiral and the Board of Admiralty', p. 138; J.R. Tanner, 'The Administration of the Navy from the Restoration to the Revolution', Part Two, *English History Review*, vol. XII (1897), pp. 679–81; Tanner, *Samuel Pepys and the Royal Navy*, p. 30.

11. R.C. Anderson, (ed.), *Journals and Narratives of the Third Dutch War* (London, 1946), pp. 371–86; *Burnet*, vol. II, p. 14 (Book III, p. 352); J. Campbell, 'The Naval History of Great Britain', vol. II (London, 1818), p. 306; Davis, *Gentlemen and Tarpaulins*, pp. 166, 169; Jones, *Anglo-Dutch Wars*, pp. 204–5; L.G.C. Laughton, 'The Vice Admiral of England', *Marriners Mirror*, vol. XVI (1928), pp. 176–8; Tanner, 'Administration of the Navy', Part Two, p. 680.

12. Davis, *Gentlemen and Tarpaulins*, p. 5; Hattendorf (ed.), *British Naval Documents*, p. 246; J.R. Tanner (ed.), *A Descriptive Catalogue of the Naval Manuscripts in the Pepysian Library*, vol. I (London, 1903), p. 39.

13. Bryant, *Samuel Pepys. The Years of Peril*, pp. 262–7; Davies, *Gentlemen and Tarpaulins*, pp. 5–8; A.M. Evans, 'The Imprisonment of Lord Danby in the Tower', *TRHS*, 4th series, vol. XII (1929), pp. 107–9; Hattendorf (ed.), *British Naval Documents*, p. 246; Hornstein, *Restoration Navy and English Foreign Trade*, pp. 11–32; Landsdowne, *Petty-Southwell Correspondence*, p. 66; *Life*, vol. I, p. 579; *Naval Minutes*, pp. 34, 181, 338.

14. Anon., *A Congratulatory Poem on his Royal Highnesses Restauration to the Dignity of Lord High Admiral of England* (London, 1684), p. 1; *Burnet*, vol. II, p. 427 (Book III, p. 582); *Evelyn Diary* (12 May 1684), p. 457; S. Pepys, *Memoires Relating to the State of the Royal Navy of England, For Ten Years Determin'd December 1688* (London, 1690), p. 12; *RPCS* (1678–80), pp. 442–4; *RPCS* (1681–2), pp. 652, 664–5; Reresby, *Memoirs*, p. 329; Tanner, *Samuel Pepys and the Royal Navy*, p. 34.

15. Hattendorf (ed.), *British Naval Documents*, p. 245; Hornstein, *Restoration Navy and English Foreign Trade*, p. 158; R. Ollard, *Pepys. A Biography* (London, 1974), pp. 278–91; Pepys, *Memoires Relating to the State of the Royal Navy*, p. 12; Tanner, *Samuel Pepys and the Royal Navy*, p. 34; Vale, 'Clarendon, Coventry, and the Sale of Naval Offices', p. 123.

16. *Naval Minutes*, pp. 62, 233.

17. *Evelyn Diary* (1 Oct. 1661), p. 278; *Pepys Diary* (3 May 1660), p. 125; Wilcox, *Mr. Pepys' Navy*, p. 153.

18. Macaulay, *History of England*, vol. I, p. 440; *Naval Minutes*, p. 338; Ollard, *Cromwell's Earl*, p. 145.

19. Quoted from Pepys, *Memoires Relating to the State of the Royal Navy*, pp. 22–3, 127. See also: Laughton, 'Vice Admiral of England', pp. 177–8; *Naval Minutes*, p. 338; *Pepys Diary* (15 Sept. 1662), vol. III, p. 198, (3 Nov. 1662), vol. III, p. 247, (17 Nov. 1662), vol. III, p. 260, (1 June 1663), vol. IV, p. 167, (30 June 1663), vol. IV, p. 204, (3 July 1663), vol. IV, p. 213, (2 Nov. 1663), vol. IV, p. 360, (7 March 1664), vol. V, p. 77, (25 July 1664), vol. V, p. 220, (21 April 1666), vol. VII, p. 105, (30 May 1666), vol. VII, pp. 136–7, (31 July 1666), vol. VII, p. 228, (28 Nov. 1666), vol. VII, p. 388, (27 Aug. 1667),

vol. VIII, p. 403, (28 Nov. 1667), vol. VIII, p. 551 and (7 Jan. 1668), vol. IX, p. 14; Turner, *James II*, p. 73.

20. Latham (ed.), *Samuel Pepys and the Second Dutch War*, pp. 45, 220, 288, 291–2, 401; *Naval Minutes*, pp. 33–4, 225, 394. See also: Anon., *English Affairs*, pp. 3–4; *CSPD* (1663–4), p. 570; Ford (ed.), *Poems on Affairs of State*, p. 52; Landsdowne, *Petty-Southwell Correspondence*, pp. xxi–xxii, 86–87; *Pepys Diary* (24 June 1663), vol. IV, p. 195; J.R. Tanner (ed.), *A Descriptive Catalogue of the Naval Manuscripts in the Pepysian Library*, vol. I (4 vols, London, 1903–23), p. 247 n. 1, 2.

21. *Naval Minutes*, pp. 159–60, 243.

22. V. Brome, *The Other Pepys* (London, 1992), pp. 164, 168, 191, 288; Bryant, *Samuel Pepys. The Years of Peril*, pp. 94–8, 267–8, 344, 371, 392; J.D. Davis, 'Pepys and the Admiralty Commission of 1679–1684', *Historical Research*, vol. LXII (1989), pp. 34–53; Hornstein, *Restoration Navy and English Foreign Trade*, pp. 18–21, 24; B. Lavery, 'The Thirty Ships of 1677', Part One, *Model Shipwright*, vol. XXXIII (1980), pp. 54–61 and Part Two, *Model Shipwright*, vol. XXXIV (1980), pp. 2–9; *Naval Minutes*, p. 181; B. Pool, 'Pepys and the Thirty Ships', *History Today*, vol. XX (1970), pp. 489–90, 493–5.

23. Hornstein, *Restoration Navy and English Foreign Trade*, pp. 11–32, 259–60, 263–4; Pool, 'Pepys and the Thirty Ships', pp. 493–5.

24. *Naval Minutes*, pp. 9, 101, 105, 107, 159, 418. See also: BL, Sloane MS, 2,439; McKie, 'James, Duke of York, F.R.S.', pp. 8–15.

25. *Pepys Diary* (1 Nov. 1665), vol. VI, p. 285.

26. *Naval Minutes*, p. 247.

27. J.S. Corbett (ed.), *Fighting Instructions, 1530–1816* (London, 1905), pp. 122–9, 146–63; National Maritime Museum, Greenwich, DAR / 9.

28. Corbett (ed.), *Fighting Instructions*, pp. 135–7, 149, 159; NMM, Greenwich, DAR / 13.

29. *Naval Minutes*, pp. 33–4.

30. Latham (ed.), *Samuel Pepys and the Second Dutch War*, pp. 291–2, 418; *Pepys Diary*, vol. IV, p. 39, (3 Jan. 1664), vol. V, p. 3, (16 March 1664), vol. V, p. 88, (26 Sept. 1664), vol. V, p. 280, (14 Aug. 1665), vol. VI, pp. 190–1, (18 Jan. 1667), vol. VIII, p. 19 and (31 Jan. 1667), vol. VIII, p. 37; Routh, *Tangier*, pp. 33–4, 72–3, 115, 130, 160, 311, 334–5, 366–8; Vale, 'Clarendon, Coventry, and the Sale of Naval Offices', pp. 107–25.

31. Anderson (ed.), *Journal of Edward Mountagu*, pp. lx and lxix.

32. *Naval Minutes*, pp. 34–5; *Pepys Diary* (Companion), vol. X, p. 210.

33. C.R. Boxer, *The Dutch Seaborne Empire* (London, 1965), pp. 102–3, 312–13; R. Davis, 'A Commercial Revolution? English Overseas Trade in the 17th, 18th Centuries', *Historical Association*, Pamphlet No. LXIV (London, 1967), *passim*; Hornstein, *Restoration Navy and English Foreign Trade*, pp. 33–5, 45–6; T. Mun, *England's Treasure by Forraign Trade* (London, 1664), *passim*; *Naval Minutes*, p. 31; J. Selden, *Mare Clausum: the Right and Dominion of the Sea in Two Books* (London, 1663), *passim*; P. Sonnio, *Louis XIV and the Origins of the Dutch War* (Cambridge, 1988), pp. 58–9; C. Wilson and D. Proctor, *1688. The Seaborne Alliance and Diplomatic Revolution* (London, 1989), pp. 76–8, 82–6.

34. Clarendon, *Life of Clarendon*, vol. II, p. 237; *Pepys Diary* (2 Feb. 1664), vol. 5, p. 35; C. Wilson, *Profit and Power* (Cambridge, 1957), pp. 99–103. See also: Boxer, *Dutch Seaborne Empire*, p. 94; 'Navigation Act, 1660' in Browning (ed.), *English Historical Documents*, pp. 533–7; Jones, *Anglo-Dutch Wars*, pp. 12, 144; *Life*, vol. I, p. 450; A.T. Mahan, *The Influence of Sea Power Upon History, 1660–1783* (Boston, Massachusetts, 1890), p. 107; *Pepys Diary*

(22 Feb. 1664), vol. V, p. 59, (4 April 1664), vol. V, p. 111, (29 May 1664), vol. V, pp. 159–60 and (18 July 1664), vol. V, p. 212; J.M. Sosin, *English America and the Restoration Monarchy of Charles II. Transatlantic Politics, Commerce, and Kinship* (Lincoln, USA and London, 1980), pp. 49–50, 54–8, 61–2.

35. *Life*, vol. I, pp. 399–401, 450; *Life*, vol. II, pp. 609, 611–12, 634; *Pepys Diary* (17 April 1663), vol. IV, p. 105; Selden, *Mare Clausum*, pp. i–v, 486–97.

36. Anderson, *Journal of Edward Mountagu*, p. 293; Anderson, *Journals and Narratives of the Third Dutch War*, p. 5; Jones, *Anglo-Dutch Wars*, p. 160; *Life*, vol. I, p. 446; Wilson, *Profit and Power*, p. 120.

37. The italics used to emphasize the quotation are those of the present author; Clarendon, *Life of Clarendon*, vol. II, p. 236.

38. *Naval Minutes*, pp. 36–7.

39. Boxer, *Dutch Seaborne Empire*, pp. 103, 105, 116–17, 312–13; C.R. Boxer, 'Ledger and Sword: Cornelis Speelman and the Growth of Dutch Power in Indonesia, 1666–1684', *History Today*, vol. VII (1958), pp. 145–54; Hornstein, *Restoration Navy and English Foreign Trade*, pp. 3–8, 47–52, 209–58; F.T. Jane, *The British Battle Fleet*, vol. I (London, 1915), pp. 79–81; J. Keay, *The Honourable Company. A History of the English East India Company* (London, 1993), pp. 130–68; B. Lavery (ed.), *Deane's Doctrine of Naval Architecture, 1670* (London, 1981), pp. 11–12, 21–2, 25–6, 28–9, 104–13; Pool, 'Pepys and the Thirty Ships', p. 489; H.C.B. Rogers, *The Dutch in the Medway* (London and New York, 1970), p. 25; Wilson, *Profit and Power*, pp. 128, 145–6.

40. Mignet quoted in Turner, *James II*, p. 76. See also: Boxer, *Dutch Seaborne Empire*, pp. 117–18, 162, 303–4, 312–13; Hornstein, *Restoration Navy and English Foreign Trade*, pp. 259–64; *Life*, vol. I, pp. 399–401; *Life*, vol. II, pp. 609, 611–12, 634; Wilson, *Profit and Power*, pp. 149–51; Wilson and Proctor, *1688. Seaborne Alliance and Diplomatic Revolution*, pp. 100–10.

41. Boxer, *Dutch Seaborne Empire*, pp. 94–101; Hornstein, *Restoration Navy and English Foreign Trade*, p. 253; Jones, *Anglo-Dutch Wars*, pp. 182–3; Lavery (ed.), *Deane's Doctrine*, pp. 13–14; Mahan, *Influence of Sea Power*, pp. 103–7; Sonnio, *Louis XIV and the Origins of the Dutch War*, pp. 65–6, 82–3, 143–6, 177–8; Wolf, *Louis XIV*, pp. 277, 282, 288–9, 316, 323.

42. Davies, 'Pepys and the Admiralty Commission', pp. 39–46, 52–3; Hornstein, *Restoration Navy and English Foreign Trade*, pp. 155–208.

CHAPTER EIGHT

1. Corbett (ed.), *Fighting Instructions*, pp. 122–9, 146–7, 152–63; G. Parker, *The Military Revolution. Military Innovation and the Rise of the West, 1500–1800* (Cambridge, 1988), pp. 102–3.

2. *CSPD* (1664–5), pp. 403–4, 408; Hartmann, *The King My Brother*, pp. 161–2; Tedder, *Navy of the Restoration*, pp. 120–1.

3. *CSPD* (1664–5), pp. 404, 408–9, 412; W.L. Clowes (ed.), *The Royal Navy* (London, 1898), vol. II, p. 263; Hartmann, *The King My Brother*, pp. 162–3; Jones, *Anglo-Dutch Wars*, pp. 156–7; *Life*, vol. I, pp. 388, 410; Ollard, *Cromwell's Earl*, pp. 129–30; *Pepys Diary* (5 June 1665), vol. VI, pp. 117–18 and (8 June 1665), vol. VI, p. 122; Tedder, *Navy of the Restoration*, pp. 121–2.

4. *CSPD* (1664–5), pp. 403, 407–9; *Life*, vol. I, pp. 410–15; Hartmann, *The King My Brother*, pp. 162–3; *Pepys Diary* (8 June 1665), vol. VI, p. 122.

5. *CSPD* (1664–5), pp. 407–9; *Evelyn Diary* (23 June 1665), p. 308; *Life*, vol. I, pp. 410–15; *Pepys Diary* (23 June 1665), vol. VI, p. 135.

6. Anderson (ed.), *Journal of Edward Mountagu*, pp. 223–30; Tedder, *Navy of the Restoration*, p. 124.

7. *CSPD* (1664–5), pp. 405–9, 411; *Naval Minutes*, p. 242; *Pepys Diary* (8 June 1665), vol. VI, pp. 122–3, (16 June 1665), vol. VI, pp. 129–30 and (23 June 1665), vol. VI, p. 135; Tedder, *Navy of the Restoration*, p. 124; Turner, *James II*, p. 80.

8. *Burnet*, vol. I, pp. 397–9 (Book II, pp. 218–19); *CSPD* (1664–5), pp. 406, 411; Clarendon, *Life of Clarendon*, vol. II, pp. 396–9; *Evelyn Diary* (8 June 1665), p. 307; G. de F. Ford (ed.), *Poems on Affairs of State, Augustan Satirical Verse, 1660–1714*, vol. I (New Haven and London), pp. 46–7; A. Grey (ed.), *Debates of the House of Commons from the Year 1667 to the Year 1694*, vol. I (London, 1769), pp. 139–41, 144; *Life*, vol. I, pp. 415–17, 421; *Pepys Diary* (20 Oct. 1667), vol. VIII, pp. 489–90, (21 Oct. 1667), vol. VIII, pp. 491–2 and (20 Feb. 1668), vol. IX, p. 80; Tedder, *Navy of the Restoration*, p. 125.

9. Anderson (ed.), *Journal of Edward Mountagu*, p. 294; *Burnet*, vol. I, p. 399 (Book II, p. 219); *CSPD* (1664–5), pp. 407–8; Clarendon, *Life of Clarendon*, vol. II, p. 399; *Life*, vol. I, pp. 415–33.

10. *CSPD* (1664–5), pp. 408, 415; *Evelyn Diary* (8 and 12 June 1665), p. 307 and (1 July 1665), p. 308; Hartmann, *The King My Brother*, p. 170; *Life*, vol. I, pp. 420–2; *Pepys Diary* (6 Nov. 1665), vol. VI, p. 291.

11. Anon., *An Essay Upon the Late Victory Obtained by His Royal Highness the Duke of York, Against the Dutch, Upon June 3rd 1665* (London, 1665), p. 1; *CSPD* (1664–5), pp. 403, 408; Clarendon, *Life of Clarendon*, vol. II, pp. 396–9; Ford, *Poems on Affairs of State*, vol. I, pp. 20–33; Higham, *King James II*, p. 103; *Life*, vol. I, pp. 415–33; *Pepys Diary* (23 June 1665), vol. VI, p. 135, (21 Oct. 1667), vol. VIII, p. 491, (31 March 1668), vol. IX, p. 142 and (18 April 1668), vol. IX, pp. 166–7.

12. *Burnet*, vol. I, p. 591 (Book II, p. 323); *CSPD* (May–Sept. 1672), pp. 83–4, 86–7, 89, 94, 97, 102–3, 109, 111, 132.

13. *CSPD* (May–Sept. 1672), pp. 92–3, 95, 103, 110, 132, 211; Churchill, *Marlborough*, vol. I, pp. 81–2; *Life*, vol. I, pp. 464–74.

14. R.C. Anderson (ed.), *The Journals and Narratives of the Third Dutch War* (London, 1946), pp. 18–20; *CSPD* (May–Sept. 1672), pp. 92, 95, 103, 108–9, 113, 132–3, 135; *Life*, vol. I, pp. 464–74.

15. *CSPD* (May–Sept. 1672), pp. 93, 95, 103, 110–11, 133–5, 170–1, 173–4.

16. Anderson (ed.), *Journals and Narratives of the Third Dutch War*, pp. 20–1; *Burnet*, vol. I, p. 591 (Book II, p. 323); *CSPD* (May–Sept. 1672), pp. 104, 108, 134–5, 171, 174.

17. James to the Count d'Estrées, 11 September 1673, quoted in Anderson, *Journals and Narratives of the Third Dutch War*, pp. 407–8. See also: *CSPD* (May–Sept. 1672), pp. 95–7.

18. Anderson, *Journals and Narratives of the Third Dutch War*, p. 15.

19. *CSPD* (1664–5), p. 403; *CSPD* (May–Sept. 1672), pp. 85, 94, 173; *English Affairs*, pp. ix–x; Hattendorf (ed.), *British Naval Documents*, pp. 194–7; *Life*, vol. I, pp. 405–21, 464–74; A.T. Mahan, *The Influence of Sea Power Upon History, 1660–1783* (London, 1890, rpt 1965), pp. 147–8.

20. *Burnet*, vol. I, p. 442 (Book II, pp. 241–2); *CSPD* (1667), p. 189; *Evelyn Diary* (29 July 1667), p. 331; Hattendorf (ed.), *British Naval Documents*, pp. 241–2; *Life*, vol. I, p. 425; Ollard, *Pepys*, p. 159; Rogers, *Dutch in the Medway*, pp. 63, 71.

21. *Burnet*, vol. I, pp. 457–8 (Book II, p. 250); *CSPD* (1667), pp. 186, 189; *Pepys Diary* (31 Jan. 1667), vol. VIII, p. 38, (17 Feb. 1667), vol. VIII, pp. 66, 68, (24 Feb. 1667), vol. VIII, pp. 80–1, (27 Feb. 1667), vol. VIII, p. 84, (28 Feb. 1667), vol. VIII, p. 88, (6 March 1667), vol. VIII, pp. 97–8, (17 March 1667), vol. VIII, p. 115, (24 March 1667), vol. VIII, p. 127, (21 Dec. 1667), vol. VIII, p. 585, (27 Dec. 1667), vol. VIII, p. 592 and (30 Dec. 1667), vol. VIII, p. 597; Vale, 'Clarendon, Coventry, and the Sale of Naval Offices', pp. 123–5.

22. Jones, *Anglo-Dutch Wars*, p. 174; *Pepys Diary* (27 Feb. 1667), vol. VIII, p. 84, (17 March 1667), vol. VIII, p. 115, (22 March 1667), vol. VIII, p. 125, (23 March 1667), vol. VIII, pp. 125–7, (18 April 1667), vol. VIII, p. 171 and (20 April 1667), vol. VIII, p. 173; Rogers, *Dutch in the Medway*, pp. 56–7, 59.

23. *Burnet*, vol. II, p. 442 (Book II, p. 242); *CSPD* (1667), pp. xxi–xxii, 167–9.

24. *CSPD* (1667), pp. xxi–xxiii, 167–8, 171–2, 177, 179, 185; *Evelyn Diary* (11 June 1667), p. 162; *Pepys Diary* (11 June 1667), vol. VIII, p. 259; Rogers, *Dutch in the Medway*, pp. 80–2.

25. *CSPD* (1667), pp. 175, 178–9, 207; F. Hussey, *Suffolk Invasion. The Dutch Attack on Landguard Fort, 1667* (Lavenham, Suffolk, 1983), pp. 47–8, 89–103; *Pepys Diary* (9 June 1667), vol. VIII, p. 255.

26. James's movements during these crucial days are not documented in the pages of the *CSPD*. He was expected to join the Duke of Monmouth – who was mustering the local gentry at Harwich – on 12 June, but there is no record of his arrival. Despite all of Pepys' scoffing, the young Monmouth really does seem to have been more active in the defence of the Royal Dockyards than his uncle. The Duke of York appears to have overseen the disastrous attempt to sink merchantmen at Barking Creek, in the early hours of 13 June. He spent the rest of the day riding 'up and down all the day here and there' in the City of London, but to little obvious effect.
Burnet, vol. I, pp. 457–9 (Book II, p. 250); *CSPD* (1667), pp. 171, 185; *Evelyn Diary* (14–28 June 1667), pp. 329–30; *Life*, vol. I, pp. 421–2; Ollard, *Pepys*, p. 165; *Pepys Diary* (9 June 1667), vol. VIII, p. 255, (10 June 1667), vol. VIII, p. 256, (13 June 1667), vol. VIII, pp. 263–4, (28 June 1667), vol. VIII, p. 298 and (29 July 1667), vol. VIII, pp. 358–9; Tedder, *Navy of the Restoration*, pp. 181–2.

27. *CSPD* (1667), p. 185.

28. *Evelyn Diary* (28 June 1667), p. 330. See also: *Burnet*, vol. I, pp. 458–9 (Book II, p. 250); *CSPD* (1667), pp. xxii–xxiii, 188; *Evelyn Diary* (17 and 24 June 1667), pp. 329–30; Ford (ed.), *Poems on Affairs of State*, pp. 98, 124–39; *Life*, vol. I, pp. 421–2; *Pepys Diary* (10 June 1667), vol. VIII, p. 256; Turner, *James II*, p. 82; Wilcox, *Mr. Pepys's Navy*, p. 50.

29. Quoted in Barbour, *Henry Bennet, Earl of Arlington*, p. 109. See also: Rogers, *Dutch in the Medway*, pp. 122, 128.

30. Rogers, *Dutch in the Medway*, pp. 57–8, 83, 138–9, 145–6, 164; J.H. Rose, 'The Influence of James II on the Navy', *Fighting Forces*, vol. I (1924), p. 220.

31. *CSPD* (1667), p. 207; Ollard, *Man of War*, pp. 165–6; Ollard, *Pepys*, pp. 161–2; 163, *Pepys Diary* (16 Dec. 1666), vol. VII, pp. 409–10, (3 June 1667), vol. VIII, p. 248, (12–13 June 1667), vol. VIII, pp. 261–3, (27 June 1667), vol. VIII, p. 298, (28 Oct. 1667), vol. VIII, p. 505 and (8 Dec. 1667), vol. VIII, pp. 570–1.

32. *CSPD* (1682), p. 210; Reresby, *Memoirs*, p. 248.

33. *CSPD* (1682), pp. 206, 210; P.M. Cowburn, 'Christopher Gunman and the Wreck of the Gloucester', Part I, *Marriners Mirror*, vol. XLII (1956), pp. 114–15; *Evelyn Diary* (16 March 1685), p. 282; S. Pepys, *Letters and the Second Diary of Samuel Pepys*, ed. R.G. Howarth (London and Toronto, 1932), p. 134.

34. *Naval Minutes*, p. 145.

35. Cowburn, 'Christopher Gunman', Part I, pp. 115, 122; *Naval Minutes*, pp. 149–50, 314; Pepys, *Letters*, p. 134; G. Robinson, 'The Casting Away of the Gloucester, 1682', *History Today*, vol. V (1955), pp. 246–7, 249.

36. Berry quoted in Cowburn, 'Christopher Gunman', Part I, p. 118. See also: H. Arthur (ed.), 'Some Familiar Letters of Charles II and James, Duke of York addressed to their daughter and niece, the Countess of Litchfield', *Archaeologia*, vol. LVIII (1902), p. 168; *Burnet*, vol. II, pp. 323–5 (Book III, p. 523); *CSPD* (1682), p. 200; Cowburn, 'Christopher Gunman', Part I, p. 121; Churchill, *Marlborough*, vol. I, pp. 153–4; *Life*, vol. I, pp. 730–3; Pepys, *Letters*, p. 134.

37. Henry Legge's letter to Erasmus Lewis, 25 January 1725, reprinted in Airy (ed.), *Burnet's History*, vol. II, p. 327 n. 2. See also: Churchill, *Marlborough*, vol. I, p. 153; Cowburn, 'Christopher Gunman', Part I, pp. 121, 124; Pepys, *Letters*, pp. 134–5; Robinson, 'Casting Away of the Gloucester', p. 251; Webb, *Lord Churchill's Coup*, pp. 63–4.

38. Airy (ed.), *Burnet's History*, vol. II, p. 327 n. 2; Anon., *The Life of James II. Late King of England*, p. 80; Arthur (ed.), 'Familiar Letters', p. 168; Cowburn, 'Christopher Gunman', Part I, pp. 119–20, 123; Pepys, *Letters*, p. 135; Reresby, *Memoirs*, p. 250.

39. *CSPD* (1682), p. 206; *Naval Minutes*, pp. 131, 146, 150, 314; Robinson, 'Casting Away of the Gloucester', p. 248.

40. P.M. Cowburn, 'Christopher Gunman and the Wreck of the Gloucester', *Marriners Mirror*, Part II, vol. XLII (1956), pp. 221–3; *Evelyn Diary* (16 March, 1685), p. 474; Robinson, 'Casting Away of the Gloucester', pp. 248, 251.

41. Anon., *An Anniversary Poem on the Sixth of May. His Royal Highness Miraculous Deliverance, then at Sea, from the Shipwreck of the Gloucester* (London, 1683); Anon., *Life of James II. Late King of England*, pp. 79–80, 82; Arthur (ed.), 'Familiar Letter', p. 168; Carrel, *History of the Counter-Revolution*, p. 1; Hawkins, *Medallic Illustrations*, vol. I, p. 586; *Life*, vol. I, p. 731; Macpherson, *Original Papers*, vol. I, p. 730.

42. N.F. Dixon, *On the Psychology of Military Incompetence* (London, 1976), pp. 152–3, 258; J. Keegan, *The Mask of Command* (London, 1987), pp. 1–11, 311–51.

CHAPTER NINE

1. G. Bryce, *The Remarkable History of the Hudson's Bay Company* (London, 1900), pp. 29–30; *CSPD* (1663–4), pp. 513, 549; *Life*, vol. I, pp. 399–401; *Life*, vol. II, pp. 609, 611, 633–4; Miller, *James II*, p. 168.

2. Ashley, Haswell, Lane and Trevor all return very favourable verdicts on James's involvement with the joint-stock companies. All of their findings are firmly based upon the accounts of the Duke's business interests given in the *Life*. It is interesting to note that Webb, despite his wide researches, seems to implicitly agree with their findings. Of

James's biographers only Miller and Turner look at sources other than the *Life*, and are consequently more dismissive of his impact upon foreign trade.

Ashley, *James II*, pp. 79–80; Haswell, *James II*, pp. 150–1; Lane, *King James the Last*, p. 74; Miller, *James II*, pp. 43–4; Trevor, *Shadow of a Crown*, p. 36; Turner, *James II*, pp. 82–3; Webb, 'Brave Men and Servants', pp. 63–4; Webb, *Lord Churchill's Coup*, pp. 3–4, 268.

3. N.P. Canny, 'The Ideology of English Colonization: From Ireland to America', *W&MQ*, 3rd series, vol. XXX (1973), pp. 575–98; K.G. Davies, *The Royal African Company* (London, 1957), pp. 71, 103, 123–4; R.S. Dunn, *Sugar and Slaves* (London, 1977), p. 232; M.I. Finley, 'Colonies – An Attempt at a Typology', *TRHS*, 5th series, vol. XXVI (1976), pp. 167–88; A. Jones, 'Semper aliquid veteris: Printed Sources for the History of the Ivory and Gold Coasts, 1500–1700', *Journal of African History*, vol. XXVII (1986), pp. 216–35; Morrah, *Prince Rupert*, p. 382; D.B. Quinn, 'Renaissance Influences in English Colonization', *TRHS*, 5th series, vol. XXVI (1976), pp. 73–93.

4. Hamilton, *Memoirs of the Count de Grammont*, p. 362; Morrah, *Prince Rupert*, pp. 266–7, 380–1; Ollard, *Man of War*, pp. 62–3; *Pepys Diary* (3 Oct. 1660), vol. I, p. 258; Wilson, *Profit and Power*, p. 112; G.F. Zook, *The Company of Royal Adventurers Trading into Africa* (Lancaster, Pennsylvania, 1919), p. 8.

5. E.W. Bovill, *The Golden Trade of the Moors* (London and New York, 1968), p. 128; *Documents Illustrative*, p. 86; *Pepys Diary* (3 Oct. 1660), vol. I, p. 258; *Select Charters*, p. 173; Wilson, *Profit and Power*, p. 112; Zook, *Company of Royal Adventurers*, p. 8.

6. *Documents Illustrative*, p. 190; *Pepys Diary* (3 Oct. 1660), vol. I, p. 258; Ritchie, 'Duke of York's Commission', pp. 177–8; *Select Charters*, p. 173.

7. *CSPD* (1663–4), p. 184; K.G. Davies, *Royal African Company*, p. 41; *Documents Illustrative*, pp. 169–72; J.R. Jones, *Anglo-Dutch Wars*, p. 150; *Select Charters*, pp. 173–4.

8. Anon., *The Several Declarations of the Company of Royal Adventurers of England Trading into Africa, inviting all his Majesties Native Subjects in general to subscribe, and become sharers in their Joynt-stock* (London, 1667), pp. 1–2, 11; *CSPC* (1661–8), no. 1721; *Documents Illustrative*, pp. 158, 160; Morrah, *Prince Rupert*, p. 381; *Select Charters*, pp. xlv n. 10, 173, 175; Zook, *Company of Royal Adventurers*, pp. iii, 12–16.

9. *CSPC* (1661–8), nos 609, 618; *CSPD* (1663–4), pp. 168, 184, 266, 328, 513, 617; *CSPD* (March 1676–Feb. 1677), pp. 530–1; *Documents Illustrative*, pp. 158, 160, 164, 169–72; Haley, *Shaftesbury*, p. 234; *Life*, vol. I, p. 400; *Pepys Diary* (14 Oct. 1663), vol. IV, p. 335; *Select Charters*, p. 173; *The Several Declarations*, p. 2; Wilson, *Profit and Power*, pp. 112–13; Zook, *Company of Royal Adventurers*, p. 16.

10. *CSPC* (1661–8), no. 615; *Pepys Diary* (2 Sept. 1668), vol. IX, p. 313; *Select Charters*, pp. 174, 176–7.

11. *CSPC* (1669–74), no. 936. PRO, T 70 / 10, ff. 1–2; J.J. Scarisbrick and P.L. Carter, 'An Expedition to Wangara', *Ghana Notes and Queries*, no. 1 (1961), pp. 4–5.

12. Bovill, *Golden Trade*, pp. 123, 128–9; *Documents Illustrative*, p. 237; PRO, T 70 / 1, ff. 5–6.

13. *CSPC* (1661–8), nos 170, 383, 407, 417, 609, 618; *CSPC* (1669–74), no. 936; *CSPD* (1663–4), p. 617; *CSPD* (March 1677–Feb. 1678), p. 489; *Documents Illustrative*, pp. 150–3, 155, 167; PRO, T 70 / 1, ff. 6, 46; *Select Charters*, pp. 172–6.

14. Anon., *Certain Considerations Relating to the Royal African Company of England* (London, 1680), p. 5; *CSPC* (1669–74), nos 178, 407, 985; *CSPC* (1677–80), nos 31, 234; *CSPD* (March 1675–Feb. 1676), pp. 291, 509; *Documents Illustrative*, pp. 168–9, 174.

15. *CSPC* (1661–8), no. 407; *Documents Illustrative*, pp. 74, 156–7, 161–2, 188, 226–8, 234, 238, 242, 249, 259–60; PRO, T 70 / 1, ff. 5–15, 19, 24–6, 46, 68; PRO, T 70 / 10, ff. 1–34

16. *Documents Illustrative*, pp. 199–209, 228–33, 250, 271; J. Walvin, *Black Ivory. A History of British Slavery* (Washington DC, 1994), p. 34.

17. *Documents Illustrative*, pp. 188, 217–20; J.D. Fage and R. Oliver, R. (eds), *The Cambridge History of Africa* (London, 1975), vol. 4, *c.* 1600–*c.* 1790, p. 589.

18. 'Mr. James York', originally known as *Hamet* or more properly Muhammad, was a Moorish slave and a particular favourite of the Duke's. James had him educated at his own expense and sent him on a Grand Tour in 1671. After studying siege craft in Germany and the Low Countries, he was sent back to North Africa to act as a specialist aide to the Governor of Tangier. However, *Hamet* immediately betrayed his former masters and led the garrison into an ambush. He subsequently helped the Moorish commanders besiege Tangier and was reported killed shortly before the end of the English occupation, although this last point may well be purely apocryphal.
    Evelyn Diary (16 Sept. 1685), p. 486; J. Luke, *Tangier at High Tide. The Journal of John Luke, 1670–1673*, eds H.A. and P. Kaufman (Geneva and Paris, 1958), p. 53; J. Ross, *Tanger's Rescue* (London, 1680), p. 21; Routh, *Tangier*, pp. 168–9.

19. *CSPD* (March 1677–Feb. 1678), pp. 34, 503–4; Fage and Oliver, *Cambridge History of Africa*, p. 220; PRO, T 70 / 1, ff. 5, 62; *Select Charters*, pp. 174, 178, 186, 191–2; Routh, *Tangier*, pp. 4–6, 10–11, 15, 27, 117–21, 266, 271.

20. *Documents Illustrative*, p. 194; Hamilton, *Memoirs of the Count de Grammont*, p. 362; A.W. Lawrence, *Trade Castles and Forts of West Africa* (London, 1963), p. 185; PRO, T 70 / 1, ff. 55, 100–1; Walvin, *Black Ivory*, p. 32.

21. PRO, T 70 / 1, ff. 5, 9, 60, 62.

22. *CSPD* (1682), p. 332; PRO, T 70 / 1, ff. 98–100, 102.

23. *CSPD* (March 1676–Feb. 1677), p. 34; *Certain Considerations*, p. 6; *Documents Illustrative*, p. 194; Hamilton, *Memoirs of the Count de Grammont*, p. 362; Lawrence, *Trade Castles*, p. 185; PRO, T 70 /1, ff. 5, 15, 68.

24. James may well have been attempting to counteract a very successful Dutch propaganda campaign, begun the year before, to win over the 'hearts and minds' of the African warriors. Ships from the States General had given out 'daily great presents to the King of Futton and . . . told the King of Ardra that they had conquered the Portugals ... turned out the Dane and Swede, and in a short time should do the same to the English'; Ardra, itself, is now known as Allada.
    C.R. Boxer, *De Ruyter* (Amsterdam, 1974), p. 45; *CSPC* (1661–8), no. 507; *Certain Considerations*, p. 8; Fage and Oliver, *Trade Castles*, pp. 226–7.

25. Boxer, *De Ruyter*, pp. 44–5.

26. *Certain Considerations*, p. 7.

27. *CSPC* (1661–8), nos 407, 618; *CSPC* (1669–74), no. 936; K.G. Davies, *Royal African Company*, p. 284; *Documents Illustrative*, p. 73; Ollard, *Man of War*, pp. 66–7; Walvin, *Black Ivory*, p. 34; Wilson, *Profit and Power*, pp. 9, 110, 123; Zook, *Company of Royal Adventurers*, pp. 11–12.

28. Boxer, *Dutch Seaborne Empire*, p. 113; *CSPC* (1661–8), no. 954; Ollard, *Man of War*, pp. 85–6; Vale, 'Clarendon, Coventry, and the Sale of Naval Offices', p. 113 n. 33; Zook, *Company of Royal Adventurers*, p. 50.

29. *CSPC* (1661–8), no. 737; Ollard, *Man of War*, pp. 93–5, 101–2, 106–8, 110–18.

30. *CSPC* (1661–8), nos 829, 986; J.R. Jones, *Anglo-Dutch Wars*, p. 150; *Pepys Diary* (22 Dec. 1664), vol. V, p. 353.

31. *CSPC* (1661–8), nos 902–3, 1294; *Certain Considerations*, pp. 3–4; *Select Charters*, pp. 186–7.

32. *CSPC* (1661–8), nos 902–3; *CSPD* (1664–5), p. 7; *Certain Considerations*, pp. 3–4; *Life*, vol. I, pp. 399–401; Morrah, *Prince Rupert*, p. 382; Zook, *Company of Royal Adventurers*, pp. 20–6.

33. Clarendon, *Life of Clarendon*, vol. II, pp. 234, 236–7.

34. R. Blackburn, *The Making of New World Slavery. From the Baroque to the Modern, 1492–1800* (London, 1997), p. 255; *CSPC* (1669–74), nos 934–6; *CSPD* (March 1676–Feb. 1677), pp. 35, 105; *Certain Considerations*, p. 4; K.G. Davies, *Royal African Company*, pp. 59, 264–5; *Documents Illustrative*, pp. 174–6, 177–92; Hartmann, *The King My Brother*, pp. 241–2, 247; *Life*, vol. I, p. 443; Routh, *Tangier*, p. 19; *Select Charters*, pp. 186–92.

35. *CSPD* (Oct. 1672–Feb. 1673), p. 262; K.G. Davies, *Royal African Company*, pp. 65–6; *Documents Illustrative*, pp. 178–82; R.S. Dunn, *Sugar and Slaves*, p. 232; *Select Charters*, pp. 187–9.

36. K.G. Davies, *Royal African Company*, pp. 62, 64–6; *Documents Illustrative*, p. 156; R.S. Dunn, *Sugar and Slaves*, p. 232; Haley, *Shaftesbury*, p. 233.

37. *Documents Illustrative*, pp. 182–3; Haley, *Shaftesbury*, p. 233; *Select Charters*, p. 189.

38. *CSPD* (Oct. 1672–Feb. 1673), p. 207; *CSPD* (Jan. 1679–Aug. 1680), p. 80; *CSPD* (Sept. 1680–Dec. 1681), p. 690; *CSPD* (Addenda 1660–85), pp. 470–1, 485; K.G. Davies, *Royal African Company*, pp. 61, 63, 68, 265; *Documents Illustrative*, p. 215; R.S. Dunn, *Sugar and Slaves*, pp. 232–3; Walvin, *Black Ivory*, p. 255.

39. Blackburn, *Making of New World Slavery*, p. 255; K.G. Davies, *Royal African Company*, pp. 70–4; R.S. Dunn, *Sugar and Slaves*, pp. 95–6, 102, 190, 232; Davies, K.G., *op.cit.* (1957), pp. 70–4.

40. *CSPD* (March 1675–Feb. 1676), p. 560; K.G. Davies, *Royal African Company*, pp. 65, 104; Haley, *Shaftesbury*, pp. 233–4, 234 n. 1, 259; M. Priestley, 'London Merchants and Opposition Politics in Charles II's Reign', *Bulletin of the Institute of Historical Research*, vol. XXIX (1956), pp. 205, 217–19; E.E. Rich, 'The First Earl of Shaftesbury's Colonial Policy', *TRHS*, vol. VII (1957), pp. 53–4.

41. *CSPD* (March 1675–Feb. 1676), pp. 378–9; *CSPD* (July–Sept. 1683), p. 393; *Pepys Diary* (23 May 1663), vol. IV, pp. 152–3; Priestley, 'London Merchants', pp. 205–19.

42. E.H.H. Archibald, *The Wooden Fighting Ship in the Royal Navy, A.D. 897–1860* (London, 1968), pp. 129, 131; K.G. Davies, *Royal African Company*, p. 106.

43. K.G. Davies, *Royal African Company*, p. 107; PRO, T 70 / 78, ff. 54 d, 55 d, 56 d.

44. *CSPD* (March 1676–Feb. 1677), pp. 530–1; PRO, T 70 /1, ff. 24–6, 42 d., 50, 53, 77, 80, 88, 103–4; PRO, T 70 / 10, ff. 18–19, 23, 34.

45. *CSPD* (Nov. 1673–Feb. 1675), p. 291; *CSPD* (Jan.–June 1683), p. 241; *CSPD* (Oct. 1683–April 1684), pp. 41–2, 57, 82, 297, 318–19, 329; *CSPD* (May 1684–Feb. 1685), pp. 102–3; *Certain Considerations*, pp. 1–2; *Documents Illustrative*, p. 222.

46. Blackburn, *Making of New World Slavery*, p. 255; P.J. Helm, *Jeffreys* (London, 1966), p. 109; J. Keay, *The Honourable Company. A History of the English East India Company* (London, 1993), pp. 174–5; S.A. Khan, *The East India Trade in the XVIIth Century, in its Political and Economic Aspects* (London, 1923), p. 182.

47. M.M. Balfour, 'An Incident in the Life of a Great Lawyer', *Law Quarterly Review*, vol. XLI (1925), p. 71; *Burnet*, vol. II, pp. 422–3 (Book III, p. 580); Helm, *Jeffreys*, pp. 46, 55, 109, 116, 146; Keay, *The Honourable Company*, p. 175; W.G. Keeton, 'Judge Jeffreys as Chief Justice of Chester, 1680–1683', *Law Quarterly Review*, vol. LXXVII (1961), pp. 36–7, 48, 52–5; Khan, *East India Company*, p. 182; R. Milne-Tyte, *Bloody Jeffreys. The Hanging Judge* (London, 1989), pp. 17, 21–3.

48. K.G. Davies, *Royal African Company*, pp. 73–4, 76–7, 79, 106; *Documents Illustrative*, pp. 217–21; P. Kolchin, *American Slavery* (London, 1993), p. 12; Miller, *James II*, p. 168; PRO, T 70 / 1, ff. 6–8, 14–15, 24–6, 46, 50, 53; PRO, T 70 / 10, ff. 12–13, 19; Walvin, *Black Ivory*, p. 34.

49. Boxer, *Dutch Seaborne Empire*, pp. 48, 75–6; *CSPD* (1651–2), p. 255; J.R. Elder, *The Royal Fishery Companies of the Seventeenth Century* (Glasgow, 1912), pp. 85–8, 93–4, 97, 106; J.T. Jenkins, *The Herring and the Herring Fisheries* (London, 1927), pp. 81–3; *Select Charters*, p. 182; Wilson, *Profit and Power*, pp. 100, 144.

50. *CSPC* (1675–6), no. 669; *CSPD* (1663–4), pp. 513, 515, 549; Elder, *Royal Fishery Companies*, pp. 98, 100; *Pepys Diary* (10 March 1664), vol. V, p. 79, (7 July 1664), vol. V, p. 198 and (Companion) vol. X, p. 360; *Select Charters*, pp. 182–6; Wilson, *Profit and Power*, p. 121.

51. *CSPD* (1664–5), p. 412; *Pepys Diary* (20 Sept. 1664), vol. V, p. 276, (10 Oct. 1664), vol. V, pp. 293–4.

52. Elder, *Royal Fishery Companies*, pp. 105, 107, 110–13; Jenkins, *Herring and the Herring Fisheries*, p. 84; *Pepys Diary* (6 Nov. 1663), vol. IV, pp. 365–6, (13 Sept. 1664), vol. V, p. 269 and (3 Dec. 1664), vol. V, p. 336.

53. V. Barbour, 'Dutch and English Merchant Shipping in the Seventeenth Century', *Economic History Review*, vol. II (1930), pp. 278–9, 286–7; Elder, *Royal Fishery Companies*, p. 114; Jenkins, *Herring and the Herring Fisheries*, pp. 84, 87.

54. Byrce, *Remarkable History*, pp. 28–9; *Minutes*, pp. xxiii, xxxi, 307–8; E.E. Rich, *The Hudson's Bay Company, 1670–1870*, vol. I, 1670–1763 (London, 1958), pp. 38, 53, 85.

55. *Letters Outward*, p. 70; Rich, *Hudson's Bay Company*, vol. I, pp. 29, 32–3, 38, 55, 69, 94, 98–9, 107, 147, 163.

56. James had already been angered by the indiscretion of his colleagues on one City board, and swore that he would 'commit no more secrets to the merchants of the Royall Company'.
    Haley, *Shaftesbury*, p. 232; *Letters Outward*, pp. 69, 82, 84–5, 89, 113; *Minutes*, p. xxi, xxiii–xxiv; *Pepys Diary* (18 Oct. 1664), vol. V, p. 300; Rich, *Hudson's Bay Company*, vol. I, pp. 39, 86–7, 89–90, 162, 164, 186.

57. The Company's only major achievement in its early years was in the hunting and trapping of beavers. Unfortunately, they were so successful that the price of beaver skins plunged as their produce glutted the nascent market. In an attempt to stimulate demand, the Company tried to find new uses for their furs and suggested that they might be used to make winter stockings. Consequently, in 1684 the Company's commercial representatives duly presented the Duke of York with a pair. Unfortunately, James does not seem to have been impressed with his new hairy socks and the fashion, unsurprisingly, never did catch on at Court.
    Bryce, *Remarkable History*, p. 28; Rich, *Hudson's Bay Company*, vol. I, p. 167.

58. Anon., *An Elegy on that Illustrious and High-Born Prince Rupert* (London, 1682), p. 1; Bryce, *Remarkable History*, p. 29; G. Martin, 'Prince Rupert and the Surgeons', *History*

Today, vol. 40 (Dec. 1990), p. 43; Morrah, *Prince Rupert*, pp. 424–5; Rich, *Hudson's Bay Company*, vol. I, pp. 105, 164.

59. Quoted in Rich, *Hudson's Bay Company*, vol. I, p. 144.
60. *Letters Outward*, pp. 73–4, 79, 90–2, 128–9, 246–9, 328–9; *Minutes*, pp. xlii–xliv, 308; Webb, *Lord Churchill's Coup*, pp. 4, 114–23.
61. Bryce, *Remarkable History*, p. 30; Churchill, *Marlborough*, vol. I, pp. 399–400; Rich, *Hudson's Bay Company*, vol. I, p. 172; Webb, *Lord Churchill's Coup*, pp. 3–4.
62. K.G. Davies, *Royal African Company*, p. 65; *Minutes*, pp. xxiii–xxiv, 307–8; Morrah, *Prince Rupert*, pp. 424–5; *Pepys Diary* (3 June 1664), vol. V, p. 167; Rich, *Hudson's Bay Company*, vol. I (1958), pp. 29, 84–5, 105, 131, 144–6, 161, 164, 174; G.M. Thomson, *Warrior Prince. The Life of Prince Rupert of the Rhine* (London,1976), p. 226.
63. *CSPD* (July–Sept. 1683), p. 393; K.G. Davies, *Royal African Company*, pp. 67–8; *Letters Outward*, pp. 82–3; Rich, *Hudson's Bay Company*, vol. I, p. 145.
64. In the early years of his service under the Duke of York, Pepys writes favourably of his master's administrative skills and application towards business. However, towards the close of the Diary he is far more scathing and portrays James as an absentee Prince. It may simply be that familiarity had bred contempt, but the records of those chartered companies with which the Duke was associated do not bear the stamp of his involvement in the minutiae of their affairs.
   CSPD (March 1676–Feb. 1677), p. 510; *Letters Outward*, pp. 72–86, 89–90, 328–9; *Minutes*, pp. xxiii–xxvii, xxxv–xl and *passim* pp. 1–306; *Pepys Diary* (14 Oct. 1663), vol. IV, p. 335 (6 Nov. 1663), vol. IV, p. 367 (11 Jan. 1664), vol. V, p. 11 (20 Jan. 1664), vol. V, p. 21 (3 June 1664), vol. V, p. 167 (21 June 1664), vol. V, pp. 185–6 (13 Oct. 1666), vol. VII, p. 320 (15 Oct. 1666), vol. VII, p. 323 (31 Oct. 1666), vol. VII, p. 350 and (5 Nov. 1668), vol. IX, p. 350; Rich, *Hudson's Bay Company*, vol. I, pp. 144, 146, 155, 659; Ritchie, 'Duke of York's Commission', pp. 177–8.
65. Bryce, *Remarkable History*, p. 29; *Minutes*, p. 308; Rich, *Hudson's Bay Company*, vol. I, pp. 38, 155.
66. *Life*, vol. I, pp. 399–401.
67. *Life*, vol. II, pp. 609, 633–4.

CHAPTER TEN

1. J.B.A. Carrel, *History of the Counter-Revolution in England* (London, 1846), p. 158; Churchill, *Marlborough*, vol. I, pp. 140–54; J. Miller, 'The Potential for Absolutism in later Stuart England', *History*, vol. 69 (1984), p. 196; D. Ogg, *England in the Reign of Charles II* (London, 1934), vol. II, p. 419; A.L. Rowse, *The Early Churchills* (London, 1956), pp. 181–3.
2. C.M. Andrews, *The Colonial Period of American History*, vol. III (New Haven, Connecticut, 1937), p. 54; M.K. Geiter, 'The Incorporation of Pennsylvania and Late Stuart Politics' (unpublished Ph.D. thesis, University of Cambridge, 1993), p. 25; R.C. Ritchie, *The Duke's Province* (Chapel Hill, North Carolina, 1977), pp. 12–17; R.C. Ritchie, 'London Merchants, the New York Market, and the Recall of Sir Edmund Andros', *New York History*, vol. LVII (1976), pp. 6–7; H. and B. van der Zee, *A Sweet and Alien Land. The Story of Dutch New York* (New York and London, 1978), pp. 437–8.

3. Andrews, *Colonial Period*, vol. I, p. 255, vol. II, pp. 23–4 and vol. III, pp. 54–5, 71–96; *CSPC* (1661–8), nos 593, 597, 603, 825; *Documents Relative*, pp. 46–8; *Life*, vol. I, p. 400; G.L. Smith, *Religion and Trade in New Netherland. Dutch Origins and American Development* (Ithaca, USA and London, 1973), pp. 235, 241–2; Wilson, *Profit and Power*, p. 116; Zee, *Sweet and Alien Land*, pp. 83–96.

4. Andrews, *Colonial Period*, vol. I, p. 493 and vol. III, pp. 59, 96; *CSPC* (1661–8), nos 672–3, 679, 686, 695; *Pepys Diary* (Companion), vol. X, p. 53; Ritchie, *Duke's Province*, p. 19; D.G. Shomette and R.D. Haslach, *Raid on America. The Dutch Naval Campaign of 1672–1674* (Columbia, South Carolina, 1988), pp. 16–17; Webb, *Governors-General*, p. 497; Zee, *Sweet and Alien Land*, pp. 383, 427, 445–8.

5. Andrews, *Colonial Period*, vol. III, p. 57; *CSPC* (1661–8), nos 675–7, 683–5, 711; *Documents Relative*, pp. 51–61; W. Smith, Jnr, *The History of the Province of New-York. Volume One – From the First Discovery to the Year 1732*, ed. M. Kammen (Cambridge, Massachusetts, 1757, rpt 1972), p. 22; Shomette and Haslach, *Raid on America*, p. 17; J. Spicer, *The Grants, Concessions, and Original Constitutions of the Province of New Jersey* (Philadelphia, 1752), pp. 3–8.

6. Andrews, *Colonial Period*, vol. I, p. 341 and vol. III, pp. 56–7, 63–5; *CSPC* (1661–8), nos 685, 924, 1000, 1091, 1626; *CSPC* (1669–74), no. 69; *Documents Relative*, pp. 61–3; Ritchie, *Duke's Province*, p. 19; R.C. Ritchie, 'London Merchants', p. 7 and p. 7 n. 4; Wilson, *Profit and Power*, p. 117.

7. Andrews, *Colonial Period*, vol. III, pp. 60, 63; T.J. Archdeacon, *New York City, 1664–1710. Conquest and Change* (Ithaca, USA and London, 1976), p. 37; *CSPC* (1661–8), nos 788, 794, 808, 846, 1602–3; *CSPC* (1669–74), no. 126; *Documents Relative*, pp. 65–6; M. Kammen, *Colonial New York. A History* (New York, 1975), p. 72; Ritchie, *Duke's Province*, p. 21; Smith, *Religion and Trade*, p. 236; J.M. Sosin, *English America and the Restoration Monarchy of Charles II. Transatlantic Politics, Commerce, and Kinship* (Lincoln, USA and London, 1980), p. 140.

8. Despite the Duke's orders that the settlers should be treated with 'humanity and gentleness', Carr went on a rampage along the Delaware River, destroying Dutch townships almost at will. It is worth remembering that at this time England and the States General were not officially at war.
    CSPC (1661–8), no. 828; *Documents Relative*, pp. 71, 73–4; Smith, *Trade and Religion*, p. 234.

9. Andrews, *Colonial Period*, vol. II, p. 192; *CSPC* (1661–8), nos 1660, 1829; *CSPC* (1669–74), nos 1305, 1338; P.R. and F.A. Christoph (eds), *The Andros Papers, 1674–1676* (Syracuse, USA, 1989), p. 5; J.E. Pomfret, *Colonial New Jersey. A History* (New York, 1973), pp. 22–3.

10. Andrews, *Colonial Period*, vol. II, p. 192; Bliss, *Revolution and Empire*, pp. 204–5; *CSPC* (1661–8), nos 921, 1184, 1660, 1829; *CSPC* (1669–74), no. 1305; *CSPC* (1677–80), nos 1123, 1579; *CSPC* (1681–5), no. 1411; Pomfret, *Colonial New Jersey*, p. 22; Ritchie, 'Duke of York's Commission', pp. 177–8, 186–7; Sosin, *English America*, pp. 138–9, 147.

11. Andrews, *Colonial Period*, vol. III, pp. 108, 138, 160, 169–70, 176–7, 251; *CSPC* (1669–74), no. 1305; Pomfret, *Colonial New Jersey*, pp. 30–1; Sosin, *English America*, p. 148.

12. *CSPC* (1661–8), nos 1095, 1169, 1829; Pomfret, *Colonial New Jersey*, p. 7; Sosin, *English America*, p. 148.

13. *CSPC* (1661–8), nos 1660, 1829; *CSPC* (1677–80), no. 1123; *CSPC* (1681–5), no. 2078; P.S. Haffenden, 'The Crown and the Colonial Charters, 1675–1688', *W&MQ,* 3rd series, vol. 15 (Oct. 1958), part II, p. 454; Kammen, *Colonial New York,* p. 75; Pomfret, *Colonial New Jersey,* p. 9.

14. Andrews, *Colonial Period,* vol. III, pp. 120, 123; Bliss, *Revolution and Empire,* pp. 221, 224, 237; *CSPC* (1677–80), no. 1123; *CSPC* (1681–5), no. 1847; Sosin, *English America,* p. 145.

15. Andrews, *Colonial Period,* vol. III, pp. 102 , 102 n. 2, 118; *CSPC* (1661–8), nos 1026, 1184, 1874; *CSPC* (1669–74), nos 137, 285; B. Fernow (ed.), *The Records of New Amsterdam* (New York, 1897), vol. V, pp. 160–1; Kammen, *Colonial New York,* p. 74; Sosin, *English America,* p. 141.

16. *CSPC* (1661–8), no. 1602; *CSPC* (1669–74), nos 137, 1279.

17. *CSPD* (1661–8), nos 794, 851, 1304, 1602–3, 1628, 1874; *CSPD* (1669–74), nos 28–9, 136, 1279; Ritchie, 'London Merchants', p. 7; Routh, *Tangier,* p. 15.

18. Archdeacon, *New York City,* pp. 34–5, 38–9; *CSPC* (1661–8), nos 803, 828; *CSPC* (1669–74), nos 936, 985; *CSPC* (1675–6), no. 1167; *CSPC* (1677–80), nos 31, 234.

19. Andrews, *Colonial Period,* vol. III, pp. 96–8; *CSPC* (1661–8), nos 683–5, 920, 1260, 1292, 1295, 1378–9, 1533; *CSPC* (1669–74), no. 137.

20. Andrews, *Colonial Period,* vol. III, pp. 71, 97–8; *CSPC* (1661–8), nos 951, 1304; *CSPC* (1675–6), no. 513.

21. Anon. (ed.), 'Lawes establisht by the authority of his Majesties Letters Patent, granted to H.R.H. James, Duke of Yorke and Albany . . . and . . . given to Col. R. Nicolls, Deputy Governor', *New York Historical Society,* vol. I (1811), pp. 307–428; Bliss, *Revolution and Empire,* pp. 202–3; *CSPC* (1661–8), nos 685, 1623; *CSPC* (1669–74), no. 137; *CSPC* (1677–80), no. 660.

22. *CSPC* (1661–8), no. 1304; *CSPC* (1669–74), nos 42–3, 51, 82, 208, 1330, 1345; Geiter, 'Incorporation of Pennsylvania', p. 15; 'Lawes establisht', pp. 332–3; Ritchie, *Duke's Province,* p. 34; Smith, *Religion and Trade,* p. 236.

23. C.M. Andrews, *British Committees, Commissions, and Councils of Trade and Plantations, 1622–1675* (New York, 1908, rpt 1970), pp. 63–5; Bliss, *Revolution and Empire,* pp. 203–4; *CSPC* (1661–8), nos 834–5; *CSPC* (1669–74), nos 43, 50–1, 646, 875, 1328; *CSPC* (1675–6), no. 513; *CSPC* (1677–80), no. 222; W.F. Craven, *The Colonies in Transition, 1660–1713* (New York, 1968), pp. 73–5; *Documents Illustrative,* p. 171 and p. 171 n. 17; Fernow (ed.), *Records of New Amsterdam,* vol. V, pp. 160–1; Sosin, *English America,* pp. 141–2, 144–5.

24. *CSPC* (1661–8), nos 1603, 1829; Kammen, *Colonial New York,* p. 79; Ritchie, *Duke's Province,* p. 8; Sosin, *English America,* p. 145.

25. *CSPC* (1661–8), no. 1834; *CSPC* (1669–74), nos 136, 208, 646; Ritchie, 'London Merchants', pp. 11–12, 15; Webb, *Governors-General,* pp. 497–8.

26. *CSPC* (1661–8), nos 1874–5; *CSPC* (1669–75), no. 1175.

27. *CSPC* (1669–74), nos 1138.I, 1138.VII, 1140, 1143; Shomette and Haslach, *Raid on America,* pp. 32–4, 37.

28. Quoted in Shomette and Haslach, *Raid on America,* p. 167. See also: *CSPC* (1669–74), nos 1143–4, 1175; *Documents Relative,* pp. 198–9.

29. J.R. Brodhead, *The History of the State of New York, 1609–1691,* vol. II (New York, 1853), pp. 204–8; *CSPC* (1669–74), nos 1122, 1138.II–IV, 1140, 1144–5, 1175; *Documents Relative,* pp. 199–203.

30. Archdeacon, *New York City*, p. 37; *CSPC* (1669–74), nos 1140, 1143–4, 1156; Shomette and Haslach, *Raid on America*, p. 253; Sosin, *English America*, p. 149; Zee, *Sweet and Alien Land*, pp. 486, 488.

31. Archdeacon, *New York City*, p. 38; Boxer, *Dutch Seaborne Empire*, p. 256; *CSPC* (1669–74), nos 423, 603, 1145, 1148, 1157, 1159–60, 1164–5, 1308, 1332, 1339, 1382; *CSPC* (1675–6), nos 400, 721; *CSPC* (1677–80), nos 1255, 1280–1; Ritchie, *Duke's Province* p. 93; Zee, *Sweet and Alien Land*, pp. 486–7, 489, 492.

32. *CSPC* (1669–74), nos 1311, 1330, 1332, 1339–43, 1346, 1382; *CSPC* (1675–6), nos 441–2, 513, 530; *Documents Relative*, pp. 235, 246; Kammen, *Colonial New York*, p. 86; Webb, *Governors-General*, p. 498.

33. *CSPC* (1669–74), no. 1299; *CSPC* (1675–6), nos 436, 669, 1026; *CSPC* (1677–80), no. 222; *Documents Relative*, pp. 228–9, 232–4, 236–40, 245–7; Ritchie, 'Duke of York's Commission', p. 178.

34. *CSPC* (1669–74), no. 1313; *CSPC* (1675–6), nos 436, 803; R. Middleton, *Colonial America. A History, 1585–1776*, 2nd edn (Oxford, 1996), p. 132; Ritchie, *Duke's Province*, p. 43; Ritchie, 'London Merchants', p. 16.

35. *CSPC* (1669–74), nos 1279, 1331; *CSPC* (1675–6), nos 436, 603, 795–6, 1024; *CSPC* (1677–80), nos 222, 502; *CSPC* (1681–5), nos 880, 2078; Pomfret, *Colonial New Jersey*, pp. 33–4.

36. *CSPC* (1675–6), no. 669; *CSPC* (1675–6), no. 669; *CSPC* (1681–5), no. 1106; Ritchie, 'London Merchants', pp. 22–3.

37. *CSPC* (1669–74), no. 1328; *CSPC* (1677–80), nos 1365–7, 1419; *CSPC* (1681–5), nos 64, 103, 348, 352; Ritchie, 'London Merchants', pp. 24–5.

38. *CSPC* (1677–80), no. 1365; Kammen, *Colonial New York*, p. 98; Middleton, *Colonial America*, p. 134; Ritchie, 'London Merchants', pp. 25, 27–9; Webb, *Governors-General*, p. 498.

39. *CSPC* (1681–85), nos 155, 591.

40. *CSPC* (1681–5), no. 348; Ritchie, 'London Merchants', p. 27.

41. *CSPC* (1681–5), nos 591, 1415.

42. *CSPC* (1675–6), no. 795; Kammen, *Colonial New York*, p. 75; A.P. Thornton, 'Charles II and the American Colonies', *History Today*, vol. VI (1956), p. 8.

43. In the light of John Lewin's suggestion, in his report to the Duke, that the economy of New York was no longer sustainable in its present form, the creation of a Parliament as a means to extract surplus revenues from the colonists was an extremely practical and lucrative solution to an intractable problem. James's sudden tactical switch, over the question of calling an assembly, would appear to mirror his later willingness to abandon his Anglican allies in favour of the Dissenters, in 1687.
   Andrews, *Colonial Period*, vol. I, p. 243; *CSPC* (1675–6), no. 795; *CSPC* (1681–5), nos 413, 449, 1848, 1910, 2079, 2085–6; Haffenden, 'The Crown and the Colonial Charters', Part II, pp. 452–3; Mullet, *James II*, pp. 1–2; Ogg, *England in the Reign of Charles II*, vol. II, p. 632; Ritchie, 'London Merchants', p. 29; Turner, *James II*, pp. 233–4; Zee, *William and Mary*, pp. 58–9.

44. Bliss, *Revolution and Empire*, pp. 208–9, 224–7; *CSPC* (1681–5), no. 1372; Geiter, 'Incorporation of Pennsylvania', pp. 28–9; Haffenden, 'The Crown and the Colonial Charters', Part II, p. 461; Middleton, *Colonial America*, pp. 134, 172–3.

45. Andrews, *Colonial Period*, vol. III, pp. 118–21; Haffenden, 'The Crown and the Colonial

Charters', Part II, pp. 452–3; Middleton, *Colonial America*, pp. 170, 172–7; Ritchie, 'Duke of York's Commission', pp. 184–5.

46. Ashley, *James II*, pp. 9, 12; Bliss, *Revolution and Empire*, p. 204; *Burnet*, vol. I, p. 297 (Book II, p. 170); *Evelyn Diary*, (19 Sept. 1685), p. 487; Haffenden, 'The Crown and the Colonial Charters', Part II, p. 465; *Life*, vol. I, pp. 399–400; *Life*, vol. II, pp. 609, 633–4.

47. *CSPC* (1669–74), nos 42, 133, 566, 1312–16; *CSPC* (1677–80), nos 202, 502, 809, 1305; *CSPC* (1681–5), nos 1735, 1746, 1979; R.R. Johnson, 'The Imperial Webb: the Thesis of Garrison Government in Early America Considered', *W&MQ*, 3rd series, vol. XLIII (1986), pp. 410–30; E.E. Rich, 'The Earl of Shaftesbury's Colonial Policy', *TRHS*, vol. VII (1957), pp. 50–2, 70; Webb, 'Brave Men and Servants', pp. 56, 59–64, 66–80; Webb, *Governors-General*, pp. 3–4, 95, 101, 112–13, 136–7, 214, 233–4, 228–9; S.S. Webb, 'The Data and Theory of Restoration Empire', *W&MQ*, 3rd series, vol. XLIII (1986), pp. 449, 454–9.

48. R.P. Beiber, 'The British Plantation Councils of 1670–1674', *English Historical Review*, vol. XL (1925), p. 97; *CSPC* (1669–74), nos 432–3, 514; Haffenden, 'The Crown and the Colonial Charters', Part II, p. 452; Routh, *Tangier*, p. 243.

49. Beiber, 'British Plantation Councils', p. 103; *CSPC* (1669–74), no. 285; A. Pagden, *Lords of all the World. Ideologies of Empire in Spain, Britain and France, c.1492–c.1800* (New Haven, USA and London, 1995), pp. 12–15, 36–7, 132–3; D.K. Richter, 'War and Culture: the Iroquois Experience', *W&MQ*, 3rd series, vol. XL (1983), p. 545; W.T. Root, 'The Lords of Trade and Plantations, 1675–1696', *American History Review*, vol. XXIII (1917), p. 37.

50. For a proprietorial colony to flourish, it primarily required the financial support of its proprietor. James, having spent all of his Parliamentary grants on entertaining himself, could simply not afford to expend his last reserves in this way.
    Ritchie, 'Duke of York's Commission', pp. 177, 179–80, 182, 186–7.

51. *CSPC* (1669–74), no. 1328.

52. Carrel, *History of the Counter-Revolution*, pp. 181–2; Hutton, *Charles II*, pp. 374–6; *Life*, vol. I, p. 574; Oman, *Mary of Modena*, pp. 64–5; Miller, *James II*, p. 100; *RPCS*, vol. VI, pp. 255–6, 259, 565; Turner, *James II*, p. 171.

53. Anon., *A Faithful Compendium, of . . . the Illustrious Prince James, Duke of York. As also the Full and Just Account of his Kind Reception, and High Entertainment by the Scotch Nobility at Edinburgh, the Metropolitan City of Scotland* (London, 1679), pp. 3–4; Her Majesty's Stationary Office, *The Manuscripts of the Right Honourable F.J. Savile Foljambe, of Osberton* (London, 1897), pp. 139–40; *Life*, vol. I, p. 702; Reresby, *Memoirs*, pp. 180–1.

54. Anon., *A Faithful Compendium*, p. 4; Anon., *A True narrative of the reception of their Royal Highnesses at their Arrival in Scotland* (Edinburgh, 1680), pp. 1–4; Hay, *Enigma of James II*, pp. 12–13; HMSO, *Manuscripts of . . . Foljambe*, p. 140; *RPCS*, vol. VI, p. 331; Reresby, *Memoirs*, p. 180.

55. *RPCS*, vol. VI, p. 344.

56. *RPCS*, vol. VI, pp. viii–ix.

57. W. Scott, *Tales of a Grandfather* (London, 1869), p. 241; A. Smellie, *Men of the Covenant* (London, 1903), p. 294; R. Wodrow, *The History of the Sufferings of the Church in Scotland*, ed. R. Burns (4 vols, Glasgow, 1828–32), vol. III, p. 174.

58. James writing from Edinburgh to George Legge, 14 December 1679, quoted in J. Dalrymple, *Memoirs of Great Britain and Ireland* (London, 1790), vol. I, p. 332. See also: *Burnet*, vol. II, p. 300 (Book III, p. 511); *RPCS*, vol. VI, pp. 77–82.

59. Hay, *Enigma of James II*, p. 14; *RPCS*, vol. VII, pp. 252–3.

60. *RPCS*, vol. VI, pp. 55–6, 77–82, 565, 576; *RPCS*, vol. VII, pp. 352–3; Turner, *James II*, pp. 180–2; T. Thomson (ed.), *Acts of the Parliaments of Scotland*, vol. VIII, 1670–86 (Sunderland, 1820), pp. 233–4.

61. Hutton, *Charles II*, pp. 387–8; W.C. Mackenzie, *The Life and Times of John Maitland, Duke of Lauderdale* (London, 1923), pp. 476, 478–80, 483–4; Miller, *James II*, pp. 106–7; *RPCS*, vol. VI, p. 568; *RPCS*, vol. VII, p. vii.

62. C.C.P. Lawson, *A History of the Uniforms of the British Army*, vol. I (London, 1940), pp. 38, 57–8; Middleton, *Life of Charles, 2nd Earl of Middleton*, p. 76; *RPCS*, vol. VII, pp. vii–viii, 204–5, 425–6, 429–30.

63. Bryant, *Samuel Pepys. The Years of Peril*, pp. 380–1; Colvin (ed.), *History of the King's Works*, vol. V, p. 23; J. Lauder of Fountainhall, *Historical Observer . . . 1680 to 1686*, (Edinburgh, 1840), p. 5.

64. H. Arthur (ed.), 'Some Familiar Letters of Charles II and James Duke of York Addressed to their Daughter and Niece, the Countess of Litchfield', *Archaeologia*, vol. LVIII (1902), pp. 159–60; J. Barr, *The Scottish Covenanters* (Glasgow, 1946), pp. 52–3; *Burnet*, vol. II, pp. 301–3 (Book III, pp. 511–12); *CSPD*, (1682), p. 141; S.H.F. Johnston, *The History of the Cameronians (Scottish Rifles)*, vol. I, 1689–1910 (Aldershot, 1957), pp. 18–19; M. Linklater and C. Hesketh, *Bonnie Dundee. John Graham of Claverhouse – For King and Conscience* (Edinburgh, 1992), pp. 66, 70–2, 74–8; *RPCS*, vol. VII, pp. 4, 34, 326–7, 333–4, 358, 366, 368–9, 373, 384, 435–6, 451, 456–8, 488, 497–9; Wodrow, *Sufferings of the Church of Scotland*, vol. III, pp. 217–21.

65. Whytford to Innes, December 2nd 1680, quoted by Hay, *Enigma of James II*, p. 17. See also: Arthur (ed.), 'Familiar Letters', pp. 159–64; *Burnet*, vol. II, p. 303 (Book III, p. 512); Hay, *Enigma of James II*, pp. 15, 17–18; *RPCS*, vol. VI, p. 393; *RPCS*, vol. VII, p. 39. For Highland troubles, and the 'frequent thefts and robberies' which attended them, see: *RPCS*, vol. VI, pp. 1–2; *RPCS*, vol. VII, pp. 65, 68.

66. I.B. Cowan, *The Scottish Covenanters, 1660–1688* (London, 1976), pp. 52, 107, 110–11, 118–19.

67. *CSPD* (1682), p. 283; J. Prebble, *Glencoe* (London, 1966), p. 66; *Life*, vol. I, p. 705; *RPCS*, vol. VII, pp. 65, 71–81, 88–9.

68. *RPCS*, vol. VII, pp. 74–84, 88–9.

69. *RPCS*, vol. VII, pp. 82–4, 590, 599.

70. *RPCS*, vol. VII, pp. 191–6, 204–5, 362.

71. Hay, *Enigma of James II*, pp. 18–19; *Life*, vol. I, p. 710; F. McLynn, *The Jacobites* (London and New York, 1985), pp. 66–7; Petrie, *The Jacobite Movement. The First Phase*, pp. 109–11; Prebble, *Glencoe*, pp. 66, 72–3.

72. Anon. (ed.), *His Majesties Gracious Letter to His Parliament of Scotland: With the Speech of his Royal Highness the Duke of York, His Majesties High Commissioner, at the opening of the Parliament at Edinburgh, the 28th Day of July, 1681* (London, 1681), pp. 3–4; Arthur, 'Familiar Letters', p. 160; Middleton, *Life of Charles, 2nd Earl of Middleton*, p. 74; *RPCS*, vol. VII, p. 170; J. Spottiswoode, *The History of the Church of Scotland* (London, 1677 edn), Appendix pp. 33–4; Thomson (ed.), *Acts of the Parliaments of Scotland*, vol. VIII, pp. 233–4.

73. *His Majesties Gracious Letter*, pp. 4–5; *RPCS*, vol. VII, pp. 148–9. See also: Hay, *Enigma of James II*, pp. 24, 26; Hay, *Winston Churchill and James II*, p. 54; HMSO, *Manuscripts of . . .*

Foljambe, p. 140; Spurr, *Restoration Church of England*, p. 81; *RPCS*, vol. VI, pp. xvi, 207–53; *RPCS*, vol. VII, pp. 177, 310; Reresby, *Memoirs*, pp. 217–18, 126.

74. *RPCS*, vol. VI, pp. 442–4; *RPCS*, vol. VII, pp. xxii, 45–6, 97–105, 110, 416, 423–4, 431, 443, 651–2, 664–5; Thomson (ed.), *Acts of the Parliaments of Scotland*, vol. VIII, pp. 234–43, 247, 348–9, 360–1.

75. Middleton, *Life of Charles, 2nd Earl of Middleton*, p. 76; *RPCS*, vol. VII, pp. 110, 597–8; Thomson (ed.), *Acts of the Parliaments of Scotland*, vol. VIII, p. 350.

76. *RPCS*, vol. VII, pp. 7, 18, 42, 93–4, 144–5, 162, 310–13; Thomson (ed.), *Acts of the Parliaments of Scotland*, vol. VIII, pp. 350, 242–3.

77. Thomson (ed.), *Acts of the Parliaments of Scotland*, vol. VIII, pp. 238–9.

78. Hutton, *Charles II*, p. 443; Mullett, *James II*, p. 45; *RPCS*, vol. VII, pp. 122, 196, 198, 239; Thomson (ed.), *Acts of the Parliaments of Scotland*, vol. VIII, pp. 243–5.

79. Hay, *Enigma of James II*, p. 29; Thomson (ed.), *Acts of the Parliaments of Scotland*, vol. VIII, pp. 244–5; Turner, *James II*, p. 189.

80. *RPCS*, vol. VII, p. 239; Thomson (ed.), *Acts of the Parliaments of Scotland*, vol. VIII, p. 245.

81. *RPCS*, vol. VII, pp. 239–40; Thomson (ed.), *Acts of the Parliaments of Scotland*, vol. VIII, pp. 243–5, 355; Turner, *James II*, pp. 189–90.

82. *Burnet*, vol. II, pp. 304–5 (Book III, p. 513); Dalrymple, *Memoirs of Great Britain and Ireland*, vol. I, p. 344; Hay, *Enigma of James II*, p. 20; *Life*, vol. I, pp. 706–7; *RPCS*, vol. VI, p. 446; *RPCS*, vol. VII, pp. 196, 198, 238, 471; Turner, *James II*, p. 191.

83. *RPCS*, vol. VII, pp. ix, 219, 233, 294–5, 304, 306, 730.

84. *Burnet*, vol. II, p. 317 (Book III, p. 519); *RPCS*, vol. II, pp. 238, 471.

85. *Burnet*, vol. II, pp. 303–4, 317–20 (Book III, pp. 512, 519–21); G.H. Jones, *Charles Middleton. The Life and Times of a Restoration Politician* (Chicago and London, 1967), p. 59; *RPCS*, vol. VII, pp. 238, 242–3; Turner, *James II*, pp. 191–2; J. Willcock, *A Scots Earl in Covenanting Times: Being the Life and Times of Archibald 9th Earl of Argyll* (Edinburgh, 1907), pp. 268–77; Wodrow, *Sufferings of the Church of Scotland*, vol. III, pp. 314, 318.

86. O. Airy (ed.), *Burnet's History of My Own*, vol. II (2 vols, Oxford, 1897 and 1900), pp. 322–3 n. 3; *Burnet*, vol. II, pp. 320–1 (Book III, pp. 521–2); *RPCS*, vol. VII, pp. 238, 242–3.

87. James to William of Orange, 24 December 1681, quoted in G.G. van Prinsterer, *Archives de la Maison Orange-Nassau*, vol. V (The Hague, 1861), p. 538. See also: Ashley, *James II*, p. 139; *Burnet*, vol. II, pp. 320–1 (Book III, pp. 521–2); Hay, *Enigma of James II*, pp. 30–1; Jones, *Charles Middleton*, pp. 59–60; *Life*, vol. I, pp. 707–12; Miller, *James II*, pp. 108–9; Turner, *James II*, p. 193; Willcock, *Scots Earl*, pp. 277–80, 294, 403–10.

88. *Life*. vol. I, p. 702; R.K. Marshall (ed.), *Dynasty: The Royal House of Scotland* (Edinburgh, 1990), p. 84; H. Ouston, '"From Thames to Tweed Departed": The Court of James, Duke of York in Scotland, 1679–82', in E. Cruickshanks (ed.), *The Stuart Courts* (Stroud, Gloucestershire, 2000), pp. 275–7.

CONCLUSION

1. R. Crawfurd, *The Last Days of Charles II* (Oxford, 1909), p. 23; Hutton, *Charles II*, p. 443; Macaulay, *History of England*, vol. I, pp. 422–4.

2. Ailesbury quoted in Crawfurd, *Last Days of Charles II*, pp. 27–9; Oman, *Mary of Modena*, p. 79.

3. Barrillon quoted in Crawfurd, *Last Days of Charles II*, p. 37.
4. PRO, SP.8. 3. f. 228.
5. *Pepys Diary* (4 June 1664), vol. V, pp. 170–1 and (24 March 1667), vol. VIII, p. 127.
6. Kroll (ed.), *Letters from Liselotte*, pp. 57, 59–60, 93; Sells (ed.), *Memoirs of James II*, pp. 52–3, 75, 104, 162–3, 228–42, 255–75.
7. Macaulay, *History of England*, vol. I, pp. 260–1.
8. *Pepys Diary* (19 March 1665), vol. VI, p. 60 and (6 April 1668), vol. IX, pp. 154–5 and p. 155 n. 1.
9. Ashley, *James II*, pp. 106–7, 109; Miller, *James II*, p. 64; Trevor, *Shadow of a Crown*, pp. 62–5; Turner, *James II*, pp. 103–4.
10. Alger, 'Posthumous Vicissitudes of James II', pp. 105–6; Jones, 'James the Second, His Remains', pp. 243–4.
11. BL, Add. MS. 14,007, f. 337; Clarendon, *Life of Clarendon*, vol. II, p. 236; *Pepys Diary* (13 Oct. 1666), vol. VII, p. 320, (15 Oct. 1666), vol. VII, p. 323 and (31 Oct. 1666), vol. VII, p. 350; PRO, SP.8. 3. ff. 26, 30, 33, 43, 47, 53; Rich, *Hudson's Bay Company*, vol. I, p. 144.
12. For two equally damning estimates of James's political acumen, drawn from opposite ends of the political spectrum, see: M. Ffinch, *Cardinal Newman. The Second Spring* (London, 1991), pp. 94–5; A.L. Morton, *A People's History of England*, 3rd edn (London, 1989), pp. 240–5.

Select Bibliography

ABBREVIATIONS

Burnet	Burnet, G., *History of His Own Time*, ed. M.J. Routh, 2nd edn, 6 vols (Oxford, 1833)
CSPC	Sainsbury, W.N. et al. (eds), *Calendar of States Papers, Colonial series, America and West Indies, 1574–1736*, vols VII–IX, 1661–76 (London, 1880–93)
CSPD	Green, M.A.E. et al. (eds), *Calendar of States Papers, Domestic, of the Reign of Charles II*, 28 vols, 1660–85 (London, 1860–1938)
CSPI	Mahaffy, R.P. (ed.), *Calendar of the State Papers relating to Ireland*, vols I–IV, 1660–70 (London, 1905–10)
Devotions	Davies, G. (ed.), *Papers of Devotion of James II* (Oxford, 1925)
Documents Illustrative	Donnan, E. (ed.), *Documents Illustrative of the History of the Slave Trade to America*, vol. I, 1441–1700 (Washington, USA, 1930)
Documents Relative	Brodhead, J.R. (ed.), *Documents Relative to the Colonial History of the State of New York*, vol. III, (Albany, USA, 1853)
Evelyn Diary	Evelyn, J., *Diary and Letters of John Evelyn*, ed. W. Bray, 2nd edn (London, 1819, rpt 1871)
JSAHR	*Journal of the Society for Army Historical Research*
Letters Outward	Rich, E.E. (ed.), *Copy-Book of Letters Outward of the Hudson's Bay Company, 1680–1687* (London, 1948)
Life	Clarke, J.S. (ed.), *The Life of James the Second, King of England, Memoirs Collected out of Writ of his own Hand, together with the King's Advice to his Son, and His Majesty's Will*, 2 vols (London, 1816)
Minutes	Rich, E.E. (ed.), *Minutes of the Hudson's Bay Company, 1679–1684*, First part 1679–82 (London, 1945)
Naval Minutes	Tanner, J.R. (ed.), *Samuel Pepys's Naval Minutes* (London, 1926)
Pepys Diary	Latham, R. and Mathews, W. (eds), *The Diary of Samuel Pepys*, 10 vols (London, 1970–83)
RPCS	Brown, P.H. (ed.), *Register of the Privy Council of Scotland*, 3rd series, vols VI–VIII, 1678–84 (Edinburgh, 1914–15)

Select Bibliography

Select Charters	Carr, C.T. (ed.), *Select Charters of Trading Companies, A.D. 1530–1707* (London, 1913)
TRHS	*Transactions of the Royal Historical Society*
W&MQ	*William and Mary Quarterly*

(a) PRIMARY MANUSCRIPT SOURCES

Bodleian Library, Oxford, Eng. hist., c. 44 f. 11, Letter from the Earl of Clarendon to the Duke of York, 4 April 1671

——, Eng. hist. c. 44 f. 12, Letter from the Earl of Clarendon to the Duchess of York, 3 April 1671

——, MSS. Add., C. 106–7, Paper relating to Mary of Modena

——, Ms. Bodl., 891, Goods of his RH the Duke of York in the Custody and Charge of Philip Kinnersley, yeom[an] of his R. Highness Wardrobe of Beds: 1 June 1674

——, MSS. Carte, 180–1, Thomas Carte's notes for an unfinished biography of James II

——, MS. Carte, 198, Thomas Carte's notes from James's autobiography; later used by Macpherson

——, MSS. Carte, 208–11, Thomas Carte's notes on the House of Stuart in exile, post 1685

——, MS. Jones, 24, Transcript of Philax Verax's *A Letter to his Royal Highness the Duke of York, c.* 1681

——, MS. Montagu, d. 20 f. 190, Letter to Prince Rupert from Louis XIV, July 1673

——, MS. Pigott, d. 10, The Duke of York's Correspondence with Lady Belasyse, 1673–88

——, MS. Rawl. Letters, 107 f. 16, Letter from Anne Hyde to Bishop Cosin of Durham, from York, 10 Sept. 1665

——, MS. Rawl. Letters, 108 f. 2, Letter from the Duke of York to Bishop Cosin of Durham, from York, 10 Aug. 1665

British Library, Add. MS., 12,093, Letter from the Duke of York to Henri de la Tour d'Auvergne [Turenne], from St James's Palace, 13 Sept. 1662

——, Add. MS., 14,007 f. 337, The disadvantages of appointing James, Duke of York, as Governor of Flanders

——, Add. MS., 18,958, Establishment in his RH Household, Michaelmas, 1682

——, Add. MSS., 22,062–3, Sir Henry Jermyn's household accounts and rent roll, 1662–3, 1676

——, Add. MS., 38,863, Establishment of the Duke of York's Household, beginning Christmas 1667

——, Add. MS., 61,484, Memorial relating to the Duke of York's service in the Spanish Army, 1657

——, Sloane MS., 3,511 f. 12, Memorial to the Duke of York by Lord Middleton

——, Sloane MS., 2,439, A Journal or Relation of a Voyage from England into the Streights or Mediterranean sea . . . [Manuscript dedicated to the Duke of York], February 1673

John Rylands Library, Manchester, ENG. MS., 294 ff. 1–17, Items relating to the revenue and Household of the Duke of York, 1662–77, and to Povey's service with Henrietta Maria, 1667–9

Public Record Office, Kew, BH1, Microfilm copies of the records of the Hudson's Bay Company

——, SP. 8. 3., ff. 1–228, The King's Chest. Letters from the Duke of York to William of Orange, written from Whitehall, Feb. 1674–Feb. 1685

——, T 48, Papers on the Royal Household and Wardrobe, 1674–91

——, T 70, Records of the Company of Royal Adventurers of England trading with Africa, 1663–72

Records of the Royal African Company of England, 1672–85

Stonyhurst College Archive, Clitheroe, Lancashire, James II's Holy Week Book, *L' Office de la Semaine Sainte Connadnent du Roy* (Paris, Privately printed and bound, *c.* 1690s)

——, Princess Louise Marie Stuart's Prayer Book, *Missale Romanum* (Paris, Privately printed and bound, *c.* 1690s)

(b) Primary Printed Sources

Ailesbury, T. Bruce, Lord, *Memoirs,* 2 vols (London, 1890)

Anderson, R.C. (ed.), *The Journal of Edward Mountagu, First Earl of Sandwich* (London, 1929)

——, *Journals and Narratives of the Third Dutch War* (London, 1946)

Anonymous, *An Answer to a late Pamphlet; Entituled* [sic], *A Character of a Popish Successor, and what England May Expect from such a One* (London, 1681)

——, *The Case Put Concerning the Succession of His Royal Highness the Duke of York* (London, 1679)

——, *Certain Considerations Relating to the Royal African Company of England* (London, 1680)

——, *A Congratulatory Poem on His Royal Highnesses Restauration* [sic] *to the Dignity of Lord High Admiral of England* (London, 1684)

——, *A Discourse on Monarchy* (London, 1684)

——, *Dux Redux: or, London's Thanksgiving* (London, 1672)

——, *An Essaye Upon his Royal Highness the Duke of York. His Adventure against the Dutch* (London, 1672)

——, *A Faithful Compendium, of the Birth, Education, Heroick Exploits and Victories of his Royal Highness, the Illustrious Prince James, Duke of York. As also the Full and Just Account of his Kind Reception, and High Entertainment by the Scotch Nobility at Edinburgh, the Metropolitan City of Scotland* (London, 1679)

——, *His Majesties Gracious Letter to His Parliament of Scotland: With the Speech of His Royal Highness the Duke, His Majesties High Commissioner, At the opening of the Parliament at Edinburgh the 28th Day of July, 1681* (London, 1681)

——, *The Life of James II. Late King of England* (London, 1702)

——, *The Memoirs of King James II – Containing an Account of the Transactions of the Last Twelve Years of His Life: with the Circumstances of his Death. Translated from the French Original* (London, 1702)

——, *The Life of James II. Late King of England – Containing Accounts of his Birth, Education, Religion and Enterprises both at home and abroad – In Peace and War* (London, 1702)

——, *Memoirs of the English Affairs, Chiefly Naval, from the Year 1660, to 1673. Written by his Royal Highness James, Duke of York. Under his Administration as Lord High Admiral* (London, 1729)

—— , *Memoirs of the Most Remarkable Enterprises and Actions of James Duke of York, Albany and Ulster* (London, 1681)

——, *A Panegyrick to His Royal Highness. Upon His Majesties late Declaration* (London, 1680)

——, *Pereat Papa: or, Reasons why a Presumptive Heir, or Popish Successor should not Inherit the Crown* (London, c. 1681)

——, *The Several Declarations of the Company of Royal Adventurers of England Trading into Africa* (London, 1669)

——, *A Short View of the Life and Actions of the Most Illustrious James, Duke of York, Together with His Character* (London, 1660)

Aquino, C. de, *Sacra Exequialia in Funere Jacobi II* (Rome, 1702)

Aulnoy, M.C., Baron d', *Memoirs of the Court of England in 1675*, ed. G.A. Gilbert (London, 1913)

Bloxam, J.R. (ed.), *Magdalen College and King James II, 1686–1688. A series of Documents* (Oxford, 1886)

Buisson, M. de, (pseudonym of S. de Courtilz), *La Vie du Vicomte de Turenne* (Cologne, 1687)

Burnet, G., *History of His Own Time*, ed. M.J. Routh, 2nd edn, 6 vols (Oxford, 1833)

Chappell, E. (ed.), *The Tangier Papers of Samuel Pepys* (London, 1935)

Christoph, P.R. and A.A., *The Andros Papers, 1674–1676. Files of the Provincial Secretary during the Administration of Governor Sir Edmund Andros, 1674–1680* (Syracuse, USA, 1989)

Clarendon, E. Hyde, Earl of, *Clarendon's Four Portraits*, ed. R. Ollard (London, 1989)

——, *The History of the Rebellion and Civil Wars in England, Begun in the Year 1641*, ed. W.D. Macray, 6 vols (Oxford, 1888)

——, *The Life of Edward Earl of Clarendon*, 3 vols (Oxford, 1827)

Clarke, J.S. (ed.), *The Life of James the Second, King of England, Memoirs Collected out of Writ of his Own Hand, together with the King's Advice to his Son, and His Majesty's Will*, 2 vols (London, 1816)

Corbett, J.S. (ed.), *Fighting Instructions, 1530–1816* (London, 1905)

Davies, G. (ed.), *Papers of Devotion of James II* (Oxford, 1925)

Estrange, R. L', *An Essay Upon the Late Victory obtained by the Duke of York, Against the Dutch, upon 3. June 1665* (London, 1665)

Evelyn, J., *Diary and Letters of John Evelyn*, ed. W. Bray, 2nd edn (London, 1819, rpt 1871)

Fitz-James, J., *Memoirs of the Marshal Duke of Berwick. Written by himself*, ed. C.L. Montesquieu, 2 vols (London, 1779)

Foxcroft, H.C. (ed.), *A Supplement to Burnet's History of My Own Times* (London, 1902)

Hamilton, A., *Memoirs of the Count de Grammont*, trans. and ed. H. Walpole and Mrs. Jameson, (London, n.d., *c.* 1900)

Hattendorf. J.B. et al. (eds), *British Naval Documents, 1204–1960* (Aldershot and Vermont, USA, 1993)

Historical Manuscripts Commission, *The Manuscripts of the Right Honourable F.J. Savile Foljambe of Osberton* (London, 1897)

Historical Manuscripts Commission, *Stuart Papers of H.M. the King*, Part I, vol. 51 (London, 1902)

Hyde, A., *A Paper Written by the Late Dutchess* [sic] *of York* (London, 1670, rpt Dublin, *c.* 1685–8)

Johnson, S., *Julian the Apostate: Being a short Account of the Life; The Sense of Primitive Christians about his Succession; and their behaviour towards him. Together with a Comparison of Popery and Paganism* (London, 1682)

Jusserand, J.J., *A French Ambassador at the Court of Charles the Second. Le Comte de Cominges from his unpublished Correspondence* (London, 1892)

Kenyon, J.P. (ed.), *Halifax. Complete Works* (Harmondsworth, Middlesex, 1969)

Kroll, M. (ed.), *Letters from Liselotte. Elizabeth Charlotte, Princess Palatine and Duchess of Orléans, 'Madame', 1652–1722* (London, 1970)

Lansdowne, Marquis of (ed.), *The Petty-Southwell Correspondence, 1676–1687* (London, 1928)

Latham, R. and Mathews, W. (eds), *The Diary of Samuel Pepys*, 10 vols (London, 1970–83)

Latham, R. (ed)., *Samuel Pepys and the Second Dutch War. Pepys's Navy White Book and Brooke House Papers* (Aldershot and Vermont, USA, 1995)

Lee, N., *To the Duke on his Return* (London, 1682)

Macpherson, J. (ed.), *Original Papers containing the Secret History of Great Britain, from the Restoration to the Accession of the House of Hanover. To which are prefixed Extracts from the Life of James II, as written by himself*, 2 vols (London, 1775)

Magalotti, L., *Lorenzo Magalotti at the Court of Charles II. His Relazione d'Inghilterra of 1668*, ed. W.E.K. Middleton (Waterloo, Canada, 1980)

Matthews, W. (ed.), *Charles II's Escape from Worcester. A Collection of Narratives Assembled by Samuel Pepys* (Berkeley and Los Angeles, 1966)

Mun, T., *England's Treasure by Forraign Trade* (London, 1664)

Norrington, R. (ed.), *My Dearest Minette. The Letters between Charles II and his sister, Henrietta, Duchesse d'Orléans* (London and Chester Springs, USA, 1996)

Pepys, S., *Letters and the Second Diary of Samuel Pepys*, ed. R.G. Howarth (London, 1932)

——, *Memoires Relating to the State of the Royal Navy of England, For Ten Years Determin'd December 1688* (London, 1690)

Powell, J.R. and Timings, E.K. (eds), *The Rupert and Monck Letter Book, 1666* (London, 1969)

Ramsay, A.M., *The History of Henri de la Tour d'Auvergne*, 2 vols (London, 1740)

Reresby, J., *The Memoirs of Sir John Reresby, 1634–1689*, ed. J.A. Cartwright, (London, 1875)

Rich, E.E. (ed.), *Copy-Book of Letters Outward of the Hudson's Bay Company, 1680–1687* (London, 1948)

——, *Minutes of the Hudson's Bay Company, 1679–1684, First Part, 1679–82* (London, 1945)

Sandford, F., *The History of the Coronation of . . . James II* (London, 1687)

Selden, J., *Mare Clausum; the Right and Dominion of the Sea in Two Books* (London, 1663)

Sells, A.L. (ed.), *The Memoirs of James II. His Campaigns as Duke of York, 1652–1660* (London, 1962)

Tanner. J.R. (ed.), *Samuel Pepys's Naval Minutes* (London, 1926)

Tayler, A. and H. (eds), *The Stuart Papers at Windsor* (London, 1939)

Thorogood (pseudonym), *Captain Thorogood. His Opinion on the Point of Succession to a Brother of the Blade in Scotland* (London, 3 Feb. 1679)

Verax, P. (pseudonym), *A Letter to His Royal Highness the Duke of York, touching his Revolt from, or Return to the Protestant Religion. By an Old Cavalier, and faithful Son of the Church of England, as Establish'd by Law* (London, 1681)

(c) SECONDARY PRINTED WORKS

Anon., *An Impartial History of the Life and Death of James the Second* (London, 1746)

Ashley, M., *James II* (London, 1977)

——, 'Is there a Case for James II?', *History Today*, vol. 13 (1963), pp. 347–52

Aubrey, P., *The Defeat of James Stuart's Armada, 1692* (Leicester, 1979)

Barclay, A.P., 'The Impact of James II on the Departments of the Royal Household' (unpublished Ph.D. thesis, University of Cambridge, 1994)

Belloc, H., *James the Second* (London, 1928)

Bliss, R.M., *Revolution and Empire. English Politics and the American Colonies in the Seventeenth Century* (Manchester and New York, 1990)

Boxer, C.R., *The Anglo-Dutch Wars of the 17th Century, 1652–1674* (London, 1974)

Browning, A., *Thomas Osborne, Earl of Danby and Duke of Leeds, 1632–1712*, 3 vols, (Glasgow, 1951)

Bryant, A., *Samuel Pepys. The Man in the Making* (London, 1933)

——, *Samuel Pepys. The Saviour of the Navy* (London, 1938)

——, *Samuel Pepys. The Years of Peril* (London, 1935)

Buranelli, V., *The King and the Quaker. A Study of William Penn and James II* (Philadelphia, 1962)

Burke, P., *The Fabrication of Louis XIV* (New Haven and London, 1992)

Callow, J., 'The Noble Duke of York. James Duke of York and Albany: The Early Modern Prince as Lord High Admiral, Imperialist and Entrepreneur, 1660–1685' (unpublished Ph.D. thesis, University of Lancaster, 1998)

Carrel, A., *History of the Counter-Revolution in England*, trans. W. Hazlitt (London, 1846)

Churchill, W.S., *Marlborough. His Life and Times*, vol. I (London, 1933)

Corp, E., 'James II and Toleration: The Years in Exile at Saint-Germain-en-Laye', *Royal Stuart Society*, Occasional Papers No. LI (1997)

Crawfurd, R., *The Last Days of Charles II* (Oxford, 1909)

Davies, K.G., *The Royal African Company* (London, 1957)

Earle, P., *The Life and Times of James II* (London, 1972)

Fea, A., *James II and his Wives* (London, 1908)

Fox, C.J., *A History of the Early Part of the Reign of James the Second* (London, 1808)

George, R.H., 'The Financial Relations of Louis XIV and James II', *Journal of Modern History*, vol. 3 (1931), pp. 392–413

Gieter, M.K., 'The Incorporation of Pennsylvania and Late Stuart Politics' (unpublished Ph.D. thesis, University of Cambridge, 1993)

Glassey, L.K.J. (ed.), *The Reigns of Charles II and James VII and II* (Basingstoke and London, 1997)

Goldie, M., 'James II and the Dissenters' Revenge', *Bulletin of the Institute of Historical Research*, vol. 66 (1993), pp. 53–8

——, 'John Locke's Circle and James II', *Historical Journal*, vol. 35 (1992), pp. 557–86

Grew, E. and M.S., *The English Court in Exile. James II at Saint-Germain* (London, 1911)

Grose, C.L., 'The Anglo-Dutch Alliance of 1678', *English Historical Review*, vol. 39 (July–Oct. 1924), pp. 349–72, 526–61

——, 'The Dunkirk Money, 1662', *Journal of Modern History*, vol. V (1933), pp. 1–18

Gwynn, R.D., 'James II in the Light of his Treatment of Huguenot Refugees in England, 1685', *English Historical Review*, vol. 92 (1977), pp. 820–33

Haile, M., *Mary of Modena. Her Life and Letters* (London and New York, 1905)

Haley, K.D.H., *The First Earl of Shaftesbury* (Oxford, 1968)

Harris, T., *Politics under the Later Stuarts. Party conflict in a divided society, 1660–1715* (London and New York, 1993)

Hartmann, C.H., *The King My Brother* (London, 1954)

Haswell, J., *James II. Soldier and Sailor* (London, 1972)

Hay, M.V., *The Enigma of James II* (London, 1938)

——, *Winston Churchill and James II of England* (London, 1934)

Head, F.W., *The Fallen Stuarts* (Cambridge, 1901)

Henslowe, J.R., *Anne Hyde, Duchess of York* (London, 1915)

Higham, F.M.G., *King James the Second* (London, 1934)

Hornstein, S., *A Study in the Restoration Navy and English Foreign Trade, 1674–1688* (London, 1991)

Hutton, R., *Charles II. King of England, Scotland and Ireland* (Oxford and New York, 1991)

——, *The Restoration. A Political and Religious History of England and Wales, 1658–1667* (Oxford and New York, 1985)

Israel, J.I., *The Dutch Republic. Its Rise, Greatness, and Fall, 1477–1806* (Oxford, 1995)

Johnson, R.R., 'The Imperial Webb: The thesis of Garrison Government in early America considered', *William and Mary Quarterly*, 3rd series, vol. XLIII (1986), pp. 408–30

Jones, J.R., *The Anglo-Dutch Wars of the Seventeenth Century* (London and New York, 1996)

——, *Charles II. Royal Politician* (London, 1987)

——, *The First Whigs. The Politics of the Exclusion Crisis, 1678–1683* (London, 1961)

—— (ed.), *The Restored Monarchy 1660–1688* (London and Basingstoke, 1979)

——, *The Revolution of 1688 in England* (London, 1972)

Kenyon, J.P., *The Popish Plot* (London, 1972)

——, *The Stuarts. A Study in English Kingship* (Glasgow, 1958)

Knights, M., *Politics and Opinion in Crisis, 1678–81* (Cambridge, 1994)

Lane, J., *King James the Last* (London, 1942)

Longueville, T., *The Adventures of King James II of England* (London, 1904)

Macaulay, T.B., *The History of England. From the Accession of James the Second*, ed. C.H. Firth, 6 vols (London, 1913–15)

McKie, D., 'James, Duke of York, F.R.S.', *Notes and Records of the Royal Society London*, vol. XIII (1958), pp. 6–18

Miller, J., *Charles II* (London, 1991)

——, *James II. A Study in Kingship* (London, 1978)

——, *Popery and Politics in England, 1660–1688* (London, 1973)

——, 'The Potential for "Absolutism" in later Stuart England', *History*, vol. 69 (1984), pp. 187–207

Mullett, M., *James II and English Politics, 1678–1688* (London and New York, 1994)

Oman, C., *Mary of Modena* (Suffolk, 1962)

Petrie, C., *The Jacobite Movement. The First Phase, 1688–1716* (London, 1948)

——, 'James the Second: a revaluation', *Nineteenth Century*, vol. 114 (1933), pp. 475–84

Ranke, L. von, *A History of England, Principally in the Seventeenth Century*, 6 vols (Oxford, 1875)

Ritchie, R.C., *The Duke's Province: A Study of New York Politics and Society, 1661–1691* (Chapel Hill, North Carolina, 1977)

——, 'The Duke of York's Commission of Revenue', *New York Historical Society Quarterly*, vol. 58 (1974), pp. 177–87

Rose, J.H., 'The Influence of James II on the Navy', *Fighting Forces*, vol. I (1924), pp. 211–21

Royal Academy, *The Age of Charles II* (London, 1960)

Scott, E., *The King in Exile. The Wanderings of Charles II from June 1646 to July 1654* (London, 1905)

——, *The Travels of the King. Charles II in Germany and Flanders, 1654–1660* (London, 1907)

Scott, G., 'Sacredness of Majesty: the English Benedictines and the Cult of King James II', *Royal Stuart Society*, Occasional Papers No. XXIII (1984)

Seaward, P., *The Cavalier Parliament and the Reconstruction of the Old Regime, 1661–1667* (Cambridge, 1989)

Shomette, D.G. and Haslach, R.D., *Raid on America. The Dutch Naval Campaign of 1672–1674* (Columbia, South Carolina, 1988)

Simms, J.G., *Jacobite Ireland, 1685–1691* (London and Toronto, 1969)

Speck, W.A., *Reluctant Revolutionaries. Englishmen and the Revolution of 1688* (Oxford, 1988)

Spurr, J., *The Restoration Church of England, 1646–1689* (New Haven and London, 1991)

Steele, I., 'Governor's or Generals? A Note on Martial Law and the Revolution of 1689 in English America', *William and Mary Quarterly*, 3rd series, vol. XLVI (1989), pp. 304–14

Tanner, J.R., *Samuel Pepys and the Royal Navy* (Cambridge, 1920)

Tedder, A.W., *The Navy of the Restoration* (London and Edinburgh, 1919)

Trevor, M., *The Shadow of a Crown. The Life Story of James II of England and VII of Scotland* (London, 1988)

Turner, F.C., *James II* (London, 1948)

Webb, S.S., *The Governors-General. The English Army and the Definition of the Empire, 1569–1681* (Chapel Hill, North Carolina, 1979)

——, *Lord Churchill's Coup. The Anglo-American Empire and the Glorious Revolution Reconsidered* (New York, 1995)

——, *1676. The End of American Independence* (New York, 1984)

——, 'Brave Men and Servants to His Royal Highness. The Household of James Stuart', *Perspectives in American History*, vol. VIII (1974), pp. 55–80

——, 'The Data and Theory of Restoration Empire', *William and Mary Quarterly*, 3rd series, vol. XLIII (1986), pp. 431–59

Wilson, C., *Profit and Power. A Study of England and the Dutch Wars* (London, 1957)

Zook, G.F., *The Company of Royal Adventurers Trading into Africa* (Lancaster, Pennsylvania, 1919)

Index

Cameron, Richard 287
Capel, Sir Henry 199
Caracena, Alonso, Marquis of 73,
    75–9, 82–3, 85–6
Carew, John 116
Cargill, Donald 287–8
Carr, C.T. 29
Carte, Thomas 4–6
Carteret, Sir George 193, 253, 260,
    265, 267–8, 278
Carteret, Captain James 268
Carteret, Philip 268, 277
Castlemaine, Barbara Palmer,
    Countess of 170–1
Castlemaine, Roger Palmer, Earl of
    232
Catherine of Braganza 89, 96, 129, 140,
    163, 168–71, 175, 180, 190, 272
Chaise, Père La 177
Chandler, David 10
Charles I 32–49, 51–2, 55–7, 71–2, 85,
    90, 100, 111, 127, 129, 132,
    140–1, 153, 170, 179, 192–3
Charles II 6, 10, 20, 32–6, 38, 41–2, 44,
    47, 49, 51, 53–9, 61–2, 67, 69–73,
    75, 80, 82–94, 96, 98, 100, 102–3,
    105, 107–8, 111–13, 122, 126,
    128–31, 134–7, 140, 144, 152–3,
    160, 162–72, 174–8, 180–7,
    189–90, 192, 197–202, 205–6,
    209, 212, 228–30, 232, 241–2,
    244, 246–8, 250–1, 254, 256–9,
    264–6, 271–2, 275, 280–1, 283,
    285, 290–2, 294–6, 298, 305
Charles XI, King of Sweden 135
Charles Louis, Elector Palatine 31, 37
Charlotte, Duchess of Albany 5–6
Charpentier, Madame 2, 4
Charpentier, Monsieur 1, 2
Child, Sir Josiah 156
Churchill, Arabella 141
Churchill, Captain George 106, 162
Churchill, Sir John (later Duke of
    Marlborough) 13, 15, 29, 106,
    108, 110, 113–14, 149, 157, 162,
    171, 173, 225, 235, 261, 279, 283,
    286, 300

Churchill, Sir Winston (*c.* 1620–1688)
    122, 162, 172
Churchill, Sir Winston Spencer
    (1874–1965) 13–16, 19, 300, 303
Clarendon, 1st Earl of *see* Hyde,
    Edward
Clarke, James Stanier 4–6, 21
Claverhouse, John Graham of 173,
    290
Cleagh, Sir William 125
Clement X, Pope 152
Clerke, Sir Samuel 108, 117
Clifford, Thomas, Lord 152
Codrington, Christopher 252
Colbert, Jean-Baptiste 143, 212
Coleman, Edward 156, 176–7, 181
Colleton, Sir Peter 253
Colt, John Dutton 159
Committee for Trade and Plantations
    281, 285
Compton, Henry, Bishop of London
    177
Condé, Louis II Bourbon, Prince de
    62, 65–7, 73, 75–6, 78–80, 83, 85,
    128
Conway, Edward, Earl of 183
Cook, Thomas 260
Corbett, Miles 116
Corbett, Thomas 211
Corbetta, Francesco 127
Cortenaer, Egbert Meüssen,
    Lieutenant-Admiral 219–20
Cosyevox, Antoine 134
Council of Foreign Plantations 265
Courland, Duke of 247
Covenanters 10, 105, 188, 284–5, 287,
    291–2, 295–6, 301
Coventry, Sir William 29, 66, 101, 103,
    113, 161–7, 172–3, 185, 194, 197,
    201, 207, 216, 228, 233, 251, 265,
    299
Cox, Sir John 225
Craven, Sir William, 1st Lord 240, 251,
    253, 257
Creed, John 114
Cromwell, Oliver 45, 69–70, 77, 81,
    102, 110, 127, 144, 193

guilt of 91, 148
High Admiral of Spain 85
household of 60, 71, 110–15, 165,
    173, 177
hunting and sports 114–15, 127,
    184, 304
Imperialism 12, 15, 17, 23, 134, 173,
    209, 238, 242, 265, 281–2
and Ireland 54, 116, 172
leader of War Party 208–10, 250
Lord High Admiral 26, 29, 33–4,
    52–4, 86, 101, 112, 117, 130, 135,
    154, 192–213, 215, 225, 233, 247,
    254
marriages 91–4
memoirs 1–7, 21–7, 30, 63–4, 301,
    303
nationalism and 54, 162, 210
personal imagery 32–3, 125–6,
    128–38, 156, 158–9, 169, 222,
    236–7
as politician 160–74, 182–4, 186–7,
    189–91
religion and 8–9, 18, 31–2, 39, 47,
    85–6, 106, 138, 140–59, 183, 197,
    292, 305
the Restoration and 86–9
Royal Commissioner in Scotland
    199, 264, 280, 282–97, 303
sex drive 91–2, 114, 148
slave trade and 242, 244, 262–3, 305
as a sailor 29, 192, 200–1, 203–5,
    215, 222, 227–9, 234–7
as a soldier 21–2, 58, 62–4, 66–8,
    73–81, 88, 101–2, 106, 108, 110,
    114, 128, 130–2, 136–8, 158, 184,
    213–14, 222, 232, 237, 281, 286–7
toleration and 151, 207
and trade 12, 15, 17, 23, 25–7, 29,
    150, 208–9, 238–63, 291, 297
Warden of the Cinque Ports 101, 160
Janzoon, Jan 203
Jeffreys, Judge George 173, 188,
    190–1, 256
Jennings, Sir William 207
Jermyn, Henry (the elder), Earl of St
    Albans 51, 58

Jermyn, Henry (the younger), later
    Earl of Dover 29, 70, 72, 106, 115,
    122, 149, 165, 171, 240, 300
Johnson, Cornelius 33
Jonson, Ben 122
Juan-José of Austria, Don 72–3, 75–6,
    78–80, 82
Julian II, Emperor of Rome 155

Kennett, White, Bishop of
    Peterborough 8
Kenyon, J.P. 112
Killigrew, Anne 130
Kirke, Colonel Percy 149, 151, 173
Kneller, Sir Godfrey 129–30, 135–7,
    149

Lambert, John 81, 87
Laud, William, Archbishop of
    Canterbury 31, 35
Lauderdale, John Maitland, Duke of
    153, 170, 179, 283, 286, 288,
    296–7
Lawson, Sir John 216, 218
Legge, Colonel George (later Earl of
    Dartmouth) 3, 29, 104, 106–7,
    149, 157, 190, 206, 230, 235–6,
    285
Lely, Sir Peter 47, 128, 130–2
Lewin, John 276–80
Ligne, Prince de 73, 80
Lingard, Father John 11–12
Littleton, Sir Charles 29, 106, 173, 230
Livesey, Sir Michael 116
Lockhart, Sir George 295
Lockhart, Sir William 77
Loebb, Emmanuel *see* Simeon, Father
Longueville, Duc de 61
Lorraine, Charles, Duke of 58–9, 64
Louis XIII, King of France 148
Louis XIV, King of France 14, 26,
    59–61, 65, 68, 93, 100, 107, 109,
    125, 134–5, 144, 153, 176–7, 181,
    199, 204, 211–12, 226, 259, 261
Louis, Grand Dauphin of France 26
Lovelace, Colonel Francis 274–6
Lovelace, Thomas 274